INTRODUCTION TO THE
LITERATURE OF EUROPE IN THE
15th, 16th, AND 17th CENTURIES

INTRODUCTION
TO THE LITERATURE
OF EUROPE
IN THE 15th, 16th, AND
17th CENTURIES

HENRY HALLAM

Volume III

FREDERICK UNGAR PUBLISHING CO.
NEW YORK

Printed in the United States of America

Library of Congress Catalog Card No. 74-118869

ISBN (3-volume set) 0-8044-2331-8
Volume I 0-8044-2332-6
Volume II 0-8044-2333-4
Volume III 0-8044-2334-2

CONTENTS

OF

THE THIRD VOLUME.

CHAPTER VI.

HISTORY OF DRAMATIC LITERATURE FROM 1600 TO 1650.

CHAPTER VII.

HISTORY OF POLITE LITERATURE IN PROSE FROM 1600 TO 1650.

CHAPTER VIII.

HISTORY OF MATHEMATICAL AND PHYSICAL SCIENCE FROM 1600 TO 1650.

CHAPTER IX.

HISTORY OF SOME OTHER PROVINCES OF LITERATURE FROM 1600 TO 1650.

PART IV.

ON THE LITERATURE OF THE SECOND HALF OF THE SEVENTEENTH CENTURY.

CHAPTER I.

HISTORY OF ANCIENT LITERATURE IN EUROPE FROM 1650 TO 1700.

CHAPTER II.

HISTORY OF THEOLOGICAL LITERATURE FROM 1650 TO 1700.

CHAPTER III.

HISTORY OF SPECULATIVE PHILOSOPHY FROM 1650 TO 1700.

CHAPTER IV.

HISTORY OF MORAL AND POLITICAL PHILOSOPHY AND OF JURISPRUDENCE
FROM 1650 TO 1700.

CHAPTER V.

HISTORY OF POETRY FROM 1650 TO 1700.

CHAPTER VI.

HISTORY OF DRAMATIC LITERATURE FROM 1650 TO 1700.

CHAPTER VII.

HISTORY OF POLITE LITERATURE IN PROSE FROM 1650 TO 1700.

CHAPTER VIII.

HISTORY OF PHYSICAL AND OTHER LITERATURE FROM 1650 TO 1700.

PART III.—*continued.*

ON THE LITERATURE OF THE FIRST HALF OF THE SEVENTEENTH CENTURY.

CHAPTER V.

HISTORY OF POETRY FROM 1600 TO 1650.

SECT I.—ON ITALIAN POETRY.

Characters of the Poets of the Seventeenth Century—Sometimes too much depreciated—Marini—Tassoni—Chiabrera.

1. AT the close of the sixteenth century, few remained in Italy to whom posterity has assigned a considerable reputation for their poetry. But the ensuing period has stood lower, for the most part, in the opinion of later ages than any other since the revival of letters. The *seicentisti*, the writers of the seventeenth century, were stigmatised in modern criticism, till the word has been associated with nothing but false taste and everything that should be shunned and despised. Those who had most influence in leading the literary judgment of Italy went back, some almost exclusively to the admiration of Petrarch and his contemporaries, some to the various writers who cultivated their native poetry in the sixteenth century. Salvini is of the former class, Muratori of the latter.[a]

Low estimation of the seicentisti.

2. The last age, that is, the concluding twenty years of the eighteenth century, brought with it, in many respects, a change of public sentiment in Italy. A masculine turn of thought, an expanded grasp of philosophy, a thirst, ardent to excess, for great exploits and noble praise, has distinguished the Italian people of the last fifty years from their progenitors of several preceding generations. It is possible that the enhanced relative importance of the

Not quite so great as formerly.

---

[a] Muratori, Della Perfetta Poesia, is one of the best books of criticism in the Italian language; in the second volume are contained some remarks by Salvini, a bigoted Florentine.

Lombards in their national literature may have not been without its influence in rendering the public taste less fastidious as to purity of language, less fine in that part of æsthetic discernment which relates to the grace and felicity of expression, while it became also more apt to demand originality, nervousness, and the power of exciting emotion. The writers of the seventeenth century may, in some cases, have gained by this revolution; but those of the preceding ages, especially the Petrarchists whom Bembo had led, have certainly lost ground in national admiration.

3. Rubbi, editor of the voluminous collection called Parnaso Italiano, had the courage to extol the 'seicentisti' for their genius and fancy, and even to place them, in all but style, above their predecessors. 'Give them,' he says, 'but grace and purity, take from them their capricious exaggerations, their perpetual and forced metaphors, you will think Marini the first poet of Italy, and his followers, with their fulness of imagery and personification, will make you forget their monotonous predecessors. I do not advise you to make a study of the seicentisti; it would spoil your style, perhaps your imagination; I only tell you that they were the true Italian poets; they wanted a good style, it is admitted, but they were so far from wanting genius and imagination, that these perhaps tended to impair their style.' [b]

Praise of them by Rubbi.

4. It is probable that every native critic would think some parts of this panegyric, and especially the strongly hyperbolical praise of Marini, carried too far. But I am not sure that we should be wrong in agreeing with Rubbi, that there is as much *catholic* poetry, by which I mean that which is good in all ages and countries, in some of the minor productions of the seventeenth as in those of the sixteenth age. The sonnets, especially, have more individuality and more meaning. In this, however, I should wish to include the latter portion of the seventeenth century. Salfi, a writer of more taste and judgment than Rubbi, has recently taken the same side, and remarked the superior originality,

Also by Salfi.

---

[b] Parnaso Italiano, vol. xli. (Avvertimento.) Rubbi, however, gives but two out of his long collection in fifty volumes, to the writers of the seventeenth century.

the more determined individuality, the greater variety of
subjects, above all, what the Italians now most value, the
more earnest patriotism of the later poets.[c] Those immediately before us, belonging to the first half of the century,
are less numerous than in the former age ; the sonnetteers
especially have produced much less; and in the collections of
poetry, even in that of Rubbi, notwithstanding his eulogy,
they take up very little room. Some, however, have obtained
a durable renown, and are better known in Europe than any,
except the Tassos, that flourished in the last fifty years of
the golden age.

5. It must be confessed that the praise of a masculine
genius, either in thought or language, cannot be Adone of
bestowed on the poet of the seventeenth century Marini.
whom his contemporaries most admired, Giovanni Battista
Marini. He is, on the contrary, more deficient than all the
rest in such qualities, and is indebted to the very opposite
characteristics for the sinister influence which he exerted on
the public taste. He was a Neapolitan by birth, and gave to
the world his famous Adone in 1623. As he was then fifty-
four years old, it may be presumed, from the character of the
poem, that it was in great part written long before; and he
had already acquired a considerable reputation by his other
works. The Adone was received with an unbounded and ill-
judging approbation ; ill-judging in a critical sense, because
the faults of this poem are incapable of defence; but not
unnatural, as many parallel instances of the world's enthusiasm have shown. No one had before carried the corruption
of taste so far; extravagant metaphors, false thoughts, and
conceits on equivocal words, are very frequent in the Adone ;
and its author stands accountable in some measure for his
imitators, who during more than half a century looked up
to Marini with emulous folly, and frequently succeeded in
greater deviations from pure taste without his imagination
and elegance.

6. The Adone is one of the longest poems in the world,
containing more than 45,000 lines. He has shown Its charac-
some ingenuity in filling up the canvas of so slight ter.

---

[c] Salfi, Hist. Litt. de l'Italie (continuation de Ginguéné), vol. xii. p. 424.

a story by additional incidents from his own invention, and by long episodes allusive to the times in which he lived. But the subject, expanded so interminably, is essentially destitute of any superior interest, and fit only for an enervated people, barren of high thoughts and high actions, the Italy, notwithstanding some bright exceptions, of the seventeenth century. If we could overcome this essential source of weariness, the Adone has much to delight our fancy and our ear. Marini is, more than any other poet, the counterpart of Ovid; his fertility of imagination, his ready accumulation of circumstances and expressions, his easy flow of language, his harmonious versification, are in no degree inferior; his faults are also the same; for in Ovid we have all the overstrained figures and false conceits of Marini. But the Italian poet was incapable of imitating the truth to nature and depth of feeling which appear in many parts of his ancient prototype, nor has he as vigorous an expression. Never does Marini rise to any high pitch; few stanzas, perhaps, are remembered by natives for their beauty, but many are graceful and pleasing, all are easy and musical.[d] ' Perhaps,' says Salfi, ' with the exception of Ariosto, no one has been more a poet by nature than he;'[e] a praise, however, which may justly seem hyperbolical to those who recall their attention to the highest attributes of poetry.

7. Marini belongs to that very numerous body of poets who, delighted with the spontaneity of their ideas, never reject any that arise; their parental love forbids all preference and an impartial law of gavelkind

And popularity.

---

[d] Five stanzas of the seventh canto, being a choral song of satyrs and bacchanti, are thrown into *versi sdruccioli*, and have been accounted by the Italians an extraordinary effort of skill, from the difficulty of sustaining a metre which is not strong in rhymes with so much spirit and ease. Each verse also is divided into three parts, themselves separately *sdruccioli*, though not rhyming. One stanza will make this clear :—

Hor d' ellera s' adornino, e di pampino
I giovani, e le vergini più tenere,
E gemine nell' anima si stampino
L' imagine di Libero, e di Venere.
Tutti ardano, s' accendano, ed avampino,
Qual Semele, ch' al folgore fù cenere ;

E cantino a Cupidine, ed a Bromio,
Con numeri poetici un encomio.
                    Cant. vii. st. 118.
Though this metrical skill may not be of the highest merit in poetry, it is no more to be slighted than facility of touch in a painter.

[e] Vol. xiv. p. 147. The character of Marini's poetry which this critic has given, is in general very just, and in good taste. Corniani (vii. 123) has also done justice, and no more than justice, to Marini. Tiraboschi has hardly said enough in his favour ; and as to Muratori, it was his business to restore and maintain a purity of taste, which rendered him severe towards the excesses of such poets as Marini.

shares their page among all the offspring of their brain. Such were Ovid and Lucan, and such have been some of our own poets of great genius and equal fame. Their fertility astonishes the reader, and he enjoys for a time the abundant banquet; but satiety is too sure a consequence, and he returns with less pleasure to a second perusal. The censure of criticism falls invariably, and sometimes too harshly, on this sort of poetry; it is one of those cases where the critic and the world are most at variance; but the world is apt, in this instance, to reverse its own judgment, and yield to the tribunal it had rejected. 'To Marini,' says an eminent Italian writer, 'we owe the lawlessness of composition: the ebullition of his genius, incapable of restraint, burst through every bulwark, enduring no rule but that of his own humour, which was all for sonorous verse, bold and ingenious thoughts, fantastical subjects, a phraseology rather Latin than Italian, and in short aimed at pleasing by a false appearance of beauty. It would almost pass belief how much this style was admired, were it not so near our own time that we hear as it were the echo of its praise; nor did Dante or Petrarch, or Tasso, or perhaps any of the ancient poets, obtain in their lives so much applause.'[f] But Marini, who died in 1625, had not time to enjoy much of this glory. The length of this poem, and the diffuseness which produces its length, render it nearly impossible to read through the Adone; and it wants that inequality which might secure a preference to detached portions. The story of Psyche in the fourth canto may perhaps be as fair a specimen of Marini as could be taken; it is not easy to destroy the beauty of that fable, nor was he unfitted to relate it with grace and interest; but he has displayed all the blemishes of his own style.[g]

8. The Secchia Rapita of Alessandro Tassoni, published at

---

[f] Crescimbeni, ii. 470.

[g] The Adone has been frequently charged with want of decency. It was put to the ban of the Roman inquisition, and grave writers have deemed it necessary to protest against its licentiousness. Andrès even goes so far as to declare, that no one can read the Adone whose heart as well as taste is not corrupt; and that, both for the sake of good morals and good poetry, it should be taken out of every one's hands. After such invectives, it may seem extraordinary that, though the poem of Marini must by its nature be rather voluptuous, it is by far less open to such an objection than the Orlando Furioso, nor more, I believe, than the Faery Queen. No charge is apt to be made so capriciously as this.

Paris in 1622, is better known in Europe than might have
been expected from its local subject, idiomatic
style, and unintelligible personalities. It turns, as
the title imports, on one of the petty wars, frequent among
the Italian cities as late as the beginning of the fourteenth
century, wherein the Bolognese endeavoured to recover the
bucket of a well, which the citizens of Modena in a prior in-
cursion had carried off. Tassoni, by a poetical anachronism,
mixed this with an earlier contest of rather more dignity
between the little republics, wherein Enzio, king of Sardinia,
a son of Frederic II., had been made prisoner. He has been
reckoned by many the inventor, or at least the reproducer in
modern times of the mock-heroic style.[h] Pulci, however,
had led the way; and when Tassoni claims originality, it
must be in a very limited view of the execution of his poem.
He has certainly more of parody than Pulci could have
attempted; the great poems of Ariosto and Tasso, especially
the latter, supply him with abundant opportunities for this
ingenious and lively, but not spiteful, exercise of wit, and he
has adroitly seized the ridiculous side of his contemporary
Marini. The combat of the cities, it may be observed, is
serious enough, however trifling the cause, and has its due
proportion of slaughter; but Tassoni, very much in the
manner of the Morgante Maggiore, throws an air of ridicule
over the whole. The episodes are generally in a still more
comic style. A graceful facility and a light humour, which
must have been incomparably better understood by his countrymen and contemporaries, make this a very amusing poem.
It is exempt from the bad taste of the age; and the few portions where the burlesque tone disappears are versified with
much elegance. Perhaps it has not been observed, that the
Count de Culagne, one of his most ludicrous characters,
bears a certain resemblance to Hudibras, both by his awk-

Secchia Rapita of Tassoni.

---

[h] Boileau seems to acknowledge himself indebted to Tassoni for the Lutrin;
and Pope may have followed both in the
first sketch of the Rape of the Lock,
though what he has added is a purely
original conception. But in fact the
mock-heroic or burlesque style, in a general sense, is so natural, and moreover
so common, that it is idle to talk of its
inventor. What else is Rabelais, Don
Quixote, or, in Italian, the romance of
Bertoldo, all older than Tassoni? What
else are the popular tales of children,
John the Giganticide, and many more?
The poem of Tassoni had a very great
reputation. Voltaire did it injustice,
though it was much in his own line.

ward and dastardly appearance as a knight, and by his ridiculous addresses to the lady whom he woos.[i] None, however, will question the originality of Butler.

9. But the poet of whom Italy has, in later times, been far more proud than of Marini or Tassoni was Chia- Chiabrera.
brera. Of his long life the greater part fell within the sixteenth century; and some his poems were published before its close; but he has generally been considered as belonging to the present period. Chiabrera is the founder of a school in the lyric poetry of Italy, rendered afterwards more famous by Guidi, which affected the name of Pindaric. It is the Theban lyre which they boast to strike: it is from the fountain of Dirce that they draw their inspiration; and these allusions are as frequent in their verse, as those to Valclusa and the Sorga in the followers of Petrarch. Chiabrera borrowed from Pindar that grandeur of sound, that pomp of epithets, that rich swell of imagery, that unvarying majesty of conception, which distinguish the odes of both poets. He is less frequently harsh or turgid, though the latter blemish has been sometimes observed in him, but wants also the masculine condensation of his prototype; nor does he deviate so frequently, or with so much power of imagination, into such digressions as those which generally shade from our eyes, in a skilful profusion of ornament, the victors of the Grecian games whom Pindar professes to celebrate. The poet of the house of Medici and of other princes of Italy, great at least in their own time, was not so much compelled to desert his immediate subject, as he who was paid for an ode by some wrestler or boxer, who could only become worthy of heroic song by attaching his name to the ancient glories of his native city. The profuse employment of mythological allusions, frigid as it appears at present, was so customary, that we can hardly impute to it much blame; and it seemed peculiarly appropriate to a style which was studiously formed on the Pindaric model.[k] The odes of

---

[i] Cantos X. and XI. It was intended as a ridicule on Marini, but represents a real personage. Salfi, xiii. 147.

[k] Salfi justifies the continual introduction of mythology by the Italian poets, on the ground that it was a part of their national inheritance, associated with the monuments and recollections of their glory. This would be more to the purpose if their mythology had not been almost exclusively Greek. But perhaps all that was of classical antiquity might be blended in their sentiments with the memory of Rome.

Chiabrera are often panegyrical, and his manner was well
fitted for that style, though sometimes we have ceased to
admire those whom he extols. But he is not eminent for
purity of taste, nor, I believe, of Tuscan language; he
endeavoured to force the idiom, more than it would bear, by
constructions and inversions borrowed from the ancient
tongues; and these odes, splendid and noble as they are,
bear, in the estimation of critics, some marks of the seventeenth century.[m] The satirical epistles of Chiabrera are
praised by Salfi as written in a moral Horatian tone, abounding with his own experience and allusions to his time.[n] But
in no other kind of poetry has he been so highly successful
as in the lyric; and, though the Grecian robe is never cast
away, he imitated Anacreon with as much skill as Pindar.
' His lighter odes,' says Crescimbeni, ' are most beautiful
and elegant, full of grace, vivacity, spirit, and delicacy,
adorned with pleasing inventions, and differing in nothing
but language from those of Anacreon. His dithyrambics I
hold incapable of being excelled, all the qualities required in
such compositions being united with a certain nobleness of
expression which elevates all it touches upon.'[o]

10. The greatest lyric poet of Greece was not more the
model of Chiabrera than his Roman competitor was of Testi.
' Had he been more attentive to the choice of his expression,'
says Crescimbeni, ' he might have earned the name of the
Tuscan Horace.' The faults of his age are said to be frequently discernible in Testi; but there is, to an ordinary
reader, an Horatian elegance, a certain charm of grace and
ease in his canzoni, which render them pleasing. One of
these, beginning, Ruscelletto orgoglioso, is highly admired
by Muratori, the best, perhaps, of the Italian critics, and
one not slow to censure any defects of taste. It apparently
alludes to some enemy in the court of Modena.[p] The character of Testi was ambitious and restless, his life spent in
seeking and partly in enjoying public offices, but terminated
in prison. He had taken, says a later writer, Horace for his
model; and perhaps like him he wished to appear sometimes

---

[m] Salfi, xii. 250.
[n] Id. xiii. 2012.
[o] Storia della Volgar Poesia, ii. 483.

[p] This canzone is in Mathias, Compo-
nimenti Lirici, ii. 190.

a stoic, sometimes an epicurean; but he knew not like him how to profit by the lessons either of Zeno or Epicurus, so as to lead a tranquil and independent life.[q]

11. The imitators of Chiabrera were generally unsuccessful; they became hyperbolical and exaggerated. His followers. The Translation of Pindar by Alessandro Adimari, though not very much resembling the original, has been praised for its own beauty. But these poets are not to be confounded with the Marinists, to whom they are much superior. Ciampoli, whose Rime were published in 1628, may perhaps be the best after Chiabrera.[r] Several obscure epic poems, some of which are rather to be deemed romances, are commemorated by the last historian of Italian literature. Among these is the Conquest of Granada by Graziani, published in 1650. Salfi justly observes that the subject is truly epic; but the poem itself seems to be nothing but a series of episodical intrigues without unity. The style, according to the same writer, is redundant, the similes too frequent and monotonous; yet he prefers it to all the heroic poems which had intervened since that of Tasso.[s]

Sect. II.—On Spanish Poetry.

Romances—The Argensolas—Villegas—Gongora, and his School.

12. The Spanish poetry of the sixteenth century might be arranged in three classes. In the first we might place that which was formed in the ancient school, The styles of Spanish Poetry. though not always preserving its characteristics; the short trochaic metres, employed in the song or the ballad, altogether national, or aspiring to be such, either in their subjects or in their style. In the second would stand that to which the imitation of the Italians had given rise, the school of Boscan and Garcilasso; and with these we might place also the epic poems, which do not seem to be essentially different from similar productions of Italy. A third and not

---

[q] Salfi, xii. 281.
[r] Salfi, p. 303. Tiraboschi, xi. 364. Baillet, on the authority of others, speaks less honourably of Ciampoli. N. 1451.
[s] Id. vol. xiii. 94—129.

inconsiderable division, though less extensive than the others, is composed of the poetry of good sense ; the didactic, semi-satirical, Horatian style, of which Mendoza was the founder, and several specimens of which occur in the Parnaso Español of Sedano.

13. The romances of the Cid and many others are referred The ro- by the most competent judges to the reign of Philip mances. III.[t] These are by no means among the best of Spanish romances, and we should naturally expect that so artificial a style as the imitation of ancient manners and sentiments by poets in wholly a different state of society, though some men of talent might succeed in it, would soon degenerate into an affected mannerism. The Italian style continued to be cultivated ; under Philip III., the decline of Spain in poetry, as in arms and national power, was not so striking as afterwards. Several poets belong to the age of that prince, and even that of Philip IV. was not destitute of The bro- men of merited reputation.[u] Among the best were thers Ar- gensola. two brothers, Lupercio and Bartholomew Argensola. These were chiefly distinguished in what I have called the third or Horatian manner of Spanish poetry, though they by no means confined themselves to any peculiar style. 'Lupercio,' says Bouterwek, 'formed his style after Horace with no less assiduity than Luis de Leon ; but he did not

---

[t] Duran, Romançero de romances doctrinales, amatorios, festivos, &c. 1829. The Moorish romances, with a few exceptions, and those of the Cid, are ascribed by this author to the latter part of the sixteenth and the first half of the seventeenth century. In the preface to a former publication, Romances Moriscos, this writer has said, Casi todos los romances que publicamos en este libro pertenecen al siglo 16mo, y algunos pocos á principio del 17mo. Los autores son desconocidos, pero sus obras han llegado, y merecido llegar á la posteridad. It seems manifest from internal evidence, without critical knowledge of the language, that those relating to the Cid are not of the middle ages, though some seem still inclined to give them a high antiquity. It is not sufficient to say that the language has been modernised ; the whole structure of these ballads is redolent of a low age ; and if the Spanish

critics agree in this, I know not why foreigners should strive against them.— [It is hardly, perhaps, necessary to warn the reader, that the celebrated long poem on the Cid is not reckoned among these romances.—1842.]

[u] Antonio bestows unbounded praise on a poem of the epic class, the Bernardo of Balbuena, published at Madrid in 1624, though he complains that in his own age it lay hid in the corners of booksellers' shops. Balbuena, in his opinion, has left all Spanish poets far behind him. The subject of his poem is the very common fable of Roncesvalles. Dieze, while he denies this absolute pre-eminence of Balbuena, gives him a respectable place among the many epic writers of Spain. But I do not find him mentioned in Bouterwek ; in fact, most of these poems are very scarce, and are treasures for the bibliomaniacs.

possess the soft enthusiasm of that pious poet, who in the religious spirit of his poetry is so totally unlike Horace. An understanding at once solid and ingenious, subject to no extravagant illusion, yet full of true poetic feeling, and an imagination more plastic than creative, impart a more perfect Horatian colouring to the odes, as well as to the canciones and sonnets of Lupercio. He closely imitated Horace in his didactic satires, a style of composition in which no Spanish poet had preceded him. But he never succeeded in attaining the bold combination of ideas which characterises the ode style of Horace ; and his conceptions have therefore seldom anything like the Horatian energy. On the other hand, all his poems express no less precision of language than the models after which he formed his style. His odes, in particular, are characterised by a picturesque tone of expression which he seems to have imbibed from Virgil rather than from Horace. The extravagant metaphors by which some of Herrera's odes are deformed were uniformly avoided by Lupercio.'[x] The genius of Bartholomew Argensola was very like that of his brother, nor are their writings easily distinguishable ; but Bouterwek assigns, on the whole, a higher place to Bartholomew. Dieze inclines to the same judgment, and thinks the eulogy of Nicolas Antonio on these brothers, extravagant as it seems, not beyond their merits.

14. But another poet, Manuel Estevan de Villegas, whose poems, written in very early youth, entitled Amatorias or Eroticas, were published in 1620, has attained a still higher reputation, especially in other parts of Europe. Dieze calls him 'one of the best lyric poets of Spain, excellent in the various styles he has employed, but above all in his odes and songs. His original poems are full of genius; his translations of Horace and Anacreon might often pass for original. Few surpass him in harmony of verse; he is the Spanish Anacreon, the poet of the Graces.'[y] Bouterwek, a more discriminating judge than Dieze, who is perhaps rather valuable for research than for taste, has observed, that 'the graceful luxuriance of the poetry of Villegas has

Villegas.

---

[x] History of Spanish Literature, p. 396.   [y] Geschichte der Spanischen Dichtkunst, p. 210.

no parallel in modern literature; and, generally speaking, no modern writer has so well succeeded in blending the spirit of ancient poetry with the modern. But constantly to observe that correctness of ideas, which distinguished the classical compositions of antiquity, was by Villegas, as by most Spanish poets, considered too rigid a requisition, and an unnecessary restraint on genius. He accordingly sometimes degenerates into conceits and images, the monstrous absurdity of which is characteristic of the author's nation and age. For instance, in one of his odes, in which he entreats Lyda to suffer her tresses to flow, he says that "agitated by Zephyr, her locks would occasion a thousand deaths, and subdue a thousand lives ;" and then he adds, in a strain of extravagance, surpassing that of the Marinists, "that the sun himself would cease to give light, if he did not snatch beams from her radiant countenance to illumine the East." But faults of this glaring kind are by no means frequent in the poetry of Villegas, and the fascinating grace with which he emulates his models, operates with so powerful a charm, that the occasional occurrence of some little affectations, from which he could scarcely be expected entirely to abstain, is easily overlooked by the reader.' [z]

15. Quevedo, who having borne the surname of Villegas, has sometimes been confounded with the poet we have just named, is better known in Europe for his prose than his verse; but he is the author of numerous poems, both serious and comic or satirical. The latter are by much the more esteemed of the two. He wrote burlesque poetry with success, but it is frequently unintelligible except to natives. In satire he adopted the Juvenalian style.[a] A few more might perhaps be added, especially Espinel, a poet of the classic school, Borja de Esquillace, once viceroy of Peru, who is called by Bouterwek the last representative of that style in Spain, but more worthy of praise for withstanding the bad taste of his contemporaries than for any vigour of genius, and Christopher de la Mena.[b] No Portuguese poetry about this time seems to be worthy of notice in

Quevedo.

---

[z] Bouterwek, i. 479.   [a] Id., p. 468.   [b] Id., p. 488.

European literature, though Manuel Faria y Sousa and a few more might attain a local reputation by sonnets and other amatory verse.

16. The original blemish of Spanish writing both in prose and verse had been an excess of effort to say everything in an unusual manner, a deviation from the beaten paths of sentiment and language in a wider curve than good taste permits. Taste is the presiding faculty which regulates, in all works within her jurisdiction, the struggling powers of imagination, emotion, and reason. Each has its claim to mingle in the composition; each may sometimes be allowed in a great measure to predominate; and a phlegmatic application of what men call common sense in æsthetic criticism is almost as repugnant to its principles as a dereliction of all reason for the sake of fantastic absurdity. Taste also must determine, by an intuitive sense of right somewhat analogous to that which regulates the manners of polished life, to what extent the most simple, the most obvious, the most natural, and therefore, in a popular meaning, the most true, is to be modified by a studious introduction of the new, the striking, and the beautiful, so that neither what is insipid and trivial, nor yet what is forced and affected, may displease us. In Spain, as we have observed, the latter was always the prevailing fault. The public taste had been formed on bad models, on the Oriental poetry, metaphorical beyond all perceptible analogy, and on that of the Provençals, false in sentiment, false in conception, false in image and figure. The national character, proud, swelling, and ceremonious, conspired to give an inflated tone; it was also grave and sententious rather than lively or delicate, and therefore fond of a strained and ambitious style. These vices of writing are carried to excess in romances of chivalry, which became ridiculous in the eyes of sensible men, but were certainly very popular; they affect also, though in a different manner, much of the Spanish prose of the sixteenth century, and they belong to a great deal of the poetry of that age, though it must be owned that much appears wholly exempt from them, and written in a very pure and classical spirit. Cervantes strove by example and by precept to maintain good taste; and some of his contemporaries

Defects of taste in Spanish verse.

took the same line.[c]　But they had to fight against the predominant turn of their nation, which soon gave the victory to one of the worst manners of writing that ever disgraced public favour.

17. Nothing can be more opposite to what is strictly called a classical style, or one formed upon the best models of Greece and Rome, than pedantry. This was nevertheless the weed that overspread the face of literature in those ages when Greece and Rome were the chief objects of veneration. Without an intimate discernment of their beauty it was easy to copy allusions that were no longer intelligible, to counterfeit trains of thought that belonged to past times, to force reluctant idioms into modern form, as some are said to dress after a lady for whom nature has done more than for themselves. From the revival of letters downwards this had been more or less observable in the learned men of Europe, and after that class grew more extensive, in the current literature of modern languages. Pedantry, which consisted in unnecessary, and perhaps unintelligible, references to ancient learning, was afterwards combined with other artifices to obtain the same end, farfetched metaphors and extravagant conceits. The French versifiers of the latter end of the sixteenth century were eminent in both, as the works of Ronsard and Du Bartas attest. We might, indeed, take the Creation of Du Bartas more properly than the Euphues of our English Lilly, which though very affected and unpleasing, does hardly such violence to common speech and common sense, for the type of the style which, in the early part of the seventeenth century, became popular in several countries, but especially in Spain, through the misplaced labours of Gongora.

Pedantry and farfetched allusions.

18. Luis de Gongora, a man of very considerable talents, and capable of writing well, as he has shown, in different styles of poetry, was unfortunately led by an ambitious desire of popularity to introduce one which should render his name immortal, as it has done in a mode which he did not design. This was his *estilo culto*, as it was usually called, or highly polished phraseology, wherein every

Gongora.

---

[c] Cervantes, in his Viage del Parnaso, praises Gongora, and even imitates his style; but this, Dieze says, is all ironical. Gesch. der Dichtkunst, p. 250.

word seems to have been out of its natural place. 'In
fulfilment of this object,' says Bouterwek, 'he formed for
himself, with the most laborious assiduity, a style as uncommon as affected, and opposed to all the ordinary rules of
the Spanish language, either in prose or verse. He particularly endeavoured to introduce into his native tongue
the intricate constructions of the Greek and Latin, though
such an arrangement of words had never been attempted in
Spanish composition. He consequently found it necessary
to invent a particular system of punctuation, in order to
render the sense of his verses intelligible. Not satisfied
with this patchwork kind of phraseology, he affected to attach an extraordinary depth of meaning to each word, and
to diffuse an air of superior dignity over his whole style.
In Gongora's poetry the most common words received a
totally new signification; and in order to impart perfection
to his *estilo culto,* he summoned all his mythological learning
to his aid.'[d] 'Gongora,' says an English writer, 'was
the founder of a sect in literature. The style called in
Castilian *cultismo* owes its origin to him. This affectation
consists in using language so pedantic, metaphors so strained,
and constructions so involved, that few readers have the
knowledge requisite to understand the words, and still fewer
ingenuity to discover the allusion, or patience to unravel
the sentences. These authors do not avail themselves of
the invention of letters for the purpose of conveying but of
concealing their ideas.'[e]

19. The Gongorists formed a strong party in literature,
and carried with them the public voice. If we were   The schools
to believe some writers of the seventeenth century,   formed by
he was the greatest poet of Spain.[f] The age of Cervantes   him.
was over, nor was there vitality enough in the criticism of
the reign of Philip IV. to resist the contagion. Two sects
soon appeared among these *cultoristos :* one who retained that

---

[d] Bouterwek, p. 434.
  [e] Lord Holland's Lope de Vega,
p. 64.
  [f] Dieze, p. 250. Nicolas Antonio,
to the disgrace of his judgment, maintains this with the most extravagant
eulogy on Gongora; and Baillet copies
him; but the next age unhesitatingly

reversed the sentence. The Portuguese
have laid claim to the estilo culto as
their property, and one of their writers
who practises it, Manuel de Faria y
Sousa, gives Don Sebastian the credit of
having been the first who wrote it in
prose.

name, and, like their master, affected a certain precision of
style; another, called *conceptistos*, which went still greater
lengths in extravagance, desirous only, it might seem, of
expressing absurd ideas in unnatural language.[g] The prevalence of such a disease, for no other analogy can so fitly
be used, would seem to have been a bad presage for Spain;
but in fact, like other diseases, it did but make the tour of
Europe, and rage worse in some countries than in others.
It had spent itself in France, when it was at its height in
Italy and England. I do not perceive the close connexion
of the *estilo culto* of Gongora with that of Marini, whom both
Bouterwek and Lord Holland suppose to have formed his
own taste on the Spanish school. It seems rather too severe
an imputation on that most ingenious and fertile poet, who,
as has already been observed, has no fitter parallel than Ovid.
The strained metaphors of the Adone are easily collected by
critics, and seem extravagant in juxtaposition, but they recur
only at intervals; while those of Gongora are studiously
forced into every line, and are besides incomparably more
refined and obscure. His style, indeed, seems to be like
that of Lycophron, without the excuse of that prophetical
mystery which breathes a certain awfulness over the symbolic
language of the Cassandra. Nor am I convinced that our
own metaphysical poetry in the reigns of James and Charles
had much to do with either Marini or Gongora, except as it
bore marks of the same vice, a restless ambition to excite
wonder by overstepping the boundaries of nature.

Sect. III.

Malherbe—Regnier—Other French Poets.

20. Malherbe, a very few of whose poems belong to the last
century, but the greater part to the first twenty years
Malherbe. of the present, gave a polish and a grace to the lyric
poetry of France which has rendered his name celebrated in
her criticism. The public taste of that country is (or I should

---

[g] Bouterwek, p. 438.

rather say, used to be) more intolerant of defects in poetry
than rigorous in its demands of excellence. Malherbe, therefore, who substituted a regular and accurate versification, a
style pure and generally free from pedantic or colloquial
phrases, and a sustained tone of what were reckoned elevated
thoughts, for the more unequal strains of the sixteenth century, acquired a reputation which may lead some of his
readers to disappointment.   And this is likely to be increased
by a very few lines of great beauty which are known by heart.
These stand too much alone in his poems.   In general, we
find in them neither imagery nor sentiment that yield us
delight.   He is less mythological, less affected, less given to
frigid hyperboles than his predecessors, but far too much so
for any one accustomed to real poetry.   In the panegyrical
odes Malherbe displays some felicity and skill; the poet of
kings and courtiers, he wisely, perhaps, wrote, even when he
could have written better, what kings and courtiers would
understand and reward.   Polished and elegant, his lines
seldom pass the conventional tone of poetry; and while he
is never original he is rarely impressive.   Malherbe may
stand in relation to Horace as Chiabrera does to Pindar : the
analogy is not very close ; but he is far from deficient in that
calm philosophy which forms the charm of the Roman poet,
and we are willing to believe that he sacrificed his time reluctantly to the praises of the great.   It may be suspected
that he wrote verses for others ; a practice not unusual, I
believe, among these courtly rhymers; at least his Alcandre
seems to be Henry IV., Chrysanthe or Oranthe the Princess
of Condé.   He seems himself in some passages to have
affected gallantry towards Mary of Medicis, which at that
time was not reckoned an impertinence.

21. Bouterwek has criticised Malherbe with some justice,
but with greater severity. [h]   He deems him no poet, Criticisms
which in a certain sense is surely true. But we narrow upon his
poetry.
our definition of poetry too much, when we exclude from it
the versification of good sense and select diction.   This may
probably be ascribed to Malherbe; though Bouhours, an
acute and somewhat rigid critic, has pointed out some passages which he deems nonsensical.   Another writer of the

---

[h] Vol. y. p. 238.

same age, Rapin, whose own taste was not very glowing,
observes that there is much prose in Malherbe; and that,
well as he merits to be called correct, he is a little too desirous
of appearing so, and often becomes frigid.[i] Boileau has
extolled him, perhaps, somewhat too highly, and La Harpe
is inclined to the same side; but in the modern state of
French criticism, the danger is that the Malherbes will be
too much depreciated.

22. The satires of Regnier have been highly praised by
Boileau, a competent judge, no doubt, in such
matters. Some have preferred Regnier even to
himself, and found in this old Juvenal of France a certain
stamp of satirical genius which the more polished critic
wanted.[k] These satires are unlike all other French poetry of
the age of Henry IV. ; the tone is vehement, somewhat rugged
and coarse, and reminds us a little of his contemporaries
Hall and Donne, whom, however, he will generally and justly
be thought much to excel. Some of his satires are borrowed
from Ovid or from the Italians.[m] They have been called
gross and licentious ; but this only applies to one, the rest
are unexceptionable. Regnier, who had probably some quarrel
with Malherbe, speaks with contempt of his elaborate polish.
But the taste of France, and especially of that highly cultivated nobility who formed the court of Louis XIII. and his
son, no longer endured the rude, though sometimes animated
versification of the older poets. Next to Malherbe in reputation stood Racan and Maynard, both more or less
of his school. Of these it was said by their master
that Racan wanted the diligence of Maynard, as Maynard
did the spirit of Racan, and that a good poet might be made
out of the two.[n] A foreigner will in general prefer the former,
who seems to have possessed more imagination and sensibility, and a keener relish for rural beauty. Maynard's

Satires of Regnier.

Racan— Maynard.

---

[i] Réflexions sur la Poëtique, p. 147.
Malherbe a esté le premier qui nous a
remis dans le bon chemin, joignant la
pureté au grand style ; mais comme il
commença cette manière, il ne put la
porter jusques dans sa perfection; il y a
bien de la prose dans ses vers. In another place he says, Malherbe est exact
et correct ; mais il ne hasarde rien, et
par l'envie qu'il a d'être trop sage, il est
souvent froid. P. 209.
[k] Bouterwek, p. 246. La Harpe.
Biogr. univ.
[m] Niceron, xi. 397.
[n] Pelisson, Hist. de l'Académie, i.
260. Baillet, Jugemens des Savans
(Poëtes), n. 1510. La Harpe, Cours de
Littérature. Bouterwek, v. 260.

verses, according to Pelisson, have an ease and elegance
that few can imitate, which proceeds from his natural and
simple construction.[o] He had more success in epigram than
in his sonnets, which Boileau has treated with little respect.
Nor does he speak better of Malleville, who chose no other
species of verse, but seldom produced a finished piece, though
not deficient in spirit and delicacy. Viaud, more frequently
known by the name of Théophile, a writer of no great elevation of style, is not destitute of imagination. Such at least
is the opinion of Rapin and Bouterwek. [p]

23. The poems of Gombauld were, in general, published
before the middle of the century; his epigrams, which
are most esteemed, in 1657. These are often lively   Voiture.
and neat. But a style of playfulness and gaiety had been introduced by Voiture. French poetry under Ronsard and his
school, and even that of Malherbe, had lost the lively tone of
Marot, and became serious almost to severity. Voiture, with
an apparent ease and grace, though without the natural air
of the old writers, made it once more amusing. In reality,
the style of Voiture is artificial and elaborate, but, like his
imitator Prior among us, he has the skill to disguise this
from the reader. He must be admitted to have had, in verse
as well as prose, a considerable influence over the taste of
France. He wrote to please women, and women are grateful
when they are pleased. Sarrazin, says his biographer,
though less celebrated than Voiture, deserves perhaps   Sarrazin.
to be rated above him; with equal ingenuity, he is far more
natural.[q] The German historian of French literature has
spoken less respectfully of Sarrazin, whose verses are the
most insipid rhymed prose, such as he not unhappily calls
toilet-poetry.[r] This is a style which finds little mercy on the
right bank of the Rhine; but the French are better judges of
the merit of Sarrazin.

---

[o] Idem.

[p] Bouterwek, 252. Rapin says, Théophile a l'imagination grande et le sens
petit. Il a des hardiesses heureuses à
force de se permettre tout. Réflexions
sur la Poëtique, p. 209.

[q] Biogr. univ. Baillet, n. 1532.

[r] Bouterwek, v. 256. Specimens of
all these poets will be found in the collection of Augnis, vol. vi.: and I must
own, that, with the exceptions of Malherbe, Regnier, and one or two more,
my own acquaintance with them extends
little farther.

Rise of Poetry in Germany—Opitz and his followers—Dutch Poets.

24. The German language had never been more despised by
<small>Low state</small> the learned and the noble than at the beginning of the
<small>of German</small>
<small>literature.</small> seventeenth century, which seems to be the lowest
point in its native literature. The capacity was not wanting; many wrote Latin verse with success; the collection
made by Gruter is abundant in these cultivators of a foreign
tongue, several of whom belong to the close of the preceding
age. But among these it is said that whoever essayed to
write their own language did but fail, and the instances
adduced are very few. The upper ranks began about this
time to speak French in common society; the burghers, as
usual, strove to imitate them; and, what was far worse, it
became the mode to intermingle French words with German,
not singly and sparingly, as has happened in other times
and countries, but in a jargon affectedly piebald and macaronic. Some hope might have been founded on the literary
<small>Literary</small> academies, which, in emulation of Italy, sprung up
<small>Societies.</small> in this period. The oldest is The Fruitful Society
(Die fruchtbringende Gesellschaft), known also as the order
of Palms, established at Weimar in 1617.[s] Five princes
enrolled their names at the beginning. It held forth the
laudable purpose of purifying and correcting the mother
tongue and of promoting its literature, after the manner of
the Italian academies. But it is not unusual for literary
associations to promise much and fail of performance; one
man is more easily found to lay down a good plan, than many
to co-operate in its execution. Probably this was merely the
scheme of some more gifted individual, perhaps Werder, who
translated Ariosto and Tasso;[t] for little good was effected
by the institution. Nor did several others which at different
times in the seventeenth century arose over Germany deserve
more praise. They copied the academies of Italy in their
quaint names and titles, in their by-laws, their petty cere-

---

[s] Bouterwek, x. 35.   [t] Bouterwek, x. 29.

monials and symbolic distinctions, to which, as we always find
in these self-elected societies, they attached vast importance,
and thought themselves superior to the world by doing
nothing for it.   'They are gone,' exclaims Bouterwek,
' and have left no clear vestige of their existence.' Such
had been the meister-singers before them, and little else in
effect were the academies, in a more genial soil, of their own
age.   Notwithstanding this, though I am compelled to follow
the historian of German literature, it must strike us that
these societies seem to manifest a public esteem for something intellectual, which they knew not precisely how to
attain; and it is to be observed that several of the best poets
in the seventeenth century belong to them.

25. A very small number of poets, such as Meckerlin and
Spee, in the early part of the seventeenth century,   Opitz.
though with many faults in point of taste, have been
commemorated by the modern historians of literature.   But
they were wholly eclipsed by one whom Germany regards as
the founder of her poetic literature, Martin Opitz, a native of
Silesia, honoured with a laurel crown by the emperor in
1628, and raised to offices of distinction and trust in several
courts.   The national admiration of Opitz seems to have
been almost enthusiastic; yet Opitz was far from being the
poet of enthusiasm.   Had he been such his age might not
have understood him.   His taste was French and Dutch;
two countries of which the poetry was pure and correct, but
not imaginative.   No great elevation, no energy of genius,
will be found in this German Heinsius or Malherbe.   Opitz
displayed, however, another kind of excellence.   He wrote
the language with a purity of idiom, in which Luther alone,
whom he chose as his model, was superior; he gave more
strength to the versification, and paid a regard to the collocation of syllables according to their quantity, or length of
time required for articulation, which the earlier poets had
neglected.   He is, therefore, reckoned the inventor of a rich
and harmonious rhythm; and he also rendered the Alexandrine verse much more common than before.[u]   His sense

---

[u] Bouterwek (p. 94) thinks this no   of the seventeenth and first part of the
advantage; a rhymed prose in Alexan-   eighteenth century.
drines overspread the German literature

is good; he writes as one conversant with the ancients, and with mankind; if he is too didactic and learned for a poet in the higher import of the word, if his taste appears fettered by the models he took for imitation, if he even retarded, of which we can hardly be sure, the development of a more genuine nationality in German literature, he must still be allowed, in a favourable sense, to have made an epoch in its history.[x]

26. Opitz is reckoned the founder of what was called the first Silesian school, rather so denominated from him than as determining the birthplace of its poets. They were chiefly lyric, but more in the line of songs and short effusions in trochaic metre than of the regular ode, and sometimes display much spirit and feeling. The German song always seems to bear a resemblance to the English; the identity of metre and rhythm conspires with what is more essential, a certain analogy of sentiment. Many, however, of Opitz's followers, like himself, took Holland for their Parnassus, and translated their songs from Dutch. Fleming was distinguished by a genuine feeling for lyric poetry; he made Opitz his model, but had he not died young, would probably have gone beyond him, being endowed by nature with a more poetical genius. Gryph, or Gryphius, who belonged to the Fruitful Society, and bore in that the surname of the immortal, with faults that strike the reader in every page, is also superior in fancy and warmth to Opitz. But Gryph is better known in German literature by his

His follow-
ers.

---

[x] Bouterwek, x. 89—119, has given an elaborate critique of the poetry of Opitz. 'He is the father, not of German poetry, but of the modern German language of poetry, der neueren deutschen Dichtersprache,' p. 93. The fame of Opitz spread beyond his country, little as his language was familiar. Non periit Germania, Grotius writes to him, in 1631, Opiti doctissime, quæ te habet locupletissimum testem, quid lingua Germanica, quid ingenia Germanica valeant. Epist. 272. And afterwards, in 1638, thanking him for the present of his translation of the Psalms: Dignus erat rex poeta interprete Germanorum poetarum rege; nihil enim tibi blandiens dico; ita sentio à te primum Germanicæ

poesi formam datam et habitum quo cum aliis gentibus possit contendere. Ep. 999. Baillet observes, that Opitz passes for the best of German poets, and the first who gave rules to that poetry, and raised it to the state it had since reached; so that he is rather to be accounted its father than its improver. Jugemens des Savans (Poëtes), n. 1436. But reputation is transitory; though ten editions of the poems of Opitz were published within the seventeenth century, which Bouterwek thinks much for Germany at that time, though it would not be so much in some countries, scarce any one, except the lovers of old literature, now asks for these obsolete productions. P. 90.

tragedies. The hymns of the Lutheran church are by no
means the lowest form of German poetry. They have been
the work of every age since the Reformation; but Dach and
Gerhard, who, especially the latter, excelled in these devotional songs, lived about the middle of the seventeenth
century. The shade of Luther seemed to protect the church
from the profanation of bad taste; or, as we should rather
say, it was the intense theopathy of the German nation, and
the simple majesty of their ecclesiastical music.[y]

27. It has been the misfortune of the Dutch, a great
people, a people fertile of men of various ability and   Dutch
erudition, a people of scholars, of theologians and   poetry.
philosophers, of mathematicians, of historians, of painters,
and, we may add, of poets, that these last have been the
mere violets of the shade, and have peculiarly suffered by
the narrow limits within which their language has been
spoken or known. The Flemish dialect of the southern
Netherlands might have contributed to make up something
like a national literature, extensive enough to be respected
in Europe, if those provinces, which now affect the name of
Belgium, had been equally fertile of talents with their
neighbours.

28. The golden age of Dutch literature is this first part
of the seventeenth century. Their chief poets are
Spiegel, Hooft, Cats, and Vondel. The first, who   Spiegel.
has been styled the Dutch Ennius, died in 1612; his principal poem, of an ethical kind, is posthumous, but may probably have been written towards the close of the preceding
century. 'The style is vigorous and concise; it is rich in
imagery and powerfully expressed, but is deficient in elegance and perspicuity.'[z] Spiegel had rendered much service
to his native tongue, and was a member of a literary academy
which published a Dutch grammar in 1584. Koornhert and
Dousa, with others known to fame, were his colleagues; and
be it remembered, to the honour of Holland, that in Germany,
or England, or even in France, there was as yet no institution
of this kind. But as Holland, at the end of the sixteenth
century, and for many years afterwards, was pre-eminently

[y] Bouterwek, x. 218. Eichhorn, iv. 888.   [z] Biogr. univ.

the literary country of Europe, it is not surprising that some endeavours were made, though unsuccessfully as to European renown, to cultivate the native language. This language is also more soft, though less sonorous than the German.

29. Spiegel was followed by a more celebrated poet, Peter Hooft, who gave sweetness and harmony to Dutch verse. 'The great creative power of poetry,' it has been said, 'he did not possess; but his language is correct, his style agreeable, and he did much to introduce a better epoch.' [a] His amatory and anacreontic lines have never been excelled in the language; and Hooft is also distinguished both as a dramatist and an historian. He has been called the Tacitus of Holland. But here again his praises must by the generality be taken upon trust. Cats is a poet of a different class; ease, abundance, simplicity, clearness, and purity are the qualities of his style: his imagination is gay, his morality popular and useful. No one was more read than Father Cats, as the people call him; but he is often trifling and monotonous. Cats, though he wrote for the multitude, whose descendants still almost know his poems by heart, was a man whom the republic held in high esteem; twice ambassador in England, he died great pensionary of Holland, in 1651. Vondel, a native of Cologne, but the glory, as he is deemed, of Dutch poetry, was best known as a tragedian. In his tragedies, the lyric part, the choruses which he retained after the ancient model, have been called the sublimest of odes. But some have spoken less highly of Vondel. [b]

(margin note: Hooft, Cats, Vondel.)

30. Denmark had no literature in the native language, except a collection of old ballads, full of Scandinavian legends, till the present period; and in this it does not appear that she had more than one poet, a Norwegian bishop, named Arrebo. Nothing, I believe, was written in Swedish. Sclavonian, that is, Polish and Russian, poets there were; but we know so little of those languages, that they cannot enter, at least during so distant a period, into the history of European literature.

(margin note: Danish poetry.)

---

[a] Biogr. univ.
[b] Foreign Quart. Rev. vol. iv. p. 49. For this short account of the Dutch poets I am indebted to Eichhorn, vol. iv. part I., and to the Biographie universelle.

SECT. V.—ON ENGLISH POETRY.

Imitators of Spenser—The Fletchers—Philosophical Poets—Denham—
   Donne—Cowley—Historical and Narrative Poets—Shakspeare's Sonnets
   —Lyric Poets—Milton's Lycidas, and other Poems.

31. THE English poets of these fifty years are very numerous, and though the greater part are not familiar to the general reader, they form a favourite study of those who cultivate our poetry, and are sought by all collectors of scarce and interesting literature. Many of them have within half a century been reprinted separately, and many more in the useful and copious collections of Anderson, Chalmers, and other editors. Extracts have also been made by Headley, Ellis, Campbell, and Southey. It will be convenient to arrange them rather according to the schools to which they belonged, than in mere order of chronology.

32. Whatever were the misfortunes of Spenser's life, whatever neglect he might have experienced at the hands of a statesman grown old in cares which render a man insensible to song, his spirit might be consoled by the prodigious reputation of the Faery Queen. He was placed at once by his country above all the great Italian names, and next to Virgil among the ancients; it was a natural consequence that some should imitate what they so deeply reverenced. An ardent admiration for Spenser inspired the genius of two young brothers, Phineas and Giles Fletcher. The first, very soon after the Queen's death, as some allusions to Lord Essex seem to denote, composed, though he did not so soon publish, a poem, entitled The Purple Island. By this strange name he expressed a subject more strange; it is a minute and elaborate account of the body and mind of man. Through five cantos the reader is regaled with nothing but allegorical anatomy, in the details of which Phineas seems tolerably skilled, evincing a great deal of ingenuity in diversifying his metaphors, and in presenting the delineation of his imaginary island with as much justice as possible to the

allegory without obtruding it on the reader's view. In the sixth canto he rises to the intellectual and moral faculties of the soul, which occupy the rest of the poem. From its nature it is insuperably wearisome; yet his language is often very poetical, his versification harmonious, his invention fertile. But that perpetual monotony of allegorical persons, which sometimes displeases us even in Spenser, is seldom relieved in Fletcher; the understanding revolts at the confused crowd of inconceivable beings in a philosophical poem ; and the justness of analogy which had given us some pleasure in the anatomical cantos, is lost in tedious descriptions of all possible moral qualities, each of them personified, which can never co-exist in the Purple Island of one individual.

33. Giles Fletcher, brother of Phineas, in Christ's Victory Giles Fletcher. and Triumph, though his subject has not all the unity that might be desired, had a manifest superiority in its choice. Each uses a stanza of his own; Phineas one of seven lines, Giles one of eight. This poem was published in 1610. Each brother alludes to the work of the other, which must be owing to the alterations made by Phineas in his Purple Island, written probably the first, but not published, I believe, till 1633. Giles seems to have more vigour than his elder brother, but less sweetness, less smoothness, and more affectation in his style. This, indeed, is deformed by words neither English nor Latin, but simply barbarous, such as *elamping, eblazon, deprostrate, purpured, glitterand,* and many others. They both bear much resemblance to Spenser : Giles sometimes ventures to cope with him, even in celebrated passages, such as the description of the Cave of Despair. [c] And he has had the honour, in turn, of being followed by Milton, especially in the first meeting of our Saviour with Satan in the Paradise Regained. Both of these brothers are deserving of much praise; they were endowed with minds eminently poetical, and not inferior in imagination to any of their contemporaries. But an injudicious taste, and an excessive fondness for a style which the public was rapidly abandoning, that of allegorical personification, prevented their powers from being effectively displayed.

---

[c] Christ's Vict. and Triumph, ii. 23.

34. Notwithstanding the popularity of Spenser, and the general pride in his name, that allegorical and ima- Philoso-
phical
poetry. ginative school of poetry, of which he was the greatest ornament, did not by any means exclude a very different kind. The English, or such as by their education gave the tone in literature, had become, in the latter years of the queen, and still more under her successor, a deeply thinking, a learned, a philosophical people. A sententious reasoning, grave, subtle and condensed, or the novel and remote analogies of wit, gained praise from many whom the creations of an excursive fancy could not attract. Hence much of the poetry of James's reign is distinguished from that of Elizabeth, except perhaps her last years, by partaking of the general character of the age; deficient in simplicity, grace, and feeling, often obscure and pedantic, but impressing us with a respect for the man, where we do not recognise the poet. From this condition of public taste arose two schools of poetry, different in character, if not unequal in merit, but both appealing to the reasoning more than to the imaginative faculty as their judge.

35. The first of these may own as its founder Sir John Davies, whose poem on the Immortality of the Soul, Lord
Brooke. published in 1599, has had its due honour in our last volume.   Davies is eminent for perspicuity; but this cannot be said for another philosophical poet, Sir Fulke Greville, afterwards Lord Brooke, the bosom friend of Sir Philip Sidney, and once the patron of Jordano Bruno.   The titles of Lord Brooke's poems, A Treatise of Human Learning, *A* Treatise of Monarchy, A Treatise of Religion, An Inquisition upon Fame and Honour, lead us to anticipate more of sense than fancy.   In this we are not deceived; his mind was pregnant with deep reflection upon multifarious learning, but he struggles to give utterance to thoughts which he had not fully endowed with words, and amidst the shackles of rhyme and metre which he had not learned to manage. Hence of all our poets he may be reckoned the most obscure; in aiming at condensation he becomes elliptical beyond the bounds of the language, and his rhymes, being forced for the sake of sound, leave all meaning behind.   Lord Brooke's poetry is chiefly worth notice as an indication of that think-

ing spirit upon political science which was to produce the
riper speculations of Hobbes, and Harrington, and Locke.

36. This argumentative school of verse was so much in
unison with the character of that generation, that Daniel, a
poet of a very different temper, adopted it in his panegyric
addressed to James soon after his accession, and in some
other poems. It had an influence upon others who trod
generally in a different track, as is especially perceived in
Denham's Giles Fletcher. The Cooper's Hill of Sir John
Cooper's Denham, published in 1643, belongs in a consider-
Hill. able degree to this reasoning class of poems. It is also
descriptive, but the description is made to slide into philosophy. The plan is original, as far as our poetry is concerned, and I do not recollect any exception in other languages. Placing himself upon an eminence not distant from
Windsor, he takes a survey of the scene; he finds the tower
of St. Paul's on his farthest horizon, the Castle much nearer,
and the Thames at his feet. These, with the ruins of an
abbey, supply in turn materials for a reflecting rather than
imaginative mind, and, with a stag-hunt, which he has very
well described, fill up the canvas of a poem of no great length,
but once of no trifling reputation.

37. The epithet, *majestic* Denham, conferred by Pope,
conveys rather too much; but Cooper's Hill is no ordinary
poem. It is nearly the first instance of vigorous and rhythmical couplets, for Denham is incomparably less feeble than
Browne, and less prosaic than Beaumont. Close in thought,
and nervous in language like Davies, he is less hard and less
monotonous; his cadences are animated and various, perhaps
a little beyond the regularity that metre demands; they have
been the guide to the finer ear of Dryden. Those who cannot
endure the philosophic poetry, must ever be dissatisfied with
Cooper's Hill; no personification, no ardent words, few metaphors beyond the common use of speech, nothing that warms,
or melts, or fascinates the heart. It is rare to find lines of
eminent beauty in Denham; and equally so to be struck by any
one as feeble or low. His language is always well chosen
and perspicuous, free from those strange turns of expression,
frequent in our older poets, where the reader is apt to suspect
some error of the press, so irreconcilable do they seem with

grammar or meaning. The expletive *do*, which the best of his predecessors use freely, seldom occurs in Denham ; and he has in other respects brushed away the rust of languid and ineffective redundancies which have obstructed the popularity of men with more native genius than himself.[d]

38. Another class of poets in the reign of James and his son were those whom Johnson has called the meta- *Poets called* physical; a name rather more applicable, in the ordi- *metaphysical.* nary use of the word, to Davies and Brooke. These were such as laboured after conceits, or novel turns of thought, usually false, and resting upon some equivocation of language, or exceedingly remote analogy. This style Johnson supposes to have been derived from Marini. But Donne, its founder, as Johnson imagines, in England, wrote before Marini. It is, in fact, as we have lately observed, the style which, though Marini has earned the discreditable reputation of perverting the taste of his country by it, had been gaining ground through the latter half of the sixteenth century. It was, in a more comprehensive view, one modification of that vitiated taste which sacrificed all ease and naturalness of writing and speaking for the sake of display. The mythological erudition and Grecisms of Ronsard's school, the euphuism of that of Lilly, the ' estilo culto ' of Gongora, even the pedantic quotations of Burton and many similar writers, both in England and on the Continent, sprang like the concetti of the Italians, and of their English imitators, from the same source, a dread of being overlooked if they paced on like their neighbours. And when a few writers had set the example of successful faults, a bad style, where no sound principles of criticism had been established, readily

---

[d] The comparison by Denham between the Thames and his own poetry was once celebrated :—

O could I flow like thee, and make thy stream
My bright example, as it is my theme ;
Though deep, yet clear ; though gentle, yet not dull ;
Strong without rage, without o'erflowing full.

Johnson, while he highly extols these lines, truly observes, that ' most of the words thus artfully opposed, are to be understood simply on one side of the comparison, and metaphorically on the other ; and if there be any language

which does not express intellectual operations by material images, into that language they cannot be translated.' Perhaps these metaphors are so naturally applied to style, that no language of a cultivated people is without them. But the ground of objection is, in fact, that the lines contain nothing but wit, and that wit which turns on a play of words. They are rather ingenious in this respect, and remarkably harmonious, which is probably the secret of their popularity ; but, as poetry, they deserve no great praise.

gaining ground, it became necessary that those who had not vigour enough to rise above the fashion, should seek to fall in with it. Nothing is more injurious to the cultivation of verse than the trick of desiring, for praise or profit, to attract those by poetry whom nature has left destitute of every quality which genuine poetry can attract. The best, and perhaps the only secure basis for *public* taste, for an æsthetic appreciation of beauty, in a court, a college, a city, is so general a diffusion of classical knowledge, as by rendering the finest models familiar, and by giving them a sort of authority, will discountenance and check at the outset the vicious novelties which always exert some influence over uneducated minds. But this was not yet the case in England. Milton was perhaps the first writer who eminently possessed a genuine discernment and feeling of antiquity; though it may be perceived in Spenser, and also in a very few who wrote in prose.

39. Donne is generally esteemed the earliest, as Cowley was afterwards the most conspicuous, model of this manner. Many instances of it, however, occur in the lighter poetry of the queen's reign. Donne is the most inharmonious of our versifiers, if he can be said to have deserved such a name by lines too rugged to seem metre. Of his earlier poems many are very licentious; the later are chiefly devout. Few are good for much; the conceits have not even the merit of being intelligible; it would perhaps be difficult to select three passages that we should care to read again.

Donne.

40. The second of these poets was Crashaw, a man of some imagination and great piety, but whose softness of heart, united with feeble judgment, led him to admire and imitate whatever was most extravagant in the mystic writings of Saint Teresa. He was more than Donne a follower of Marini, one of whose poems, The Massacre of the Innocents, he translated with success. It is difficult, in general, to find anything in Crashaw that bad taste has not deformed. His poems were first published in 1646.

Crashaw.

41. In the next year, 1647, Cowley's Mistress appeared; the most celebrated performance of the miscalled metaphysical poets. It is a series of short amatory poems, in the Italian style of the age, full of analogies that

Cowley.

have no semblance of truth, except from the double sense of words, and thoughts that unite the coldness of subtilty with the hyperbolical extravagance of counterfeited passion. A few anacreontic poems, and some other light pieces of Cowley, have a spirit and raciness very unlike these frigid conceits; and in the ode on the death of his friend Mr. Harvey, he gave some proofs of real sensibility and poetic grace. The Pindaric odes of Cowley were not published within this period. But it is not worth while to defer mention of them. They contain, like all his poetry, from time to time, very beautiful lines, but the faults are still of the same kind; his sensibility and good sense, nor has any poet more, are choked by false taste; and it would be difficult to fix on any one poem in which the beauties are more frequent than the blemishes. Johnson has selected the elegy on Crashaw as the finest of Cowley's works. It begins with a very beautiful couplet, but I confess that little else seems, to my taste, of much value. The 'Complaint,' probably better known than any other poem, appears to me the best in itself. His disappointed hopes give a not unpleasing melancholy to several passages. But his Latin ode in a similar strain is much more perfect. Cowley, perhaps, upon the whole, has had a reputation more above his deserts than any English poet; yet it is very easy to perceive that some who wrote better than he did not possess so fine a genius. Johnson has written the life of Cowley with peculiar care; and as his summary of the poet's character is more favourable than my own, it may be candid to insert it in this place, as at least very discriminating, elaborate, and well expressed.

42. ' It may be affirmed, without any encomiastic fervour, that he brought to his poetic labours a mind replete [Johnson's character of him.] with learning, and that his pages are embellished with all the ornaments which books could supply; that he was the first who imparted to English numbers the enthusiasm of the greater ode, and the gaiety of the less;[c] that he was equally qualified for sprightly sallies and for lofty flights; that he was among those who freed translation from

---

[c] Was not Milton's Ode on the Nativity written as early as any of Cowley's? And would Johnson have thought Cowley superior in gaiety to Sir John Suckling?

servility, and instead of following his author at a distance, walked by his side; and that, if he left versification yet improvable, he left likewise, from time to time, such specimens of excellence as enabled succeeding poets to improve it.'

43. The poets of historical or fabulous narrative belong to Narrative another class. Of these the earliest is Daniel, whose poets. Daniel. minor poems fall partly within the sixteenth century. His history of the Civil Wars between York and Lancaster, a poem in eight books, was published in 1604. Faithfully adhering to truth, which he does not suffer so much as an ornamental episode to interrupt, and equally studious to avoid the bolder figures of poetry, it is not surprising that Daniel should be little read. It is, indeed, certain that much Italian and Spanish poetry, even by those whose name has once stood rather high, depends chiefly upon merits which he abundantly possesses, a smoothness of rhythm, and a lucid narration in simple language. But that which from the natural delight in sweet sound is enough to content the ear in the southern tongues, will always seem bald and tame in our less harmonious verse. It is the chief praise of Daniel, and must have contributed to what popularity he enjoyed in his own age, that his English is eminently pure, free from affectation of archaism and from pedantic innovation, with very little that is now obsolete. Both in prose and in poetry, he is, as to language, among the best writers of his time, and wanted but a greater confidence in his own power, or, to speak less indulgently, a greater share of it, to sustain his correct taste, calm sense, and moral feeling.

44. Next to Daniel in time, and much above him in reach Drayton's of mind, we place Michael Drayton, whose ' Barons' Polyolbion. Wars ' have been mentioned under the preceding period, but whose more famous work was published partly in 1613, and partly in 1622. Drayton's Polyolbion is a poem of about 30,000 lines in length, written in Alexandrine couplets, a measure from its monotony, and perhaps from its frequency in doggerel ballads, not at all pleasing to the ear. It contains a topographical description of England, illustrated with a prodigality of historical and legendary erudition. Such a poem is essentially designed to instruct, and speaks to the understanding more than to the fancy. The powers

displayed in it are, however, of a high cast. It has generally been a difficulty with poets to deal with a necessary enumeration of proper names. The catalogue of ships is not the most delightful part of the Iliad, and Ariosto never encountered such a roll of persons or places without sinking into the tamest insipidity. Virgil is splendidly beautiful upon similar occasions; but his decorative elegance could not be preserved, nor would continue to please, in a poem that kept up through a great length the effort to furnish instruction. The style of Drayton is sustained, with extraordinary ability, on an equable line, from which he seldom much deviates, neither brilliant nor prosaic; few or no passages could be marked as impressive, but few are languid or mean. The language is clear, strong, various, and sufficiently figurative; the stories and fictions interspersed, as well as the general spirit and liveliness, relieve the heaviness incident to topographical description. There is probably no poem of this kind in any other language, comparable together in extent and excellence to the 'Polyolbion;' nor can any one read a portion of it without admiration for its learned and highly-gifted author. Yet, perhaps, no English poem, known as well by name, is so little known beyond its name; for while its immense length deters the common reader, it affords, as has just been hinted, no great harvest for selection, and would be judged very unfairly by partial extracts. It must be owned, also, that geography and antiquities may, in modern times, be taught better in prose than in verse; yet, whoever consults the 'Polyolbion' for such objects, will probably be repaid by petty knowledge which he may not have found anywhere else.

45. Among these historical poets I should incline to class William Browne, author of a poem with the quaint title of Britannia's Pastorals, though his story, one of little interest, seems to have been invented by himself. Browne, indeed, is of no distinct school among the writers of that age; he seems to recognise Spenser as h⸗ master, but his own manner is more to be traced among later than earlier poets. He was a native of Devonshire; and his principal poem, above mentioned, relating partly to the local scenery of that county, was printed in 1613. Browne is truly a poet, full of

imagination, grace, and sweetness, though not very nervous or rapid. I know not why Headley, favourable enough for the most part to this generation of the sons of song, has spoken of Browne with unfair contempt. Justice, however, has been done to him by later critics.[f] But I have not observed that they take notice of what is remarkable in the history of our poetical literature, that Browne is an early model of ease and variety in the regular couplet. Many passages in his unequal poem are hardly excelled in this respect, by the fables of Dryden. It is manifest that Milton was well acquainted with the writings of Browne.

46. The commendation of improving the rhythm of the couplet is due also to Sir John Beaumont, author of a short poem on the battle of Bosworth Field. It was not written, however, so early as the Britannia's Pastorals of Browne. In other respects it has no pretensions to a high rank. But it may be added that a poem of Drummond on the visit of James I. to Scotland in 1617 is perfectly harmonious; and what is very remarkable in that age, he concludes the verse at every couplet with the regularity of Pope.

Sir John Beaumont.

47. Far unlike the poem of Browne was Gondibert, published by Sir William Davenant in 1650. It may probably have been reckoned by himself an epic; but in that age the practice of Spain and Italy had effaced the distinction between the regular epic and the heroic romance. Gondibert belongs rather to the latter class by the entire want of truth in the story, though the scene is laid at the court of the Lombard kings, by the deficiency of unity in the action, by the intricacy of the events, and by the resources of the fable, which are sometimes too much in the style of comic fiction. It is so imperfect, only two books and part of the third being completed, that we can hardly judge of the termination it was to receive. Each book, however, after

Davenant's Gondibert.

---

[f] 'Browne,' Mr. Southey says, ' is a poet who produced no slight effect upon his contemporaries. George Wither in his happiest pieces has learned the manner of his friend, and Milton may be traced to him. And in our days his peculiarities have been caught and his beauties imitated, by men who will themselves find admirers and imitators hereafter.' ' His poetry,' Mr. Campbell, a far less indulgent judge of the older bards, observes, 'is not without beauty; but it is the beauty of mere landscape and allegory, without the manners and passions that constitute human interest.' Specimens of English Poetry, iv. 323.

the manner of Spenser, is divided into several cantos. It contains about 6,000 lines. The metre is the four-lined stanza of alternate rhymes; one capable of great vigour, but not perhaps well adapted to poetry of imagination or of passion. These, however, Davenant exhibits but sparingly in Gondibert; they are replaced by a philosophical spirit, in the tone of Sir John Davies, who had adopted the same metre, and, as some have thought, nourished by the author's friendly intercourse with Hobbes. Gondibert is written in a clear, nervous English style; its condensation produces some obscurity, but pedantry, at least that of language, will rarely be found in it; and Davenant is less infected by the love of conceit and of extravagance than his contemporaries, though I would not assert that he is wholly exempt from the former blemish. But the chief praise of Gondibert is due to masculine verse in a good metrical cadence; for the sake of which we may forgive the absence of interest in the story, and even of those glowing words and breathing thoughts which are the soul of genuine poetry. Gondibert is very little read; yet it is better worth reading than the Purple Island, though it may have less of that which distinguishes a poet from another man.

48. The sonnets of Shakspeare, for we now come to the minor, that is the shorter and more lyric, poetry of Sonnets of the age, were published in 1609, in a manner as Shakspeare. mysterious as their subject and contents. They are dedicated by an editor (Thomas Thorpe, a bookseller) 'to Mr. W. H., the only begetter of these sonnets.' [g] No one, as far as I remember, has ever doubted their genuineness; no one can doubt that they express not only real but intense emotions of the heart; but when they were written, who was the W. H. quaintly called their begetter, by which we can only understand the cause of their being written, and to what persons or circumstances they allude, has of late years been

---

[g] The precise words of the dedication are the following :—

To the only Begetter
Of these ensuing Sonnets,
　　Mr. W. H.
　　All happiness
And that eternity promised
By our ever living poet

Wisheth the
Well-wishing Adventurer
In setting forth.
　　T. T.

The title-page runs : Shakspeare's Sonnets, never before imprinted, 4to. 1609, G. Eld for T. T.

the subject of much curiosity.   These sonnets were long
overlooked; Steevens spoke of them with the utmost scorn,
as productions which no one could read; but a very different
suffrage is generally given by the lovers of poetry, and perhaps there is now a tendency, especially among young men
of poetical tempers, to exaggerate the beauties of these remarkable productions.   They rise, indeed, in estimation, as
we attentively read and reflect upon them; for I do not think
that at first they give us much pleasure.   No one ever
entered more fully than Shakspeare into the character of
this species of poetry, which admits of no expletive imagery,
no merely ornamental line.   But though each sonnet has
generally its proper unity, the sense, I do not mean the
grammatical construction, will sometimes be found to spread
from one to another, independently of that repetition of the
leading idea, like variations of an air, which a series of them
frequently exhibits, and on account of which they have
latterly been reckoned by some rather an integral poem than
a collection of sonnets.   But this is not uncommon among
the Italians, and belongs, in fact, to those of Petrarch himself.   They may easily be resolved into several series according
to their subjects;[h] but when read attentively, we find them
relate to one definite, though obscure, period of the poet's
life; in which an attachment to some female, which seems
to have touched neither his heart nor his fancy very sensibly,
was overpowered, without entirely ceasing, by one to a
friend; and this last is of such an enthusiastic character,
and so extravagant in the phrases that the author uses, as to
have thrown an unaccountable mystery over the whole work.
It is true that in the poetry as well as in the fictions of early
ages we find a more ardent tone of affection in the language of
friendship than has since been usual; and yet no instance has
been adduced of such rapturous devotedness, such an idolatry
of admiring love, as one of the greatest beings whom nature

---

[h] This has been done in a late publication, 'Shakspeare's Auto-biographical
Poems, by George Armitage Brown'
(1838).   It might have occurred to any
attentive reader, but I do not know that
the analysis was ever so completely
made before, though almost every one
has been aware that different persons
are addressed in the former and latter
part of the sonnets.   Mr. Brown's work
did not fall into my hands till nearly the
time that these sheets passed through
the press, which I mention on account
of some coincidences of opinion, especially as to Shakspeare's knowledge of
Latin.

ever produced in human form pours forth to some unknown youth in the majority of these sonnets.

49.   The notion that a woman was their general object is totally untenable, and it is strange that Cole- The person whom they ridge should have entertained it.[i]   Those that address. were evidently addressed to a woman, the person above hinted, are by much the smaller part of the whole, but twenty-eight out of one hundred and fifty-four.   And this mysterious Mr. W. H. must be presumed to be the idolised friend of Shakespeare.   But who could he be? No one recorded as such in literary history or anecdote answers the description.   But if we seize a clue which innumerable passages give us, and suppose that they allude to a youth of high rank as well as personal beauty and accomplishment, in whose favour and intimacy, according to the base prejudices of the world, a player and a poet, though he were the author of Macbeth, might be thought honoured, something of the strangeness, as it appears to us, of Shakespeare's humiliation in addressing him as a being before whose feet he crouched, whose frown he feared, whose injuries, and those of the most insulting kind, the seduction of the mistress to whom we have alluded, he felt and bewailed without resenting; something, I say, of the strangeness of this humiliation, and at best it is but little, may be lightened and in a certain sense rendered intelligible.   And it has been ingeniously conjectured within a few years by inquirers independent of each other, that William Herbert, Earl of Pembroke, born in 1580, and afterwards a man of noble and gallant character, though always of a licentious life, was shadowed under the initials of Mr. W. H.   This hypothesis is not strictly proved, but sufficiently so, in my opinion, to demand our assent.[k]

---

[i] 'It seems to me that the sonnets could only have come from a man deeply in love, and in love with a woman; and there is one sonnet which from its incongruity I take to be a purposed blind.' Table Talk, vol. ii. p. 180. This sonnet the editor supposes to be the twentieth, which certainly could not have been addressed to a woman; but the proof is equally strong as to most of the rest. Coleridge's opinion is absolutely untenable; nor do I conceive that any one else is likely to maintain it after reading the sonnets of Shakspeare; but to those who have not done this, the authority may justly seem imposing.

[k] In the Gentleman's Magazine for 1832, p 217 et post, it will be seen that this occurred both to Mr. Boaden and Mr. Heywood Bright.   And it does not

50. Notwithstanding the frequent beauties of these sonnets, the pleasure of their perusal is greatly diminished by
these circumstances; and it is impossible not to wish that
Shakespeare had never written them. There is a weakness
and folly in all excessive and misplaced affection, which is
not redeemed by the touches of nobler sentiments that abound
in this long series of sonnets. But there are also faults of a
merely critical nature. The obscurity is often such as only
conjecture can penetrate; the strain of tenderness and adora-
tion would be too monotonous, were it less unpleasing; and
so many frigid conceits are scattered around, that we might
almost fancy the poet to have written without genuine
emotion, did not such a host of other passages attest the
contrary.

51. The sonnets of Drummond of Hawthornden, the most
Sonnets of celebrated in that class of poets, have obtained, pro-
Drummond
and others. bably, as much praise as they deserve.[m] But they
are polished and elegant, free from conceit and bad taste, in

---

appear that Mr. Brown, author of the
work above quoted, had any knowledge
of their priority.

Drake has fixed on Lord Southampton
as the object of these sonnets, induced
probably by the tradition of his friendship with Shakspeare, and by the latter's
having dedicated to him his Venus and
Adonis, as well as by what is remarkable on the face of the series of sonnets,
that Shakspeare looked up to his friend
'with reverence and homage.'   But,
unfortunately, this was only the reverence and homage of an inferior to one
of high rank, and not such as the virtues of Southampton might have challenged. Proofs of the low moral character of 'Mr. W. H.' are continual.
It was also impossible that Lord Southampton could be called 'beauteous and
lovely youth,' or 'sweet boy.'   Mrs.
Jameson, in her 'Loves of the Poets,'
has adopted the same hypothesis, but is
forced in consequence to suppose some
of the earlier sonnets to be addressed to
a woman.

Pembroke succeeded to his father in
1601: I incline to think that the sonnets were written about that time, some
probably earlier, some later. That they
were the same as Meres, in 1598, has
mentioned among the compositions of
Shakspeare ' his sugred sonnets among

his private friends,' I do not believe,
both on account of the date, and from
the peculiarly personal allusions they
contain.

[Much has been written lately on the
subject of Shakspeare's sonnets, and a
natural reluctance to admit any failings
in such a man has led some to fancy
that his mistress was no other than his
wife, Ann Hathaway, and others to
conjecture that he lent his pen to the
amours of a friend. But I have seen no
ground to alter my own view of the
case; except that possibly some other
sonnets may have been meant by Meres.
—1842.]

[m] I concur in this with Mr. Campbell,
iv. 343. Mr. Southey thinks Drummond
'has deserved the high reputation he
has obtained;' which seems to say the
same thing, but is in fact different.
He observes that Drummond ' frequently borrows and sometimes trans-
lates from the Italian and Spanish
poets.' Southey's British poets, p. 798.
The furious invective of Gifford against
Drummond for having written private
memoranda of his conversations with Ben
Jonson, which he did not publish, and
which, for aught we know, were perfectly faithful, is absurd. Any one else
would have been thankful for so much
literary anecdote.

pure unblemished English; some are pathetic or tender in sentiment, and if they do not show much originality, at least would have acquired a fair place among the Italians of the sixteenth century. Those of Daniel, of Drayton, and of Sir William Alexander, afterwards Earl of Stirling, are perhaps hardly inferior. Some may doubt, however, whether the last poet should be placed on such a level.[n] But the difficulty of finding the necessary rhymes in our language has caused most who have attempted the sonnet to swerve from laws which cannot be transgressed, at least to the degree they have often dared, without losing the unity for which that complex mechanism was contrived. Certainly three quatrains of alternate rhymes, succeeded by a couplet, which Drummond, like many other English poets, has sometimes given us, is the very worst form of the sonnet, even if, in deference to a scanty number of Italian precedents, we allow it to pass as a sonnet at all.[o] We possess indeed noble poetry in the form of sonnet; yet with us it seems more fitted for grave than amatory composition; in the latter we miss the facility and grace of our native English measures, the song, the madrigal, or the ballad.

---

[n] Lord Stirling is rather monotonous, as sonnetteers usually are, and he addresses his mistress by the appellation 'Fair tygress.' Campbell observes that there is elegance of expression in a few of Stirling's shorter pieces. Vol. iv. p. 206. The longest poem of Stirling is entitled Domesday, in twelve books, or, as he calls them, hours. It is written in the Italian octave stanza, and has somewhat of the condensed style of the philosophical school, which he seems to have imitated, but his numbers are harsh.

[o] The legitimate sonnet consists of two quatrains and two tercets; as much skill, to say the least, is required for the management of the latter as of the former. The rhymes of the last six lines are capable of many arrangements; but by far the worst, and also the least common in Italy, is that we usually adopt, the fifth and sixth rhyming together, frequently after a full pause, so that the sonnet ends with the point of an epigram. The best form, as the Italians hold, is the rhyming together of the three uneven, and the three even lines, but as our language is less rich in consonant terminations, there can be no objection to what has abundant precedents even in theirs, the rhyming of the first and fourth, second and fifth, third and sixth, lines. This, with a break in the sense at the third line, will make a real sonnet, which Shakspeare, Milton, Bowles, and Wordsworth, have often failed to give us, even where they have given us something good instead.

[The common form of the Italian sonnet is called *rima chiusa;* where the rhymes of the two quatrains are 1, 4, 5, 8—2, 3, 6, 7; but the alternate rhyme sometimes, though less regularly, occurs. The tercets are either in *rima incatenata*, or *rima alternata;* and great variety is found in these, even among the early poets. Quadrio prefers the order a, b, a, b, a, b, where there are only two rhyming terminations; but does not object to a, b, c, a, b, c; or even a, b, c, b, a, c. The couplet termination he entirely condemns. Quadrio, Storia d' ogni poesia, iii. 25.—1842.]

52.   Carew is the most celebrated among the lighter poets,
though no collection has hitherto embraced his entire
writings.   Headley has said, and Ellis echoes the
praise, that 'Carew has the ease without the pedantry of
Waller, and perhaps less conceit.   Waller is too exclusively
considered as the first man who brought versification to anything like its present standard.   Carew's pretensions to the
same merit are seldom sufficiently either considered or
allowed.'   Yet, in point of versification, others of the same
age seem to have surpassed Carew, whose lines are often very
harmonious, but not so artfully constructed or so uniformly
pleasing as those of Waller.   He is remarkably unequal; the
best of his little poems (none of more than thirty lines are good)
excel all of his time ; but, after a few lines of great beauty,
we often come to some ill-expressed, or obscure, or weak, or
inharmonious passage.   Few will hesitate to acknowledge
that he has more fancy and more tenderness than Waller,
but less choice, less judgment and knowledge where to stop,
less of the equability which never offends, less attention to
the unity and thread of his little pieces.   I should hesitate
to give him, on the whole, the preference as a poet, taking
collectively the attributes of that character ; for we must not,
in such a comparison, overlook a good deal of very inferior
merit which may be found in the short volume of Carew's
poems.   The best have great beauty, but he has had in late
criticism, his full share of applause.   Two of his most pleasing
little poems appear also among those of Herrick ; and as
Carew's were, I believe, published posthumously, I am rather
inclined to prefer the claim of the other poet, independently
of some internal evidence as to one of them.   In all ages
these very short compositions circulate for a time in polished
society, while mistakes as to the real author are natural.[p]

---

[p] One of these poems begins—

Amongst the myrtles as I walk'd,
Love and my sighs thus intertalk'd.

Herrick wants four good lines which are
in Carew; and as they are rather more
likely to have been interpolated than
left out, this leads to a sort of inference
that he was the original ; there are also
some other petty improvements.   The
second poem is that beginning—

Ask me why I send you here
This firstling of the infant year.

Herrick gives the second line strangely,

This sweet infanta of the year,

which is little else than nonsense ; and
all the other variations are for the worse.
I must leave it in doubt, whether he
borrowed, and disfigured a little, or was
himself improved upon.   I must own
that he has a trick of spoiling what he

53. The minor poetry of Ben Jonson is extremely beautiful. This is partly mixed with his masques and
Ben Jonson.
interludes, poetical and musical rather than dramatic pieces, and intended to gratify the imagination by the
charms of song, as well as by the varied scenes that were
brought before the eye; partly in very short effusions of a
single sentiment, among which two epitaphs are known by
heart. Jonson possessed an admirable taste and feeling in
poetry, which his dramas, except the Sad Shepherd, do not
entirely lead us to value highly enough; and when we consider how many other intellectual excellences distinguished
him, wit, observation, judgment, memory, learning, we must
acknowledge that the inscription on his tomb, O rare Ben
Jonson! is not more pithy than it is true.

54. George Wither, by siding with the less poetical,
though more prosperous party in the civil war, and
Wither.
by a profusion of temporary writings to serve the
ends of faction and folly, has left a name which we were
accustomed to despise, till Ellis did justice to 'that playful
fancy, pure taste, and artless delicacy of sentiment which
distinguish the poetry of his early youth.' His best poems
were published in 1622 with the title ' Mistress of Philarete.'
Some of them are highly beautiful, and bespeak a mind
above the grovelling puritanism into which he afterwards
fell. I think there is hardly anything in our lyric poetry of
this period equal to Wither's lines on his Muse, published
by Ellis.[q]

55. The poetry of Habington is that of a pure and amiable
mind, turned to versification by the custom of
Habington.
the age, during a real passion for a lady of birth
and virtue, the Castara whom he afterwards married; but
it displays no great original power, nor is it by any means
exempt from the ordinary blemishes of hyperbolical compliment and far-fetched imagery. The poems of
Earl of
Pembroke.
William Earl of Pembroke, long known by the

---

takes. Suckling has an incomparable
image, on a lady dancing—

　Her feet beneath the petticoat,
　Like little mice, stole in and out,
　　As if they feared the light—

Herrick has it thus—

Her pretty feet, *like snails*, did creep
　A little out;

a most singular parallel for an elegant
dancer.

　[q] Ellis's Specimens of Early English
Poets, iii. 96.

character drawn for him by Clarendon, and now as the
object of Shakspeare's doting friendship, were ushered into
the world after his death, with a letter of extravagant flattery
addressed by Donne to Christiana, Countess of Devonshire.[r]
But there is little reliance to be placed on the freedom from
interpolation of these posthumous editions. Among these
poems attributed to Lord Pembroke, we find one of the best
known of Carew's,[s] and even the famous lines addressed to
the Soul which some have given to Silvester. The poems, in
general, are of little merit; some are grossly indecent; nor
would they be mentioned here except for the interest recently
attached to the author's name. But they throw no light
whatever on the sonnets of Shakespeare.

56. Sir John Suckling is acknowledged to have left far
behind him all former writers of song in gaiety and
ease; it is not equally clear that he has ever since
been surpassed. His poetry aims at no higher praise; he
shows no sentiment or imagination, either because he had
them not, or because he did not require either in the style
he chose. Perhaps the Italians may have poetry in that
style equal to Suckling's; I do not know that they have, nor
do I believe that there is any in French; that there is none
in Latin I am convinced.[t] Lovelace is chiefly
known by a single song; his other poetry is much
inferior; and indeed it may be generally remarked that the
flowers of our early verse, both in the Elizabethan and the
subsequent age, have been well culled by good taste and a
friendly spirit of selection. We must not judge of them, or
shall judge of them very favourably, by the extracts of
Headley or Ellis.

Suckling.

Lovelace.

57. The most amorous, and among the best of our amorous
poets, was Robert Herrick, a clergyman ejected
from his living in Devonshire by the Long Parliament, whose 'Hesperides, or Poems Human and Divine,'
were published in 1648. Herrick's divine poems are, of

Herrick.

---

[r] The only edition that I have seen,
or that I find mentioned, of Lord Pembroke's poems, is in 1660. But as
Donne died in 1631, I conceive that
there must be one of earlier date. The
Countess of Devonshire is not called
dowager; her husband died in 1643.

[s] Ask me no more whither do stray
The golden atoms of the day.

[t] Suckling's Epithalamium, though
not written for those 'Qui musas co-
litis severiores,' has been read by almost
all the world, and is a matchless piece
of liveliness and facility.

course, such as might be presumed by their title and by his calling; of his human, which are poetically much superior, and probably written in early life, the greater portion is light and voluptuous, while some border on the licentious and indecent. A selection was published in 1815, by which, as commonly happens, the poetical fame of Herrick does not suffer; a number of dull epigrams are omitted, and the editor has a manifest preference for what must be owned to be the most elegant and attractive part of his author's rhymes. He has much of the lively grace that distinguishes Anacreon and Catullus, and approaches also, with a less cloying monotony, to the Basia of Joannes Secundus. Herrick has as much variety as the poetry of kisses can well have; but his love is in a very slight degree that of sentiment, or even any intense passion; his mistresses have little to recommend them, even in his own eyes, save their beauties, and none of these are omitted in his catalogues. Yet he is abundant in the resources of verse; without the exuberant gaiety of Suckling, or perhaps the delicacy of Carew, he is sportive, fanciful, and generally of polished language. The faults of his age are sometimes apparent; though he is not often obscure, he runs, more perhaps for the sake of variety than any other cause, into occasional pedantry; he has his conceits and false thoughts, but these are more than redeemed by the numerous very little poems (for those of Herrick are frequently not longer than epigrams), which may be praised without much more qualification than belongs to such poetry.

58. John Milton was born in 1609. Few are ignorant of his life, in recovering and recording every circumstance of which no diligence has been spared, nor Milton. has it often been unsuccessful. Of his Latin poetry some was written at the age of seventeen; in English we have nothing, I believe, the date of which is known to be earlier than the sonnet on entering his twenty-third year. In 1634 he wrote Comus, which was published in 1637. Lycidas was written in the latter year, and most of his shorter pieces soon afterwards, except the sonnets, some of which do not come within the first half of the century.

59. Comus was sufficient to convince any one of taste

and feeling that a great poet had arisen in England, and
one partly formed in a different school from his
contemporaries.   Many of them had produced
highly beautiful and imaginative passages; but none had
evinced so classical a judgment, none had aspired to so
regular a perfection.   Jonson had learned much from the
ancients; but there was a grace in their best models which
he did not quite attain.   Neither his Sad Shepherd nor the
Faithful Shepherdess of Fletcher have the elegance or
dignity of Comus.   A noble virgin and her young brothers,
by whom this masque was originally represented, required
an elevation, a purity, a sort of severity of sentiment, which
no one in that age could have given but Milton.   He
avoided, and nothing loth, the more festive notes which
dramatic poetry was wont to mingle with its serious strain.
But for this he compensated by the brightest hues of fancy
and the sweetest melody of song.   In Comus we find nothing
prosaic or feeble, no false taste in the incidents, and not
much in the language, nothing over which we should desire
to pass on a second perusal.   The want of what we may
call personality, none of the characters having names, except Comus himself, who is a very indefinite being, and the
absence of all positive attributes of time and place, enhance
the ideality of the fiction by a certain indistinctness not unpleasing to the imagination.

His Comus.

60. It has been said, I think very fairly, that Lycidas is a
good test of a real feeling for what is peculiarly
called poetry.   Many, or perhaps we might say,
most readers, do not taste its excellence; nor does it follow
that they may not greatly admire Pope and Dryden, or even
Virgil and Homer.   It is, however, somewhat remarkable
that Johnson, who has committed his critical reputation by
the most contemptuous depreciation of this poem, had in an
earlier part of his life selected the tenth eclogue of Virgil for
peculiar praise; [u] the tenth eclogue, which, beautiful as it is,
belongs to the same class of pastoral and personal allegory,
and requires the same sacrifice of reasoning criticism as the
Lycidas itself.   In the age of Milton the poetical world had

Lycidas.

---

[u] Adventurer, No. 92.

been accustomed by the Italian and Spanish writers to a
more abundant use of allegory than has been pleasing to their
posterity; but Lycidas is not so much in the nature of an
allegory as of a masque : the characters pass before our eyes
in imagination, as on the stage; they are chiefly mythological, but not creations of the poet. Our sympathy with
the fate of Lycidas may not be much stronger than for the
desertion of Gallus by his mistress; but many poems will
yield an exquisite pleasure to the imagination that produce
no emotion in the heart; or none at least except through
associations independent of the subject.

61. The introduction of St. Peter after the fabulous deities
of the sea has appeared an incongruity deserving of censure
to some admirers of this poem.   It would be very reluctantly
that we could abandon to this criticism the most splendid
passage it presents. But the censure rests, as I think, on
too narrow a principle. In narrative or dramatic poetry,
where something like illusion or momentary belief is to be
produced, the mind requires an objective possibility, a capacity of real existence, not only in all the separate portions of
the imagined story, but in their coherency and relation to a
common whole. Whatever is obviously incongrous, whatever shocks our previous knowledge of possibility, destroys
to a certain extent that acquiescence in the fiction, which it
is the true business of the fiction to produce. But the case
is not the same in such poems as Lycidas. They pretend to
no credibility, they aim at no illusion ; they are read with the
willing abandonment of the imagination to a waking dream,
and require only that general possibility, that combination
of images which common experience does not reject as incompatible, without which the fancy of the poet would be only
like that of the lunatic. And it had been so usual to blend
sacred with mythological personages in allegory, that no
one probably in Milton's age would have been struck by the
objection.

62. The Allegro and Penseroso are perhaps more familiar
to us than any part of the writings of Milton. They *Allegro and*
satisfy the critics, and they delight mankind. The *Penseroso.*
choice of images is so judicious, their succession so rapid, the
allusions are so various and pleasing, the leading distinction

of the poems is so felicitously maintained, the versification is so animated, that we may place them at the head of that long series of descriptive poems which our language has to boast. It may be added, as in the greater part of Milton's writings, that they are sustained at an uniform pitch, with few blemishes of expression and scarce any feebleness; a striking contrast, in this respect, to all the contemporaneous poetry, except perhaps that of Waller. Johnson has thought that, while there is no mirth in his melancholy, he can detect some melancholy in his mirth. This seems to be too strongly put; but it may be said that his Allegro is rather cheerful than gay, and that even his cheerfulness is not always without effort. In these poems he is indebted to Fletcher, to Burton, to Browne, to Wither, and probably to more of our early versifiers; for he was a great collector of sweets from those wild flowers.

63. The Ode on the Nativity, far less popular than most of the poetry of Milton, is perhaps the finest in the English language. A grandeur, a simplicity, a breadth of manner, an imagination at once elevated and restrained by the subject, reign throughout it. If Pindar is a model of lyric poetry, it would be hard to name any other ode so truly Pindaric; but more has naturally been derived from the Scriptures. Of the other short poems, that on the death of the Marchioness of Winchester deserves particular mention. It is pity that the first lines are bad, and the last much worse; for rarely can we find more feeling or beauty than in some other passages.

Ode on the Nativity.

64. The sonnets of Milton have obtained of late years the admiration of all real lovers of poetry. Johnson has been as impotent to fix the public taste in this instance as in his other criticisms on the smaller poems of the author of Paradise Lost. These sonnets are indeed unequal; the expression is sometimes harsh, and sometimes obscure; sometimes too much of pedantic allusion interferes with the sentiment, nor am I reconciled to his frequent deviations from the best Italian structure. But such blemishes are lost in the majestic simplicity, the holy calm, that ennoble many of these short compositions.

His Sonnets.

65. Many anonymous songs, many popular lays, both of

Scottish and English minstrelsy, were poured forth in this period of the seventeenth century. Those of Scotland became, after the union of the crowns, and the consequent cessation of rude border frays, less warlike than before; they are still, however, imaginative, pathetic, and natural. It is probable that the best even of this class are a little older; but their date is seldom determinable with much precision. The same may be said of the English ballads, which, so far as of a merely popular nature, appear, by their style and other circumstances, to belong more frequently to the reign of James I. than any other period.

Anonymous poetry.

Sect. VI.—On Latin Poetry.

Latin Poets of France—And other Countries—Of England—May—Milton.

66. FRANCE, in the latter part of the sixteenth century, had been remarkably fruitful of Latin poetry; it was the pride of her scholars, and sometimes of her statesmen. In the age that we have now in review we do not find so many conspicuous names; but the custom of academical institutions, and especially of the seminaries conducted by the Jesuits, kept up a facility of Latin versification, which it was by no means held pedantic or ridiculous to exhibit in riper years. The French enumerate several with praise: Guijon, Bourbon (Borbonius), whom some have compared with the best of the preceding century, and among whose poems that on the death of Henry IV. is reckoned the best; Cerisantes, equal, as some of his admirers think, to Sarbievius, and superior, as others presume, to Horace; and Petavius, who having solaced his leisure hours with Greek and Hebrew, as well as Latin versification, has obtained in the last the general suffrage of critics.[x] I can speak of none

Latin poets of France.

---

[x] Baillet, Jugemens des Sçavans, has criticised all these and several more. Rapin's opinion on Latin poetry is entitled to much regard from his own excellence in it. He praises three lyrists, Casimir, Magdelenet, and Cerisantes; the two latter being French. Sarbieuski a de l'élévation mais sans pureté; Magdelenet est pur mais sans élévation. Cerisantes a joint dans ses odes l'un et l'autre; car il écrit noblement, et d'un style assez pur. Après tout, il n'a pas tant de feu que Casimir, lequel avoit bien de l'esprit, et de cet esprit heureux

of these from direct knowledge, except of Borbonius, whose
Diræ on the death of Henry have not appeared to my judgment deserving of so much eulogy.

67. The Germans wrote much in Latin, especially in the
In Germany earlier decads of this period. Melissus Schedius,
and Italy. not undistinguished in his native tongue, might
have been mentioned as a Latin poet in the last volume,
since most of his compositions were published in the sixteenth century. In Italy we have not many conspicuous
names. The bad taste that infested the school of Marini
spread also, according to Tiraboschi, over Latin poetry.
Martial, Lucan, and Claudian became in their eyes better
models than Catullus and Virgil. Baillet, or rather those
whom he copies, and among whom Rossi, author of the
Pinacotheca Virorum illustrium, under the name of Ery-
thræus, a profuse and indiscriminating panegyrist, for the
most part, of his contemporaries, furnishes the chief materials, bestows praise on Cesarini, on Querenghi, whom even
Tiraboschi selects from the crowd, and on Maffei Barberini,
best known as Pope Urban VIII.

68. Holland stood at the head of Europe in this line of
In Holland. poetry. Grotius has had the reputation of writing
Heinsius. with spirit, elegance, and imagination.[y] But he is
excelled by Heinsius, whose elegies, still more than his
hexameters, may be ranked high in modern Latin. The
habit, however, of classical imitation has so much weakened
all individual originality in these versifiers, that it is often
difficult to distinguish them, or to pronounce of any twenty
lines that they might not have been written by some other
author. Compare, for example, the elegies of Buchanan
with those of Heinsius, wherever there are no proper names
to guide us; a more finished and continued elegance belongs,
on the whole (as at least I should say), to the latter, but in

---

qui fait les poètes. Bucanan a des odes
dignes de l'antiquité, mais il a de grandes
inégalités par le mélange de son caractère
qui n'est pas assez uni. Réflexions sur
la Poëtique, p. 208.

[y] [The Adamus Exul of Grotius, which,
after going through several editions in
Holland before the middle of the 17th

century, has lately been retranslated by
Mr. Barham, is not only of considerable
poetical merit, but deserving of notice,
as having suggested much to Milton.
Lauder perceived this, but was strangely
led to exaggerate the resemblance by
forgery.—1847.]

a short passage this may not be perceptible, and I believe few would guess with much confidence between the two. Heinsius, however, like most of the Dutch, is remarkably fond of a polysyllabic close in the pentameter; at least in his Juvenilia, which, notwithstanding their title, are perhaps better than his later productions. As it is not necessary to make a distinct head for the Latin drama, we may here advert to a tragedy by Heinsius, Herodes Infanticida. This has been the subject of a critique by Balzac, for the most part very favourable; and it certainly contains some highly beautiful passages. Perhaps the description of the Virgin's feelings on the nativity, though praised by Balzac, and exquisitely classical in diction, is not quite in the best taste.[z]

69. Sidonius Hoschius, a Flemish Jesuit, is extolled by Baillet and his authorities. But another of the same order, Casimir Sarbievius, a Pole, is far better known, and, in lyric poetry, which he almost exclusively cultivated, obtained a much higher reputation. He had lived some years at Rome, and is full of Roman allusion. He had read Horace, as Sannazarius had Virgil, and Heinsius Ovid, till the style and tone became spontaneous; but he has more of centonism than the other two. Yet while he constantly reminds us of Horace, it is with as constant an inferiority; we feel that his Rome was not the same Rome, that Urban VIII. was not Augustus, nor the Polish victories on the Danube like those of the sons of Livia. Hence his flattery of the great, though not a step beyond that of his master, seems rather more displeasing, because we have it only on his word that they were truly great. Sarbievius seldom rises high or pours out an original feeling; but he is free from conceits, never becomes prosaic, and knows how to put in good language the common-places with which his

Casimir
Sarbievius.

---

[z] Oculosque nunc huc pavida nunc illuc jacit,
Interque matrem virginemque hærent adhuc
Suspensa matris gaudia, ac trepidus pudor.
* * * sæpe, cum blandas puer,
Aut a sopore languidas jactat manus,
Tenerisque labris pectus intactum petit,
Virginea subitus ora perfundit rubor,
Laudemque matris virginis crimen putat.

A critique on the poems of Heinsius will be found in the Retrospective Review, vol. i. p. 49; but notwithstanding the laudatory spirit, which is for the most part too indiscriminating in that publication, the reviewer has not done justice to Heinsius, and hardly seems, perhaps, a very competent judge of Latin verse. The suffrages of those who were so, in favour of this Batavian poet, are collected by Baillet, n. 1482.

subject happens to furnish him. He is, to a certain degree, in Latin poetry what Chiabrera is in Italian, but does not deserve so high a place. Sarbievius was perhaps the first who succeeded much in the Alcaic stanza, which the earlier poets seemed to avoid, or to use unskilfully. But he has many unwarrantable licenses in his metre, and even false quantities, as is common to the great majority of these Latin versifiers.

70. Gaspar Barlæus had as high a name, perhaps, as any Latin poet of this age. His rhythm is indeed excellent, but if he ever rises to other excellence, I have not lighted on the passages. A greater equality I have never found than in Barlæus ; nothing is bad, nothing is striking. It was the practice with Dutchmen on their marriage to purchase epithalamiums in hexameter verse ; and the muse of Barlæus was in request. These nuptial songs are of course about Peleus and Thetis, or similar personages, interspersed with fitting praises of the bride and bridegroom. Such poetry is not likely to rise high. The epicedia, or funeral lamentations, paid for by the heir, are little, if at all, better than the epithalamia ; and the panegyrical effusions on public or private events rather worse. The elegies of Barlæus, as we generally find, are superior to the hexameters ; he has here the same smoothness of versification, and a graceful gaiety which gives us pleasure. In some of his elegies and epistles he counterfeits the Ovidian style extremely well, so that they might pass for those of his model. Still there is an equability, a recurrence of trivial thoughts and forms, which in truth is too much characteristic of modern Latin to be a reproach to Barlæus. He uses the polysyllabic termination less than earlier Dutch poets. One of the epithalamia of Barlæus, it may be observed before we leave him, is entitled Parádisus, and recounts the nuptials of Adam and Eve. It is possible that Milton may have seen this ; the fourth book of the Paradise Lost compresses the excessive diffuseness of Barlæus, but the ideas are in great measure the same. Yet since this must naturally be the case, we cannot presume imitation. Few of the poems of Barlæus are so redundant as this ; he has the gift of stringing together mythological parallels and descriptive poetry

Barlæus.

without stint, and his discretion does not inform him where
to stop.

71. The eight books of Sylvæ by Balde, a German ecclesiastic, are extolled by Baillet and Bouterwek far Balde.
above their value; the odes are tumid and unclassi- Greek poem
of Heinsius.
cal; yet some have called him equal to Horace. Heinsius
tried his skill in Greek verse. His Peplus Græcorum Epi-
grammatum was published in 1613. These are what our
schoolboys would call very indifferent in point of elegance, and, as I should conceive, of accuracy: articles and
expletives (as they used to be happily called) are perpetually employed for the sake of the metre, not of the
sense.

72. Scotland might perhaps contend with Holland in this
as well as the preceding age. In the Deliciæ Poe- Latin poets
tarum Scotorum, published in 1637 by Arthur Jon- of Scotland
Jonston's
ston, we find about an equal produce of each cen- Psalms.
tury, the whole number being thirty-seven. Those of Jonston
himself, and some elegies by Scot of Scotstarvet, are among
the best. The Scots certainly wrote Latin with a good ear
and considerable elegance of phrase. A sort of critical controversy was carried on in the last century as to the versions
of the Psalms by Buchanan and Jonston. Though the
national honour may seem equally secure by the superiority of
either, it has, I believe, been usual in Scotland to maintain the
older poet against all the world. I am nevertheless inclined
to think that Jonston's Psalms, all of which are in elegiac
metre, do not fall short of those of Buchanan, either in elegance of style or in correctness of Latinity. In the 137th,
with which Buchanan has taken much pains, he may be
allowed the preference, but not at a great interval, and he
has attained this superiority by too much diffuseness.

73. Nothing good, and hardly tolerable, in a poetical sense,
had appeared in Latin verse among ourselves till Owen's epi-
this period. Owen's epigrams (Audoeni Epigram- grams.
mata), a well-known collection, were published in 1607;
unequal enough, they are sometimes neat and more often
witty: but they scarcely aspire to the name of poetry. Alabaster, a man of recondite Hebrew learning, pub- Alabaster's
lished in 1632 his tragedy of Roxana, which as Roxana.

he tells us, was written about forty years before for one night's representation, probably at college, but had been lately printed by some plagiary as his own. He forgets, however, to inform the reader, and thus lays himself open to some recrimination, that his tragedy is very largely borrowed from the Dalida of Groto, an Italian dramatist of the sixteenth century.[a] The story, the characters, the incidents, almost every successive scene, many thoughts, descriptions, and images, are taken from this original; but it is a very free translation, or rather differs from what can be called a translation. The tragedy of Groto is shortened, and Alabaster has thrown much into another form, besides introducing much of his own. The plot is full of all the accumulated horror and slaughter in which the Italians delighted on their stage. I rather prefer the original tragedy. Alabaster has spirit and fire with some degree of skill; but his notion of tragic style is of the 'King Cambyses' vein;' he is inflated and hyperbolical to excess, which is not the case with Groto.

74. But the first Latin poetry which England can vaunt May's Supplement to Lucan. is May's Supplement to Lucan, in seven books, which carry down the history of the Pharsalia to the death of Cæsar. This is not only a very spirited poem, but in many places at least, an excellent imitation. The versification, though it frequently reminds us of his model, is somewhat more negligent. May seems rarely to fall into Lucan's tumid extravagances, or to emulate his philosophical grandeur; but the narration is almost as impetuous and rapid, the images as thronged; and sometimes we have rather a happy imitation of the ingenious sophisms Lucan is apt to employ. The death of Cato and that of Cæsar are among the passages well worthy of praise. In some lines on Cleopatra's intrigue with Cæsar, while married to her brother, he has seized, with felicitous effect, not only the

---

[a] I am indebted for the knowledge of this to a manuscript note I found in the copy of Alabaster's Roxana in the British Museum: Haud multum abest hæc tragedia a pura versione tragediæ Italicæ Ludovici Groti Cæci Hadriensis cui titulus Dalida. This induced me to read the tragedy of Groto, which I had not previously done.

The title of Roxana runs thus:— Roxana tragedia a plagiarii unguibus vindicata aucta et agnita ab autore Gul. Alabastro. Lond. 1632.

broken cadences, but the love of moral parodox we find in Lucan.[b]

75. Many of the Latin poems of Milton were written in early life, some even at the age of seventeen. His Milton's name, and the just curiosity of mankind to trace Latin poems. the development of a mighty genius, would naturally attract our regard. They are in themselves full of classical elegance, of thoughts natural and pleasing, of a diction culled with taste from the gardens of ancient poetry, of a versification remarkably well cadenced and grateful to the ear. There is in them without a marked originality, which Latin verse can rarely admit but at the price of some incorrectness or impropriety, a more individual display of the poet's mind than we usually find. 'In the elegies,' it is said by Warton, a very competent judge of Latin poetry, 'Ovid was professedly Milton's model for language and versification. They are not, however, a perpetual and uniform tissue of Ovidian phraseology. With Ovid in view he has an original manner and character of his own, which exhibit a remarkable perspicuity of contexture, a native facility and fluency. Nor does his observation of Roman models oppress or destroy our great poet's inherent powers of invention and sentiment. I value these pieces as much for their fancy and genius as for their style and expression. That Ovid, among the Latin poets, was Milton's favourite, appears not only from his elegiac but his hexametric poetry. The versification of our author's hexameters has yet a different structure from that of the Metamorphoses: Milton's is more clear, intelligible, and flowing; less desultory, less familiar, and less embarrassed, with a frequent recurrence of periods. Ovid is at once rapid and abrupt.'[c] Why Warton should have at once supposed Ovid to be Milton's favourite model in hexameters, and yet so totally different as he represents him to be, seems hard to say. The structure of our poet's hexameters is much more Virgilian, nor do I see the least resemblance in them to the

---

[b] . . . Nec crimen inesse
Concubitu nimium tali, Cleopatra, putabunt
Qui Ptolemæorum thalamos, consuetaque jura
Incestæ novere domûs, fratemque sorori
Conjugio junctum, sacræ sub nomine tædæ
Majus adulterio delictum ; turpius isset,
Quis credat ? justi ad thalamos Cleopatra
    mariti,

Utque minus lecto peccaret, adultera facta
    est.

[c] Warton's essay on the Latin poetry of Milton, inserted at length in Todd's edition.

manner of Ovid. These Latin poems of Milton bear some traces of juvenility, but for the most part, such as please us for that very reason; it is the spring-time of an ardent and brilliant fancy, before the stern and sour spirit of polemical puritanism had gained entrance into his mind, the voice of the Allegro and of Comus.

CHAPTER VI.

HISTORY OF DRAMATIC LITERATURE FROM 1600 TO 1650.

SECT. I.

ON THE ITALIAN AND SPANISH DRAMA.

Character of the Italian Theatre in this Age—Bonarelli—The Spanish Theatre—Calderon—Appreciation of his Merits as a Dramatic Poet.

1. THE Italian theatre, if we should believe one of its historians, fell into total decay during the whole course of the seventeenth century, though the number of dramatic pieces of various kinds was by no means small. He makes a sort of apology for inserting in a copious list of dramatic performances any that appeared after 1600, and stops entirely with 1650.[d] But in this he seems hardly to have done justice to a few, which, if not of remarkable excellence, might be selected from the rest. Andreini is perhaps best known by name in England, and that for one only of his eighteen dramas, the Adamo, which has been supposed, on too precarious grounds, to have furnished the idea of Paradise Lost in the original form, as it was planned by its great author. The Adamo was first published in 1613, and afterwards with amplification in 1641. It is denominated 'A Sacred Representation;' and as Andreini was a player by profession, must be presumed to have been brought upon the stage. It is, however, asserted by Riccoboni, that those who wrote regular tragedies did not cause them to be represented; probably he might have scrupled to give that epithet to the Adamo. Hayler and Walker have reckoned it a composition of considerable beauty.

> Decline of the Italian theatre.

---

[d] Riccoboni, Hist. du Théâtre Italien, vol. i.

2. The majority of Italian tragedies in the seventeenth century were taken, like the Adamo, from sacred subjects, including such as ecclesiastical legends abundantly supplied. Few of these gave sufficient scope, either by action or character, for the diversity of excitement which the stage demands. Tragedies more truly deserving that name were the Solimano of Bonarelli, the Tancredi of Campeggio, the Demetrio of Rocco, which Salfi prefers to the rest, and the Aristodemo of Carlo de' Dottori. A drama by Testi, L'Isola di Alcina, had some reputation ; but in this, which the title betrays not to be a legitimate tragedy, he introduced musical airs, and thus trod on the boundaries of a rival art.[e] It has been suggested, and with no inconsiderable probability, that in her passion for the melodrame Italy lost all relish for the graver tone of tragedy. Music, at least the music of the opera, conspired with many more important circumstances to spread an effeminacy over the public character.

3. The pastoral drama had always been allied to musical sentiment, even though it might be without accompaniment. The feeling it inspired was nearly that of the opera. In this style we find one imitation of Tasso and Guarini, inferior in most qualities, yet deserving some regard, and once popular even with the critics of Italy. This was the Filli di Sciro of Bonarelli, published at Ferrara, a city already fallen into the hands of priests, but round whose deserted palaces the traditions of poetical glory still lingered, in 1607, and represented by an academy in the same place soon afterwards. It passed through numerous editions, and was admired, even beyond the Alps, during the whole century, and perhaps still longer. It displays much of the bad taste and affectation of that period. Bonarelli is as strained in the construction of history, and in his characters, as he is in his style. Celia, the heroine of this pastoral, struggles with a double love, the original idea, as he might truly think, of his drama, which he wrote a long dissertation in order to justify. It is, however, far less conformable to the truth of nature than to the sophisticated

Filli di Sciro.

---

[e] Salfi, continuation de Ginguéné, vol. xii. chap. ix. Besides this larger work, Salfi published in 1829 a short essay on the Italian stage, Saggio Storico-Critico della Commedia Italiana.

society for which he wrote. A wanton capricious court
lady might perhaps waver, with some warmth of inclination
towards both, between two lovers, 'Alme dell' alma mia,'
as Celia calls them, and be very willing to possess either.
But what is morbid in moral affection seldom creates sympathy, or is fit either for narrative poetry or the stage.
Bonarelli's diction is studied and polished to the highest
degree ; and though its false refinement and affected graces
often displease us, the real elegance of insulated passages
makes us pause to admire. In harmony and sweetness of
sound he seems fully equal to his predecessors, Tasso and
Guarini ; but he has neither the pathos of the one, nor the
fertility of the other. The language and turn of thought
seems, more than in the Pastor Fido, to be that of the opera,
wanting, indeed, nothing but the intermixture of air to be
perfectly adapted to music. Its great reputation, which
even Crescimbeni does his utmost to keep up, proves the
decline of good taste in Italy, and the lateness of its revival.[f]

4. A new fashion, which sprung up about 1620, both
marks the extinction of a taste for genuine tragedy, Translations of Spanish dramas.
and, by furnishing a substitute, stood in the way of
its revival. Translations from Spanish tragedies and tragi-
comedies, those of Lope de Vega and his successors, replaced
the native muse of Italy. These were in prose and in three
acts, irregular of course, and with very different characteristics from those of the Italian school. 'The very name
of tragedy,' says Riccoboni, 'became unknown in our
country ; the *monsters* which usurped the place did not
pretend to that glorious title. Tragi-comedies rendered
from the Spanish, such as Life is a Dream (of Calderon), the
Samson, the Guest of Stone, and others of the same class,
were the popular ornaments of the Italian stage.'[g]

5. The extemporaneous comedy had always been the
amusement of the Italian populace, not to say of Extempo- raneous comedy.
all who wished to unbend their minds.[h] An epoch

---

[f] Istoria della volgar Poesia, iv. 147.
He places the Filli di Sciro next to the
Aminta.

[g] Hist. du Théâtre Italien, i. 47.

[h] The extemporaneous comedy was
called commedia dell' arte. 'It consisted,' says Salfi, 'in a mere sketch or
plan of a dramatic composition, the parts
in which, having been hardly shadowed
out, were assigned to different actors who

in this art was made in 1611 by Flaminio Scala, who first
published the outline or canvas of a series of these pieces,
the dialogue being of course reserved for the ingenious
performers.[i] This outline was not quite so short as that
sometimes given in Italian play-bills : it explained the drift
of each actor's part in the scene, but without any distinct
hint of what he was to say. The construction of these
fables is censured by Riccoboni as weak; but it would not be
reasonable to expect that it should be otherwise. The talent
of the actors supplied the deficiency of writers. A certain quickness of wit, and tact in catching the shades of
manner, comparatively rare among us, are widely diffused
in Italy. It would be, we may well suspect, impossible to
establish an extemporaneous theatre in England, which
should not be stupidly vulgar.[k] But Bergamo sent out
many Harlequins, and Venice many Pantaloons. They were
respected, as brilliant wit ought to be. The emperor Mathias
ennobled Cecchini, a famous Harlequin, who was, however,
a man of letters. These actors sometimes took the plot of
old comedies as their outline, and disfigured them, so as
hardly to be known, by their extemporaneous dialogue.[m]

6. Lope de Vega was at the height of his glory at the
beginning of this century. Perhaps the majority
of his dramas fall within it; but enough has been
said on the subject in the last volume. His contemporaries

Spanish stage.

---

were to develop them in extemporaneous
dialogue.' Such a sketch was called a
scenario, containing the subject of each
scene, and those of Flaminio Scala were
celebrated. Saggio Storico-Critico, p. 38.
The pantomime, as it exists among us,
is the descendant of this extemporaneous
comedy, but with little of the wit and
spirit of its progenitor.

[i] Salfi, p. 40.

[k] This is only meant as to dialogue
and as to the public stage. The talent
of a single actor, like the late Charles
Mathews, is not an exception ; but even
the power of strictly extemporaneous
comedy, with the agreeable poignancy
that the minor theatre requires, is not
wanting among some whose station and
habits of life restrain its exercise to the
most private circles.

[m] Riccoboni, Hist. du Théâtre Ita-

lien. Salfi, xii. 518. An elaborate disquisition on the extemporaneous comedy
by Mr. Panizzi, in the Foreign Review
for 1829 (not the Foreign Quarterly,
but one early extinguished), derives it
from the mimes and Atellanian comedies
of ancient Italy, tracing them through
the middle ages. The point seems sufficiently proved. The last company of
performers in this old, though plebeian,
family, existed within about thirty years
in Lombardy. A friend of mine at that
time witnessed the last of the Harlequins. I need hardly say that this character was not a mere skipper over the
stage, as we have seen him, but a very
honest and lively young Bergamasque.
The plays of Carlo Gozzi, if plays they
are, are mere hints to guide the wit of
extemporaneous actors.

and immediate successors were exceedingly numerous; the
effulgence of dramatic literature in Spain corresponding
exactly in time to that of England.   Several are named by
Bouterwek and Velasquez; but one only, Pedro ^{Calderon.}
Calderon de la Barca, must be permitted to arrest ^{Number of his pieces.}
us.   This celebrated man was born in 1600, and died in
1683.   From an early age till after the middle of the century
when he entered the church, he contributed, with a fertility
only eclipsed by that of Lope, a long list of tragic, historic,
comic, and tragi-comic dramas to the Spanish stage.   In
the latter period of his life he confined himself to the
religious pieces called Autos Sacramentales.   Of these, 97
are published in the collective edition of 1726, besides 127 of
his regular plays.   In one year, 1635, it is said that twelve
of his comedies appeared; but the authenticity of so large
a number has been questioned.   He is said to have given a
list of his sacred plays, at the age of eighty, consisting of
only 68.   No collection was published by himself.   Some of
his comedies, in the Spanish sense of the word, it may be
observed, turn more or less on religious subjects, as their
titles show: El Purgatorio de San Patricio—La Devocion de
la Cruz—Judas Maccabeus—La Cisma de Inghilterra.   He
did not dislike contemporary subjects.   In El Sitio de Breda,
we have Spinola, Nassau, and others then living, on the
scene.   Calderon's metre is generally trochaic, of eight or
seven syllables, not always rhyming; but verses de arte
mayor, as they were called, or anapæstic lines of eleven or
twelve syllables, and also hendecasyllables, frequently occur.

7. The comedies, those properly so called *de capa y
espada*, which represent manners, are full of inci- ^{His come-dies.}
dent, but not perhaps crowded so as to produce any
confusion; the characters have nothing very salient, but
express the sentiments of gentlemen with frankness and
spirit.   We find in every one a picture of Spain; gallantry,
jealousy, quick resentment of insult, sometimes deep revenge.   The language of Calderon is not unfrequently
poetical, even in these lighter dramas, but hyperbolical
figures and insipid conceits deform its beauty.   The gra-
cioso, or witty servant, is an unfailing personage; but I do
not know (my reading, however, being extremely limited)

that Calderon displays much brilliancy or liveliness in his
sallies.

8. The plays of Calderon required a good deal of theatrical apparatus, unless the good nature of the audience dispensed with it. But this kind of comedy must have led to
scenical improvements. They seem to contain no indecency, nor do the intrigues ever become criminal, at least
in effect; most of the ladies, indeed, are unmarried. Yet
they have been severely censured by later critics on the
score of their morality, which is no doubt that of the stage,
but considerably purified in comparison with the Italian
and French of the sixteenth century. Calderon seems to
bear no resemblance to any English writer of his age,
except, in a certain degree, to Beaumont and Fletcher. And
as he wants their fertility of wit and humour, we cannot, I
presume, place the best of his comedies on a level with
even the second class of theirs. But I should speak perhaps with more reserve of an author, very few of whose
plays I have read, and with whose language I am very imperfectly acquainted; nor should I have ventured so far,
if the opinion of many European critics had not seemed to
warrant my frigid character of one who has sometimes been
so much applauded.

9. La Vida es Sueno rises, in its subject as well as style,
La Vida es   above the ordinary comedies of Calderon. Basilius,
Sueno.   King of Poland, a deep philosopher, has, by consulting the stars, had the misfortune of ascertaining that his
unborn son Sigismund would be under some extraordinary
influences of evil passion. He resolves in consequence to
conceal his birth, and to bring him up in a horrible solitude,
where, it hardly appears why, he is laden with chains, and
covered with skins of beasts, receiving meantime an excellent education, and becoming able to converse on every
subject, though destitute of all society but that of his
keeper Clotaldo. The inheritance of the crown of Poland
is supposed to have devolved on Astolfo, duke of Moscovy,
or on his cousin Estrella, who, as daughter of an elder
branch, contests it with him. The play opens by a scene,
in which Rosaura, a Moscovite lady, who having been
betrayed by Astolfo, has fled to Poland in man's attire,

descends the almost impassable precipices which overhang
the small castle wherein Sigismund is confined. This
scene and that in which he first appears, are impressive and
full of beauty, even now that we are become accustomed in
excess to these theatrical wonders. Clotaldo discovers the
prince in conversation with a stranger, who by the king's
general order must be detained, and probably for death.
A circumstance leads him to believe that this stranger is his
son ; but the Castilian loyalty transferred to Poland forbids
him to hesitate in obeying his instructions. The king, however, who has fortunately determined to release his son, and
try an experiment upon the force of the stars, coming in, at
this time, sets Rosaura at liberty.

10. In the next act Sigismund, who by the help of a
sleeping potion, has been conveyed to the palace, wakes in a
bed of down, and in the midst of royal splendour. He has
little difficulty in understanding his new condition, but preserves a not unnatural resentment of his former treatment.
The malign stars prevail ; he treats Astolfo with the utmost
arrogance ; reviles and threatens his father, throws one of
his servants out of the window, attempts the life of Clotaldo
and the honour of Rosaura. The king, more convinced than
ever of the truth of astrology, directs another soporific
draught to be administered; and in the next scene we find
the prince again in his prison. Clotaldo once more at his
side, persuades him that his late royalty has passed in a
dream, wisely observing, however, that asleep or awake we
should always do what is right.

11. Sigismund, after some philosophical reflections, pre-
pares to submit to the sad reality which has displaced his
vision. But in the third act an unforeseen event recalls him
to the world. The army, become acquainted with his rights,
and indignant that the king should transfer them to Astolfo,
break into his prison and place him at their head. Clotaldo
expects nothing but death. A new revolution, however, has
taken place. Sigismund, corrected by the dismal consequences of giving way to passion in his former dream, and
apprehending a similar waking once more, has suddenly
overthrown the sway of the sinister constellations that had
enslaved him; he becomes generous, mild, and master of

himself; and the only pretext for his disinheritance being
removed, it is easy that he should be reconciled to his father,
that Astolfo, abandoning a kingdom he can no longer claim,
should espouse the injured Rosaura, and that the reformed
prince should become the husband of Estrella. The incidents which chiefly relate to these latter characters have
been omitted in this slight analysis.

12. This tragi-comedy presents a moral not so contemptible in the age of Calderon as it may now appear:
that the stars may influence our will, but do not oblige it.
If we could extract an allegorical meaning from the chimeras of astrology, and deem the stars but names for the
circumstances of birth and fortune which affect the character as well as condition of every man, but yield to the per-
severing energy of self-correction, we might see in this fable
the shadow of a permanent and valuable truth. As a play it
deserves considerable praise ; the events are surprising without excessive improbability, and succeed each other without
confusion; the thoughts are natural and poetically expressed;
and it requires, on the whole, less allowance for the different
standard of national taste than is usual in the Spanish drama.

13. A secreto Agravio secreta Vengança is a domestic
tragedy which turns on a common story—a husband's revenge on one whom he erroneously be-
lieves to be still a favoured, and who had been
once an accepted, lover. It is something like Tancred and
Sigismunda, except that the lover is killed instead of the
husband. The latter puts him to death secretly, which gives
name to the play. He afterwards sets fire to his own
house, and in the confusion designedly kills his wife. A
friend communicates the fact to his sovereign, Sebastian,
King of Portugal, who applauds what has been done. It is
an atrocious play, and speaks terrible things as to the state
of public sentiment in Spain, but abounds with interesting
and touching passages.

A secreto Agravio se-creta Ven-gança.

14. It has been objected to Calderon, and the following
defence of Bouterwek seems very insufficient, that
his servants converse in a poetical style like their
masters. 'The spirit, on these particular occasions,' says
that judicious but lenient critic, 'must not be misunder-

Style of Calderon.

stood. The servants in Calderon's comedies always imitate
the language of their masters. In most cases they express
themselves like the latter, in the natural language of real
life, and often divested of that colouring of the ideas, without which a dramatic work ceases to be a poem. But whenever romantic gallantry speaks in the language of tenderness, admiration, or flattery, then, according to Spanish
custom, every idea becomes a metaphor ; and Calderon, who
was a thorough Spaniard, seized these opportunities to give
the reins to his fancy, and to suffer it to take a bold lyric
flight beyond the boundaries of nature. On such occasions
the most extravagant metaphoric language, in the style of
the Italian Marinists, did not appear unnatural to a Spanish
audience ; and even Calderon himself had for that style a
particular fondness, to the gratification of which he sacrificed a chaster taste. It was his ambition to become a more
refined Lope de Vega or a Spanish Marini. Thus in his
play, Bien vengas Mal si vengas solo, a waiting maid, addressing her young mistress who has risen in a gay humour,
says—"Aurora would not have done wrong had she slumbered that morning in her snowy crystal, for that the sight
of her mistress's charms would suffice to draw aside the
curtains from the couch of Sol." She adds that, using a
Spanish idea, "it might then, indeed, be said that the sun
had risen in her lady's eyes." Valets, on the like occasion,
speak in the same style ; and when lovers address compliments to their mistresses, and these reply in the same
strain, the play of far-fetched metaphors is aggravated by
antitheses to a degree which is intolerable to any but a
Spanish-formed taste. But it must not be forgotten that
this language of gallantry was in Calderon's time spoken
by the fashionable world, and that it was a vernacular property of the ancient national poetry.'[n] What is this but to
confess that Calderon had not genius to raise himself above
his age, and that he can be read only as a 'Triton of the
minnows ;' one who is great but in comparison with his

---

[n] P. 507. It has been ingeniously
hinted in the 'Quarterly Review,' vol.
xxv., that the high-flown language of
servants in Spanish dramas is a parody
on that of their masters, and designed
to make it ridiculous. But this is probably too refined an excuse.

neighbours? It will not convert bad writing into good to
tell us, as is perpetually done, that we must place ourselves
in the author's position, and make allowances for the taste
of his age, or the temper of his nation. All this is true
relatively to the author himself, and may be pleaded against
a condemnation of his talents; but the excuse of the man is
not that of the work.

15. The fame of Calderon has been latterly revived in
His merits
sometimes
overrated. Europe through the praise of some German
critics, but especially the unbounded panegyric
of one of their greatest men, William Schlegel. The passage is well known for its brilliant eloquence. Every one
must differ with reluctance and respect from this accomplished writer; and an Englishman, acknowledging with
gratitude and admiration what Schlegel has done for the
glory of Shakspeare, ought not to grudge the laurels he
showers upon another head. It is however rather as a poet
than a dramatist that Calderon has received this homage;
and in his poetry, it seems to be rather bestowed on the
mysticism, which finds a responsive chord in so many
German hearts, than on what we should consider a more
universal excellence, a sympathy with, and a power over,
all that is true and beautiful in nature and in man. Sismondi (but the distance between Weimar and Geneva in
matters of taste is incomparably greater than by the public
road) dissenting from this eulogy of Schlegel, which he
fairly lays before the reader, stigmatises Calderon as eminently the poet of the age wherein he lived, the age of
Philip IV. Salfi goes so far as to say we can hardly read
Calderon without indignation; since he seems to have had
no view but to make his genius subservient to the lowest
prejudices and superstitions of his country.° In the twenty-
fifth volume of the Quarterly Review an elaborate and able
critique on the plays of Calderon seems to have estimated
him without prejudice on either side. 'His boundless and
inexhaustible fertility of invention, his quick power of seizing and prosecuting everything with dramatic effect, the
unfailing animal spirits of his dramas, if we may venture on

° Hist. Litt. de Ginguéné, vol. xii. p. 499.

the expression, the general loftiness and purity of his sentiments, the rich facility of his verse, the abundance of his
language, and the clearness and precision with which he
embodies his thoughts in words and figures, entitle him to a
high rank as to the imagination and creative faculty of a
poet, but we cannot consent to enrol him among the mighty
masters of the human breast.'[p] His total want of truth
to nature, even the ideal nature which poetry embodies,
justifies at least this sentence. 'The wildest flights of
Biron and Romeo,' it is observed, ' are tame to the heroes
of Calderon; the Asiatic pomp of expression, the exuberance
of metaphor, the perpetual recurrence of the same figures,
which the poetry of Spain derived from its intercourse with
the Arabian conquerors of the peninsula, are lavished by him
in all their fulness. Every address of a lover to a mistress
is thickly studded with stars and flowers; her looks are
always nets of gold, her lips rubies, and her heart a rock,
which the rivers of his tears attempt in vain to melt. In
short, the language of the heart is entirely abandoned for
that of the fancy; the brilliant but false concetti which have
infected the poetical literature of every country, and which
have been universally exploded by pure taste, glitter in every
page and intrude into every speech.' [q]

Sect. II.—On the French Drama.

Early French Dramatists of this Period—Corneille—His principal Tragedies
—Rotrou.

16. Among the company who performed at the second
theatre of Paris, that established in the Marais,   Plays of
was Hardy, who, like Shakspeare, uniting both   Hardy.
arts, was himself the author of 600, or, as some say, 800
dramatic pieces. It is said that forty-one of these are
extant in the collection of his works, which I have never
seen. Several of them were written, learned by heart, and
represented within a week. His own inventions are the

---

[p] P. 24.   P. 14.

worst of all; his tragedies and tragi-comedies are borrowed
with as close an adherence to the original text as possible
from Homer or Plutarch or Cervantes. They have more
incident than those of his predecessors, and are somewhat
less absurd; but Hardy is a writer of little talent. The
Marianne is the most tolerable of his tragedies. In these
he frequently abandoned the chorus, and even where he
introduces it, does not regularly close the act with an ode.[r]

17. In the comedies of Hardy, and in the many burlesque
farces represented under Henry IV. and Louis XIII., no
regard was paid to decency, either in the language or the
circumstances. Few persons of rank, especially ladies,
attended the theatres.[s] These were first attracted by pastoral representations, of which Racan gave a successful
example in his Artenice. It is hardly, however, to be called
a drama.[t] But the stage being no longer abandoned to the
populace, and a more critical judgment in French literature
gaining ground, encouraged by Richelieu, who built a large
room in his palace for the representation of Mirame, an
indifferent tragedy, part of which was suspected to be his
own,[u] the ancient theatre began to be studied, rules were
laid down and partially observed, a perfect decorum replaced
the licentiousness and gross language of the old writers.
Mairet and Rotrou, though without rising, in their first
plays, much above Hardy, just served to prepare the way
for the father and founder of the national theatre.[x]

18. The Melite of Corneille, his first production, was
represented in 1629, when he was twenty-three years of age.
This is only distinguished, as some say, from those of Hardy

---

[r] Fontenelle, Hist. du Théâtre François (in Œuvres de Fontenelle, iii. 72).
Suard, Mélanges de Littérature, vol. iv.
[s] Suard, p. 134. Rotrou boasts that
since he wrote for the theatre, it had become so well regulated that respectable
women might go to it with as little
scruple as to the Luxembourg garden.
Corneille, however, has, in general, the
credit of having purified the stage; after
his second piece, Clitandre, he admitted
nothing licentious in his comedies. The
only remain of grossness, Fontenelle observes, was that the lovers *se tutoyoient*;
but as he gravely goes on to remark, le

tutoyement ne choque pas les bonnes
mœurs; il ne choque que la politesse et
la vraie galanterie. P. 91. But the last
instance of this heinous offence is in Le
Menteur.
[t] Suard, ubi suprà.
[u] Fontenelle, p. 84, 96.
[x] Id. p. 78. It is difficult in France,
as it is with us, to ascertain the date of
plays, because they were often represented for years before they came from
the press. It is conjectured by Fontenelle that one or two pieces of Mairet
and Rotrou may have preceded any by
Corneille.

by a greater vigour of style; but Fontenelle gives a very
different opinion. It had at least a success which caused a
new troop of actors to be established in the Marais. His
next, Clitandre, it is agreed, is not so good. But La
Veuve is much better; irregular in action, but with spirit,
character, and well-invented situations, it is the first model
of the higher comedy.[y] These early comedies must in fact
have been relatively of considerable merit since they raised
Corneille to high reputation, and connected him with the
literary men of his time. The Medea, though much borrowed from Seneca, gave a tone of grandeur and dignity
unknown before to French tragedy. This appeared in 1635,
and was followed by the Cid next year.

19. Notwithstanding the defence made by La Harpe, I
cannot but agree with the French Academy, in
their criticism on this play, that the subject is   The Cid.
essentially ill-chosen. No circumstances can be imagined,
no skill can be employed, that will reconcile the mind to the
marriage of a daughter with one that has shed her father's
blood. And the law of unity of time, which crowds every
event of the drama within a few hours, renders the promised
consent of Chimène (for such it is) to this union still more
revolting and improbable.[z] The knowledge of this termination re-acts on the reader during a second perusal, so as
to give an irresistible impression of her insincerity in her
previous solicitations for his death. She seems, indeed, in
several passages, little else than a tragic coquette, and one
of the most odious kind.[a] The English stage at that time
was not exempt from great violations of nature and decorum;
yet had the subject of the Cid fallen into the hands of
Beaumont and Fletcher, and it is one which they would
have willingly selected, for the sake of the effective situa-

---

[y] Suard. Fontenelle. La Harpe.

[z] La Harpe has said that Chimène
does not promise at last to marry Rodrigue, though the spectator perceives
that she will do so. He forgets that she
has commissioned her lover's sword in
the duel with Don Sancho :—

Sors vainqueur d'un combat dont Chimène est
le prix.—Act v. sc. 1.

[a] In these lines, for examp'e, of the
third act, scene 4th :—

Malgré les feux si beaux qui rompent ma colère
Je ferai mon possible à bien venger mon père ;
Mais malgré la rigueur d'un si cruel devoir,
Mon unique souhait est de ne rien pouvoir

It is true that he found this in his
Spanish original, but that does not render the imitation judicious, or the sentiment either moral, or even theatrically
specious.

tions and contrasts of passion it affords, the part of Chimène
would have been managed by them with great warmth and
spirit, though probably not less incongruity and extravagance; but I can scarcely believe that the conclusion would
have been so much in the style of comedy. Her death, or
retirement into a monastery, would have seemed more consonant to her own dignity and to that of a tragic subject.
Corneille was however borne out by the tradition of Spain,
and by the authority of Guillen de Castro whom he
imitated.

20. The language of Corneille is elevated, his sentiments,
Style of   if sometimes hyperbolical, generally noble, when
Corneille.   he has not to deal with the passion of love; conscious of the nature of his own powers, he has avoided
subjects wherein this must entirely predominate; it was to
be, as he thought, an accessory but never a principal source
of dramatic interest. In this, however, as a general law of
tragedy, he was mistaken; love is by no means unfit for the
chief source of tragic distress, but comes in generally with
a cold and feeble effect as a subordinate emotion. In those
Roman stories which he most affected, its expression could
hardly be otherwise than insipid and incongruous. Corneille
probably would have dispensed with it, like Shakspeare in
Coriolanus and Julius Cæsar; but the taste of his contemporaries, formed in the pedantic school of romance, has
imposed fetters on his genius in almost every drama. In
the Cid, where the subject left him no choice, he has perhaps
succeeded better in the delineation of love than on any other
occasion; yet even here we often find the cold exaggerations
of complimentary verse, instead of the voice of nature. But
other scenes of this play, especially in the first act, which
bring forward the proud Castilian characters of the two
fathers of Rodrigo and Chimène, are full of the nervous
eloquence of Corneille; and the general style, though it
may not have borne the fastidious criticism either of the
Academy or of Voltaire, is so far above anything which had
been heard on the French stage, that it was but a very frigid
eulogy in the former to say that it 'had acquired a considerable reputation among works of the kind.' It had at
that time astonished Paris; but the prejudices of Cardinal

Richelieu and the envy of inferior authors, joined perhaps
to the proverbial unwillingness of critical bodies to commit
themselves by warmth of praise, had some degree of influence on the judgment which the Academy pronounced on
the Cid, though I do not think it was altogether so unjust
and uncandid as has sometimes been supposed.

21. The next tragedy of Corneille, Les Horaces, is hardly
open to less objection than the Cid; not so much
because there is, as the French critics have dis- ^{Les Horaces.}
covered, a want of unity in the subject, which I do not quite
perceive, nor because the fifth act is tedious and uninteresting, as from the repulsiveness of the story, and the jarring
of the sentiments with our natural sympathies. Corneille
has complicated the legend in Livy with the marriage of the
younger Horatius to the sister of the Curiatii, and thus
placed his two female personages in a nearly similar situation, which he has taken little pains to diversify by any
contrast in their characters. They speak, on the contrary,
nearly in the same tone, and we see no reason why the hero
of the tragedy should not, as he seems half disposed, have
followed up the murder of his sister by that of his wife.
More skill is displayed in the opposition of character between
the combatants themselves; but the mild, though not less
courageous or patriotic, Curiatius attaches the spectator, who
cares nothing for the triumph of Rome, or the glory of the
Horatian name. It must be confessed that the elder
Horatius is nobly conceived; the Roman energy, of which
we find but a caricature in his brutish son, shines out in him
with an admiral dramatic spirit. I shall be accused, nevertheless, of want of taste, when I confess that his celebrated
Qu'il mourût, has always seemed to me less eminently sublime
than the general suffrage of France has declared it. There
is nothing very novel or striking in the proposition, that a
soldier's duty is to die in the field rather than desert his
post by flight; and in a tragedy full of the hyperboles of
Roman patriotism, it appears strange that we should be
astonished at that which is the principle of all military
honour. The words are emphatic in their position, and
calculated to draw forth the actor's energy; but this is an
artifice of no great skill; and one can hardly help thinking,

that a spectator in the pit would spontaneously have anticipated the answer of a warlike father to the feminine
question,—

'Que vouliez-vous qu'il fît contre trois ?'

The style of this tragedy is reckoned by the critics superior
to that of the Cid ; the nervousness and warmth of Corneille
is more displayed ; and it is more free from incorrect and
trivial expression.

22. Cinna, the next in order of time, is probably that
tragedy of Corneille which would be placed at the
head by a majority of suffrages. His eloquence
reached here its highest point; the speeches are longer,
more vivid in narration, more philosophical in argument,
more abundant in that strain of Roman energy, which he had
derived chiefly from Lucan, more emphatic and condensed in
their language and versification. But, as a drama, this is
deserving of little praise ; the characters of Cinna and Maximus are contemptible, that of Emilia is treacherous and
ungrateful. She is indeed the type of a numerous class
who have followed her in works of fiction, and sometimes,
unhappily, in real life ; the female patriot, theoretically, at
least, an assassin, but commonly compelled, by the iniquity
of the times, to console herself in practice with safer trans-
gressions. We have had some specimens ; and other
nations to their shame and sorrow, have had more. But
even the magnanimity of Augustus, whom we have not
seen exposed to instant danger, is uninteresting, nor do
we perceive why he should bestow his friendship as well
as his forgiveness on the detected traitor that cowers before
him. It is one of those subjects which might, by the invention of a more complex plot than history furnishes,
have better excited the spectator's attention, but not his
sympathy.

23. A deeper interest belongs to Polyeucte; and this is
the only tragedy of Corneille wherein he affects the
heart. There is, indeed, a certain incongruity
which we cannot overcome between the sanctity of Christian
martyrdom and the language of love, especially when the
latter is rather the more prominent of the two in the conduct

Cinna.

Polyeucte.

of the drama.[b]   But the beautiful character of Pauline would
redeem much greater defects than can be ascribed to this
tragedy.   It is the noblest, perhaps, on the French stage,
and conceived with admirable delicacy and dignity.[c]   In the
style, however, of Polyeucte, there seems to be some return
towards the languid tone of common-place which had been
wholly thrown off in Cinna.[d]

24. Rodogune is said to have been a favourite with the
author.   It can hardly be so with the generality of
his readers.   The story has all the atrocity of the   *Rodogune.*
older school, from which Corneille, in his earlier plays, had
emancipated the stage.   It borders even on ridicule.   Two
princes, kept by their mother, one of those furies whom our
own Webster or Marston would have delighted to draw, in
ignorance which is the elder, and consequently entitled to
the throne, are enamoured of Rodogune.   Their mother
makes it a condition of declaring the succession, that they
should shed the blood of this princess.   Struck with horror
at such a proposition, they refer their passion to the choice
of Rodogune, who, in her turn, demands the death of their
mother.   The embarassment of these amiable youths may
be conceived.   La Harpe extols the fifth act of this tragedy,
and it may perhaps be effective in representation.

25. Pompey, sometimes inaccurately called the Death of
Pompey, is more defective in construction than even
any other tragedy of Corneille.   The hero, if Pompey   *Pompey.*
is such, never appears on the stage, and his death being re-
counted at the beginning of the second act, the real subject
of the piece, so far as it can be said to have one, is the

---

[b] The Coterie at the Hôtel Rambouillet thought that Polyeucte would not
succeed on account of its religious character.   Corneille, it is said, was about
to withdraw his tragedy, but was dis-
suaded by an actor of so little reputation
that he did not even bear a part in the
performance.   Fontenelle, p. 101.

[c] Fontenelle thinks that it shows 'un
grand attachement à son devoir, et un
grand caractère' in Pauline to desire
that Severus should save her husband's
life, instead of procuring the latter to be
executed that she might marry her lover.
Réflexions sur la Poëtique, sect. 16.
This is rather an odd notion of what is

sufficient to constitute an heroic character.   It is not the conduct of Pauline,
which in every Christian or virtuous
woman must naturally be the same, but
the fine sentiments and language which
accompany it, that render her part so
noble.

[d] In the second scene of the second
act, between Severus and Pauline, two
characters of the most elevated class,
the former quits the stage with this
line,—

Adieu, trop vertueux objet, et trop charmant.

The latter replies,—

Adieu, trop malheureux, et trop parfait amant.

punishment of his assassins ; a retribution demanded by the
moral sense of the spectator, but hardly important enough
for dramatic interest. The character of Cæsar is somewhat weakened by his passion for Cleopatra, which assumes more the tone of devoted gallantry than truth or
probability warrant; but Cornelia, though with some Lu-
canic extravagance, is full of a Roman nobleness of spirit,
which renders her, after Pauline, but at a long interval, the
finest among the female characters of Corneille. The language
is not beneath that of his earlier tragedies.

26. In Heraclius we begin to find an inferiority of style.
Heraclius. Few passages, especially after the first act, are
written with much vigour ; and the plot, instead of
the faults we may ascribe to some of the former dramas, a
too great simplicity and want of action, offends by the perplexity of its situations, and still more by their nature ;
since they are wholly among the proper resources of comedy.
The true and the false Heraclius, each uncertain of his
paternity, each afraid to espouse one who may or may not
be his sister, the embarrassment of Phocas, equally irritated
by both, but aware that in putting either to death, he may
punish his own son, the art of Leontine who produces this
confusion, not by silence, but by a series of inconsistent
falsehoods, all these are in themselves ludicrous, and such as
in comedy could produce no other effect than laughter.

27. Nicomède is generally placed by the critics below
Nicomède. Heraclius, an opinion in which I should hardly
concur. The plot is feeble and improbable, but
more tolerable than the strange entanglements of Heraclius;
and the spirit of Corneille shines out more in the characters
and sentiments. None of his later tragedies deserve much
notice, except that we find one of his celebrated scenes in
Sertorius, a drama of little general merit. Nicomède and
Sertorius were both first represented after the middle of the
century.

28. Voltaire has well distinguished 'the fine scenes of
Faults and Corneille, and the fine tragedies of Racine.' It
beauties of
Corneille. can, perhaps, hardly be said that, with the exception of Polyeucte, the former has produced a single play,
which, taken as a whole, we can commend. The keys of
the passions were not given to his custody. But in the

which he introduced upon the French stage, and which long
continued to be its boast, impressive, energetic declamation,
thoughts masculine, bold, and sometimes sublime, conveyed
in a style for the most part clear, condensed, and noble, and
in a rhythm sonorous and satisfactory to the ear, he has not
since been equalled.   Lucan, it has always been said, was
the favourite study of Corneille.   No one, perhaps, can
admire one who has not a strong relish for the other.   That
the tragedian has ever surpassed the highest flights of his
Roman prototype, it might be difficult to prove ; but if his
fire is not more intense, it is accompanied by less smoke; his
hyperboles, for such he has, are less frequent and less turgid ;
his taste is more judicious, he knows better, especially in
description, what to choose and where to stop.   Lucan,
however, would have disdained the politeness of the amorous heroes of Corneille, and though often tedious, often
offensive to good taste, is never languid or ignoble.

29. The first French comedy written in polite language,
without low wit or indecency, is due to Corneille, *Le Menteur.*
or rather, in some degree, to the Spanish author
whom he copied in Le Menteur.   This has been improved
a little by Goldoni, and our own well-known farce, The Liar,
is borrowed from both.   The incidents are diverting, but it
belongs to the subordinate class of comedy, and a better
moral would have been shown in the disgrace of the principal
character.   Another comedy about the same time, Le Pedant
Joué, by Cyrano de Bergerac, had much success.   It has
been called the first comedy in prose, and the first wherein a
provincial dialect is introduced ; the remark, as to the former
circumstance, shows a forgetfulness of Larivey.   Molière has
borrowed freely from this play.

30. The only tragedies, after those of Corneille, anterior
to 1650, which the French themselves hold worthy *Other French*
of remembrance, are the Sophonisbe of Mairet ; in *tragedies.*
which some characters and some passages are vigorously
conceived, but the style is debased by low and ludicrous
thoughts, which later critics never fail to point out with
severity ;[e] the Scevole of Duryer, the best of several good
tragedies, full of lines of great simplicity in expression, but

---

[e] Suard, ubi suprà.

which seem to gain force through their simplicity, by one
who, though never sublime, adopted with success the severe
and reasoning style of Corneille; [f] the Marianne of Tristan,
which, at its appearance in 1637, passed for a rival of the
Cid, and remained for a century on the stage, but is now
ridiculed for a style alternately turgid and ridiculous; and
the Wenceslas of Rotrou, which had not ceased perhaps
thirty years since to be represented.

31. This tragedy, the best work of a fertile dramatist, who
Wenceslas did himself honour by a ready acknowledgment of
of Rotrou. the superiority of Corneille, instead of canvassing
the suffrages of those who always envy genius, is by no
means so much below that great master, as, in the unfortunate efforts of his later years, he was below himself.
Wenceslas was represented in 1647. It may be admitted
that Rotrou had conceived his plot, which is wholly original,
in the spirit of Corneille; the masculine energy of the sentiments, the delineation of bold and fierce passions, of noble
and heroic love, the attempt even at political philosophy,
are copies of that model. It seems, indeed, that in several
scenes Rotrou must, out of mere generosity to Corneille,
have determined to outdo one of his most exceptionable
passages, the consent of Chimène to espouse the Cid. His
own curtain drops on the vanishing reluctance of his heroine
to accept the hand of a monster whom she hated, and who
had just murdered her lover in his own brother. It is the
Lady Anne of Shakspeare; but Lady Anne is not a heroine.
Wenceslas is not unworthy of comparison with the second
class of Corneille's tragedies. But the ridiculous tone of
language and sentiment which the heroic romance had
rendered popular, and from which Corneille did not wholly
emancipate himself, often appears in this piece of Rotrou;
the intrigue is rather too complex, in the Spanish style, for
tragedy; the diction seems frequently obnoxious to the most
indulgent criticism; but, above all, the story is essentially
ill contrived, ending in the grossest violation of poetical
justice ever witnessed on the stage, the impunity and even
the triumph of one of the worst characters that was ever
drawn.

----

[f] Suard, p. 196.

Sect. III.—On the English Drama.

London Theatres—Shakspeare—Jonson—Beaumont and Fletcher—
Massinger—Other English Dramatists.

32. The English drama had been encouraged through the reign of Elizabeth by increasing popularity, not- *Popularity* withstanding the strenuous opposition of a party *of the stage under Eliza-* sufficiently powerful to enlist the magistracy, and, *beth.* in a certain measure, the government, on its side. A progressive improvement in dramatic writing, possibly also, though we know less of this, in the skill of the actors, ennobled, while it kept alive, the public taste; the crude and insipid compositions of an Edwards or a Whetstone, among numbers more whose very names are lost, gave way to the real genius of Green and Marlowe, and after them to Shakspeare.

33. At the beginning of this century not less than eleven regular play-houses had been erected in London *Number of* and its suburbs; several of which, it appears, were *theatres.* still in use, an order of the privy council in 1600, restraining the number to two, being little regarded. Of these the most important was that of the Black Friars, with which another, called the Globe, on the opposite side of the river, was connected; the same company performing at the former in winter, at the latter in summer. This was the company of which Burbage, the best actor of the day, was chief, and to which Shakspeare, who was also a proprietor, belonged. Their names appear in letters patent, and other legal instruments.[g]

34. James was fond of these amusements, and had encouraged them in Scotland. The puritan influence, *Encouraged* which had been sometimes felt in the council of *by James.* Elizabeth, came speedily to an end; though the representa-

---

[g] Shakspeare probably retired from the stage, as a performer, soon after 1603; his name appears among the actors of Sejanus in 1603, but not among those of Volpone in 1605. There is a tradition that James I. wrote a letter thanking Shakspeare for the compliment paid to him in Macbeth. Malone, it seems, believed this: Mr. Collier does not, and probably most people will be equally sceptical. Collier, i. 370.

tion of plays on Sundays, a constant theme of complaint, but never wholly put down, was now abandoned, and is not even tolerated by the Declaration of Sports. The several companies of players, who, in her reign, had been under the nominal protection of some men of rank, were now denominated the servants of the king, the queen, or other royal personages.[h] They were relieved from some of the vexatious control they had experienced, and subjected only to the gentle sway of the Master of the Revels. It was his duty to revise all dramatic works before they were represented, to exclude profane and unbecoming language, and specially to take care that there should be no interference with matters of state. The former of these corrective functions must have been rather laxly exercised; but there are instances in which a licence was refused on account of very recent history being touched in a play.

35. The reigns of James and Charles were the glory of our theatre. Public applause, and the favour of princes, were well bestowed on those bright stars of our literature who then appeared. In 1623, when Sir Henry Herbert became Master of the Revels, there were five companies of actors in London. This, indeed, is something less than at the accession of James, and the latest historian of the drama suggests the increase of puritanical sentiments as a likely cause of this apparent decline. But we find little reason to believe that there was any decline in the public taste for the theatre; and it may be as probable an hypothesis, that the excess of competition, at the end of Elizabeth's reign had rendered some undertakings unprofitable; the greater fishes, as usual in such cases, swallowing up the less. We learn from Howes, the continuator of Stow, that within sixty years before 1631, seventeen playhouses had been built in the metropolis. These were now

General taste for the stage.

---

[h] Collier, i. 347. But the privilege of peers to grant licences to itinerant players, given by Statute 14 Eliz. c. 5, and 39 Eliz. c. 4, was taken away by 1 Jac. I. c. 7, so that they became liable to be treated as vagrants. Accordingly there were no established theatres in any provincial city, and strollers, though dear to the lovers of the buskin, were always obnoxious to grave magistrates. The licence, however, granted to Burbage, Shakspeare, Hemmings, and others, in 1603, authorises them to act plays not only at the usual house, but in any other part of the kingdom. Burbage was reckoned the best actor of his time, and excelled as Richard III.

larger and more convenient than before. They were divided
into public and private; not that the former epithet was inapplicable to both; but those styled public were not completely roofed, nor well provided with seats, nor were the
performances by candlelight; they resembled more the rude
booths we still see at fairs, or the constructions in which
interludes are represented by day in Italy: while private
theatres, such as that of the Black Friars, were built in
nearly the present form. It seems to be the more probable
opinion that moveable scenery was unknown on these
theatres. 'It is a fortunate circumstance,' Mr. Collier has
observed, 'for the poetry of our old plays that it was so; the
imagination of the auditor only was appealed to; and we
owe to the absence of painted canvas many of the finest
descriptive passages in Shakspeare, his contemporaries, and
immediate followers. The introduction of scenery gives
the date to the commencement of the decline of our dramatic poetry.' In this remark, which seems as original
as just, I entirely concur. Even in this age the prodigality
of our theatre in its peculiar boast, scene-painting, can
hardly keep pace with the creative powers of Shakspeare; it
is well that he did not live when a manager was to estimate
his descriptions by the cost of realising them on canvas, or
we might never have stood with Lear on the cliffs of Dover,
or amidst the palaces of Venice with Shylock and Antonio.
The scene is perpetually changed in our old drama, precisely
because it was not changed at all. A powerful argument
might otherwise have been discovered in favour of the unity
of place, that it is very cheap.

36. Charles, as we might expect, was not less inclined to
this liberal pleasure than his predecessors. It was *Theatres*
to his own cost that Prynne assaulted the stage in *closed by the parlia-*
his immense volume, the Histrio-mastix. Even *ment.*
Milton, before the foul spirit had wholly entered into him,
extolled the learned sock of Jonson, and the wild wood-
notes of Shakspeare. But these days were soon to pass
away; the ears of Prynne were avenged; by an order of
the two houses of parliament, Sept. 2, 1642, the theatres
were closed, as a becoming measure during the season of
public calamity and impending civil war; but, after some

unsuccessful attempts to evade this prohibition, it was
thought expedient, in the complete success of the party
who had always abhorred the drama, to put a stop to it
altogether; and another ordinance of Jan. 22, 1648, reciting
the usual objections to all such entertainments, directed the
theatres to be rendered unserviceable. We must refer the
reader to the valuable work which has supplied the sketch of
these pages for further knowledge; [i] it is more our province
to follow the track of those who most distinguished a period
so fertile in dramatic genius: and first that of the greatest
of them all.

37. Those who originally undertook to marshal the plays
Shakspeare's of Shakspeare according to chronological order,
Twelfth
Night.   always attending less to internal evidence than to
the very fallible proofs of publication they could obtain,
placed Twelfth Night last of all, in 1612 or 1613. It afterwards rose a little higher in the list; but Mr. Collier has
finally proved that it was on the stage early in 1602, and
was at that time chosen, probably as rather a new piece, for
representation at one of the Inns of Court.[k] The general
style resembles, in my judgment, that of Much Ado about
Nothing, which is referred with probability to the year
1600. Twelfth Night, notwithstanding some very beautiful
passages, and the humorous absurdity of Malvolio, has not
the coruscations of wit and spirit of character that distinguish the excellent comedy it seems to have immediately
followed, nor is the plot nearly so well constructed. Viola
would be more interesting, if she had not indelicately, as
well as unfairly towards Olivia, determined to win the Duke's
heart before she had seen him. The part of Sebastian has
all that improbability which belongs to mistaken identity,
without the comic effect for the sake of which that is
forgiven in Plautus and in the Comedy of Errors.

38. The Merry Wives of Windsor is that work of

---

[i] I have made no particular references
to Mr. Collier's *double* work, The History
of English Dramatic Poetry, and Annals
of the Stage; it will be necessary for
the reader to make use of his index; but
few books lately published contain so
much valuable and original information,
though not entirely arranged in the
most convenient manner. He seems nevertheless to have obligations to Dods-
ley's preface to his Collection of Old
Plays, or rather perhaps to Reed's
edition of it.

[k] Vol. i. p. 327.

Shakspeare in which he has best displayed English manners ; for though there is something of this in the his- Merry Wives of Windsor. torical plays, yet we rarely see in them such a picture of actual life as comedy ought to represent. It may be difficult to say for what cause he has abstained from a source of gaiety whence his prolific invention and keen eye for the diversities of character might have drawn so much. The Masters Knowell and Wellborn, the young gentlemen who spend their money freely and make love to rich widows (an insipid race of personages, it must be owned), recur for ever in the old plays of James's reign ; but Shakspeare threw an ideality over this class of characters, the Bassanios, the Valentines, the Gratianos, and placed them in scenes which neither by dress nor manners recalled the prose of ordinary life.[m] In this play, however, the English gentleman, in age and youth, is brought upon the stage, slightly caricatured in Shallow, and far more so in Slender. The latter, indeed, is a perfect satire, and I think was so intended, on the brilliant youth of the provinces, such as we may believe it to have been before the introduction of newspapers and turnpike roads, awkward and boobyish among civil people, but at home in rude sports, and proud of exploits at which the town would laugh, yet perhaps with more courage and good-nature than the laughers. No doubt can be raised that the family of Lucy is ridiculed in Shallow ; but those who have had recourse to the old fable of the deer-stealing, forget that Shakspeare never lost sight of his native county, and went, perhaps every summer, to Stratford. It is not impossible that some arrogance of the provincial squires towards a player, whom, though a gentleman by birth and the recent grant of arms, they might not reckon such, excited his malicious wit to those admirable delineations.

39. The Merry Wives of Windsor was first printed in 1602, but very materially altered in a subsequent edition.

---

[m] 'No doubt,' says Coleridge, 'they (Beaumont and Fletcher) imitated the ease of gentlemanly conversation better than Shakspeare, who was unable not to be too much *associated* to succeed in this.' Table Talk, ii. 396. I am not quite sure that I understand this expression ; but probably the meaning is not very different from what I have said.

It is wholly comic; so that Dodd, who published the Beauties of Shakspeare, confining himself to poetry, says it is the only play which afforded him nothing to extract. This play does not excite a great deal of interest; for Anne Page is but a sample of a character not very uncommon, which under a garb of placid and decorous mediocrity is still capable of pursuing its own will. But in wit and humorous delineation no other goes beyond it. If Falstaff seems, as Johnson has intimated, to have lost some of his powers of merriment, it is because he is humiliated to a point where even his invention and impudence cannot bear him off victorious. In the first acts he is still the same Jack Falstaff of the Boar's Head. Jonson's earliest comedy, Every Man in His Humour, had appeared a few years before the Merry Wives of Windsor; they both turned on English life in the middle class, and on the same passion of jealousy. If then we compare these two productions of our greatest comic dramatists, the vast superiority of Shakspeare will appear undeniable. Kitely, indeed, has more energy, more relief, more excuse, perhaps, in what might appear to his temper matter for jealousy, than the wretched, narrow-minded Ford; he is more of a gentleman, and commands a certain degree of respect; but dramatic justice is better dealt upon Ford by rendering him ridiculous, and he suits better the festive style of Shakspeare's most amusing play. His light-hearted wife, on the other hand, is drawn with more spirit than Dame Kitely; and the most ardent admirer of Jonson would not oppose Master Stephen to Slender or Bobadil to Falstaff. The other characters are not parallel enough to admit of comparison; but in their diversity (nor is Shakspeare perhaps in any one play more fertile), and their amusing peculiarity, as well as in the construction and arrangement of the story, the brilliancy of the wit, the perpetual gaiety of the dialogue, we perceive at once to whom the laurel must be given. Nor is this comparison instituted to disparage Jonson, whom we have praised, and shall have again to praise so highly, but to show how much easier it was to vanquish the rest of Europe than to contend with Shakspeare.

40. Measure for Measure, commonly referred to the end

of 1603, is perhaps after Hamlet, Lear, and Macbeth, the play in which Shakspeare struggles, as it were, Measure for Measure. most with the over-mastering power of his own mind; the depths and intricacies of being which he has searched and sounded with intense reflection, perplex and harass him; his personages arrest their course of action to pour forth, in language the most remote from common use, thoughts which few could grasp in the clearest expression; and thus he loses something of dramatic excellence in that of his contemplative philosophy. The Duke is designed as the representative of this philosophical character. He is stern and melancholy by temperament, averse to the exterior shows of power, and secretly conscious of some unfitness for its practical duties. The subject is not very happily chosen, but artfully improved by Shakspeare. In most of the numerous stories of a similar nature, which before or since his time have been related, the sacrifice of chastity is really made, and made in vain. There is, however, something too coarse and disgusting in such a story; and it would have deprived him of a splendid exhibition of character. The virtue of Isabella, inflexible and independent of circumstance, has something very grand and elevated; yet one is disposed to ask, whether, if Claudio had been really executed, the spectator would not have gone away with no great affection for her; and at least we now feel that her reproaches against her miserable brother when he clings to life like a frail and guilty being are too harsh. There is great skill in the invention of Mariana, and without this the story could not have had anything like a satisfactory termination; yet it is never explained how the Duke had become acquainted with this secret, and being acquainted with it how he had preserved his esteem and confidence in Angelo. His intention, as hinted towards the end, to marry Isabella, is a little too common-place; it is one of Shakspeare's hasty half-thoughts. The language of this comedy is very obscure, and the text seems to have been printed with great inaccuracy. I do not value the comic parts highly; Lucio's impudent profligacy, the result rather of sensual debasement than of natural ill disposition, is well represented; but Elbow is a very inferior repetition of Dog-

berry.   In dramatic effect Measure for Measure ranks high ;
the two scenes between Isabella and Angelo, that between
her and Claudio, those where the Duke appears in disguise,
and the catastrophe in the fifth act, are admirably written
and very interesting; except so far as the spectator's knowledge of the two stratagems which have deceived Angelo
may prevent him from participating in the indignation at
Isabella's imaginary wrong which her lamentations would
excite.   Several of the circumstances and characters are
borrowed from the old play of Whetstone, Promos and
Cassandra; but very little of the sentiments or language.
What is good in Measure for Measure is Shakspeare's own.

41. If originality of invention did not so much stamp
almost every play of Shakspeare that to name

Lear.

one as the most original seems a disparagement
to others, we might say, that this great prerogative of
genius was exercised above all in Lear.   It diverges more
from the model of regular tragedy than Macbeth or Othello,
and even more than Hamlet; but the fable is better constructed than in the last of these, and it displays full as
much of the almost superhuman inspiration of the poet as
the other two.   Lear himself is, perhaps, the most wonderful of dramatic conceptions, ideal to satisfy the most
romantic imagination, yet idealised from the reality of
nature.   Shakspeare, in preparing us for the most intense
sympathy with this old man, first abases him to the ground ;
it is not Œdipus, against whose respected age the gods
themselves have conspired; it is not Orestes, noble-minded
and affectionate, whose crime has been virtue ; it is a
headstrong, feeble, and selfish being, whom, in the first act
of the tragedy, nothing seems capable of redeeming in our
eyes ; nothing but what follows, intense woe, unnatural
wrong.   Then comes on that splendid madness, not absurdly sudden, as in some tragedies, but in which the strings
that keep his reasoning power together give way one after
the other in the frenzy of rage and grief.   Then it is that
we find what in life may sometimes be seen, the intellectual energies grow stronger in calamity, and especially
under wrong.   An awful eloquence belongs to unmerited
suffering.   Thoughts burst out, more profound than Lear

in his prosperous hour could ever have conceived; inconsequent, for such is the condition of madness, but in themselves fragments of coherent truth, the reason of an unreasonable mind.

42. Timon of Athens is cast as it were in the same mould as Lear; it is the same essential character, the same generosity more from wanton ostentation than love of others, the same fierce rage under the smart of ingratitude, the same rousing ʼup, in that tempest of powers that had slumbered unsuspected in some deep recess of the soul; for had Timon or Lear known that philosophy of human nature in their calmer moments which fury brought forth, they would never have had such terrible occasion to display it. The thoughtless confidence of Lear in his children has something in it far more touching than the self-beggary of Timon; though both one and the other have prototypes enough in real life. And as we give the old king more of our pity, so a more intense abhorrence accompanies his daughters and the evil characters of that drama, than we spare for the miserable sycophants of the Athenian. Their thanklessness is anticipated, and springs from the very nature of their calling; it verges on the beaten road of comedy. In this play there is neither a female personage, except two courtezans, who hardly speak; nor is there any prominent character (the honest steward is not such) redeemed by virtue enough to be estimable; for the cynic Apemantus is but a cynic, and ill replaces the noble Kent of the other drama. The fable, if fable it can be called, is so extraordinarily deficient in action, a fault of which Shakspeare is not guilty in any other instance, that we may wonder a little how he should have seen in the single delineation of Timon a counterbalance for the manifold objections to this subject. But there seems to have been a period of Shakspeare's life when his heart was ill at ease, and ill content with the world or his own conscience; the memory of hours misspent, the pang of affection, misplaced or unrequited, the experience of man's worser nature which intercourse with unworthy associates, by choice or circumstance, peculiarly teaches;—these, as they sank down into the depths of his

great mind, seem not only to have inspired into it the conception of Lear and Timon, but that of one primary character, the censurer of mankind. This type is first seen
in the philosophic melancholy of Jaques, gazing with an
undiminished serenity, and with a gaiety of fancy, though
not of manners, on the follies of the world. It assumes a
graver cast in the exiled Duke of the same play, and next
one rather more severe in the Duke of Measure for Measure. In all these, however, it is merely contemplative
philosophy. In Hamlet this is mingled with the impulses
of a perturbed heart under the pressure of extraordinary
circumstances; it shines no longer as in the former characters, with a steady light, but plays in fitful coruscations
amidst feigned gaiety and extravagance. In Lear it is the
flash of sudden inspiration across the incongruous imagery
of madness; in Timon it is obscured by the exaggerations
of misanthropy. These plays all belong to nearly the same
period : As you Like It being usually referred to 1600,
Hamlet, in its altered form, to about 1602, Timon to the
same year, Measure for Measure to 1603, and Lear to 1604.
In the later plays of Shakspeare, especially in Macbeth and
the Tempest, much of moral speculation will be found, but
he has never returned to this type of character in the
personages. Timon is less read and less pleasing than the
great majority of Shakspeare's plays ; but it abounds with
signs of his genius. Schlegel observes that of all his works
it is that which has most satire ; comic in representation of
the parasites, indignant and Juvenalian in the bursts of
Timon himself.

43. Pericles is generally reckoned to be in part, and
only in part, the work of Shakspeare. From
the poverty and bad management of the fable,
the want of any effective or distinguishable character, for
Marina is no more than the common form of female virtue, such as all the dramatists of that age could draw, and
a general feebleness of the tragedy as a whole, I should
not believe the structure to have been Shakspeare's. But
many passages are far more in his manner than in that of
any contemporary writer with whom I am acquainted ; and
the extrinsic testimony, though not conclusive, being of

some value, I should not dissent from the judgment of
Steevens and Malone, that it was, in no inconsiderable degree, repaired and improved by his touch.   Drake has placed
it under the year 1590, as the earliest of Shakspeare's plays,
for no better reason apparently, than that he thought it
inferior to all the rest.   But if, as most will agree, it were
not quite his own, this reason will have less weight; and
the language seems to me rather that of his second or third
manner than of his first.   Pericles is not known to have
existed before 1609.

44. The majority of readers, I believe, assign to Macbeth,
which seems to have been written about 1606, the pre-eminence among the works of Shakspeare; many, however,
would rather name Othello, one of his latest, which is
referred to 1611; and a few might prefer Lear to either.
The great epic drama, as the first may be called, deserves, in
my own judgment, the post it has obtained, as being, in
the language of Drake, ' the greatest effort of our author's
genius, the most sublime and impressive drama which the
world has ever beheld.'   It will be observed that Shakspeare
had now turned his mind towards the tragic drama. No tragedy but Romeo and Juliet belongs to the sixteenth century;
ten, without counting Pericles, appeared in the first eleven
years of the present.   It is not my design to distinguish each
of his plays separately; and it will be evident that I pass
over some of the greatest.   No writer, in fact, is so well
known as Shakspeare, or has been so abundantly, and, on
the whole, so ably criticised ; I might have been warranted
in saying even less than I have done.

45. Shakspeare was, as I believe, conversant with the
better class of English literature which the reign of
Elizabeth afforded.   Among other books, the translation by North of Amyot's Plutarch seems to have
fallen into his hands about 1607.   It was the source of three
tragedies founded on the lives of Brutus, Antony, and
Coriolanus, the first bearing the name of Julius Cæsar.   In
this the plot wants even that historical unity which the
romantic drama requires; the third and fourth acts are ill
connected; it is deficient in female characters, and in that
combination which is generally apparent amidst all the

His Roman tragedies.

Julius Cæsar

intricacies of his fable. But it abounds in fine scenes and
fine passages; the spirit of Plutarch's Brutus is well seized,
the predominance of Cæsar himself is judiciously restrained,
the characters have that individuality which Shakspeare
seldom misses; nor is there, perhaps, in the whole range of
ancient and modern eloquence a speech more fully realising
the perfection that orators have striven to attain than that
of Antony.

46. Antony and Cleopatra is of rather a different order;
it does not furnish, perhaps, so many striking beauties as the last, but is at least equally redolent of
the genius of Shakspeare. Antony indeed was given him
by history, and he has but embodied in his own vivid colours
the irregular mind of the triumvir, ambitious and daring
against all enemies but himself. In Cleopatra he had less to
guide him; she is another incarnation of the same passions,
more lawless and insensible to reason and honour as they
are found in women. This character being not one that can
please, its strong and spirited delineation has not been
sufficiently observed. It has indeed only a poetical originality; the type was in the courtezan of common life, but the
resemblance is that of Michael Angelo's Sibyls to a muscular
woman. In this tragedy, like Julius Cæsar, as has been
justly observed by Schlegel, the events that do not pass on
the stage are scarcely made clear enough to one who is not
previously acquainted with history, and some of the persons
appear and vanish again without sufficient reason. He has,
in fact, copied Plutarch too exactly.

*Antony and
Cleopatra.*

47. This fault is by no means discerned in the third
Roman tragedy of Shakspeare, Coriolanus. He
luckily found an intrinsic historical unity which he
could not have destroyed, and which his magnificent delineation of the chief personage has thoroughly maintained.
Coriolanus himself has the grandeur of sculpture; his proportions are colossal, nor would less than this transcendent superiority, by which he towers over his fellow-citizens,
warrant, or seem for the moment to warrant, his haughtiness
and their pusillanimity. The surprising judgment of Shakspeare is visible in this. A dramatist of the second class (for
he alone is in the first), a Corneille, a Schiller, or an Alfieri,

Coriolanus.

would not have lost the occasion of representing the plebeian form of courage and patriotism. A tribune would have been made to utter noble speeches, and some critics would have extolled the balance and contrast of the antagonist principles. And this might have degenerated into the general saws of ethics and politics which philosophical tragedians love to pour forth. But Shakspeare instinctively perceived that to render the arrogance of Coriolanus endurable to the spectator, or dramatically probable, he must abase the plebeians to a contemptible populace. The sacrifice of historic truth is often necessary for the truth of poetry. The citizens of early Rome, ' *rusticorum mascula militum proles,*' are indeed calumniated in his scenes, and might almost pass for burgesses of Stratford ; but the unity of emotion is not dissipated by contradictory energies. Coriolanus is less rich in poetical style than the other two, but the comic parts are full of humour. In these three tragedies it is manifest that Roman character, and still more Roman manners, are not exhibited with the precision of a scholar; yet there is something that distinguishes them from the rest, something of a *grandiosity* in the sentiments and language, which shows us that Shakspeare had not read that history without entering into its spirit.

48. Othello, or perhaps the Tempest, is reckoned by many the latest of Shakspeare's works. In the zenith of his faculties, in possession of fame dis- His retirement and death. proportionate indeed to what has since accrued to his memory, but beyond that of any contemporary, at the age of about forty-seven, he ceased to write, and settled himself at a distance from all dramatic associations, in his own native town ; a home of which he had never lost sight, nor even permanently quitted, the birthplace of his children, and to which he brought what might then seem affluence in a middle station, with the hope, doubtless, of a secure decline in the yellow leaf of years. But he was cut off in 1616, not probably in the midst of any schemes for his own glory, but to the loss of those enjoyments which he had accustomed himself to value beyond it. His descendants, it is well known, became extinct in little more than half a century.

49. The name of Shakspeare is the greatest in our litera-
Greatness of his genius. ture—it is the greatest in all literature. No man
ever came near to him in the creative powers of
the mind ; no man had ever such strength at once and
such variety of imagination. Coleridge has most felicitously applied to him a Greek epithet, given before to I
know not whom, certainly none so deserving of it, μυριόνους,
the thousand-souled Shakspeare.[n] The number of characters in his plays is astonishingly great, without reckoning
those, who, although transient, have often their individuality, all distinct, all types of human life in well defined
differences. Yet he never takes an abstract quality to em-
body it, scarcely perhaps a definite condition of manners,
as Jonson does ; nor did he draw much, as I conceive,
from living models; there is no manifest appearance of
personal caricature in his comedies, though in some slight
traits of character this may not improbably have been the
case. Above all, neither he nor his contemporaries wrote
for the stage in the worse, though most literal, and of late
years, the most usual, sense ; making the servants and
handmaids of dramatic invention to lord over it, and
limiting the capacities of the poet's mind to those of the
performers. If this poverty of the representative department of the drama had hung like an incumbent fiend on
the creative power of Shakspeare, how would he have
poured forth with such inexhaustible prodigality the vast
diversity of characters that we find in some of his plays?
This it is in which he leaves far behind not the dramatists
alone, but all writers of fiction. Compare with him Homer, the tragedians of Greece, the poets of Italy, Plautus,
Cervantes, Molière, Addison, Le Sage, Fielding, Richard-
son, Scott, the romancers of the elder or later schools—
one man has far more than surpassed them all. Others
may have been as sublime, others may have been more
pathetic, others may have equalled him in grace and purity
of language, and have shunned some of its faults ; but the

---

[n] Table Talk, vol. ii. p. 301. Coleridge had previously spoken of Shakspeare's *oceanic* mind, which, if we take
it in the sense of multitudinous unity,
ποντίων κυμάτων ἀνήριθμον γέλασμα, will
present the same idea as μυριόνους in
a beautiful image.

philosophy of Shakspeare, his intimate searching out of the
human heart, whether in the gnomic form of sentence, or
in the dramatic exhibition of character, is a gift peculiarly
his own.   It is, if not entirely wanting, very little manifested in comparison with him, by the English dramatists of
his own and the subsequent period, whom we are about to
approach.

50. These dramatists, as we shall speedily perceive, are
hardly less inferior to Shakspeare in judgment. His judg-
To this quality I particularly advert, because fo- ment.
reign writers and sometimes our own, have imputed an
extraordinary barbarism and rudeness to his works.   They
belong indeed to an age sufficiently rude and barbarous in
its entertainments, and are of course to be classed with
what is called the romantic school, which has hardly yet
shaken off that reproach.   But no one who has perused the
plays anterior to those of Shakspeare, or contemporary with
them, or subsequent to them, down to the closing of the
theatres in the civil war, will pretend to deny that there is
far less regularity, in regard to everything where regula-
larity can be desired, in a large proportion of these (perhaps
in all the tragedies) than in his own.   We need only
repeat the names of the Merchant of Venice, Romeo and
Juliet, Macbeth, Othello, the Merry Wives of Windsor,
Measure for Measure.   The plots in these are excellently
constructed, and in some with uncommon artifice.   But
even where an analysis of the story might excite criticism,
there is generally an unity of interest which tones the
whole.   The Winter's Tale is not a model to follow, but
we feel that the Winter's Tale is a single story; it is even
managed as such with consummate skill.   It is another
proof of Shakspeare's judgment, that he has given action
enough to his comedies without the bustling intricacy of the
Spanish stage.   If his plots have any little obscurity in
some parts, it is from copying his novel or history too
minutely.

51. The idolatry of Shakspeare has been carried so far
of late years, that Drake and perhaps greater authorities
have been unwilling to acknowledge any faults in his plays.
This however is an extravagance rather derogatory to the

critic than honourable to the poet.   Besides the blemishes
of construction in some of his plots, which are pardonable
but still blemishes, there are too many in his style.   His
conceits and quibbles often spoil the effect of his scenes, and
take off from the passion he would excite.   In the last act
of Richard II., the Duke of York is introduced demanding
the punishment of his son Aumale for a conspiracy against
the king, while the Duchess implores mercy.   The scene
is ill conceived and worse executed throughout; but one
line is both atrocious and contemptible.   The Duchess
having dwelt on the word *pardon*, and urged the king to
let her hear it from his lips, York takes her up with this
stupid quibble:—

> Speak it in French, King; say Pardonnez-moi.

It would not be difficult to find several other instances,
though none, perhaps, quite so bad, of verbal equivocations,
misplaced and inconsistent with the person's, the author's,
the reader's sentiment.

52. Few will defend these notorious faults.   But is there
not one, less frequently mentioned, yet of more
continual recurrence; the extreme obscurity of
Shakspeare's diction? His style is full of new words and
new senses.   It is easy to pass this over as obsoleteness;
but though many expressions are obsolete, and many provincial, though the labour of his commentators has never
been so profitably, as well as so diligently, employed as in
tracing this by the help of the meanest and most forgotten
books of the age, it is impossible to deny that innumerable
lines in Shakspeare were not more intelligible in his time
than they are at present.   Much of this may be forgiven,
or rather is so incorporated with the strength of his reason
and fancy, that we love it as the proper body of Shakspeare's soul.   Still, can we justify the very numerous
passages which yield to no interpretation, knots which are
never unloosed, which conjecture does but cut, or even
those, which, if they may at last be understood, keep the
attention in perplexity till the first emotion has passed
away?   And these occur not merely in places where the
struggles of the speaker's mind may be well denoted by

*His obscu-
rity.*

some obscurities of language, as in the soliloquies of Hamlet
and Macbeth, but in dialogues between ordinary personages, and in the business of the play.   We learn Shakspeare, in fact, as we learn a language, or as we read a
difficult passage in Greek, with the eye glancing on the
commentary; and it is only after much study that we come
to forget a part, it can be but a part, of the perplexities he
has caused us.   This was no doubt one reason that he was
less read formerly, his style passing for obsolete, though in
many parts, as we have just said, it was never much more
intelligible than it is.[o]

53. It does not appear probable that Shakspeare was ever
placed below, or merely on a level with the other dramatic
writers of this period.[p]   That his plays were not so frequently
represented as those of Fletcher, is little to the pur-   His popu-
pose; they required a more expensive decoration, a   larity.
larger company of good performers, and, above all, they were
less intelligible to a promiscuous audience.   Yet it is certain
that throughout the seventeenth century, and even in the
writings of Addison and his contemporaries, we seldom or
never meet with that complete recognition of his supremacy,
that unhesitating preference of him to all the world, which
has become the faith of the last and the present century.   And
it is remarkable that this apotheosis, so to speak, of Shakspeare, was originally the work of what has been styled a,
frigid and tasteless generation, the age of George II.   Much

---

[o] 'Shakspeare's style is so pestered
with figurative expressions that it is as
affected as it is obscure.   It is true that
(in his latter plays he had worn off somewhat of this rust.'—Dryden's Works
(Malone), vol. ii. part ii. p. 252. This is
by no means the truth, but rather the
reverse of it; Dryden knew not at all
which were earlier, or which later, of
Shakspeare's plays.

[p] A certain William Cartwright, in
commendatory verses addressed to Fletcher, has the assurance to say,—

Shakspeare to thee was dull, whose best wit lies
I' th' ladies' questions and the fools' replies.

But the suffrage of Jonson himself, of
Milton, and of many more that might be
quoted, tends to prove that his genius
was esteemed beyond that of any other,

though some might compare inferior
writers to him in certain qualifications of
the dramatist.   Even Dryden, who came
in a worse period, and had no undue reverence for Shakspeare, admits that 'he
was the man who of all modern, and perhaps ancient, poets, had the largest and
most comprehensive soul. All the images
of nature were still present to him, and
he drew them not laboriously, but
luckily: when he describes any thing,
you more than see it, you feel it too.
Those who accuse him to have wanted
learning give him the greater commendation: he was naturally learned; he
needed not the spectacles of books to
read nature; he looked inwards, and
found her there.' — Dryden's Prose
Works (Malone's edition), vol. i. part ii.
p. 99.

is certainly due to the stage itself, when those appeared who could guide and control the public taste, and discover that in the poet himself which sluggish imaginations could not have reached. The enthusiasm for Shakspeare is nearly coincident with that for Garrick; it was kept up by his followers, and especially by that highly-gifted family which has but recently been withdrawn from our stage.

54. Among the commentators on Shakspeare, Warburton, always striving to display his own acuteness and scorn of others, deviates more than any one else from the meaning. Theobald was the first who did a little. Johnson explained much well, but there is something magisterial in the manner wherein he dismisses each play like a boy's exercise, that irritates the reader. His criticism is frequently judicious, but betrays no ardent admiration for Shakspeare. Malone and Steevens were two laborious commentators on the meaning of words and phrases; one dull, the other clever; but the dulness was accompanied by candour and a love of truth, the cleverness by a total absence of both. Neither seems to have had a full discernment of Shakspeare's genius. The numerous critics of the last age who were not editors have poured out much that is trite and insipid, much that is hypercritical and erroneous; yet collectively they not only bear witness to the public taste for the poet, but taught men to judge and feel more accurately than they would have done for themselves. Hurd and Lord Kaimes, especially the former, may be reckoned among the best of this class;[q] Mrs. Montagu, perhaps, in her celebrated Essay, not very far from the bottom of the list. In the present century, Coleridge and Schlegel, so nearly at the same time that the question of priority and even plagiarism has been mooted, gave a more philosophical, and at the same time a more intrinsically exact view of Shakspeare, than their

Critics on Shakspeare.

---

[q] Hurd, in his notes on Horace's Art of Poetry, vol. i. p. 52, has some very good remarks on the diction of Shakspeare, suggested by the ' callida junctura' of the Roman poet, illustrated by many instances. These remarks both serve to bring out the skill of Shakspeare, and to explain the disputed passage in Horace. Hurd justly maintains the obvious construction of that passage; ' notum si callida verbum Reddiderit junctura novum.' That proposed by Lambinus and Beattie, which begins with *novum*, is inadmissible, and gives a worse sense.

predecessors. What has since been written, has often been highly acute and æsthetic, but occasionally with an excess of refinement which substitutes the critic for the work. Mrs. Jameson's Essays on the Female Characters of Shakspeare are among the best. It was right that this province of illustration should be reserved for a woman's hand.

55. Ben Jonson, so generally known by that familiar description that some might hardly recognize him without it, was placed next to Shakspeare by his own age. They were much acquainted and belonged to the oldest, perhaps, and not the worst of clubs, formed by Sir Walter Raleigh about the beginning of the century, which met at the Mermaid in Friday Street. We may easily believe the testimony of one of its members, that it was a feast of the most subtle and brilliant wit.[r] Jonson had abundant powers of poignant and sarcastic humour, besides extensive reading, and Shakspeare must have brought to the Mermaid the brightness of his fancy. Selden and Camden, the former in early youth, are reported to have given the ballast of their strong sense and learning to this cluster of poets. There has been, however, a prevalent tradition that Jonson was not without some malignant and envious feelings towards Shakspeare. Gifford has repelled this imputation with considerable success, though we may still suspect that there was something caustic and saturnine in the temper of Jonson.

Ben Jonson.

56. The Alchemist is a play which long remained on the stage, though I am not sure that it has been represented since the days of Garrick, who was famous in Abel Drugger. Notwithstanding the indiscriminate and injudicious panegyric of Gifford, I believe there is no reader of taste but will condemn the outrageous excess of pedantry with which the first acts of this play abound ; pedantry the more intolerable, that it is not even what, however unfit for the English stage, scholars may comprehend, but the gibberish of obscure treatises on alchemy, which, whatever the commentators may choose to say, was as unintelligible to all but a few half-witted dupes of that imposture as it is at present. Much of this, it seems impossible to doubt, was omitted in

The Alchemist.

---

[r] Gifford's Life of Jonson, p. 65.   Collier, iii. 275.

representation. Nor is his pedantic display of learning confined to the part of the Alchemist, who had certainly a right
to talk in the style of his science, if he had done it with some
moderation : Sir Epicure Mammon, a worldly sensualist,
placed in the author's own age, pours out a torrent of glut-
tonous cookery from the kitchens of Heliogabalus and
Apicius; his dishes are to be camels' heels, the beards of
barbels and dissolved pearl, crowning all with the paps of a
sow. But while this habitual error of Jonson's vanity is not
to be overlooked, we may truly say, that it is much more than
compensated by the excellences of this comedy. The plot,
with great simplicity, is continually animated and interesting;
the characters are conceived and delineated with admirable
boldness, truth, spirit and variety ; the humour, especially in
the two Puritans, a sect who now began to do penance on
the stage, is amusing ; the language, when it does not smell
too much of book-learning, is forcible and clear. The Alchemist is one of the three plays which usually contest the
superiority among those of Jonson.

57. The second of these is The Fox, which, according to
Volpone or general opinion, has been placed above the Alchem-
The Fox. ist. Notwithstanding the dissent of Gifford, I should
concur in this suffrage. The fable belongs to a higher class
of comedy. Without minutely inquiring whether the Roman
hunters after the inheritance of the rich, so well described by
Horace, and especially the costly presents by which they endeavoured to secure a better return, are altogether according
to the manners of Venice, where Jonson has laid his scene,
we must acknowledge that he has displayed the base cupidity,
of which there will never be wanting examples among mankind, in such colours as all other dramatic poetry can hardly
rival. Cumberland has blamed the manner in which Volpone
brings ruin on his head by insulting, in disguise, those whom
he had duped. In this, I agree with Gifford, there is no
violation of nature. Besides their ignorance of his person,
so that he could not necessarily foresee the effects of Voltore's
rage, it has been well and finely said by Cumberland, that
there is a moral in a villain's outwitting himself. And this
is one that many dramatists have displayed.

58. In the choice of subject, The Fox is much inferior to

Tartuffe, to which it bears some very general analogy.
Though the Tartuffe is not a remarkably agreeable play, The
Fox is much less so; five of the principal characters are
wicked almost beyond any retribution that comedy can dispense; the smiles it calls forth are not those of gaiety but
scorn; and the parts of an absurd English knight and his
wife, though very humorous, are hardly prominent enough to
enliven the scenes of guilt and fraud which pass before our
eyes. But, though too much pedantry obtrudes itself, it does
not overspread the pages with nonsense as in the Alchemist;
the characters of Celia and Bonario excite some interest; the
differences, one can hardly say the gradations, of villany are
marked with the strong touches of Jonson's pen; the incidents succeed rapidly and naturally; the dramatic effect,
above all, is perceptible to every reader, and rises in a climax
through the last two acts to the conclusion.

59. The Silent Woman, which has been named by some
with the Alchemist and the Fox, falls much below   The Silent
them in vigorous delineation and dramatic effect.   Woman.
It has more diversity of manner than of character; the
amusing scenes border sometimes on farce, as where two
cowardly knights are made to receive blows in the dark, each
supposing them to come from his adversary, and the catastrophe is neither pleasing nor probable. It is written with
a great deal of spirit, and has a value as the representation
of London life in the higher ranks at that time. But upon
the whole I should be inclined to give to Every Man in his
Humour a much superior place. It is a proof of Jonson's
extensive learning, that the story of this play, and several
particular passages, have been detected in a writer so much
out of the beaten track as Libanius.[s]

60. The pastoral drama of the Sad Shepherd is the best
testimony to the poetical imagination of Jonson.   Sad Shep-
Superior in originality, liveliness, and beauty to the   herd.

---

[s] Gifford discovered this. Dryden,
who has given an examination of the
Silent Woman, in his Essay on Dramatic Poetry, takes Morose for a real character, and says that he had so been
informed. It is possible that there might
be some foundation of truth in this: the
skeleton is in Libanius, but Jonson may
have filled it up from the life. Dryden
gives it as his opinion that there is more
wit and acuteness of fancy in this play
than in any of Ben Jonson's, and that
he has described the conversation of
gentlemen with more gaiety and freedom than in the rest of his comedies.
P. 107.

Faithful Shepherdess of Fletcher, it reminds us rather, in language and imagery, of the Midsummer Night's Dream, and perhaps no other poetry has come so near to that of Shakspeare. Jonson, like him, had an extraordinary command of English, in its popular and provincial idioms, as well as what might be gained from books; and though his invincible pedantry now and then obtrudes itself into the mouths of shepherds, it is compensated by numerous passages of the most natural and graceful expression. This beautiful drama is imperfect, hardly more than half remaining, or, more probably, having ever been written. It was also Jonson's last song; age and poverty had stolen upon him; but as one has said, who experienced the same destiny, ' the life was in the leaf,' and his laurel remained verdant amidst the snow of his honoured head. The beauties of the Sad Shepherd might be reckoned rather poetical than dramatic; yet the action is both diversified and interesting to a degree we seldom find in the pastoral drama; there is little that is low in the comic speeches, nothing that is inflated in the serious.

61. Two men, once united by friendship, and for ever by Beaumont fame, the Dioscuri of our zodiac, Beaumont and and Fletcher. Fletcher, rose upon the horizon as the star of Shakspeare, though still in its fullest brightness, was declining in the sky. The first in order of time among more than fifty plays published with their joint names, is the Woman-Hater, represented, according to Langbaine, in 1607, and ascribed to Beaumont alone by Seward, though, I believe, merely on conjecture.[t] Beaumont died, at the age of thirty, in 1615; Fletcher in 1625. No difference of manner is perceptible, or, at least, no critic has perceived any, in the plays that appeared between these two epochs; in fact, the greater part were not printed till 1647, and it is only through the records of the play-house that we distinguish their dates.

---

[t] Vol. i. p. 3. He also thinks The Nice Valour exclusively Beaumont's. These two appear to me about the worst in the collection.

[The latest editor of Beaumont and Fletcher is inclined to modify this opinion, latterly prevalent, as to the respective shares of the two poets. The Woman-Hater, he thinks, was ' in all probability the unassisted composition of Fletcher.' On the other hand, he says, ' not the slightest doubt can be entertained that of the earlier plays in the present collection (and among those plays are the best) Beaumont contributed a large (perhaps the weightier) portion.' ' Some account of the Lives and Writings of Beaumont and Fletcher,' prefixed to Mr. Dyce's edition.—1847.]

The tradition, however, of their own times, as well as the earlier death of Beaumont, give us reason to name Fletcher, when we mention one singly, as the principal author of all these plays; and of late years this has perhaps become more customary than it used to be.   A contemporary copy of verses, indeed, seems to attribute the greater share in the Maid's Tragedy, Philaster, and King and No King, to Beaumont.   But testimony of this kind is very precarious.   It is sufficient that he bore a part in these three.

62. Of all our early dramatic poets, none have suffered such mangling by the printer as Beaumont and *Corrupt* Fletcher.   Their style is generally elliptical and *state of their text.* not very perspicuous; they use words in peculiar senses, and there seems often an attempt at pointed expression, in which its meaning has deserted them.   But after every effort to comprehend their language, it is continually so remote from all possibility of bearing a rational sense, that we can only have recourse to one hypothesis, that of an extensive and irreparable corruption of the text.   Seward and Simpson, who, in 1750, published the first edition in which any endeavour was made at illustration or amendment, though not men of much taste, and too fond of extolling their authors, showed some acuteness, and have restored many passages in a probable manner, though often driven out at sea to conjecture something, where the received reading furnished not a vestige which they could trace.   No one since has made any great progress in this criticism, though some have carped at these editors for not performing more.   The problem of actual restoration in most places, where the printers or transcribers have made such strange havoc, must evidently be insoluble. [u]

63. The first play in the collected works of Beaumont and Fletcher, though not the earliest, is the Maid's *The Maid's* Tragedy, and it is among the best.   None of their *Tragedy.* female characters, though they are often very successful in beautiful delineations of virtuous love, attaches our sympathy like Aspasia.   Her sorrows are so deep, so pure, so unmerited, she sustains the breach of plighted faith in Amyntor, and the

---

[u] [The recent edition of Mr. Dyce has gone far towards a restoration of the genuine text.—1847.]

taunts of vicious women, with so much resignation, so little
of that termagant resentment which these poets are apt to
infuse into their heroines, the poetry of her speeches is so
exquisitely imaginative, that, of those dramatic persons who
are not prominent in the development of a story, scarce any,
even in Shakspeare, are more interesting. Nor is the praise
due to the Maid's Tragedy confined to the part of Aspasia.
In Melantius we have Fletcher's favourite character, the
brave, honest soldier, incapable of suspecting evil till it becomes impossible to be ignorant of it, but unshrinking in its
punishment. That of Evadne well displays the audacious
security of guilt under the safeguard of power; it is highly
theatrical, and renders the success of this tragedy not surprising in times when its language and situations could be
endured by the audience. We may remark in this tragedy,
as in many others of these dramatists, that, while pouring
out the unlimited loyalty fashionable at the court of James,
they are full of implied satire, which could hardly escape observation. The warm eulogies on military glory, the scorn of
slothful peace, the pictures of dissolute baseness in courtiers,
seem to spring from a sentiment very usual among the English gentry, a rank to which they both belonged, of dislike to
that ignominious government; and though James was far
enough removed from such voluptuous tyrants as Fletcher
has portrayed in this and some other plays, they did not
serve to exemplify the advantages of monarchy in the most
attractive manner.

64. The Maid's Tragedy, unfortunately, beautiful and
essentially moral as it is, cannot be called a tragedy for
maids, and indeed should hardly be read by any respectable
woman. It abounds with that studiously protracted indecency which distinguished Fletcher beyond all our early
dramatists, and is so much incorporated with his plays, that
very few of them can be so altered as to become tolerable at
present on the stage. In this he is strikingly contrasted
with Shakspeare, whose levities of this kind are so transitory,
and so much confined to language, that he has borne the process of purification with little detriment to his genius, or
even to his wit.

65. Philaster has been, in its day, one of the best known

and most popular of Fletcher's plays.[x] This was owing
to the pleasing characters of Philaster and Bellario,
and to the frequent sweetness of the poetry. It is, _{Philaster.}
nevertheless, not a first-rate play. The plot is most absurdly
managed. It turns on the suspicion of Arethusa's infidelity.
And the sole ground of this is that an abandoned woman,
being detected herself, accuses the princess of unchastity.
Not a shadow of presumptive evidence is brought to confirm
this impudent assertion, which, however, the lady's father,
her lover, and a grave, sensible courtier, do not fail implicitly
to believe. How unlike the chain of circumstance, and the
devilish cunning, by which the Moor is wrought up to think
his Desdemona false! Bellario is suggested by Viola; there
is more picturesqueness, more dramatic importance, not, perhaps, more beauty and sweetness of affection, but a more
eloquent development of it in Fletcher; on the other hand,
there is still more of that improbability which attends a
successful concealment of sex by mere disguise of clothes,
though no artifice has been more common on the stage.
Many other circumstances in the conduct of Fletcher's story
are ill contrived. It has less wit than the greater part of his
comedies; for among such, according to the old distinction,
it is to be ranked, though the subject is elevated and serious.

66. King and No King is, in my judgment, inferior to
Philaster. The language has not so much of poe- _{King and}
tical beauty. The character of Arbaces excites no _{No King.}
sympathy; it is a compound of vain-glory and violence,
which rather demands disgrace from poetical justice than
reward. Panthea is innocent, but insipid; Mardonius a good
specimen of what Fletcher loves to exhibit, the plain, honest
courtier. As for Bessus, he certainly gives occasion to several
amusing scenes; but his cowardice is a little too glaring;
he is neither so laughable as Bobadil, nor so sprightly as
Parolles. The principal merit of this play, which rendered
it popular on the stage for many years, consists in the effective scenes where Arbaces reveals his illicit desire. That

---

[x] Dryden says, but I know not how
truly, that Philaster was 'the first play
that brought Beaumont and Fletcher in
esteem; for before that they had written two or three very unsuccessfully.'

P. 100. Philaster was not printed, according to Langbaine, till 1620 : I do
not know that we have any evidence of
the date of its representation.

especially with Mardonius is artfully and elaborately written. Shakspeare had less of this skill; and his tragedies suffer for it in their dramatic effect. The scene between John and Hubert is an exception, and there is a great deal of it in Othello; but in general he may be said not to have exerted the power of detaining the spectator in that anxious suspense, which creates almost an actual illusion, and makes him tremble at every word, lest the secret which he has learned should be imparted to the imaginary person on the stage. Of this there are several fine instances in the Greek tragedians, the famous scene in the Œdipus Tyrannus being the best; and it is possible that the superior education of Fletcher may have rendered him familiar with the resources of ancient tragedy. These scenes in the present play would have been more highly powerful if the interest could have been thrown on any character superior to the selfish braggart Arbaces. It may be said, perhaps, that his humiliation through his own lawless passions, after so much insolence of success, affords a moral; he seems, however, but imperfectly cured at the conclusion, which is also hurried on with unsatisfactory rapidity.

67. The Elder Brother has been generally reckoned among
The Elder
Brother.
the best of Fletcher's comedies. It displays in a new form an idea not very new in fiction, the power of love, on the first sight of a woman, to vivify a soul utterly ignorant of the passion. Charles, the Elder Brother, much unlike the Cymon of Dryden, is absorbed in study; a mere scholar without a thought beyond his books. His indifference, perhaps, and ignorance about the world are rather exaggerated, and border on stupidity; but it was the custom of the dramatists in that age to produce effect in representation by very sudden developments, if not changes, of character. The other persons are not ill conceived; the honest, testy Miramont, who admires learning without much more of it than enables him to sign his name, the two selfish, worldly fathers of Charles and Angelina, believing themselves shrewd, yet the easy dupes of coxcomb manners from the court, the spirited Angelina, the spoiled but not worthless Eustace, show Fletcher's great talent in dramatic invention. In none of his mere comedies has he sustained so uniformly elegant

and pleasing a style of poetry; the language of Charles is naturally that of a refined scholar, but now and then, perhaps, we find old Miramont talk above himself. The underplot hits to the life the licencious endeavours of an old man to seduce his inferior; but, as usual, it reveals vice too broadly. This comedy is of very simple construction, so that Cibber was obliged to blend it with another, The Custom of the Country, in order to compose from the two his Love Makes a Man, by no means the worst play of that age. The two plots, however, do not harmonise very well.

68. The Spanish Curate is, in all probability, taken from one of those comedies of intrigue which the fame The Spanish of Lope de Vega had made popular in Europe.[y] Curate. It is one of the best specimens of that manner; the plot is full of incident and interest, without being difficult of comprehension, nor, with fair allowance for the conventions of the stage and manners of the country, improbable. The characters are in full relief without caricature. Fletcher, with an artifice of which he was very fond, has made the fierce resentment of Violante break out unexpectedly from the calmness she had shown in the first scenes; but it is so well accounted for, that we see nothing unnatural in the development of passions for which there had been no previous call. Ascanio is again one of Fletcher's favourite delineations; a kind of Bellario in his modest, affectionate disposition; one in whose prosperity the reader takes so much pleasure that he forgets it is, in a worldly sense, inconsistent with that of the honest-hearted Don Jamie. The doting husband, Don Henrique, contrasts well with the jealous Bartolus; and both afford by their fate, the sort of moral which is looked for in comedy. The underplot of the lawyer and his wife, while it shows how licentious in principle as well as indecent in language the stage had become, is conducted with incomparable humour and amusement. Congreve borrowed part of this in the Old Bachelor without by any means equalling it. Upon the whole, as a comedy of this class, it deserves to be placed in the highest rank.

---

[y] [The Spanish Curate, Mr. Dyce informs us, is founded on 'Gerardo, the Unfortunate Spaniard,' a novel by Gonçalo de Cespides, of which an English translation, by Leonard Digges, appeared in 1622.—1847.]

69. The Custom of the Country is much deformed by
The Custom obscenity, especially the first act.   But it is full of
of the
Country.   nobleness in character and sentiment, of interesting
situations, of unceasing variety of action.   Fletcher has
never shown what he so much delights in drawing, the contrast of virtuous dignity with ungoverned passion in woman,
with more success than in Zenocia and Hippolyta.   Of these
three plays we may say, perhaps, that there is more poetry
in the Elder Brother, more interest in the Custom of the
Country, more wit and spirit in the Spanish Curate.

70. The Loyal Subject ought also to be placed in a high
The Loyal rank among the works of Beaumont and Fletcher.
Subject.   There is a play by Heywood, The Royal King and
Loyal Subject, from which the general idea of several circumstances of this has been taken.   That Heywood's was
the original, though the only edition of it is in 1637, while
the Loyal Subject was represented in 1618, cannot bear a
doubt.   The former is expressly mentioned in the epilogue
as an old play, belonging to a style gone out of date, and
not to be judged with rigour.   Heywood has therefore the
praise of having conceived the character of Earl Marshal,
upon which Fletcher somewhat improved in Archas; a brave
soldier, of that disinterested and devoted loyalty which bears
all ingratitude and outrage at the hands of an unworthy and
misguided sovereign.   In the days of James there could
be no more courtly moral.   In each play the prince, after
depriving his most deserving subject of honours and fortune,
tries his fidelity by commanding him to send two daughters,
whom he had educated in seclusion, to the court, with
designs that the father may easily suspect.   The loyalty,
however, of these honest soldiers submits to encounter this
danger; and the conduct of the young ladies soon proves
that they might be trusted in the fiery trial.   In the Loyal
Subject, Fletcher has beautifully, and with his light touch
of pencil, sketched the two virtuous sisters; one high-
spirited, intrepid, undisguised; the other shrinking with
maiden modesty, a tremulous dew-drop in the cup of a violet.
But unfortunately his original taint betrays itself, and the
elder sister cannot display her scorn of licentiousness without
borrowing some of its language.   If Shakespeare had put

these loose images into the mouth of Isabella, how differently we should have esteemed her character!

71. We find in the Loyal Subject what is neither pleasing nor probable, the disguise of a youth as a girl. This was of course not offensive to those who saw nothing else on the stage. Fletcher did not take this from Heywood. In the whole management of the story he is much superior; the nobleness of Archas and his injuries are still more displayed than those of the Earl Marshal; and he has several new characters, especially Theodore, the impetuous son of the Loyal Subject, who does not brook the insults of a prince as submissively as his father, which fill the play with variety and spirit. The language is in some places obscure and probably corrupt, but abounding with that kind of poetry which belongs to Fletcher.

72. Beggar's Bush is an excellent comedy; the serious parts interesting, the comic diverting. Every cha- Beggar's racter supports itself well: if some parts of the Bush. plot have been suggested by As You Like It, they are managed so as to be original in spirit. Few of Fletcher's plays furnish more proofs of his characteristic qualities. It might be represented with no great curtailment.

73. The Scornful Lady is one of those comedies which exhibit English domestic life, and have therefore a The Scorn-value independent of their dramatic merit. It does ful Lady. not equal Beggar's Bush, but is full of effective scenes, which, when less regard was paid to decency, must have rendered it a popular play. Fletcher, in fact, is as much superior to Shakspeare in his knowledge of the stage, as he falls below him in that of human nature.[z] His fertile invention

---

[z] [Mr. Dyce, as well as an earlier editor of Beaumont and Fletcher, thinks the greater part of this comedy written by Beaumont. Mr. Dyce adds: 'In the edition of 1750, Theobald has a note concerning the steward Savil, where he says, "The ingenious Mr. Addison, I remember, told me that he sketched out his character of Vellum, in the comedy called the Drummer, purely from this model."' It is said of some plagiaries, that they are like gypsies, who steal children, and disfigure them that they may not be known. 'The ingenious Mr. Addison' went another way to work; when he took any one's silver, he turned it into gold. I doubt whether Theobald reported his ingenious friend's words rightly; for the inimitable formality of Vellum has no prototype in Savil. But, while making this avowal, why did not he add, that the Waiting-Woman in the Scornful Lady is called Abigail? Here was a heinous theft; and after its concealment, I fear that we must refuse absolution. After all, however, there is a certain resemblance in these comedies, which may lead us

was turned to the management of his plot (always with a view to representation), the rapid succession of incidents, the surprises and embarrassments which keep the spectator's attention alive. His characters are but vehicles to the story: they are distinguished, for the most part, by little more than the slight peculiarities of manner, which are easily caught by the audience; and we do not often meet, especially in his comedies, with the elaborate delineations of Jonson, or the marked idiosyncrasies of Shakspeare. Of these his great predecessors, one formed a deliberate conception of a character, whether taken from general nature or from manners, and drew his figure, as it were, in his mind before he transferred it to the canvas; with the other the idea sprang out of the depths of his soul, and though suggested by the story he had chosen, became so much the favourite of his genius as he wrote, that in its development he sometimes grew negligent of his plot.

74. No tragedy of Fletcher would deserve higher praise than Valentinian, if he had not, by an inconceivable want of taste and judgment, descended from beauty and dignity to the most preposterous absurdities. The matron purity of the injured Lucina, the ravages of unrestrained self-indulgence on a mind not wholly without glimpses of virtue in Valentinian, the vileness of his courtiers, the spirited contrast of unconquerable loyalty in Ætius with the natural indignation at wrong in Maximus, are brought before our eyes in some of Fletcher's best poetry, though in a text that seems even more corrupt than usual. But after the admirable scene in the third act, where Lucina (the Lucretia of this story) reveals her injury, perhaps almost the only scene in this dramatist, if we except the Maid's Tragedy, that can move us to tears, her husband Maximus, who even here begins to forfeit our sympathy by his ready consent, in the Spanish style of perverted honour, to her suicide, becomes a treacherous and ambitious villain, the loyalty of Ætius turns

Valentinian.

---

to believe that Addison had his predecessors in his head. Since this was written, I have observed that Mr. Dyce, in 'Some Account of the Lives and Writings of Beaumont and Fletcher,' prefixed to his edition, p. 41, has re-

marks to the same purport. Mr. Dyce adds, that when 'the Spectator and Tatler are hastening to oblivion,' (Pudet hæc opprobria,) 'it cannot be expected that the reader will know much of The Drummer.'—1847.]

to downright folly, and the rest of the play is but such a series
of murders as Marston or the author of Andronicus might have
devised.   If Fletcher meant, which he very probably did, to
inculcate as a moral, that the worst of tyrants are to be
obeyed with unflinching submission, he may have gained
applause at court, at the expense of his reputation with
posterity.

75. The Two Noble Kinsmen is a play that has been
honoured by a tradition of Shakspeare's concern in   The Two
it.   The first evidence as to this is the title-page of   Noble Kins-
the first edition; which, though it may seem much at first
sight, is next to nothing in our old drama, full of misnomers
of this kind.   The editors of Beaumont and Fletcher have
insisted upon what they take for marks of Shakspeare's style;
and Schlegel, after 'seeing no reason for doubting so probable an opinion,' detects the spirit of Shakspeare in a
certain ideal purity which distinguishes this from other
plays of Fletcher, and in the conscientious fidelity with which
it follows the Knight's Tale in Chaucer.   The Two Noble
Kinsmen has much of that elevated sense of honour, friendship, fidelity, and love, which belongs, I think, more characteristically to Fletcher, who had drunk at the fountain of
Castilian romance, than to one in whose vast mind this
conventional morality of particular classes was subordinated
to the universal nature of man.   In this sense Fletcher is
always, in his tragic compositions, a very ideal poet.   The
subject itself is fitter for him than for Shakspeare.   In the
language and conduct of this play, with great deference to
better and more attentive critics, I see imitations of Shakspeare rather than such resemblances as denote his powerful
stamp.   The madness of the gaoler's daughter, where some
have imagined they saw the master-hand, is doubtless suggested by that of Ophelia, but with an inferiority of taste and
feeling which it seems impossible not to recognise.   The
painful and degrading symptom of female insanity, which
Shakspeare has touched with his gentle hand, is dwelt upon
by Fletcher with all his innate impurity.   Can any one
believe that the former would have written the last scene in
which the gaoler's daughter appears on the stage?   Schlegel
has too fine taste to believe that this character came from

Shakspeare, and it is given up by the latest assertor of his claim to a participation in the play.[a]

76. The Faithful Shepherdess, deservedly among the most The Faithful celebrated productions of Fletcher, stands alone in Shepherdess. its class, and admits of no comparison with any other play. It is a pastoral drama, in imitation of the Pastor Fido, at that time very popular in England. The Faithful Shepherdess, however, to the great indignation of all the poets, did not succeed on its first representation. There is nothing in this surprising; the tone of pastoral is too far removed from the possibilities of life for a stage which appealed, like ours, to the boisterous sympathies of a general audience. It is a play very characteristic of Fletcher, being a mixture of tenderness, purity, indecency, and absurdity. There is some justice in Schlegel's remark, that it is an immodest eulogy on modesty. But this critic, who does not seem to appreciate the beauty of Fletcher's poetry, should hardly have mentioned Guarini as a model whom he might have followed. It was by copying the Corisca of the Pastor Fido that Fletcher introduced the character of the vicious shepherdess Chloe; though, according to his times, and, we must own, to his own disposition, he has greatly aggravated the faults to which just exception has been taken in his original.

77. It is impossible to withhold our praise from the poetical

---

[a] The author of a 'Letter on Shakspeare's Authorship of the Drama entitled the Two Noble Kinsmen,' Edinburgh, 1833, notwithstanding this title, does not deny a considerable participation to Fletcher. He lays no great stress on the external evidence. But in arguing from the similarity of style in many passages to that of Shakspeare, the author, Mr. Spalding of Edinburgh, shows so much taste and so competent a knowledge of the two dramatists, that I should perhaps scruple to set up my own doubts in opposition. His chief proofs are drawn from the force and condensation of language in particular passages, which doubtless is one of the great distinctions between the two. But we might wish to have seen this displayed in longer extracts than such as the author of this Letter has generally given us. It is difficult to say of a man like Fletcher that he could not have written single lines in the spirit of his predecessor. A few instances, however, of longer passages will be found; and I believe that it is a subject upon which there will long be a difference of opinion.

[Coleridge has said, 'I have no doubt whatever that the first act, and the first scene of the second act, of the Two Noble Kinsmen, are Shakspeare's.' Table-Talk, vol. ii. p. 119.—1842.]

[Mr. Dyce concurs with Mr. Spalding as to the share of Shakspeare, which they both think to have been the first, and a part, if not all, of the fifth, but not much of the intermediate parts. The hypothesis of a joint production is open to much difficulty, which Mr. Dyce hardly removes.— 1847.]

beauties of this pastoral drama. Every one knows that it contains the germ of Comus; the benevolent Satyr, whose last proposition to 'stray in the middle air, and stay the sailing rack, or nimbly take hold of the moon,' is not much in the character of those sylvans, has been judiciously metamorphosed by Milton to an attendant spirit; and a more austere as well as more uniform language has been given to the speakers. But Milton has borrowed largely from the imagination of his predecessor : and by quoting the lyric parts of the Faithful Shepherdess, it would be easy to deceive any one not accurately familiar with the songs of Comus. They abound with that rapid succession of ideal scenery, that darting of the poet's fancy from earth to heaven, those picturesque and novel metaphors, which distinguish much of the poetry of this age, and which are ultimately, perhaps, in great measure referable to Shakspeare.

78. Rule a Wife and Have a Wife is among the superior comedies of its class. That it has a prototype on the Spanish theatre must appear likely; but I should be suprised if the variety and spirit of character, the vivacity of humour, be not chiefly due to our own authors.[b] Every personage in this comedy is drawn with a vigorous pencil ; so that it requires a good company to be well represented. It is indeed a mere picture of roguery ; for even Leon, the only character for whom we can feel any sort of interest, has gained his ends by stratagem ; but his gallant spirit redeems this in our indulgent views of dramatic morality, and we are justly pleased with the discomfiture of fraud and effrontery in Estifania and Margarita.

Rule a Wife and Have a Wife.

79. The Knight of the Burning Pestle is very diverting, and more successful, perhaps than any previous attempt to introduce a drama within a drama. I should hardly except the Introduction to the Taming of the Shrew. The burlesque, though very ludicrous, does not transgress all bounds of probability. The Wild-goose Chase, The Chances, the Humorous Lieutenant, Women Pleased, Wit without Money, Monsieur Thomas, and several other

Some other plays.

---

[b] [It is taken, in part, from one of the novels of Cervantes. See Mr. Dyce's Introduction, p. 7.—1847.]

comedies deserve to be praised for the usual excellences of Fletcher, his gaiety, his invention, his ever varying rapidity of dialogue and incident. None are without his defects; and we may add, what is not in fairness to be called a defect of his, since it applies perhaps to every dramatic writer except Shakspeare and Molière, that, being cast as it were in a common mould, we find both a monotony in reading several of these plays, and a difficulty of distinguishing them in remembrance.

80. The later writers, those especially after the Restoration, did not fail to appropriate many of the inventions of Fletcher. He and his colleague are the proper founders of our comedy of intrigue, which prevailed through the seventeenth century, the comedy of Wycherley, Dryden, Behn, and Shadwell. Their manner, if not their actual plots, may still be observed in many pieces that are produced on our stage. But few of those imitators came up to the sprightliness of their model. It is to be regretted that it is rarely practicable to adapt any one of his comedies to representation without such changes as destroy their original raciness, and dilute the geniality of their wit.

81. There has not been much curiosity to investigate the sources of his humorous plays. A few are historical; but it seems highly probable that the Spanish stage of Lope de Vega and his contemporaries often furnished the subject, and perhaps many of the scenes, to his comedies. These possess all the characteristics ascribed to the comedies of intrigue so popular in that country. The scene too is more commonly laid in Spain, and the costume of Spanish manners and sentiments more closely observed, than we should expect from the invention of Englishmen. It would be worth the leisure of some lover of theatrical literature to search the collection of Lope de Vega's works, and, if possible, the other Spanish writers at the beginning of the century, in order to trace the footsteps of our two dramatists. Sometimes they may have had recourse to novels. The Little French Lawyer seems to indicate such an origin. Nothing had as yet been produced, I believe, on the French stage from which it could have been derived, but the story and most of the characters are manifestly of French derivation.

Origin of Fletcher's plays.

The comic humour of La Writ in this play we may ascribe to the invention of Fletcher himself.[c]

82. It is, however, not improbable that the entire plot was sometimes original. Fertile as their invention was, Defects of their plots. to an extraordinary degree, in furnishing the incidents of their rapid and animated comedies, we may believe the fable itself to have sometimes sprung from no other source. It seems, indeed, now and then, as if the authors had gone forward with no very clear determination of their catastrophe; there is a want of unity in the conception, a want of consistency in the characters, which appear sometimes rather intended to surprise by incongruity, than framed upon a definite model. That of Ruy Diaz in the Island Princess, of whom it is hard to say whether he is a brave man or a coward, or alternately one and the other, is an instance to which many more might easily be added. In the Bloody Brother, Rollo sends to execution one of his councillors, whose daughter Edith vainly interferes in a scene of great pathos and effect. In the progress of the drama she arms herself to take away the tyrant's life; the whole of her character has been consistent and energetic; when Fletcher, to the reader's astonishment, thinks fit to imitate the scene between Richard and Lady Anne; and the ignominious fickleness of that lady, whom Shakspeare with wonderful skill, but in a manner not quite pleasing, sacrifices to the better display of the cunning crook-back, is here transferred to the heroine of the play, and the very character upon whom its interest ought to depend. Edith is on the point of giving up her purpose, when some others in the conspiracy coming in, she recovers herself enough to exhort them to strike the blow.[d]

---

[c] Dryden reckons this play with the Spanish Curate, the Chances, and Rule a Wife and Have a Wife, among those which he supposes to be drawn from Spanish novels. Essay on Dramatic Poetry, p. 204. By novels we should probably understand plays; for those which he mentions are little in the style of novels. But the Little French Lawyer has all the appearance of coming from a French novel; the scene lies in France, and I see nothing Spanish about it. Dryden was seldom well informed about the early stage.

[In this conjecture I have been mistaken: the plot, Langbaine says, is borrowed from the Spanish Rogue of Guzman d'Alfarache; and Mr. Dyce adds that this writer took it from an older novel, by Masuccio Salernitano. Beaumont and Fletcher have, however, greatly improved the story. Dyce's Beaumont and Fletcher, vol. iii. p. 459. See, too, what is said above. on the same authority, as to the Spanish Curate.—1847.]

[d] Rotrou, in his Wenceslas, as we have already observed, has done some-

83. The sentiments and style of Fletcher, where not con-

Their sen-
timents and
style dra-
matic.
cealed by obscurity, or corruption of the text, are very dramatic. We cannot deny that the depths of Shakspeare's mind were often unfathomable by an audience; the bow was drawn by a matchless hand, but the shaft went out of sight. All might listen to Fletcher's pleasing, though not profound or vigorous, language; his thoughts are noble, and tinged with the ideality of romance, his metaphors vivid, though sometimes too forced; he possesses the idiom of English without much pedantry, though in many passages he strains it beyond common use; his versification, though studiously irregular, is often rhythmical and sweet. Yet we are seldom arrested by striking beauties; good lines occur in every page, fine ones but rarely; we lay down the volume with a sense of admiration of what we have read, but little of it remains distinctly in the memory. Fletcher is not much quoted, and has not even afforded copious materials to those who cull the beauties of ancient lore.

84. In variety of character there can be no comparison

Their cha-
racters.
between Fletcher and Shakspeare. A few types return upon us in the former; an old general, proud of his wars, faithful and passionate, a voluptuous and arbitrary king (for his principles of obedience do not seem to have inspired him with much confidence in royal virtues), a supple courtier, a high-spirited youth, or one more gentle in manners but not less stout in action, a lady, fierce and not always very modest in her chastity, repelling the solicitations of licentiousness, another impudently vicious, form the usual pictures for his canvas. Add to these, for the lighter comedy, an amorous old man, a gay spendthrift, and a few more of the staple characters of the stage, and we have the materials of Fletcher's dramatic world. It must be remembered that we compare him only with Shakspeare, and that as few dramatists have been more copious than Fletcher, few have

---

thing of the same kind; it may have been meant as an ungenerous and calumnious attack on the constancy of the female sex. If lions were painters, the old fable says, they would exhibit a very different view of their contentions with men. But lionesses are become very good painters; and it is but through their clemency that we are not delineated in such a style as would avenge them for the injuries of these tragedians.

been so much called upon for inventions, in which the custom
of the theatre has not exacted much originality. The great
fertility of his mind in new combinations of circumstance
gives as much appearance of novelty to the personages themselves as an unreflecting audience requires. In works of
fiction, even those which are read in the closet, this variation
of the mere dress of a character is generally found sufficient
for the public.

85. The tragedies of Beaumont and Fletcher, by which
our ancestors seem to have meant only plays where- Their
in any one of the personages, or at least one whom tragedies;
the spectator would wish to keep alive, dies on the stage,
are not very numerous, but in them we have as copious an
effusion of blood as any contemporary dramas supply. The
conclusion, indeed, of these, and of the tragi-comedies,
which form a larger class, is generally mismanaged. A propensity to take the audience by surprise leads often to an
unnatural and unsatisfactory catastrophe ; it seems their aim
to disappoint common expectation, to baffle reasonable conjecture, to mock natural sympathy. This is frequently the
practice of our modern novelists, who find no better resource
in the poverty of their invention to gratify the jaded palate
of the world.

86. The comic talents of these authors far exceeded their
skill in tragedy. In comedy they founded a new inferior to
school, at least in England, the vestiges of which their comedies.
are still to be traced in our theatre. Their plays are at
once distinguishable from those of their contemporaries by
the regard to dramatic effect which influenced the writers'
imagination. Though not personally connected with the
stage, they had its picture ever before their eyes. Hence
their incidents are numerous and striking, their characters
sometimes slightly sketched, not drawn, like those of Jonson,
from a preconceived design, but preserving that degree of
individual distinctness which a common audience requires,
and often highly humorous without extravagance ; their
language brilliant with wit, their measure, though they do
not make great use of prose, very lax and rapid, running
frequently to lines of thirteen and fourteen syllables. Few
of their comedies are without a mixture of grave sentiments

or elevated characters; and though there is much to condemn in their indecency and even licentiousness of principle,
they never descend to the coarse buffoonery not unfrequent
in their age.   Never were dramatic poets more thoroughly
gentlemen, according to the standard of their times; and,
when we consider the court of James I., we may say that
they were above that standard.[e]

87. The best of Fletcher's characters are female; he
Their female characters. wanted that large sweep of reflection and experience which is required for the greater diversity of
the other sex.   None of his women delight us like Imogen
and Desdemona; but he has many Imogens and Desdemonas
of a fainter type.   Spacelia, Zenocia, Celia, Aspasia, Evanthe,
Lucina, Ordella, Oriana, present the picture that cannot be
greatly varied without departing from its essence, but which
never can be repeated too often to please us, of faithful,
tender, self-denying female love, superior to everything but
virtue.   Nor is he less successful, generally, in the contrast
of minds stained by guilty passion, though in this he sometimes exaggerates the outline till it borders on caricature.
But it is in vain to seek in Fletcher the strong conceptions
of Shakspeare, the Shylocks, the Lears, the Othellos.
Schlegel has well said that 'scarce anything has been
wanting to give a place to Beaumont and Fletcher among
the great dramatists of Europe but more of seriousness and
depth, and the regulating judgment which prescribes the
due limits in every part of composition.'   It was for want of
the former qualities that they conceive nothing in tragedy
very forcibly; for want of the latter that they spoil their
first conception by extravagance and incongruity.[f]

---

[e] 'Their plots were generally more
regular than Shakspeare's especially
those which were made before Beaumont's death; and they understood and
imitated the conversation of gentlemen
much better; whose wild debaucheries,
and quickness of wit in repartees, no poet
before them could paint as they have
done.   Humour, which Ben Jonson derived from particular persons, they made
it not their business to describe; they
represented all the passions very lively,
but above all, love.   I am apt to believe
the English language in them arrived
to its highest perfection; what words
have since been taken in are rather superfluous than ornamental.   Their plays
are now the most pleasant and frequent
entertainments of the stage; two of
theirs being acted through the year for
one of Shakspeare's or Jonson's: the reason is, because there is a certain gaiety
in their comedies, and pathos in their
more serious plays, which suits generally
with all men's humours.   Shakspeare's
language is likewise a little obsolete,
and Jonson's wit falls short of theirs.'
Dryden, p.101.

[f] 'Shakspeare,' says Dryden, 'writ
better between man and man, Fletcher

88. The reputation of Beaumont and Fletcher was at its height, and most of their plays had been given to the stage, when a worthy inheritor of their mantle appeared in Philip Massinger. Of his extant dramas the Virgin Martyr, published in 1622, seems to be the earliest; but we have reason to believe that several are lost; and even this tragedy may have been represented some years before. The far greater part of his remaining pieces followed within ten years; the Bashful Lover, which is the latest now known, was written in 1636. Massinger was a gentleman, but in the service, according to the language of those times, of the Pembroke family; his education was at the university, his acquaintance both with books and with the manners of the court is familiar, his style and sentiments are altogether those of a man polished by intercourse of good society.

89. Neither in his own age nor in modern times does Massinger seem to have been put on a level with Fletcher or Jonson. Several of his plays, as has been just observed, are said to have perished in manuscript; few were represented after the Restoration; and it is only in consequence of his having met with more than one editor who has published his collected works in a convenient form, that he is become tolerably familiar to the general reader. He is, however, far more intelligible than Fletcher; his text has not given so much embarrassment from corruption, and his general style is as perspicuous as we ever find it in the dramatic poets of that age. The obscure passages in Massinger, after the care that Gifford has taken, are by no means frequent.

---

betwixt man and woman; consequently the one described friendship better, the other love; yet Shakspeare taught Fletcher to write love, and Juliet and Desdemona are originals. It is true the scholar had the softest soul, but the master had the kinder. . . . Shakspeare had an universal mind, which comprehended all characters and passions; Fletcher a more confined and limited; for though he treated love in perfection, yet honour, ambition, revenge, and generally all the stronger passions, he either touched not, or not masterly. To conclude all, he was a limb of Shakspeare.'

P. 301. This comparison is rather generally than strictly just, as is often the case with the criticisms of Dryden. That Fletcher wrote better than Shakspeare 'between man and woman,' or in displaying love, will be granted when he shall be shown to have excelled Ferdinand and Miranda, or Posthumus and Imogen. And, on the other hand, it is unjust to deny him credit for having sometimes touched the stronger emotions, especially honour and ambition, with great skill, though much inferior to that of Shakspeare.

90. Five of his sixteen plays are tragedies, that is, are
General
nature of
his drama. concluded in death; of the rest, no one belongs to
the class of mere comedy, but by the depth of the
interest, the danger of the virtuous, or the atrocity of the
vicious characters, as well as the elevation of the general
style, must be ranked with the serious drama, or, as it was
commonly termed, tragi-comedy. A shade of melancholy
tinges the writings of Massinger; but he sacrifices less than
his contemporaries to the public taste for superfluous blood-
shed on the stage. In several of his plays, such as the
Picture, or the Renegado, where it would have been easy to
determine the catastrophe towards tragedy, he has preferred
to break the clouds with the radiance of a setting sun. He
consulted in this his own genius, not eminently pathetic,
nor energetic enough to display the utmost intensity of
emotion, but abounding in sweetness and dignity, apt to
delineate the loveliness of virtue, and to delight in its recompense after trial. It has been surmised that the religion of Massinger was that of the church of Rome; a conjecture not improbable, though, considering the ascetic and
imaginative piety which then prevailed in that of England,
we need not absolutely go so far for his turn of thought in
the Virgin Martyr or the Renegado.

91. The most striking excellence of this poet is his con-
His delinea-
tions of
character. ception of character; and in this I must incline to
place him above Fletcher, and, if I may venture to
say it, even above Jonson. He is free from the hard outline of the one and the negligent looseness of the other.
He has indeed no great variety, and sometimes repeats, with
such bare modifications as the story demands, the type
of his first design. Thus the extravagance of conjugal affection is portrayed, feeble in Theodosius, frantic in Domitian,
selfish in Sforza, suspicious in Mathias; and the same impulses of doting love return upon us in the guilty eulogies of
Mallefort on his daughter. The vindictive hypocrisy of Mon-
treville in the Unnatural Combat has nearly its counterpart
in that of Francesco in the Duke of Milan, and is again displayed with more striking success in Luke This last villain,
indeed, and that original, masterly, inimitable conception,
Sir Giles Overreach, are sufficient to establish the rank of

Massinger in this great province of dramatic art. But his own disposition led him more willingly to pictures of moral beauty. A peculiar refinement, a mixture of gentleness and benignity with noble daring, belong to some of his favourite characters, to Pisander in the Bondman, to Antonio in A Very Woman, to Charolois in the Fatal Dowry. It may be readily supposed that his female characters are not wanting in these graces. It seems to me that he has more variety in his women than in the other sex, and that they are less mannered than the heroines of Fletcher. A slight degree of error or passion in Sophia, Eudocia, Marcelia, without weakening our sympathy, serves both to prevent the monotony of perpetual rectitude, so often insipid in fiction, and to bring forward the development of the story.

92. The subjects chosen by Massinger are sometimes historical, but others seem to have been taken from French or Italian novels, and those so obscure that *His subjects.* his editor, Gifford, a man of much reading and industry, has seldom traced them. This, indeed, was an unusual practice of our ancient dramatists. Their works have, consequently, a romantic character, presenting as little of the regular Plautine comedy as of the Greek forms of tragedy. They are merely novels in action, following, probably, their models with no great variation, except the lower and lighter episodes which it was always more or less necessary to combine with the story. It is from this choice of subjects, perhaps, as much as from the peculiar temper of the poets, that love is the predominant affection of the mind which they display; not cold and conventional, as we commonly find it on the French stage, but sometimes, as the novelists of the South were prone to delineate its emotions, fiery, irresistible, and almost resembling the fatalism of ancient tragedy; sometimes a subdued captive at the chariot-wheels of honour or religion. The range of human passion is, consequently, far less extensive than in Shakspeare; but the variety of circumstance, and the modifications of the paramount affection itself, compensated for this deficiency.

93. Next to the grace and dignity of sentiment in Massinger, we must praise those qualities in his style. *Beauty of* Every modern critic has been struck by the peculiar *his style.*

beauty of his language. In his harmonious swell of numbers, in his pure and genuine idiom, which a text, by good fortune and the diligence of its last editor, far less corrupt than that of Fletcher, enables us to enjoy, we find an unceasing charm. The poetical talents of Massinger were very considerable, his taste superior to that of his contemporaries; the colouring of his imagery is rarely overcharged; a certain redundancy, as some may account it, gives fulness, or what the painters call *impasto*, to his style, and if it might not always conduce to effect on the stage, is on the whole suitable to the character of his composition.[g]

94. The comic powers of this writer are not on a level with the serious; with some degree of humorous conception he is too apt to aim at exciting ridicule by caricature, and his dialogue wants altogether the sparkling wit of Shakspeare and Fletcher. Whether from a consciousness of this defect, or from an unhappy compliance with the viciousness of the age, no writer is more contaminated by gross indecency. It belongs, indeed, chiefly, not perhaps exclusively, to the characters he would render odious; but upon them he has bestowed this flower of our early theatre with no sparing hand. Few, it must be said, of his plays, are incapable of representation merely on this account, and the offence is therefore more incurable in Fletcher.

Inferiority of his comic powers.

95. Among the tragedies of Massinger, I should incline to prefer the Duke of Milan. The plot borrows enough from history to give it dignity, and to counterbalance in some measure the predominance of the passion of love which the invented parts of the drama exhibit. The characters of Sforza, Marcelia, and Francesco are in Massinger's best manner; the story is skilfully and not improbably developed; the pathos is deeper than we generally find in his writings; the eloquence of language, especially in the celebrated speech of Sforza before the em-

Some of his tragedies particularised.

---

[g] [I quote the following criticism from Coleridge, without thoroughly assenting to it:—' The styles of Massinger's plays and the Samson Agonistes are the two extremes of the arc within which the diction of dramatic poetry may oscillate. Shakspeare in his great plays is the midpoint. In the Samson Agonistes, colloquial language is left at the greatest distance; yet something of it is preserved to render the dialogue probable: in Massinger the style is differenced, but differenced in the smallest degree possible, from animated conversation, by the vein of poetry.' Table Talk, vol. ii. p. 121.—1842.]

peror, has never been surpassed by him. Many, however, place the Fatal Dowry still higher. This tragedy furnished Rowe with the story of his Fair Penitent. The superiority of the original, except in suitableness for representation, has long been acknowledged. In the Unnatural Combat, probably among the earliest of Massinger's works, we find a greater energy, a bolder strain of figurative poetry, more command of terror, and perhaps of pity, than in any other of his dramas. But the dark shadows of crime and misery which overspread this tragedy belong to rather an earlier period of the English stage than that of Massinger, and were not congenial to his temper. In the Virgin Martyr he has followed the Spanish model of religious Autos, with many graces of language and a beautiful display of Christian heroism in Dorothea; but the tragedy is in many respects unpleasing.

96. The Picture, The Bondman, and A Very Woman may be reckoned among the best of the tragi-comedies of Massinger. But the general merits as well as defects of this writer are perceptible in all; and the difference between these and the rest is not such as to be apparent to every reader. Two others are distinguishable as more English than the rest: the scene lies at home, and in the age: and to these the common voice has assigned a superiority. They are A New Way to Pay Old Debts, and The City Madam. A character drawn, as it appears, from reality, and though darkly wicked, not beyond the province of the higher comedy, Sir Giles Overreach, gives the former drama a striking originality and an impressive vigour. It retains, alone among the productions of Massinger, a place on the stage. Gifford inclines to prefer the City Madam; which, no doubt, by the masterly delineation of Luke, a villain of a different order from Overreach, and a larger portion of comic humour and satire than is usual with this writer, may dispute the palm. But there seems to be more violent improbability in the conduct of the plot than in A New Way to pay Old Debts.

And of his other plays.

97. Massinger, as a tragic writer, appears to me second only to Shakspeare; in the higher comedy I can hardly think him inferior to Jonson. In wit and

Ford.

sprightly dialogue, as well as in knowledge of theatrical effect, he falls very much below Fletcher. These, however, are the great names of the English stage. At a considerable distance below Massinger we may place his contemporary, John Ford. In the choice of tragic subjects from obscure fictions which have to us the charm of entire novelty, they resemble each other; but in the conduct of their fable, in the delineation of their characters, each of these poets has his distinguishing excellencies. 'I know,' says Gifford, 'few things more difficult to account for than the deep and lasting impression made by the more tragic portions of Ford's poetry.' He succeeds, however, pretty well in accounting for it; the situations are awfully interesting, the distress intense, the thoughts and language becoming the expression of deep sorrow. Ford, with none of the moral beauty and elevation of Massinger, has, in a much higher degree, the power over tears; we sympathise even with his vicious characters, with Giovanni and Annabella and Bianca. Love, and love in guilt or sorrow, is almost exclusively the emotion he portrays; no heroic passion, no sober dignity, will be found in his tragedies. But he conducts his stories well and without confusion; his scenes are often highly wrought and effective; his characters, with no striking novelty, are well supported; he is seldom extravagant or regardless of probability. The Broken Heart has generally been reckoned his finest tragedy; and if the last act had been better prepared, by bringing the love of Calantha for Ithocles more fully before the reader in the earlier part of the play, there would be very few passages of deeper pathos in our dramatic literature. 'The style of Ford,' it is said by Gifford, 'is altogether original and his own. Without the majestic march which distinguishes the poetry of Massinger, and with little or none of that light and playful humour which characterises the dialogue of Fletcher, or even of Shirley, he is yet elegant, and easy, and harmonious; and though rarely sublime, yet sufficiently elevated for the most pathetic tones of that passion on whose romantic energies he chiefly delighted to dwell.' Yet he censures afterwards Ford's affectation of uncouth phrases, and perplexity of language. Of comic ability this writer does not display one particle. Nothing can be meaner

than those portions of his dramas which, in compliance with
the prescribed rules of that age, he devotes to the dialogue
of servants or buffoons.

98. Shirley is a dramatic writer much inferior to those
who have been mentioned, but has acquired some
degree of reputation, or at least notoriety of name,   Shirley.
in consequence of the new edition of his plays.   These are
between twenty and thirty in number ; some of them, however, written in conjunction with his fellow-dramatists. A few
of these are tragedies, a few are comedies drawn from English
manners ; but in the greater part we find the favourite style
of that age, the characters foreign and of elevated rank, the
interest serious, but not always of buskined dignity, the
catastrophe fortunate ; all, in short, that has gone under the
vague appellation of tragi-comedy.   Shirley has no originality, no force in conceiving or delineating character, little of
pathos, and less perhaps of wit ; his dramas produce no deep
impression in reading, and of course can leave none on the
memory.   But his mind was poetical; his better characters,
especially females, express pure thoughts in pure language;
he is never tumid or affected, and seldom obscure; the incidents succeed rapidly, the personages are numerous, and
there is a general animation in the scenes which causes us to
read him with some pleasure.   No very good play, nor, possibly, any very good scene, could be found in Shirley ; but he
has many lines of considerable beauty.   Among his comedies
the Gamesters may be reckoned the best.   Charles I. is said
to have declared that it was ' the best play he had seen these
seven years;' and it has even been added that the story was
of his royal suggestion.   It certainly deserves praise both for
language and construction of the plot, and it has the advantage of exposing vice to ridicule; but the ladies of that court,
the fair forms whom Vandyke has immortalised, must have
been very different indeed from their posterity if they could
sit it through.   The Ball, and also some more among the
comedies of Shirley, are so far remarkable and worthy of
being read, that they bear witness to a more polished elegance
of manners and a more free intercourse in the higher class,
than we find in the comedies of the preceding reign.   A queen
from France, and that queen Henrietta Maria, was better

fitted to give this tone than Anne of Denmark. But it is
not from Shirley's pictures that we can draw the most
favourable notions of the morals of that age.

99. Heywood is a writer still more fertile than Shirley;
between forty and fifty plays are ascribed to him.
Heywood. We have mentioned one of the best in the second
volume, ante-dating, perhaps, its appearance by a few years.
In the English Traveller he has returned to something like
the subject of A Woman killed with Kindness, but with less
success. This play is written in verse, and with that ease and
perspicuity, seldom rising to passion or figurative poetry,
which distinguishes this dramatist. Young Geraldine is a
beautiful specimen of the Platonic, or rather inflexibly virtuous lover whom the writers of this age delighted to pour-
tray. On the other hand, it is difficult to pronounce whether
the lady is a thorough-paced hypocrite in the first acts, or
falls from virtue, like Mrs. Frankfort, on the first solicitations
of a stranger. In either case the character is unpleasing,
and, we may hope, improbable. The underplot of this play
is largely borrowed from the Mostellaria of Plautus, and is
diverting, though somewhat absurd, Heywood seldom rises to
much vigour of poetry; but his dramatic invention is ready,
his style is easy, his characters do not transgress the boundaries of nature, and it is not surprising that he was popular
in his own age.

100. Webster belongs to the first part of the reign of
James. He possessed very considerable powers and
Webster. ought to be ranked, I think, the next below Ford.
With less of poetic grace than Shirley, he had incomparably
more vigour; with less of nature and simplicity than Heywood,
he had a more elevated genius, and a bolder pencil. But the
deep sorrows and terrors of tragedy were peculiarly his province. 'His imagination,' says his last editor, 'had a fond
familiarity with objects of awe and fear. The silence of the
sepulchre, the sculptures of marble monuments, the knolling
of church bells, the cerements of the corpse, the yew that
roots itself in dead men's graves are the illustrations that
most readily present themselves to his imagination.' I think
this well-written sentence a little one-sided, and hardly doing
justice to the variety of Webster's power; but in fact he

was as deeply tainted as any of his contemporaries with the savage taste of the Italian school, and in the Duchess of Malfy scarcely leaves enough on the stage to bury the dead.

101. This is the most celebrated of Webster's dramas. The story is taken from Bandello, and has all that His Duchess accumulation of wickedness and horror which the of Malfy. Italian novelists perversely described, and our tragedians as perversely imitated. But the scenes are wrought up with skill, and produce a strong impression. Webster has a superiority in delineating character above many of the old dramatists; he is seldom extravagant beyond the limits of conceivable nature ; we find the guilt, or even the atrocity, of human passions, but not that incarnation of evil spirits which some more ordinary dramatists loved to exhibit. In the character of the Duchess of Malfy herself there wants neither originality nor skill of management, and I do not know that any dramatist after Shakspeare would have succeeded better in the difficult scene where she discloses her love to an inferior. There is perhaps a little failure in dignity and delicacy, especially towards the close; but the Duchess of Malfy is not drawn as an Isabella or a Portia; she is a love-sick widow, virtuous and true-hearted, but more intended for our sympathy than our reverence.

102. The White Devil, or Vittoria Corombona, is not much inferior in language and spirit to the Duchess of Vittoria Malfy; but the plot is more confused, less interest- Corombona. ing, and worse conducted. Mr. Dyce, the late editor of Webster, praises the dramatic vigour of the part of Vittoria, but justly differs from Lamb, who speaks of 'the innocence-resembling boldness' she displays in the trial scene. It is rather a delineation of desperate guilt, losing in a counter-feited audacity all that could seduce or conciliate the tribunal. Webster's other plays are less striking; in Appius and Virginia he has done perhaps better than any one who has attempted a subject not on the whole very promising for tragedy; several of the scenes are dramatic and effective; the language, as is usually the case with Webster, is written so as to display an actor's talents, and he has followed the received history sufficiently to abstain from any excess of slaughter at the close. Webster is not without comic wit, as

well as a power of imagination, his plays have lately met
with an editor of taste enough to admire his beauties, and
not very over-partial in estimating them.

103. Below Webster we might enumerate a long list of
dramatists under the first Stuarts. Marston is a tumid and
ranting tragedian, a wholesale dealer in murders and ghosts.
Chapman, who assisted Ben Jonson and some others in comedy,
deserves but limited praise for his Bussy d'Amboise. The
style in this, and in all his tragedies, is extravagantly hyperbolical; he is not very dramatic, nor has any power of exciting
emotion except in those who sympathise with a tumid pride
and self-confidence. Yet he has more thinking than many
of the old dramatists; and the praise of one of his critics,
though strongly worded, is not without some foundation, that
we 'seldom find richer contemplations on the nature of man
and the world.' There is also a poetic impetuosity in Chapman, such as has redeemed his translation of Homer, by
which we are hurried along. His tragi-comedies, All Fools
and The Gentleman Usher, are perhaps superior to his tragedies.[h] Rowley and Le Tourneur, especially the former,
have occasionally good lines, but we cannot say that they
were very superior dramatists. Rowley, however, was often
in comic partnership with Massinger. Dekker merits a
higher rank; he co-operated with Massinger in some of his
plays, and manifests in his own some energy of passion and
some comic humour. Middleton belongs to this lower class
of dramatic writers; his tragedy entitled 'Women beware
Women' is founded on the story of Bianca Cappello; it is
full of action, but the characters are all too vicious to be
interesting, and the language does not rise much above mediocrity. In comedy, Middleton deserves more praise. 'A
Trick to catch the Old One,' and several others that bear
his name, are amusing and spirited. But Middleton wrote
chiefly in conjunction with others, and sometimes with
Jonson and Massinger.

---

[h] Chapman is well reviewed, and at length, in an article of the Retrospective
Review, vol. iv. p. 333, and again in vol. v.

CHAPTER VII.

HISTORY OF POLITE LITERATURE IN PROSE
FROM 1600 TO 1650.

Sect. I.

Italian Writers—Boccalini—Grammatical and Critical Works—Gracian—
French Writers—Balzac—Voiture—French Academy—Vaugelas—Patru
and Le Maistre—Style of English Prose—Earl of Essex—Knolles—
Several other English Writers.

1. It would be vain, probably, to inquire from what general
causes we should deduce the decline of taste in Italy. Decline of
taste in
Italy.
None at least have occurred to my mind, relating
to political or social circumstances, upon which we could
build more than one of those sophistical theories which
assume a causal relation between any concomitant events.
Bad taste, in fact, whether in literature or the arts, is always
ready to seize upon the public, being, in many cases, no more
than a pleasure in faults which are really fitted to please us,
and of which it can only be said that they hinder or impair
the greater pleasure we should derive from beauties. Among
these critical sins, none are so dangerous as the display of
ingenious and novel thoughts or turns of phrase : for as such
enter into the definition of good writing, it seems very difficult to persuade the world that they can ever be the characteristics of bad writing. The metes and bounds of ornament,
the fine shades of distinction which regulate a judicious
choice, are only learned by an attentive as well as a naturally
susceptible mind; and it is no rare case for an unprepared
multitude to prefer the worse picture, the worse building,
the worse poem, the worse speech to the better. Education,
an acquaintance with just criticism, and still more the habitual observation of what is truly beautiful in nature or art,

or in the literature of taste, will sometimes generate almost a national tact that rejects the temptations of a meretricious and false style; but experience has shown that this happy state of public feeling will not be very durable. Whatever might be the cause of it, this age of the Italian seicentisti has been reckoned almost as inauspicious to good writing in prose as in verse. 'If we except,' says Tiraboschi, 'the Tuscans and a very few more, never was our language so neglected as in this period. We can scarce bear to read most of the books that were published, so rude and full of barbarisms is their style. Few had any other aim than to exercise their wit in conceits and metaphors; and so long as they could scatter them profusely over their pages, cared nothing for the choice of phrases or the purity of grammar. Their eloquence on public occasions was intended only for admiration and applause, not to persuade or move.'[i] And this, he says, is applicable alike to their Latin and Italian, their sacred and profane harangues. The academical discourses, of which Dati has collected many in his Prose Fiorentine, are poor in comparison with those of the sixteenth.[k]

2. A later writer than Tiraboschi has thought this sentence against the seicentisti a little too severe, and condemning equally with him the bad taste characteristic of that age, endeavours to rescue a few from the general censure.[m] It is at least certain that the insipidity of the cinque cento writers, their long periods void of any but the most trivial meaning, their affectation of the faults of Cicero's manner in their own language, ought not to be overlooked or wholly pardoned, while we dwell on an opposite defect of their successors, the perpetual desire to be novel, brilliant, or profound. This may, doubtless, be the more offensive of the two; but it is, perhaps, not less likely to be mingled with something really worth reading.

3. It will not be expected that we can mention many Italian books, after what has been said, which come very precisely within the class of polite literature, or claim any praise on the ground of style. Their greatest luminary, Galileo, wrote with clearness, elegance, and spirit;

Style of Galileo.

---

[i] Vol. xi. p. 415.   [k] Id.   [m] Salfi, xiv. 11.

no one among the moderns had so entirely rejected a dry
and technical manner of teaching, and thrown such attrac-
tions round the form of truth. Himself a poet, and a critic,
he did not hesitate to ascribe his own philosophical perspicuity to the constant perusal of Ariosto. This I have
mentioned in another place; but we cannot too much remember that all objects of intellectual pursuit are as bodies
acting with reciprocal forces in one system, being all in
relation to the faculties of the mind, which is itself but one;
and that the most extensive acquaintance with the various
provinces of literature will not fail to strengthen our dominion
over those we more peculiarly deem our own. The school
of Galileo, especially Torricelli and Redi, were not less distinguished than himself for their union of elegance with
philosophy.[n]

4. The letters of Bentivoglio are commonly known. This
epistolary art was always cultivated by the Italians
first in the Latin tongue, and afterwards in their　Bentivoglio.
own. Bentivoglio has written with equal dignity and ease.
Galileo's letters are also esteemed on account of their style
as well as of what they contain. In what is more peculiarly
called eloquence, the Italians of this age are rather emulous
of success than successful; the common defects of taste in
themselves, and in those who heard or read them, as well as,
in most instances, the uninteresting nature of their subjects,
exclude them from our notice.

5. Trajan Boccalini was by his disposition inclined to
political satire, and possibly to political intrigue;　Boccalini's
but we have here only to mention the work by　News from
Parnassus.
which he is best known, Advices from Parnassus (Ragguagli
di Parnaso). If the idea of this once popular and celebrated
book is not original, which I should rather doubt, though
without immediately recognising a similarity to anything
earlier (Lucian, the common prototype, excepted), it has
at least been an original source. In the general turn of
Boccalini's fictions, and perhaps in a few particular instances,
we may sometimes perceive what a much greater man has
imitated; they bear a certain resemblance to those of Addi-

---

[n] Salfi, xiv. 12.

son, though the vast superiority of the latter in felicity of execution and variety of invention may almost conceal it. The
Ragguagli are a series of despatches from the court of Apollo
on Parnassus, where he is surrounded by eminent men of all
ages. This fiction becomes in itself very cold and monotonous; yet there is much variety in the subjects of the
decisions made by the god with the advice of his counsellors,
and some strokes of satire are well hit, though more perhaps
fail of effect. But we cannot now catch the force of every
passage. Boccalini is full of allusions to his own time, even
where the immediate subject seems ancient. This book was
published at Venice in 1612; at a time when the ambition
of Spain was regarded with jealousy by patriotic Italians,
who thought that pacific republic their bulwark and their
glory. He inveighs therefore against the military spirit and
the profession of war, 'necessary sometimes, but so fierce and
inhuman that no fine expressions can make it honourable.' °
Nor is he less severe on the vices of kings, nor less ardent
in his eulogies of liberty; the government of Venice being
reckoned, and not altogether untruly, an asylum of free
thought and action in comparison with that of Spain.
Aristotle, he reports in one of his despatches, was besieged
in his villa on Parnassus by a number of armed men belonging to different princes, who insisted on his retracting the
definition he had given of a tyrant, that he was one who
governed for his own good and not that of the people,
because it would apply to every prince, all reigning for their
own good. The philosopher, alarmed by this demand,
altered his definition; which was to run thus, that tyrants
were certain persons of old time, whose race was now quite
extinct.ᴾ Boccalini, however, takes care in general, to mix
something of playfulness with his satire, so that it could not
be resented without apparent ill-nature. It seems, indeed,
to us, free from invective, and rather meant to sting than to
wound. But this, if a common rumour be true, did not
secure him against a beating of which he died. The style
of Boccalini is said by the critics to be clear and fluent,
rather than correct or elegant; and he displays the taste of

° Ragg. 75.   ᴾ Id. 76.

his times by extravagant metaphors. But to foreigners, who regard this less, his Advices from Parnassus, unequal of course, and occasionally tedious, must appear to contain many ingenious allusions, judicious criticisms, and acute remarks.

6. The Pietra del Paragone by the same author is an odd, and rather awkward, mixture of reality and His Pietra fiction, all levelled at the court of Spain, and de- del Para- gone. signed to keep alive a jealousy of its ambition. It is a kind of episode or supplement to the Ragguagli di Parnaso, the leading invention being preserved. Boccalini is an interesting writer, on account of the light he throws on the history and sentiments of Italy. He is in this work a still bolder writer than in the former; not only censuring Spain without mercy, but even the Venetian aristocracy, observing upon the insolence of the young nobles towards the citizens, though he justifies the senate for not punishing the former more frequently with death by public execution, which would lower the nobility in the eyes of the people. They were, however, he says, as severely punished, when their conduct was bad, by exclusion from offices of trust. The Pietra del Paragone is a kind of political, as the Ragguagli is a critical, miscellany.

7. About twenty years after Boccalini, a young man appeared, by name Ferrante Pallavicino, who, with Ferrante a fame more local and transitory, with less re- Pallavicino spectability of character, and probably with inferior talents, trod to a certain degree in his steps. As Spain had been the object of satire to the one, so was Rome to the other Urban VIII., an ambitious pontiff, and vulnerable in several respects, was attacked by an imprudent and self-confident enemy, safe, as he imagined, under the shield of Venice. But Pallavicino having been trepanned into the power of the Pope, lost his head at Avignon. None of his writings have fallen in my way; that most celebrated at the time, and not wholly dissimilar in the conception to the Advices from Parnassus, was entitled The Courier Robbed; a series of imaginary letters which such a fiction gave him a pretext for bringing together. Perhaps we may consider Pallavicino as rather a counterpart to Jor-

dano Bruno, in the satirical character of the latter, than to
Boccalini.[q]

8. The Italian language itself, grammatically considered,
Dictionary   was still assiduously cultivated.   The Academicians
Della Crusca. of Florence published the first edition of their celebrated Vocabolario della Crusca in 1613.   It was avowedly
founded on Tuscan principles, setting up the fourteenth century as the Augustan period of the language, which they
disdained to call Italian; and though not absolutely excluding the great writers of the sixteenth age whom Tuscany
had not produced, giving in general a manifest preference to
their own.   Italy has rebelled against this tyranny of Florence, as she did, in the Social War, against that of Rome.
Her Lombard and Romagnol and Neapolitan writers have
claimed the rights of equal citizenship, and fairly won them
in the field of literature.   The Vocabulary itself was not received as a legislative code.   Beni assailed it by his Anti-
Crusca the same year; many invidiously published marginal
notes to point out the inaccuracies; and in the frequent revi-
sions and enlargements of this dictionary the exclusive character which it affected has, I believe, been nearly lost.

9. Buonmattei, himself a Florentine, was the first who
Grammatical completed an extensive and methodical grammar,
works.   'developing,' says Tiraboschi, 'the whole economy
Buonmattei.
Bartoli.   and system of our language.'   It was published
entire, after some previous impressions of parts, with the
title Della Lingua Toscana, in 1643.   This has been reckoned
a standard work, both for its authority and for the clearness,
precision, and elegance with which it is written; but it betrays something of an academical and Florentine spirit in the
rigour of its grammatical criticism.[r]   Bartoli, a Ferrarese
Jesuit, and a man of extensive learning, attacked that dogmatic school who were accustomed to proscribe common
phrases with Non si può (It cannot be used), in a treatise
entitled Il torto ed il diritto del Non si può.   His object was
to justify many expressions thus authoritatively condemned,
by the examples of the best writers.   This book was a little
later than the middle of the century.[s]

---

[q] Corniani, viii. 205.   Salfi, xiv. 46.   [s] Corniani, vii. 259.   Salfi, xiii. 417.
[r] Tiraboschi, xi. 409.   Salfi, xiii. 398.

10. Petrarch had been the idol, in general, of the preceding age; and, above all, he was the peculiar divinity _{Tassoni's}
of the Florentines.   But this seventeenth century ^{remarks on} Petrarch.
was in the productions of the mind a period of revolutionary
innovation; men dared to ask why, as well as what, they
ought to worship; and sometimes the same who rebelled
against Aristotle as an infallible guide, were equally contu-
macious in dealing with the great names of literature.
Tassoni published in 1609 his Observations on the Poems of
Petrarch.   They are not written, as we should now think,
adversely to one whom he professes to honour above all lyric
poets in the world, and though his critical remarks are
somewhat minute, they seem hardly unfair.   A writer like
Petrarch, whose fame has been raised so high by his style, is
surely amenable to this severity of examination.   The finest
sonnets Tassoni generally extols, but gives a preference, on
the whole, to the odes; which, even if an erroneous judgment, cannot be called unfair upon the author of both.[t]   He
produces many parallel passages from the Latin poems of
Petrarch himself, as well as from the ancients and from
the earlier Italians and Provençals.   The manner of Tassoni
is often humorous, original, intrepid, satirical on his own
times; he was a man of real taste, and no servile worshipper
of names.

11. Galileo was less just in his observations upon Tasso.
They are written with severity, and sometimes an _{Galileo's}
insulting tone towards the great poet, passing over ^{remarks on} Tasso.
generally the most beautiful verses, though he sometimes
bestows praise.   The object is to point out the imitations of
Tasso from Ariosto, and his general inferiority.   The Observations on the Art of Writing by Sforza Palla- _{Sforza Pal-}
vicino, the historian of the Council of Trent, pub- ^{lavicino;}
lished at Rome, 1646, is a work of general criticism containing many good remarks.   What he says of imitation is
worthy of being compared with Hurd; though he will be
found not to have analysed the subject with anything like so
much acuteness, nor was this to be expected in his age.

---

[t] Tutte le rime, tutti i versi in gene-   quelle, che poeta grande e famoso lo,
rale del Petrarca lo fecero poeta; ma le   fecero.   p. 46.
canzoni, per quanto a mi ne pare, furono

Pallavicino has an ingenious remark, that elegance of style
is produced by short metaphors, or *metaforette*, as he calls
them, which give us a more lively apprehension of an object
than its proper name. This seems to mean only single words
in a figurative sense, as opposed to phrases of the same
kind. He writes in a pleasing manner, and is an accomplished critic without pedantry. Salfi has given rather a
long analysis of this treatise.[u] The same writer, treading
in the steps of Corniani, has extolled some Italian critics
and other
critical
writers. of this period, whose writings I have never seen;
Beni, author of a prolix commentary in Latin on
the Poetics of Aristotle; Peregrino, not inferior, perhaps, to
Pallavicino, though less known, whose theories are just
and deep, but not expressed with sufficient perspicuity; and
Fioretti, who assumed the fictitious name of Udeno Nisieli,
and presided over an academy at Florence denominated the
Apatisti. The Progymnasmi Poetici of this writer, if we
may believe Salfi, ascend to that higher theory of criticism
which deduces its rules, not from precedents or arbitrary
laws, but from the nature of the human mind, and has,
in modern times, been distinguished by the name of
æsthetic.[x]

12. In the same class of polite letters as these Italian
Prolusiones
of Strada. writings we may place the Prolusiones Academicæ
of Famianus Strada. They are agreeably written,
and bespeak a cultivated taste. The best is the sixth of the
second book, containing the imitations of six Latin poets,
which Addison has made well known (as I hope) to every
reader in the 115th and 119th numbers of the Guardian. It
is is here that all may judge of this happy and graceful fiction; but those who have read the Latin imitations themselves, will perceive that Strada has often caught the tone of
the ancients with considerable felicity. Lucan and Ovid
are, perhaps, best counterfeited, Virgil not quite so well, and
Lucretius worst of the six. The other two are Statius and
Claudian.[y] In almost every instance the subject chosen is
appropriate to the characteristic peculiarities of the poet.

---

[u] Vol. xiii. p. 440.

[x] Corniani, vii. 156. Salfi, xiii. 426.

[y] A writer, quoted in Blount's Censura Autorum, p. 859, praises the imitation of Claudian above the rest, but
thinks all excellent.

13. The style of Gongora, which deformed the poetry of Spain, extended its influence over prose. A writer named Gracian (it seems to be doubtful which of two brothers, Lorenzo and Balthazar) excelled Gongora himself in the affectation, the refinement, the obscurity of his style. ' The most voluminous of his works,' says Bouterwek, ' bears the affected title of El Criticon. It is an allegorical picture of the whole course of human life divided into Crises, that is, sections, according to fixed points of view, and clothed in the formal garb of a pompous romance. It is scarcely possible to open any page of this book without recognising in the author a man who is in many respects far from common, but who, from the ambition of being entirely uncommon in thinking and writing studiously and ingeniously, avoids nature and good taste. A profusion of the most ambiguous subtleties expressed in ostentatious language are scattered throughout the work ; and these are the more offensive in consequence of their union with the really grand view of the relationship of man to nature and his Creator which forms the subject of the treatise. Gracian would have been an excellent writer, had he not so anxiously wished to be an extraordinary one.'[z]

14. The writings of Gracian seem in general to be the quintessence of bad taste. The worst of all, probably, is El Eroe, which is admitted to be almost unintelligible by the number of far-fetched expressions, though there is more than one French translation of it. El politico Fernando, a panegyric on Ferdinand the Catholic, seems as empty as it is affected and artificial. The style of Gracian is always pointed, emphatic, full of that which looks like profundity or novelty, though neither deep nor new. He seems to have written on a maxim he recommends to the man of the world : ' if he desires that all should look up to him, let him permit himself to be known, but not to be understood.'[a] His treatise entitled Agudeza y arte de ingenio is a system of concetti, digested under their different heads, and selected from Latin, Italian, and Spanish writers of that and the preceding age. It is said in the Biographie universelle that

margin notes: Spanish prose. Gracian.

---

[z] Hist. of Spanish Literature, p: 533.

[a] Si quiere que le veneren todos, permitase al conocimiento, no á la comprehension.

this work, though too metaphysical, is useful in the critical
history of literature.   Gracian obtained a certain degree of
popularity in France and England.

15. The general taste of French writers in the sixteenth

French
prose.
Du Vair.

century, as we have seen, was simple and lively, full
of sallies of natural wit and a certain archness of
observation, but deficient in those higher qualities of language which the study of the ancients had taught men to
admire.   In public harangues, in pleadings, and in sermons,
these characteristics of the French manner were either introduced out of place, or gave way to a tiresome pedantry.   Du
Vair was the first who endeavoured to bring in a more
elaborate and elevated diction.   Nor was this confined to
the example he gave.   In 1607 he published a treatise on
French eloquence, and on the causes through which it had
remained at so low a point.   This work relates chiefly to the
eloquence of the bar, or at least that of public speakers, and
the causes which he traces are chiefly such as would operate
on that kind alone.   But some of his observations are applicable to style in the proper sense; and his treatise has
been reckoned the first which gave France the rules of good
writing, and the desire to practise them.[b]   A modern critic
who censures the Latinisms of Du Vair's style, admits that his
treatise on eloquence makes an epoch in the language.[c]

16. A more distinguished era, however, is dated from

Balzac.

1625, when the letters of Balzac were published.[d]
There had indeed been a few intermediate works,
which contributed, though now little known, to the improvement of the language.   Among these the translation of

---

[b] Gibert, Jugemens des Savans sur
les auteurs qui ont traité de la rhéto-
rique.   This work is annexed to some
editions of Baillet.   Goujet has copied
or abridged Gibert, without distinct acknowledgment, and not always carefully
preserving the sense.

[c] Neufchâteau, préface aux Œuvres
de Pascal, p. 181.

[d] The same writer fixes on this as an
epoch, and it was generally admitted in
the seventeenth century.   The editor of
Balzac's Works in 1665 says, after
speaking of the unformed state of the
French language, full of provincial idioms
and incorrect phrases: M. de Balzac est

venu en ce temps de confusion et de dés-
ordre, où toutes les lectures qu'il faisoit
et toutes les actions qu'il entendoit lui
devoient être suspectes, où il avoit à se
défier de tous les maîtres et de tous les
exemples; et où il ne pouvoit arriver à son
but qu'en s'éloignant de tous les chemins
battus, ni marcher dans la bonne route
qu'après se l'être ouverte à lui-même.   Il
l'a ouverte en effet, et pour lui et pour
les autres ; il y a fait entrer un grand
nombre d'heureux génies, dont il étoit le
guide et le modèle : et si la France voit
aujourd'hui que ses écrivains sont plus
polis et plus réguliers que ceux d'Espagne
et d'Italie, il faut qu'elle en rende l'hon-

Florus by Coeffeteau was reckoned a masterpiece of French style, and Vaugelas refers more frequently to this than to any other book. The French were very strong in translations from the classical writers; and to this they are certainly much indebted for the purity and correctness which they reached in their own language. These translators, however, could only occupy a secondary place. Balzac himself is hardly read. 'The polite world,' it was said a hundred years since, 'knows nothing now of these works, which were once its delight.'[e] But his writings are not formed to delight those who wish either to be merry or wise, to laugh or to learn; yet he has real merits, besides those which may be deemed relative to the age in which he came. His language is polished, his sentiments are just, but sometimes common, the cadence of his periods is harmonious, but too artificial and uniform; on the whole he approaches to the tone of a languid sermon, and leaves a tendency to yawn. But in his time superficial truths were not so much proscribed as at present; the same want of depth belongs to almost all the moralists in Italian and in modern Latin. Balzac is a moralist with a pure heart, and a love of truth and virtue (somewhat alloyed by the spirit of flattery towards persons, however he may declaim about

Character of his writings.

---

neur à ce grand homme, dont la mémoire lui doit être en vénération. . . . La même obligation que nous avons à M. de Malherbe pour la poésie, nous l'avons à M. de Balzac pour la prose; il lui a prescrit des bornes et des règles; il lui a donné de la douceur et de la force, il a montré que l'éloquence doit avoir des accords, aussi bien que la musique, et il a sçu mêler si adroitement cette diversité de sons et de cadences, qu'il n'est point de plus délicieux concert que celui de ses paroles. C'est en plaçant tous les mots avec tant d'ordre et de justesse qu'il ne laisse rien de mol ni de foible dans son discours, etc. This regard to the cadence of his periods is characteristic of Balzac. It has not, in general, been much practised in France, notwithstanding some splendid exceptions, especially in Bossuet. Olivet observes, that it was the peculiar glory of Balzac to have shown the capacity of the language for this rhythm. Hist. de l'Acad. française,

p. 84. But has not Du Vair some claim also? Neufchâteau gives a much more limited eulogy of Balzac. Il avoit pris à la lettre les réflexions de Du Vair sur la trop grande bassesse de notre éloquence. Il s'en forma une haute idée; mais il se trompe d'abord dans l'application, car il porta dans le style épistolaire, qui doit être familier et léger, l'enflure hyperbolique, la pompe, et le nombre, qui ne convient qu'aux grandes déclamations et aux harangues oratoires. . . . . Ce défaut de Balzac contribua peut-être à son succès, car le goût n'étoit pas formé; mais il se corrigea dans la suite, et en parcourant son recueil on s'aperçoit des progrès sensibles qu'il faisoit avec l'âge. Ce recueil si précieux pour l'histoire de notre littérature a eu longtemps une vogue extraordinaire. Nos plus grands auteurs l'avoient bien étudié. Molière lui a emprunté quelques idées.

[e] Goujet, i. 426.

courts and courtiers in general), a competent erudition, and a good deal of observation of the world. In his Aristippe, addressed to Christina, and consequently a late work, he deals much in political precepts and remarks, some of which might be read with advantage. But he was accused of borrowing his thoughts from the ancients, which the author of an Apology for Balzac seems not wholly to deny. This apology indeed had been produced by a book on the Conformity of the eloquence of M. Balzac with that of the ancients.

17. The letters of Balzac are in twenty-seven books; they begin in 1620, and end about 1653; the first portion having appeared in 1625. 'He passed all his life,' says Vigneul-Marville, ' in writing letters, without ever catching the right characteristics of that style.'[f] This demands a peculiar ease and naturalness of expression, for want of which they seem no genuine exponents of friendship or gallantry, and hardly of polite manners. His wit was not free from pedantry, and did not come from him spontaneously. Hence he was little fitted to address ladies, even the Rambouillets; and indeed he had acquired so laboured and artificial a way of writing letters, that even those to his sister, though affectionate, smell too much of the lamp. His advocates admit that they are to be judged rather by the rules of oratorical than epistolary composition.

18. In the moral dissertations, such as that entitled the Prince, this elaborate manner is of course not less discernible, but not so unpleasant or out of place. Balzac has been called the father of the French language, the master and model of the great men who have followed him. But it is confessed by all that he wanted the fine taste to regulate his style according to the subject. Hence he is pompous and inflated upon ordinary topics; and in a country so quick to seize the ridiculous as his own, not all his nobleness and purity of style, not the passages of eloquence which we often find, have been sufficient to redeem him from the sarcasms of those who have had more power to amuse. The stateliness, however,

---

[f] Mélanges de Littérature, vol. i. p. 126. He adds, however, that Balzac had 'un talent particulier pour embellir notre langue.' The writer whom I quote under the name of Vigneul-Marville, which he assumed, was D'Argonne, a Benedictine of Rouen.

of Balzac is less offensive and extravagant than the affected
intensity of language which distinguishes the style of the
present age on both sides of the Channel, and which is in
fact a much worse modification of the same fault.

19. A contemporary and rival of Balzac, though very
unlike in most respects, was Voiture. Both one and
the other were received with friendship and admiration in a celebrated society of Paris, the first which, on this
side of the Alps, united the aristocracy of rank and of genius
in one circle, that of the Hôtel Rambouillet. Catherine de
Vivonne, widow of the Marquis de Rambouillet, was the
owner of this mansion. It was frequented, during the long
period of her life, by all that was distinguished in France, by
Richelieu and Condé, as much as by Corneille, and a long
host of inferior men of letters. The heiress of this family,
Julie d'Angennes, beautiful and highly accomplished, became the central star of so bright a galaxy. The love of
intellectual attainments, both in mother and daughter, the
sympathy and friendship they felt for those who displayed
them, as well as their moral worth, must render their names
respectable; but these were in some measure sullied by false
taste, and what we may consider an habitual affectation even
in their conduct. We can scarcely give another name to the
caprice of Julia, who, in the fashion of romance, compelled
the Duke of Montausier to carry on a twelve years' courtship,
and only married him in the decline of her beauty. This
patient lover, himself one of the most remarkable men in the
court of Louis XIV., had many years before, in 1633, presented her with what has been called the Garland of Julia,
a collection to which the poets and wits of Paris had contributed. Every flower, represented in a drawing, had its
appropriate little poem, and all conspired to the praise of
Julia.[g]

20. Voiture is chiefly known by his letters; his other
writings at least are inferior. These begin about 1627, and
are addressed to Madame de Rambouillet and to several
other persons of both sexes. Though much too laboured and

---

[g] [Two copies were made of the
Guirlande de Julie; but, in the usual
style of the Rambouillets, no one was
admitted to see either but as a remarkable favour. Huet, who tells us this,
was one. Huetiana, p. 104.—1842.]

affected, they are evidently the original type of the French epistolary school, including those in England who have formed themselves upon it. Pope very frequently imitated Voiture; Walpole not so much in his general correspondence, but he knew how to fall into it. The object was to say what meant little, with the utmost novelty in the mode, and with the most ingenious compliment to the person addressed; so that he should admire himself and admire the writer. They are of course very tiresome after a short time; yet their ingenuity is not without merit. Balzac is more solemn and dignified, and it must be owned that he has more meaning. Voiture seems to have fancied that good sense spoils a man of wit. But he has not so much wit as *esprit*; and his letters serve to exemplify the meaning of that word. Pope, in addressing ladies, was nearly the ape of Voiture. It was unfortunately thought necessary, in such a correspondence, either to affect despairing love, which was to express itself with all possible gaiety, or where love was too presumptuous, as with the Rambouillets, to pour out a torrent of nonsensical flattery, which was to be rendered tolerable by far-fetched turns of thought. Voiture has the honour of having rendered this style fashionable. But if the bad taste of others had not perverted his own, Voiture would have been a good writer. His letters, especially those written from Spain, are sometimes truly witty, and always vivacious. Voltaire, who speaks contemptuously of Voiture, might have been glad to have been the author of some of his jeux d'esprit; that, for example, addressed to the Prince of Condé in the character of a pike, founded on a game where the prince had played that fish. We should remember, also, that Voiture held his place in good society upon the tacit condition that he should always strive to be witty.[h]

21. But the Hôtel Rambouillet, with its false theories of taste derived in a great measure from the romances of Scudéry and Calprenede, and encouraged by the agreeably

---

[h] Nothing, says Olivet, could be more opposite than Balzac and Voiture. L'un se portoit toujours au sublime, l'autre toujours au délicat. L'un avoit une imagination élevée qui jetoit de la noblesse dans les moindres choses; l'autre, une imagination enjouée, qui faisoit prendre à toutes ses pensées un air de galanterie. L'un, même lorsqu'il vouloit plaisanter, étoit toujours grave; l'autre, dans les occasions même sérieuses, trouvoit à rire. Hist. de l'Académie, p. 83.

artificial manner of Voiture, would have produced, in all probability, but a transient effect. A far more important event was the establishment of the French Academy. France was ruled by a great minister, who loved her glory and his own. This indeed has been common to many statesmen, but it was a more peculiar honour to Richelieu, that he felt the dignity which letters conferred on a nation. He was himself not deficient in literary taste; his epistolary style is manly, and not without elegance ; he wrote theology in his own name, and history in that of Mezeray ; but what is most to the present purpose, his remarkable fondness for the theatre led him not only to invent subjects for other poets, but, as it has been believed, to compose one forgotten tragi-comedy, Mirame, without assistance.[i] He availed himself, fortunately, of an opportunity which almost every statesman would have disregarded, to found the most illustrious institution in the annals of polite literature.

Establishment of French Academy.

22. The French Academy sprang from a private society of men of letters at Paris, who, about the year 1629, agreed to meet once a week, as at an ordinary visit, conversing on all subjects, and especially on literature. Such among them as were authors communicated their works, and had the advantage of free and fair criticism. This continued for three or four years with such harmony and mutual satisfaction, that the old men, who remembered this period, says their historian, Pelisson, looked back upon it as a golden age. They were but nine in number, of whom Gombauld and Chapelain are the only names by any means famous, and their meetings were at first very private. More by degrees were added, among others Boisrobert, a favourite of Richelieu, who liked to hear from him the news of the town. The Cardinal, pleased with the account of this society, suggested their public establishment. This, it is said, was unpleasing to every one of them, and some proposed to refuse it ; but the consideration that the offers of such a man were not to be slighted overpowered their modesty ; and they consented to become a royal institution. They now enlarged their num-

---

[i] Fontenelle, Hist. du Théâtre, p. 96.

bers, created officers, and began to keep registers of their proceedings. These records commence on March 13, 1634, and are the basis of Pelisson's history. The name of French Academy was chosen after some deliberation. They were established by letters patent in January, 1635, which the parliament of Paris enregistered with great reluctance, requiring not only a letter from Richelieu, but an express order from the king; and when this was completed in July, 1637, it was with a singular proviso that the Academy should meddle with nothing but the embellishment and improvement of the French language, and such books as might be written by themselves, or by others who should desire their interference. This learned body of lawyers had some jealousy of the innovations of Richelieu; and one of them said it reminded him of the satire of Juvenal, where the senate, after ceasing to bear its part in public affairs, was consulted about the sauce for a turbot.[k]

23. The professed object of the Academy was to purify the language from vulgar, technical, or ignorant usages, and to establish a fixed standard. The Academicians undertook to guard scrupulously the correctness of their own works, examining the arguments, the method, the style, the structure of each particular word. It was proposed by one that they should swear not to use any word which had been rejected by a plurality of votes. They soon began to labour in their vocation, always bringing words to the test of good usage, and deciding accordingly. These decisions are recorded in their registers. Their number was fixed by the letters patent at forty, having a director, chancellor, and secretary; the two former changed every two, afterwards every three months, the last chosen for life. They read discourses weekly, which, by the titles of some that Pelisson has given us, seem rather trifling and in the style of the Italian Academies; but this practice was soon disused. Their more important and ambitious occupations were to compile a dictionary and a grammar: Chapelain drew up the scheme of the former, in which it was determined, for the sake of brevity, to give no quotations, but to form it from about

Its objects and constitution.

---

[k] Pelisson, Hist. de l'Académie française.

twenty-six good authors in prose, and twenty in verse.
Vaugelas was entrusted with the chief direction of this work.

24. The Academy was subjected, in its very infancy, to a
severe trial of that literary integrity without which It publishes
a critique on
the Cid.
such an institution can only escape from being per-
nicious to the republic of letters by becoming too despicable
and odious to produce mischief.   On the appearance of the
Cid, Richelieu, who had taken up a strong prejudice against
it, insisted that the Academy should publish their opinion
on this play.   The more prudent part of that body were very
loth to declare themselves at so early a period of their own
existence; but the Cardinal was not apt to take excuses; and
a committee of three was appointed to examine the Cid itself,
and the observations upon it which Scudéry had already published.   Five months elapsed before the Sentimens de l'Académie française sur la Tragédie du Cid were made public in
November, 1637.[m]   These are expressed with much respect
for Corneille, and profess to be drawn up with his assent, as
well as at the instance of Scudéry.   It has been not uncommon to treat this criticism as a servile homage to power.
But a perusal of it will not lead us to confirm so severe a
reproach.   The Sentimens de l'Académie are drawn up with
great good sense and dignity.   The spirit indeed of critical
orthodoxy is apparent; yet this was surely pardonable in an
age when the violation of rules had as yet produced nothing
but such pieces as those of Hardy.   It is easy to sneer at
Aristotle when we have a Shakspeare; but Aristotle formed
his rules on the practice of Sophocles.   The Academy could
not have done better than by inculcating the soundest maxims
of criticism, but they were a little too narrow in their application.   The particular judgments which they pass on each
scene of the play, as well as those on the style, seem for the
most part very just, and such as later critics have generally
adopted; so that we can really see little ground for the allegation of undue compliance with the Cardinal's prejudices,
except in the frigid tone of their praise, and in their omission to proclaim that a great dramatic genius had arisen in
France.[n]   But this is so much the common vice or blindness

---

[m] Pelisson. The printed edition bears
the date of 1638.

[n] They conclude by saying that, in
spite of the faults of this play, la naïveté

of critics, that it may have sprung less from baseness than from a fear to compromise their own superiority by vulgar admiration. The Academy had great pretensions, and Corneille was not yet the Corneille of France and of the world.

25. Gibert, Goujet, and other writers enumerate several works on the grammar of the French language in this period. But they were superseded, and we may almost say that an era was made in the national literature by the publication of Vaugelas, Remarques sur la Langue française, in 1649. Thomas Corneille, who, as well as Patru, published notes on Vaugelas, observes that the language has only been written with politeness since the appearance of these remarks. They were not at first received with general approbation, and some even in later times thought them too scrupulous; but they gradually became of established authority. Vaugelas is always clear, modest, and ingenuous in stating his opinion. His remarks are 547 in number, no gross fault being noticed, nor any one which is not found in good authors. He seldom mentions those whom he censures. His test of correct language is the manner of speaking in use with the best part (la plus saine partie) of the court, conformably with the manner of writing in the best part of contemporary authors. But though we must have recourse to good authors in order to establish an indisputably good usage, yet the court, he thinks, contributes incomparably more than books; the consent of the latter being as it were the seal and confirmation of what is spoken at court, and deciding what is there doubtful. And those who study the best authors get rid of many faults common at court, and acquire a peculiar purity of style. None, however, can dispense with a knowledge of what is reckoned good language at court, since much that is spoken there will hardly be found in books. In writing it is otherwise, and he

Vaugelas's remarks on the French language.

---

et la véhémence de ses passions, la force et la délicatesse de plusieurs de ses pensées, et cet agrément inexplicable qui se mêle dans tous ses défauts lui ont acquis un rang considérable entre les poëmes français de ce genre qui ont le plus donné de satisfaction. Si l'auteur ne doit pas toute sa réputation à son mérite, il ne la doit pas toute à son bonheur, et la nature lui a été assez libérale pour ex-

cuser la fortune si elle lui a été, prodigue.

The Academy, justly in my opinion, blame Corneille for making Chimène consent to marry Rodrigue the same day that he had killed her father. Cela surpasse toute sorte de créance, et ne peut vraisemblablement tomber dans l'âme non-seulement d'une sage fille, mais d'une qui seroit le plus dépouillée d'honneur et d'humanité, &c. p. 49.

admits that the study of good authors will enable us to write
well, though we shall write still better by knowing how to
speak well. Vaugelas tells us that his knowledge was acquired by long practice at court, and by the conversation of
Cardinal Perron and of Coeffeteau.

26. La Mothe le Vayer, in his Considérations sur l'Éloquence française, 1647, has endeavoured to steer a La Mothe le
middle course between the old and the new schools Vayer.
of French style, but with a marked desire to withstand the
latter. He blames Du Vair for the strange and barbarous
words he employs. He laughs also at the nicety of those
who were beginning to object to a number of common French
words. One would not use the conjunction *Car*; against
which folly Le Vayer wrote a separate treatise.[o] He defends
the use of quotations in a different language, which some
purists in French style had in horror. But this treatise
seems not to contain much that is valuable, and it is very
diffuse.

27. Two French writers may be reckoned worthy of a place
in this chapter, who are, from the nature of their Legal
speeches of
works, not generally known out of their own country, Patru;
and whom I cannot refer with absolute propriety to this
rather than to the ensuing period, except by a certain character and manner of writing, which belongs more to the
earlier than the later moiety of the seventeenth century.
These were two lawyers, Patru and Le Maistre. The pleadings of Patru appear to me excellent in their particular line
of forensic eloquence, addressed to intelligent and experienced
judges. They greatly resemble what are called the private
orations of Demosthenes, and those of Lysias and Isæus,
especially, perhaps, the last. No ambitious ornament, no
appeal to the emotions of the heart, no bold figures of rhetoric, are permitted in the Attic severity of this style ; or, if
they ever occur, it is to surprise us as things rather uncommon in the place where they appear than in themselves.
Patru does not even employ the exordium usual in speeches,
but rushes instantaneously, though always perspicuously, into

---

[o] This was Gomberville, in whose
immense romance, Polexandre, it is said
that this word only occurs three times ;
a discovery which does vast honour to
the person who took the pains to make
it.

his statement of the case. In the eyes of many this is no eloquence at all, and it requires perhaps some taste for legal reasoning to enter fully into its merit. But the Greek orators are masters whom a modern lawyer need not blush to follow, and to follow, as Patru did, in their respect for the tribunal they addressed. They spoke to rather a numerous body of judges; but those were Athenians, and, as we have reason to believe, the best and most upright, the salt of that vicious city. Patru again spoke to the parliament of Paris, men too well versed in the ways of law and justice to be the dupes of tinkling sound. He is therefore plain, lucid, well arranged, but not emphatic or impetuous: the subjects of his published speeches would not admit of such qualities; though Patru is said to have employed on some occasions the burning words of the highest oratory. His style has always been reckoned purely and rigidly French; but I have been led rather to praise what has struck me in the substance of his pleadings; which, whether read at this day in France or not, are, I may venture to say, worthy to be studied by lawyers, like those to which I have compared them, the strictly forensic portion of Greek oratory. In some speeches of Patru which are more generally praised, that on his own reception in the Academy, and one complimentary to Christina, it has seemed to me that he falls very short of his judicial style; the ornaments are common-place, and such as belong to the panegyrical department of oratory, in all ages less important and valuable than the other two. It should be added, that Patru was not only one of the purest writers, but one of the best critics whom France possessed.[p]

28. The forensic speeches of Le Maistre are more eloquent, in a popular sense of the word, more ardent, more imaginative, than those of Patru; the one addresses the judges alone, the other has a view to the audience; the one seeks the success of his cause alone, the other that and his own glory together. The one will be more prized by the lovers of legal reasoning, the other by the majority of man-

and of Le Maistre.

---

[p] Perrault says of Patru in his Hommes illustres de France, vol. ii. p. 66: Ses plaidoyers servent *encore aujourd'hui* de modèle pour écrire correctement en notre langue. Yet they were not much above thirty years old—so much had the language changed, as to rules of writing, within that time.

kind. The one more reminds us of the orations of Demosthenes for his private clients, the other of those of Cicero. Le Maistre is fervid and brilliant—he hurries us with him; in all his pleadings, warmth is his first characteristic, and a certain elegance is the second. In the power of statement I do not perceive that he is inferior to Patru; both are excellent. Wherever great moral or social topics or extensive views of history and human nature can be employed, Le Maistre has the advantage. Both are concise, relatively to the common verbosity of the bar; but Le Maistre has much more that might be retrenched; not that it is redundant in expression, but unnecessary in substance. This is owing to his ambitious display of general erudition; his quotations are too frequent and too ornamental, partly drawn from the ancients, but more from the fathers. Ambrose, in fact, Jerome and Augustin, Chrysostom, Basil, and Gregory were the models whom the writers of this age were accustomed to study; and hence they are often, and Le Maistre among the rest, too apt to declaim where they should prove, and to use arguments from analogy, rather striking to the common hearer, than likely to weigh much with a tribunal. He has less simplicity, less purity of taste than Patru; his animated language would, in our courts, be frequently effective with a jury, but would seem too indefinite and common-place to the judges; we should crowd to hear Le Maistre, we should be compelled to decide with Patru. They are both, however, very superior advocates, and do great honour to the French bar.

29. A sensible improvement in the general style of English writers had come on before the expiration of the sixteenth century; the rude and rough phrases, sometimes almost requiring a glossary, which lie as *Improvement in English style.* spots of rust on the pages of Latimer, Grafton, Aylmer, or even Ascham, had been chiefly polished away; if we meet in Sidney, Hooker, or the prose of Spenser, with obsolete expressions or forms, we find none that are in the least unintelligible, none that give us offence. But to this next period belong most of those whom we commonly reckon our old English writers; men often of such sterling worth for their sense, that we might read them with little regard to

their language, yet, in some instances at least, possessing much that demands praise in this respect. They are generally nervous and effective, copious to redundancy in their command of words, apt to employ what seemed to them ornament with much imagination rather than judicious taste, yet seldom degenerating into common-place and indefinite phraseology. They have, however, many defects; some of them, especially the most learned, are full of pedantry, and deform their pages by an excessive and preposterous mixture of Latinisms unknown before;[q] at other times we are disgusted by colloquial and even vulgar idioms or proverbs; nor is it uncommon to find these opposite blemishes not only in the same author, but in the same passages. Their periods, except in a very few, are ill constructed and tediously prolonged; their ears (again with some exceptions) seem to have been insensible to the beauty of rhythmical prose; grace is commonly wanting, and their notion of the artifices of style, when they thought at all about them, was not congenial to our own language. This may be deemed a general description of the English writers under James and Charles; we shall now proceed to mention some of the most famous, and who may, in a certain degree, be deemed to modify this censure.

30. I will begin with a passage of very considerable beauty,
Earl of Essex.
which is here out of place, since it was written in the year 1598. It is found in the Apology for the Earl of Essex, published among the works of Lord Bacon, and passing, I suppose, commonly for his. It seems nevertheless, in my judgment, far more probably genuine. We have nowhere in our early writers a flow of words so easy and graceful, a structure so harmonious, a series of antitheses so spirited without affectation, an absence of quaintness, pedantry, and vulgarity so truly gentlemanlike, a paragraph so worthy of the most brilliant man of his age. This could not have come from Bacon, who never divested himself of a certain didactic formality, even if he could have counterfeited that chivalrous generosity which it was not in his nature to

---

[q] In Pratt's edition of Bishop Hall's works we have a glossary of unusual words employed by him. They amount to more than eleven hundred, the greater part being of Latin or Greek origin; some are Gallicisms.

feel. It is the language of a soldier's heart, with the unstudied grace of a noble courtier.[r]

31. Knolles, already known by a spirited translation of Bodin's Commonwealth, published in 1610 a copious History of the Turks, bringing down his narrative to the most recent times. Johnson, in a paper of the Rambler, has given him the superiority over all English historians. 'He has displayed all the excellences that narration can admit. His style, though somewhat obscured by time, and vitiated by false wit, is pure, nervous, elevated, and clear. . . . . Nothing could have sunk this author into obscurity but the remoteness and barbarity of the people whose story he relates. It seldom happens that all circumstances concur to happiness or fame. The nation which produced this great historian has the grief of seeing his genius employed upon a foreign and uninteresting subject; and that writer who might have secured perpetuity to his name by a history of his own country, has exposed himself to the danger of oblivion by recounting enterprises and revolutions of which none

[r] 'A word for my friendship with the chief men of action, and favour generally to the men of war; and then I come to their main objection, which is my crossing of the treaty in hand. For most of them that are accounted the chief men of action, I do confess, I do entirely love them. They have been my companions both abroad and at home; some of them began the wars with me, most have had place under me, and many have had me a witness of their rising from captains, lieutenants, and private men to those charges which since by their virtue they have obtained. Now that I have tried them, I would choose them for friends, if I had them not; before I had tried them, God by his providence chose them for me. I love them for mine own sake; for I find sweetness in their conversation, strong assistance in their employments with me, and happiness in their friendship. I love them for their virtues' sake, and for their greatness of mind; (for little minds, though never so full of virtue, can be but a little virtuous;) and for their great understanding; for to understand little things, or things not of use, is little better than to understand nothing at all. I love them for their affections; for self-loving men love ease, pleasure, and profit; but they that love pains, danger, and fame, show that they love public profit more than themselves. I love them for my country's sake; for they are England's best armour of defence and weapons of offence. If we may have peace, they have purchased it; if we must have war, they must manage it. Yet while we are doubtful and in treaty we must value ourselves by what may be done, and the enemy will value us by what hath been done by our chief men of action.

'That generally I am affected to the men of war, it should not seem strange to any reasonable man. Every man doth love them of his own profession. The grave judges favour the students of the law; the reverend bishops the labourers in the ministry; and I (since her Majesty hath yearly used my service in her late actions) must reckon myself in the number of her men of war. Before action, Providence makes me cherish them for what they can do; in action, necessity makes me value them for the service they do; and after action, experience and thankfulness make me love them for the service they have done.'

desire to be informed.'[s]   The subject, however, appeared to
Knolles, and I know not how we can say erroneously, one
of the most splendid that he could have selected.   It was the
rise and growth of a mighty nation, second only to Rome
in the constancy of success, and in the magnitude of empire ;
a nation fierce and terrible in that age, the present scourge
of half Christendom, and though from our remoteness not
very formidable to ourselves, still one of which not the bookish
man in his closet or the statesman in council had alone
heard, but the smith at his anvil, and the husbandman at
his plough.   A long decrepitude of the Turkish empire on
one hand, and our frequent alliance with it on the other,
have since obliterated the apprehensions and interests of
every kind which were awakened throughout Europe by its
youthful fury and its mature strength.   The subject was also
new in England, yet rich in materials ; various, in comparison with ordinary history, though not perhaps so fertile of
philosophical observation as some others, and furnishing
many occasions for the peculiar talents of Knolles.   These
were displayed, not in depth of thought, or copiousness of
collateral erudition, but in a style and in a power of narration which Johnson has not too highly extolled.   His
descriptions are vivid and animated ; circumstantial, but not
to feebleness; his characters are drawn with a strong pencil.
It is indeed difficult to estimate the merits of an historian
very accurately without having before our eyes his original
sources ; he may probably have translated much that we
admire, and he had shown that he knew how to translate.
In the style of Knolles there is sometimes, as Johnson has
hinted, a slight excess of desire to make every phrase effective ; but he is exempt from the usual blemishes of his age ;
and his command of the language is so extensive, that we
should not err in placing him among the first of our elder
writers.   Comparing, as a specimen of Knolles's manner, his
description of the execution of Mustapha, son of Solyman,
with that given by Robertson, where the latter historian has
been as circumstantial as his limits would permit, we shall
perceive that the former paints better his story, and deepens
better its interest.[t]

     [s] Rambler, No. 122.   [t] Knolles, p. 515.   Robertson's Charles

32. Raleigh's History of the World is a proof of the respect for laborious learning that had long dis- Raleigh's tinguished Europe.   We should expect from the the World. prison-house of a soldier, a courtier, a busy intriguer in state affairs, a poet and a man of genius, something well worth our notice; but hardly a prolix history of the ancient world, hardly disquisitions on the site of Paradise and the travels of Cain.   These are probably translated with little alteration from some of the learned writings of the continent; they are by much the least valuable portion of Raleigh's work.   The Greek and Roman story is told more fully and exactly than by any earlier English author, and with a plain eloquence which has given this book a classical reputation in our language, though from its length, and the want of that critical sifting of facts which we now justly demand, it is not greatly read.   Raleigh has intermingled political reflections, and illustrated his history by episodes from modern times, which perhaps are now the most interesting passages. It descends only to the second Macedonian war; the continuation might have been more generally valuable; but either the death of Prince Henry, as Raleigh himself tells us, or the new schemes of ambition which unfortunately opened upon his eyes, prevented the execution of the large plan he had formed.   There is little now obsolete in the words of Raleigh, nor, to any great degree, in his turn of phrase; the periods, when pains have been taken with them, show that artificial structure which we find in Sidney and Hooker; he is less pedantic than most of his contemporaries, seldom low, never affected.

33. Daniel's History of England from the Conquest to the Reign of Edward III., published in 1618, is deserv- Daniel's ing of some attention on account of its language. England. It is written with a freedom from all stiffness and a purity of style which hardly any other work of so early a date exhibits.   These qualities are indeed so remarkable that it would require a good deal of critical observation to distin-

---

the Fifth, book xi. [The principal authority for this description appears to be Busbequius, in his excellent Legationis Turcicæ Epistolæ. It has been justly observed that I might have mentioned Busbequius in a former volume among the good Latin writers of the sixteenth century.—1842.]

guish it even from writings of the reign of Anne; and where it differs from them (I speak only of the secondary class of works, which have not much individuality of manner), it is by a more select idiom, and by an absence of the Gallicism or vulgarity which are often found in that age. It is true that the merits of Daniel are chiefly negative; he is never pedantic, or antithetical, or low, as his contemporaries were apt to be; but his periods are ill constructed; he has little vigour or elegance; and it is only by observing how much pains he must have taken to reject phrases which were growing obsolete, that we give him credit for having done more than follow the common stream of easy writing. A slight tinge of archaism, and a certain majesty of expression, relatively to colloquial usage, were thought by Bacon and Raleigh congenial to an elevated style; but Daniel, a gentleman of the king's household, wrote as the court spoke, and his facility would be pleasing if his sentences had a less negligent structure. As an historian, he had recourse only to common authorities; but his narration is fluent and perspicuous, with a regular vein of good sense, more the characteristic of his mind, both in verse and prose, than any commanding vigour.

34. The style of Bacon has an idiosyncracy which we might expect from his genius. It can rarely indeed happen, and only in men of secondary talents, that the language they use is not, by its very choice and collocation, as well as its meaning, the representative of an individuality that distinguishes their turn of thought. Bacon is elaborate, sententious, often witty, often metaphorical; nothing could be spared; his analogies are generally striking and novel; his style is clear, precise, forcible; yet there is some degree of stiffness about it, and in mere language he is inferior to Raleigh. The History of Henry VII., admirable as many passages are, seems to be written rather too ambitiously, and with too great an absence of simplicity.

Bacon.

35. The polemical writings of Milton, which chiefly fall within this period, contain several bursts of his splendid imagination and grandeur of soul. They are, however, much inferior to the Areopagitica, or Plea

Milton.

for the Liberty of Unlicensed Printing. Many passages in this famous tract are admirably eloquent; an intense love of liberty and truth glows through it; the majestic soul of Milton breathes such high thoughts as had not been uttered before; yet even here he frequently sinks in a single instant, as is usual with our old writers, from his highest flights to the ground; his intermixture of familiar with learned phraseology is unpleasing, his structure is affectedly elaborate, and he seldom reaches any harmony. If he turns to invective, as sometimes in this treatise, and more in his Apology for Smectymnuus, it is mere ribaldrous vulgarity blended with pedantry; his wit is always poor and without ease. An absence of idiomatic grace, and an use of harsh inversions violating the rules of the language, distinguish, in general, the writings of Milton, and require in order to compensate them such high beauties as will sometimes occur.

36. The History of Clarendon may be considered as belonging rather to this than to the second period of the century, both by the probable date of composi- Clarendon. tion and by the nature of its style. He is excellent in everything that he has performed with care; his characters are beautifully delineated; his sentiments have often a noble gravity, which the length of his periods, far too great in itself, seems to befit; but in the general course of his narration he is negligent of grammar and perspicuity, with little choice of words, and therefore sometimes idiomatic without ease or elegance. The official papers on the royal side, which are generally attributed to him, are written in a masculine and majestic tone, far superior to those of the parliament. The latter had, however, a writer who did them honour : May's History of the Parliament is a good model of genuine English; he is plain, terse, and vigorous, never slovenly, though with few remarkable passages, and is, in style as well as substance, a kind of contrast to Clarendon.

37. The famous Icon Basilice, ascribed to Charles I., may deserve a place in literary history. If we could The Icon trust its panegyrists, few books in our language Basilice. have done it more credit by dignity of sentiment and beauty of style. It can hardly be necessary for me to express my unhesitating conviction that it was solely written by Bishop

Gauden, who after the Restoration unequivocally claimed it as his own. The folly and impudence of such a claim, if it could not be substantiated, are not to be presumed as to any man of good understanding, fair character, and high station, without stronger evidence than has been alleged on the other side; especially when we find that those who had the best means of inquiry, at a time when it seems impossible that the falsehood of Gauden's assertion should not have been demonstrated, if it were false, acquiesced in his pretensions. We have very little to place against this, except secondary testimony, vague, for the most part, in itself, and collected by those whose veracity has not been put to the test like that of Gauden.[u] The style also of the Icon Basilice has been identified by Mr. Todd with that of Gauden by the use of several phrases so peculiar that we can hardly conceive them to have suggested themselves to more than one person. It is nevertheless superior to his acknowledged writings. A strain of majestic melancholy is well kept up; but the personated sovereign is rather too theatrical for real nature, the language is too rhetorical and amplified, the periods too artificially elaborated. None but scholars and practised writers employ such a style as this.

38. Burton's Anatomy of Melancholy belongs, by its sys-
Burton's Anatomy of Melancholy. tematic divisions and its accumulated quotations, to the class of mere erudition; it seems at first sight like those tedious Latin folios into which scholars of the sixteenth and seventeenth centuries threw the materials of their Adversaria, or common-place books, painfully selected and arranged by the labour of many years. But writing fortunately in English, and in a style not by any means devoid

---

[u] There is only one claimant, in a proper sense, for the Icon Basilice, which is Gauden himself; the king neither appears by himself nor representative. And, though we may find several instances of plagiarism in literary history (one of the grossest being the publication by a Spanish friar, under another title, of a book already in print with the name of Hyperius of Marpurg, its real author), yet I cannot call to mind any, where a man known to the world has asserted in terms his own authorship of a book not written by himself, but universally ascribed to another, and which had never been in his possession. A story is told, and I believe truly, that a young man assumed the credit of Mackenzie's Man of Feeling while it was still anonymous. But this is widely different from the case of the Icon Basilice. We have had an interminable discussion as to the Letters of Junius; but no one has ever claimed this derelict property to himself, or told the world, I am Junius.

of point and terseness, with much good sense and observation of men as well as of books, and having also the skill of choosing his quotations for their rareness, oddity, and amusing character, without losing sight of their pertinence to the subject, he has produced a work of which, as is well known, Johnson said that it was the only one which had ever caused him to leave his bed earlier than he had intended. Johnson, who seems to have had some turn for the singularities of learning which fill the Anatomy of Melancholy, may perhaps have raised the credit of Burton higher than his desert. He is clogged by excess of reading, like others of his age, and we may peruse entire chapters without finding more than a few lines that belong to himself. This becomes a wearisome style, and, for my own part, I have not found much pleasure in glancing over the Anatomy of Melancholy. It may be added that he has been a collector of stories far more strange than true, from those records of figments, the old medical writers of the sixteenth century, and other equally deceitful sources. Burton lived at Oxford, and his volumes are apparently a great sweeping of miscellaneous literature from the Bodleian Library.

39. John Earle, after the Restoration bishop of Worcester, and then of Salisbury, is author of 'Microcosmogra- *Earle's* phia, or a Piece of the Worlde discovered in Essays *Characters.* and Characters,' published anonymously in 1628. In some of these short characters, Earle is worthy of comparison with La Bruyère; in others, perhaps the greater part, he has contented himself with pictures of ordinary manners, such as the varieties of occupation, rather than of intrinsic character, supply. In all, however, we find an acute observation and a happy humour of expression. The chapter entitled the Sceptic is best known; it is witty, but an insult throughout on the honest searcher after truth, which could have come only from one that was content to take up his own opinions for ease or profit. Earle is always gay and quick to catch the ridiculous, especially that of exterior appearances; his style is short, describing well with a few words, but with much of the affected quaintness of that age. It is one of those books which give us a picturesque idea of the manners of our fathers at a period now become remote, and for this reason, were there no other, it would deserve to be read.

40. But the Microcosmography is not an original work in
_{Overbury's} its plan or mode of execution ; it is a close imitation
_{Characters.} of the Characters of Sir Thomas Overbury.   They
both belong to the favourite style of apophthegm, in which
every sentence is a point or a witticism.   Yet the entire character so delineated produces a certain effect; it is a Dutch
picture, a Gerard Dow, somewhat too elaborate.   Earle has
more natural humour than Overbury, and hits his mark more
neatly; the other is more satirical, but often abusive and
vulgar.   The ' Fair and Happy Milkmaid,' often quoted, is
the best of his characters.   The wit is often trivial and flat;
the sentiments have nothing in them general or worthy of
much remembrance; praise is only due to the graphic skill
in delineating character.   Earle is as clearly the better, as
Overbury is the more original, writer.

41. A book by Ben Jonson, entitled ' Timber, or Dis-
_{Jonson's} coveries made upon Men and Matter,'[x] is altogether
_{Discoveries.} miscellaneous, the greater part being general moral
remarks, while another portion deserves notice as the only
book of English criticism in the first part of the seventeenth
century.   The observations are unconnected, judicious, sometimes witty, frequently severe.   The style is what was called
pregnant, leaving much to be filled up by the reader's reflection.   Good sense and a vigorous manner of grappling
with every subject will generally be found in Jonson, but he
does not reach any very profound criticism.   His English
Grammar is said by Gifford to have been destroyed in the
conflagration of his study.   What we have therefore under
that name is, he thinks, to be considered as properly the
materials of a more complete work that is lost.   We have, as
I apprehend, no earlier grammar upon so elaborate a plan ;
every rule is illustrated by examples, almost to redundance ;
but he is too copious on what is common to other languages,
and perhaps not full enough as to our peculiar idiom.

---

[x] [' Timber,' I suppose, is meant as a ludicrous translation of Sylva.—1842.]

SECT. II.—ON FICTION.

Cervantes—French Romances—Calprenède—Scuderi—Latin and English
Works of Fiction.

42. THE first part of Don Quixote was published in 1605.
We have no reason, I believe, to suppose that it Publication
was written long before. It became immediately of Don Quixote.
popular; and the admiration of the world raised up envious
competitors, one of whom, Avellenada, published a continuation in a strain of invective against the author. Cervantes,
who cannot be imagined to have ever designed the leaving
his romance in so unfinished a state, took time about the
second part, which did not appear till 1615.

43. Don Quixote is almost the only book in the Spanish
language which can now be said to possess so much Its reputa-
of an European reputation as to be popularly read tion.
in every country. It has, however, enjoyed enough to compensate for the neglect of the rest. It is to Europe in general
what Ariosto is to Italy, and Shakspeare to England; the
one book to which the slightest allusions may be made without affectation, but not missed without discredit. Numerous
translations and countless editions of them, in every language, bespeak its adaptation to mankind; no critic has
been paradoxical enough to withhold his admiration, no
reader has ventured to confess a want of relish for that in
which the young and old, in every climate, have age after
age taken delight. They have doubtless believed that they
understood the author's meaning; and, in giving the reins
to the gaiety that his fertile invention and comic humour
inspired, never thought of any deeper meaning than he announces, or delayed their enjoyment for any metaphysical
investigation of his plan.

44. A new school of criticism, however, has of late years
arisen in Germany, acute, ingenious, and sometimes New views of
eminently successful in philosophical, or, as they its design.
denominate it, æsthetic analysis of works of taste, but glid-
ing too much into refinement and conjectural hypothesis,

and with a tendency to mislead men of inferior capacities for
this kind of investigation into mere paradox and absurdity.
An instance is supplied, in my opinion, by some remarks of
Bouterwek, still more explicitly developed by Sismondi, on
the design of Cervantes in Don Quixote, and which have
been repeated in other publications.   According to these
writers, the primary idea is that of a 'man of elevated character, excited by heroic and enthusiastic feelings to the extravagant pitch of wishing to restore the age of chivalry;
nor is it possible to form a more mistaken notion of this
work than by considering it merely as a satire, intended by
the author to ridicule the absurd passion for reading old romances.'[y]   'The fundamental principle of Don Quixote,'
says Sismondi, 'is the eternal contrast between the spirit of
poetry and that of prose.   Men of an elevated soul propose
to themselves as the object of life to be the defenders of the
weak, the support of the oppressed, the champions of justice
and innocence.   Like Don Quixote, they find on every side
the image of the virtues they worship; they believe that
disinterestedness, nobleness, courage, in short, knight-
errantry, are still prevalent; and with no calculation of their
own powers, they expose themselves for an ungrateful world,
they offer themselves as a sacrifice to the laws and rules of
an imaginary state of society.'[z]

45. If this were a true representation of the scheme of
Don Quixote, we cannot wonder that some persons should,
as M. Sismondi tells us they do, consider it as the most melancholy book that has ever been written.   They consider it
also, no doubt, one of the most immoral, as chilling and pernicious in its influence on the social converse of mankind, as
the Prince of Machiavel is on their political intercourse.
'Cervantes,' he proceeds, 'has shown us in some measure the
vanity of greatness of soul and the delusion of heroism.   He
has drawn in Don Quixote a perfect man (un homme accompli),
who is nevertheless the constant object of ridicule.   Brave
beyond the fabled knights he imitates, disinterested, honourable, generous, the most faithful and respectful of lovers, the
best of masters, the most accomplished and well educated of
gentlemen, all his enterprises end in discomfiture to himself,

---

[y] Bouterwek, p. 334.   [z] Littérature du Midi, vol. iii. p. 339.

and in mischief to others.' M. Sismondi descants upon the perfections of the Knight of La Mancha with a gravity which it is not quite easy for his readers to preserve.

46. It might be answered by a phlegmatic observer, that a mere enthusiasm for doing good, if excited by vanity, and not accompanied by common sense, will Probably erroneous. seldom be very serviceable to ourselves or to others ; that men who in their heroism and care for the oppressed would throw open the cages of lions, and set galley-slaves at liberty, not forgetting to break the limbs of harmless persons whom they mistake for wrong-doers, are a class of whom Don Quixote is the real type; and that the world being much the worse for such heroes, it might not be immoral, notwithstanding their benevolent enthusiasm, to put them out of countenance by a little ridicule. This, however, is not, as I conceive, the primary aim of Cervantes ; nor do I think that the exhibition of one great truth, as the predominant, but concealed, moral, of a long work, is in the spirit of his age. He possessed a very thoughtful mind and a profound knowlege of humanity : yet the generalisation which the hypothesis of Bouterwek and Sismondi requires for the leading conception of Don Quixote, besides its being a little inconsistent with the valorous and romantic character of its author, belongs to a more advanced period of philosophy than his own. It will at all events, I presume, be admitted, that we cannot reason about Don Quixote except from the book ; and I think it may be shown in a few words that these ingenious writers have been chiefly misled by some want of consistency which circumstances produced in the author's delineation of his hero.

47. In the first chapter of this romance, Cervantes, with a few strokes of a great master, sets before us the Difference between the two parts. pauper gentleman, an early riser and keen sportsman, who ' when he was idle, which was most part of the year,' gave himself up to reading books of chivalry till he lost his wits. The events that follow are in every one's recollection ; his lunacy consists no doubt only in one idea ; but this is so absorbing that it perverts the evidence of his senses, and predominates in all his language. It is to be observed, therefore, in relation to the nobleness of soul ascribed to Don

Quixote, that every sentiment he utters is borrowed with a
punctilious rigour from the romances of his library; he
resorts to them on every occasion for precedents; if he is
intrepidly brave, it is because his madness and vanity have
made him believe himself unconquerable; if he bestows
kingdoms, it is because Amadis would have done the same;
if he is honourable, courteous, a redresser of wrongs, it is in
pursuance of these prototypes, from whom, except that he
seems rather more scrupulous in chastity, it is his only boast
not to diverge. Those who talk of the exalted character of
Don Quixote seem really to forget that, on these subjects, he
has no character at all; he is the echo of romance; and to
praise him is merely to say that the tone of chivalry, which
these productions studied to keep up, and, in the hands of
inferior artists, foolishly exaggerated, was full of moral dignity, and has, in a subdued degree of force, modelled the character of a man of honour in the present day. But throughout
the first two volumes of Don Quixote, though in a few unimportant passages he talks rationally, I cannot find more than
two in which he displays any other knowledge or strength of
mind than the original delineation of the character would
lead us to expect.

48. The case is much altered in the last two volumes.
Cervantes had acquired an immense popularity, and perceived
the opportunity, of which he had already availed himself,
that this romance gave for displaying his own mind. He had
become attached to a hero who had made him illustrious, and
suffered himself to lose sight of the clear outline he had once
traced for Quixote's personality. Hence we find in all this
second part that, although the lunacy as to knights errant
remains unabated, he is, on all other subjects, not only rational in the low sense of the word, but clear, acute, profound,
sarcastic, cool-headed. His philosophy is elevated but not
enthusiastic, his imagination is poetical, but it is restrained
by strong sense. There are, in fact, two Don Quixotes: one,
whom Cervantes first designed to draw, the foolish gentleman
of La Mancha, whose foolishness had made him frantic; the
other, a highly gifted, accomplished model of the best chivalry, trained in all the court, the camp, or the college could
impart, but scathed in one portion of his mind by an inex-

plicable visitation of monomania. One is inclined to ask why
this Don Quixote, who is Cervantes, should have been more
likely to lose his intellects by reading romances than Cervantes himself. As a matter of bodily disease, such an event
is doubtless possible; but nothing can be conceived more
improper for fiction, nothing more incapable of affording a
moral lesson, than the insanity which arises wholly from
disease. Insanity is, in no point of view, a theme for ridicule; and this is an inherent fault of the romance (for those
who have imagined that Cervantes has not rendered Quixote
ridiculous have a strange notion of the word); but the
thoughtlessness of mankind, rather than their insensibility
(for they do not connect madness with misery), furnishes
some apology for the first two volumes. In proportion as we
perceive below the veil of mental delusion a noble intellect,
we feel a painful sympathy with its humiliation: the character becomes more complicated and interesting, but has less
truth and naturalness; an objection which might also be
made, comparatively speaking, to the incidents in the latter
volumes, wherein I do not find the admirable probability
that reigns through the former. But this contrast of wisdom
and virtue with insanity in the same subject would have
been repulsive in the primary delineation; as I think any one
may judge, by supposing that Cervantes had, in the first
chapter, drawn such a picture of Quixote as Bouterwek and
Sismondi have drawn for him.

49. I must therefore venture to think, as I believe the
world has generally thought for two centuries, that Cervantes
had no more profound aim than he proposes to the reader.
If the fashion of reading bad romances of chivalry perverted
the taste of his contemporaries, and rendered their language
ridiculous, it was natural that a zealous lover of good literature should expose this folly to the world by exaggerating
its effects on a fictitious personage. It has been said by
some modern writer, though I cannot remember by whom,
that there was a *prose side* in the mind of Cervantes. There
was indeed a side of calm strong sense, which some take for
unpoetical. He thought the tone of those romances extravagant. It might naturally occur how absurd any one must
appear who should attempt to realise in actual life the ad-

ventures of Amadis. Already a novelist, he perceived the
opportunities this idea suggested. It was a necessary consequence that the hero must be represented as literally insane,
since his conduct would have been extravagant beyond the
probability of fiction on any other hypothesis; and from this
happy conception germinated in a very prolific mind the
whole history of Don Quixote. Its simplicity is perfect : no
limit could be found save the author's discretion, or sense
that he had drawn sufficiently on his imagination ; but the
death of Quixote, which Cervantes has been said to have
determined upon, lest some one else should a second time
presume to continue the story, is in fact the only possible
termination that could be given, after he had elevated the
character to that pitch of mental dignity which we find in
the last two volumes.

50. Few books of moral philosophy display as deep an
insight into the mechanism of the mind as Don
Quixote. And when we look also at the fertility
of invention, the general probability of the events, and the
great simplicity of the story, wherein no artifices are practised to create suspense, or complicate the action, we shall
think Cervantes fully deserving of the glory that attends this
monument of his genius. It is not merely that he is superior
to all his predecessors and contemporaries. This, though it
might account for the European fame of his romance, would
be an inadequate testimony to its desert. Cervantes stands
on an eminence, below which we must place the best of his
successors. We have only to compare him with Le Sage or
Fielding, to judge of his vast superiority. To Scott, indeed,
he must yield in the variety of his power ; but in the line of
comic romance, we should hardly think Scott his equal.

*Excellence
of this
romance.*

51. The moral novels of Cervantes, as he calls them (No-
vellas Exemplares), are written, I believe, in a good
style, but too short, and constructed with too little
artifice to rivet our interest. Their simplicity and truth, as
in many of the old novels, have a certain charm;
but in the present age our sense of satiety in works
of fiction cannot be overcome but by excellence. Of the
Spanish comic romances, in the *picaresque* style, several
remain : Justina was the most famous. One that does not

*Minor
novels of
Cervantes.*

*Other
novels—
Spanish.*

strictly belong to this lower class is the Marcos de Obregon
of Espinel.   This is supposed to have suggested much to Le
Sage in Gil Blas ; in fact, the first story we meet with is that
of Mergellina, the physician's wife.   The style, though not
dull, wants the grace and neatness of Le Sage.   This is
esteemed one of the best novels that Spain has produced.
Italy was no longer the seat of this literature.   A romance
of chivalry by Marini (not the poet of that name), entitled
Il Caloandro (1640), was translated but indiffer-   And Italian.
ently into French by Scuderi, and has been praised
by Salfi as full of imagination, with characters skilfully diversified, and an interesting, well-conducted story.[a]

52. France in the sixteenth century, content with Amadis
de Gaul and the numerous romances of the Spanish   French ro-
school, had contributed very little to that literature.   Astrée.
But now she had native writers of both kinds, the pastoral
and heroic, who completely superseded the models they had
before them.   Their earliest essay was the Astrée of D'Urfé.
Of this pastoral romance the first volume was published in
1610 ; the second in 1620 ; three more came slowly forth,
that the world might have due leisure to admire.   It contains about 5,500 pages.   It would be almost as discreditable
to have read such a book through at present, as it was to be
ignorant of it in the age of Louis XIII.   Allusions, however, to real circumstances served in some measure to lessen
the insipidity of a love story which seems to equal any in
absurdity and want of interest.   The style, and I can judge
no farther, having read but a few pages, seems easy and not
unpleasing ; but the pastoral tone is insufferably puerile, and
a monotonous solemnity makes us almost suspect that one
source of its popularity was its gentle effect, when read in
small portions before retiring to rest.   It was nevertheless
admired by men of erudition, like Camus and Huet, or even
by men of the world like Rochefoucault.[b]

53. From the union of the old chivalrous romance with
this newer style, the courtly pastoral, sprang   Heroic ro-
another kind of fiction, the French heroic romance.   Gomber-
Three nearly contemporary writers, Gomberville,   ville.

---

[a] Salfi, vol. xiv. p. 88.   p. 184.   Biographie universelle.   Bou-
[b] Dunlop's History of Fiction, vol. iii.   terwek, vol. v. p. 295.

Calprenède, Scuderi, supplied a number of voluminous stories, frequently historical in some of their names, but utterly destitute of truth in circumstances, characters, and manners. Gomberville led the way in his Polexandre, first published in 1632, and reaching in later editions to about 6,000 pages. ' This,' says a modern writer, ' seems to have been the model of the works of Calprenède and Scuderi. This ponderous work may be regarded as a sort of intermediate production between the later compositions and the ancient fables of chivalry. It has, indeed, a close affinity to the heroic romance ; but many of the exploits of the hero are as extravagant as those of a paladin or knight of the round table.'[c]   No romance in the language has so complex an intrigue, insomuch that it is followed with difficulty ; and the author has in successive editions capriciously remodelled parts of his story, which is wholly of his own invention.[d]

54. Calprenède, a poet of no contemptible powers of imagination, poured forth his stores of rapid invention

Calprenède.

in several romances more celebrated than that of Gomberville.   The first, which is contained in ten octavo volumes, is the Cassandra.   This appeared in 1642, and was followed by the Cleopatra, published, according to the custom of romancers, in successive parts, the earliest in 1646.   La Harpe thinks this unquestionably the best work of Calprenède ; Bouterwek seems to prefer the Cassandra.   Pharamond is not wholly his own ; five out of twelve volumes belong to one De Vaumorière, a continuator.[e]   Calprenède, like many others, had but a life estate in the temple of fame, and more happy, perhaps, than greater men, lived out the whole favour of the world, which, having been largely showered on his head, strewed no memorials on his grave.   It became, soon after his death, through the satire of Boileau and the influence of a new style in fiction, a matter of course to turn him into ridicule.   It is impossible that his romances should be read again ; but those who, for the purposes of general criticism, have gone back to these volumes, find not a little to praise in his genius, and in some measure to explain his popularity.   ' Calprenède,' says Bouterwek, ' belonged to the extravagant party, which endeavoured to give a triumph to

[c] Dunlop, iii. 230.   [d] Biogr. univ.   [e] Dunlop, iii. 259.

genius at the expense of taste, and by that very means played into the hands of the opposite party, which saw nothing so laudable as the observation of rules which taste prescribed. We have only to become acquainted with any one of the prolix romances of Calprenède, such, for instance, as the Cassandra, to see clearly the spirit which animates the whole invention. We find there again the heroism of chivalry, the enthusiastic raptures of love, the struggle of duty with passion, the victory of magnanimity, sincerity, and humanity, over force, fraud, and barbarism, in the genuine characters and circumstances of romance. The events are skilfully interwoven, and a truly poetical keeping belongs to the whole, however extended it may be. The diction of Calprenède is a little monotonous, but not at all trivial, and seldom affected. It is like that of old romance, grave, circumstantial, somewhat in the chronicle style, but picturesque, agreeable, full of sensibility and simplicity. Many passages might, if versified, find a place in the most beautiful poem of this class.' [f]

55. The honours of this romantic literature have long been shared by the female sex. In the age of Richelieu and Mazarin, this was represented by Mademoiselle de Scuderi, a name very glorious for a season, but which unfortunately did not, like that of Calprenède, continue to be such during the whole lifetime of her who bore it. The old age of Mademoiselle de Scuderi was ignominiously treated by the pitiless Boileau ; and reaching more than her ninetieth year, she almost survived her only offspring, those of her pen. In her youth she had been the associate of the Rambouillet circle, and caught perhaps in some measure from them what she gave back with interest, a tone of perpetual affectation, and a pedantic gallantry, which could not withstand the first approach of ridicule. Her first romance was Ibrahim, published in 1635; but the more celebrated were the Grand Cyrus and the Clélie. Each of these two romances is in ten volumes. [g] The persons chiefly connected with the Hôtel Rambouillet sat for their pictures, as Persians or Babylonians, in Cyrus. Julie d'Angennes herself bore the name of Arte-

Scuderi.

---

[f] Bouterwek, vi. 230.   [g] Biogr. univ. Dunlop. Bouterwek.

nice, by which she was afterwards distinguished among her
friends; and it is a remarkable instance not only of the popularity of these romances, but of the respectful sentiment,
which, from the elevation and purity no one can deny them
to exhibit, was always associated in the gravest persons with
their fictions, that a prelate of eminent fame for eloquence,
Fléchier, in his funeral sermon on this lady, calls her ' the
incomparable Artenice.' [h] Such an allusion would appear to
us misplaced; but we may presume that it was not so thought.
Scuderi's romances seem to have been remarkably the favourites of the clergy; Huet, Mascaron, Godeau, as much as Fléchier, were her ardent admirers. ' I find,' says the second of
these, one of the chief ornaments of the French pulpit, in
writing to Mademoiselle de Scuderi, ' so much in your works
calculated to reform the world, that in the sermons I am now
preparing for the court, you will often be on my table by the
side of St. Augustin and St. Bernard.' [i] In the writings
of this lady we see the last footstep of the old chivalrous
romance. She, like Calprenède, had derived from this source
the predominant characteristics of her personages, an exalted
generosity, a disdain of all selfish considerations, a courage
which attempts impossibilities and is rewarded by achieving
them, a love outrageously hyperbolical in pretence, yet intrinsically without passion, all, in short, that Cervantes has
bestowed on Don Quixote. Love, however, or its counterfeit, gallantry, plays a still more leading part in the French
romance than in its Castilian prototype; the feats of heroes,
though not less wonderful, are less prominent on the canvas,
and a metaphysical pedantry replaces the pompous metaphors
in which the knight of sorrowful countenance had taken so
much delight. The approbation of many persons, far superior
judges to Don Quixote, makes it impossible to doubt that
the romances of Calprenède and Scuderi were better than
his library. But as this is the least possible praise, it will

---

[h] Sermons de Fléchier, ii. 325 (edit.
1690). But probably Bossuet would
not have stooped to this allusion.

[i] Biogr. univ. Mademoiselle de
Scuderi was not gifted by nature with
beauty, or, as this biographer more
bluntly says, était d'une extrême laideur.
She would probably have wished this to

have been otherwise, but carried off the
matter very well, as appears by her epigram on her own picture by Nanteuil:

Nanteuil, en faisant mon image,
A de son art divin signalé le pouvoir;
Je haïs mes yeux dans mon miroir,
Je les aime dans son ouvrage.

certainly not tempt any one away from the rich and varied repast of fiction which the last and present century have spread before him. Mademoiselle de Scuderi has perverted history still more than Calprenède, and changed her Romans into languishing Parisians. It is not to be forgotten that the taste of her party, though it did not, properly speaking, infect Corneille, compelled him to weaken some of his tragedies. And this must be the justification of Boileau's cutting ridicule upon this truly estimable woman. She had certainly kept up a tone of severe and high morality, with which the aristocracy of Paris could ill dispense; but it was one not difficult to feign, and there might be Tartuffes of sentiment as well as of religion. Whatever is false in taste is apt to be allied to what is insincere in character.

56. The Argenis of Barclay, a son of the defender of royal authority against republican theories, is a Latin ro- Argenis mance, superior, perhaps, to those, after Cervantes, of Barclay. which the Spanish or French language could boast. It has indeed always been reckoned among political allegories. That the state of France in the last years of Henry III. is partially shadowed in it, can admit of no doubt; several characters are faintly veiled either by anagram or Greek translation of their names; but whether to avoid the insipidity of servile allegory, or to excite the reader by perplexity, Barclay has mingled so much of mere fiction with his story, that no attempts at a regular key to the whole work can be successful, nor in fact does the fable of this romance run in any parallel stream with real events. His object seems in great measure to have been the discussion of political questions in feigned dialogue. But though in these we find no want of acuteness or good sense, they have not at present much novelty in our eyes; and though the style is really pleasing, or, as some have judged, excellent,[k] and the incidents not ill contrived, it might be hard to go entirely through a Latin romance of 700 pages, unless indeed we had no alternative

---

[k] Coleridge has pronounced an ardent, and rather excessive, eulogy on the language of the Argenis, preferring it to that of Livy or Tacitus. Coleridge's Remains, vol. i. p. 257. I cannot by any means go this length; it has struck me that the Latinity is more that of Petronius Arbiter, but I am not well enough acquainted with that writer to speak confidently. The same observation seems applicable to the Euphormio.

given but the perusal of the similar works in Spanish or French. The Argenis was published at Rome in 1622 ; some of the personages introduced by Barclay are his own contemporaries ; a proof that he did not intend a strictly historical allegory of the events of the last age. The His Euphormio of the same author resembles in some degree the Argenis, but, with less of story and character, has a more direct reference to European politics. It contains much political disquisition, and one whole book is employed in a description of the manners and laws of different countries with no disguise of names.

His Euphormio.

57. Campanella gave a loose to his fanciful humour in a fiction entitled The City of the Sun, published at Frankfort in 1623, in imitation, perhaps, of the Utopia. The City of the Sun is supposed to stand upon a mountain situated at Ceylon, under the equator. A community of goods and women is established in this republic ; the principal magistrate of which is styled Sun, and is elected after a strict examination in all kinds of science. Campanella has brought in so much of his own philosophical system, that we may presume that to have been the object of this romance. The Solars, he tells us, abstained at first from flesh, because they thought it cruel to kill animals. ' But afterwards considering that it would be equally cruel to kill plants, which are not less endowed with sensation, so that they must perish by famine, they understood that ignoble things were created for the use of nobler things, and now eat all things without scruple.' Another Latin romance had some celebrity in its day, the Monarchia Solipsorum, a satire on the Jesuits in the fictitious name of Lucius Cornelius Europeus. It has been ascribed to more than one person ; the probable author is one Scotti, who had himself belonged to the order.[m] This book did not seem to me in the least interesting ; if it is so in any degree, it must be not as mere fiction, but as a revelation of secrets.

Campanella's City of the Sun.

58. It is not so much an extraordinary as an unfortunate deficiency in our own literary annals, that England should have been destitute of the comic romance, or that derived from real life, in this period; since in fact we

Few books of fiction in England.

---

[m] Biogr. univ.: arts. Scotti and Inchoffer. Niceron, vols. xxxv. and xxxix.

may say the same, as has been seen, of France. The *picaresque* novels of Spain were thought well worthy of translation; but it occurred to no one, or no one had the gift of genius, to shift the scene, and imitate their delineation of native manners. Of how much value would have been a genuine English novel, the mirror of actual life in the various ranks of society, written under Elizabeth or under the Stuarts! We should have seen, if the execution had not been very coarse, and the delineation absolutely confined to low characters, the social habits of our forefathers better than by all our other sources of that knowledge, the plays, the letters, the traditions and anecdotes, the pictures or buildings of the time. Notwithstanding the interest which all profess to take in the history of manners, our notions of them are generally meagre and imperfect; and hence modern works of fiction are but crude and inaccurate designs when they endeavour to represent the living England of two centuries since. Even Scott, who had a fine instinctive perception of truth and nature, and who had read much, does not appear to have seized the genuine tone of conversation, and to have been a little misled by the style of Shakspeare. This is rather elaborate and removed from vulgar use by a sort of archaism in phrase, and by a pointed turn in the dialogue, adapted to theatrical utterance, but wanting the ease of ordinary speech.

59. I can only produce two books by English authors in this first part of the seventeenth century which fall properly under the class of novels or romances; and of these one is written in Latin. This is the *Mundus Alter et Idem of Hall.* Mundus Alter et Idem of Bishop Hall, an imitation of the latter and weaker volumes of Rabelais. A country in Terra Australis is divided into four regions, Crapulia, Viraginia, Moronea, and Lavernia. Maps of the whole land and of particular regions are given; and the nature of the satire, not much of which has any especial reference to England, may easily be collected. It is not a very successful effort.

60. Another prelate, or one who became such, Francis Godwin, was the author of a much more curious *Godwin's Journey to the Moon.* story. It is called the Man in the Moon, and relates the journey of one Domingo Gonzalez to that planet. This

was written by Godwin, according to Antony Wood, while
he was a student at Oxford.[n] By some internal proofs, it
must have been later than 1599, and before the death of
Elizabeth in 1603.   But it was not published till 1638.   It
was translated into French, and became the model of Cyrano
de Bergerac, as he was of Swift.   Godwin himself had no
prototype, as far as I know, but Lucian.   He resembles those
writers in the natural and veracious tone of his lies.   The
fiction is rather ingenious and amusing throughout; but the
most remarkable part is the happy conjectures, if we must
say no more, of his philosophy.   Not only does the writer
declare positively for the Copernican system, which was uncommon at that time, but he has surprisingly understood the
principle of gravitation, it being distinctly supposed that the
earth's attraction diminishes with the distance.   Nor is the
following passage less curious:—' I must let you understand
that the globe of the moon is not altogether destitute of an
attractive power; but it is far weaker than that of the earth;
as if a man do but spring upwards with all his force, as dan-
cers do when they show their activity by capering, he shall
be able to mount fifty or sixty feet high, and then he is quite
beyond all attraction of the moon.'   By this device Gonzalez
returns from his sojourn in the latter, though it required a
more complex one to bring him thither.   ' The moon,' he
observes, ' is covered with a sea, except the parts which seem
somewhat darker to us, and are dry land.'   A contrary
hypothesis came afterwards to prevail; but we must not expect everything from our ingenious young student.

61. Though I can mention nothing else in English which
comes exactly within our notions of a romance, we
may advert to the Dodona's Grove of James Howell.
This is a strange allegory, without any ingenuity in maintaining the analogy between the outer and inner story, which
alone can give a reader any pleasure in allegorical writing.
The subject is the state of Europe, especially of England,
about 1640, under the guise of animated trees in a forest.
The style is like the following:—' The next morning the

Howell's
Dodona's
Grove.

---

[n] Athenæ Oxonienses, vol. ii. col. 558.
It is remarkable that Mr. Dunlop has
been ignorant of Godwin's claim to this
work, and takes Dominic Gonzalez for
the real author. Hist. of Fiction, iii.
394.

royal olives sent some prime elms to attend Prince Rocolino
in quality of officers of state; and a little after he was
brought to the royal palace in the same state Elaiana's kings
use to be attended the day of their coronation.' The contrivance is all along so clumsy and unintelligible, the invention so poor and absurd, the story, if story there be, so dull
an echo of well-known events, that it is impossible to reckon
Dodona's Grove anything but an entire failure. Howell has
no wit, but he has abundance of conceits, flat and common-
place enough. With all this he was a man of some sense
and observation. His letters are entertaining, but they
scarcely deserve consideration in this volume.

62. It is very possible that some small works belonging to
this extensive class have been omitted, which my   Adventures
                                                    of Baron
readers, or myself on second consideration, might   de Fæneste.
think not unworthy of notice. It is also one so miscellaneous
that we might fairly doubt as to some which have a certain
claim to be admitted into it. Such are the Adventures of
the Baron de Fæneste, by the famous Agrippa d'Aubigné
(whose autobiography, by the way, has at least the liveliness
of fiction); a singular book, written in dialogue, where an
imaginary Gascon baron recounts his tales of the camp and
the court. He is made to speak a patois not quite easy for
us to understand, and not perhaps worth the while; but it
seems to contain much that illustrates the state of France
about the beginning of the seventeenth century. Much in
this book is satirical; and the satire falls on the Catholics,
whom Fæneste, a mere foolish gentleman of Gascony, is
made to defend against an acute Huguenot.

CHAPTER VIII.

HISTORY OF MATHEMATICAL AND PHYSICAL SCIENCE
FROM 1600 TO 1650.

Sect. I.

Invention of Logarithms by Napier—New Geometry of Kepler and Cavalieri
—Algebra—Harriott—Descartes—Astronomy—Kepler—Galileo —Copernican System begins to prevail—Cartesian Theory of the World—Mechanical Discoveries of Galileo—Descartes—Hydrostatics—Optics.

1. In the last part of this work we have followed the progress of mathematical and physical knowledge down
to the close of the sixteenth century.   The ancient
geometers had done so much in their own province
of lines and figures, that little more of importance could be
effected, except by new methods extending the limits of the
science, or derived from some other source of invention.
Algebra had yielded a more abundant harvest to the genius
of the sixteenth century; yet something here seemed to be
wanting to give that science a character of utility and reference to general truth; nor had the formulæ of letters and
radical signs that perceptible beauty which often wins us to
delight in geometrical theorems of as little apparent usefulness in their results.   Meanwhile the primary laws, to which
all mathematical reasonings, in their relation to physical
truths, must be accommodated, lay hidden, or were erroneously conceived; and none of these latter sciences, with
the exception of astronomy, were beyond their mere infancy,
either as to observation or theory.

State of
science in
sixteenth
century.

ᵃ In this chapter my obligations to
Montucla are so numerous that I shall
seldom make particular references to his
Histoire des Mathématiques, which must
be understood to be my principal authority as to *facts*.

2. Astronomy, cultivated in the latter part of the sixteenth century with much industry and success, Tediousness
was repressed, among other more insuperable ob- of calcula-
stacles, by the laborious calculations that it required. The
trigonometrical tables of sines, tangents, and secants, if they
were to produce any tolerable accuracy in astronomical observation, must be computed to six or seven places of decimals, upon which the regular processes of multiplication and
division were perpetually to be employed. The consumption
of time as well as risk of error which this occasioned, was a
serious evil to the practical astronomer.

3. John Napier, laird of Merchiston, after several attempts
to diminish this labour by devices of his invention, Napier's
was happy enough to discover his famous method invention of
of logarithms. This he first published at Edinburgh in 1614,
with the title, Mirifici Logarithmorum Canonis Descriptio,
seu Arithmeticarum Supputationum Mirabilis Abbreviatio.
He died in 1618, and in a posthumous edition, entitled
Mirifici Logarithmorum Canonis Constructio, 1619, the
method of construction, which had been at first withheld, is
given; and the system itself, in consequence perhaps of the
suggestion of his friend Briggs, underwent some change.

4. The invention of logarithms is one of the rarest instances of sagacity in the history of mankind; and Their
it has been justly noticed as remarkable, that it nature.
issued complete from the mind of its author, and has not received any improvement since his time. It is hardly necessary to say, that logarithms are a series of numbers arranged
in tables parallel to the series of natural numbers, and of
such a construction that by adding the logarithms of two of
the latter we obtain the logarithm of their product; by sub-
tracting the logarithm of one number from that of another
we obtain that of their quotient. The longest processes
therefore of multiplication and division are spared, and
reduced to one of mere addition or subtraction.

5. It has been supposed that an arithmetical fact, said to
be mentioned by Archimedes, and which is certainly Property of
pointed out in the work of an early German writer, numbers
Michael Stifelius, put Napier in the right course by Stifelius.
for this invention. It will at least serve to illustrate the

principle of logarithms. Stifelius shows that if in a geometrical progression we add the indices of any terms in the series, we shall obtain the index of the products of those terms. Thus if we compare the geometrical progression, 1, 2, 4, 8, 16, 32, 64, with the arithmetical one which numbers the powers of the common ratio, namely, 0, 1. 2, 3, 4, 5, 6, we see that by adding two terms of the latter progression, as 2 and 3, to which 4 and 8 correspond in the geometrical series, we obtain 5, to which 32, the product of 4 by 8, corresponds; and the quotient would be obtained in a similar manner. But though this, which becomes self-evident when algebraical expressions are employed for the terms of a series, seemed at the time rather a curious property of numbers in geometrical progression, it was of little value in facilitating calculation.

6. If Napier had simply considered numbers in themselves, as repetitions of unity, which is their only intelligible definition, it does not seem that he could ever have carried this observation upon progressive series any farther. Numerically understood, the terms of a geometrical progression proceed *per saltum* ; and in the series 2, 4, 8, 16, it is as unmeaning to say that 3, 5, 6, 7, 9, in any possible sense, have a place, or can be introduced to any purpose, as that $\frac{1}{2}$, $\frac{1}{4}$, $\frac{1}{8}$, $\frac{1}{16}$, or other fractions, are true numbers at all.[b] The case, however, is widely different when we use numbers as merely the signs of something capable of continuous increase or decrease ; of space, of duration, of velocity. These are, for our convenience, divided by arbitrary intervals, to which the numerical unit is made to correspond. But as these intervals are indefinitely divisible, the unit is supposed capable of division into fractional parts, each of them a repre-

Extended to magnitudes.

[b] Few books of arithemetic, or even algebra, draw the reader's attention at the outset to this essential distinction between discrete and continuous quantity, which is almost sure to be overlooked in all their subsequent reasonings. Wallis has done it properly : after stating very clearly that there are no proper numbers but integers, he meets the objection, that fractions are called intermediate numbers. Concedo quidem sic responderi posse ; concedo etiam numeros quos frac-tos vocant, sive fractiones, esse quidam uni et nulli quasi intermedios. Sed addo, quod jam transitur εἰς ἀλλὸ γένος. Respondetur enim non de *quot*, sed de *quanto*. Pertinet igitur hæc responsio propriè loquendo, non tam ad quantitatem discretam, seu numerum, quam ad continuam : prout hora supponitur esse quid continuum in partes divisibile, quamvis quidem harum partium ad totum ratio numeris exprimatur. Mathesis Universalis, c. 1.

sentation of the ratio which a portion of the interval bears to
the whole.   And thus also we must see, that as fractions of
the unit bear a relation to uniform quantity, so all the integral
numbers, which do not enter into the terms of a geometrical
progression, correspond to certain portions of variable quantity.   If a body falling down an inclined plane acquires a
velocity at one point which would carry it through two feet
in a second, and at a lower point one which would carry it
through four feet in the same time, there must, by the nature
of a continually accelerated motion, be some point between
these where the velocity might be represented by the number
three.   Hence, wherever the numbers of a common geometrical series, like 2, 4, 8, 16, represent velocities at certain intervals, the intermediate numbers will represent velocities at
intermediate intervals; and thus it may be said that all
numbers are terms of a geometrical progression, but one
which would always be considered as what it is—a progression of continuous, not discrete quantity, capable of being
indicated by number, but not number itself.

7. It was a necessary consequence, that if all numbers
could be treated as terms of a progression, and if
their indices could be found like those of an ordinary By Napier.
series, the method of finding products of terms by addition
of indices would be universal.   The means that Napier
adopted for this purpose were surprisingly ingenious; but it
would be difficult to make them clear to those who are likely
to require it, especially without the use of lines.   It may
suffice to say that his process was laborious in the highest
degree, consisting of the interpolation of 6931472 mean pro-
portionals between 1 and 2, and repeating a similar and still
more tedious operation for all prime numbers. The logarithms
of other numbers were easily obtained, according to the
fundamental principle of the invention, by adding their
factors.   Logarithms appear to have been so called because
they are the sum of these mean ratios, λόγων ἀριθμός.

8. In the original tables of Napier the logarithm of 10 was
2.3025850.   In those published afterwards (1618), Tables of
Napier and
Briggs.
he changed this for 1.0000000, making of course
that of 100, 2.0000000, and so forth.   This construction has
been followed since; but those of the first method are not

wholly neglected; they are called hyperbolical logarithms, from expressing a property of that curve. Napier found a coadjutor well worthy of him in Henry Briggs, professor of geometry at Gresham College. It is uncertain from which of them the change in the form of logarithms proceeded. Briggs, in 1618, published a table of logarithms up to 1000, calculated by himself. This was followed in 1624 by his greater work, Arithmetica Logarithmica, containing the logarithms of all natural numbers as high as 20,000, and again from 90,000 to 100,000. These are calculated to fourteen places of decimals, thus reducing the error, which, strictly speaking, must always exist from the principle of logarithmical construction, to an almost infinitesimal fraction. He had designed to publish a second table, with the logarithms of sines and tangents to the 100th part of a degree. This he left in a considerably advanced state; and it was published by Gellibrand in 1633. Gunter had as early as 1620 given the logarithms of sines and tangents on the sexagesimal scale, as far as seven decimals. Vlacq, a Dutch bookseller, printed in 1628 a translation of Briggs's Arithmetica Logarithmica, filling up the interval from 20,000 to 90,000 with logarithms calculated to eleven decimals. He published also in 1633 his Trigonometrica Artificialis, the most useful work, perhaps, that had appeared, as it incorporated the labours of Briggs and Gellibrand. Kepler came like a master to the subject; and observing that some foreign mathematicians disliked the theory upon which Napier had explained the nature of logarithms, as not rigidly geometrical, gave one of his own to which they could not object. But it may probably be said, that the very novelty to which the disciples of the ancient geometry were averse, the introduction of the notion of velocity into mathematical reasoning, was that which linked the abstract science of quantity with nature, and prepared the way for that expansive theory of infinites, which bears at once upon the subtlest truths that can exercise the understanding, and the most evident that can fall under the senses.

9. It was indeed at this time that the modern geometry, Kepler's new geometry. which, if it deviates something from the clearness and precision of the ancient, has incomparably the

advantage over it in its reach of application, took its rise.
Kepler was the man that led the way. He published in
1615 his Nova Stereometria Doliorum, a treatise on the
capacity of casks. In this he considers the various solids
which may be formed by the revolution of a segment of a
conic section round a line which is not its axis, a condition
not unfrequent in the form of a cask. Many of the problems
which he starts he is unable to solve. But what is most remarkable in this treatise is that he here suggests the bold
idea, that a circle may be deemed to be composed of an
infinite number of triangles, having their bases in their circumference, and their common apex in the centre; a cone, in
like manner, of infinite pyramids, and a cylinder of infinite
prisms.[c] The ancients had shown, as is well known, that a
polygon inscribed in a circle, and another described about it,
may by continual bisection of their sides be made to approach nearer to each other than by any assignable difference.
The circle itself lay of course between them. Euclid contents
himself with saying, that the circle is greater than any polygon that can be inscribed in it, and less than any polygon
that can be described about it. The method by which they
approximated to the curve space by continual increase or
diminution of the rectilineal figure was called exhaustion,
and the space itself is properly called by later geometers the
limit. As curvilineal and rectilineal spaces cannot possibly
be compared by means of superposition, or by showing that
their several constituent portions could be made to coincide,
it had long been acknowledged by the best geometers impossible to quadrate by a direct process any curve surface.
But Archimedes had found, as to the parabola, that there
was a rectilineal space, of which he could indirectly demonstrate that it was equal, that is, could not be unequal, to
the curve itself.

10. In this state of the general problem, the ancient
methods of indefinite approximation having pre- Its differ-
pared the way, Kepler came to his solution of the ancient.
questions which regarded the capacity of vessels. According
to Fabroni, he supposed solids to consist of an infinite num-

---

[c] Fabroni, Vitæ Italorum, i. 272.

ber of surfaces, surfaces of an infinity of lines, lines of infinite points.[d] If this be strictly true, he must have left little, in point of invention, for Cavalieri. So long as geometry is employed as a method of logic, an exercise of the understanding on those modifications of quantity which the imagination cannot grasp, such as points, lines, infinites, it must appear almost an offensive absurdity to speak of a circle as a polygon with an infinite number of sides. But when it becomes the handmaid of practical art, or even of physical science, there can be no other objection than always arises from incongruity and incorrectness of language. It has been found possible to avoid the expressions attributed to Kepler; but they seem to denote, in fact, nothing more than those of Euclid or Archimedes; that the difference between a magnitude and its limit may be regularly diminished, till without strictly vanishing it becomes less than any assignable quantity, and may consequently be disregarded in reasoning upon actual bodies.

11. Galileo, says Fabroni, trod in the steps of Kepler, and

Adopted by Galileo.

in his first dialogue on mechanics, when treating of a cylinder cut out of an hemisphere, became conversant with indivisibles (familiarem habere cœpit cum indivisibilibus usum). But in that dialogue he confused the metaphysical notions of divisible quantity, supposing it to be composed of unextended indivisibles; and not venturing to affirm that infinites could be equal or unequal to one another, he preferred to say, that words denoting equality or excess could only be used as to finite quantities. In his fourth dialogue on the centre of gravity, he comes back to the exhaustive method of Archimedes.[e]

12. Cavalieri, professor of mathematics at Bologna, the generally reputed father of the new geometry, though

Extended by Cavalieri.

Kepler seems to have so greatly anticipated him, had completed his Method of Indivisibles in 1626. The book was not published till 1635. His leading principle is that

---

[d] Idem quoque solida cogitavit ex infinito numero superficierum existere, superficies autem ex lineis infinitis, ac lineis ex infinitis punctis. Ostendit ipse quantum ea ratione brevior fieri via possit ad vera quædam captu difficiliora, cum antiquarum demonstrationum circuitus ac methodus inter se comparandi figuras circumscriptas et inscriptas iis planis aut solidis, quæ mensuranda essent, ita declinarentur. Fabroni, Vitæ Italorum, i. 272.

[e] Ibid.

solids are composed of an infinite number of surfaces placed
one above another as their indivisible elements. Surfaces
are formed in like manner by lines, and lines by points.
This, however, he asserts with some excuse and explanation;
declaring that he does not use the words so strictly, as to
have it supposed that divisible quantities truly and literally
consist of indivisibles, but that the ratio of solids is the same
as that of an infinite number of surfaces, and the ratio of
surfaces the same as that of an infinite number of lines; and
to put an end to cavil, he demonstrated that the same consequences would follow if a method should be adopted, borrowing nothing from the consideration of indivisibles.[f] This
explanation seems to have been given after his method had
been attacked by Guldin in 1640.

13. It was a main object of Cavalieri's geometry to demonstrate the proportions of different solids. This Applied to
is partly done by Euclid, but generally in an indi- of solids.
rect manner. A cone, according to Cavalieri, is composed of
an infinite number of circles decreasing from the base to the
summit, a cylinder of an infinite number of equal circles.
He seeks therefore the ratio of the sum of all the former to
that of all the latter. The method of summing an infinite
series of terms in arithmetical progression was already known.
The diameters of the circles in the cone decreasing uniformly
were in arithmetical progression, and the circles would be as
their squares. He found that when the number of terms is
infinitely great, the sum of all the squares described on lines
in arithmetical progression is exactly one third of the greatest
square multiplied by the number of terms. Hence the cone
is one third of a cylinder of the same base and altitude, and
similar proof may be given as to the ratios of other solids.

---

[f] Non eo rigore a se voces adhiberi, ac
si dividuæ quantitates verè ac propriè ex
indivisibilibus existerent; verumtamen
id sibi duntaxat velle, ut proportio solid-
orum eadem esset ac ratio superficierum
omnium numero infinitarum, et proportio superficierum eadem ac illa infinitarum linearum: denique ut omnia, quæ
contra dici poterant, in radice præcideret,
demonstravit, easdem omnino consecu-
tiones erui, si methodi aut rationes ad-
hiberentur omnino diversæ, quæ nihil ab
indivisibilium consideratione penderent.

Fabroni.
Il n'est aucun cas dans la géométrie
des indivisibles, qu'on ne puisse facile-
ment réduire à la forme ancienne de démonstration. Ainsi, c'est s'arrêter à
l'écorce que de chicaner sur le mot d'indivisibles. Il est impropre si l'on veut,
mais il n'en résulte aucun danger pour
la géométrie; et loin de conduire à l'erreur, cette méthode, au contraire, a été
utile pour atteindre à des vérités qui
avoient échappé jusqu'alors aux efforts
des géomètres. Montucla, vol. ii. p. 39.

14. This bolder geometry was now very generally applied in difficult investigations. A proof was given in the celebrated problems relative to the cycloid, which served as a test of skill to the mathematicians of that age. The cycloid is the curve described by a point in a circle, while it makes one revolution along an horizontal base, as in the case of a carriage wheel. It was far more difficult to determine its area. It was at first taken for the segment of a circle. Galileo considered it, but with no success. Mersenne, who was also unequal to the problem, suggested it to a very good geometer, Roberval, who after some years, in 1634, demonstrated that the area of the cycloid is equal to thrice the area of the generating circle. Mersenne communicated this discovery to Descartes, who, treating the matter as easy, sent a short demonstration of his own. On Roberval's intimating that he had been aided by a knowledge of the solution, Descartes found out the tangents of the curve, and challenged Roberval and Fermat to do the same. Fermat succeeded in this; but Roberval could not achieve the problem, in which Galileo also and Cavalieri failed; though it seems to have been solved afterwards by Viviani. 'Such,' says Montucla, 'was the superiority of Descartes over all the geometers of his age, that questions which most perplexed them cost him but an ordinary degree of attention.' In this problem of the tangents (and it might not perhaps have been worth while to mention it otherwise in so brief a sketch) Descartes made use of the principle introduced by Kepler, considering the curve as a polygon of an infinite number of sides, so that an infinitely small arc is equal to its chord. The cycloid has been called by Montucla the Helen of geometers. This beauty was at least the cause of war, and produced a long controversy. The Italians claim the original invention as their own; but Montucla seems to have vindicated the right of France to every solution important in geometry. Nor were the friends of Roberval and Fermat disposed to acknowledge so much of the exclusive right of Descartes as was challenged by his disciples. Pascal, in his history of the cycloid, enters the lists on the side of Roberval. This was not published till 1658.

15. Without dwelling more minutely on geometrical trea-

tises of less importance, though in themselves valuable, such
as that of Gregory St. Vincent in 1647, or the Cy- Progress of
clometricus of Willebrod Snell in 1621, we come to algebra.
the progress of analysis during this period. The works of
Vieta, it may be observed, were chiefly published after the
year 1600. They left, as must be admitted, not much in
principle for the more splendid generalisations of Harriott
and Descartes. It is not unlikely that the mere employment
of a more perfect notation would have led the acute mind of
Vieta to truths which seem to us who are acquainted with
them but a little beyond what he discovered.

16. Briggs, in his Arithmetica Logarithmica, was the first
who clearly showed what is called the Binomial Briggs.
Theorem, or a compendious method of involution, Girard.
by means of the necessary order of co-efficients in the successive powers of a binomial quantity. Cardan had partially,
and Vieta more clearly, seen this, nor, as far as his notation
went, was it likely to escape the profound mind of the latter.
Albert Girard, a Dutchman, in his Invention Nouvelle en
Algèbre, 1629, conceived a better notion of negative roots
than his predecessors. Even Vieta had not paid attention
to them in any solution. Girard, however, not only assigns
their form, and shows that in a certain class of cubic equations there must always be one or two of this description,
but uses this remarkable expression: 'A negative solution
means in geometry that the *minus* recedes as the *plus* advances.'[g] It seems manifest that till some such idea suggested itself to the minds of analysts, the consideration of
negative roots, though they could not possibly avoid perceiving their existence, would merely have confused their
solutions. It cannot therefore be surprising that not only
Cardan and Vieta, but Harriott himself, should have paid
little attention to them.

17. Harriott, the companion of Sir Walter Raleigh in Virginia, and the friend of the Earl of Northumberland,
in whose house he spent the latter part of his life, Harriott.
was destined to make the last great discovery in the pure
science of algebra. Though he is mentioned here after

---

[g] La solution par moins s'explique en recule où le plus avance. Montucla, p.
géométrie en rétrogradant, et le moins   112.

Girard, since the Artis Analyticæ Praxis was not published till 1631, this was ten years after the author's death. Harriott arrived at a complete theory of the genesis of equations, which Cardan and Vieta had but partially conceived. By bringing all the terms on one side, so as to make them equal to zero, he found out that every unknown quantity in an equation has as many values as the index of its powers in the first term denotes ; and that these values, in a necessary sequence of combinations, form the co-efficients of the succeeding terms into which the decreasing powers of the unknown quantity enter, as they do also, by their united product, the last or known term of the equation. This discovery facilitated the solution of equations, by the necessary composition of their terms which it displayed. It was evident, for example, that each integral root of an equation must be a factor, and consequently a divisor, of the last term.[h]

18. Harriott introduced the use of small letters instead of capitals in algebra ; he employed vowels for unknown, consonants for known quantities, and joined them to express their product.[i] There is certainly not much in this ; but its evident convenience renders it wonderful that it should have been reserved for so late an æra. Wallis, in his History of Algebra, ascribes to Harriott a long list of discoveries, which have been reclaimed for Cardan and Vieta, the great founders of the higher algebra, by Cossali and Montucla.[k] The latter of these writers has been charged, even by foreigners, with similar injustice towards our countryman ; and that he has been provoked by what he thought the unfairness of Wallis

---

[h] Harriott's book is a thin folio of 180 pages, with very little besides examples ; for his principles are shortly and obscurely laid down. Whoever is the author of the preface to this work cannot be said to have suppressed or extenuated the merits of Vieta, or to have claimed anything for Harriott but what he is allowed to have deserved. Montucla justly observes, that Harriott *very rarely* makes an equation equal to zero, by bringing all the quantities to one side of the equation.

[i] Oughtred, in his Clavis Mathematica, published in 1631, abbreviated the rules of Vieta, though he still used capital letters. He also gave succinctly the praxis of algebra, or the elementary rules we find in our common books, which, though what are now first learned, were, from the singular course of algebraical history, discovered late. They are however given also by Harriott. Wallisii Algebra.

[k] These may be found in the article Harriott of the Biographia Britannica. Wallis however does not suppress the honour due to Vieta quite as much as is intimated by Montucla.

to something like a depreciation of Harriott, seems as clear as that he has himself robbed Cardan of part of his due credit in swelling the account of Vieta's discoveries. From the general integrity, however, of Montucla's writings, I am much inclined to acquit him of any wilful partiality.

19. Harriott had shown what were the hidden laws of algebra, as the science of symbolical notation. But one man, the pride of France, and wonder of his contemporaries, was destined to flash light upon the labours of the analyst, and to point out what those symbols, so darkly and painfully traced, and resulting commonly in irrational or even impossible forms, might represent and explain. The use of numbers, or of letters denoting numbers, for lines and rectangles capable of division into aliquot parts, had long been too obvious to be overlooked, and is only a compendious abbreviation of geometrical proof. The next step made was the perceiving that irrational numbers, as they are called, represent incommensurable quantities; that is, if unity be taken for the side of a square, the square root of two will represent its diagonal. Gradually the application of numerical and algebraical calculation to the solution of problems respecting magnitude became more frequent and refined.[m] It is certain, however, that no one before Descartes had employed algebraic formulæ in the construction of curves; that is, had taught the inverse process, not only how to express diagrams by algebra, but how to turn algebra into diagrams. The ancient geometers, he observes, were scrupulous about using the language of arithmetic in geometry, which could only proceed from their not perceiving the relation between the two; and this has produced a great deal of obscurity and embarrassment in some of their demonstrations.[n]

20. The principle which Descartes establishes is, that every curve of those which are called geometrical has its fundamental equation expressing the constant relation between the absciss and the ordinate. Thus the rectangle under the abscisses of a diameter of the circle is equal to the square of the ordinate, and the other conic sections, as well as higher curves, have each their leading pro-

Descartes.

His application of algebra to curves.

---

[m] See note in vol. ii. p. 223.   [n] Œuvres de Descartes, v. 323.

perty, which determines their nature, and shows how they may be generated. A simple equation can only express the relation of straight lines : the solutions of a quadratic must be found in one of the four conic sections ; and the higher powers of an unknown quantity lead to curves of a superior order. The beautiful and extensive theory developed by Descartes in this short treatise displays a most consummate felicity of genius. That such a man, endowed with faculties so original, should have encroached on the just rights of others, is what we can only believe with reluctance.

21. It must, however, be owned that, independently of the suspicions of an unacknowledged appropriation of what others had thought before him, which unfortunately hang over all the writings of Descartes, he has taken to himself the whole theory of Harriott on the nature of equations in a manner which, if it is not a remarkabl? case of simultaneous invention, can only be reckoned a very unwarrantable plagiarism. For not only he does not name Harriott, but he evidently introduces the subject as an important discovery of his own, and in one of his letters asserts his originality in the most positive language.[o] Still it

Suspected plagiarism from Harriott.

---

[o] Tant s'en faut que les choses que j'ai écrites puissent être aisément tirées de Viète, qu'au contraire ce qui est cause que mon traité est difficile à entendre, c'est que j'ai tâché à n'y rien mettre que ce que j'ai crû n'avoir point été su ni par lui ni par aucun autre ; comme on peut voir si on confère ce que j'ai écrit du nombre des racines qui sont en chaque équation, dans la page 372, qui est l'endroit où je commence à donner les règles de mon algèbre, avec ce que Viète en a écrit tout à la fin de son livre, De Emendatione Æquationum ; car on verra que je le détermine généralement en toutes équations, au lieu que lui n'en ayant donné que quelques exemples particuliers, dont il fait toutefois si grand état qu'il a voulu conclure son livre par là, il a montré qu'il ne le pouvoit déterminer en général. Et ainsi, j'ai commencé où il avoit achevé, ce que j'ai fait toutefois sans y penser ; car j'ai plus feuilleté Viète depuis que j'ai reçu votre dernière que je n'avois jamais fait auparavant, l'ayant trouvé ici par hasard entre les mains d'un de mes amis ; et entre nous je ne trouve pas qu'il en ait tant su que je pensois, nonobstant qu'il fût fort habile. This is in a letter to Mersenne in 1637. Œuvres de Descartes, vol. vi. p. 300.

The charge of plagiarism from Harriott was brought against Descartes in his lifetime : Roberval, when an English gentleman showed him the Artis Analyticæ Praxis, exclaimed eagerly, ' Il l'a vu ! il l'a vu ! ' It is also a very suspicious circumstance, if true, as it appears to be, that Descartes was in England the year (1631) that Harriott's work appeared. Carcavi, a friend of Roberval, in a letter to Descartes in 1649, plainly intimates to him that he has only copied Harriott as to the nature of equations. Œuvres de Descartes, vol. x. p. 373. To this accusation Descartes made no reply. See Biographia Britannica, art Harriott. The Biographie universelle unfairly suppresses all mention of this, and labours to depreciate Harriott.

See Leibnitz's catalogue of the supposed thefts of Descartes in vol. ii. p. 465 of this work.

is quite possible that, prepared as the way had been by Vieta,
and gifted as Descartes was with a wonderfully intuitive
acuteness in all mathematical reasoning, he may in this, as
in other instances, have divined the whole theory by himself. Montucla extols the algebra of Descartes, that is, so
much of it as can be fairly claimed for him without any precursor, very highly ; and some of his inventions in the treatment of equations have long been current in books of that
science. He was the first who showed what were called impossible or imaginary roots, though he never assigns them,
deeming them no quantities at all. He was also, perhaps,
the first who fully understood negative roots, though he still
retains the appellation, false roots, which is not so good as
Harriott's epithet, privative. According to his panegyrist,
he first pointed out that in every equation (the terms being
all on one side) which has no imaginary roots, there are as
many changes of signs as positive roots, as many continua-
tions of them as negative.

22. The geometer next in genius to Descartes, and perhaps
nearer to him than to any third, was Fermat, a man
of various acquirements, of high rank in the parlia- *Fermat.*
ment of Toulouse, and of a mind incapable of envy, forgiving
of detraction, and delighting in truth, with almost too much
indifference to praise. The works of Fermat were not published till long after his death in 1665 ; but his frequent discussions with Descartes, by the intervention of their common
correspondent Mersenne, render this place more appropriate
for the introduction of his name. In these controversies
Descartes never behaved to Fermat with the respect due to
his talents ; in fact, no one was ever more jealous of his
own pre-eminence, or more unwilling to acknowledge the
claims of those who scrupled to follow him implicitly, and who
might in any manner be thought rivals of his fame. Yet it
is this unhappy temper of Descartes which ought to render
us more slow to credit the suspicions of his designed plagiarism from the discoveries of others ; since this, combined
with his unwillingness to acknowledge their merits, and
affected ignorance of their writings, would form a character
we should not readily ascribe to a man of great genius, and
whose own writings give many apparent indications of sincerity

and virtue.   But in fact there was in this age a great probability of simultaneous invention of science, from developing
principles that had been partially brought to light.   Thus
Roberval discovered the same method of indivisibles as Cavalieri, and Descartes must equally have been led to his theory
of tangents by that of Kepler.   Fermat also, who was in possession of his principal discoveries before the geometry of
Descartes saw the light, derived from Kepler his own celebrated method, *de maximis et minimis :* a method of discovering the greatest or least value of a variable quantity, such as
the ordinate of a curve.   It depends on the same principle
as that of Kepler.   From this he deduced a rule for drawing
tangents to curves different from that of Descartes.   This
led to a controversy between the two geometers, carried on
by Descartes, who yet is deemed to have been in the wrong,
with his usual quickness of resentment.   Several other discoveries, both in pure algebra and geometry, illustrate the
name of Fermat.[p]

23. The new geometry of Descartes was not received with
Algebraic   the universal admiration it deserved.   Besides its
geometry   conciseness and the inroad it made on old prejudices
not successful at first.   as to geometrical methods, the general boldness of
the author's speculations in physical and metaphysical
philosophy, as well as his indiscreet temper, alienated many
who ought to have appreciated it ; and it was in his own
country, where he had ceased to reside, that Descartes had
the fewest admirers.   Roberval made some objections to his
rival's algebra, but with little success.   A commentary on the
treatise of Descartes by Schooten, professor of geometry at
Leyden, first appeared in 1649.

24. Among those who devoted themselves ardently and
Astronomy   successfully to astronomical observations at the end
—Kepler.   of the sixteenth century, was John Kepler, a native
of Wirtemburg, who had already shown that he was likely to
inherit the mantle of Tycho Brahe.   He published some astronomical treatises of comparatively small importance in the
first years of the present period.   But in 1609 he made an
epoch in that science by his Astronomia Nova αἰτιολογητός,

---

[p] A good article on Fermat by M. Maurice will be found in the Biographie
universelle.

or Commentaries on the Planet Mars. It had been always assumed that the heavenly bodies revolve in circular orbits round their centre, whether this were taken to be the sun or the earth. There was, however, an apparent eccentricity or deviation from this circular motion, which it had been very difficult to explain, and for this Ptolemy had devised his complex system of epicycles. No planet showed more of this eccentricity than Mars; and it was to Mars that Kepler turned his attention. After many laborious researches he was brought by degrees to the great discovery, that the motion of the planets, among which, having adopted the Copernican system, he reckoned the earth, is not performed in circular but in elliptical orbits, the sun not occupying the centre but one of the foci of the curve; and, secondly, that it is performed with such a varying velocity, that the areas described by the radius vector, or line which joins this focus to the revolving planet, are always proportional to the times. A planet, therefore, moves less rapidly as it becomes more distant from the sun. These are the first and second of the three great laws of Kepler. The third was not discovered by him till some years afterwards. He tells us himself that, on the 8th of May, 1618, after long toil in investigating the proportion of the periodic times of the planetary movements to their orbits, an idea struck his mind, which, chancing to make a mistake in the calculation, he soon rejected. But a week after, returning to the subject, he entirely established his grand discovery, that the squares of the times of revolution are as the cubes of the mean distances of the planets. This was first made known to the world in his Mysterium Cosmographicum, published in 1619; a work mingled up with many strange effusions of a mind far more eccentric than any of the planets with which it was engaged. In the Epitome Astronomiæ Copernicanæ, printed the same year, he endeavours to deduce this law from his theory of centrifugal forces. He had no small insight into the principles of universal gravitation, as an attribute of matter; but several of his assumptions as to the laws of motion are not consonant to truth. There seems indeed to have been a considerable degree of good fortune in the discoveries of Kepler; yet this may be deemed the reward of his indefatigable laboriousness,

and of the ingenuousness with which he renounced any hypothesis that he could not reconcile with his advancing knowledge of the phænomena.

25. The appearance of three comets in 1618 called once
more the astronomers of Europe to speculate on the
nature of those anomalous bodies. They still passed
for harbingers of worldly catastrophes ; and those who feared
them least could not interpret their apparent irregularity.
Galileo, though Tycho Brahe had formed a juster notion,
unfortunately took them for atmospheric meteors. Kepler,
though he brought them from the far regions of space, did
not suspect the nature of their orbits, and thought that,
moving in straight lines, they were finally dispersed and
came to nothing. But a Jesuit, Grassi, in a treatise, De
Tribus Cometis, Rome, 1619, had the honour of explaining
what had baffled Galileo, and first held them to be planets
moving in vast ellipses round the sun.[q]

Conjectures as to comets.

26. But long before this time the name of Galileo had
become immortal by discoveries which, though they
would certainly have soon been made by some other,
perhaps far inferior, observer, were happily reserved
for the most philosophical genius of the age. Galileo assures
us that, having heard of the invention of an instrument in
Holland which enlarged the size of distant objects, but
knowing nothing of its construction, he began to study the
theory of refractions, till he found by experiment, that by
means of a convex and concave glass in a tube he could
magnify an object threefold. He was thus encouraged to
make another which magnified thirty times; and this he
exhibited in the autumn of 1609 to the inhabitants of Venice.
Having made a present of his first telescope to the senate,
who rewarded him with a pension, he soon constructed
another; and in one of the first nights of January, 1610,
directing it towards the moon, was astonished to see her
surface and edges covered with inequalities. These he considered to be mountains, and judged by a sort of measurement that some of them must exceed those of the earth.
His next observation was of the milky way ; and this he

Galileo's discovery of Jupiter's satellites.

---

[q] The Biographie universelle, art. Grassi, ascribes this opinion to Tycho.

found to derive its nebulous lustre from myriads of stars not
distinguishable, through their remoteness, by the unassisted
sight of man. The nebulæ in the constellation Orion he
perceived to be of the same character. Before his delight
at these discoveries could have subsided, he turned his telescope to Jupiter, and was surprised to remark three small
stars, which, in a second night's observation had changed
their places. In the course of a few weeks he was able to
determine by their revolutions, which are very rapid, that
these are secondary planets, the moons or satellites of Jupiter;
and he had added a fourth to their number. These marvellous
revelations of nature he hastened to announce in a work,
aptly entitled Sidereus Nuncius, published in March, 1610.
In an age when the fascinating science of astronomy had
already so much excited the minds of philosophers, it may
be guessed with what eagerness this intelligence from the
heavens was circulated. A few, as usual, through envy or
prejudice, affected to contemn it. But wisdom was justified
of her children. Kepler, in his Narratio de observatis a se
Quatuor Jovis Satellitibus, 1610, confirmed the discoveries of
Galileo. Peiresc, an inferior name, no doubt, but deserving
of every praise for his zeal in the cause of knowledge, having
with difficulty procured a good telescope, saw the four
satellites in November, 1610, and is said by Gassendi to have
conceived at that time the ingenious idea that their occulta-
tions might be used to ascertain the longitude.[r]

27. This is the greatest and most important of the discoveries of Galileo. But several others were of the Other dis-
deepest interest. He found that the planet Venus coveries by
him.
had phases, that is, periodical differences of apparent form,
like the moon; and that these are exactly such as would
be produced by the variable reflection of the sun's light on
the Copernican hypothesis; ascribing also the faint light on
that part of the moon which does not receive the rays of the
sun to the reflection from the earth, called by some late
writers earth-shine; which though it had been suggested by
Mæstlin, and before him by Leonardo da Vinci, was not
generally received among astronomers. Another striking

---

[r] Gassendi, Vita Peirescii, p. 77.

phænomenon, though he did not see the means of explaining
it, was the triple appearance of Saturn, as if smaller stars
were conjoined as it were like wings to the planet. This
of course was the ring.

28. Meantime the new auxiliary of vision which had re-
Spots of the sun discovered. vealed so many wonders could not lie unemployed in
the hands of others. A publication by John Fabricius
at Wittenberg in July, 1611, De Maculis in Sole visis, announced a phænomena in contradiction of common prejudice.
The sun had passed for a body of liquid flame, or, if thought
solid, still in a state of perfect ignition. Kepler had some
years before observed a spot, which he unluckily mistook for
the orb of Mercury in its passage over the solar orb. Fabricius
was not permitted to claim this discovery as his own.
Scheiner, a Jesuit, professor of mathematics at Ingolstadt,
asserts in a letter dated 12th of November, 1611, that he
first saw the spots in the month of March in that year, but
he seems to have paid little attention to them before that of
October. Both Fabricius, however, and Scheiner may be put
out of the question. We have evidence that Harriott observed the spots on the sun as early as December 8th, 1610.[s]
The motion of the spots suggested the revolution of the sun
round its axis completed in twenty-four days, as it is now
determined; and their frequent alterations of form as well
as occasional disappearance could only be explained by the
hypothesis of a luminous atmosphere in commotion, a sea of
flame, revealing at intervals the dark central mass of the
sun's body which it envelopes.

29. Though it cannot be said, perhaps, that the discoveries
Copernican system held by Galileo. of Galileo would fully prove the Copernican system
of the world to those who were already insensible
to reasoning from its sufficiency to explain the phænomena,
and from the analogies of nature, they served to familiarise
the mind to it, and to break down the strong rampart of prejudice which stood in its way. For eighty years, it has been
said, this theory of the earth's motion had been maintained
without censure; and it could only be the greater boldness

* [Montucla, ii. 106. Hutton's Dic-   Harriott had been established by Zach
tionary, art. Harriott. The claim of   in Berlin Transactions for 1788.—1842.]

of Galileo in its assertion which drew down upon him the notice of the church. But, in these eighty years since the publication of the treatise of Copernicus, his proselytes had been surprisingly few. They were now becoming more numerous : several had written on that side ; and Galileo had begun to form a school of Copernicans who were spreading over Italy. The Lincean society, one of the most useful and renowned of Italian academies, founded at Rome by Frederic Cesi, a young man of noble birth, in 1603, had as a fundamental law to apply themselves to natural philosophy ; and it was impossible that so attractive and rational a system as that of Copernicus could fail of pleasing an acute and ingenious nation strongly bent upon science. The church, however, had taken alarm ; the motion of the earth was conceived to be as repugnant to Scripture as the existence of antipodes had once been reckoned ; and in 1616 Galileo, though respected, and in favour with the court of Rome, was compelled to promise that he would not maintain that doctrine in any manner. Some letters that he had published on the subject were put, with the treatise of Copernicus and other works, into the Index Expurgatorius, where, I believe, they still remain.[1]

30. He seems, notwithstanding this, to have flattered himself that after several years had elapsed, he might elude the letter of this prohibition by throwing the arguments in favour of the Ptolemaic and Copernican systems into the form of a dialogue. This was published in 1632 ; and he might, from various circumstances, not unreasonably hope for impunity. But his expectations were deceived. It is well known that he was compelled by the Inquisition at Rome, into whose hands he fell, to retract in the most solemn

His dialogues and persecution.

---

[1] Drinkwater Bethune's Life of Galileo. Fabroni, Vitæ Italorum, vol. i. The former seems to be mistaken in supposing that Galileo did not endeavour to prove his system compatible with Scripture. In a letter to Christina, the Grand Duchess of Tuscany, the author (Brenna) of the Life in Fabroni's work tells us, he argued very elaborately for that purpose. In eâ videlicit epistolâ philosophus noster ita disserit, ut nihil etiam ab hominibus, qui omnem in sa-crarum literarum studio consumpsissent ætatem, aut subtilius aut verius aut etiam accuratius explicatum expectari potuerit. P. 118. It seems, in fact, to have been this over-desire to prove his theory orthodox, which incensed the church against it. See an extraordinary article on this subject in the eighth number of the Dublin Review (1838). Many will tolerate propositions inconsistent with orthodoxy, when they are not brought into immediate juxtaposition with it.

and explicit manner the propositions he had so well proved,
and which he must have still believed. It is unnecessary to
give a circumstantial account, especially as it has been so
well done in the Life of Galileo, by the late Mr. Drinkwater
Bethune. The papal court meant to humiliate Galileo, and
through him to strike an increasing class of philosophers with
shame and terror; but not otherwise to punish one of whom
even the inquisitors must, as Italians, have been proud: his
confinement, though Montucla says it lasted for a year, was
very short. He continued, nevertheless, under some restraint
for the rest of his life, and though he lived at his own villa
near Florence, was not permitted to enter the city.[u]

31. The church was not mistaken in supposing that she
should intimidate the Copernicans, but very much
so in expecting to suppress the theory. Descartes
was so astonished at hearing of the sentence on Galileo,
that he was almost disposed to burn his papers, or at least
to let no one see them. ‘I cannot collect,’ he says, ‘that he
who is an Italian, and a friend of the pope, as I understand,
has been criminated on any other account than for having
attempted to establish the motion of the earth. I know that
this opinion was formerly censured by some cardinals, but I
thought I had since heard that no objection was now made
to its being publicly taught even at Rome.’[x] It seems not
at all unlikely that Descartes was induced, on this account,
to pretend a greater degree of difference from Copernicus
than he really felt, and even to deny, in a certain sense of
his own, the obnoxious tenet of the earth’s motion.[y] He
was not without danger of a sentence against truth nearer
at hand; Cardinal Richelieu having had the intention of
procuring a decree of the Sorbonne to the same effect, which

Descartes alarmed by this.

---

[u] Fabroni. His Life is written in
good Latin, with knowledge and spirit,
more than Tiraboschi has ventured to
display.

It appears from some of Grotius’s
Epistles that Galileo had thoughts,
about 1635, of seeking the protection of
the United Provinces. But on account
of his advanced age he gave this up:
fessus senio constituit manere in quibus
est locis, et potius quæ ibi sunt incom-

moda perpeti, quam malæ ætati migrandi
onus, et novas parandi amicitias imponere. The very idea shows that he
must have deeply felt the restraint imposed upon him in his country. Epist.
Grot., 407, 446.

[x] Vol. vi. p. 239: he says here of the
motion of the earth, Je confesse que s’il
est faux, tous les fondemens de ma
philosophie le sont aussi.

[y] Vol. vi. p. 50.

through the good sense of some of that society fell to the ground.[z]

32. The progress, however, of the Copernican theory in Europe, if it may not actually be dated from its condemnation at Rome, was certainly not at all slower after that time. Gassendi rather cautiously took that side; the Cartesians brought a powerful reinforcement; Bouillaud and several other astronomers of note avowed themselves favourable to a doctrine which, though in Italy it lay under the ban of the papal power, was readily saved on this side of the Alps by some of the salutary distinctions long in use to evade that authority.[a] But in the middle of the seventeenth century and long afterwards, there were mathematicians of no small reputation, who struggled staunchly for the immobility of the earth; and except so far as Cartesian theories might have come in vogue, we have no reason to believe that any persons unacquainted with astronomy, either in this country or on the Continent, had embraced the system of Copernicus. Hume has censured Bacon for rejecting it; but if Bacon had not done so, he would have anticipated the rest of his countrymen by a full quarter of a century.

Progress of Copernican system.

33. Descartes, in his new theory of the solar system, aspired to explain the secret springs of nature, while Kepler and Galileo had merely showed their effects. By what force the heavenly bodies were impelled, by what law they were guided, was certainly a very different question from that of the orbit they described, or the period of their revolution. Kepler had evidently some notion of that universally mutual gravitation which Hooke saw more clearly, and Newton established on the basis of his geometry.[p] But Descartes rejected this with contempt. 'For,' he says, 'to conceive this we must not only suppose that every portion of matter in the universe is animated, and animated by several different souls which do not obstruct one another, but that

Descartes denies general gravitation.

---

[z] Montucla, ii. 297.

[a] Id., p. 50.

[p] 'If the earth and moon,' he says, 'were not retained in their orbits, they would fall one on another, the moon moving about $\frac{33}{34}$ of the way, the earth the rest, supposing them equally dense. By this attraction of the moon, he accounts for tides. He compares the attraction of the planet towards the sun to that of heavy bodies towards the earth.

those souls are intelligent, and even divine; that they may know what is going on in the most remote places without any messenger to give them notice, and that they may exert their powers there.'[q] Kepler, who took the world for a single animal, a leviathan that roared in caverns and breathed in the ocean tides, might have found it difficult to answer this, which would have seemed no objection at all to Campanella. If Descartes himself had been more patient towards opinions which he had not formed in his own mind, that constant divine agency, to which he was, on other occasions, apt to resort, could not but have suggested a sufficient explanation of the gravity of matter, without endowing it with self-agency. He had, however, fallen upon a complicated and original scheme, the most celebrated, perhaps, though not the most admirable, of the novelties which Descartes brought into philosophy.

34. In a letter to Mersenne, Jan. 9th, 1639, he shortly states that notion of the material universe which he afterwards published in the Principia Philosophiæ. 'I will tell you,' he says, 'that I conceive, or rather I can demonstrate, that besides the matter which composes terrestrial bodies, there are two other kinds: one very subtle, of which the parts are round or nearly round like grains of sand, and this not only occupies the pores of terrestrial bodies, but constitutes the substance of all the heavens; the other incomparably more subtle, the parts of which are so small, and move with such velocity, that they have no determinate figure, but readily take at every instant that which is required to fill all the little intervals which the other does not occupy.'[r] To this hypothesis of a double ether he was driven by his aversion to admit any vacuum in nature; the rotundity of the former corpuscles having been produced, as he fancied, by their continual circular motions, which had rubbed off their angles. This seems at present rather a clumsy hypothesis, but it is literally that which Descartes presented to the world.

Cartesian theory of the world.

35. After having thus filled the universe with different sorts of matter, he supposes that the subtler particles, formed

[q] Vol. ix. p. 560.

[r] Vol. viii. p. 73.

by the perpetual rubbing off of the angles of the larger in their progress towards sphericity, increased by degrees till there was a superfluity that was not required to fill up the intervals; and this, flowing towards the centre of the system, became the sun, a very subtle and liquid body, while in like manner the fixed stars were formed in other systems. Round these centres the whole mass is whirled in a number of distinct vortices, each of which carries along with it a planet. The centrifugal motion impels every particle in these vortices at each instant to fly off from the sun in a straight line; but it is retained by the pressure of those which have already escaped, and form a denser sphere beyond it. Light is no more than the effect of particles seeking to escape from the centre, and pressing one on another, though perhaps without actual motion.[s] The planetary vortices contain sometimes smaller vortices, in which the satellites are whirled round their principal.

36. Such, in a few words, is the famous Cartesian theory, which, fallen in esteem as it now is, stood its ground on the continent of Europe for nearly a century, till the simplicity of the Newtonian system, and above all, its conformity to the reality of things, gained an undisputed predominance. Besides the arbitrary suppositions of Descartes, and the various objections that were raised against the absolute plenum of space and other parts of his theory, it has been urged that his vortices are not reconcilable, according to the laws of motion in fluids, with the relation, ascertained by Kepler, between the periods and distances of the planets; nor does it appear why the sun should be in the focus, rather than in the centre of their orbits. Yet within a few years it has seemed not impossible that a part of his bold conjectures will enter once more with soberer steps into the schools of philosophy. His doctrine as to the nature of light, improved as it was by Huygens, is daily gaining ground over that of Newton; that of a subtle ether pervading space, which in

---

[s] J'ai souvent averti que par la lumière je n'entendois pas tant le mouvement que cette inclination ou propension que ces petits corps ont à se mouvoir, et que ce que je dirois du mouvement, pour être plus aisément entendu, se devoit rapporter à cette propension; d'où il est manifeste que selon moi l'on ne doit entendre autre chose par les couleurs que les différentes variétés qui arrivent en ces propensions. Vol. vii. p. 193.

fact is nearly the same thing, is becoming a favourite speculation, if we are not yet to call it an established truth; and
the affirmative of a problem which an eminent writer has
started, whether this ether has a vorticose motion round the
sun, would not leave us very far from the philosophy which
it has been so long our custom to turn into ridicule.

37. The passage of Mercury over the sun was witnessed
Transits of
Mercury
and Venus. by Gassendi in 1631. This phænomenon, though it
excited great interest in that age, from its having
been previously announced, so as to furnish a test of astronomical accuracy, recurs too frequently to be now considered
as of high importance. The transit of Venus is much more
rare. It occurred on Dec. 4, 1639, and was then only seen
by Horrox, a young Englishman of extraordinary mathematical genius. There is reason to ascribe an invention of great
importance, though not perhaps of extreme difficulty, that of
the micrometer, to Horrox.

38. The satellites of Jupiter and the phases of Venus are
Laws of
Mechanics. not so glorious in the scutcheon of Galileo as his
discovery of the true principles of mechanics. These,
as we have seen in the preceding volume, were very imperfectly known till he appeared; nor had the additions to that
science since the time of Archimedes been important. The
treatise of Galileo, Della Scienza Mecanica, has been said, I
know not on what authority, to have been written in 1592.
It was not published, however, till 1634, and then only in a
French translation by Mersenne, the original not appearing
till 1649. This is chiefly confined to statics, or the doctrine
of equilibrium; it was in his dialogues on motion, Della
Nuova Scienza, published in 1638, that he developed his
Statistics of
Galileo. great principles of the science of dynamics, the
moving forces of bodies. Galileo was induced to
write his treatise on mechanics, as he tells us, in consequence
of the fruitless attempts he witnessed in engineers to raise
weights by a small force, 'as if with their machines they
could cheat nature, whose instinct as it were by fundamental
law is that no resistance can be overcome except by a superior
force.' But as one man may raise a weight to the height of
a foot by dividing it into equal portions, commensurate to his
power, which many men could not raise at once, so a weight,
which raises another greater than itself, may be considered

as doing so by successive instalments of force, during each
of which it traverses as much space as a corresponding
portion of the larger weight. Hence the velocity, of which
space uniformly traversed in a given time is the measure, is
inversely as the masses of the weights, and thus the equilibrium of the straight lever is maintained, when the weights
are inversely as their distance from the fulcrum. As this
equilibrium of unequal weights depends on the velocities
they would have if set in motion, its law has been called the
principle of virtual velocities. No theorem has been of more
important utility to mankind. It is one of those great truths
of science, which, combating and conquering enemies from
opposite quarters, prejudice and empiricism, justify the name
of philosophy against both classes. The waste of labour and
expense in machinery would have been incalculably greater
in modern times, could we imagine this law of nature not to
have been discovered; and as their misapplication prevents
their employment in a proper direction, we owe, in fact, to
Galileo the immense effect which a right application of it has
produced. It is possible that Galileo was ignorant of the
demonstration given by Stevinus of the law of equilibrium in
the inclined plane. His own is different; but he seems only
to consider the case when the direction of the force is parallel
to that of the plane.

39. Still less was known of the principles of dynamics than
of those of statics, till Galileo came to investigate His Dyna-
them. The acceleration of falling bodies, whether mics.
perpendicularly or on inclined planes, was evident; but in
what ratio this took place, no one had succeeded in determining, though many had offered conjectures. He showed
that the velocity acquired was proportional to the time from
the commencement of falling. This might now be demonstrated from the laws of motion; but Galileo, who did not
perhaps distinctly know them, made use of experiment. He
then proved by reasoning that the spaces traversed in falling
were as the squares of the times or velocities; that their increments in equal times were as the uneven numbers, 1, 3, 5,
7, and so forth; and that the whole space was half what
would have been traversed uniformly from the beginning
with the final velocity. These are the great laws of accele-

rated and retarded motion, from which Galileo deduced most important theorems. He showed that the time in which bodies roll down the length of inclined planes is equal to that in which they would fall down the height, and in different planes is proportionate to the height; and that their acquired velocity is in the same ratios. In some propositions he was deceived; but the science of dynamics owes more to Galileo than to any one philosopher. The motion of projectiles had never been understood; he showed it to be parabolic; and in this he not only necessarily made use of a principle of vast extent, that of compound motion, (which, though it is clearly mentioned in one passage by Aristotle,[t] and may probably be implied, or even asserted, in the reasonings of others, as has been observed in another place with respect to Jordano Bruno, does not seem to have been explicitly laid down by modern writers on mechanical science,) but must have seen the principle of curvilinear deflection by forces acting in infinitely small portions of time. The ratio between the times of vibration in pendulums of unequal length had early attracted Galileo's attention. But he did not reach the geometrical exactness of which this subject is capable.[u] He developed a new principle as to the resistance of solids to the fracture of their parts, which, though Descartes as usual treated it with scorn, is now established in philosophy. 'One forms, however,' says Playfair, 'a very imperfect idea of this philosopher from considering the discoveries and inventions, numerous and splendid as they are, of which he was the undisputed author. It is by following his reasonings, and by pursuing the train of his thoughts, in his own elegant, though somewhat diffuse exposition of them, that we become acquainted with the fertility of his genius, with the sagacity, penetration, and comprehensiveness of his mind. The service which he rendered to real knowledge is to be estimated not only from the truths which he discovered, but from the errors which he detected; not merely from the sound principles which he established, but from the pernicious idols which he overthrew. Of all the writers who have lived in an age which was yet only emerging from ignorance and barbarism,

---

[t] Drinkwater's Life of Galileo, p. 80.　　　　　[u] Fabroni.

Galileo has most entirely the tone of true philosophy, and is most free from any contamination of the times, in taste, sentiment, and opinion.' [x]

40. Descartes, who left nothing in philosophy untouched turned his acute mind to the science of mechanics Mechanics sometimes with signal credit, sometimes very un- cartes. successfully. He reduced all statics to one principle, that it requires as much force to raise a body to a given height, as to raise a body of double weight to half the height. This is the theorem of virtual velocities in another form. In many respects he displays a jealousy of Galileo, and an unwillingness to acknowledge his discoveries, which puts himself often in the wrong. ' I believe,' he says, ' that the velocity of very heavy bodies which do not move very quickly in descending increases nearly in a duplicate ratio; but I deny that this is exact, and I believe that the contrary is the case when the movement is very rapid.' [y] This recourse to the air's resistance, a circumstance of which Galileo was well aware, in order to diminish the credit of a mathematical theorem, is unworthy of Descartes; but it occurs more than once in his letters. He maintained also, against the theory of Galileo, that bodies do not begin to move with an infinitely small velocity, but have a certain degree of motion at the first instance which is afterwards accelerated. [z] In this too, as he meant to extend his theory to falling bodies, the consent of philosophers has decided the question against him. It was a corollary from these notions that he denies the increments of spaces to be according to the progression of uneven numbers. [a] Nor would he allow that the velocity of a body augments its force, though it is a concomitant. [b]

---

[x] Preliminary Dissertation to Encyclop. Britan.

[y] Œuvres de Descartes, vol. viii. p. 24.

[z] Il faut savoir, quoique Galilée et quelques autres disent au contraire, que les corps qui commencent à descendre, ou à se mouvoir en quelque façon que ce soit, ne passent point par tous les degrés de tardiveté; mais que dès le premier moment ils ont certaine vîtesse qui s'augmente après de beaucoup, et c'est de cette augmentation que vient la force de la percussion. viii. 181.

[a] Cette proportion d'augmentation selon les nombres impairs, 1, 3, 5, 7, &c., qui est dans Galilée, et que je crois vous avoir aussi écrite autrefois, ne peut être vraie, qu'en supposant deux ou trois choses qui sont très-fausses, dont l'une est que le mouvement croisse par degrés depuis le plus lent, ainsi que le songe Galilée, et l'autre que la résistance de l'air n'empêche point. vol. ix. p. 349.

[b] Je pense que la vîtesse n'est pas la

41. Descartes, however, is the first who laid down the laws
Laws of mo- of motion; especially that all bodies persist in their
tion laid   present state of rest or uniform rectilineal motion
down by
Descartes.   till affected by some force. Many had thought, as
the vulgar always do, that a continuance of rest was natural
to bodies, but did not perceive that the same principle of
inertia or inactivity was applicable to them in rectilineal
motion. Whether this is deducible from theory, or depends
wholly on experience, by which we ought to mean experiment, is a question we need not discuss. The fact, however,
is equally certain; and hence Descartes inferred that every
curvilinear deflection is produced by some controlling force,
from which the body strives to escape in the direction of
a tangent to the curve. The most erroneous part of his
mechanical philosophy is contained in some propositions as
to the collision of bodies, so palpably incompatible with
obvious experience that it seems truly wonderful he could
ever have adopted them. But he was led into these paradoxes by one of the arbitrary hypotheses which always
governed him. He fancied it a necessary consequence from
the immutability of the divine nature that there should be at
all times the same quantity of motion in the universe; and
rather than abandon this singular assumption he did not
hesitate to assert, that two hard bodies striking each other
in opposite directions would be reflected with no loss of
velocity; and, what is still more outrageously paradoxical,
that a smaller body is incapable of communicating motion to
a greater; for example, that the red billiard-ball cannot put
the white into motion. This manifest absurdity he endeavoured to remove by the arbitrary supposition, that when
we see, as we constantly do, the reverse of his theorem
take place, it is owing to the air, which, according to him,
renders bodies more susceptible of motion than they would
naturally be.

42. Though Galileo, as well as others, must have been
acquainted with the laws of the composition of moving

---

cause de l'augmentation de la force, encore qu'elle l'accompagne toujours. Id.,
p. 356. See also vol. viii. p. 14. He
was probably perplexed by the metaphysical notion of causation, which he knew
not how to ascribe to mere velocity.
The fact that increased velocity is a
condition or antecedent of augmented
force could not be doubted.

forces, it does not appear that they had ever been so distinctly
enumerated as by Descartes, in a passage of his Di- Also those
optrics.[c] That the doctrine was in some measure of compound
forces.
new may be inferred from the objections of Fermat; and
Clerselier, some years afterwards, speaks of persons 'not
much versed in mathematics, who cannot understand an
argument taken from the nature of compound motion.'[d]

43. Roberval demonstrated what seems to have been
assumed by Galileo, and is immediately deducible Other dis-
from the composition of forces, that weights on an coveries in
mechanics.
oblique or crooked lever balance each other, when they are
inversely as the perpendiculars drawn from the centre of
motion to their direction.   Fermat, more versed in geometry than physics, disputed this theorem, which is now
quite elementary.   Descartes, in a letter to Mersenne, un-
graciously testifies his agreement with it.[e]   Torricelli, the
most illustrious disciple of Galileo, established that when
weights balance each other in all positions, their common
centre of gravity does not ascend or descend, and conversely.

44. Galileo, in a treatise entitled Delle Cose che stanno
nell' Acqua, lays down the principles of hydrostatics In hydro-
already established by Stevin, and among others statics and
pneumatics.
what is called the hydrostatical paradox.   Whether he was
acquainted with Stevin's writings may be perhaps doubted;
it does not appear that he mentions them.   The more difficult
science of hydraulics was entirely created by two disciples of
Galileo, Castellio and Torricelli.   It is one everywhere of
high importance, and especially in Italy.   The work of
Castellio, Della Misura dell' Acque Correnti, and a continuation, were published at Rome, in 1628.   His practical skill
in hydraulics, displayed in carrying off the stagnant waters
of the Arno, and in many other public works, seems to have
exceeded his theoretical science.   An error into which he

---

[c] Vol. v. p. 18.
[d] Vol. vi. p. 508.

[e] Je suis de l'opinion, says Descartes,
de ceux qui disent que *pondera sunt in
æquilibrio quando sunt in ratione reci-
proca linearum perpendicularium*, &c.
vol. ix. p. 357. He would not name
Roberval; one of those littlenesses
which appear too frequently in his
letters, and in all his writings. Des-

cartes, in fact, could not bear to think
that another, even though not an enemy,
had discovered anything. In the preceding page he says, C'est une chose
ridicule que de vouloir employer la
raison du levier dans la poulie, ce qui
est, si j'ai bonne mémoire, une imagination de Guide Ubalde. Yet this imagination is demonstrated in all our
elementary books on mechanics.

fell, supposing the velocity of fluids to be as the height down
which they had descended, led to false results. Torricelli
proved that it was as the square root of the altitude. The
latter of these two was still more distinguished by his discovery of the barometer. The principle of the syphon or
sucking pump, and the impossibility of raising water in it
more than about thirty-three feet, were both well known ;
but even Galileo had recourse to the clumsy explanation that
Nature limited her supposed horror of a vacuum to this altitude. It occurred to the sagacity of Torricelli, that the
weight of the atmospheric column pressing upon the fluid
which supplied the pump was the cause of this rise above its
level ; and that the degree of rise was consequently the
measure of that weight. That the air had weight was known
indeed to Galileo and Descartes ; and the latter not only had
some notion of determining it by means of a tube filled with
mercury, but, in a passage which seems to have been much
overlooked, distinctly suggests as one reason why water will
not rise above eighteen *brasses* in a pump, ' the weight of the
water which counterbalances that of the air.'[f] Torricelli
happily thought of using mercury, a fluid thirteen times
heavier, instead of water, and thus invented a portable
instrument by which the variations of the mercurial column
might be readily observed. These he found to fluctuate
between certain well-known limits, and in circumstances
which might justly be ascribed to the variations of atmospheric gravity. This discovery he made in 1643 ; and in
1648, Pascal, by his celebrated experiment on the Puy de
Dôme, established the theory of atmospheric pressure beyond
dispute. He found a considerable difference in the height of
the mercury at the bottom and the top of that mountain ;
and a smaller yet perceptible variation was proved on taking
the barometer to the top of one of the loftiest churches in
Paris.

45. The science of optics was so far from falling behind
Optics. Dis-   other branches of physics in this period, that, in-
coveries of
Kepler.   cluding the two great practical discoveries which

---

[f] Vol. vii. p. 437.
[This seems an error of the press, or
of the writer ; for the French *brasse*
being of six feet, water does not rise
much more than five *brasses*.—1847.]

illustrate it, no former or later generation has witnessed such an advance.   Kepler began, in the year 1604, by one of his first works, Paralipomena ad Vitellionem, a title somewhat more modest than he was apt to assume.   In this supplement to the great Polish philosopher of the middle ages, he first explained the structure of the human eye, and its adaptation to the purposes of vision.   Porta and Maurolycus had made important discoveries, but left the great problem untouched. Kepler had the sagacity to perceive the use of the retina as the canvas on which images were painted.   In his treatise, says Montucla, we are not to expect the precision of our own age; but it is full of ideas novel and worthy of a man of genius.   He traced the causes of imperfect vision in its two principal cases, where the rays of light converge to a point before or behind the retina.   Several other optical phænomena are well explained by Kepler; but he was unable to master the great enigma of the science, the law of refraction. To this he turned his attention again in 1611, when he published a treatise on Dioptrics.   He here first laid the foundation of that science.   The angle of refraction, which Maurolycus had supposed equal to that of incidence, Descartes assumed to be one third of it; which, though very erroneous as a general theorem, was sufficiently accurate for the sort of glasses he employed.   It was his object to explain the principle of the telescope; and in this he well succeeded. Invention of the telescope. That admirable invention was then quite recent. Whatever endeavours have been made to carry up the art of assisting vision by means of a tube to much more ancient times, it seems to be fully proved that no one had made use of combined lenses for that purpose.   The slight benefit which a hollow tube affords by obstructing the lateral ray must have been early familiar, and will account for passages which have been construed to imply what the writers never dreamed of.[g]   The real inventor of the telescope is not certainly known.   Metius of Alkmaar long enjoyed that honour; but the best claim seems to be that of Zachary Jens, a dealer in spectacles at Middleburg.   The date of the invention, or

---

[g] Even Dutens, whose sole aim is to show that the ancients made use of depreciate those whom modern science glasses to assist vision.   Origine des has most revered, cannot pretend to Découvertes, i. 218.

at least of its publicity, is referred beyond dispute to 1609.
The news of so wonderful a novelty spread rapidly through
Europe; and in the same year Galileo, as has been mentioned,
having heard of the discovery, constructed, by his own sagacity, the instrument which he exhibited at Venice. It is,
however, unreasonable to regard himself as the inventor;
and in this respect his Italian panegyrists have gone too far.
The original sort of telescope, and the only one employed in
Europe for above thirty years, was formed of a convex object
glass with a concave eye-glass. This, however, has the dis-
advantage of diminishing too much the space which can be
taken in at one point of view; 'so that,' says Montucla,
'one can hardly believe that it could render astronomy such
service as it did in the hands of a Galileo or a Scheiner.'
Kepler saw the principle upon which another kind might be
framed with both glasses convex. This is now called the
astronomical telescope, and was first employed a little before
the middle of the century. The former, called the Dutch
telescope, is chiefly used for short spying glasses.

46. The microscope has also been ascribed to Galileo; and
so far with better cause, that we have no proof of his
Of the mi-
croscope.   having known the previous invention. It appears,
however, to have originated, like the telescope, in Holland,
and perhaps at an earlier time. Cornelius Drebbel, who
exhibited the microscope in London about 1620, has often
passed for the inventor. It is suspected by Montucla that
the first microscopes had concave eye-glasses; and that the
present form with two convex glasses is not older than the
invention of the astronomical telescope.

47. Antonio de Dominis, the celebrated archbishop of
Antonio de
Dominis.   Spalato, in a book published in 1611, though written
several years before, De Radiis Lucis in Vitris Per-
spectivis et Iride, explained more of the phænomena of the
rainbow than was then understood. The varieties of colour
had baffled all inquirers, though the bow itself was well
known to be the reflection of solar light from drops of rain.
Antonio de Dominis, to account for these varieties, had recourse
to refraction, the known means of giving colour to the solar
ray; and guiding himself by the experiment of placing
between the eye and the sun a glass bottle of water, from the

lower side of which light issued in the same order of colours
as in the rainbow, he inferred that after two refractions and
one intermediate reflection within the drop, the ray came to
the eye tinged with different colours, according to the angle
at which it had entered. Kepler, doubtless ignorant of De
Dominis's book, had suggested nearly the same. This,
though not a complete theory of the rainbow, and though it
left a great deal to occupy the attention, first of Descartes,
and afterwards of Newton, was probably just, and carried the
explanation as far as the principles then understood allowed
it to go. The discovery itself may be considered as an ano-
maly in science, as it is one of a very refined and subtle
nature, made by a man who has given no other indication of
much scientific sagacity or acuteness. In many things his
writings show great ignorance of principles of optics well
known in his time, so that Boscovich, an excellent judge in
such matters, has said of him, ' Homo opticarum rerum supra
quod patiatur ea ætas imperitissimus.' [h] Montucla is hardly
less severe on De Dominis, who in fact was a man of more
ingenious than solid understanding.

48. Descartes announced to the world in his Dioptrics,
1637, that he had at length solved the mystery
which had concealed the law of refraction. He
showed that the sine of the angle of incidence at
which the ray enters, has, in the same medium, a constant
ratio to that of the angle at which it is refracted, or bent in
passing through. But this ratio varies according to the
medium; some having a much more refractive power than
others. This was a law of beautiful simplicity as well as
extensive usefulness; but such was the fatality, as we would
desire to call it, which attended Descartes, that this discovery
had been indisputably made twenty years before by a Dutch
geometer of great reputation, Willebrod Snell. The treatise
of Snell had never been published; but we have the evidence
both of Vossius and Huygens, that Hortensius, a Dutch professor, had publicly taught the discovery of his countryman.
Descartes had long lived in Holland; privately, it is true,
and by his own account reading few books; so that in this,
as in other instances, we may be charitable in our suspicions;

Marginal note: Dioptrics of Descartes. Law of re-fraction;

---

[h] Playfair, Dissertation on Physical Philosophy, p. 119.

yet it is unfortunate that he should perpetually stand in need
of such indulgence.

49. Fermat did not inquire whether Descartes was the
original discoverer of the law of refraction, but
disputed its truth. Descartes, indeed, had not
contented himself with experimentally ascertaining it, but,
in his usual manner, endeavoured to show the path of the
ray by direct reasoning. The hypothesis he brought forward seemed not very probable to Fermat, nor would it be
permitted at present. His rival, however, fell into the
same error; and starting from an equally dubious supposition of his own, endeavoured to establish the true law of
refraction. He was surprised to find that, after a calculation founded upon his own principle, the real truth of a constant ratio between the sines of the angles came out according to the theorem of Descartes. Though he did not the
more admit the validity of the latter's hypothetical reasoning,
he finally retired from the controversy with an elegant compliment to his adversary.

50. In the Dioptrics of Descartes, several other curious
theorems are contained. He demonstrated that
there are peculiar curves, of which lenses may be
constructed, by the refraction from whose superficies all the
incident rays will converge to a focal point, instead of being
spread, as in ordinary lenses, over a certain extent of surface,
commonly called its spherical aberration. The effect of
employing such curves of glass would be an increase of
illumination, and a more perfect distinctness of image.
These curves were called the ovals of Descartes; but the
elliptic or hyperbolic speculum would answer nearly the
same purpose. The latter kind has been frequently attempted; but, on account of the difficulties in working them,
if there were no other objection, none but spherical lenses
are in use. In Descartes's theory, he explained the equality
of the angles of incidence and reflection in the case of light,
correctly as to the result, though with the assumption of a
false principle of his own, that no motion is lost in the collision of hard bodies such as he conceived light to be. Its
perfect elasticity makes his demonstration true.

disputed by Fermat.

Curves of Descartes.

51. Descartes carried the theory of the rainbow beyond
the point where Antonio de Dominis had left it. Theory of
He gave the true explanation of the outer bow, by the rainbow.
a second intermediate reflection of the solar ray within the
drop: and he seems to have answered the question most
naturally asked, though far from being of obvious solution,
why all this refracted light should only strike the eye in two
arches with certain angles and diameters, instead of pouring
its prismatic lustre over all the rain-drops of the cloud. He
found that no pencil of light continued, after undergoing the
processes of refraction and reflection in the drop, to be composed of parallel rays, and consequently to possess that
degree of density which fits it to excite sensation in our eyes,
except the two which make those angles with the axis drawn
from the sun to an opposite point at which the two bows are
perceived.

CHAPTER IX.

HISTORY OF SOME OTHER PROVINCES OF LITERATURE FROM 1600 TO 1650.

Sect. I.—On Natural History.

Zoology—Fabricius on Language of Brutes—Botany.

1. The vast collections of Aldrovandus on zoology, though
Aldrovandus. they may be considered as representing to us the
knowledge of the sixteenth century, were, as has
been seen before, only published in a small part before its
close. The fourth and concluding part of his Ornithology
appeared in 1603; the History of Insects in 1604. Aldrovandus himself died in 1605. The posthumous volumes
appeared at considerable intervals; that on molluscous animals and zoophytes in 1606; on fishes and cetacea in 1613;
on whole-hoofed quadrupeds in 1616; on digitate quadrupeds
both viviparous and oviparous, in 1637; on serpents in 1640;
and on cloven-hoofed quadrupeds in 1642. There are also
volumes on plants and minerals. These were all printed at
Bologna, and most of them afterwards at Frankfort; but a
complete collection is very rare.

2. In the Exotica of Clusius, 1605, a miscellaneous volume
Clusius. on natural history, chiefly, but not wholly, consisting of translations or extracts from older works, we
find several new species of simiæ, the manis, or scaly ant-
eater of the old world, the three-toed sloth, and one or two
armadillos. We may add also the since extinguished race,
that phœnix of ornithologists, the much-lamented dodo.
This portly bird is delineated by Clusius, such as it then
existed in the Mauritius.

3. In 1648, Piso on the Materia Medica of Brazil, together with Marcgraf's Natural History of the same country, was published at Leyden, with notes by De Laet. The descriptions of Marcgraf are good, and enable us to identify the animals. They correct the imperfect notions of Gesner, and add several species which do not appear in his work, or perhaps in that of Aldrovandus: such as the tamandua, or Brazilian ant-eater; several of the family of cavies; the coati-mondi, which Gesner had perhaps meant in a defective description; the lama, the pacos, the jaguar, and some smaller feline animals; the prehensile porcupine, and several ruminants. But some, at least, of these had been already described in the histories of the West Indies, by Hernandez d'Oviedo, Acosta, and Herrera.

Piso and Marcgraf.

4. Jonston, a Pole of Scots origin, collected the information of his predecessors in a Natural History of Animals, published in successive parts from 1648 to 1652. The History of Quadrupeds appeared in the latter year. 'The text,' says Cuvier, 'is extracted, with some taste, from Gesner, Aldrovandus, Marcgraf, and Mouffet; and it answered its purpose as an elementary work in natural history, till Linnæus taught a more accurate method of classifying, naming, and describing animals. Even Linnæus cites him continually.'[i] I find in Jonston a pretty good account of the chimpanzee (Orang-otang Indorum, ab Angola delatus), taken perhaps from the Observationes Medicæ of Tulpius.[k] The delineations in Jonston being from copper-plates, are superior to the coarse wood-cuts of Gesner, but fail sometimes very greatly in exactness. In his notions of classification, being little else than a compiler, it may be supposed that he did not advance a step beyond his predecessors. The Theatrum Insectorum by Mouffet, an

Jonston.

---

[i] Biogr. univ.

[k] Grotius, Epist. ad Gallos, p. 21, gives an account of a chimpanzee, monstrum hominis dicam an bestiæ? and refers to Tulpius. The doubt of Grotius as to the possible humanity of this quam similis turpissima bestia nobis, is not so strange as the much graver language of Linnæus.

[In the description of Homo Tro-glodytes, as Linnæus denominates the chimpanzee of Angola, we find alarming intimations, Cogitat, ratiocinatur, credit sui causa factam tellurem, se aliquando iterum fore imperantem, si unquam fides peregrinatoribus multis. Systema Naturæ, Holm, 1766. I rather believe this has been left out by Gmelin. But perhaps it was only a dry way of turning travellers into ridicule.—1842.]

English physician of the preceding century, was published in 1634; it seems to be compiled in a considerable degree from the unpublished papers of Gesner and foreign naturalists, whom the author has rather too servilely copied. Haller, however, is said to have placed Mouffet above all entomologists before the age of Swammerdam.[m]

5. We may place under the head of zoology a short essay by Fabricius de Aquapendente on the language of brutes; a subject very curious in itself, and which has by no means sufficiently attracted notice even in this experimental age. It cannot be said that Fabricius enters thoroughly into the problem, much less exhausts it. He divides the subject into six questions:—1. Whether brutes have a language, and of what kind: 2. How far it differs from that of man, and whether the languages of different species differ from one another: 3. What is its use: 4. In what modes animals express their affections: 5. What means we have of understanding their language: 6. What is their organ of speech. The affirmative of the first question he proves by authority of several writers, confirmed by experience, especially of hunters, shepherds, and cowherds, who know by the difference of sounds what animals mean to express. It may be objected that brutes utter sounds, but do not speak. But this is merely as we define speech; and he attempts to show that brutes, by varying their utterance, do all that we do by *literal* sounds. This leads to the solution of the second question. Men agree with brutes in having speech, and in forming elementary sounds of determinate time; but ours is more complex; these elementary sounds, which he calls *articulos,* or joints of the voice, being quicker and more numerous. Man, again, forms his sounds more by means of the lips and tongue, which are softer in him than they are in brutes. Hence his speech runs into great variety

Fabricius on the language of brutes.

---

[m] Biogr. univ. Chalmers. I am no judge of the merits of the book; but if the following sentence of the English translation does it no injustice, Mouffet must have taken little pains to do more than transcribe:—' In Germany and England I do not hear that there are any *grasshoppers* at all; but if there be, they are *in both countries* called Bowkrickets, or Baulm-krickets.' P. 989. This translation is subjoined to Topsell's History of Four-Footed Beasts, collected out of Gesner and others, in an edition of 1658. The first edition of Topsell's very ordinary composition was in 1608.

and complication, which we call language, while that of animals within the same species is much more uniform.

6. The question as to the use of speech to brutes is not
difficult. But he seems to confine this utility to the expression of particular emotions, and does not meddle with the
more curious inquiry, whether they have a capacity of communicating specific facts to one another; and if they have,
whether this is done through the organs of the voice. The
fourth question is, in how many modes animals express their
feelings. These are by look, by gesture, by sound, by voice,
by language. Fabricius tells us that he had seen a dog,
meaning to expel another dog from the place he wished himself to occupy, begin by looking fierce, then use menacing
gestures, then growl, and finally bark. Inferior animals,
such as worms, have only the two former sorts of communication. Fishes, at least some kinds, have a power of emitting
a sound, though not properly a voice; this may be by the
fins or gills. To insects also he seems to deny voice, much
more language, though they declare their feelings by sound.
Even of oxen, stags, and some other quadrupeds, he would
rather say that they have voice than language. But cats,
dogs, and birds have a proper language. All, however, are
excelled by man, who is truly called μέροψ, from his more
clear and distinct articulations.

7. In the fifth place, however difficult it may appear to
understand the language of brutes, we know that they understand what is said to them; how much more therefore ought
we, superior in reason, to understand them! He proceeds
from hence to an analysis of the passions, which he reduces
to four: joy, desire, grief, and fear. Having thus drawn our
map of the passions, we must ascertain by observation what
are the articulations of which any species of animals is
capable, which cannot be done by description. His own experiments were made on the dog and the hen. Their articulations are sometimes complex; as, when a dog wants to come
into his master's chamber, he begins by a shrill small yelp,
expressive of desire, which becomes deeper, so as to denote
a mingled desire and annoyance, and ends in a lamentable
howl of the latter feeling alone. Fabricius gives several other
rules deducted from observation of dogs, but ends by confess-

ing that he has not fully attained his object, which was to furnish every one with a compendious method of understanding the language of animals : the inquirer must therefore proceed upon these rudiments, and make out more by observation and good canine society. He shows finally, from the different structure of the organs of speech, that no brute can ever rival man ; the chief instrument being the throat, which we use only for vowel sounds. Two important questions are hardly touched in this little treatise : first, as has been said, whether brutes can communicate specific facts to each other ; and, secondly, to what extent they can associate ideas with the language of man. These ought to occupy our excellent naturalists.

8. Columna, belonging to the Colonna family, and one of

Botany—
Columna. the greatest botanists of the sixteenth century, maintained the honour of that science during the present period, which his long life embraced. In the academy of the Lincei, to which the revival of natural philosophy is greatly due, Columna took a conspicuous share. His Ecphrasis, a history of rare plants, was published in two parts at Rome, in 1606 and 1616. In this he laid down the true basis of the science, by establishing the distinction of genera, which Gesner, Cæsalpin, and Joachim Camerarius had already conceived, but which it was left for Columna to confirm and employ. He alone, of all the contemporary botanists, seems to have appreciated the luminous ideas which Cæsalpin had bequeathed to posterity.[n] In his posthumous observations on the natural history of Mexico by Hernandez, he still further developed the philosophy of botanical arrangements. Columna is the first who used copper instead of wood to delineate plants ; an improvement which soon became general. This was in the Φυτοβάσανος, sive Plantarum aliquot Historia, 1594. There are errors in this work ; but it is remarkable for the accuracy of the descriptions, and for the correctness and beauty of the figures.[o]

9. Two brothers, John and Gaspar Bauhin, inferior in phi-

John and
Gaspar
Bauhin. losophy to Columna, made more copious additions to the nomenclature and description of plants. The elder, who was born in 1541, and had acquired some celebrity

<hr>

[n] Biogr. univ.   [o] Id. Sprengel.

as a botanist in the last century, lived to complete, but not
to publish, an Historia Plantarum Universalis, which did not
appear till 1650. It contains the descriptions of 5000 species,
and the figures of 3577, but small and ill-executed. His
brother, though much younger, had preceded him, not only
by the Phytopinax in 1596, but by his chief work, the Pinax
Theatri Botanici, in 1623. ' Gaspar Bauhin,' says a modern
botanist, ' is inferior to his brother in his descriptions and in
sagacity; but his delineations are better, and his synonyms
more complete. They are both below Clusius in description,
and below several older botanists in their figures. In their
arrangement they follow Lobel, and have neglected the
lights which Cæsalpin and Columna had held out. Their
chief praise is to have brought together a great deal of knowledge acquired by their predecessors, but the merit of both
has been exaggerated.'[p]

10. Johnson, in 1636, published an edition of Gerard's
Herbal. But the Theatrum Botanicum of Parkin-
son, in 1640, is a work, says Pulteney, of much   Parkinson.
more originality than Gerard's, and it contains abundantly
more matter. We find in it near 3800 plants; but many
descriptions recur more than once. The arrangement is in
seventeen classes, partly according to the known or supposed
qualities of the plant, and partly according to their external
character.[q] ' This heterogeneous classification, which seems
to be founded on that of Dodoens, shows the small advances
that had been made towards any truly scientific distribution;
on the contrary, Gerard, Johnson, and Parkinson had rather
gone back, by not sufficiently pursuing the example of Lobel.'

---

[p] Biogr. univ. Pulteney speaks more
highly of John Bauhin : ' That which
Gesner performed for zoology, John
Bauhin effected in botany. It is, in
reality, a repository of all that was valuable in the ancients, in his immediate
predecessors, and in the discoveries of
his own time, relating to the history of
vegetables, and is executed with that
accuracy and critical judgment which
can only be exhibited by superior
talents.'—Hist. of Botany in England,
i. 190.
[q] P. 146.

Sect. II.—On Anatomy and Medicine.

Claims of early Writers to the Discovery of the Circulation of the Blood—
Harvey—Lacteal Vessels discovered by Asellius—Medicine.

11. The first important discovery that was made public in
Valves of this century was that of the valves of the veins;
the veins
discovered. which is justly ascribed to Fabricius de Aquapendente, a professor at Padua; because though some of these
valves are described even by Berenger, and further observations
were made on the subject by Sylvius, Vesalius, and other
anatomists, yet Fallopius himself had in this instance thrown
back the science by denying their existence, and no one before
Fabricius had generalised the discovery. This he did in his
public lectures as early as 1524; but his tract De Venarum
Ostiolis appeared in 1603. This discovery, as well as that of
Harvey, has been attributed to Father Paul Sarpi, whose immense reputation in the north of Italy accredited every tale
favourable to his glory. But there seems to be no sort of
ground for either supposition.

12. The discovery of a general circulation in the blood has
Theory of done such honour to Harvey's name, and has been
the blood's
circulation, claimed for so many others, that it deserves more
consideration than we can usually give to anatomical science.
According to Galen, and the general theory of anatomists
formed by his writings, the arterial blood flows from the
heart to the extremities, and returns again by the same
channels, the venous blood being propelled, in like manner,
to and from the liver. The discovery attributed to Harvey
was, that the arteries communicate with the veins, and that
all the blood returns to the heart by the latter vessels. Besides
this general or systemic circulation, there is one called the
pulmonary, in which the blood is carried by certain arteries
through the lungs, and returned again by corresponding veins
preparatory to its being sent into the general sanguineous
system; so that its course is through a double series of
ramified vessels, each beginning and terminating at the heart,
but not at the same side of the heart; the left side, which

from a cavity called its ventricle throws out the arterial blood
by the aorta, and by another called its auricle receives that
which has passed through the lungs by the pulmonary vein,
being separated by a solid septum from the right side, which,
by means of similar cavities, receives the blood of all the
veins, excepting those of the lungs, and throws it out into
the pulmonary artery.   It is thus evident that the word
pulmonary circulation is not strictly proper, there being only
one for the whole body.

13. The famous work of Servetus, Christianismi Restitutio,
has excited the attention of the literary part of the *sometimes
ascribed to*
world, not only by the unhappy fate it brought upon *Servetus;*
the author, and its extreme scarcity, but by a remarkable
passage wherein he has been supposed to describe the circulation of the blood.   That Servetus had a just idea of the
pulmonary circulation and the aeration of the blood in the
lungs, is manifest by this passage, and is denied by no one;
but it has been the opinion of anatomists that he did not
apprehend the return of the mass of the blood through the
veins to the right auricle of the heart.[r]

---

[r] In the first edition of this work I
remarked, vol. i. p. 456, that Levasseur
had come much nearer to the theory
of a general circulation than Servetus.
But the passage in Levasseur, which I
knew only from the quotation in Portal,
Hist. de l'Anatomie, i. 373, does not,
on consulting the book itself, bear out
the inference which Portal seems to
deduce; and he has, not quite rightly,
omitted all expressions which he thought
erroneous.   Thus. Levasseur precedes
the first sentence of Portal's quotation
by the following : Intus (in corde) sunt
sinus seu ventriculi duo tantum, septo
quodam medio discreti, *per cujus fora-
mina* sanguis et spiritus communicatur.
In utroque duo vasa habentur.   For
this he quotes Galen ; and the perforation of the septum of the heart is known
to be one of Galen's errors.   Upon the
whole there seems no ground for believing that Levasseur was acquainted with
the general circulation; and though his
language may at first lead us to believe
that he speaks of that through the
lungs, even this is not distinctly made
out.   Sprengel, in his History of Medicine, does not mention the name of

Levasseur (or Vassæus, as he was called
in Latin) among those who anticipated
in any degree the discovery of circulation.   The book quoted by Portal is
Vassæus in Anatomen Corporis Humani
Tabulæ Quatuor, several times printed
between 1540 and 1560.

Andrès (Origine e Progresso d' ogni
Litteratura, vol. xiv. p. 37) has put in
a claim for a Spanish farrier, by name
Reyna, who, in a book printed in 1552,
but of which there seems to have been
an earlier edition (Libro de Maniscal-
cheria hecho y ordenado por Francisco
de la Reyna), asserts in few and plain
words, as Andrès quotes them in Italian,
that the blood goes in a circle through
all the limbs.   I do not know that the
book has been seen by any one else ; and
it would be desirable to examine the
context, since other writers have seemed
to know the truth without really apprehending it.

That Servetus was only acquainted
with the pulmonary circulation has been
the general opinion.   Portal, though in
one place he speaks with less precision,
repeatedly limits the discovery to this ;
and Sprengel does not entertain the least

14. Columbus is acknowledged to have been acquainted
_{to Colum-bus} with the pulmonary circulation. He says of his
own discovery that no one had observed or consigned
it to writing before. Arantius, according to Portal, has
described the pulmonary circulation still better than Columbus, while Sprengel denies that he has described it at all.
It is perfectly certain, and is admitted on all sides, that
Columbus did not know the systemic circulation: in what
manner he disposed of the blood does not very clearly appear;
but as he conceived a passage to exist between the ventricles
of the heart, it is probable, though his words do not lead to
this inference, that he supposed the aerated blood to be
transmitted back in this course.[s]

suspicion that it went farther. Andrès
(xiv. 38), not certainly a medical authority, but conversant with such, and
very partial to Spanish claimants, asserts
the same. If a more general language
may be found in some writers, it may be
ascribed to their want of distinguishing
the two circulations. A medical friend
who, at my request, perused and considered the passage in Servetus, as it is
quoted in Allwoerden's life, says in a
letter, 'All that this passage implies
which has any reference to the greater
circulation, may be comprised in the
following points:—1. That the heart
transmits a vivifying principle along
the arteries and the blood which they
contain to the anastomosing veins; 2.
That this living principle vivifies the
liver and the venous system generally;
3. That the liver produces the blood
itself, and transmits it through the vena
cava to the heart, in order to obtain the
vital principle, by performing the lesser
circulation, which Servetus seems perfectly to comprehend.
'Now, according to this view of the
passage, all the movement of the blood
implied is that which takes place from
the liver, through the vena cava to the
heart, and that of the lesser circulation.
It would appear to me that Servetus is
on the brink of the discovery of the circulation ; but that his notions respecting
the transmission of his 'vitalis spiritus'
diverted his attention from that great
movement of the blood itself which Harvey discovered. . . . It is clear that the
quantity of blood sent to the heart for
the elaboration of the vitalis spiritus is,

according to Servetus, only that furnished by the liver to the vena cava inferior. But the blood thus introduced
is represented by him as performing the
circulation through the lungs very regularly.'
It appears singular that, while Servetus distinctly knew that the septum
of the heart, paries ille medius, as he
calls it, is closed, which Berenger had
discovered, and Vesalius confirmed
(though the bulk of anatomists long
afterwards adhered to Galen's notion
of perforation), and consequently that
some other means must exist for restoring the blood from the left division
of the heart to the right, he should not
have seen the necessity of a system of
vessels to carry forward this communication.
[s] The leading passage in Columbus
(De Re Anatomica, lib. vii. p. 177, edit.
1559), which I have not found quoted
by Portal or Sprengel, is as follows :—
Inter hos ventriculos septum adest,
per quod fere omnes existimant san-
guini a dextro ventriculo ad sinistrum
aditum patefieri ; id ut fieret facilius, in
transitu ob vitalium spirituum gener-
ationem demum reddi ; sed longa errant
via ; nam sanguis per arteriosam venam
ad pulmonem fertur ; ibique attenuatur ;
deinde cum aere una per arteriam venalem ad sinistrum cordis ventriculum
defertur ; quod nemo hactenus aut animadvertit aut scriptum reliquit ; licet
maximè et ab omnibus animadverten-
dum. He afterwards makes a remark,
in which Servetus had preceded him,
that the size of the pulmonary artery

15. Cæsalpin, whose versatile genius entered upon every field of research, has, in more than one of his treatises relating to very different topics, and especially in that upon plants, some remarkable passages on the same subject, which approach more nearly than any we have seen to a just notion of the general circulation, and have led several writers to insist on his claim as a prior discoverer to Harvey. Portal admits that this might be regarded as a fair pretension, if he were to judge from such passages ; but there are others which contradict this supposition, and show Cæsalpin to have had a confused and imperfect idea of the office of the veins. Sprengel, though at first he seems to incline more towards the pretensions of Cæsalpin, comes ultimately almost to the same conclusion ; and giving the reader the words of most importance, leaves him to form his own judgment. The Italians are more confident: Tiraboschi and Corniani, neither of whom are medical authorities, put in an unhesitating claim for Cæsalpin as the discoverer of the circulation of the blood, not without unfair reflections on Harvey.[t]

and to Cæsalpin.

(vena arteriosa) is greater than would be required for the nutrition of the lungs alone. Whether he knew of the passages in Servetus or no, notwithstanding his claim of originality, is not perhaps manifest ; the coincidence as to the function of the lungs in aerating the blood is remarkable ; but if Columbus had any direct knowledge of the Christianismi Restitutio, he did not choose to follow it in the remarkable discovery that there is no perforation in the septum between the ventricles.

[t] Tiraboschi, x. 49. Corniani, vi. 8. He quotes, on the authority of another Italian writer, il giudizio di due illustri Inglesi, i fratelli Hunter, i quali, esaminato bene il processo di questa causa, *si maravigliano della sentenza data in favore del loro concittadino.* I must doubt, till more evidence is produced, whether this be true.

The passage in Cæsalpin's Quæstiones Peripateticæ is certainly the most resembling a statement of the entire truth that can be found in any writer before Harvey. I transcribe it from Dutens's Origine des Découvertes, vol. ii. p. 23 : Idcirco pulmo per venam arteriis similem ex dextro cordis ventriculo fervidum hauriens sanguinem, eumque per anastomosin arteriæ venali reddens, quæ in sinistrum cordis ventriculum tendit, transmisso interim aere frigido per asperæ arteriæ canales, qui juxta arteriam venalem protenduntur, non tamen osculis communicantes, ut putavit Galenus, solo tactu temperat. Huic sanguinis circulationi ex dextro cordis ventriculo per pulmones in sinistrum ejusdem ventriculum optimè respondent ea quæ ex dissectione apparent. Nam duo sunt vasa in dextrum ventriculum desinentia, duo etiam in sinistrum; duorum autem unum intromittit tantum, alterum educit, membranis eo ingenio constitutis. Vas igitur intromittens vena est magna quidem in dextro, quæ cava appellatur ; parva autem in sinistro ex pulmone introducens, cujus unica est tunica, ut cæterarum venarum. Vas autem educens arteria est magna quidem in sinistro, quæ aorta appellatur ; parva autem in dextro ad pulmones derivans, cujus similiter duæ sunt tunicæ, ut in cæteris arteriis.

In the treatise De Plantis we have a similar, but shorter, passage : Nam in animalibus videmus alimentum per venas duci ad cor tanquam ad officinam caloris

16. It is thus manifest that several anatomists of the six-
Generally unknown before Harvey. teenth century were on the verge of completely de-
tecting the law by which the motion of the blood is
governed; and the language of one is so strong,
that we must have recourse, in order to exclude his claim,
to the irresistible fact that he did not confirm by proof his
own theory, nor proclaim it in such a manner as to attract
the attention of the world. Certainly, when the doctrine of
a general circulation was advanced by Harvey, he both announced it as a paradox, and was not deceived in expecting
that it would be so accounted. Those again who strove to
depreciate his originality, sought intimations in the writings
of the ancients, and even spread a rumour that he had stolen
the papers of Father Paul; but it does not appear that they
talked, like some moderns, of plagiarism from Levasseur or
Cæsalpin.

17. William Harvey first taught the circulation of the
His dis-covery. blood in London in 1619; but his Exercitatio de
Motu Cordis was not published till 1628. He was
induced, as is said, to conceive the probability of this great
truth, by reflecting on the final cause of those valves, which
his master, Fabricius de Aquapendente, had demonstrated in
the veins; valves whose structure was such as to prevent the
reflux of the blood towards the extremities. Fabricius himself seems to have been ignorant of this structure, and certainly of the circulation; for he presumes that they serve to
prevent the blood from flowing like a river towards the feet
and hands, and from collecting in one part. Harvey followed his own happy conjecture by a long inductive process
of experiments on the effects of ligatures, and on the observed motion of the blood in living animals.

18. Portal has imputed to Harvey an unfair silence as to
Unjustly doubted to be original. Servetus, Columbus, Levasseur, and Cæsalpin, who
had all preceded him in the same track. Tiraboschi
copies Portal, and Corniani speaks of the appropriation of
Cæsalpin's discovery by Harvey. It may be replied, that no
one can reasonably presume Harvey to have been acquainted

---

insiti, et adepta inibi ultima perfectione,
per arterias in universum corpus distri-
bui agente spiritu, qui ex eodem ali-
mento in corde gignitur. I have taken,
this from the article on Cæsalpin in the
Biographie universelle.

with the passage in Servetus. But the imputation of suppressing the merits of Columbus is grossly unjust, and founded upon ignorance or forgetfulness of Harvey's celebrated Exercitation. In the prooemium to this treatise, he observes, that almost all anatomists have hitherto supposed with Galen, that the mechanism of the pulse is the same as that of respiration. But he not less than three times makes an exception for Columbus, to whom he most expressly refers the theory of a pulmonary circulation.[u] Of Cæsalpin he certainly says nothing ; but there seems to be no presumption that he was acquainted with that author's writings. Were it even true that he had been guided in his researches by the obscure passages we have quoted, could this set aside the merit of that patient induction by which he established his own theory? Cæsalpin asserts at best, what we may say he divined, but did not know to be true : Harvey asserts what he had demonstrated. The one is an empiric in a philosophical sense, the other a legitimate minister of truth. It has been justly said, that he alone discovers who proves ; nor is there a more odious office, or a more sophistical course of reasoning, than to impair the credit of great men, as Dutens wasted his erudition in doing, by hunting out equivocal and insulated passages from older writers, in order to depreciate the originality of the real teachers of mankind.[x] It may

---

[u] Pæne omnes huc usque anatomici medici et philosophi supponunt cum Galeno eundem usum esse pulsus, quam respirationis. But though he certainly claims the doctrine of a general circulation as wholly his own, and counts it a paradox which will startle every one, he as expressly refers (pp. 38 and 41 of the Exercitatio) that of a pulmonary transmission of the blood to Columbus, peritissimo doctissimoque anatomico; and observes, in his prooemium, as an objection to the received theory, quomodo probabile est (*uti notavit Rualdus Columbus*) tanto sanguine opus esse ad nutritionem pulmonum, cum hoc vas, vena videlicet arteriosa [id est, arteria pulmonalis] exsuperet magnitudine utrumque ramum distribitionis venæ cavæ descendentis cruralem. P. 16.

[x] This is the general character of a really learned and interesting work by Dutens, Origine des Découvertes attri-

buées aux Modernes. Justice is due to those who have first struck out, even without following up, original ideas in any science ; but not at the expense of those who, generally without knowledge of what had been said before, have deduced the same principles from reasoning or from observation, and carried them out to important consequences. Pascal quotes Montaigne for the shrewd remark, that we should try a man who says a wise thing, for we may often find that he does not understand it. Those who entertain a morbid jealousy of modern philosophy are glad to avail themselves of such hunters into obscure antiquity as Dutens, and they are seconded by all the envious, the uncandid, and by many of the unreflecting among mankind. With respect to the immediate question, the passages which Dutens has quoted from Hippocrates and Plato have certainly an appearance

indeed be thought wonderful that Servetus, Columbus, or Cæsalpin should not have more distinctly apprehended the consequences of what they maintained, since it seems difficult to conceive the lesser circulation without the greater; but the defectiveness of their views is not to be alleged as a counterbalance to the more steady sagacity of Harvey. The solution of their falling so short is that they were right, not indeed quite by guess, but upon insufficient proof; and that the consciousness of this embarrassing their minds prevented them from deducing inferences which now appear irresistible. In every department of philosophy, the researches of the first inquirers have often been arrested by similar causes.[y]

19. Harvey is the author of a treatise on generation, Harvey's treatise on Generation. wherein he maintains that all animals, including men, are derived from an egg. In this book we first find an argument maintained against spontaneous generation, which, in the case of the lower animals had been generally received. Sprengel thinks this treatise prolix, and not equal to the author's reputation.[z] It was first published in 1651.

20. Next in importance to the discovery of Harvey is Lacteals discovered by Asellius. that of Asellius as to the lacteal vessels. Eustachius had observed the thoracic duct in a horse. But Asellius, more by chance, as he owns, than by sagacity, perceived the lacteals in a fat dog whom he opened soon after it had eaten. This was in 1622, and his treatise De Lacteis Venis was published in 1627.[a] Harvey did not

---

of expressing a real circulation of the blood by the words περίοδος and περίφερομένου αἵματος; but others, and especially one from Nemesius, on which some reliance has been placed, mean nothing more than the flux and reflux of the blood, which the contraction and dilatation of the heart was supposed to produce. See Dutens, vol. ii. pp. 8–13. Mr. Coleridge has been deceived in the same manner by some lines of Jordano Bruno, which he takes to describe the circulation of the blood; whereas they merely express its movement to and fro, *meat et remeat*, which might be by the same system of vessels.

[y] The biographer of Harvey in the Biographie universelle strongly vindicates his claim. Tous les hommes in-

struits conviennent aujourd'hui que Harvey est le véritable auteur de cette belle découverte. . . . Césalpin pressentoit la circulation artérielle, en supposant que le sang retourne des extrémités au cœur; mais ces assertions ne furent point prouvées; elles ne se trouvèrent étayées par aucune expérience, par aucun fait; et l'on peut dire de Césalpin qu'il divina presque la grande circulation dont les lois lui furent totalement inconnues; la découverte en était réservée à Guillaume Harvey.

[z] Hist. de la Médecine, iv. 299. Portal, ii. 477.

[a] Portal, ii. 461. Sprengel, iv. 201. Peiresc soon after this got the body of a man fresh hanged after a good supper, and had the pleasure of confirming the

assent to this discovery, and endeavoured to dispute the use
of the vessels; nor is it to his honour that even to the end
of his life he disregarded the subsequent confirmation that
Pecquet and Bartholin had furnished.[b] The former detected
the common origin of the lacteal and lymphatic vessels in
1647, though his work on the subject was not published till
1651. But Olaus Rudbeck was the first who clearly distinguished these two kinds of vessels.

21. Scheiner proved that the retina is the organ of sight,
and that the humours serve only to refract the rays   Optical dis-
which paint the object on the optic nerve.   This   coveries of Scheiner.
was in a treatise entitled Oculus, hoc est, Fundamentum
Opticum, 1619.[c] The writings of several anatomists of this
period, such as Riolan, Vesling, Bartholin, contain partial
accessions to the science; but it seems to have been less
enriched by great discoveries, after those already named,
than in the preceding century.

22. The mystical medicine of Paracelsus continued to have
many advocates in Germany. A new class of   Medicine—
enthusiasts sprung from the same school, and calling   Van Hel-mont.
themselves Rosicrucians, pretended to cure diseases by faith
and imagination. A true Rosicrucian, they held, had only
to look on a patient to cure him. The analogy of magnetism,
revived in the last and present age, was commonly employed.[d]
Of this school the most eminent was Van Helmont, who
combined the Paracelsian superstitions with some original
ideas of his own. His general idea of medicine was that its
business was to regulate the archæus, an immaterial principle
of life and health; to which, like Paracelsus, he attributed a
mysterious being and efficacy. The seat of the archæus is in
the stomach; and it is to be affected either by a scheme of
diet or through the imagination. Sprengel praises Van
Helmont for overthrowing many current errors, and for
announcing principles since pursued.[e] The French physicians

discovery of Asellius by his own eyes.
Gassendi, Vita Peirescii, p. 177.

[b] Sprengel, iv. 203.

[c] Id. 270.

[d] All in nature, says Croll of Hesse,
one of the principal theosophists in
medicine, is living; all that lives has
its vital force, or astrum, which cannot
act without a body, but passes from one
to another. All things in the macro-
cosm are found also in the microcosm.
The inward or astral man is Gabalis,
from which the science is named. This
Gabalis or imagination is as a magnet
to external objects, which it thus attracts. Medicines act by a magnetic
force. Sprengel, iii. 362.

[e] Vol. v. p. 22.

adhered to the Hippocratic school, in opposition to what Sprengel calls the Chemiatric, which more or less may be reckoned that of Paracelsus. The Italians were still renowned in medicine. Sanctorius, De Medicina Statica, 1614, seems the only work to which we need allude. It is loaded with eulogy by Portal, Tiraboschi, and other writers.[f]

Sect. III.

On Oriental Literature—Hebrew Learning—Arabic and other Eastern Languages.

23. During no period of equal length since the revival of letters, has the knowledge of the Hebrew language *Diffusion of Hebrew.* been, apparently, so much diffused among the literary world as in that before us. The frequent sprinkling of its characters in works of the most miscellaneous erudition will strike the eye of every one who habitually consults them. Nor was this learning by any means so much confined to the clergy as it has been in later times, though their order naturally furnished the greater portion of those who laboured in that field. Some of the chief Hebraists of this age were laymen. The study of this language prevailed most in the Protestant countries of Europe, and it was cultivated with much zeal in England. The period between the last years of Elizabeth and the Restoration may perhaps be reckoned that in which a knowledge of Hebrew has been most usual among our divines.

24. Upon this subject I can only assert what I collect to be the verdict of judicious critics.[g]   It seems that the Hebrew *Language not studied in the best method.* language was not yet sufficiently studied in the method most likely to give an insight into its principles by comparing it with all the cognate

---

[f] Portal, ii. 391. Tiraboschi, xi. 270. Biogr. univ.

[g] The fifth volume of Eichhorn's Geschichte der Cultur is devoted to the progress of Oriental literature in Europe, not very full in characterising the various productions it mentions, but analytically arranged, and highly useful for reference. Jenisch, in his preface to Meninski's Thesaurus (Vienna, 1780) has traced a sketch of the same subject. We may have trusted in some respects to Simon, Histoire Critique du Vieux Testament. The biographical dictionaries, English and French, have of course been resorted to.

tongues, latterly called Semitic, spoken in the neighbouring parts of Asia, and manifestly springing from a common source. Postel, indeed, had made some attempts at this in the last century, but his learning was very slight; and Schindler published in 1612 a Lexicon Pentaglottum, in which the Arabic, as well as Syriac and Chaldaic, were placed in apposition with the Hebrew text. Louis de Dieu, whose ' Remarks on all the books of the Old Testament' were published at Leyden in 1648, has frequently recourse to some of the kindred languages, in order to explain the Hebrew.[h] But the first instructors in the latter had been Jewish rabbis; and the Hebraists of the sixteenth age had imbibed a prejudice, not unnatural though unfounded, that their teachers were best conversant with the language of their forefathers.[i] They had derived from the same source an extravagant notion of the beauty, antiquity, and capacity of the Hebrew; and, combining this with still more chimerical dreams of a mystical philosophy, lost sight of all real principles of criticism.

25. The most eminent Hebrew scholars of this age were the two Buxtorfs of Basle, father and son, both devoted to the rabbinical school. The elder, who had become distinguished before the end of the preceding century, published a grammar in 1609, which long continued to be reckoned the best, and a lexicon of Hebrew, Chaldee and Syriac, in 1623, which was not superseded for more than a hundred years. Many other works relating to these three dialects, as well as to that of the later Jews, do honour to the erudition of the elder Buxtorf; but he is considered as representing a class of Hebraists which in the more comprehensive orientalism of the eighteenth century has lost much of its credit. The son trod closely in his father's footsteps, whom he succeeded as professor of Hebrew at Basle. They held this chair between them more than seventy years. The younger Buxtorf was engaged in controversies which had not begun in his father's lifetime. Morin, one of those learned

The Bux-
torfs.

---

[h] Simon, Hist. critique du Vieux Testament, p. 494.

[i] This was not the case with Luther, who rejected the authority of the rabbis, and thought none but Christians could understand the Old Testament. Simon, p. 375. But Munster, Fagius, and several others, who are found in the Critici Sacri, gave way to the prejudice in favour of rabbinical opinions, and their commentaries are consequently too Judaical. P. 496.

Protestants who had gone over to the church of Rome, systematically laboured to establish the authority of those versions which the church had approved, by weakening that of the text which passed for original.[k] Hence he endeavoured to show, though this could not logically do much for his object, that the Samaritan Pentateuch, then lately brought to Europe, which is not in a different language, but merely the Hebrew written in Samaritan characters, is deserving of preference above what is called the Masoretic text, from which the Protestant versions are taken. The variations between these are sufficiently numerous to affect a favourite hypothesis, borrowed from the rabbis, but strenuously maintained by the generality of Protestants, that the Hebrew text of the Masoretic recension is perfectly incorrupt.[m] Morin's opinion was opposed by Buxtorf and Hottinger, and by other writers even of the Romish church. It has, however, been countenanced by Simon and Kennicott. The integrity, at least, of the Hebrew copies was gradually given up, and it has since been shown that they differ greatly among themselves. The Samaritan Pentateuch was first published in 1645, several years after this controversy began, by Sionita, editor of the Parisian Polyglott. This edition, sometimes called by the name of Le Jay, contains most that is in the Polyglott of Antwerp, with the addition of the Syriac and Arabic versions of the Old Testament.

26. An epoch was made in Hebrew criticism by a work of Louis Cappel, professor of that language at Saumur, the Arcanum Punctuationis Revelatum, in 1624. He maintained in this an opinion promulgated by Elias Levita, and held by the first reformers and many other Protestants of the highest authority, though contrary to that vulgar orthodoxy which is always omnivorous, that the vowel-points of Hebrew were invented by certain Jews of Tiberias in the sixth century. They had been generally deemed coeval with the language, or at least brought in by Esdras through divine inspiration. It is not surprising that such an hypothesis clashed with the prejudices of mankind, and Cappel was obliged to publish his work in Holland. The Protes-

Vowel points rejected by Cappel.

---

[k] Simon, p. 522.   [m] Id. p. 522. Eichhorn, v. 464.

testants looked upon it as too great a concession in favour of the Vulgate; which having been translated before the Masoretic punctuation, on Cappel's hypothesis, had been applied to the text, might now claim to stand on higher ground, and was not to be judged by these innovations. After twenty years the younger Buxtorf endeavoured to vindicate the antiquity of vowel-points; but it is now confessed that the victory remained with Cappel, who has been styled the father of Hebrew criticism. His principal work is the Critica Sacra, published at Paris in 1650, wherein he still farther discredits the existing manuscripts of the Hebrew Scriptures, as well as the Masoretic punctuation.[n]

27. The rabbinical literature, meaning as well the Talmud and other ancient books, as those of the later ages since the revival of intellectual pursuits among the Jews of Spain and the East, gave occupation to a considerable class of scholars. Several of these belong to England, such as Ainsworth, Godwin, Lightfoot, Selden, and Pococke. The antiquities of Judaism were illustrated by Cunæus in Jus Regium Hebræorum, 1623, and especially by Selden, both in the Uxor Hebraica and in the treatise De Jure Naturali et Gentium juxta Hebræos. But no one has left a more durable reputation in this literature than Bochart, a Protestant minister at Caen. His Geographia Sacra, published in 1646, is not the most famous of his works, but the only one which falls within this period. It displays great learning and sagacity; but it was impossible, as has been justly observed, that he could thoroughly elucidate this subject at a time when we knew comparatively little of modern Asia, and had few good books of travels. A similar observation might of course be applied to his Hierozoicon, on the animals mentioned in Scripture. Both these works, however, were much extolled in the seventeenth century.

(marginal note: Hebrew scholars.)

---

[n] Simon, Eichhorn, &c. A detailed account of this controversy about vowel-points between Cappel and the Buxtorfs will be found in the 12th volume of the Bibliothèque universelle; and a shorter précis in Eichhorn's Einleitung in das alte Testament, vol i. p. 242.

[It is not universally agreed that Cappel was altogether in the right about Hebrew vowels. Schultens was the first, according to Dathe, who proved that neither party could be reckoned wholly victorious. It seems, however, that the points now in use are acknowledged to be comparatively modern. Dathe, præfatio ad Waltoni Prolegomena, Lips. 1777, p. 27.—1847.]

28. In the Chaldee and Syriac languages, which approach
Chaldee and so closely to Hebrew that the best scholars in the
Syriac.   latter are rarely unacquainted with them, besides
the Buxtorfs, we find Ferrari, author of a Syriac lexicon,
published at Rome in 1622; Louis de Dieu of Leyden,
whose Syriac grammar appeared in 1626; and the Syriac
translation of the Old Testament in the Parisian Polyglott,
edited by Gabriel Sionita, in 1642. A Syriac college for the
Maronites of Libanus had been founded at Rome by
Gregory XIII.; but it did not as yet produce anything of
importance.

29. But a language incomparably more rich in literary
         treasures, and long neglected by Europe, began now
Arabic. to take a conspicuous place in the annals of learning.
Scaliger deserves the glory of being the first real Arabic
scholar; for Postel, Christman, and a very few more of the
sixteenth century, are hardly worth notice. His friend
Casaubon, who extols his acquirements, as usual, very highly,
devoted himself some time to this study. But Scaliger made
use of the language chiefly to enlarge his own vast sphere of
erudition. He published nothing on the subject; but his
collections became the base of Rapheling's Arabic lexicon;
and it is said that they were far more extensive than what
appears in that work. He who properly added this language
         to the domain of learning, was Erpenius, a native
Erpenius. of Gorcum, who, at an early age, had gained so unrivalled an acquaintance with the Oriental languages as to be
appointed professor of them at Leyden, in 1613. He edited
the same year the above-mentioned lexicon of Rapheling, and
published a grammar, which might not only be accounted
the first composed in Europe that deserved the name, but
became the guide to most later scholars. Erpenius gave
several other works to the world, chiefly connected with the
         Arabic version of the Scriptures.[o] Golius, his suc-
Golius. cessor in the Oriental chair at Leyden, besides
publishing a lexicon of the language, which is said to be
still the most copious, elaborate, and complete that has
appeared,[p] and several editions of Arabic writings, poetical

---

[o] Biogr. univ.
[p] Jenisch, Præfatio in Meninski Thesaurus Linguarum Orientalium, p. 110.

and historical, contributed still more extensively to bring the range of Arabian literature before the world. He enriched with a hundred and fifty manuscripts, collected in his travels, the library of Leyden, to which Scaliger had bequeathed forty.[q] The manuscripts belonging to Erpenius found their way to Cambridge; while, partly by the munificence of Laud, partly by later accessions, the Bodleian Library at Oxford became extremely rich in this line. The much larger collection in the Escurial seems to have been chiefly formed under Philip III. England was now as conspicuous in Arabian as in Hebrew learning. Selden, Greaves, and Pococke, especially the last, who was probably equal to any Oriental scholar whom Europe had hitherto produced, by translations of the historical and philosophical writings of the Saracenic period, gave a larger compass to general erudition.[r]

30. The remaining languages of the East are of less importance. The Turkish had attracted some degree of attention in the sixteenth century; but the first grammar was published by Megiser, in 1612, a very slight performance; and a better at Paris, by Du Ryer, in 1630.[s] The Persic grammar was given at Rome by Raimondi, in 1614; by Dieu, at Leyden, in 1639; by Greaves, at London, in 1641 and 1649.[t] An Armenian dictionary, by Rivoli, 1621, seems the only accession to our knowledge of that ancient language during this period.[u] Athanasius Kircher, a man of immense erudition, restored the Coptic, of which Europe had been wholly ignorant. Those farther eastward had not yet begun to enter into the studies of Europe. Nothing was known of the Indian; but some Chinese manuscripts had been brought to Rome and Madrid as early as 1580; and not long afterwards, two Jesuits, Roger and Ricci, both missionaries in China, were the first who acquired a sufficient knowledge of the language to translate from it.[x] But scarcely any farther advance took place before the middle of the century.

Other Eastern languages.

---

q Biogr. univ.
r Jenisch. Eichhorn. Biogr. universelle. Biogr. Britannica.
s Eichhorn, v. 367.
t Id. 320.
u Id. 351.
x Id. 64.

Sect. IV.

On Geography and History.

31. Purchas, an English clergyman, imbued by nature, like
Purchas's Hakluyt, with a strong bias towards geographical
Pilgrim. studies, after having formed an extensive library in
that department, and consulted, as he professes, above 1200
authors, published the first volume of his Pilgrim, a collection of voyages in all parts of the world, in 1613; four more
followed in 1625. The accuracy of this useful compiler has
been denied by those who have had better means of knowledge, and probably is inferior to that of Hakluyt; but his
labour was far more comprehensive. The Pilgrim was at all
events a great source of knowledge to the contemporaries
of Purchas.[y]

32. Olearius was ambassador from the Duke of Holstein to
Olearius and Muscovy and Persia from 1633 to 1639. His travels,
Pietro della
Valle. in German, were published in 1647, and have been
several times reprinted and translated. He has well described
the barbarism of Russia and the despotism of Persia; he is
diffuse and episodical, but not wearisome; he observes well
and relates faithfully; all who have known the countries he
has visited are said to speak well of him.[z] Pietro della Valle
is a far more amusing writer. He has thrown his travels
over Syria and Persia into the form of letters written from
time to time, and which he professes to have recovered from
his correspondents. This perhaps is not a very probable
story, both on account of the length of the letters, and the
want of that reference to the present time and to small passing events, which such as are authentic commonly exhibit.
His observations, however, on all the countries he visited,
especially Persia, are apparently consistent with the knowledge we have obtained from later travellers. Gibbon says
that none have better observed Persia, but his vanity and
prolixity are insufferable. Yet I think that Della Valle can

---

[y] Biogr. univ.   Pinkerton's Collection of Voyages and Travels.   The latter
does not value Purchas highly for correctness.
[z] Biogr. universelle.

hardly be reckoned tedious; and if he is a little egotistical, the usual and almost laudable characteristic of travellers, this gives a liveliness and racy air to his narrative. What his wife, the Lady Maani, an Assyrian Christian, whom he met with at Bagdad, and who accompanied him through his long wanderings, may really have been, we can only judge from his eulogies on her beauty, her fidelity, and her courage; but she throws an air of romance over his adventures, not unpleasing to the reader. The travels of Pietro della Valle took place from 1614 to 1626; but the book was first published at Rome in 1650, and has been translated into different languages.

33. The Lexicon Geographicum of Ferrari, in 1627, was the chief general work on geography; it is alphabetical, and contains 9600 articles. The errors have Lexicon of Ferrari. been corrected in later editions, so that the first would probably be required in order to estimate the knowledge of its author's age.[a]

34. The best measure, perhaps, of geographical science, are the maps published from time to time, as perfectly for the most part, we may presume, as their Maps of Blaew. editors could render them. If we compare the map of the world in the 'Theatrum Orbis Terrarum sive Novus Atlas' of Blaew in 1648 with that of the edition of Ortelius published at Antwerp in 1612, the improvements will not appear exceedingly great. America is still separated from Asia by the straits of Anian, about lat. 60; but the coast to the south is made to trend away more than before; on the N.E. coast we find Davis's Sea, and Estotiland has vanished to give way to Greenland. Canada continues to be most inaccurately laid down, though there is a general idea of lakes and rivers better than in Ortelius. Scandinavia is far better, and tolerably correct. In the South, Tierra del Fuego terminates in Cape Horn, instead of being united to Terra Australis; but in the East, Corea appears as an oblong island; the Sea of Aral is not set down, and the wall of China is placed north of the fiftieth parallel. India is very much too small, and the shape of the Caspian Sea is wholly inaccurate. But a

---

[a] Salfi, xi. 418. Biogr. universelle.

comparison with the map of Hakluyt, mentioned in our second volume, will not exhibit so much superiority of Blaew's Atlas. The latter, however, shows more knowledge of the interior country, especially in North America, and a better outline in many parts of the Asiatic coast. The maps of particular regions in Europe are on a large scale, and numerous. Speed's maps, 1646, appear by no means inferior to those of Blaew; but several of the errors are the same. Considering the progress of commerce, especially that of the Dutch, during this half century, we may rather be surprised at the defective state of these maps.

35. Two histories of general reputation were published in the Italian language during these fifty years; one of the civil wars in France by Davila, in 1630, and another of those in Flanders by Cardinal Bentivoglio. Both of these had the advantage of interesting subjects; they had been sufficiently conversant with the actors to know much and to judge well, without that particular responsibility which tempts an historian to prevaricate. They were both men of cool and sedate tempers, accustomed to think policy a game in which the strong play with the weak, obtuse, especially the former, in moral sentiment, but on this account not inclined to calumniate an opposite party, or to withhold admiration from intellectual power. Both these histories may be read over and over with pleasure; if Davila is too refined, if he is not altogether faithful, if his style wants the elegance of some older Italians, he more than redeems all this by the importance of his subject, the variety and picturesqueness of his narration, and the acuteness of his reflections. Bentivoglio is reckoned, as a writer, among the very first of his age.

Davila and Bentivoglio.

36. The History of the War of Granada, that is, the rebellion of the Moriscos in 1565, by the famous Diego de Mendoza, was published posthumously in 1610. It is placed by the Spaniards themselves on a level with the most renowned of the ancients. The French have now their first general historian, Mezeray, a writer esteemed for his lively style and bold sense, but little read, of course, in an age like the last or our own, which have demanded an exactness in matter of fact, and an extent

Mendoza's Wars of Granada.

Mezeray.

of historical erudition, which was formerly unknown. We
now began, in England, to cultivate historical com- English
position, and with so much success, that the present historians.
period was far more productive of such works as deserve
remembrance than a whole century that next followed.
But the most considerable of these have already English
been mentioned. Lord Herbert of Cherbury's His- histories.
tory of Henry VIII. ought here to be added to the list, as a
book of good authority, relatively at least to any that preceded, and written in a manly and judicious spirit.[b] Camden's
Life of Elizabeth is also a solid and valuable history. Bacon's
Life of Henry VII. is something more; it is the first instance
in our language of the application of philosophy to reasoning
on public events in the manner of the ancients and the
Italians. Praise upon Henry is too largely bestowed; but it
was in the nature of Bacon to admire too much a crafty and
selfish policy; and he thought also, no doubt, that so near
an ancestor of his own sovereign should not be treated with
severe impartiality.

Sect. V.

On the General State of Literature.

37. Of the Italian and other continental universities, we have
little to say beyond what may be collected from the Universi-
general tenor of this literary history, that they ties.
contributed little to those departments of knowledge to which
we have paid most attention, and adhering pertinaciously
to their ancient studies, were left behind in the advance of
the human mind. They were, indeed, not less crowded with
scholars than before, being the necessary and prescribed road
to lucrative professions. In theology, law, and medicine,

---

[b] [Lord Herbert's Life of Henry VIII.
was composed with great assistance from
Thomas Masters, of a Gloucestershire
family, who collected materials; whether
he wrote any part is not clear. Wood's
Athenæ Oxonienses (Bliss's edition), vol.
iii. p. 79.—1853.]

sciences, the two former of which, at least, did not claim to be progressive, they might sustain a respectable posture; in philosophy, and even in polite letters, they were less prominent.

38. The English universities are in one point of view very different from those of the rest of Europe. Their great endowments created a resident class, neither teachers nor students, who might devote an unbroken leisure to learning with the advantage of that command of books which no other course of life could have afforded. It is true that in no age has the number of these been great; but the diligence of a few is enough to cast a veil over the laziness of many. The century began with an extraordinary piece of fortune to the university of Oxford, which formed in the seventeenth century, whatever it may since have been, one great cause of her literary distinction. Sir Thomas Bodley, with a munificence which has rendered his name more immortal than the foundation of a family could have done, bestowed on the university a library collected by him at great costs, building a magnificent room for its reception, and bequeathed large sums for its increase. The building was completed in 1606; and Casaubon has, very shortly afterwards, given such an account of the university itself, as well as of the Bodleian library, as will perhaps be interesting to the reader, though it contains some of those mistakes into which a stranger is apt to fall.

Bodleian library founded.

39. 'I wrote you word,' he says in July, 1613, to one of his correspondents, ' a month since, that I was going to Oxford in order to visit that university and its library, of which I had heard much. Every thing proved beyond my expectation. The colleges are numerous, most of them very rich. The revenues of these colleges maintain above two thousand students, generally of respectable parentage, and some even of the first nobility; for what we call the habits of pedagogues (pædagogica vitæ ratio) is not found in these English colleges. Learning is here cultivated in a liberal style; the heads of houses live handsomely, even splendidly, like men of rank. Some of them can spend ten thousand livres [about 1000l. at that time, if I mistake not] by the year. I much approved the mode in which pecuniary

Casaubon's account of Oxford.

concerns are kept distinct from the business of learning.[c] Many still are found, who emulate the liberality of their predecessors. Hence new buildings rise every day; even some new colleges are raised from the foundation; some are enlarged, such as that of Merton, over which Saville presides, and several more. There is one begun by Cardinal Wolsey, which if it should be completed, will be worthy of the greatest admiration. But he left at his death many buildings which he had begun in an unfinished state, and which no one expects to see complete. None of the colleges, however, attracted me so much as the Bodleian library, a work rather for a king than a private man. It is certain that Bodley, living or dead, must have expended 200,000 livres on that building. The ground plot is the figure of the letter T. The part which represents the perpendicular stem was formerly built by some prince, and is very handsome; the rest was added by Bodley with no less magnificence. In the lower part is a divinity school, to which perhaps nothing in Europe is comparable. It is vaulted with peculiar skill. The upper story is the library itself, very well built, and fitted with an immense quantity of books. Do not imagine that such plenty of manuscripts can be found here, as in the royal library (of Paris); there are not a few manuscripts in England, but nothing to what the king possesses. But the number of printed books is wonderful, and increasing every year; for Bodley has bequeathed a considerable revenue for that purpose. As long as I remained at Oxford, I passed whole days in the library; for books cannot be taken out, but the library is open to all scholars for seven or eight hours every day. You might always see therefore many of these greedily enjoying the banquet prepared for them, which gave me no small pleasure.'[d]

40. The Earl of Pembroke, Selden, and above all, Archbishop Laud, greatly improved the Bodleian library. It became, especially through the munificence of that prelate, extremely rich in Oriental manuscripts. The Duke of Buckingham presented a collection made by Erpenius to the public

---

[c] Res studiosorum et rationes separatæ sunt, quod valde probavi. I have given the translation which seemed best; but I may be mistaken.
[d] Casaub. Epist. 899.

library at Cambridge, which, though far behind that of the
sister university, was enriched by many donations, and became very considerable.   Usher formed the library of Trinity
College, Dublin ; an university founded on the English model,
with noble revenues, and a corporate body of fellows and
scholars to enjoy them.

41. A catalogue of the Bodleian library was published by
Catalogue   James in 1620.   It contains about 20,000 articles.
of Bodleian
library.   Of these, no great number are in English, and such
as there are chiefly of a later date than the year 1600 ; Bodley, perhaps, had been rather negligent of poetry and plays.
The editor observes that there were in the library three or
four thousand volumes in modern languages.   This catalogue
not classed, but alphabetical; which James mentions as
something new, remarking at the same time the difficulty of
classification, and that in the German catalogues we find
grammars entered under the head of philosophy.   One published by Draud, Bibliotheca Classica, sive Catalogus Offici-
nalis, Frankfort, 1625, is hardly worth mention.   It professes
to be a general list of printed books ; but as the number
seems to be not more than 30,000, all in Latin, it must be
very defective.   About two-fifths of the whole are theological.
A catalogue of the library of Sion College, founded in 1631,
was printed in 1650 ; it contains eight or nine thousand
volumes.[e]

42. The library of Leyden had been founded by the first
Continental   prince of Orange.   Scaliger bequeathed his own to
libraries.   it ; and it obtained the oriental manuscripts of Golius.   A catalogue had been printed by Peter Bertius as early
as 1597.[f]   Many public and private libraries either now began
to be formed in France, or received great accessions ; among
the latter, those of the historian De Thou, and the president
Seguier.   No German library, after that of Vienna, had been
so considerable as one formed in the course of several ages
by the Electors Palatine at Heidelberg.   It contained many
rare manuscripts.   On the capture of the city by Tilly in
1622, he sent a number of these to Rome, and they long
continued to sleep in the recesses of the Vatican.   Napoleon,

---

• In Museo Britannico.   f Jugler, Hist. Litteraria, c. 3.   g Id. ibid.

emulous of such a precedent, obtained thirty-eight of the
Heidelberg manuscripts by the treaty of Tolentino, which
were transmitted to Paris. On the restitution of these in
1815, it was justly thought that prescription was not to be
pleaded by Rome for the rest of the plunder, especially when
she was recovering what she had lost by the same right of
spoliation; and the whole collection has been replaced in the
library of Heidelberg.

43. The Italian academies have been often represented as
partaking in the alleged decline of literary spirit Italian aca-
during the first part of the seventeenth century. demies.
Nor is this reproach a new one. Boccalini, after the commencement of this period, tells us that these institutions once
so famous had fallen into decay, their ardent zeal in literary
exercises and discussions having abated by time, so that while
they had once been frequented by private men, and esteemed
by princes, they were now abandoned and despised by all.
They petition Apollo, therefore, in a chapter of his Ragguagli
di Parnasso, for a reform. But the god replies that all things
have their old age and decay, and as nothing can prevent the
neatest pair of slippers from wearing out, so nothing can rescue academies from a similar lot; hence he can only advise
them to suppress the worst, and to supply their places by
others.[h] If only such a counsel were required, the institution of academies in general would not perish. And in fact
we really find that while some societies of this class came to
nothing, as is always the case with self-constituted bodies,
the seventeenth century had births of its own to boast, not
inferior to the older progeny of the last age. The Academy
of Humorists at Rome was one of these. It arose casually
at the marriage of a young nobleman of the Mancini family,
and took the same line as many have done, reciting verses
and discourses, or occasionally representing plays. The tragedy of Demetrius, by Rocco, one of this academy, is reckoned
among the best of the age. The Apatisti of Florence took
their name from Fioretti, who had assumed the appellation
of Udeno Nisielo, Academico Apatista. The Rozzi of Siena,
whom the government had suppressed in 1568, revived again

---

[h] Ragg. xviii. c. 1.

in 1605, and rivalled another society of the same city, the Intronati. The former especially dedicated their time to pastoral in the rustic dialect (commedia rusticale), a species of dramatic writing that might amuse at the moment, and was designed for no other end, though several of these farces are extant.[i]

44. The Academy Della Crusca, which had more solid objects for the advantage of letters in view, has been mentioned in another place. But that of the Lincei, founded by Frederic Cesi, stands upon a higher ground than any of the rest. This young man was born at Rome in 1585, son of the Duke of Acqua Sparta, a father and a family known only for their pride and ignorance. But nature had created in Cesi a philosophic mind; in conjunction with a few of similar dispositions, he gave his entire regard to science, and projected himself, at the age of eighteen, an academy, that is, a private association of friends for intellectual pursuits, which, with reference to their desire of piercing with acute discernment into the depths of truth, he denominated the Lynxes. Their device was that animal, with its eyes turned towards heaven, and tearing a Cerberus with its claws; thus intimating that they were prepared for war against error and falsehood. The church, always suspicious, and inclined to make common cause with all established tenets, gave them some trouble, though neither theology nor politics entered into their scheme. This embraced, as in their academies, poetry and elegant literature, but physical science was their peculiar object. Porta, Galileo, Colonna, and many other distinguished men, both of Italy and the Transalpine countries, were enrolled among the Lynxes; and Cesi is said to have framed rather a visionary plan of a general combination of philosophers, in the manner of the Pythagoreans, which should extend itself to every part of Europe. The constitutions of this imaginary order were even published in 1624; they are such as could not have been realised, but from the organisation and secrecy that seem to have been their elements, might not improbably have drawn down a prosecution upon themselves, or even rendered the name of philosophy

The Lincei.

---

[i] Salfi, vol. xii.

obnoxious.   Cesi died in 1630, and his academy of Lynxes
did not long survive the loss of their chief.[k]

45. The tide of public opinion had hitherto set regularly
in one direction; ancient times, ancient learning, Prejudice
ancient wisdom and virtue, were regarded with un- for antiquity di-
qualified veneration; the very course of nature was minished.
hardly believed to be the same, and a common degeneracy
was thought to have overspread the earth and its inhabitants.
This had been at its height in the first century after the
revival of letters, the prejudice in favour of the past, always
current with the old, who affect to dictate the maxims of experience, conspiring with the genuine lustre of classical
literature and ancient history, which dazzled the youthful
scholar.   But this aristocracy of learning was now assailed
by a new power which had risen up in sufficient strength to dispute the pre-eminence. We, said Bacon, are the true ancients ;
what we call the antiquity of the world was but its infancy.
This thought, equally just and brilliant, was caught up and
echoed by many; it will be repeatedly found in later works.
It became a question whether the moderns had not really
left behind their progenitors; and though it has been hinted,
that a dwarf on a giant's shoulders sees farther than the
giant, this is, in one sense, to concede the point in dispute.[m]

46. Tassoni was one of the first who combated the established prejudice by maintaining that modern times are not
inferior to ancient; it well became his intrepid disposition.[n]
But Lancilotti, an Italian ecclesiastic, and member of several
academies, pursued this subject in an elaborate work, intended to prove—first, that the world was neither morally
worse nor more afflicted by calamities than it had been ;
secondly, that the intellectual abilities of mankind had not
degenerated.   It bears the general title, L'Hoggidi, To-Day;
and is throughout a ridicule of those whom he calls Hoggi-
diani, perpetual declaimers against the present state of
things.   He is a very copious and learned writer, and no

---

[k] Salfi, xi. 102. Tiraboschi, xi. 42, 243.
[m] Ac quemamodum pygmæus hu-
meris gigantis insidens longius quam
gigas prospicere, neque tamen se gigante
majorem habere aut sibi multum tri-
buere potest, ita nos veterum laboribus

vigiliisque in nostros usus conversis
adjicere aliquid, non supercilia tollere,
aut parvi facere, qui ante nos fuerunt,
debemus. Cyprianus, Vita Campanellæ,
p. 15.
[n] Salfi, xi. 381.

friend to antiquity; each chapter being entitled Disinganno,
and intended to remove some false prejudice. The first part
of this work appeared in 1623, the second, after the author's
death, not till 1658. Lancilotti wrote another book with
somewhat a similar object, entitled Farfalloni degl' Antichi
Istorici, and designed to turn the ancient historians into
ridicule; with a good deal of pleasantry, but chiefly on
account of stories which no one in his time would have
believed. The same ground was taken soon afterwards by
an English divine, George Hakewill, in his ' Apology, or
Declaration of the Power and Providence of God in the
Government of the World,' published in 1627. This is designed to prove that there is not that perpetual and universal
decay in nature which many suppose. It is an elaborate
refutation of many absurd notions which seem to have prevailed; some believing that even physical nature, the sun
and stars, the earth and waters, were the worse for wear.
A greater number thought this true of man; his age, his
size, his strength, his powers of mind, were all supposed to
have been deteriorated. Hakewill patiently and learnedly
refuted all this. The moral character of antiquity he shows
to be much exaggerated, animadverting especially on the
Romans. The most remarkable, and certainly the most disputable chapters, are those which relate to the literary merits
of ancient and modern times. He seems to be one of the
first who ventured to put in a claim for the latter. In this
he anticipates Wotton, who had more to say. Hakewill goes
much too far in calling Sidney's Arcadia ' nothing inferior
to the choicest piece among the ancients; ' and even thinks
' he should not much wrong Virgil by matching him with
Du Bartas.' The learning shown in this treatise is very
extensive, but Hakewill has no taste, and cannot perceive
any real superiority in the ancients. Compared with Lancilotti, he is much inferior in liveliness, perhaps even in
learning; but I have not observed that he has borrowed
anything from the Italian, whose publication was but four
years earlier.

47. Browne's Inquiry into Vulgar Errors displays a great
deal of erudition, but scarcely raises a high notion
of Browne himself as a philosopher, or of the state

Browne's
Vulgar
Errors.

of physical knowledge in England. The errors he indicates
are such as none but illiterate persons, we should think, were
likely to hold; and I believe that few on the continent, so
late as 1646, would have required to have them exploded
with such an ostensation of proof. Who did not know that
the phœnix is a fable? Browne was where the learned in
Europe had been seventy years before, and seems to have
been one of those who saturate their minds with bad books
till they have little room for anything new that is better. A
man of so much credulity and such an irregular imagination
as Browne was almost sure to believe in witchcraft and all
sorts of spiritual agencies. In no respect did he go in
advance of his age, unless we make an exception for his
declaration against persecution. He seems to have been
fond of those trifling questions which the bad taste of the
schoolmen and their contemporaries introduced; as whether
a man has fewer ribs than a woman, whether Adam and Eve
had navels, whether Methusaleh was the oldest man; the
problems of children put to adults. With a strong curiosity
and a real love of truth, Browne is a striking instance of a
merely empirical mind; he is at sea with sails and a rudder,
but without a compass or log-book; and has so little notion
of any laws of nature, or of any inductive reasoning either
as to efficient or final causes, that he never seems to judge
anything to be true or false except by experiment.

48. In concluding our review of the sixteenth century, we
selected Pinelli, as a single model of the literary cha- Life and
racter which, loving and encouraging knowledge, character of Peiresc.
is yet too little distinguished by any writings to fall naturally
within the general subject of these volumes. The period
which we now bring to a close will furnish us with a much
more considerable instance. Nicolas Peiresc was born in
1580, of an ancient family in Provence, which had for some
generations held judicial offices in the parliament of Aix.
An extraordinary thirst for every kind of knowledge characterised Peiresc from his earliest youth, and being of a weak
constitution, as well as ample fortune, though he retained,
like his family, an honourable post in the parliament, his
time was principally devoted to the multifarious pursuits of
an enlightened scholar. Like Pinelli, he delighted in the

rarities of art and antiquity; but his own superior genius, and the vocation of that age towards science, led him on to a far more extensive field of inquiry. We have the life of Peiresc written by his countryman and intimate friend Gassendi; and no one who has any sympathy with science or with a noble character will read it without pleasure. Few books, indeed, of that period are more full of casual information.

49. Peiresc travelled much in the early part of his life; he was at Rome in 1600, and came to England and Holland in 1606. The hard drinking, even of our learned men,[o] disconcerted his southern stomach; but he was repaid by the society of Camden, Saville, and Cotton. The king received Peiresc courteously, and he was present at the opening of parliament. On returning to his native province, he began to form his extensive collections of marbles and medals, but especially of natural history in every line. He was, perhaps, the first who observed the structure of zoophytes, though he seems not to have suspected their animal nature. Petrifactions occupied much of his time; and he framed a theory of them which Gassendi explains at length, but which, as might be expected, is not the truth.[p] Botany was among his favourite studies, and Europe owes to him, according to Gassendi, the Indian jessamine, the gourd of Mecca, the real Egyptian papyrus, which is not that described by Prosper Alpinus. He first planted ginger, as well as many other Oriental plants, in an European garden, and also the cocoanut, from which, however, he could not obtain fruit.

50. Peiresc was not less devoted to astronomy: he had no sooner heard of the discoveries of Galileo than he set himself to procure a telescope, and had in the course of the same year, 1610, the pleasure of observing the moons of Jupiter. It even occurred to him that these might serve to ascertain the longitude, though he did not follow up the idea. Galileo indeed, with a still more inventive mind, and with more of mathematics, seems to have stood in the way of Peiresc. He took, as far as appears, no great pains to publish his researches, contenting himself with the intercourse of literary

---

• Gassendi, Vita Peirescii, p. 51.   [p] P. 147.

men who passed near him, or with whom he could maintain correspondence. Several discoveries are ascribed to him by Gassendi; of their originality I cannot venture to decide. 'From his retreat,' says another biographer, 'Peiresc gave more encouragement to letters than any prince, more even than the Cardinal de Richelieu, who some time afterwards founded the French Academy. Worthy to have been called by Bayle the *attorney-general* of literature, he kept always on the level of progressive science, published manuscripts at his own expense, followed the labours of the learned throughout Europe, and gave them an active impulse by his own aid.' Scaliger, Salmasius, Holstenius, Kircher, Mersenne, Grotius, Valois, are but some of the great names of Europe whom he assisted by various kinds of liberality.[q] He published nothing himself, but some of his letters have been collected.

51. The character of Peiresc was amiable and unreserved among his friends; but he was too much absorbed in the love of knowledge for insipid conversation. For the same reason, his biographer informs us, he disliked the society of women, gaining nothing valuable from the trifles and scandal upon which alone they could converse.[r] Possibly the society of both sexes at Aix, in the age of Peiresc, was such as, with no excessive fastidiousness, he might avoid. In his eagerness for new truths, he became somewhat credulous; an error not perhaps easy to be avoided, while the accumulation of facts proceeded more rapidly than the ascertainment of natural laws. But for a genuine liberality of mind and extensive attainments in knowledge very few can be compared to Peiresc; nor among those who have resembled him in this employment of weath and leisure, do I know that any names have descended to posterity with equal lustre, except our two countrymen of the next generation, who approached so nearly to his character and course of life, Boyle and Evelyn.

q Biogr. universelle.   r Gassendi, p. 219.

PART IV.

ON THE LITERATURE OF THE SECOND HALF OF THE
SEVENTEENTH CENTURY.

CHAPTER I.

HISTORY OF ANCIENT LITERATURE IN EUROPE, FROM
1650 TO 1700.

SECT. I.

Dutch Scholars—Jesuit and Jansenist Philologers—Delphin Editions—
French Scholars—English Scholars—Bentley.

1. THE death of Salmasius about the beginning of this period left a chasm in critical literature which no one was James Frederic Gronovius. equal to fill. But the nearest to this giant of philology was James Frederic Gronovius, a native of Hamburg, but drawn, like several more of his countrymen, to the universities of Holland, the peculiarly learned state of Europe through the seventeenth century. The principal labours of Gronovius were those of correcting the text of Latin writers; in Greek we find very little due to him.[a] His notes form an useful and considerable part of those which are collected in what are generally styled the Variorum editions, published, chiefly after 1660, by the Dutch booksellers. These contain selections from the older critics, some of them, especially those first edited, indifferently made and often mutilated; others with more attention to preserve entire the original notes. These however are for the most part only critical, as if explanatory observations were below the notice of an editor; though, as Le Clerc says, those of Manutius on Cicero's epistles cost him much more time than modern editors have given to their conjectures.[b] In general, the Variorum editions were not greatly prized, with the exception of those by the two Gronovii and Grævius.[c]

---

[a] Baillet, Critiques Grammairiens, n. 548. Blount. Biogr. univ.
[b] Parrhasiana, i. 233.

[c] A list of the Variorum editions will be found in Baillet, Critiques Grammairiens, n. 604.

2. The place of the elder Gronovius, in the latter part of
James Gro- this present period, was filled by his son. James
novius. Gronovius, by indefatigable labour, and by a greater
number of editions which bear his name, may be reckoned,
if not a greater philologer, one not less celebrated than his
father. He was at least a better Greek critic, and in this
language, though far below those who were about to arise,
and who did in fact eclipse him long before his death, Bentley
and Burman, he kept a high place for several years.[d] Græ-
Grævius. vius, another German, whom the Dutch universities
had attracted and retained, contributed to the Variorum editions, chiefly those of Latin authors, an erudition
not less copious than that of any contemporary scholar.

3. The philological character of Gerard Vossius himself,
Isaac if we might believe some partial testimonies, fell
Vossius. short of that of his son Isaac; whose observations
on Pomponius Mela, and an edition of Catullus, did him extraordinary credit, and have placed him among the first philologers of this age. He was of a more lively genius, and perhaps
hardly less erudition, than his father, but with a paradoxical
judgment, and has certainly rendered much less service to
letters.[e] Another son of a great father, Nicolas Heinsius,
has by none been placed on a level with him; but his editions
of Prudentius and Claudian are better than any that had
preceded them.

4. Germany fell lower and lower in classical literature. A
Decline of writer as late as 1714 complains, that only modern
German books of Latin were taught in the schools, and that
learning. the students in the universities despised all grammatical
learning. The study 'not of our own language, which we
entirely neglect, but of French,' he reckons among the causes
of this decay in ancient learning; the French translations of
the classics led many to imagine that the original could be
dispensed with.[f] Ezekiel Spanheim, envoy from the court of
Brandenburg to that of Louis XIV., was a distin-
Spanheim. guished exception; his edition of Julian, and his
notes on several other writers, attest an extensive learning,

---

[d] Baillet, n. 548. Niceron, ii. 177.
[e] Niceron, vol. xiii.

[f] Burckhardt, De Linguæ Latinæ
hodie neglectæ Causis Oratio, p. 34.

which has still preserved his name in honour.   As the century
drew nigh to its close, Germany began to revive ; a few men
of real philological learning, especially Fabricius, appeared as
heralds of those greater names which adorn her literary annals
in the next age.

5. The Jesuits had long been conspicuously the classical
scholars of France; in their colleges the purest and   Jesuit col-
most elegant Latinity was supposed to be found;   leges in
France.
they had early cultivated these graces of literature, while all
polite writing was confined to the Latin language, and they
still preserved them in its comparative disuse.   'The Jesuits,'
Huet says, ' write and speak Latin well, but their style is
almost always too rhetorical.   This is owing to their keeping
regencies [an usual phrase for academical exercises] from
their early youth, which causes them to speak incessantly in
public, and become accustomed to a sustained and polished
style, above the tone of common subjects.'[g]   Jouvancy, whose
Latin orations were published in 1700, has had no equal, if
we may trust a panegyrist, since Maffei and Muretus.[h]

6. The Jansenists appeared ready at one time to wrest this
palm from their inveterate foes.   Lancelot threw   Port Royal
some additional lustre round Port Royal by the   writers.
Lancelot.
Latin and Geeek grammars, which are more frequently called
by the name of that famous cloister than by his own.   Both
were received with great approbation in the French schools,
except, I suppose, where the Jesuits predominated, and their
reputation lasted for many years.   They were never so popular, though well known, in this country.   'The public,' says
Baillet of the Greek grammar, which is rather the more
eminent of the two, 'bears witness that nothing of its kind
has been more finished.   The order is clear and concise.   We
find in it many remarks, both judicious and important for
the full knowledge of the language.   Though Lancelot has
chiefly followed Caninius, Sylburgius, Sanctius, and Vossius,
his arrangement is new, and he has selected what is most
valuable in their works.'[i]   In fact, he professes to advance
nothing of his own, being more indebted, he says, to Caninius
than to any one else.   The method of Clenardus he disap-

---

[g] Huetiana, p. 71.   [h] Biogr. univ.   [i] Baillet, n. 714.

proves, and thinks that of Ramus intricate. He adopts the
division into three declensions. But his notions of the proper
meaning of the tenses are strangely confused and erroneous :
several other mistakes of an obvious nature, as we should
now say, will occur in his syntax; and upon the whole the
Port Royal grammar does not give us a high idea of the
critical knowledge of the seventeenth century, as to the more
difficult language of antiquity.

7. The Latin, on the other hand, had been so minutely
Latin gram- and laboriously studied, that little more than glean-
mars.
Perizonius. ings after a great harvest could be obtained. The
Aristarchus of Vossius, and his other grammatical works,
though partly not published till this period, have been mentioned in the last volume. Perizonius, a professor at Frane-
ker, and in many respects one of the most learned of this
age, published a good edition of the Minerva of Sanctius in
1687. This celebrated grammar had become very scarce, as
well as that of Scioppius, which contained nothing but remarks upon Sanctius. Perizonius combined the two with
notes more ample than those of Scioppius, and more bold in
differing from the Spanish grammarian.

8. If other editions of the classical authors have been pre-
Delphin   ferred by critics, none, at least of this period, have
editions.   been more celebrated than those which Louis XIV.,
at the suggestion of the Duke de Montausier, caused to be
prepared for the use of the Dauphin. The object in view was
to elucidate the Latin writers, both by a continual gloss in the
margin, and by such notes as should bring a copious mass of
ancient learning to bear on the explanation, not of the more
difficult passages alone, but of all those in which an ordinary
reader might require some aid. The former of these is less
useful and less satisfactorily executed than the latter ; as for
the notes, it must be owned that, with much that is superfluous even to tolerable scholars, they bring together a great
deal of very serviceable illustration. The choice of authors
as well as of editors was referred to Huet, who fixed the
number of the former at forty. The idea of an index, on a
more extensive plan than in any earlier editions, was also due
to Huet, who had designed to fuse those of each work into

one more general, as a standing historical analysis of the
Latin language.[k] These editions are of very unequal merit,
as might be expected from the number of persons employed;
a list of whom will be found in Baillet.[m]

9. Tanaquil Faber, thus better known than by his real name,
Tanneguy le Fevre, a man learned, animated, not
fearing the reproach of paradox, acquired a considerable name among French critics by several editions, as well
as by other writings in philology. But none of his literary
productions were so celebrated as his daughter, Anne le Fevre,
afterwards Madame Dacier. The knowledge of Greek, though
once not very uncommon in a woman, had become prodigious
in the days of Louis XIV.; and when this distinguished
lady taught Homer and Sappho to speak French prose, she
appeared a phœnix in the eyes of her countrymen. She was
undoubtedly a person of very rare talents and estimable character; her translations are numerous and reputed to be
correct, though Niceron has observed that she did not raise
Homer in the eyes of those who were not prejudiced in his
favour.[n] Her husband was a scholar of kindred mind and
the same pursuits. Their union was facetiously called the
wedding of Latin and Greek. But each of this learned
couple was skilled in both languages. Dacier was a great
translator; his Horace is perhaps the best known of his versions; but the Poetics of Aristotle have done him most
honour. The Daciers had to fight the battle of antiquity
against a generation both ignorant and vain-glorious, yet
keen-sighted in the detection of blemishes, and disposed to
avenge the wrongs of their fathers, who had been trampled
upon by pedants, with the help of a new pedantry, that of the
court and the mode. With great learning they had a competent share of good sense, but not perhaps a sufficiently
discerning taste, or liveliness enough of style, to maintain a
cause that had so many prejudices of the world now enlisted
against it.[o]

Marginal note: Le Fevre and the Daciers.

[k] Huetiana, p. 92.

[m] Critiques Grammairiens, n. 605.

[n] [It has been remarked, that her
edition of Callimachus, with critical
notes, ought to have been mentioned, as

the *chef-d'œuvre* of one whom Bentley
calls ' fœminarum doctissima.'—1847.]

[o] Baillet. Niceron, vol. iii. Bibliothèque universelle, x. 295, xxii. 176,
xxiv. 241, 261. Biogr. univ.

10. Henry Valois might have been mentioned before for
his edition of Ammianus Marcellinus in 1636, which
established his philological reputation. Many other
works in the same line of criticism followed. He is
among the great ornaments of learning in this period.
Nor was France destitute of others that did her honour.
Cotelier, it is said, deserved by his knowledge of Greek to be
placed on a level with the great scholars of former times.
Yet there seems to have been some decline, at least towards
the close of the century, in that prodigious erudition which
had distinguished the preceding period. 'For we know no
one,' says Le Clerc, about 1699, ' who equals in learning, in
diligence, and in the quantity of his works, the Scaligers,
the Lipsii, the Casaubons, the Salmasii, the Meursii, the
Vossii, the Seldens, the Gronovii, and many more of former
times.'p Though perhaps in this reflection there was something of the customary bias against the present generation,
we must own that the writings of scholars were less massive,
and consequently gave less apparent evidence of industry,
than formerly. But in classical philology, at least, a better
day was about to arise, and the first omen of it came from a
country not yet much known in that literature.

Henry Valois. Complaints of decay of learning.

11. It has been observed in a former passage, that while
England was very far from wanting men of extensive
erudition, she had not been at all eminent in ancient
or classical literature. The proof which the absence of critical writings, or even of any respectable editions, furnishes,
appears weighty; nor can it be repelled by sufficient testimony. In the middle of the century James Duport, Greek
professor at Cambridge, deserves honour by standing almost
alone. 'He appears,' says a late biographer, ' to have been
the main instrument by which literature was upheld in this
university during the civil disturbances of the seventeenth
century; and though little known at present, he enjoyed an
almost transcendent reputation for a great length of time
among his contemporaries as well as in the generation which

English learning. Duport.

---

p Parrhasiana, vol. i. p. 225. Je viens
d'apprendre, says Charles Patin in one
of his letters, que M. Gronovius est
mort à Leyden. Il restoit presque tout
seul du nombre des savans d'Hollande.
Il n'est plus dans ce pais-là des gens
faits comme Jos. Scaliger, Baudius,
Heinsius, Salmasius, et Grotius. (P. 582.)

immediately succeeded.'[q]   Duport, however, has little claim
to this reputation, except by translations of the writings of
Solomon, the book of Job, and the Psalms, into Greek hexameters; concerning which his biographer gently intimates
that 'his notions of versification were not formed in a severe
or critical school;' and by what has certainly been more
esteemed, his Homeri Gnomologia, which Le Clerc and Bishop
Monk agree to praise, as very useful to the student of Homer.
Duport gave also some lectures on Theophrastus about 1656,
which were afterwards published in Needham's edition of
that author. 'In these,' says Le Clerc, 'he explains words
with much exactness, and so as to show that he understood
the analogy of the language.'[r]   'They are, upon the whole,
calculated,' says the Bishop of Gloucester, 'to give no unfavourable opinion of the state of Greek learning in the university at that memorable crisis.'

12. It cannot be fairly said that our universities declined
in general learning under the usurpation of Crom-   Greek not
well. They contained, on the contrary, more extra-   much
                                                      studied.
ordinary men than in any earlier period, but not generally
well affected to the predominant power. Greek however
seems not much to have flourished, even immediately after
the Restoration. Barrow, who was chosen Greek professor
in 1660, complains that no one attended his lectures. 'I sit
like an Attic owl,' he says, 'driven out from the society of
all other birds.'[s]   According indeed to the scheme of study
retained from a more barbarous age, no knowledge of the
Greek language appears to have been required from the students, as necessary for their degrees. And if we may believe
a satirical writer of the time of Charles II., but one whose
satire had great circulation and was not taxed with falsehood,

---

[q] Museum Criticum, vol. ii. p. 672
(by the Bishop of Gloucester and
Bristol).

[r] Bibliothèque choisie, xxv. 18.

[s] See a biographical memoir of Barrow prefixed to Hughes's edition of his
works. This contains a sketch of studies
pursued in the university of Cambridge
from the twelfth to the seventeenth century, brief indeed, but such as I should
have been glad to have seen before.
P. 62. No alteration in the statutes,

so far as they related to study, was
made after the time of Henry VIII. or
Edward VI.

['The studies of the Cambridge
schools about 1680 consisted of logic,
ethics, natural philosophy, and mathematics; the latter branch of knowledge,
which was destined subsequently to take
the lead, and almost swallow up the
rest, had then but recently become an
object of much attention.' Monk's Life
of Bentley, p. 6.—1842.]

the general state of education, both in the schools and universities, was as narrow, pedantic, and unprofitable as can be conceived.[t]

13. We were not, nevertheless, destitute of men distin-
Gataker's Cinnus and Antoninus. guished for critical skill, even from the commencement of this period. The first was a very learned divine, Thomas Gataker, one whom a foreign writer has placed among the six Protestants most conspicuous, in his judgment, for depth of reading. His Cinnus, sive Adversaria Miscellanea, published in 1651, to which a longer work, entitled Adversaria Posthuma, is subjoined in later editions, may be introduced here; since, among a far greater number of Scriptural explanations, both of these miscellanies contain many relating to profane antiquity. He claims a higher place for his edition of Marcus Antoninus the next year. This is the earliest edition, if I am not mistaken, of any classical writer published in England with original annotations. Those of Gataker evince a very copious learning, and the edition is still, perhaps, reckoned the best that has been given of this author.

14. Thomas Stanley, author of the History of Ancient
Stanley's Æschylus. Philosophy, undertook a more difficult task, and gave in 1663 his celebrated edition of Æschylus. It was, as every one has admitted, by far superior to any that had preceded it; nor can Stanley's real praise be effaced, though it may be diminished, by an unfortunate charge that has been brought against him, of having appropriated to himself the conjectures, most of them unpublished, of Casaubon, Dorat, and Scaliger, to the number of at least three hundred emendations of the text. It will hardly be reckoned a proof of our nationality, that a living English scholar was the first to detect and announce this plagiarism of a critic, in whom we had been accustomed to take pride, from these foreigners.[u] After these plumes have been withdrawn Stanley's Æschylus will remain a great monument of critical learning.

15. Meric Casaubon, by his notes on Persius, Antoninus,

---

[t] Eachard's Grounds and Occasions of the Contempt of the Clergy. This little tract was published in 1670, and went through ten editions by 1696.

[u] Edinburgh Review, xix. 494. Museum Criticum, ii. 498 (both by the Bishop of London).

and Diogenes Laertius, Pearson by those on the last author, Gale on Iamblichus, Price on Apuleius, Hudson by his editions of Thucydides and Josephus, Potter by that of Lycophron, Baxter of Anacreon, attested the progress of classical learning in a soil so well fitted to give it nourishment. The same William Baxter published the first grammar, not quite elementary, which had appeared in England, entitled De Analogia, seu Arte Latinæ Linguæ Commentarius. It relates principally to etymology, and to the deduction of the different parts of the verb from a stem, which he conceives to be the imperative mood. Baxter was a man of some ability, but, in the style of critics, offensively contemptuous towards his brethren of the craft.

Other English philologers.

16. We must hasten to the greatest of English critics in this, or possibly any other age, Richard Bentley. His first book was the epistle to Mill, subjoined to the latter's edition of the chronicle of John Malala, a Greek writer of the Lower Empire.[x] In a desultory and almost garrulous strain, Bentley pours forth an immense store of novel learning and of acute criticism, especially on his favourite subject, which was destined to become his glory, the scattered relics of the ancient dramatists. The style of Bentley, always terse and lively, sometimes humorous and drily sarcastic, whether he wrote in Latin or in English, could not but augment the admiration which his learning challenged. Grævius and Spanheim pronounced him the rising star of British literature, and a correspondence with the former began in 1692, which continued in unbroken friendship till his death.

Bentley. His epistle to Mill.

17. But the rare qualities of Bentley were more abundantly displayed, and before the eyes of a more numerous tribunal, in his famous dissertation on the epistles ascribed to Phalaris. This was provoked, in the first instance, by a few lines of eulogy on these epistles by Sir William Temple, who pretended to find in them indubitable marks

Dissertation on Phalaris.

---

[x] [I am indebted to Mr. Dyce for reminding me, that Mill only superintended the publication of Malala; the prolegomena having been written by Hody, the notes and Latin translation by Chilmead in the reign of Charles I. The notes, indeed, appear to have been written by John Gregory, whom Bishop Monk calls 'a man of prodigious learning,' not long before the Civil War. See a full account of this edition of Malala in Life of Bentley, i. 25.—1847.]

of authenticity. Bentley, in a dissertation subjoined to
Wotton's Reflections on Modern and Ancient Learning, gave
tolerably conclusive proofs of the contrary. A young man of
high family and respectable learning, Charles Boyle, had
published an edition of the Epistles of Phalaris, with some
reflection on Bentley for personal incivility ; a charge which
he seems to have satisfactorily disproved. Bentley animadverted on this in his dissertation. Boyle the next year, with
the assistance of some leading men at Oxford, Aldrich, King,
and Atterbury, published his Examination of Bentley's Dissertation on Phalaris ; a book generally called, in familiar
brevity, Boyle against Bentley.[y] The Cambridge giant of
criticism replied in an answer which goes by the name of
Bentley against Boyle. It was the first great literary war
that had been waged in England ; and like that of Troy, it
has still the prerogative of being remembered, after the
Epistles of Phalaris are almost as much buried as the walls
of Troy itself. Both combatants were skilful in wielding the
sword : the arms of Boyle, in Swift's language, were given
him by all the gods ; but his antagonist stood forward in no
such figurative strength, master of a learning to which nothing parallel had been known in England, and that directed
by an understanding prompt, discriminating, not idly sceptical, but still farther removed from trust in authority, sagacious in perceiving corruptions of language, and ingenious,
at the least, in removing them, with a style rapid, concise,
amusing, and superior to Boyle in that which he had chiefly
to boast, a sarcastic wit.[z]

18. It may now seem extraordinary to us, even without
looking at the anachronisms or similar errors which Bentley

---

[y] 'The principal share in the undertaking fell to the lot of Atterbury; this
was suspected at the time, and has since
been placed beyond all doubt by the
publication of a letter of his to Boyle.'
—Monk's Life of Bentley, p. 69.

[z] 'In point of classical learning the
joint stock of the confederacy bore no
proportion to that of Bentley; their
acquaintance with several of the books
upon which they comment appears only
to have begun upon that occasion, and
sometimes they are indebted for their
knowledge of them to their adversary;
compared with his boundless erudition

their learning was that of school-boys,
and not always sufficient to preserve
them from distressing mistakes. But
profound literature was at that period
confined to few, while wit and raillery
found numerous and eager readers. It
may be doubtful whether Busby himself, by whom every one of the con-
federated band had been educated, possessed knowledge which would have
qualified him to enter the lists in such
a controversy.'—Monk's Bentley, p. 69.
Warburton has justly said that Bentley
by his wit foiled the Oxford men at
their own weapons.

has exposed, that any one should be deceived by the Epistles of Phalaris. The rhetorical common-places, the cold declamation of the sophist, the care to please the reader, the absence of that simplicity with which a man who has never known restraint in disguising his thoughts or choosing his words is sure to express himself, strike us in the pretended letters of this buskined tyrant, the Icon Basilice of the ancient world. But this was doubtless thought evidence of their authenticity by many who might say, as others have done, in a happy vein of metaphor, that they seemed 'not written with a pen but with a sceptre.' The argument from the use of the common dialect by a Sicilian tyrant, contemporary with Pythagoras, is of itself conclusive, and would leave no doubt in the present day.

19. 'It may be remarked,' says the Bishop of Gloucester, 'that a scholar at that time possessed neither the aids nor the encouragements which are now presented to smooth the paths of literature. The grammars of the Latin and Greek languages were imperfectly and erroneously taught; and the critical scholar must have felt severely the absence of sufficient indexes, particularly of the voluminous scholiasts, grammarians, and later writers of Greece, in the examination of which no inconsiderable portion of a life might be consumed. Bentley, relying upon his own exertions and the resources of his own mind, pursued an original path of criticism, in which the intuitive quickness and subtlety of his genius qualified him to excel. In the faculty of memory, so important for such pursuits, he has himself candidly declared that he was not particularly gifted. Consequently he practised throughout life the precaution of noting in the margin of his books the suggestions and conjectures which rushed into his mind during their perusal. To this habit of laying up materials in store, we may partly attribute the surprising rapidity with which some of his most important works were completed. He was also at the trouble of constructing for his own use indexes of authors quoted by the principal scholiasts, by Eustathius and other ancient commentators, of a nature similar to those afterwards published by Fabricius in his Bibliotheca Græca; which latter were the produce of the joint labour of various hands.' [a]

Disadvantages of scholars in that age.

---

[a] Monk's Life of Bentley, p. 12.

SECT. II.—ON ANTIQUITIES.

Grævius and Gronovius—Fabretti—Numismatic Writers—Chronology.

20. THE two most industrious scholars of their time, Grævius and Gronovius, collected into one body such of
the numerous treatises on Roman and Greek antiquities as they thought most worthy of preservation
in an uniform and accessible work. These form the Thesaurus
Antiquitatum Romanarum, by Grævius, in twelve volumes,
the Thesaurus Antiquitatum Græcarum, by Gronovius, in
thirteen volumes; the former published in 1694, the first
volumes of the latter in 1697. They comprehend many of the
labours of the older antiquaries already commemorated from
the middle of the sixteenth to that of the seventeenth century, and some also of a later date. Among these, in the
collection of Grævius, are a treatise of Albert Rubens, son of
the great painter, on the dress of the Romans, particularly
the laticlave (Antwerp, 1665), the enlarged edition of Octavius Ferrarius on the same subject, several treatises by Spanheim and Ursatus, and the Roma Antica of Nardini, published
in 1666. Gronovius gave a place in his twelfth volume
(1702) to the very recent work of a young Englishman,
Potter's Antiquities, which the author, at the request of the
veteran antiquary, had so much enlarged, that the Latin
translation in Gronovius is nearly double in length the first
edition of the English.[b] The warm eulogies of Gronovius
attest the merit of this celebrated work. Potter was but
twenty-three years of age; he had of course availed himself
of the writings of Meursius, but he has also contributed to
supersede them. It has been said that he is less exact in
attending to the difference of times and places than our finer
criticism requires.[c]

21. Bellori in a long list of antiquarian writings, Falconieri
in several more, especially his Inscriptiones Athle-
ticæ, maintained the honour of Italy in this province, so justly claimed as her own.[d] But no one has been

(margin notes: Thesauri of Grævius and of Gronovius. — Fabretti.)

---

[b] The first edition of Potter's Antiquities was published in 1697 and 1698.

[c] Biogr. univ.
[d] Salfi, vol. xi. p. 364.

accounted equal to Raphael Fabretti, by judges so competent
as Maffei, Gravina, Fabroni, and Visconti.[e] His diligence in
collecting inscriptions was only surpassed by his sagacity in
explaining them ; and his authority has been preferred to
that of any other antiquary.[f] His time was spent in delving
among ruins and vaults, to explore the subterranean treasures
of Latium ; no heat, nor cold, nor rain, nor badness of road,
could deter him from these solitary peregrinations. Yet the
glory of Fabretti must be partly shared with his horse. This
wise and faithful animal, named Marco Polo, had acquired,
it is said, the habit of standing still, and as it were *pointing*,
when he came near an antiquity ; his master candidly owning
that several things which would have escaped him had been
detected by the antiquarian quadruped.[g] Fabretti's principal works are three dissertations on the Roman aqueducts, and
one on the Trajan column. Little, says Fabroni, was known
before about the Roman galleys or their naval affairs in
general.[h] Fabretti was the first who reduced lapidary remains
into classes, and arranged them so as to illustrate each other ;
a method, says one of his most distinguished successors,
which has laid the foundations of the science.[i] A profusion
of collateral learning is mingled with the main stream of all
his investigations.

22. No one had ever come to the study of medals with such
stores of erudition as Ezekiel Spanheim. The earlier Numis-
writers on the subject, Vico, Erizzo, Angeloni, were matics.
Spanheim—
not comparable to him, and had rather dwelt on the Vaillant.
genuineness or rarity of coins than on their usefulness in
illustrating history. Spanheim's Dissertations on the Use of
Medals, the second improved edition of which appeared in
1671, first connected them with the most profound and critical research into antiquity.[k] Vaillant, travelling into the
Levant, brought home great treasures of Greek coinage, especially those of the Seleucidæ, at once enriching the cabinets
of the curious and establishing historical truth. Medallic
evidence, in fact, may be reckoned among those checks upon

[e] Fabretti's life has been written by
two very favourable biographers, Fabroni, in Vitæ Italorum, vol. vi., and
Visconti, in the Biographie universelle.
[f] F broni, p. 187. Biogr. univ.

[g] Fabroni, p. 192.
[h] P. 201.
[i] Biogr. univ.
[k] Bibl. choisie, vol. xxii.

the negligence of historians, that, having been retrieved by industrious antiquaries, have created a cautious and discerning spirit which has been exercised in later times upon facts, and which, beginning in scepticism, passes onward to a more rational, and therefore more secure, conviction of what can fairly be proved. Jobert, in 1692, consolidated the researches of Spanheim, Vaillant, and other numismatic writers, in his book entitled La Science des Médailles, a better system of the science than had been published.[m]

23. It would of course not be difficult to fill these pages Chronology. with brief notices of other books that fall within the Usher. extensive range of classical antiquity. But we have no space for more than a mere enumeration, which would give little satisfaction. Chronology has received some attention in former volumes. Our learned Archbishop Usher might there have been named, since the first part of his Annals of the Old Testament, which goes down to the year of the world 3828, was published in 1650. The second part followed in 1654. This has been the chronology generally adopted by English historians, as well as by Bossuet, Calmet, and Rollin, so that for many years it might be called the orthodox scheme of Europe. No former annals of the world had been so exact in marking dates and collating sacred history with profane. It was therefore exceedingly convenient for those who, possessing no sufficient leisure or learning for these inquiries, might very reasonably confide in such authority.

24. Usher, like Scaliger and Petavius, had strictly conformed to the Hebrew chronology in all Scriptural Pezron. dates. But it is well known that the Septuagint version, and also the Samaritan Pentateuch, differ greatly from the Hebrew and from each other, so that the age of the world has nearly 2000 years more antiquity in the Greek than in the original text. Jerome had followed the latter in the Vulgate; and in the seventeenth century it was usual to maintain the incorrupt purity of the Hebrew manuscripts, so that when Pezron, in his Antiquité des Temps dévoilée, 1687, attempted to establish the Septuagint chronology, it excited

---

[m] Biogr. univ.

a clamour in some of his church, as derogatory to the Vulgate translation. Martianay defended the received chronology, and the system of Pezron gained little favour in that age.[n] It has since become more popular, chiefly, perhaps, on account of the greater latitude it gives to speculations on the origin of kingdoms and other events of the early world, which are certainly somewhat cramped in the common reckoning. But the Septuagint chronology is not free from its own difficulties, and the internal evidence seems rather against its having been the original. Where two must be wrong, it is possible that all three may be so; and the most judicious inquirers into ancient history have of late been coming to the opinion, that, with certain exceptions, there are no means of establishing an entire accuracy in dates before the Olympiads. While much of the more ancient history itself, even in leading and important events, is so precarious as must be acknowledged, there can be little confidence in chronological schemes. They seem, however, to be very seducing, so that those who enter upon the subject as sceptics become believers in their own theory.

25. Among those who addressed their attention to particular portions of chronology, Sir John Marsham ought to be mentioned. In his Canon Chronicus Ægyptiacus he attempted, as the learned were still more prone than they are now, to reconcile conflicting authorities without rejecting any. He is said to have first started the ingenious idea that the Egyptian dynasties, stretching to such immense antiquity, were not successive but collateral.[o] Marsham fell, like many others after him, into the unfortunate mistake of confounding Sesostris with Sesac. But in times when discoveries that Marsham could not have anticipated were yet at a distance, he is extolled by most of those who had laboured, by help of the Greek and Hebrew writers alone, to fix ancient history on a stable foundation, as the restorer of the Egyptian annals.

Marsham.

---

[n] Biogr. univ.: arts. Pezron and Martianay. Bibliothèque univ. xxiv. 103.
[o] Biograph. Britannica.

CHAPTER II.

HISTORY OF THEOLOGICAL LITERATURE FROM
1650 to 1700.

Sect. I.

Papal Power limited by the Gallican Church—Dupin—Fleury—Protestant
Controversy—Bossuet—His Assaults on Protestantism—Jansenism—
Progress of Arminianism in England—Trinitarian Controversy—De-
fences of Christianity—Pascal's Thoughts—Toleration—Boyle—Locke
—French Sermons—And English—Other Theological Works.

1. It has been observed in the last volume, that while little
Decline of or no decline could be perceived in the general
papal in-
fluence. church of Rome at the conclusion of that period
which we then had before us, yet the papal authority itself
had lost a part of that formidable character which, through
the Jesuits, and especially Bellarmin, it had some years
before assumed. This was now still more decidedly manifest: the temporal power over kings was not, certainly,
renounced, for Rome never retracts any thing; nor was it
perhaps without Italian Jesuits to write in its behalf; but
the common consent of nations rejected it so strenuously,
that on no occasion has it been brought forward by any
accredited or eminent advocate. There was also a growing
disposition to control the court of Rome; the treaty of
Westphalia was concluded in utter disregard of her protest.
But such matters of history do not belong to us, when they
do not bear a close relation to the warfare of the pen. Some
events there were which have had a remarkable influence
on the theological literature of France, and indirectly of
the rest of Europe.

2. Louis XIV., more arrogant, in his earlier life, than
bigoted, became involved in a contest with Innocent XI.,

by a piece of his usual despotism and contempt of his
subjects' rights. He extended in 1673 the ancient Dispute of
prerogative, called the regale, by which the king Louis XIV.
with In-
enjoyed the revenues of vacant bishoprics, to all nocent XI.
the kingdom, though many sees had been legally exempt
from it. Two bishops appealed to the pope, who interfered
in their favour more peremptorily than the times would
permit. Innocent, it is but just to say, was maintaining
the fair rights of the church, rather than any claim of his
own. But the dispute took at length a different form.
France was rich in prelates of eminent worth, and among
such, as is evident, the Cisalpine theories had never lain
wholly dormant since the councils of Constance and Basle.
Louis convened the famous assembly of the Gallican clergy
in 1682. Bossuet, who is said to have felt some apprehensions lest the spirit of resistance should become one of
rebellion, was appointed to open this assembly; and his
sermon on that occasion is among his most splendid works.
His posture was indeed magnificent: he stands forward
not so much the minister of religion as her arbitrator; we
see him poise in his hands earth and heaven, and draw that
boundary line which neither was to transgress; he speaks
the language of reverential love towards the mother-church,
that of St. Peter, and the fairest of her daughters to which
he belongs, conciliating their transient feud; yet in this
majestic tone which he assumes, no arrogance betrays itself,
no thought of himself as one endowed with transcendant
influence; he speaks for his church, and yet we feel that
he raises himself above those for whom he speaks.[p]

3. Bossuet was finally entrusted with drawing up the
four articles, which the assembly, rather at the in- Four articles
stigation perhaps of Colbert than of its own of 1682.
accord, promulgated as the Gallican creed on the limitations of papal authority. These declare: 1. That kings are
subject to no ecclesiastical power in temporals, nor can be
deposed directly or indirectly by the chiefs of the church:
2. That the decrees of the council of Constance as to the
papal authority are in full force and ought to be observed:

---

[p] This sermon will be found in Œuvres de Bossuet, vol. ix.

3. That this authority can only be exerted in conformity with the canons received in the Gallican church: 4. That though the pope has the principal share in determining controversies of faith, and his decrees extend to all churches, they are not absolutely final, unless the consent of the catholic church be superadded. It appears that some bishops would have willingly used stronger language, but Bossuet foresaw the risk of an absolute schism. Even thus the Gallican church approached so nearly to it that, the pope refusing the usual bulls to bishops nominated by the king according to the concordat, between thirty and forty sees, at last, were left vacant. No reconciliation was effected till 1693, in the pontificate of Innocent XII. It is to be observed, whether the French writers slur this over or not, that the pope gained the honours of war; the bishops who had sat in the assembly of 1682 writing separately letters which have the appearance of regretting, if not retracting, what they had done. These were however worded with intentional equivocation; and as the court of Rome yields to none in suspecting the subterfuges of words, it is plain that it contented itself with an exterior humiliation of its adversaries. The old question of the regale was tacitly settled; Louis enjoyed all that he had desired, and Rome might justly think herself not bound to fight for the privileges of those who had made her so bad a return.[q]

4. The doctrine of the four articles gained ground perhaps Dupin on the ancient discipline. in the church of France through a work of great boldness, and deriving authority from the learning and judgment of its author, Dupin. In the height of the contest, while many were considering how far the Gallican church might dispense with the institution of bishops at Rome, that point in the established system which evidently secured the victory to their antagonist, in the year 1686, he published a treatise on the ancient discipline of the church. It is written in Latin, which he probably chose as less obnoxious than his own language. It may be true,

---

[q] I have derived most of this account from Bausset's Life of Bossuet, vol. ii. Both the bishop and his biographer shuffle a good deal about the letter of the Gallican prelates in 1693. But when the Roman legions had passed under the yoke at the Caudine Forks, they were ready to take up arms again.

which I cannot affirm or deny, that each position in this
work had been advanced before; but the general tone
seems undoubtedly more adverse to the papal supremacy
than any book which could have come from a man of
reputed orthodoxy. It tends, notwithstanding a few necessary admissions, to represent almost all that can be called
power or jurisdiction in the see of Rome as acquired, if not
abusive, and would leave, in a practical sense, no real pope
at all; mere primacy being a trifle, and even the right of
interfering by admonition being of no great value, when
there was no definite obligation to obey. The principle of
Dupin is, that the church having reached her perfection in
the fourth century, we should endeavour, as far as circumstances will admit, to restore the discipline of that age. But,
even in the Gallican church, it has generally been held
that he has urged his argument farther than is consistent
with a necessary subordination to Rome.[r]

5. In the same year Dupin published the first volume of
a more celebrated work, his Nouvelle Bibliothèque Dupin's Ec-
des Auteurs ecclésiastiques, a complete history of Library.
theological literature, at least within the limits of the church,
which, in a long series of volumes, he finally brought down
to the close of the seventeenth century. It is unquestionably the most standard work of that kind extant, whatever
deficiencies may have been found in its execution. The
immense erudition requisite for such an undertaking must
have rendered it inevitable to take some things at second
hand, or to fall into some errors; and we may add other
causes less necessary, the youth of the writer in the first
volumes, and the rapidity with which they appeared. Integrity, love of truth, and moderation distinguish this
ecclesiastical history, perhaps beyond any other. Dupin is
often near the frontier of orthodoxy, but he is careful, even
in the eyes of jealous Catholics, not quite to overstep it.
This work was soon translated into English, and furnished
a large part of such knowledge on the subject as our own
divines possessed. His free way of speaking, however, on

---

[r] Bibliothèque universelle, vi. 109.
The book is very clear, concise, and
learned, so that it is worth reading
through by those who would understand
such matters. I have not observed that
it is much quoted by English writers.

the Roman supremacy and some other points, excited the animadversion of more rigid persons, and among others of Bossuet, who stood on his own vantage-ground, ready to strike on every side. The most impartial critics have been of Dupin's mind; but Bossuet, like all dogmatic champions of orthodoxy, never sought truth by an analytical process of investigation, assuming his own possession of it as an axiom in the controversy.[s]

6. Dupin was followed a few years afterwards by one *Fleury's* not his superior in learning and candour (though *Ecclesiasti-* deficient in neither), but in skill of narration and *cal History.* beauty of style, Claude Fleury. The first volume of his Ecclesiastical History came forth in 1691; but a part only of the long series falls within this century. The learning of Fleury has been said to be frequently not original, and his prolixity to be too great for an elementary historian. The former is only blamable when he has concealed his immediate authorities; few works of great magnitude have been written wholly from the prime sources; with regard to his diffuseness, it is very convenient to those who want access to the original writers, or leisure to collate them. Fleury has been called by some credulous and uncritical; but he is esteemed faithful, moderate, and more respectful or cautious than Dupin. Yet many of his volumes are a continual protest against the vices and ambition of the mediæval popes, and his Ecclesiastical History must be reckoned among the causes of that estrangement, in spirit and affection, from the court of Rome, which leavens the theological literature of France in the eighteenth century.

7. The dissertations of Fleury, interspersed with his his-*His Dis-* tory, were more generally read and more conspi-*sertations.* cuously excellent. Concise, but neither dry nor superficial; luminous, yet appearing simple; philosophical without the affectation of profundity, seizing all that is most essential in their subject without the tediousness of detail or the pedantry of quotation; written, above all, with

---

* Bibliothèque universelle, iii. 39, vii. 335, xxii. 120. Biogr. universelle. Œuvres de Bossuet, vol. xxx. Dupin seems not to have held the superiority of bishops to priests jure divino, which provokes the prelate of Méaux. Ces grands critiques sont peu favorables aux supériorités ecclésiastiques, et n'aiment guère plus celles desévê ques que celles du pape. p. 491.

that clearness, that ease, that unaffected purity of taste, which belong to the French style of that best age, they present a contrast not only to the inferior writings on philosophical history with which our age abounds, but, in some respects, even to the best. It cannot be a crime that these dissertations contain a good deal which, after more than a century's labour in historical inquiry, has become more familiar than it was.

8. The French Protestants, notwithstanding their disarmed condition, were not, I apprehend, much oppressed under Richelieu and Mazarin. But soon afterwards an eagerness to accelerate what was taking place through natural causes, their return into the church, brought on a series of harassing edicts, which ended in the revocation of that of Nantes. During this time they were assailed by less terrible weapons, yet such as required no ordinary strength to resist, the polemical writings of the three greatest men in the church of France—Nicole, Arnauld, and Bossuet. The two former were desirous to efface the reproaches of an approximation to Calvinism, and of a disobedience to the Catholic church, under which their Jansenist party was labouring. Nicole began with a small treatise, entitled La Perpétuité de la Foi de l'Église catholique, touchant l'Eucharistie, in 1664. This aimed to prove that the tenet of transubstantiation had been constant in the church. Claude, the most able controvertist among the French Protestants, replied in the next year. This led to a much more considerable work by Nicole and Arnauld conjointly, with the same title as the former; nor was Claude slow in combating his double-headed adversary. Nicole is said to have written the greater portion of this second treatise, though it commonly bears the name of his more illustrious colleague.[t]

9. Both Arnauld and Nicole were eclipsed by the most distinguished and successful advocate of the Catholic church, Bossuet. His Exposition de la Foi catholique was written in 1668, for the use of two brothers of the Dangeau family; but having been commu-

Protestant controversy in France.

Bossuet's exposition of Catholic faith.

---

[t] Biogr. univ.

nicated to Turenne, the most eminent Protestant that
remained in France, it contributed much to his conversion.
It was published in 1671; and though enlarged from the
first sketch, does not exceed eighty pages in octavo.
Nothing can be more precise, more clear, or more free
from all circuity and detail than this little book; every
thing is put in the most specious light; the authority of
the ancient church, recognised, at least nominally, by the
majority of Protestants, is alone kept in sight. Bossuet
limits himself to doctrines established by the council of
Trent, leaving out of the discussion not only all questionable points, but, what is perhaps less fair, all rites and
usages, however general, or sanctioned by the regular discipline of the church, except so far as formally approved
by that council. Hence he glides with a transient step over
the invocation of saints and the worship of images, but
presses with his usual dexterity on the inconsistencies and
weak concessions of his antagonists. The Calvinists, or
some of them, had employed a jargon of words about real
presence, which he exposes with admirable brevity and
vigour.[u] Nor does he gain less advantage in favour of
tradition and church authority from the assumption of
somewhat similar claims by the same party. It has often
been alleged that the Exposition of Bossuet was not well
received by many on his own side. And for this there
seems to be some foundation, though the Protestant con-
trovertists have made too much of the facts. It was
published at Rome in 1678, and approved in the most
formal manner by Innocent XI. the next year. But it must
have been perceived to separate the faith of the church, as
it rested on dry propositions, from the same faith living
and embodied in the every-day worship of the people.[x]

---

[u] Bossuet observes, that most other
controversies are found to depend more
on words than substance, and the difference becomes less the more they are examined; but in that of the Eucharist the
contrary is the case, since the Calvinists
endeavour to accommodate their phraseology to the Catholics, while essentially
they differ. Vol. xviii. p. 135.

[x] The writings of Bossuet against

the Protestants occupy nine volumes,
xviii.—xxvi., in the great edition of his
works, Versailles, 1816. The Exposition de la Foi is in the eighteenth.
Bausset, in his Life of Bossuet, appears
to have refuted the exaggerations of
many Protestants as to the ill reception
of this little book at Rome. Yet there
was a certain foundation for them. See
Bibliothèque universelle, vol. xi. p. 455.

10. Bossuet was now the acknowledged champion of the Roman church in France; Claude was in equal His confer-
ence with
Claude. pre-eminence on the other side. These great ad- versaries had a regular conference in 1678. Mademoiselle de Duras, a Protestant lady, like most others of her rank at that time, was wavering about religion, and in her presence the dispute was carried on. It entirely turned on church authority. The arguments of Bossuet differ only from those which have often been adduced by the spirit and conciseness with which he presses them. We have his own account, which of course gives himself the victory. It was almost as much of course that the lady was con- verted; for it is seldom that a woman can withstand the popular argument on that side, when she has once gone far enough to admit the possibility of its truth, by giving it a hearing. Yet Bossuet deals in sophisms which, though always in the mouths of those who call themselves ortho- dox, are contemptible to such as know facts as well as logic. ' I urged,' he says, ' in a few words, what presumption it was to believe that we can better understand the word of God than all the rest of the church, and that nothing would thus prevent there being as many religions as persons.'ʸ But there can be no presumption in supposing that we may understand anything better than one who has never examined it at all; and if this rest of the church, so magnificently brought forward, have commonly acted on Bossuet's principle, and thought it presumptuous to judge for themselves; if out of many millions of persons a few only have deliberately reasoned on religion, and the rest have been, like true zeros, nothing in themselves, but much in sequence; if also, as is most frequently the case, this presumptuousness is not the assertion of a paradox or no- velty, but the preference of one denomination of Christians, or of one tenet maintained by respectable authority, to an- other, we can only scorn the emptiness, as well as resent the effrontery, of this common-place that rings so often in our ears. Certainly reason is so far from condemning a defer- ence to the judgment of the wise and good, that nothing is

---

ʸ Œuvres de Bossuet, xxiii. 290.

more irrational than to neglect it; but when this is claimed
for those whom we need not believe to have been wiser and
better than ourselves, nay, sometimes whom without vain
glory we may esteem less, and that so as to set aside the
real authority of the most philosophical, unbiassed, and judicious of mankind, it is not pride or presumption, but a sober
use of our faculties that rejects the jurisdiction.

11. Bossuet once more engaged in a similar discussion
about 1691. Among the German Lutherans there
seems to have been for a long time a lurking notion
that on some terms or other a reconciliation with
the church of Rome could be effected; and this was most
countenanced in the dominions of Brunswick, and above all
in the University of Helmstadt. Leibnitz himself, and
Molanus, a Lutheran divine, were the negotiators on that side
with Bossuet. Their treaty, for such it was apparently
understood to be, was conducted by writing; and when we
read their papers on both sides, nothing is more remarkable
than the tone of superiority which the Catholic plenipoten-
tiary, if such he could be deemed without powers from any
one but himself, has thought fit to assume. No concession
is offered, no tenet explained away; the sacramental cup to
the laity, and a permission to the Lutheran clergy already
married to retain their wives after their reordination, is all
that he holds forth; and in this, doubtless, he had no authority from Rome. Bossuet could not veil his haughty
countenance, and his language is that of asperity and contemptuousness instead of moderation. He dictates terms of
surrender as to a besieged city when the breach is already
practicable, and hardly deigns to show his clemency by
granting the smallest favour to the garrison. It is curious
to see the strained constructions, the artifices of silence
to which Molanus has recourse, in order to make out some
pretence for his ignominious surrender. Leibnitz, with
whom the correspondence broke off in 1693, and was renewed
again in 1699, seems not quite so yielding as the other; and
the last biographer of Bossuet suspects that the German
philosopher was insincere or tortuous in the negotiation. If
this were so, he must have entered upon it less of his own
accord than to satisfy the Princess Sophia, who, like many

Correspond-
dence with
Molanus and
Leibnitz.

of her family, had been a little wavering, till our Act of
Settlement became a true settlement to their faith. This
bias of the court of Hanover is intimated in several passages.
The success of this treaty of union, or rather of subjection,
was as little to be expected as it was desirable ; the old spirit
of Lutheranism was much worn out, but there must surely
have been a determination to resist so unequal a compromise.
Rome negotiated as a conqueror with these beaten Cartha-
ginians ; yet no one had beaten them but themselves.[z]

12. The warfare of the Roman church may be carried on
either in a series of conflicts on the various doctrines   His Varia-
wherein the reformers separated from her, or by one   tions of
pitched battle on the main question of a conclusive   Protestant
Churches.
authority somewhere in the church. Bossuet's temper, as
well as his inferiority in original learning, led him in preference to the latter scheme of theological strategy. It was
also manifestly that course of argument which was most
likely to persuade the unlearned. He followed up the blow
which he had already struck against Claude in his famous
work on the Variations of Protestant Churches. Never did
his genius find a subject more fit to display its characteristic
impetuosity, its arrogance, or its cutting and merciless spirit of
sarcasm. The weaknesses, the inconsistent evasions, the ex-
travagancies of Luther, Zwingle, Calvin, and Beza, pass, one
one after another, before us, till these great reformers seem
like victim prisoners to be hewn down by the indignant prophet. That Bossuet is candid in statement, or even faithful
in quotation. I should much doubt ; he gives the words of
his adversaries in his own French, and the references are not
made to any specified edition of their voluminous writings.
The main point, as he contends it to be, that the Protestant
churches (for he does not confine this to persons) fluctuated
much in the sixteenth century, is sufficiently proved ; but it
remained to show that this was a reproach. Those who have
taken a different view from Bossuet may perhaps think that
a little more of this censure would have been well incurred ;
that they have varied too little rather than too much ; and
that it is far more difficult, even in controversy with the church

---

[z] Œuvres de Bossuet, vols. xxv. and xxvi.

of Rome, to withstand the inference which their long creeds
and confessions, as well as the language too common with
their theologians, have furnished to her more ancient and
catholic claim of infallibility, than to vindicate those successive variations which are analogous to the necessary course
of human reason on all other subjects. The essential fallacy
of Romanism, that truth must ever exist visibly on earth,
is implied in the whole strain of Bossuet's attack on the
variances of Protestantism : it is evident that variance of
opinion proves error somewhere ; but unless it can be shown
that we have any certain method of excluding it, this should
only lead us to be more indulgent towards the judgment of
others, and less confident of our own. The notion of an
intrinsic moral criminality in religious error is at the root of
the whole argument ; and till Protestants are well rid of this,
there seems no secure mode of withstanding the effect which
the vast weight of authority asserted by the Latin church,
even where it has not the aid of the Eastern, must produce
on timid and scrupulous minds.

13. In no period has the Anglican church stood up so
Anglican
writings
against
popery. powerfully in defence of the Protestant cause as in
that before us.   From the æra of the Restoration to
the close of the century the war was unremitting
and vigorous.   And it is particularly to be remarked, that
the principal champions of the church of England threw off
that ambiguous syncretism which had displayed itself under
the first Stuarts, and, comparatively at least with their immediate predecessors, avoided every admission which might
facilitate a deceitful compromise. We can only mention a few
of the writers who signalized themselves in this controversy.

14. Taylor's Dissuasive from Popery was published in
Taylor's
Dissuasive. 1664 ; and in this his latest work we find the same
general strain of Protestant reasoning, the same
rejection of all but Scriptural authority, the same free exposure of the inconsistencies and fallacies of tradition, the
same tendency to excite a sceptical feeling as to all except
the primary doctrines of religion, which had characterised
the Liberty of Prophesying. These are mixed, indeed, in
Taylor's manner, with a few passages, (they are, I think,
but few,) which, singly taken, might seem to breathe not

quite this spirit; but the tide flows for the most part the same way, and it is evident that his mind had undergone no change. The learning, in all his writings, is profuse; but Taylor never leaves me with the impression that he is exact and scrupulous in its application. In one part of this Dissuasive from Popery, having been reproached with some inconsistency, he has no scruple to avow that in a former work he had employed weak arguments for a laudable purpose.[a]

15. Barrow, not so extensively learned as Taylor, who had read rather too much, but inferior, perhaps, Barrow. even in that respect to hardly any one else, and Stillingfleet. above him in closeness and strength of reasoning, maintained the combat against Rome in many of his sermons, and especially in a long treatise on the papal supremacy. Stillingfleet followed, a man deeply versed in ecclesiastical antiquity, of an argumentative mind, excellently fitted for polemical dispute, but perhaps by those habits of his life rendered too much of an advocate to satisfy an impartial reader. In the critical reign of James II., he may be considered as the leader on the Protestant side; but Wake, Tillotson, and several more, would deserve mention in a fuller history of ecclesiastical literature.

16. The controversies always smouldering in the church of Rome, and sometimes breaking into flame, to which the Anti-Pelagian writings of Augustin had Jansenius. originally given birth, have been slightly touched in our former volumes. It has been seen that the rigidly predestinarian theories had been condemned by the court of Rome in Baius, that the opposite doctrine of Molina had narrowly escaped censure, that it was safest to abstain from any language not verbally that of the church or of Augustin, whom the church held incontrovertible. But now a more serious and celebrated controversy, that of the Jansenists, pierced as it were to the heart of the church. It arose before the middle of the century. Jansenius, Bishop of Ypres, in his Augustinus, published after his death, in 1640, gave, as he professed, a faithful statement of the

---

[a] Taylor's Works, x. 304. This is not surprising, as in his Ductor Dubitantium, xi. 484, he maintains the right of using arguments and authorities in controversy which we do not believe to be valid.

tenets of that father. 'We do not inquire,' he says, 'what men ought to believe on the powers of human nature, or on the grace and predestination of God, but what Augustin once preached with the approbation of the church, and has consigned to writing in many of his works.' This book is in three parts; the first containing a history of the Pelagian controversy, the second and third an exposition of the tenets of Augustin. Jansenius does not, however, confine himself so much to mere analysis, but that he attacks the Jesuits Lessius and Molina, and even reflects on the bull of Pius V. condemning Baius, which he cannot wholly approve.[b]

17. Richelieu, who is said to have retained some animosity against Jansenius on account of a book called Mars Gallicus, which he had written on the side of his sovereign the king of Spain, designed to obtain the condemnation of the Augustinus by the French clergy. The Jesuits, therefore, had gained ground so far that the doctrines of Augustin were out of fashion, though few besides themselves ventured to reject his nominal authority. It is certainly clear that Jansenius offended the greater part of the church. But he had some powerful advocates, and especially Antony Arnauld, the most renowned of a family long conspicuous for eloquence, for piety, and for opposition to the Jesuits. In 1649, after several years of obscure dispute, Cornet, syndic of the faculty of theology in the University of Paris, brought forward for censure seven propositions, five of which became afterwards so famous, without saying that they were found in the work of Jansenius. The faculty condemned them, though it had never been reckoned favourable to the Jesuits; a presumption that they were at least expressed in a manner repugnant to the prevalent doctrine. Yet Le Clerc declares his own opinion

Marginal note: Condemnation of his Augustinus in France,

---

[b] A very copious history of Jansenism, taking it up from the Council of Trent, will be found in the fourteenth volume of the Bibliothèque universelle, p. 139–398, from which Mosheim has derived most of what we read in his Ecclesiastical History. And the History of Port-Royal was written by Racine in so perspicuous and neat a style, that, though we may hardly think with Olivet that it places him as high in prose writing as his tragedies do in verse, it entitles him to rank in the list of those who have succeeded in both. Is it not probable that in some scenes of Athalie he had Port-Royal before his eyes? The history and the tragedy were written about the same time. Racine, it is rather remarkable, had entered the field against Nicole in 1666, chiefly indeed to defend theatrical representations, but not without many sarcasms against Jansenism.

that there may be some ambiguity in the style of the first, but that the other four are decidedly conformable to the theology of Augustin.

18. The Jesuits now took the course of calling in the authority of Rome. They pressed Innocent X. to _{and at} condemn the five propositions, which were main- _{Rome.} tained by some doctors in France. It is not the policy of that court to compromise so delicate a possession as infallibility by bringing it to the test of that personal judgment, which is of necessity the arbiter of each man's own obedience. The popes have, in fact, rarely taken a part, independently of councils, in these school debates, The bull of Pius V., (a man too zealous by character to regard prudence,) in which he condemned many tenets of Baius, had not, nor could it, give satisfaction to those who saw with their own eyes that it swerved from the Augustinian theory. Innocent was, at first, unwilling to meddle with a subject which, as he owned to a friend, he did not understand. But after hearing some discussions, he grew more confident of his knowledge, which he ascribed, as in duty bound, to the inspiration of the Holy Ghost, and went so heartily along with the Anti-Jansenists that he refused to hear the deputies of the other party. On the 31st of May, 1653, he condemned the five propositions, four as erroneous, and the fifth in stronger language, declaring, however, not in the bull, but orally, that he did not condemn the tenet of efficacious grace (which all the Dominicans held), nor the doctrine of St. Augustin, which was, and ever would be, that of the church.

19. The Jansenists were not bold enough to hint that they did not acknowledge the infallibility of the pope in _{The Janse-} an express and positive declaration. Even if they _{nists take a distinction;} had done so, they had an evident recognition of this censure of the five propositions by their own church, and might dread its being so generally received as to give the sanction which no Catholic can withstand. They had recourse, unfortunately, to a subterfuge which put them in the wrong. They admitted that the propositions were false, but denied that they could be found in the book of Jansenius. Thus each party rested on the denial of a matter of fact, and each erroneously, according at least to the judgment of the most

learned and impartial Protestants. The five propositions express the doctrine of Augustin himself; and if they do this, we can hardly doubt that they express that of Jansenius. In a short time this ground of evasion was taken from their party. An assembly of French prelates in the first place, and afterwards Alexander VII., successor of Innocent X., condemned the propositions as in Jansenius, and in the sense intended by Jansenius.

20. The Jansenists were now driven to the wall: the Sorbonne in 1655, in consequence of some propositions of Arnauld, expelled him from the theological faculty; a formulary was drawn up to be signed by the clergy, condemning the propositions of Jansenius, which was finally established in 1661; and those who refused, even nuns, underwent a harassing persecution. The most striking instance of this, which still retains an historical character, was the dissolution of the famous convent of Port-Royal, over which Angelica Arnauld, sister of the great advocate of Jansenism, had long presided with signal reputation. This nunnery was at Paris, having been removed in 1644 from an ancient Cistertian convent of the same name about six leagues distant, and called for distinction Port-Royal des Champs. To this now unfrequented building some of the most eminent men repaired for study, whose writings being anonymously published, have been usually known by the name of their residence. Arnauld, Pascal, Nicole, Lancelot, De Sacy, are among the Messieurs de Port-Royal, an appellation so glorious in the seventeenth century. The Jansenists now took a distinction, very reasonable, as it seems, in its nature, between the authority which asserts or denies a proposition, and that which does the like as to a fact. They refused to the pope, that is, in this instance, to the church, the latter infallibility. We cannot prosecute this part of ecclesiastical history farther: if writings of any literary importance had been produced by the controversy, they would demand our attention; but this does not appear to have been the case. The controversy between Arnauld and Malebranche may perhaps be an exception. The latter, carried forward by his original genius, attempted to deal with the doctrines of theology as

and are persecuted.

with metaphysical problems, in his Traité de la Nature et de la Grâce. Arnauld animadverted on this in his Réflexions philosophiques et théologiques. Malebranche replied in Lettres du Père Malebranche à un de ses Amis. This was published in 1686, and the controversy between such eminent masters of abstruse reasoning began to excite attention. Malebranche seems to have retired first from the field. His antagonist had great advantages in the dispute, according to received systems of theology, with which he was much more conversant, and perhaps on the whole in the philosophical part of the question. This however cannot be reckoned entirely a Jansenistic controversy, though it involved those perilous difficulties which had raised that flame.[c]

21. The credit of Augustin was now as much shaken in the Protestant as in the Catholic regions of Europe. Episcopius had given to the Remonstrant party a reputation which no sect so inconsiderable in its separate character has ever possessed. *Progress of Arminianism.* The Dutch Arminians were at no time numerous: they took no hold of the people; they had few churches, and though not persecuted by the now lenient policy of Holland, were still under the ban of an orthodox clergy, as exclusive and bigoted as before. But their writings circulated over Europe, and made a silent impression on the adverse party. It became less usual to bring forward the Augustinian hypothesis in prominent or unequivocal language. Courcelles, born at Geneva, *Courcelles.* and the successor of Episcopius in the Remonstrant congregation at Amsterdam, with less genius than his predecessor, had perhaps a more extensive knowledge of ecclesiastical antiquity. His works were much in esteem with the theologians of that way of thinking; but they have not fallen in my way.

22. Limborch, great-nephew of Episcopius, seems more than any other Arminian divine to have inherited his mantle. His most important work is the Theologia *Limborch.* Christiana, containing a system of divinity and morals, in seven books and more than 900 pages, published. in 1686.

---

[c] An account of this controversy will be found at length in the second volume of the Bibliothèque universelle.

It is the fullest delineation of the Arminian scheme; but as
the Arminians were by their principle free inquirers, and
not, like other churches, bondsmen of symbolical formularies,
no one book can strictly be taken as their representative.
The tenets of Limborch are, in the majority of disputable
points, such as impartial men have generally found in the
primitive or Ante-Nicene fathers; but in some he probably
deviates from them, steering far away from all that the Protestants of the Swiss reform had abandoned as superstitious
or unintelligible.

23. John Le Clerc, in the same relationship to Courcelles
Le Clerc. that Limborch was to Episcopius, and like him trans-
planted from Geneva to the more liberal air, at that
time, of the United Provinces, claims a high place among the
Dutch Arminians; for though he did not maintain their
cause either in systematic or polemical writings, his commentary on the Old Testament, and still more his excellent
and celebrated reviews, the Bibliothèques universelle, choisie,
and ancienne et moderne, must be reckoned a perpetual combat on that side. These journals enjoyed an extraordinary
influence over Europe, and deserved to enjoy it. Le Clerc
is generally temperate, judicious, appeals to no passion, displays a very extensive, though not perhaps a very deep
erudition, lies in wait for the weakness and temerity of those
he reviews, thus sometimes gaining the advantage over more
learned men than himself. He would have been a perfect
master of that sort of criticism, then newly current in literature, if he could have repressed an irritability in matters
personal to himself, and a degree of prejudice against the
Romish writers, or perhaps those styled orthodox in general,
which sometimes disturbs the phlegmatic steadiness with
which a good reviewer, like a practised sportsman, brings
down his game.[d]

___

[d] Bishop Monk observes that Le Clerc
'seems to have been the first person who
understood the power which may be
exercised over literature by a reviewer.'
Life of Bentley, p. 209. This may be
true, especially as he was nearly the first
reviewer, and certainly better than his
predecessors. But this remark is followed by a sarcastic animadversion upon
Le Clerc's ignorance of Greek metres,
and by the severe assertion, that 'by an
absolute system of terror he made himself a despot in the republic of letters.'
[The former is certainly just: Le
Clerc was not comparable to Bentley, or
to many who have followed, in his
critical knowledge of Greek metres;
which, at the present day, would be held

24. The most remarkable progress made by the Arminian theology was in England. This had begun under Sancroft's Fur Prædestinatus. James and Charles; but it was then taken up in conjunction with that patristic learning which adopted the fourth and fifth centuries as the standard of orthodox faith. Perhaps the first very bold and unambiguous attack on the Calvinistic system which we shall mention came from this quarter. This was in an anonymous Latin pamphlet entitled Fur Prædestinatus, published in 1651, and generally ascribed to Sancroft, at that time a young man. It is a dialogue between a thief under sentence of death and his attendant minister, wherein the former insists upon his assurance of being predestinated to salvation. In this idea there is nothing but what is sufficiently obvious; but the dialogue is conducted with some spirit and vivacity. Every position in the thief's mouth is taken from eminent Calvinistic writers; and what is chiefly worth notice is, that Sancroft, for the first time, has ventured to arraign the greatest heroes of the Reformation; not only Calvin, Beza, and Zanchius, but, who had been hitherto spared, Luther and Zwingle. It was in the nature of a manifesto from the Arminian party, that they would not defer in future to any modern authority.[e]

---

very cheap. He is however to be judged relatively to his predecessors; and, in the particular department of metrical rules, few had known much more than he did: as we may perceive by the Greek compositions of Casaubon and other eminent scholars. Le Clerc might have been more prudent in abstaining from interference with what he did not well understand; but this cannot warrant scornful language towards so general a scholar, and one who served literature so well. That he made himself a despot in the republic of letters by a system of terror, is a charge not made out, as it seems to me, by the general character of Le Clerc's criticisms, which, where he has no personal quarrel, is temperate and moderate, neither traducing men, nor imputing motives. I adhere to the character of his reviews given in the text; and having early in life become acquainted with them, and having been accustomed, by books then esteemed, to think highly of Le Clerc, I must be excused from following a change of fashion. This note has been modified on the complaint of the learned prelate quoted in it, whom I had not the slightest intention of offending, but who might take some expressions, with respect to periodical criticism, as personal to himself; which neither were so meant, nor, as far as I know, could apply to any reputed writings of his composition.—1847.]

[e] The Fur Prædestinatus is reprinted in D'Oyly's Life of Sancroft. It is much the best proof of ability that the worthy archbishop ever gave.

[The superiority of this little piece to anything else ascribed to Sancroft is easily explained. It was not his own; of which his biographers have been ignorant. Leibnitz informs us that it is a translation from a Dutch tract, published at the beginning of the Arminian controversy. Bayle, he says, was not aware of this, and quotes it as written in English, Theodicea, sect. 167. Sancroft, as appears by D'Oyly's Life of him, was in Holland from 1657 to 1659.—1853.]

25. The loyal Anglican clergy, suffering persecution at the
Arminian- hands of Calvinistic sectaries, might be naturally
ism in
England. expected to cherish the opposite principles. These
are manifest in the sermons of Barrow, rather perhaps by his
silence than his tone, and more explicitly in those of South.
But many exceptions might be found among leading men,
such as Sanderson; while in an opposite quarter, among
the younger generation who had conformed to the times,
arose a more formidable spirit of Arminianism, which changed
the face of the English church. This was displayed among
those who, just about the epoch of the Restoration, were denominated Latitude-men, or more commonly Latitudinarians,
trained in the principles of Episcopius and Chillingworth,
strongly averse to every compromise with popery; and thus
distinguished from the high church party ; learned rather in
profane philosophy than in the fathers, more full of Plato
and Plotinus than Jerome or Chrysostom, great maintainers
of natural religion, and of the eternal laws of morality, not
very solicitous about systems of orthodoxy, and limiting very
considerably beyond the notions of former ages the fundamental tenets of Christianity. This is given as a general
character, but varying in the degree of its application to particular persons. Burnet enumerates as the chief of this body
of men, More, Cudworth, Whichcot, Tillotson, Stillingfleet;
some, especially the last, more tenacious of the authority of
the fathers and of the church than others, but all concurring
in the adoption of an Arminian theology.[f] This became
so predominant before the Revolution, that few English
divines of eminence remained, who so much as endeavoured
to steer a middle course, or to dissemble their renunciation
of the doctrines which had been sanctioned at the synod of
Dort by the delegates of their church. ' The Theological
Institutions of Episcopius,' says a contemporary writer, ' were
at that time (1685) generally in the hands of our students of
divinity in both universities, as the best system of divinity that
had appeared.'[g]   And he proceeds afterwards : ' The Remon-

---

[f] Burnet's History of His Own Times,   499.
i. 187. ' Account of the new Sect called   [g] Nelson's Life of Bull, in Bull's
Latitudinarians,' in the collection of   Works, vol. viii. p. 257.
tracts, entitled The Phœnix, vol. ii. p.

strant writers, among whom there were men of excellent learning and parts, had now acquired a considerable reputation in our universities by the means of some great men among us.' This testimony seems irresistible; and as one hundred years before the Institutes of Calvin were read in the same academical studies, we must own, unless Calvin and Episcopius shall be maintained to have held the same tenets, that Bossuet might have added a Chapter to the Variations of Protestant Churches.

26. The methods adopted in order to subvert the Augustinian theology were sometimes direct, by explicit controversy, or by an opposite train of Scriptural interpretation in regular commentaries ; more frequently perhaps indirect, by inculcating moral duties, and especially by magnifying the law of nature. Among the first class the Harmonia Apostolica of Bull seems to be reckoned the principal work of this period. It was published in 1669, and was fiercely encountered at first not merely by the presbyterian party, but by many of the church, the Lutheran tenets as to justification by faith being still deemed orthodox. Bull establishes as the groundwork of his harmony between the apostles Paul and James, on a subject where their language apparently clashes in terms, that we are to interpret St. Paul by St. James, and not St. James by St. Paul, because the latest authority, and that which may be presumed to have explained what was obscure in the former, ought to prevail ;[h] a rule doubtless applicable in many cases, whatever it may be in this. It at least turned to his advantage ; but it was not so easy for him to reconcile his opinions with those of the reformers, or with the Anglican articles.

Bull's Harmonia Apostolica.

27. The Paraphrase and Annotations of Hammond on the New Testament give a different colour to the Epistles of St. Paul from that which they display in the hands of Beza and the other theologians of the sixteenth century. And the name of Hammond stood so high with the Anglican clergy, that he naturally turned the tide of interpretation his own way. The writings of Fowler, Wilkins, and Whichcot are chiefly intended to exhibit the moral lustre

Hammond— Locke— Wilkins.

---

[h] Nelson's Life of Bull.

of Christianity, and to magnify the importance of virtuous life. Wilkins left an unfinished work on the Principles and Duties of Natural Religion. Twelve chapters only, about half the volume, were ready for the press at his death; the rest was compiled by Tillotson as well as the materials left by the author would allow; and the expressions employed lead us to believe that much was due to the editor. The latter's preface strongly presses the separate obligation of natural religion, upon which both the disciples of Hobbes, and many of the less learned sectaries, were at issue with him.

28. We do not find much of importance written on the Trinitarian controversy before the middle of the seventeenth century, except by the Socinians themselves. But the case was now very different. Though the Polish or rather German Unitarians did not produce more distinguished men than before, they came more forward in the field of dispute. Finally expelled from Poland in 1660, they sought refuge in more learned as well as more tolerant regions, and especially in the genial soil of religious liberty, the United Provinces. Even here they enjoyed no avowed toleration; but the press, with a very slight concealment of place, under the attractive words Eleutheropolis, Irenopolis, or Freystadt, was ready to serve them with its natural impartiality. They began to make a slight progress in England; the writings of Biddle were such as even Cromwell, though habitually tolerant, did not overlook; the author underwent an imprisonment both at that time and after the Restoration. In general, the Unitarian writers preserved a disguise. Milton's treatise, not long since brought to light, goes on the Arian hypothesis, which had probably been countenanced by some others. It became common, in the reign of Charles II., for the English divines to attack the Anti-Trinitarians of each denomination.

Socinians in England.

29. An epoch is supposed to have been made in this controversy by the famous work of Bull, Defensio Fidei Nicenæ. This was not primarily directed against the heterodox party. In the Dogmata Theologica of Petavius, published in 1644, that learned Jesuit, laboriously compiling passages from the fathers, had come to the conclusion,

Bull's Defensio Fidei Nicenæ.

that most of those before the Nicene council had seemed, by
their language, to run into nearly the same heresy as that
which the council had condemned, and this inference appeared to rest on a long series of quotations. The Arminian
Courcelles, and even the English philosopher Cudworth, the
latter of whom was as little suspected of an heterodox lean-
ing as Petavius himself, had arrived at the same result; so
that a considerable triumph was given to the Arians, in
which the Socinians, perhaps at that time more numerous,
seem to have thought themselves entitled to partake. Bull
had therefore to contend with authorities not to be despised
by the learned.

30. The Defensio Fidei Nicenæ was published in 1685.
It did not want answerers in England; but it obtained a
great reputation, and an assembly of the French clergy,
through the influence of Bossuet, returned thanks to the
author. It was indeed evident that Petavius, though he had
certainly formed his opinion with perfect honesty, was preparing the way for an inference, that if the primitive fathers
could be heterodox on a point of so great magnitude, we
must look for infallibility not in them nor in the diffusive
church, but in general councils presided over by the pope, or
ultimately in the pope himself. This, though not unsuitable
to the notions of some Jesuits, was diametrically opposite to
the principles of the Gallican church, which professed to
repose on a perpetual and catholic tradition.

31. Notwithstanding the popularity of this defence of the
Nicene faith, and the learning it displays, the author **Not satis-**
was far from ending the controversy, or from satis- **factory to
all.**
fying all his readers. It was alleged that he does not meet
the question with which he deals; that the word ὁμοούσιος,
being almost new at the time of the council, and being
obscure and metaphysical in itself, required a precise definition to make the reader see his way before him, or at least
one better than Bull has given, which the adversary might
probably adopt without much scruple; that the passages
adduced from the fathers are often insufficient for his purpose; that he confounds the eternal essence with the eternal
personality or distinctness of the Logos, though well aware,
of course, that many of the early writers employed different

names (ἐνδιάθετος and προφορικὸς) for these; and that he does
not repel some of the passages which can hardly bear an
orthodox interpretation. It was urged, moreover, that his
own hypothesis, taken altogether, is but a palliated Arianism,
that by insisting for more than one hundred pages on the
subordination of the Son to the Father, he came close to
what since has borne that name, though it might not be
precisely what had been condemned at Nice, and could not
be reconciled with the Athanasian creed, except by such an
interpretation of the latter as is neither probable, nor has
been reputed orthodox.

32. Among the theological writers of the Roman church,
and in a less degree among Protestants, there has
always been a class not inconsiderable for numbers
or for influence, generally denominated mystics, or, when
their language has been more unmeasured, enthusiasts and
fanatics. These may be distinguished into two kinds, though
it must readily be understood that they may often run much
into one another; the first believing that the soul, by immediate communion with the Deity, receives a peculiar illumination and knowledge of truths not cognisable by the understanding; the second less solicitous about intellectual
than moral light, and aiming at such pure contemplation of
the attributes of God, and such an intimate perception of
spiritual life, as may end in a sort of absorption into the
divine essence. But I should not probably have alluded to
any writings of this description, if the two most conspicuous
luminaries of the French church, Bossuet and Fenelon, had not clashed with each other in that famous
controversy of Quietism, to which the enthusiastic writings
of Madame Guyon gave birth. The 'Maximes des Saints'
of Fenelon I have never seen; some editions of his entire
works, as they affect to be, do not include what the church
has condemned; and the original book has probably become
scarce.[i] Fenelon appears to have been treated by his friend,
(shall we call him?) or rival, with remarkable harshness.
Bossuet might have felt some jealousy at the rapid elevation
of the Archbishop of Cambray; but we need not have re-

Mystics.

Fenelon.

[It is reprinted in the edition of Fenelon's works, Versailles, 1820.—1847.]

course to this; the rigour of orthodoxy in a temper like his will account for all. There could be little doubt but that many saints honoured by the church had uttered things quite as strong as any that Fenelon's work contained. Bossuet however succeeded in obtaining its condemnation at Rome. Fenelon was of the second class above mentioned among the mystics, and seems to have been absolutely free from such pretences to illumination as we find in Behmen or Barclay. The pure disinterested love of God was the main spring of his religious theory. The Divine Œconomy of Poiret, 1686, and the writings of a German quietist, Spener, do not require any particular mention.[k]

33. This later period of the seventeenth century was marked by an increasing boldness in religious inquiry; we find more disregard of authority, more disposition to question received tenets, a more suspicious criticism, both as to the genuineness and the credibility of ancient writings, a more ardent love of truth, that is, of perceiving and understanding what is true, instead of presuming that we possess it without any understanding at all. Much of this was associated, no doubt, with the other revolutions in literary opinion; with the philosophy of Bacon, Descartes, Gassendi, Hobbes, Bayle, and Locke, with the spirit which a slightly learned, yet acute generation of men rather conversant with the world than with libraries, (to whom the appeal in modern languages must be made,) was sure to breathe, with that incessant reference to proof which the physical sciences taught mankind to demand. Hence quotations are comparatively rare in the theological writings of this age; they are better reduced to their due office of testimony as to fact, sometimes of illustration or better statement of an argument, but not so much alleged as argument or authority in themselves. Even those who combated on the side of established doctrines were compelled to argue more from themselves, lest the public, their umpire, should reject, with an opposite prejudice, what had enslaved the prejudices of their fathers.

Change in the character of theological literature.

34. It is well known that a disbelief in Christianity became

---

[k] Bibl. universelle, v. 412, xvi. 224.

very frequent about this time. Several books more or less ap-
Freedom of
many
writings. pear to indicate this spirit, but the charge has often
been made with no sufficient reason. Of Hobbes
enough has been already said, and Spinosa's place as a metaphysician will be in the next chapter. His Tractatus Theo-
logico-Politicus, published anonymously at Amsterdam, with
the false date of Hamburg, in 1670, contains many observations on the Old Testament, which, though they do not really
affect its general authenticity and truth, clashed with the
commonly received opinion of its absolute inspiration. Some
of these remarks were, if not borrowed, at least repeated in
a book of more celebrity, Sentimens de quelques Théologiens
de Hollande sur l'Histoire critique du Père Simon. This
work is written by Le Clerc, but it has been doubted whether
he is the author of those acute, but hardy, questions on the
inspiration of Scripture which it contains. They must however be presumed to coincide for the most part with his own
opinion ; but he has afterwards declared his dissent from the
hypothesis contained in these volumes, that Moses was not
the author of the Pentateuch. The Archæologia Philosophica
of Thomas Burnet is intended to dispute the literal history
of the creation and fall. But few will pretend that either
Le Clerc or Burnet were disbelievers in Revelation.

35. Among those who sustained the truth of Christianity
Thoughts
of Pascal. by argument rather than authority, the first place
both in order of time and of excellence is due to
Pascal, though his Thoughts were not published till 1670,
some years after his death, and, in the first edition, not
without suppressions. They have been supposed to be fragments of a more systematic work that he had planned, or
perhaps only reflections committed to paper, with no design
of publication in their actual form. But, as is generally the
case with works of genius, we do not easily persuade ourselves that they could have been improved by any such alteration as would have destroyed their type. They are at
present bound together by a real coherence through the predominant character of the reasonings and sentiments, and
give us everything that we could desire in a more regular
treatise without the tedious verbosity which regularity is apt
to produce. The style is not so polished as in the Provincial

Letters, and the sentences are sometimes ill-constructed and elliptical. Passages almost transcribed from Montaigne have been published by careless editors as Pascal's.

36. But the Thoughts of Pascal are to be ranked, as a monument of his genius, above the Provincial Letters, though some have asserted the contrary. They burn with an intense light; condensed in expression, sublime, energetic, rapid, they hurry away the reader till he is scarcely able or willing to distinguish the sophisms from the truth which they contain. For that many of them are incapable of bearing a calm scrutiny is very manifest to those who apply such a test. The notes of Voltaire, though always intended to detract, are sometimes unanswerable; but the splendour of Pascal's eloquence absolutely annihilates, in effect on the general reader, even this antagonist.

37. Pascal had probably not read very largely, which has given an ampler sweep to his genius. Except the Bible and the writings of Augustin, the book that seems most to have attracted him was the Essays of Montaigne. Yet no men could be more unlike in personal dispositions and in the cast of their intellect. But Pascal, though abhorring the religious and moral carelessness of Montaigne, found much that fell in with his own reflections in the contempt of human opinions, the perpetual humbling of human reason, which runs through the bold and original work of his predecessor. He quotes no book so frequently; and indeed, except Epictetus, and once or twice Descartes, he hardly quotes any other at all. Pascal was too acute a geometer, and too sincere a lover of truth, to countenance the sophisms of mere Pyrrhonism; but like many theological writers, in exalting faith he does not always give reason her value, and furnishes weapons which the sceptic might employ against himself. It has been said that he denies the validity of the proofs of natural religion. This seems to be in some measure an error, founded on mistaking the objections he puts in the mouths of unbelievers for his own. But it must, I think, be admitted that his arguments for the being of a God are too often *à tutiori*, that it is the safer side to take.

38. The Thoughts of Pascal on miracles abound in proofs of his acuteness and originality; an originality much more

striking when we recollect that the subject had not been discussed as it has since, but with an intermixture of some sophistical and questionable positions. Several of them have a
secret reference to the famous cure of his niece, Mademoiselle
Perier, by the holy thorn. But he is embarrassed with the
difficult question whether miraculous events are sure tests of
the doctrine which they support, and is not wholly consistent
in his reasoning, or satisfactory in his distinctions. I am
unable to pronounce whether Pascal's other observations on
the rational proofs of Christianity are as original as they are
frequently ingenious and powerful.

39. But the leading principle of Pascal's theology, that
from which he deduces the necessary truth of Revelation, is
the fallen nature of mankind ; dwelling less upon Scriptural
proofs, which he takes for granted, than on the evidence
which he supposes man himself to supply. Nothing, however,
can be more dissimilar than his beautiful visions to the vulgar
Calvinism of the pulpit. It is not the sordid, grovelling, degraded Caliban of that school, but the ruined archangel that
he delights to paint. Man is so great, that his greatness is
manifest even in his knowledge of his own misery. A tree
does not know itself to be miserable. It is true that to know
we are miserable is misery ; but still it is greatness to know
it. All his misery proves his greatness ; it is the misery of
a great lord, of a king, dispossessed of their own. Man is
the feeblest branch of nature, but it is a branch that thinks.
He requires not the universe to crush him. He may be killed
by a vapour, by a drop of water. But if the whole universe
should crush him, he would be nobler than that which causes
his death, because he knows that he is dying, and the universe would not know its power over him. This is very
evidently sophistical and declamatory ; but it is the sophistry
of a fine imagination. It would be easy, however, to find
better passages. The dominant idea recurs in almost every
page of Pascal. His melancholy genius plays in wild and
rapid flashes, like lightning round the scathed oak, about
the fallen greatness of man. He perceives every characteristic quality of his nature under these conditions. They are
the solution of every problem, the clearing up of every inconsistency that perplexes us. ' Man,' he says very finely, ' has

a secret instinct that leads him to seek diversion and employment from without; which springs from the sense of his continual misery, And he has another secret instinct, remaining from the greatness of his original nature, which teaches him that happiness can only exist in repose. And from these two contrary instincts there arises in him an obscure propensity, concealed in his soul, which prompts him to seek repose through agitation, and even to fancy that the contentment he does not enjoy will be found, if by struggling yet a little longer he can open a door to rest.'[m]

40. It can hardly be conceived that any one would think the worse of human nature or of himself by reading these magnificent lamentations of Pascal. He adorns and ennobles the degeneracy that he exaggerates. The ruined aqueduct, the broken column, the desolated city, suggest no ideas but of dignity and reverence. No one is ashamed of a misery which bears witness to his grandeur. If we should persuade a labourer that the blood of princes flows in his veins, we might spoil his contentment with the only lot he has drawn, but scarcely kill in him the seeds of pride.

41. Pascal, like many others who have dwelt on this alleged degeneracy of mankind, seems never to have disentangled his mind from the notion, that what we call human nature has not merely an arbitrary and grammatical, but an intrinsic objective reality. The common and convenient forms of language, the analogies of sensible things, which the imagination readily supplies, conspire to delude us into this fallacy. Yet though each man is born with certain powers and dispositions which constitute his own nature, and the resemblance of these in all his fellows produces a general idea, or a collective appellation, whichever we may prefer to say, called the nature of man, few would in this age explicitly contend for the existence of this as a substance capable of qualities, and those qualities variable, or subject to mutation. The corruption of human nature is therefore a phrase which may convey an intelligible meaning, if it is acknowledged to be merely analogical and inexact, but will mislead those who do not keep this in mind. Man's nature, as it now is, that

---

[m] Œuvres de Pascal, vol. i. p. 121.

which each man and all men possess, is the immediate workmanship of God, as much as at his creation ; nor is any other
hypothesis consistent with theism.

42. This notion of a real universal in human nature presents to us in an exaggerated light those anomalies from
which writers of Pascal's school are apt to infer some vast
change in our original constitution.   Exaggerated, I say, for
it cannot be denied that we frequently perceive a sort of in-
coherence, as it appears at least to our defective vision, in
the same individual; and, like threads of various hues shot
through one web, the love of vice and of virtue, the strength
and weakness of the heart, are wonderfully blended in self-
contradictory and self-destroying conjunction.   But even if
we should fail altogether in solving the very first steps of this
problem, there is no course for a reasonable being, except to
acknowledge the limitations of his own faculties; and it
seems rather unwarrantable, on the credit of this humble
confession, that we do not comprehend the depths of what
has been withheld from us, to substitute something far more
incomprehensible and revolting to our moral and rational
capacities in its place.   'What,' says Pascal, ' can be more
contrary to the rules of our wretched justice, than to damn
eternally an infant incapable of volition, for an offence
wherein he seems to have had no share, and which was committed six thousand years before he was born ?   Certainly,
nothing shocks us more rudely than this doctrine ; and yet,
without this mystery, the most incomprehensible of all,
we are incomprehensible to ourselves.   Man is more inconceivable without this mystery, than the mystery is inconceivable to man.'

43. It might be wandering from the proper subject of these
volumes, if we were to pause, even shortly, to inquire whether,
while the creation of a world so full of evil must ever remain
the most inscrutable of mysteries, we might not be led some
way in tracing the connexion of moral and physical evil in
mankind with his place in that creation ; and especially,
whether the law of continuity, which it has not pleased his
Maker to break with respect to his bodily structure, and
which binds that, in the unity of one great type, to the lower
forms of animal life by the common conditions of nourish-

ment, reproduction, and self-defence, has not rendered necessary both the physical appetites and the propensities which
terminate in self; whether, again, the superior endowments
of his intellectual nature, his susceptibility of moral emotion, and of those disinterested affections which, if not exclusively, he far more intensely possesses than any inferior being ;
above all, the gifts of conscience, and a capacity to know God,
might not be expected, even beforehand, by their conflict with
the animal passions, to produce some partial inconsistencies,
some anomalies at least, which he could not himself explain,
in so compound a being.   Every link in the long chain of
creation does not pass by easy transition into the next.
There are necessary chasms, and, as it were, leaps, from one
creature to another, which, though not exceptions to the law
of continuity, are accommodations of it to a new series of
being.   If man was made in the image of God, he was also
made in the image of an ape.   The framework of the body of
him who has weighed the stars, and made the lightning his
slave, approaches to that of a speechless brute, who wanders
in the forests of Sumatra.   Thus standing on the frontier
land between animal and angelic natures, what wonder that
he should partake of both !   But these are things which it is
difficult to touch ; nor would they have been here introduced,
but in order to weaken the force of positions so confidently
asserted by many, and so eloquently by Pascal.

44. Among the works immediately designed to confirm the
truth of Christianity, a certain reputation was ac- Vindications
quired, through the known erudition of its author, of Christian-
                                                      ity.
by the Demonstratio Evangelica of Huet, Bishop of Avranches.   This is paraded with definitions, axioms, and propositions, in order to challenge the name it assumes.   But the
axioms, upon which so much is to rest, are often questionable or equivocal ; as, for instance : Omnis prophetia est
verax, quæ prædixit res eventu deinde completas,—equivocal
in the word *verax*.   Huet also confirms his axioms by argument, which shows that they are not truly such.   The whole
book is full of learning ; but he frequently loses sight of the
points he would prove, and his quotations fall beside the
mark.   Yet he has furnished much to others, and possibly no
earlier work on the same subject is so elaborate and compre-

hensive.   The next place, if not a higher one, might be given
to the treatise of Abbadie, a French refugee, published in
1684.   His countrymen bestow on it the highest eulogies,
but it was never so well known in England, and is now almost
forgotten.   The oral conferences of Limborch with Orobio,
a Jew of considerable learning and ability, on the prophecies
relating to the Messiah, were reduced into writing and published; they are still in some request.   No book of this period,
among many that were written, reached so high a reputation
in England as Leslie's Short Method with the Deists, published in 1694 ; in which he has started an argument, pursued
with more critical analysis by others, on the peculiarly distinctive marks of credibility that pertain to the Scriptural
miracles.   The authenticity of this little treatise has been
idly questioned on the Continent, for no better reason than
that a translation of it has been published in a posthumous
edition (1732) of the works of Saint Real, who died in 1692.
But posthumous editions are never deemed of sufficient authority to establish a literary title against possession; and
Prosper Marchand informs us that several other tracts, in
this edition of Saint Real, are erroneously ascribed to him.
The internal evidence that the Short Method was written by
a Protestant should be conclusive.[n]

45.   Every change in public opinion which this period wit-
Progress of nessed, confirmed the principles of religious tolera-
tolerant
principles.   tion, that had taken root in the earlier part of the
century ; the progress of a larger and more catholic theology,

---

[n] The   Biographie   universelle, art.
Leslie, says, Cet ouvrage, qui passe pour
ce qu'il a fait de mieux, lui a été con-
testé.   Le docteur Gleigh [sic] a fait de
grands efforts pour prouver qu'il ap-
partenait à Leslie, quoiqu'il fût publié
parmi les ouvrages de l'abbé de Saint-
Real, mort en 1692.   It is melancholy
to see this petty spirit of cavil against
an English writer in so respectable a
work as the Biographie universelle.   No
grands efforts could be required from
Dr. Gleig or any one else to prove that
a book was written by Leslie, which
bore his name, which was addressed to
an English peer, and had gone through
many editions, when there is literally
no claimant on the other side; for a
posthumous edition, forty years after

the supposed author's death, without
attestation, is no literary evidence at all,
even where the book is published for the
first time, much less where it has a known
status as the production of a certain
author.   This is so manifest to any one
who has the slightest tincture of critical
judgment, that we need not urge the
palpable improbability of ascribing to
Saint Real, a Romish ecclesiastic, an
argument which turns peculiarly on the
distinction between the Scriptural miracles and those alleged upon inferior evidence.   I have lost, or never made, the
reference to Prosper Marchand ; but the
passage will be found in his Dictionnaire
historique, which contains a full article
on Saint Real.

the weakening of bigotry in the minds of laymen, and the
consequent disregard of ecclesiastical clamour, not only in
England and Holland, but to a considerable extent in
France; we might even add, the violent proceedings of the
last government in the revocation of the Edict of Nantes
and the cruelties which attended it. Louis XIV., at a time
when mankind were beginning to renounce the very theory
of persecution, renewed the ancient enormities of its practice, and thus unconsciously gave the aid of moral sympathy
and indignation to the adverse argument. The Protestant
refugees of France, scattered among their brethren, brought
home to all minds the great question of free conscience; not
with the stupid and impudent limitation which even Protestants had sometimes employed, that truth indeed might not
be restrained, but that error might; a broader foundation
was laid by the great advocates of toleration in this period,
Bayle, Limborch, and Locke, as it had formerly been by
Taylor and Episcopius.[o]

46. Bayle, in 1686, while yet the smart of his banishment
was keenly felt, published his Philosophical Com- Bayle's Phi-
mentary on the text in Scripture, 'Compel them to losophical
Commen-
come in;' a text which some of the advocates of tary.
persecution were accustomed to produce. He gives in the
first part nine reasons against this literal meaning, among
which none are philological. In the second part he replies
to various objections. This work of Bayle does not seem to
me as subtle and logical as he was wont to be, notwithstanding the formal syllogisms with which he commences each of
his chapters. His argument against compulsory conversions,
which the absurd interpretation of the text by his adversaries required, is indeed irresistible; but this is far from sufficiently establishing the right of toleration itself. It appears
not very difficult for a skilful sophist, and none was more so
than Bayle himself, to have met some of his reasoning with
a specious reply. The sceptical argument of Taylor, that we

[o] The Dutch clergy, and a French
minister in Holland, Jurieu, of great
polemical fame in his day, though now
chiefly known by means of his adversaries, Bayle and Le Clerc, strenuously
resisted both the theory of general toleration, and the moderate or liberal principles in religion which were connected
with it. Le Clerc passed his life in
fighting this battle, and many articles
in the Bibliothèque universelle relate
to it.

can rarely be sure of knowing the truth ourselves, and consequently of condemning in others what is error, he touches but slightly; nor does he dwell on the political advantages which experience has shown a full toleration to possess. In the third part of the Philosophical Commentary, he refutes the apology of Augustin for persecution; and a few years afterwards he published a supplement answering a book of Jurieu, which had appeared in the mean time.

47. Locke published anonymously his Letter on Toleration Locke's in 1689. The season was propitious; a legal tole-
Letter on
Toleration. rance of public worship had first been granted to the dissenters after the Revolution, limited indeed to such as held most of the doctrines of the church, but preparing the nation for a more extensive application of its spirit. In the Liberty of Prophesying, Taylor had chiefly in view to deduce the justice of tolerating a diversity in religion, from the difficulty of knowing the truth. He is not very consistent as to the political question, and limits too narrowly the province of tolerable opinions. Locke goes more expressly to the right of the civil magistrate, not omitting, but dwelling less forcibly on the chief arguments of his predecessor. His own theory of government came to his aid. The clergy in general, and perhaps Taylor himself, had derived the magistrate's jurisdiction from paternal power. And as they apparently assumed this power to extend over adult children, it was natural to give those who succeeded to it in political communities a large sway over the moral and religious behaviour of subjects. Locke, adopting the opposite theory of compact, defines the commonwealth to be a society of men constituted only for the procuring, preserving, and advancing their own civil interests. He denies altogether that the care of souls belongs to the civil magistrate, as it has never been committed to him. 'All the power of civil government relates only to men's civil interests, is confined to the things of this world, and hath nothing to do with the world to come.'[p]

---

[p] [This principle, that the civil magistrate is not concerned with religion as true, but only as useful, was strenuously maintained by Warburton, in his Alliance of Church and State. It is supported on Scriptural grounds by Hoadly, in his famous sermon which produced the Bangorian controversy, and by Archbishop Whately, in a sermon on the same text as Hoadly's, 'My kingdom is not of this world;' but with more closeness, though not less

48. The admission of this principle would apparently decide the controversy, so far as it rests on religious grounds. But Locke has recourse to several other arguments independent of it. He proves, with no great difficulty, that the civil power cannot justly, or consistently with any true principle of religion, compel men to profess what they do not believe. This, however, is what very few would, at present, be inclined to maintain. The real question was as to the publicity of opinions deemed heterodox, and especially in social worship; and this is what those who held the magistrate to possess an authority patriarchal, universal, and arbitrary, and who were also rigidly tenacious of the necessity of an orthodox faith, as well as perfectly convinced that it was no other than their own, would hardly be persuaded to admit by any arguments that Locke has alleged. But the tendency of public opinion had begun to manifest itself against all these tenets of the high-church party, so that, in the eighteenth century, the principles of general tolerance became too popular to be disputed with any chance of attention. Locke was engaged in a controversy through his first Letter on Toleration, which produced a second and a third; but it does not appear to me that these, though longer than the first, have considerably modified its leading positions.[q] It is to be observed that he pleads for the universal toleration of all modes of worship not immoral in their nature, or involving doctrines inimical to good government; placing in the latter category some tenets of the church of Rome.

49. It is confessed by Goujet that, even in the middle of the seventeenth century, France could boast very French little of pulpit eloquence. Frequent quotations sermons. from heathen writers, and from the schoolmen, with little

---

decision and courage. I cannot, nevertheless, admit the principle as a conclusion from their premises, though very desirous to preserve it on other grounds. The late respected Dr. Arnold was exceedingly embarrassed by denying its truth, while he was strenuous for toleration in the amplest measure; which leaves his writings on the subject unsatisfactory, and weak against an adversary.—1847.]

[q] Warburton has fancied that Locke's real sentiments are only discoverable in his first Letter on Toleration, and that in the two latter he ' combats his intolerant adversary quite through the controversy with his own principles, well foreseeing, that at such a time of prejudice arguments built on received opinions would have greatest weight, and make quickest impression on the body of the people whom it was his business to gain.' Biogr. Britannica, art. Locke.

solid morality and less good reasoning, make up the sermons
of that age.[r] But the revolution in this style, as in all
others, though perhaps gradual, was complete in the reign of
Louis XIV. A slight sprinkling of passages from the fathers,
and still more frequently from the Scriptures, but always
short, and seeming to rise out of the preacher's heart, rather
than to be sought for in his memory, replaced that intolerable parade of a theological common-place book, which had
been as customary in France as in England. The style was
to be the perfection of French eloquence, the reasoning persuasive rather than dogmatic, the arrangement more methodical and distributive than at present, but without the excess
we find in our old preachers. This is the general character
of French sermons ; but those who most adorned the pulpit
had of course their individual distinctions. Without delay-
ing to mention those who are now not greatly remembered,
such as La Rue, Hubert, Mascaron, we must confine ourselves to three of high reputation, Bourdaloue, Bossuet, and
Fléchier.

50. Bourdaloue, a Jesuit, but as little of a Jesuit in the
worst acceptation of the word as the order has produced, is remarkably simple, earnest, practical ; he
convinces rather than commands, and by convincing he persuades ; for his discourses tend always to some duty, to something that is to be done or avoided. His sentences are short,
interrogative, full of plain and solid reasoning, unambitious
in expression, and wholly without that care in the choice of
words and cadences which we detect in Bossuet and Fléchier.
No one would call Bourdaloue a rhetorician, and though he
continually introduces the fathers, he has not caught their
vices of language.[s]

Bourdaloue.

---

[r] Bibliothèque française, vol. ii. p.
283.

[s] The public did justice to Bourdaloue,
as they generally do to a solid and impressive style of preaching. 'Je crois,'
says Goujet, p. 300, ' que tout le monde
convient qu'aucun autre ne lui est supé-
rieur. C'est le grand maître pour l'éloquence de la chaire ; c'est le prince des
prédicateurs. Le public n'a jamais été
partagé sur son sujet ; la ville et la cour

l'ont également estimé et admiré. C'est
qu'il avoit réuni en sa personne tous les
grands caractères de la bonne éloquence ;
la simplicité du discours chrétien avec
la majesté et la grandeur, le sublime
avec l'intelligible et le populaire, la force
avec la douceur, la véhémence avec
l'onction, la liberté avec la justesse, et
la plus vive ardeur avec la plus pure
lumière.'

51. Bourdaloue is almost in the same relation to Bossuet as Patru to Le Maistre, though the two orators compared of the pulpit are far above those of the bar. As the with Bossuet. one is short, condensed, plain, reasoning, and though never feeble, not often what is generally called eloquent, so the other is animated, figurative, rather diffuse and prodigal of ornament, addressing the imagination more than the judgment, rich and copious in cadence, elevating the hearer to the pitch of his own sublimity. Bossuet is sometimes too declamatory ; and Bourdaloue perhaps sometimes borders on dryness. Much in the sermons of the former is true poetry ; but he has less of satisfactory and persuasive reasoning than the latter. His tone is also, as in all his writings, too domineering and dogmatical for those who demand something beyond the speaker's authority when they listen.

52. The sermons however of Bossuet, taken generally, are not reckoned in the highest class of his numerous Funeral writings; perhaps scarcely justice has been done to discourses of Bossuet. them. His genius, on the other hand, by universal confession, never shone higher than in the six which bear the name of Oraisons Funèbres. They belong in substance so much more naturally to the province of eloquence than of theology, that I should have reserved them for another place if the separation would not have seemed rather unexpected to the reader. Few works of genius perhaps in the French language are better known, or have been more prodigally extolled. In that style of eloquence which the ancients called demonstrative, or rather descriptive (ἐπιδεικτικὸς), the style of panegyric or commemoration, they are doubtless superior to those justly celebrated productions of Thucydides and Plato that have descended to us from Greece; nor has Bossuet been equalled by any later writer. Those on the queen of England, on her daughter the Duchess of Orleans, and on the Prince of Condé, outshine the rest ; and if a difference is to be made among these, we might perhaps, after some hesitation, confer the palm on the first. The range of topics is so various, the thoughts so just, the images so noble and poetical, the whole is in such perfect keeping, the tone of awful contemplation is so uniform, that if it has not any passages of such extraor-

dinary beauty as occur in the other two, its general effect on the mind is more irresistible.[t]

53. In this style, much more of ornament, more of what speaks in the spirit, and even the very phrase, of poetry, to the imagination and the heart, is permitted by a rigorous criticism, than in forensic or in deliberative eloquence. The beauties that rise before the author's vision are not renounced; the brilliant colours of his fancy are not subdued; the periods assume a more rhythmical cadence, and emulate, like metre itself, the voluptuous harmony of musical intervals ; the whole composition is more evidently formed to delight ; but it will delight to little purpose, or even cease, in any strong sense of the word, to do so at all, unless it is ennobled by moral wisdom. In this Bossuet was pre-eminent; his thoughts are never subtle or far fetched; they have a sort of breadth, a generality of application, which is peculiarly required in those who address a mixed assembly, and which many that aim at what is profound and original are apt to miss. It may be confessed, that these funeral discourses are not exempt from some defects, frequently inherent in panegyrical eloquence ; they are sometimes too rhetorical, and do not appear to show so little effort as some have fancied ; the amplifications are sometimes too unmeasured, the language sometimes borders too nearly on that of the stage ; above all, there is a tone of adulation not quite pleasing to a calm posterity.

54. Fléchier, (the third name of the seventeenth century), for Massillon belongs only to the next,) like Bossuet, has been more celebrated for his funeral sermons than for any others; but in this line it is unfortunate for him to enter into unavoidable competition with one whom

Fléchier.

---

[t] An English preacher of conspicuous renown for eloquence was called upon, within no great length of time, to emulate the funeral discourse of Bossuet on the sudden death of Henrietta of Orleans. He had before him a subject incomparably more deep in interest, more fertile in great and touching associations —he had to describe, not the false sorrow of courtiers, not the shriek of sudden surprise that echoed by night in the halls of Versailles, not the apocryphal penitence of one so tainted by the world's intercourse, but the manly grief of an entire nation in the withering of those visions of hope which wait upon the untried youth of royalty, in its sympathy with grandeur annihilated, with beauty and innocence precipitated into the tomb. Nor did he sink beneath his subject, except as compared with Bossuet. The sermon to which my allusion will be understood is esteemed by many the finest effort of this preacher; but if read together with that of its prototype, it will be laid aside as almost feeble and unimpressive.

he cannot rival. The French critics extol Fléchier for the
arrangement and harmony of his periods; yet even in this,
according to La Harpe, he is not essentially superior to
Bossuet; and to an English ear, accustomed to the long
swell of our own writers and of the Ciceronian school in
Latin, he will probably not give so much gratification. He
does not want a moral dignity, or a certain elevation of
thought, without which the funeral panegyric must be contemptible; but he has not the majestic tone of Bossuet; he
does not, like him, raise the heroes and princes of the earth
in order to abase them by paintings of mortality and weakness, or recall the hearer in every passage to something more
awful than human power, and more magnificent than human
grandeur. This religious solemnity, so characteristic in
Bossuet, is hardly felt in the less emphatic sentences of
Fléchier. Even where his exordium is almost worthy of comparison, as in the funeral discourse on Turenne, we find him
degenerate into a trivial eulogy, and he flatters both more
profusely and with less skill. His style is graceful, but not
without affectation and false taste.[u] La Harpe has compared
him to Isocrates among the orators of Greece, the place of
Demosthenes being of course reserved for Bossuet.[x]

---

[u] [La Harpe justly ridicules an expression of Fléchier, in his funeral sermon on Madame de Montausier: Un
ancien disait autrefois que les hommes
étaient nés pour l'action et pour la con-
duite du monde, et que les *dames* n'étaient nées que pour le repos et pour la
retraite.—1842.]

[x] The native critics ascribe a reform in
the style of preaching to Paolo Segneri,
whom Corniani does not hesitate to call,
with the sanction, he says, of posterity,
the father of Italian eloquence. It is to
be remembered that in no country has
the pulpit been so much degraded by
empty declamation, and even by a stupid
buffoonery. 'The language of Segneri,'
the same writer observes, 'is always full
of dignity and harmony. He inlaid it
with splendid and elegant expressions,
and has thus obtained a place among
the authors to whom authority has
been given by the Della Crusca dictionary. His periods are flowing, natural, and intelligible, without the affec-

tation of obsolete Tuscanisms, which
pass for graces of the language with
many.' Tiraboschi, with much commendation of Segneri, admits that we
find in him some vestiges of the false
taste he endeavoured to reform. The
very little that I have seen of the sermons of Segneri gives no impression of
any merit that can be reckoned more
than relative to the miserable tone of
his predecessors. The following specimen is from one of his most admired
sermons:—E Cristo non potrà ottenere
da voi che gli rimettiate un torto, un
affronto, un aggravio, una parolina? Che
vorreste da Cristo? Vorreste ch' egli
vi si gettasse supplichevole a piedi a
chiedervi questa grazia? Io son quasi
per dire ch' egli il farebbe; perchè se
non dubiti di prostrarsi a piedi di un
traditore, qual' era Giuda, di lavarglieli,
di asciugarglieli, di baciarglieli, non si
vergognerebbe, cred' io, di farsi vedere
ginocchioni a piè vostri. Ma vi fa biso-
gno di tanto per muovervi a compia-

55. The style of preaching in England was less ornamental, and spoke less to the imagination and affections, than these celebrated writers of the Gallican
church ; but in some of our chief divines it had its own excellences. The sermons of Barrow display a strength of mind,
a comprehensiveness and fertility, which have rarely been
equalled. No better proof can be given than his eight sermons on the government of the tongue; copious and exhaustive without tautology or superfluous declamation, they
are, in moral preaching, what the best parts of Aristotle are
in ethical philosophy, with more of development and a more
extensive observation. It would be said of these sermons,
and indeed, with a few exceptions, of all those of Barrow,
that they are not what is now called evangelical; they indicate the ascendancy of an Arminian party, dwelling far more
than is usual in the pulpit on moral and rational, or even
temporal inducements, and sometimes hardly abstaining
from what would give a little offence in later times.ʸ His
quotations also from ancient philosophers, though not so
numerous as in Taylor, are equally uncongenial to our ears.
In his style, notwithstanding its richness and occasional
vivacity, we may censure a redundancy and excess of apposition : it is not sufficient to avoid strict tautology ; no second
phrase (to lay down a general rule not without exception)
should be so like the first, that the reader would naturally
have understood it to be comprised therein. Barrow's language is more antiquated and formal than that of his age ;
and he abounds too much in uncommon words of Latin de-

---

cerlo ? Ah Cavalieri, Cavalieri, io non
vorrei questa volta farvi arrossire. Nel
resto io so di certo, che se altrettanto
fosse a voi domandato da quella donna
che chiamate la vostra dama, da quella,
di cui forsennati idolatrate il volto, indo-
vinate le voglie, ambite le grazie, non
vi farete pregar tanto a concedergli elo.
E poi vi fate pregar tanto da un Dio per
voi crocefisso ? O confusione ! O vitu-
pero ! O vergogna !—Raccolta di Prose
Italiane (in Classici Italiani), vol. ii.
p. 345.
  This is certainly not the manner of
Bossuet, and more like that of a third-
rate Methodist among us.
  ʸ Thus, in his sermon against evil

speaking (xvi.), Barrow treats it as fit
‘ for rustic boors or men of coarsest
education and employment, who having
their minds debased by being conversant
in meanest affairs, do vent their sorry
passions, and bicker about their petty
concernments in such strains, who also,
not being capable of a fair reputation, or
sensible of disgrace to themselves, do
little value the credit of others, or care
for aspersing it. But such language is
unworthy of those persons, and cannot
easily be drawn from them, who are
wont to exercise their thoughts about
nobler matters,’ &c. No one would
venture this now from the pulpit.

rivation, frequently such as appear to have no authority but
his own.

56. South's sermons begin, in order of date, before the
Restoration, and come down to nearly the end of
the century. They were much celebrated at the ^{South.} South.
time, and retain a portion of their renown. This is by no
means surprising. South had great qualifications for that
popularity which attends the pulpit, and his manner was at
that time original. Not diffuse, not learned, not formal in
argument like Barrow, with a more natural structure of sentences, a more pointed, though by no means a more fair and
satisfactory turn of reasoning, with a style clear and English,
free from all pedantry, but abounding with those colloquial
novelties of idiom, which, though now become vulgar and
offensive, the age of Charles II. affected, sparing no personal
or temporary sarcasm, but, if he seems for a moment to tread
on the verge of buffoonery, recovering himself by some stroke
of vigorous sense and language ; such was the witty Dr.
South, whom the courtiers delighted to hear. His sermons
want all that is called unction, and sometimes even earnest-
ness, which is owing, in a great measure, to a perpetual
tone of gibing at rebels and fanatics; but there is a masculine spirit about them, which, combined with their peculiar
characteristics, would naturally fill the churches where he
might be heard. South appears to bend towards the Arminian theology, without adopting so much of it as some of his
contemporaries.

57. The sermons of Tillotson were for half a century more
read than any in our language. They are now
bought almost as waste paper, and hardly read at ^{Tillotson.} Tillotson.
all. Such is the fickleness of religious taste, as abundantly
numerous instances would prove. Tillotson is reckoned
verbose and languid. He has not the former defect in nearly
so great a degree as some of his eminent predecessors; but
there is certainly little vigour or vivacity in his style. Full
of the Romish controversy, he is perpetually recurring to
that 'world's debate;' and he is not much less hostile to
all the Calvinistic tenets. What is most remarkable in
the theology of Tillotson is his strong assertion, in almost all
his sermons, of the principles of natural religion and morality,

not only as the basis of all revelation, without a dependence
on which it cannot be believed, but as nearly coincident with
Christianity in their extent; a length to which few at present would be ready to follow him. Tillotson is always of a
tolerant and catholic spirit, enforcing right actions rather
than orthodox opinions, and obnoxious, for that and other
reasons, to all the bigots of his own age.

58. It has become necessary to draw towards a conclusion
Expository of this chapter; the materials are far from being
theology. exhausted. In expository, or, as some call it, exe-
getical theology, the English divines had already taken a
conspicuous station. Andrès, no partial estimator of Protestant writers, extols them with marked praise.[z] Those who
belonged to the earlier part of the century form a portion of
a vast collection, the Critici Sacri, published by one Bee, a
bookseller, in 1660. This was in nine folio volumes; and in
1669, Matthew Pool, a nonconforming minister, produced
his Synopsis Criticorum in five volumes, being in great measure an abridgment and digest of the former. Bee complained of the infraction of his copyright, or rather his
equitable interest; but such a dispute hardly pertains to our
history.[a] The work of Pool was evidently a more original
labour than the former. Hammond, Patrick, and other commentators, do honour to the Anglican church in the latter
part of the century.

59. Pearson's Exposition of the Apostles' Creed, published
Pearson on in 1659, is a standard book in English divinity.
the Creed. It expands beyond the literal purport of the creed
itself to most articles of orthodox belief, and is a valuable
summary of arguments and authorities on that side. The
closeness of Pearson, and his judicious selection of proofs,
distinguish him from many, especially the earlier, theologians. Some might surmise that his undeviating adherence
to what he calls the Church is hardly consistent with independence of thinking; but, considered as an advocate, he is
one of much judgment and skill. Such men as Pearson and

---

[z] I soli Inglesi, che ampio spazio non   i più degni della nostra stima ? Vol. xix.
dovrebbono occupare in questo capo dell'   p. 253.
esegetica sacra, se l' istituto della nostr'   [a] Chalmers.
opera ci permettesse tener dietro a tutti

Stillingfleet would have been conspicuous at the bar, which we could not quite affirm of Jeremy Taylor.

60. Simon, a regular priest of the congregation called The Oratory, which has been rich in eminent men, owes much of his fame to his Critical History of the Old Testament. This work, bold in many of its positions, as it then seemed to both the Catholic and Protestant orthodox, after being nearly strangled by Bossuet in France, appeared at Rotterdam in 1685. Bossuet attacked it with extreme vivacity, but with a real inferiority to Simon both in learning and candour.[b] Le Clerc on his side carped more at the Critical History than it seems to deserve. Many paradoxes, as they then were called, in this famous work, are now received as truth, or at least pass without reproof. Simon may possibly be too prone to novelty, but a love of truth as well as great acuteness are visible throughout. His Critical History of the New Testament was published in 1689, and one or two more works of a similar description before the close of the century.

Simon's Critical Histories.

61. I have on a former occasion adverted, in a corresponding chapter, to publications on witchcraft and similar superstitions. Several might be mentioned at this time; the belief in such tales was assailed by a prevalent scepticism which called out their advocates. Of these the most unworthy to have exhibited their great talents in such a cause were our own philosophers Henry More and Joseph Glanvil. The Sadducismus Triumphatus, or Treatise on Apparitions, by the latter, has passed through several editions, while his Scepsis Scientifica has hardly been seen, perhaps, by six living persons. A Dutch minister, by name Bekker, raised a great clamour against himself by a downright denial of all power to the devil, and consequently to his supposed instruments, the ancient beldams of Holland and other countries. His Monde enchanté, originally published in Dutch, is in four volumes, written in a systematic manner, and with tedious prolixity. There was no ground for imputing infidelity to the author, except the usual ground of calumniating every

---

[b] Défense de la Tradition des Saints Pères. Œuvres de Bossuet, vol. v., and Instructions sur la Version du N. T., imprimée à Trévoux, Id. vol. iv. p. 313. Bausset, Vie de Bossuet, iv. 276.

one who quits the beaten path in theology; but his explanations of Scripture in the case of the demoniacs and the like are, as usual with those who have taken the same line, rather forced. The fourth volume, which contains several curious stories of imagined possession, and some which resemble what is now called magnetism, is the only part of Bekker's once celebrated book that can be read with any pleasure. Bekker was a Cartesian, and his theory was built too much on Cartesian assumptions of the impossibility of spirit *acting* on body.

CHAPTER III.

HISTORY OF SPECULATIVE PHILOSOPHY FROM 1650 TO 1700.

Aristotelians—Logicians—Cudworth—Sketch of the Philosophy of Gassendi
—Cartesianism—Port-Royal Logic—Analysis of the Search for Truth
of Malebranche, and of the Ethics of Spinosa—Glanvil—Locke's Essay
on the Human Understanding.

1. THE Aristotelian and scholastic metaphysics, though shaken on every side, and especially by the rapid progress of the Cartesian theories, had not lost their hold over the theologians of the Roman church, or even the Protestant universities, at the beginning of this period, and hardly at its close. Brucker enumerates several writers of that class in Germany;[a] and we find, as late as 1693, a formal injunction by the Sorbonne, that none who taught philosophy in the colleges under its jurisdiction should introduce any novelties, or swerve from the Aristotelian doctrine.[b] The Jesuits, rather unfortunately for their credit, distinguished themselves as strenuous advocates of the old philosophy, and thus lost the advantage they had obtained in philology as enemies of barbarous prejudice, and encouragers of a progressive spirit in their disciples. Rapin, one of their most accomplished men, after speaking with little respect of the Novum Organum, extols the disputations of the schools as the best method in the education of young men, who, as he fancies, have too little experience to delight in physical science.[c]

Aristotelian metaphysics.

---

[a] Vol. iv. See his long and laborious chapter on the Aristotelian philosophers of the sixteenth and seventeenth centuries; no one else seems to have done more than copy Brucker.

[b] Cum relatum esset ad Societatem (Sorbonicam) nonnullos philosophiæ professores, ex iis etiam aliquando qui ad Societatem anhelant, novas quasdam doctrinas in philosophicis sectari, minusque Aristotelicæ doctrinæ studere, quam hactenus usurpatum fuerit in Academiâ Parisiensi, censuit Societas injungendum esse illis, imo et iis qui docent philosophiam in collegiis suo regimini creditis, ne deinceps novitatibus studeant, aut ab Aristotelica doctrina deflectant. 31 Dec. 1693. Argentré, Collectio Judiciorum, ii. 150.

[c] Réflexions sur la Poëtique, p. 368. He admits, however, that to introduce more experiment and observation would

2. It is a difficult and dangerous choice, in a new state of public opinion, (and we have to make it at present,) between that which may itself pass away, and that which must efface what has gone before. Those who clung to the ancient philosophy believed that Bacon and Descartes were the idols of a transitory fashion, and that the wisdom of long ages would regain its ascendancy. They were deceived, and their own reputation has been swept off with the systems to which they adhered. Thomas White, an English catholic priest, whose Latin appellation is Albius, endeavoured to maintain the Aristotelian metaphysics and the scholastic terminology in several works, and especially in an attack upon Glanvil's Vanity of Dogmatising. This book, entitled Sciri, I know only through Glanvil's reply in his second edition, by which White appears to be a mere Aristotelian. He was a friend of Sir Kenelm Digby, who was himself, though a man of considerable talents, incapable of disentangling his mind from the Peripatetic hypotheses. The power of words indeed is so great, the illusions of what is called realism, or of believing that general terms have an objective exterior being, are so natural, and especially so bound up both with our notions of essential, especially theological, truth, and with our popular language, that no man could in that age be much censured for not casting off his fetters, even when he had heard the call to liberty from some modern voices. We find that even after two centuries of a better method, many are always ready to fall back into a verbal process of theorising.

Their decline. Thomas White.

3. Logic was taught in the Aristotelian method, or rather in one which, with some change for the worse, had been gradually founded upon it. Burgersdicius, in this and in other sciences, seems to have been in repute; Smiglecius also is mentioned with praise.[d] These lived

Logic.

---

be an improvement. Du reste il y a apparence que les loix, qui ne souffrent point d'innovation dans l'usage des choses universellement établies, n'autoriseront point d'autre méthode que celle qui est aujourd'hui en usage dans les universités; afin de ne pas donner trop de licence à la passion qu'on a naturellement pour les nouvelles opinions, dont le cours

est d'une dangereuse conséquence dans un état bien réglé; vu particulièrement que la philosophie est un des organes dont se sert la religion pour s'expliquer dans ses décisions.

[d] La Logique de Smiglecius, says Rapin, est un bel ouvrage. The same writer proceeds to observe that the Spaniards of the preceding century had

both in the former part of the century. But they were
superseded, at least in England, by Wallis, whose Institutio
Logicæ ad Communes Usus Accommodata was published in
1687. He claims as an improvement upon the received
system, the classifying singular propositions among universals.[e] Ramus had made a third class of them, and in this
he seems to have been generally followed. Aristotle, though
it does not appear that he is explicit on the subject, does not
rank them as particular. That Wallis is right will not be
doubted by any one at present; but his originality we must
not assert. The same had been perceived by the authors of
the Port-Royal Logic; a work to which he has made no
allusion.[f] Wallis claims also as his own the method of reducing hypothetical to categorical syllogisms, and proves it
elaborately in a separate dissertation. A smaller treatise,
still much used at Oxford, by Aldrich, Compendium Artis
Logicæ, 1691, is clear and concise, but seems to contain
nothing very important; and he alludes to the Art de Penser
in a tone of insolence, which must rouse indignation in those
who are acquainted with that excellent work. Aldrich's
censures are, in many instances, mere cavil and misrepresentation; I do not know that they are right in any.[g] Of
the Art de Penser itself we shall have something to say in
the course of this chapter.

---

corrupted logic by their subtilties. En
se jetant dans des spéculations creuses
qui n'avoient rien de réel, leurs philo-
sophes trouvèrent l'art d'avoir de la
raison malgré le bon sens, et de donner
de la couleur, et même je ne sçais quoi
de spécieux, à ce qui étoit de plus dé-
raisonnable. p. 382. But this must have
been rather the fault of their metaphysics than of what is strictly called
logic.

[e] Atque hoc signanter notatum velim,
quia novus forte hic videar, et præter
aliorum loquendi formulam hæc dicere.
Nam plerique logici propositionem quam
vocant singularem, hoc est, de subjecto
individuo sive singulari, pro particulari
habent, non universali. Sed perperam
hoc faciunt, et præter mentem Aristotelis, (qui, quantum memini, nunquam
ejusmodi singularem, τὴν κατὰ μέρος ap-
pellat aut pro tali habet,) et præter rei
naturam: Non enim hic agitur de par-

ticularitate subjecti (quod ἄτομον vocat
Aristotelis, non κατὰ μέρος) sed de partia-
litate prædicationis. . . . Neque ego interim novator censendus sum qui hæc
dixerim, sed illi potius novatores qui ab
Aristotelica doctrina recesserint: eoque
multa introduxerint incommoda de quibus suo loco dicetur. p. 125. He has
afterwards a separate dissertation or
thesis to prove this more at length. It
seems that the Ramists held a third class
of propositions, neither universal nor
particular, to which they gave the name
of *propria*, equivalent to singular.

[f] Art de Penser, part ii. chap. iii.

[g] One of Aldrich's charges against
the author of the Art de Penser is, that
he brings forward as a great discovery
the equality of the angles of a chiliagon
to 1996 right angles; and another is,
that he gives as an example of a regular
syllogism one that has obviously five
terms; thus expecting the Oxford stu-

4. Before we proceed to those whose philosophy may be
Stanley's reckoned original, or at least modern, a very few
History of
Philosophy. deserve mention who have endeavoured to maintain
or restore that of antiquity. Stanley's History of Philosophy,
in 1655, is in great measure confined to biography, and comprehends no name later than Carneades. Most is derived
from Diogenes Laertius; but an analysis of the Platonic
philosophy is given from Alcinous, and the author has compiled one of the Peripatetic system from Aristotle himself.
The doctrine of the Stoics is also elaborately deduced from
various sources. Stanley, on the whole, brought a good deal
from an almost untrodden field; but he is merely an historian, and never a critic of philosophy.[h]

5. Gale's Court of the Gentiles, which appeared partly in
Gale's Court 1669 and partly in later years, is incomparably a
of Gentiles. more learned work than that of Stanley. Its aim
is to prove that all heathen philosophy, whether barbaric
or Greek, was borrowed from the Scriptures, or at least from
the Jews. The first part is entitled Of Philology, which
traces the same leading principle by means of language; the
second, Of Philosophy; the third treats of the Vanity of
Philosophy, and the fourth of Reformed Philosophy, ' wherein
Plato's moral and metaphysic or prime philosophy is reduced
to an usual form and method.' Gale has been reckoned
among Platonic philosophers, and indeed he professes to find
a great resemblance between the philosophy of Plato and his
own. But he is a determined Calvinist in all respects, and
scruples not to say, ' Whatever God wills is just, because he
wills it ; ' and again, ' God willeth nothing without himself
because it is just, but it is therefore just because he willeth
it. The reasons of good and evil extrinsic to the divine
essence are all dependent on the divine will, either decernent
or legislative.'[i] It is not likely that Plato would have
acknowledged such a disciple.

---

dents for whom he wrote, to believe that
Antony Arnauld neither knew the first
book of Euclid, nor the mere rudiments
of common logic.

[h] [In former editions, through an
oversight altogether inexplicable by me
at present, I had said that Stanley does
not mention Epicurus, who occupies a

considerable space in the History of
Philosophy. I have searched my notes
in vain for the source of this mistake,
which was courteously pointed out to
me; but I think it fitter to make this
public acknowledgment, than silently
to withdraw the sentence.—1847.]
[i] Part iv. p. 339.

6. A much more eminent and enlightened man than Gale, Ralph Cudworth, by his Intellectual System of the Universe, published in 1678, but written several years before, placed himself in a middle point between the declining and rising schools of philosophy; more independent of authority, and more close, perhaps, in argument than the former, but more prodigal of learning, more technical in language, and less conversant with analytical and inductive processes of reasoning than the latter. Upon the whole, however, he belongs to the school of antiquity, and probably his wish was to be classed with it. Cudworth was one of those whom Hobbes had roused by the atheistic and immoral theories of the Leviathan; nor did any antagonist perhaps of that philosopher bring a more vigorous understanding to the combat. This understanding was not so much obstructed in its own exercise by a vast erudition, as it is sometimes concealed by it from the reader. Cudworth has passed more for a recorder of ancient philosophy, than for one who might stand in a respectable class among philosophers; and his work, though long, being unfinished, as well as full of digression, its object has not been fully apprehended.

Cudworth's Intellectual System.

7. This object was to establish the liberty of human actions against the fatalists. Of these he lays it down that there are three kinds: the first atheistic; the second admitting a Deity, but one acting necessarily and without moral perfections: the third granting the moral attributes of God, but asserting all human actions to be governed by necessary laws which he has ordained. The first book of the Intellectual System, which alone is extant, relates wholly to the proofs of the existence of a Deity against the atheistic fatalists, his moral nature being rarely or never touched; so that the greater and more interesting part of the work, for the sake of which the author projected it, is wholly wanting, unless we take for fragments of it some writings of the author preserved in the British Museum.

Its object.

8. The first chapter contains an account of the ancient corpuscular philosophy, which, till corrupted by Leucippus and Democritus, Cudworth takes to have been not only theistic, but more consonant to theistic principles than any other. These two, however, brought in a

Sketch of it.

fatalism grounded on their own atomic theory. In the second chapter he states very fully and fairly all their arguments, or rather all that have ever been adduced on the atheistic side. In the third he expatiates on the hylozoic atheism, as he calls it, of Strato, which accounts the universe to be animated in all its parts, but without a single controlling intelligence, and adverts to another hypothesis, which gives a vegetable but not sentient life to the world.

9. This leads Cudworth to his own famous theory of a plastic nature, a device to account for the operations of physical laws without the continued agency of the Deity. Of this plastic energy he speaks in rather a confused and indefinite manner, giving it in one place a sort of sentient life, or what he calls 'a drowsy unawakened cogitation,' and always treating it as an entity or real being. This language of Cudworth, and indeed the whole hypothesis of a plastic nature, was unable to stand the searching eye of Bayle, who, in an article of his dictionary, pointed out its unphilosophical and dangerous assumptions. Le Clerc endeavoured to support Cudworth against Bayle, but with little success.[n] It has had, however, some partisans, though rather among physiologists than metaphysicians. Grew adopted it to explain vegetation; and the plastic nature differs only, as I conceive, from what Hunter and Abernethy have called life in organised bodies by its more extensive agency; for if we are to believe that there is a vital power, not a mere name for the sequence of phænomena, which marshals the molecules of animal and vegetable substance, we can see no reason why a similar energy should not determine other molecules to assume geometrical figures in crystallisation. The error or paradox consists in assigning a real unity of existence, and a real power of causation, to that which is unintelligent.

His plastic nature.

10. The fourth chapter of the Intellectual System, of vast length, and occupying half the entire work, launches into a sea of old philosophy, in order to show the unity of a supreme God to have been a general belief of antiquity. 'In this fourth chapter,' he says, ' we were neces-

His account of old philosophy.

---

[n] Bibliothèque choisie, vol. v.

sitated by the matter itself to run out into philology and
antiquity, as also in the other parts of the book we do often
give an account of the doctrine of the ancients ; which, however some over-severe philosophers may look upon fastidiously
or undervalue and depreciate, yet as we conceived it often
necessary, so possibly may the variety thereof not be ungrateful to others, and this mixture of philology throughout
the whole sweeten and allay the severity of philosophy to
them; the main thing which the book pretends to, in the
meantime, being the philosophy of religion. But for our
part we neither call philology, nor yet philosophy our mistress, but serve ourselves of either as occasion requireth.' [o]

11. The whole fourth chapter may be reckoned one great
episode, and as it contains a store of useful knowledge on
ancient philosophy, it has not only been more read than the
remaining part of the Intellectual System, but has been the
cause, in more than one respect, that the work has been
erroneously judged. Thus Cudworth has been reckoned, by
very respectable authorities, in the Platonic school of philosophers, and even in that of the later Platonists ; for which
I perceive little other reason than that he has gone diffusely
into a supposed resemblance between the Platonic and
Christian Trinity. Whether we agree with him in this or
no, the subject is insulated, and belongs only to the history
of theological opinion ; in Cudworth's own philosophy he appears to be an eclectic, not the vassal of Plato, Plotinus, or
Aristotle, though deeply versed in them all.[p]

12. In the fifth and last chapter of the first and only book
of the Intellectual System, Cudworth, reverting to His argu-
the various atheistical arguments which he had ments
against
stated in the second chapter, answers them at great atheism.
length, and though not without much erudition, perhaps
more than was requisite, yet depending chiefly on his own

---

[o] Preface, p. 37.

[p] [' Cudworth,' says a late very learned
and strong-minded writer, ' should be
read with the notes of Mosheim ; unless,
indeed, one be so acquainted with the
philosophy and religion of the ancients,
and so accustomed to reasoning, and to
estimating the power and the ambiguity
of language, as to be able to correct for
himself his deceptive representations.
He deserves the highest praise for integrity as a writer, his learning was su-
perabundant, and his intellect vigorous
enough to wield it to his purpose. But
he transfers his own conceptions to the
heathen philosophers and religionists,'
&c.   Norton on Genuineness of Gospels,
vol. ii. p. 215.—1847.]

stores of reasoning. And inasmuch as even a second-rate philosopher ranks higher in literary precedence than the most learned reporter of other men's doctrine, it may be unfortunate for Cudworth's reputation that he consumed so much time in the preceding chapter upon mere learning, even though that should be reckoned more useful than his own reasonings. These, however, are frequently valuable, and, as I have intimated above, he is partially tinctured by the philosophy of his own generation, while he endeavours to tread in the ancient paths. Yet he seems not aware of the place which Bacon, Descartes, and Gassendi were to hold ; and not only names them sometimes with censure, hardly with praise, but most inexcusably throws out several intimations that they had designedly served the cause of atheism. The disposition of the two former to slight the argument from final causes, though it might justly be animadverted upon, could not warrant this most uncandid and untrue aspersion. But justice was even-handed ; Cudworth himself did not escape the slander of bigots ; it was idly said by Dryden, that he had put the arguments against a Deity so well, that some thought he had not answered them ; and if Warburton may be believed, the remaining part of the Intellectual System was never published, on account of the world's malignity in judging of the first.[q] Probably it was never written.

13. Cudworth is too credulous and uncritical about ancient writings, defending all as genuine, even where his own age had been sceptical. His terminology is stiff and pedantic, as is the case with all our older metaphysicians, abounding in words which the English language has not recognised. He is full of the ancients, but rarely quotes the schoolmen. Hobbes is the adversary with whom he most grapples ; the materialism, the resolving all ideas into sensation, the low morality of that writer, were obnoxious to the animadversion of so strenuous an advocate of a more elevated philosophy. In some respects Cudworth has, as I conceive, much the advantage ; in others, he will generally be thought by our metaphysicians to want precision and logical reasoning ; and

---

[q] Warburton's preface to Divine Legation, vol. ii.

upon the whole we must rank him, in philosophical acumen, far below Hobbes, Malebranche, and Locke, but also far above any mere Aristotelians or retailers of Scotus and Aquinas.[r]

14. Henry More, though by no means less eminent than Cudworth in his own age, ought not to be placed on the same level. More fell not only into the mystical *More.* notions of the later Platonists, but even of the Cabalistic writers. His metaphysical philosophy was borrowed in great measure from them; and though he was in correspondence with Descartes, and enchanted with the new views that opened upon him, yet we find that he was reckoned much less of a Cartesian afterwards, and even wrote against parts of the theory.[s] The most peculiar tenet of More was the extension of spirit; acknowledging and even striving for the soul's immateriality, he still could not conceive it to be unextended. Yet it seems evident that if we give extension as well as figure, which is implied in finite extension, to the single self-conscious monad, qualities as heterogeneous to thinking as material impenetrability itself, we shall find it in vain to deny the possibility at least of the latter. Some indeed might question whether what we call matter is any real being at all, except as extension under peculiar conditions. But this conjecture need not here be pressed.

15. Gassendi himself, by the extensiveness of his erudition, may be said to have united the two schools of speculative philosophy, the historical and the *Gassendi.* experimental, though the character of his mind determined him far more towards the latter. He belongs in point of time rather to the earlier period of the century; but his Syntagma Philosophicum having been published in 1658, we have deferred the review of it for this volume. This posthumous work, in two volumes folio, and nearly 1600 pages closely printed in double columns, is divided into three parts, the

---

[r] [The inferiority of Cudworth to Hobbes is not at present very manifest to me.—1847.]

[s] Baillet, Vie de Descartes, liv. vii. It must be observed that More never wholly agreed with Descartes. Thus they differed about the omnipresence of the Deity; Descartes thought that he was partout à raison de sa puissance, et qu'à raison de son essence il n'a absolument aucune relation au lieu. More, who may be called a lover of extension, maintained a strictly local presence. Œuvres de Descartes, vol. x. p. 239.

Logic, the Physics, and the Ethics; the second occupying
more than five-sixths of the whole. The Logic is introduced
by two procemial books; one containing a history of the
science from Zeno of Elea, the parent of systematic logic, to
Bacon and Descartes;[t] the other, still more valu-
His Logic. able, on the criteria of truth; shortly criticising
also, in a chapter of this book, the several schemes of logic
which he had merely described in the former. After stating
very prolixly, as is usual with him, the arguments of the
sceptics against the evidence of the senses, and those of the
dogmatics, as he calls them, who refer the sole criterion of
truth to the understanding, he propounds a sort of middle
course. It is necessary, he observes, before we can infer
truth, that there should be some sensible sign, αἰσθητὸν
σημεῖον; for, since all the knowledge we possess is derived
from the sense, the mind must first have some sensible
image, by which it may be led to a knowledge of what is latent and not perceived by sense. Hence we may distinguish
in ourselves a double criterion; one by which we perceive the
sign, namely, the senses; another, by which we understand
through reasoning the latent thing, namely, the intellect or
rational faculty.[u] This he illustrates by the pores of the
skin, which we do not perceive, but infer their existence by
observing the permeation of moisture.

16. In the first part of the treatise itself on Logic, to which
His theory these two books are introductory, Gassendi lays
of ideas, down again his favourite principle, that every idea
in the mind is ultimately derived from the senses. But
while what the senses transmit are only singular ideas, the

---

[t] Prætereundum porro non est ob
eam, quâ est, celebritatem Organum,
sive logica Francisci Baconis Verulamii.
He extols Bacon highly, but gives an analysis of the Novum Organum without
much criticism. De Logicæ Origine,
c. x.

Logica Verulamii, Gassendi says in
another place, tota ac per se ad physi-
cam, atque adeo ad veritatem notitiamve
rerum germanam habendam contendit.
Præcipuè autem in eo est, ut bene ima-
ginemur, quatenus vult esse imprimis
exuenda omnia præjudicia, ac novas deinde notiones ideasve ex novis debitèque

factis experimentis inducendas. Logica
Cartesii rectè quidem Verulamii imita-
tione ab eo exorditur, quod ad bene
imaginandum prava præjudicia exuenda,
recta vero induenda vult, &c. p. 90.

[u] P. 81. If this passage be well attended to, it will show how the philosophy of Gassendi has been misunderstood by those who confound it with the
merely sensual school of metaphysicians.
No one has more clearly, or more at
length, distinguished the αἰσθητὸν σημεῖον,
the sensible associated sign, from the
unimaginable objects of pure intellect,
as we shall soon see.

mind has the faculty of making general ideas out of a number of these singular ones when they resemble each other.[x]
In this part of his Logic he expresses himself clearly and
unequivocally a conceptualist.

17. The Physics were expanded with a prodigality of learning upon every province of nature.   Gassendi is full of quotation, and his systematic method manifests the comprehensiveness of his researches.   In the third book of the second
part of the third section of the Physics, he treats of the
immateriality, and, in the fourteenth, of the immortality of
the soul, and maintains the affirmative of both propositions.
This may not be what those who judge of Gassendi merely
from his objections to the Meditations of Descartes have
supposed.   But a clearer insight into his metaphysical theory
will be obtained from the ninth book of the same part of
the Physics, entitled De Intellectu, on the Human Understanding.

18. In this book, after much display of erudition on the
tenets of philosophers, he determines the soul to be and of the
an incorporeal substance, created by God, and in- the soul.
fused into the body, so that it resides in it as an informing
and not merely a present nature, forma informans, et non
simpliciter assistens.[y] He next distinguishes intellection or
understanding from imagination or perception; which is
worthy of particular notice, because in his controversy with
Descartes he had thrown out doubts as to any distinction
between them.   We have in ourselves a kind of faculty
which enables us, by means of reasoning, to understand that
which by no endeavours we can imagine or represent to the
mind.[z]   Of this the size of the sun, or innumerable other

---

[x] P. 93.
[y] P. 440.
[z] Itaque est in nobis intellectûs species, qua ratiocinando eo provehimur,
ut aliquid intelligamus, quod imaginari,
vel cujus habere obversantem imaginem,
quantumcunque animi vires contenderi-
mus, non possimus. . . . After instancing
the size of the sun, possunt consimilia
sexcenta afferri. . . . Verum quidem istud
sufficiat, ut constet quidpiam nos intelligere quod imaginari non liceat, et intel-
lectum ita esse distinctum a phantasia, ut
cum phantasia habeat materiales species,

sub quibus res imaginatur, non habeat
tamen intellectus, sub quibus res intel-
ligat : neque enim ullam, v.g. habet illius
magnitudinis quam in sole intelligit;
sed tantum vi propria, seu ratiocinando,
eam esse in sole magnitudinem compre-
hendit, ac pari modo cætera.   Nempe ex
hoc efficitur, ut rem sine specie materiali
intelligens, esse immaterialis debeat ; si-
cuti phantasia ex eo materialis arguitur,
quod materiali specie utatur.   Ac utitur
quidem etiam intellectus speciebus phantasia perceptis, tanquam gradibus, ut ratiocinando assequatur ea, quæ deinceps

examples might be given; the mind having no idea suggested
by the imagination of the sun's magnitude, but knowing it
by a peculiar operation of reason. And hence we infer that
the intellectual soul is immaterial, because it understands
that which no material image presents to it, as we infer also
that the imaginative faculty is material, because it employs
the images supplied by sense. It is true that the intellect
makes use of these sensible images, as steps towards its
reasoning upon things which cannot be imagined; but the
proof of its immateriality is given by this, that it passes
beyond all material images, and attains a true knowledge of
that whereof it has no image.

19. Buhle observes that in what Gassendi has said on the
power of the mind to understand what it cannot conceive,
there is a forgetfulness of his principle, that nothing is in
the understanding which has not been in the sense. But,
unless we impute repeated contradictions to this philosopher,
he must have meant that axiom in a less extended sense than
it has been taken by some who have since employed it. By
that which is 'in the understanding,' he could only intend
definite images derived from sense, which must be present
before the mind can exercise any faculty, or proceed to
reason up to unimaginable things. The fallacy of the sensualist school, English and French, has been to conclude that
we can have no knowledge of that which is not 'in the understanding;' an inference true in the popular sense of words,
but false in the metaphysical.

20. There is, moreover, Gassendi proceeds, a class of reflex
operations, whereby the mind understands itself and
its own faculties, and is conscious that it is exercis-
ing such acts. And this faculty is superior to any
that a material substance possesses: for no body can act re-
flexly on itself, but must move from one place to another.[a]
Our observation therefore of our own imaginings must be by

Distin-
guishes
ideas of
reflection.

---

sine speciebus phantasmatisve intelligit:
sed hoc ipsum est quod illius imma-
terialitatem arguit, quod ultra omnem
speciem materialem se provehat, quid-
piamque cujus nullam habeat phantasma
revera agnoscat.

[a] Alterum est genus reflexarum ac-
tionum, quibus intellectus seipsum, suas-

que functiones intelligit, ac speciatim se
intelligere animadvertit. Videlicet hoc
munus est omni facultate corporea su-
perius; quoniam quicquid corporeum
est, ita certo loco, sive permanenter, sive
succedenter alligatum est, ut non versus
se, sed solum versus aliud diversum a se
procedere possit.

a power superior to imagination itself; for imagination is employed on the image, not on the perception of the image, since there is no image of the act of perception.

21. The intellect also not only forms universal ideas, but perceives the nature of universality. And this seems peculiar to mankind; for brutes do not show anything more than a power of association by resemblance. In our own conception of an universal, it may be urged, there is always some admixture of singularity, as of a particular form, magnitude, or colour; yet we are able, Gassendi thinks, to strip the image successively of all these particular adjuncts.[b] He seems therefore, as has been remarked above, to have held the conceptualist theory in the strictest manner, admitting the reality of universal ideas even as images present to the mind.

22. Intellection being the proper operation of the soul, it is needless to inquire whether it does this by its own nature, or by a peculiar faculty called under- standing, nor should we trouble ourselves about the Aristotelian distinction of the active and passive intellect.[c] We have only to distinguish this intellection from mere conception derived from the phantasy, which is necessarily associated with it. We cannot conceive God in this life, except under some image thus supplied; and it is the same with all other incorporeal things. Nor do we comprehend infinite quantities, but have a sort of confused image of indefinite extension. This is surely a right account of the matter; and if Stewart had paid any attention to these and several other passages, he could not have so much misconceived the philosophy of Gassendi.

Also intellect from imagination.

23. The mind, as long as it dwells in the body, seems to have no intelligible species, except phantasms derived from sense. These he takes for impressions on the brain, driven to and fro by the animal spirits till they reach the *phantasia*, or imaginative faculty, and cause it to imagine sensible things. The soul, in Gassendi's theory, consists of an incor-

---

[b] Et ne instes in nobis quoque, dum universale concipimus, admisceri semper aliquid singularitatis, ut certæ magnitudinis, certæ figuræ, certi coloris, &c. experimur tamen, nisi [sic] simul, saltem successivè spoliari à nobis naturam qualibet speciali magnitudine, qualibet speciali figurâ, quolibet speciali colore; atque ita de cæteris.

[c] P. 446.

poreal part or intellect, and of a corporeal part, the phantasy or sensitive soul, which he conceives to be diffused throughout the body. The intellectual soul instantly perceives, by its union with the phantasy, the images impressed upon the latter, not by impulse of these sensible and material species, but by intuition of their images in the phantasy.[d] Thus, if I rightly apprehend his meaning, we are to distinguish; first, the species in the brain, derived from immediate sense or reminiscence; secondly, the image of these conceived by the phantasy; thirdly, the act of perception in the mind itself, by which it knows the phantasy to have imagined these species, and knows also the species themselves to have, or to have had, their external archetypes. This distinction of the *animus*, or reasonable, from the *anima*, or sensitive soul, he took, as he did a great part of his philosophy, from Epicurus.

24. The phantasy and intellect proceed together, so that they might appear at first to be the same faculty. Not only, however, are they different in their operation even as to objects which fall under the senses, and are represented to the mind, but the intellect has certain operations peculiar to itself. Such is the apprehension of things which cannot be perceived by sense, as the Deity, whom though we can only imagine as corporeal, we apprehend or understand to be otherwise.[e] He repeats a good deal of what he had before said on the distinctive province of the understanding, by which we reason on things incapable of being imagined; drawing several instances from the geometry of infinites, as in asymptotes, wherein, he says, something is always inferred by reasoning which we presume to be true, and yet cannot reach by any effort of the imagination.[f]

---

[d] Eodem momento intellectus ob intimam sui præsentiam cohærentiamque cum phantasia rem eandem contuetur. p. 450.

[e] Hoc est autem præter phantasiæ cancellos, intellectûsque ipsius proprium, potestque adeo talis apprehensio non jam imaginatio, sed intelligentia vel intellectio dici. Non quod intellectus non accipiat ansam ab ipsa phantasia ratiocinandi esse aliquid ultra id, quod specie imagineve repræsentatur, neque non si-

mul comitantem talem speciem vel imaginationem habeat; sed quod apprehendat, intelligatve aliquid, ad quod apprehendendum sive percipiendum assurgere phantasia non possit, ut quæ omnino terminetur ad corporum speciem, seu imaginem, ex qua illius operatio imaginatio appellatur. Ibid.

[f] In quibus semper aliquid argumentando colligitur, quod et verum esse intelligimus et imaginando non assequimur tamen.

25. I have given a few extracts from Gassendi in order to
confirm what has been said, his writings being little His philoso-
read in England, and his philosophy not having phy misun-
been always represented in the same manner.   De- Stewart.
gerando has claimed, on two occasions, the priority for
Gassendi in that theory of the generation of ideas which
has usually been ascribed to Locke.[g]   But Stewart protests
against this alleged similarity in the tenets of the French
and English philosophers. 'The remark,' he says, 'is certainly just, if restrained to Locke's doctrine as interpreted
by the greater part of philosophers on the Continent; but it
is very wide of the truth, if applied to it as now explained
and modified by the most intelligent of his disciples in this
country. The main scope, indeed, of Gassendi's argument
against Descartes is to materialise that class of our ideas
which the Lockists as well as the Cartesians consider as the
exclusive objects of the power of *reflection*, and to show that
these ideas are all ultimately resolvable into images or conceptions borrowed from things external. It is not therefore
what is sound and valuable in this part of Locke's system,
but the errors grafted on it in the comments of some of his
followers, that can justly be said to have been borrowed from
Gassendi.   Nor has Gassendi the merit of originality even in

---

[Bernier well and clearly expressed the
important distinction between αἰσθητὰ
and νούμενα, which separates the two
schools of philosophy; and thus places
Gassendi far apart from Hobbes. The
passage, however, which I shall give in
French, cannot be more decisive than
the Latin sentence just quoted. Il ne faut
pas confondre l'imagination, ou, pour
parler ainsi, l'intellection intuitive, ou
directe, et qui se fait par l'application
seule de l'entendement aux phantômes
ou idées de la phantasie, avec l'intellection pure que nous avons par le
raisonnement, et que nous tirons par
conséquence. D'où vient que ceux qui
se persuadent qu'il n'y a aucune substance incorporelle, parce qu'ils ne con-
çoivent rien que dans une espèce ou
image corporelle, se trompent en ce
qu'ils ne reconnoissent pas qu'il y a une
sorte d'intelligence qui n'est pas imagination, à savoir celle par laquelle
nous connoissons par raisonnement qu'il

y a quelque chose outre ce qui tombe
sous l'imagination. Abrégé du Système
de Gassendi, vol. iii. p. 14. Gassendi
plainly confines idea to phantasy or imagination, and so far differs from Locke.
—1847.]

[g] Histoire comparée des Systèmes,
1804, vol. i. p. 301; and Biogr. universelle, art. Gassendi. Yet in neither of
these does M. Degerando advert expressly to the peculiar resemblance between the systems of Gassendi and
Locke, in the account they give of ideas
of reflection. He refers however to a
more particular essay of his own on the
Gassendian philosophy, which I have not
seen. As to Locke's positive obligations
to his predecessor, I should be perhaps
inclined to doubt whether he, who was
no great lover of large books, had read
so unwieldly a work as the Syntagma
Philosophicum; but the abridgment of
Bernier would have sufficed.

these errors; for scarcely a remark on the subject occurs in
his works, but what is copied from the accounts transmitted
to us of the Epicurean metaphysics.'[h]

26. It will probably appear to those who consider what I
have quoted from Gassendi, that in his latest writings he did
not differ so much from Locke, and lead the way so much
to the school of the French metaphysicians of the eighteenth
century, as Stewart has supposed. The resemblance to the
Essay on the Human Understanding in several points, especially in the important distinction of what Locke has called
ideas of reflection from those of sense, is too evident to be
denied. I am at the same time unable to account in a satisfactory manner for the apparent discrepancy between the
language of Gassendi in the Syntagma Philosophicum, and
that which we find in his objections to the Meditations of
Descartes. No great interval of time had intervened between
the two works; for his correspondence with Descartes bears
date in 1641, and it appears by that with Louis, Count of
Angoulême, in the succeeding year, that he was already employed on the first part of the Syntagma Philosophicum.[i]
Whether he urged some of his objections against the Cartesian metaphysics with a regard to victory rather than truth,
or, as would be the more candid and perhaps more reasonable hypothesis, he was induced by the acuteness of his great
antagonist, to review and reform his own opinions, I must
leave to the philosophical reader.[k]

27. Stewart had evidently little or no knowledge of the
Bernier's
epitome of
Gassendi. Syntagma Philosophicum. But he had seen an
Abridgment of the Philosophy of Gassendi by Ber-
nier, published at Lyons in 1678, and finding in this the doctrine of Locke on ideas of reflection, conceived that it did not

---

[h] Preliminary Dissertation to Encyclopædia.

[i] Gassendi Opera, vol. vi. p. 130.
These letters are interesting to those who
would study the philosophy of Gassendi.

[k] Baillet, in his Life of Descartes,
would lead us to think that Gassendi
was too much influenced by personal
motives in writing against Descartes,
who had mentioned the phænomena of
parhelia, without alluding to a dissertation of Gassendi on the subject. The

latter, it seems, owns in a letter to Rivet,
that he should not have examined so
closely the metaphysics of Descartes, if
he had been treated by him with as
much politeness as he had expected.
Vie de Descartes, liv. vi. The retort of
Descartes, O caro! (see Vol. II. of this
work, p. 449) offended Gassendi, and
caused a coldness; which, according to
Baillet, Sorbière aggravated, acting a
treacherous part in exasperating the
mind of Gassendi.

faithfully represent its own original.   But this was hardly
a very plausible conjecture; Bernier being a man of considerable ability, an intimate friend of Gassendi, and his epitome
being so far from concise that it extends to eight small
volumes. Having not indeed collated the two books, but read
them within a short interval of time, I can say that Bernier
has given a faithful account of the philosophy of Gassendi,
as it is contained in the Syntagma Philosophicum, for he
takes notice of no other work; nor has he here added anything of his own.   But in 1682 he published another little
book, entitled Doutes de M. Bernier sur quelques-uns des
principaux Chapitres de son Abrégé de la Philosophie de
Gassendi.   One of these doubts relates to the existence of
space; and in another place he denies the reality of eternity
or abstract duration.   Bernier observes, as Descartes had
done, that it is vain and even dangerous to attempt a definition of evident things, such as motion, because we are apt to
mistake a definition of the word for one of the thing; and
philosophers seem to conceive that motion is a real being,
when they talk of a billiard-ball communicating or losing it.[m]

28. The Cartesian philosophy, which its adversaries had
expected to expire with its founder, spread more Process of
and more after his death, nor had it ever depended Cartesian
philosophy.
on any personal favour or popularity of Descartes, since he
did not possess such except with a few friends. The churches
and schools of Holland were full of Cartesians.   The old
scholastic philosophy became ridiculous; its distinctions, its
maxims were laughed at, as its adherents complain; and probably a more fatal blow was given to the Aristotelian system
by Descartes than even by Bacon.   The Cartesian theories
were obnoxious to the rigid class of theologians; but two
parties of considerable importance in Holland, the Arminians
and the Coccejans, generally espoused the new philosophy.
Many speculations in theology were immediately connected
with it, and it acted on the free and scrutinising spirit which
began to sap the bulwarks of established orthodoxy.   The

---

[m] Even Gassendi has defined duration
' an incorporeal flowing extension,' which
is a good instance of the success that can
attend such definitions of simple ideas.

[Though this is not a proper definition
of duration, it is, perhaps, not ill expressed as an analogy.—1847.]

Cartesians were denounced in ecclesiastical synods, and were
hardly admitted to any office in the church. They were condemned by several universities, and especially by that of
Leyden in 1678,[n] for the position that the truth of Scripture
must be proved by reason. Nor were they less exposed to
persecution in France.[o]

29. The Cartesian philosophy, in one sense, carried in
itself the seeds of its own decline; it was the Scylla of many
dogs; it taught men to think for themselves, and to think
often better than Descartes had done. A new eclectic philosophy, or rather the genuine spirit of free inquiry, made Cartesianism cease as a sect, though it left much that had been
introduced by it. We owe thanks to these Cartesians of the
seventeenth century for their strenuous assertion of reason
against prescriptive authority: the latter part of this age
was signalised by the overthrow of a despotism which had
fought every inch in its retreat, and it was manifestly after
a struggle, on the Continent, with this new philosophy, that
it was ultimately vanquished.[p]

---

[n] Leyden had condemned the whole
Cartesian system as early as 1651, on the
ground that it was an innovation on the
Aristotelian philosophy, so long received;
and ordained, ut in Academia intra Aristotelicæ philosophiæ limites, quæ hic
hactenus recepta fuit, nos contineamus,
utque in posterum nec philosophiæ, neque nominis Cartesiani in disputationibus,
lectionibus aut publicis aliis exercitiis,
nec pro nec contra mentio fiat. Utrecht,
in 1644, had gone farther, and her decree
is couched in terms which might have
been used by any one who wished to ridicule university prejudice by a forgery.
Rejicere novam istam philosophiam,
primo quia veteri philosophiæ, quam
Academiæ toto orbi terrarum hactenus
optimo consilio docuere, adversatur, ejus-
que fundamenta subvertit; deinde quia
juventutem a veteri et sana philosophia
avertit, impeditque quo minus ad *culmen
eruditionis provehatur*; eo quod istius
præsumptæ philosophiæ adminiculo *tech-
nologemata in auctorum libris professorum-
que lectionibus et disputationibus usitata,
percipere nequit;* postremo quod ex
eadem variæ falsæ et absurdæ opiniones
partim consignantur, partim ab impro-
vida juventute deduci possint pugnantes

cum cæteris disciplinis et facultatibus,
atque imprimis cum orthodoxa theologia;
censere igitur et statuere omnes philosophiam in hac Academia docentes impos-
terum a tali instituto et incepto absti-
nere debere, contentos *modica libertate
dissentiendi* in singularibus nonnullis
opinionibus ad aliarum celebrium Aca-
demiarum exemplum hic usitata, ita ut
veteris et receptæ philosophiæ fundamenta non labefactent. Tepel. Hist.
Philos. Cartesianæ, p. 75.

[o] An account of the manner in which
the Cartesians were harassed through the
Jesuits is given by M. Cousin in the
Journal des Savans, March, 1838.

[p] For the fate of the Cartesian philosophy in the life of its founder, see the
life of Descartes by Baillet, 2 vols. in
quarto, which he afterwards abridged in
12mo. After the death of Descartes, it
may be best traced by means of Brucker.
Buhle, as usual, is a mere copyist of his
predecessor. He has however given a
fuller account of Regis. A contemporary History of Cartesian Philosophy by
Tepel contains rather a neatly written
summary of the controversies it excited
both in the lifetime of Descartes and for
a few years afterwards.

30. The Cartesian writers of France, the Low Countries, and Germany, were numerous and respectable. La La Forge. Regis. Forge of Saumur first developed the theory of occasional causes to explain the union of soul and body, wherein he was followed by Geulinx, Regis, Wittich, and Malebranche.[q] But this and other innovations displeased the stricter Cartesians who did not find them in their master. Clauberg in Germany, Clerselier in France, Le Grand in the Low Countries, should be mentioned among the leaders of the school. But no one has left so comprehensive a statement and defence of Cartesianism as Jean Silvain Regis, whose Système de la Philosophie, in three quarto volumes, appeared at Paris in 1690. It is divided into four parts, on Logic, Metaphysics, Physics, and Ethics. In the three latter Regis claims nothing as his own except some explanations. 'All that I have said being due to M. Descartes, whose method and principles I have followed, even in explanations that are different from his own.' And in his Logic he professes to have gone little beyond the author of the Art de Penser.[r] Notwithstanding this rare modesty, Regis is not a writer unworthy of being consulted by the studious of philosophy, nor deficient in clearer and fuller statements than will always be found in Descartes. It might even be said that he has many things which would be sought in vain through his master's writings, though I am unable to prove that they might not be traced in those of the intermediate Cartesians. Though our limits will not permit any further account of Regis, I will give a few passages in a note.[s]

---

[q] Tennemann (Manuel de la Philosophie, ii. 99) ascribes this theory to Geulinx. See also Brucker, v. 704.

[r] It is remarkable that Regis says nothing about figures and modes of syllogism: Nous ne dirons rien des figures ni des syllogismes en général; car bien que tout cela puisse servir de quelque chose pour la spéculation de la logique, il n'est au moins d'aucun usage pour la pratique, laquelle est l'unique but que nous nous sommes proposés dans ce traité. p. 37.

[s] Regis, in imitation of his master, and perhaps with more clearness, observes that our knowledge of our own existence is not derived from reasoning,

mais par une connoissance simple et intérieure, qui précède toutes les connoissances acquises, et que j'appelle *conscience*. En effet, quand je dis que je connois ou que je crois connoître, ce *je* présuppose lui-même mon existence, étant impossible que je connoisse, ou seulement que je croie connoître, et que je ne sois pas quelque chose d'existant. p. 68. The Cartesian paradox, as it at first appears, that thinking is the essence of the soul, Regis has explained away. After coming to the conclusion, Je suis donc une pensée, he immediately corrects himself: Cependant je crains encore de me définir mal, quand je dis que je suis une pensée, qui a la propriété de douter et d'avoir de

31. Huet, Bishop of Avranches, a man of more general eruditionthan philosophical acuteness, yet not quite without this, arraigned the whole theory in his Censura Philosophiæ Cartesianæ. He had been for many years, as he tells us, a favourer of Cartesianism, but his retraction is very complete. It cannot be denied that Huet strikes well at the vulnerable parts of the Cartesian metaphysics, and exposes their alternate scepticism and dogmatism with some justice. In other respects he displays an inferior know-

Huet's Censure of Cartesianism.

---

la certitude ; car quelle apparence y a-t-il que ma nature, qui doit être une chose fixe et permanente, consiste dans la pensée, puisque je sais par expérience que mes pensées sont dans un flux continuel, et que je ne pense jamais à la même chose deux momens de suite ? mais quand je considère la difficulté de plus près, je conçois aisément qu'elle vient de ce que le mot de *pensée* est équivoque, et que je m'en sers indifféremment pour signifier la pensée qui constitue ma nature, et pour désigner les différentes manières d'être de cette pensée ; ce qui est une erreur extrême, car il y a cette différence entre la pensée qui constitue ma nature, et les pensées qui n'en sont que les manières d'être, que la première est une pensée fixe et permanente, et que les autres sont des pensées changeantes et passagères. C'est pourquoi, afin de donner une idée exacte de ma nature, je dirai que je suis une pensée qui existe en elle-même, et qui est le sujet de toutes mes manières de penser. Je dis que je suis une pensée pour marquer ce que la pensée qui constitue ma nature a de commun avec la pensée en général qui comprend sous soi toutes les manières particulières de penser : et j'ajoute, qui existe en elle-même, et qui est le sujet de différentes manières de penser, pour désigner ce que cette pensée a de particulier qui la distingue de la pensée en général, vu qu'elle n'existe que dans l'entendement de celui qui la conçoit ainsi que toutes les autres natures universelles. p. 70.

Every mode supposes a substance wherein it exists. From this axiom Regis deduces the objective being of space, because we have the ideas of length, breadth, and depth, which cannot belong to ourselves, our souls having none of these properties ; nor could the ideas be suggested by a superior being,

if space did not exist, because they would be the representations of nonentity, which is impossible. But this transcendental proof is too subtle for the world.

It is an axiom of Regis that we only know things without us by means of ideas, and that things of which we have no ideas are in regard to us as if they did not exist at all. Another axiom is that all ideas, considered in respect to their representative property, depend on objects as their types, or *causes exemplaires*. And a third, that the 'cause exemplaire' of ideas must contain all the properties which the ideas represent. These axioms, according to him, are the bases of all certainty in physical truth. From the second axiom he deduces the objectivity or 'cause exemplaire' of his idea of a perfect being ; and his proof seems at least more clearly put than by Descartes. Every idea implies an objective reality ; for otherwise there would be an effect without a cause. Yet in this we have the sophisms and begging of questions of which we may see many instances in Spinosa.

In the second part of the first book of his metaphysics, Regis treats of the union of soul and body, and concludes that the motions of the body only act on the soul by a special will of God, who has determined to produce certain thoughts simultaneously with certain bodily motions. p. 124. God is the efficient first cause of all effects, his creatures are but secondarily efficient. But as they act immediately, we may ascribe all modal beings to the efficiency of second causes. And he prefers this expression to that of occasional causes, usual among the Cartesians, because he fancies the latter rather derogatory to the fixed will of God.

ledge of the human mind and of the principles of reasoning
to Descartes. He repeats Gassendi's cavil that, Cogito, ergo
sum, involves the truth of Quod cogitat, est. The Cartesians, Huet observes, assert the major, or universal, to be
deduced from the minor; which, though true in things
known by induction, is not so in propositions necessarily
known, or as the schools say, à priori, as that the whole is
greater than its part. It is not, however, probable that
Descartes would have extended his reply to Gassendi's criticism so far as this; some have referred our knowledge of
geometrical axioms to mere experience, but this seems not
agreeable to the Cartesian theory.

32. The influence of the Cartesian philosophy was displayed in a treatise of deserved reputation, L'Art   Port-Royal
de Penser, often called the Port-Royal Logic. It   Logic.
seems to have been the work of Anthony Arnauld, with some
assistance, perhaps, by Nicole. Arnauld was not an entire
Cartesian; he had himself been engaged in controversy with
Descartes, but his understanding was clear and calm, his
love of truth sincere, and he could not avoid recognising the
vast superiority of the new philosophy to that received in the
schools. This logic, accordingly, is perhaps the first regular
treatise on that science that contained a protestation, though
in very moderate language, against the Aristotelian method.
The author tells us that after some doubt he had resolved to
insert a few things rather troublesome, and of little value,
such as the rules of conversion and the demonstration of the
syllogistic figures, chiefly as exercises of the understanding,
for which difficulties are not without utility. The method of
syllogism itself he deems little serviceable in the discovery
of truth; while many things dwelt upon in books of logic,
such as the ten categories, rather injure than improve the
reasoning faculties, because they accustom men to satisfy
themselves with words, and to mistake a long catalogue of
arbitrary definitions for real knowledge. Of Aristotle he
speaks in more honourable terms than Bacon had done before,
or than Malebranche did afterwards: acknowledging the
extraordinary merit of some of his writings, but pointing out
with an independent spirit his failings as a master in the art
of reasoning.

33. The first part of L'Art de Penser is almost entirely metaphysical, in the usual sense of that word. It considers ideas in their nature and origin, in the chief differences of the objects they represent, in their simplicity or composition, in their extent, as universal, particular, or singular, and, lastly, in their distinctness or confusion. The word idea, it is observed, is among those which are so clear that we cannot explain them by means of others, because none can be more clear and simple than themselves.[t] But here it may be doubtful whether the sense in which the word is to be taken must strike every one in the same way. The clearness of a word does not depend on its association with a distinct conception in our own minds, but on the generality of this same association in the minds of others.

34. No follower of Descartes has more unambiguously than this author distinguished between imagination and intellection, though he gives the name of idea to both. Many suppose, he says, that they cannot conceive a thing when they cannot imagine it. But we cannot imagine a figure of 1,000 sides, though we can conceive it and reason upon it. We may indeed get a confused image of a figure with many sides, but these are no more 1,000 than they are 999. Thus also we have ideas of thinking, affirming, denying, and the like, though we have no imagination of these operations. By ideas therefore we mean not images painted in the fancy, but all that is in our minds when we say that we conceive anything, in whatever manner we may conceive it. Hence it is easy to judge of the falsehood of some opinions held in this age. One philosopher has advanced that we have no idea of God; another that all reasoning is but an assemblage of words connected by an affirmation. He glances here at Gassendi and Hobbes.[u] Far from all our ideas coming from the senses, as the Aristotelians have said, and as Gassendi asserts in his Logic, we may say, on the contrary, that no

---

[t] C. 1.

[u] The reflection on Gassendi is a mere cavil, as will appear by remarking what he has really said, and which we have quoted a few pages above. The Cartesians were resolute in using one sense of the word idea, while Gassendi used another. He had himself been to blame in this controversy with the father of the new philosophy, and the disciples (calling the author of L'Art de Penser such in a general sense) retaliated by equal captiousness.

idea in our minds is derived from the senses except occasionally (par occasion) ; that is, the movements of the brain, which is all that the organs of sense can affect, give occasion to the soul to form different ideas which it would not otherwise form, though these ideas have scarce ever any resemblance to what occurs in the organs of sense and in the brain, and though there are also very many ideas which, deriving nothing from any bodily image, cannot without absurdity be referred to the senses.[x] This is perhaps a clearer statement of an important truth than will be found in Malebranche or in Descartes himself.

35. In the second part Arnauld treats of words and propositions. Much of it may be reckoned more within the province of grammar than of logic. But as it is inconvenient to refer the student to works of a different class, especially if it should be the case that no good grammars, written with a regard to logical principles, were then to be found, this cannot justly be made an objection. In the latter chapters of this second part, he comes to much that is strictly logical, and taken from ordinary books on that science. The third part relates to syllogisms, and notwithstanding the author's low estimation of that method, in comparison with the general regard for it in the schools, he has not omitted the common explanations of mood and figure, ending with a concise but good account of the chief sophisms.

36. The fourth and last part is entitled, On Method, and contains the principles of connected reasoning, which he justly observes to be more important than the rules of single syllogisms, wherein few make any mistake. The laws of demonstration given by Pascal are here laid down with some enlargement. Many observations not wholly bearing on merely logical proof are found in this part of the treatise.

37. The Port-Royal Logic, though not, perhaps, very much read in England, has always been reckoned among the best works in that science, and certainly had a great influence in rendering it more metaphysical, more ethical (for much is said by Arnauld on the moral discipline of the mind in order

---

to fit it for the investigation of truth), more exempt from technical barbarisms and trifling definitions and divisions. It became more and more acknowledged that the rules of syllogism go a very little way in rendering the mind able to follow a course of inquiry without error, much less in assisting it to discover truth; and that even their vaunted prerogative of securing us from fallacy is nearly ineffectual in exercise. The substitution of the French language, in its highest polish, for the uncouth Latinity of the Aristotelians, was another advantage of which the Cartesian school legitimately availed themselves.

38. Malebranche, whose Recherche de la Vérité was published in 1674, was a warm and almost enthusiastic admirer of Descartes, but his mind was independent, searching, and fond of its own inventions; he acknowledged no master, and in some points dissents from the Cartesian school. His natural temperament was sincere and rigid; he judges the moral and intellectual failings of mankind with a severe scrutiny, and a contemptuousness not generally unjust in itself, but displaying too great confidence in his own superiority. This was enhanced by a religious mysticism, which enters, as an essential element, into his philosophy of the mind. The fame of Malebranche, and still more the popularity in modern times of his Search for Truth, has been affected by that peculiar hypothesis, so mystically expressed, the seeing all things in God, which has been more remembered than any other part of that treatise. 'The union,' he says, 'of the soul to God is the only means by which we acquire a knowledge of truth. This union has indeed been rendered so obscure by original sin, that few can understand what it means; to those who follow blindly the dictates of sense and passion it appears imaginary. The same cause has so fortified the connexion between the soul and body that we look on them as one substance, of which the latter is the principal part. And hence we may all fear that we do not well discern the confused sounds with which the senses fill the imagination from that pure voice of truth which speaks to the soul. The body speaks louder than God himself; and our pride makes us presumptuous enough to judge without waiting for those

words of truth, without which we cannot truly judge at all. And the present work,' he adds, ' may give evidence of this; for it is not published as being infallible.   But let my readers judge of my opinions according to the clear and distinct an- swers they shall receive from the only Lord of all men, after they shall have interrogated him by paying a serious atten- tion to the subject.'   This is a strong evidence of the enthu- siastic confidence in supernatural illumination which belongs to Malebranche, and which we are almost surprised to find united with so much cool and acute reasoning as his writings contain.

39. The Recherche de la Vérité is in six books; the first five on the errors springing from the senses, from the imagination, from the understanding, from the natural inclinations, and from the passions.   The sixth con- tains the method of avoiding these, which however has been anticipated in great measure throughout the preceding. Malebranche has many repetitions, but little, I think, that can be called digressive, though he takes a large range of illustration, and dwells rather diffusely on topics of subor- dinate importance.   His style is admirable; clear, precise, elegant, sparing in metaphors, yet not wanting them in due place, warm, and sometimes eloquent, a little redundant, but never passionate or declamatory.

His style.

40. Error, according to Malebranche, is the source of all human misery; man is miserable because he is a sinner, and he would not sin if he did not consent to err.   For the will alone judges and reasons, the under- standing only perceives things and their relations—a devia- tion from common language, to say the least, that seems quite unnecessary.[y]   The will is active and free; not that we can avoid willing our own happiness; but it possesses a power of turning the understanding towards such objects as please us, and commanding it to examine everything thoroughly, else we should be perpetually deceived, and without remedy, by the appearances of truth.   And this liberty we should use on every occasion : it is to become slaves, against the will of God, when we acquiesce in false

Sketch of his theory.

---

[y] L. i. c. 2.

appearances; but it is in obedience to the voice of eternal truth which speaks within us, that we submit to those secret reproaches of reason, which accompany our refusal to yield to evidence. There are, therefore, two fundamental rules, one for science, the other for morals; never to give an entire consent to any propositions, except those which are so evidently true that we cannot refuse to admit them without an internal uneasiness and reproach of our reason; and, never fully to love anything which we can abstain from loving without remorse. We may feel a great inclination to consent absolutely to a probable opinion; yet, on reflection, we shall find that we are not compelled to do so by any tacit self-reproach if we do not. And we ought to consent to such probable opinions for the time until we have more fully examined the question.

41. The sight is the noblest of our senses; and if they had been given us to discover truth, it is through vision that we should have done it. But it deceives us in all that it represents; in the size of bodies, their figures and motions, in light and colours. None of these are such as they appear, as he proves by many obvious instances. Thus we measure the velocity of motion by duration of time and extent of space; but of duration the mind can form no just estimate, and the eye cannot determine equality of spaces. The diameter of the moon is greater by measurement when she is high in the heavens; it appears greater to our eyes in the horizon.[z] On all sides we are beset with error through our senses. Not that the sensations themselves, properly speaking, deceive us. We are not deceived in supposing that we see an orb of light before the sun has risen above the horizon, but in supposing that what we see is the sun itself. Were we even delirious, we should see and feel what our senses present to us, though our judgment as to its reality would be erroneous. And this judgment we may withhold by assenting to nothing without perfect certainty.

42. It would have been impossible for a man endowed with such intrepidity and acuteness as Malebranche to overlook the question, so naturally raised by this sceptical theory,

---

[z] L. i. c. 9. Malebranche was engaged afterwards in a controversy with Regis on this particular question of the horizontal moon.

as to the objective existence of an external world.   There is
no necessary connexion, he observes, between the presence of
an idea in the soul and the existence of the thing which it
represents, as dreams and delirium prove.   Yet we may be
confident that extension, figure, and movement do generally
exist without us when we perceive them.   These are not
imaginary ; we are not deceived in believing their reality,
though it is very difficult to prove it.   But it is far otherwise
with colours, smells, or sounds, for these do not exist at all
beyond the mind.   This he proceeds to show at considerable
length.[a]   In one of the illustrations subsequently written in
order to obviate objections, and subjoined to the Recherche
de la Vérité, Malebranche comes again to this problem of the
reality of matter, and concludes by subverting every argument in its favour, except what he takes to be the assertion
of Scripture.   Berkeley, who did not see this in the same
light, had scarcely a step to take in his own famous theory,
which we may consider as having been anticipated by Malebranche, with the important exception that what was only
scepticism and denial of certainty in the one, became a positive and dogmatic affirmation in the other.

43. In all our sensations, he proceeds to show, there are
four things distinct in themselves, but which, examined as
they arise simultaneously, we are apt to confound ; these are
the action of the object, the effect upon the organ of sense,
the mere sensation, and the judgment we form as to its cause.
We fall into errors as to all these, confounding the sensation
with the action of bodies, as when we say there is heat in the
fire or colour in the rose, or confounding the motion of the
nerves with sensation, as when we refer heat to the hand ;
but most of all, in drawing mistaken inferences as to the
nature of objects from our sensations.[b]   It may be here remarked, that what Malebranche has properly called the judgment of the mind as to the cause of its sensations, is precisely
what Reid denominates perception ; a term less clear, and
which seems to have led some of his school into important
errors.   The language of the Scottish philosopher appears
to imply that he considered perception as a distinct and

---

[a] L. i. c. 10.   [b] C. 12.

original faculty of the mind, rather than what it is, a complex operation of the judgment and memory, applying knowledge already acquired by experience.   Neither he, nor his disciple Stewart, though aware of the mistakes that have arisen in this province of metaphysics by selecting our instances from the phænomena of vision instead of the other senses, have avoided the same source of error.   The sense of sight has the prerogative of enabling us to pronounce instantly on the external cause of our sensation ; and this perception is so intimately blended with the sensation itself, that it does not imply in our minds, whatever may be the case with young children, the least consciousness of a judgment.   But we need only make our experiment upon sound or smell, and we shall at once acknowledge that there is no sort of necessary connexion between the sensation and our knowledge of its corresponding external object.   We hear sounds continually, which we are incapable of referring to any particular body ; nor does anyone, I suppose, deny that it is by experience alone we learn to pronounce, with more or less of certainty according to its degree, on the causes from which these sensations proceed.[c]

---

[c] [The word 'perception' has not, in this passage, been used in its most approved sense; but the language of philosophers is not uniform. Locke often confounds perception with sensation, so as to employ the words indifferently. But this is not the case when he writes with attention. 'The ideas,' he says, 'we receive from sensation are often in grown people altered by the judgment without our taking notice of it ;' instancing a globe, 'of which the idea imprinted in our own mind is of a flat circle variously shadowed ; but we, having been by use accustomed to perceive what kind of appearance convex bodies are wont to make in us, what alterations are made in the reflections of light by the difference of the sensible figures of bodies, the judgment presently, by an habitual custom, alters the appearances of things into their causes ; so that, from that which truly is variety of shadow or colour, collecting the figure, it makes it pass for a mark of a figure, and frames to itself the *perception* of a convex figure and an uniform colour, when the idea we receive from thence is only a plane variously coloured.' B. ii. ch. 9. M. Cousin, therefore, is hardly just in saying that 'perception, according to Locke, does nothing but perceive the sensation—it is hardly more than an effect of the sensation.' Cours de l'Hist. de la Philosophie, vol. ii. p. 136, edit. 1829. Doubtless perception is the *effect* of sensation ; but Locke extends the word, in this passage at least, to much of which *mere* sensation has only furnished the materials, to the inferences derived from experience. Later metaphysicians limit more essentially the use of the word. La perception, says M. de Rémusat, dans sa plus grande complicité, n'est que la distinction mentale de l'objet de la sensation. Essais de Philosophie, vol. ii. p. 372. Kant, with his usual acuteness of discrimination, analyses the process. We have, first, the phænomenon, or appearance of the object, under which he comprehends the impression made on the organ of sense ;

44. Sensation he defines to be 'a modification of the soul
in relation to something which passes in the body to which
she is united.' These sensations we know by experience; it
is idle to go about defining or explaining them; this cannot
be done by words. It is an error, according to Malebranche,
to believe that all men have like sensations from the same objects. In this he goes farther than Pascal, who thinks it
probable that they have; while Malebranche holds it indubitable, from the organs of men being constructed differently,
that they do not receive similar impressions, instancing music,
some smells and flavours, and many other things of the same
kind. But it is obvious to reply that he has argued from the
exception to the rule; the great majority of mankind agreeing as to musical sounds (which is the strongest case that
can be put against his paradox), and most other sensations.
That the sensations of different men, subject to such excep-

---

secondly, the sensation itself; thirdly,
the representation of the object by the
mind; fourthly, the reference of this representation to the object. And there
may be, but not necessarily, the conception or knowledge of what the object
is. Id. vol. i. p. 270. Locke sometimes
seems to use the word perception for
the third of these; Reid very frequently
for the fourth. In his first work, indeed,
the Inquiry into the Human Mind, he
expressly distinguishes perception from
'that knowledge of the objects of sense,
which is got by reasoning. There is no
reasoning in perception. The belief
which is implied in it is the effect of
instinct.' Chap. vi. § 20. But, in fact,
he limits the strict province of perception to the primary qualities of matter,
and to the idea of space. Both Locke
and Reid, however, sometimes extend
it to the conception or knowledge of the
actual object. We have just quoted a
passage from Locke. ' In two of our
senses,' says Reid, ' touch and taste,
there must be an immediate application
of the object to the organ ; in the other
three the object is *perceived* at a distance,
but still by means of a medium by which
some impression is made upon the organ.'
Intellect. Powers, Essay II. ch. ii. But
perception of the object, through the
organs of sound, smell, and taste, must
of necessity imply a knowledge of it

derived from experience Those senses,
by themselves, give us no perception of
external things. But the word has one
meaning in modern philosophy, and
another in popular usage, which philosophers sometimes inadvertently follow.
In the first it is a mere reference of the
sensation to some external object, more
definite in sight, somewhat less so in
touch, and not at all in the three other
senses. In the other it is a reference of
the sensation to a known object, and in
all the senses; we *perceive* an oak-tree,
the striking of the clock, the perfume
of a violet. The more philosophical
sense of the word perception limits
greatly the extent of the faculty. ' We
perceive,' says Sir W. Hamilton, on the
passage last quoted from Reid, ' nothing
but what is in relation to the organ ;
and nothing is in relation to the organ
that is not present to it. All the senses
are, in fact, modifications of touch, as
Democritus of old taught. We reach
the distant reality, not by sense, not by
perception, but by inference.' Brown
had said the same. This has been, in
the case of sight, controverted by Dr.
Whewell ; but whether we see objects,
strictly speaking, at a distance, or on
the retina, it is evident that we do not
know *what* they are, till we have been
taught by experience.—1847.]

tions, if not strictly alike, are, so to say, in a constant ratio, seems as indisputable as any conclusion we can draw from their testimony.

45. The second book of Malebranche's treatise relates to the imagination, and the errors connected with it. ' The imagination consists in the power of the mind to form images of objects by producing a change in the fibres of that part of the brain, which may be called principal because it corresponds with all parts of the body, and is the place where the soul, if we may so speak, immediately resides.' This he supposes to be where all the filaments of the brain terminate: so difficult was it, especially in that age, for a philosopher who had the clearest perception of the soul's immateriality to free himself from the analogies of extended presence and material impulse. The imagination, he says, comprehends two things; the action of the will and the obedience of the animal spirits which trace images on the brain. The power of conception depends partly upon the strength of those animal spirits, partly on the qualities of the brain itself. For just as the size, the depth, and the clearness of the lines in an engraving depend on the force with which the graver acts, and on the obedience which the copper yields to it, so the depth and clearness of the traces of the imagination depend on the force of the animal spirits, and on the constitution of the fibres of the brain; and it is the difference of these which occasions almost the whole of that vast inequality which we find in the capacities of men.

46. This arbitrary, though rather specious hypothesis, which in the present more advanced state of physiology a philosopher might not in all points reject, but would certainly not assume, is spread out by Malebranche over a large part of his work, and especially the second book. The delicacy of the fibres of the brain, he supposes, is one of the chief causes of our not giving sufficient application to difficult subjects. Women possess this delicacy, and hence have more intelligence than men as to all sensible objects; but whatever is abstract is to them incomprehensible. The fibres are soft in children, and become stronger with age, the greatest perfection of the understanding being between thirty and fifty; but with prejudiced men, and especially

when they are advanced in life, the hardness of the cerebral fibre confirms them in error.   For we can understand nothing without attention, nor attend to it without having a strong image in the brain, nor can that image be formed without a suppleness and susceptibility of motion in the brain itself. It is therefore highly useful to get the habit of thinking on all subjects, and thus to give the brain a facility of motion analogous to that of the fingers in playing on a musical instrument.   And this habit is best acquired by seeking truth in difficult things while we are young, because it is then that the fibres are most easily bent in all directions.[d]

47. This hypothesis, carried so far as it has been by Malebranche, goes very great lengths in asserting not merely a connexion between the cerebral motions and the operations of the mind, but something like a subordination of the latter to a plastic power in the animal spirits of the brain.   For if the differences in the intellectual powers of mankind, and also, as he afterwards maintains, in their moral emotions, are to be accounted for by mere bodily configuration as their regulating cause, little more than a naked individuality of consciousness seems to be left to the immaterial principle. No one, however, whether he were staggered by this difficulty or not, had a more decided conviction of the essential distinction between mind and matter than this disciple of Descartes.   The soul, he says, does not become body, nor the body soul, by their union.   Each substance remains as it is, the soul incapable of extension and motion, the body incapable of thought and desire.   All the alliance between soul and body which is known to us consists in a natural and mutual correspondence of the thoughts of the former with the traces on the brain, and of its emotions with the traces of the animal spirits.   As soon as the soul receives new ideas, new traces are imprinted on the brain; and as soon as external objects imprint new traces, the soul receives new ideas.   Not that it contemplates these traces, for it has no knowledge of them ; nor that the traces contain the ideas, since they have no relation to them ; nor that the soul receives her ideas from the traces, for it is inconceivable that

---

[d] L. ii. c. 1.

the soul should receive anything from the body, and become
more enlightened, as some philosophers (meaning Gassendi)
express it, by turning itself towards the phantasms in the
brain. Thus, also, when the soul wills that the arm should
move, the arm moves, though she does not even know what
else is necessary for its motion; and thus, when the animal
spirits are put into movement, the soul is disturbed, though
she does not even know that there are animal spirits in the
body.

48. These remarks of Malebranche it is important to familiarise to our minds; and those who reflect upon them will
neither fall into the gross materialism to which many physiologists appear prone; nor, on the other hand, out of fear of
allowing too much to the bodily organs, reject any sufficient
proof that may be adduced for the relation between the cerebral system and the intellectual processes. These opposite
errors are by no means uncommon in the present age. But,
without expressing an opinion on that peculiar hypothesis
which is generally called phrenology, we might ask whether
it is not quite as conceivable, that a certain state of portions
of the brain may be the antecedent condition of memory or
imagination, as that a certain state of nervous filaments may
be, what we know it is, an invariable antecedent of sensation.
In neither instance can there be any resemblance or proper
representation of the organic motion transferred to the soul;
nor ought we to employ, even in metaphor, the analogies of
impulse or communication. But we have two phenomena,
between which, by the constitution of our human nature, and
probably by that of the very lowest animals, there is a perpetual harmony and concomitance; an ultimate fact, according to the present state of our faculties, which may in some
senses be called mysterious, inasmuch as we can neither fully
apprehend its final causes, nor all the conditions of its operation, but one which seems not to involve any appearance of
contradiction, and should therefore not lead us into the useless perplexity of seeking a solution that is almost evidently
beyond our reach.

49. The association of ideas is far more extensively developed by Malebranche in this second book than by any of
the old writers, not even, I think, with the exception of

Hobbes; though he is too fond of mixing the psychological
facts which experience furnishes with his precarious, however
plausible, theory of cerebral traces. Many of his remarks
are acute and valuable. Thus he observes that writers who
make use of many new terms in science, under the notion of
being more intelligible, are often not understood at all, whatever care they may take to define their words. We grant in
theory their right to do this ; but nature resists. The new
words, having no ideas previously associated with them, fall
out of the reader's mind, except in mathematics, where they
can be rendered evident by diagrams. In all this part, Malebranche expatiates on the excessive deference shown to authority, which, because it is great in religion, we suppose equally
conclusive in philosophy, and on the waste of time which
mere reading of many books entails; experience, he says,
having always shown that those who have studied most are
the very persons who have led the world into the greatest
errors. The whole of the chapters on this subject is worth
perusal.

50. In another part of this second book, Malebranche has
opened a new and fertile vein, which he is far from having
exhausted, on what he calls the contagiousness of a powerful
imagination. Minds of this character, he observes, rule those
which are feebler in conception; they give them by degrees
their own habit, they impress their own type; and as men of
strong imagination are themselves for the most part very
unreasonable, their brains being cut up, as it were, by deep
traces, which leave no room for anything else, no source of
human error is more dangerous than this contagiousness of
their disorder. This he explains, in his favourite physiology,
by a certain natural sympathy between the cerebral fibres of
different men, which being wanting in anyone with whom we
converse, it is vain to expect that he will enter into our views,
and we must look for a more sympathetic tissue elsewhere.

51. The moral observations of Malebranche are worth more
than these hypotheses with which they are mingled. Men of
powerful imagination express themselves with force and vivacity, though not always in the most natural manner, and
often with great animation of gesture; they deal with subjects that excite sensible images, and from all this they

acquire a great power of persuasion. This is exercised especially over persons in subordinate relations; and thus children, servants, or courtiers adopt the opinions of their superiors. Even in religion nations have been found to take up the doctrines of their rulers, as has been seen in England. In certain authors, who influence our minds without any weight of argument, this despotism of a strong imagination is exercised, which he particularly illustrates by the examples of Tertullian, Seneca, and Montaigne. The contagious power of imagination is also manifest in the credulity of mankind as to apparitions and witchcraft; and he observes that where witches are burned, there is generally a great number of them, while, since some parliaments have ceased to punish for sorcery, the offence has diminished within their jurisdiction.

52. The application which these striking and original views will bear spreads far into the regions of moral philosophy in the largest sense of that word. It is needless to dwell upon, and idle to cavil at the physiological theories to which Malebranche has had recourse. False let them be, what is derived from the experience of human nature will always be true. No one general phenomenon in the intercommunity of mankind with each other is more worthy to be remembered, or more evident to an observing eye, than this contagiousness, as Malebranche phrases it, of a powerful imagination, especially when assisted by any circumstances that secure and augment its influence. The history of every popular delusion, and even the petty events of every day in private life, are witnesses to its power.

53. The third book is entitled, Of the Understanding or Pure Spirit (l'Esprit pur). By the pure understanding he means the faculty of the soul to know the reality of certain things without the aid of images in the brain. And he warns the reader that the inquiry will be found dry and obscure. The essence of the soul, he says, following his Cartesian theory, consists in thought, as that of matter does in extension; will, imagination, memory, and the like, are modifications of thought or forms of the soul, as water, wood, or fire are modifications of matter. This sort of expression has been adopted by our metaphysicians of the Scots school in

preference to the ideas of reflection, as these operations are
called by Locke. But by the word thought (pensée) Malebranche, like Regis, does not mean these modifications, but
the soul or thinking principle absolutely, capable of all these
modifications, as extension is neither round nor square,
though capable of either form. The power of volition, and,
by parity of reasoning we may add, of thinking, is insepar-
able from the soul, but not the acts of volition or thinking
themselves; as a body is always movable, though it be not
always in motion.

54. In this book it does not seem that Malebranche has
been very successful in distinguishing the ideas of pure intellect from those which the senses or imagination present
to us; nor do we clearly see what he means by the former,
except those of existence and a few more. But he now
hastens to his peculiar hypothesis as to the mode of perception. By ideas he understands the immediate object of the
soul, which all the world, he supposes, will agree not to be
the same with the external objects of sense. Ideas are real
existences; for they have properties, and represent very different things; but nothing can have no property.[e] How
then do they enter into the mind, or become present to it?
Is it, as the Aristotelians hold, by means of species transmitted from the external objects? Or are they produced
instantaneously by some faculty of the soul? Or have they
been created and posited as it were in the soul, when it began
to exist? Or does God produce them in us whenever we
think or perceive? Or does the soul contain in herself in
some transcendental manner whatever is in the sensible
world? These hypotheses of elder philosophers, some of
which are not quite intelligibly distinct from each other,
Malebranche having successfully refuted, comes to what he

---

[e] [Cudworth uses the same argument
for the reality of ideas. 'It is a ridiculous conceit of a modern atheistic
writer that universals are nothing else
but names, attributed to many singular
bodies, because whatever is, is singular.
For though whatever exists without the
mind be singular, yet it is plain that
there are conceptions in our minds objectively universal. Which universal objects
of our mind, though they exist not as such
any where without it, yet are they not
therefore nothing, but have an intelligible entity, for this very reason, because they are conceivable; for since
nonentity is not conceivable, whatever
is conceivable as an object of the mind
is therefore something.' Intellectual
System, p. 731.—1842.]

considers the only possible alternative; namely, that the soul
is united to an all-perfect Being, in whom all that belongs
to his creatures is contained. Besides the exclusion of every
other supposition which he conceives himself to have given,
he subjoins several direct arguments in favour of his own
theory, but in general so obscure and full of arbitrary assumption that they cannot be stated in this brief sketch.[f]

55. The mysticism of this eminent man displays itself
throughout this part of his treatise, but rarely leading him
into that figurative and unmeaning language from which the
inferior class of enthusiasts are never free. His philosophy,
which has hitherto appeared so sceptical, assumes now the
character of intense irresistible conviction. The scepticism
of Malebranche is merely ancillary to his mysticism. His
philosophy, if we may use so quaint a description of it, is
subjectivity leading objectivity in chains. He seems to
triumph in his restoration of the inner man to his pristine
greatness, by subduing those false traitors and rebels, the
nerves and brain, to whom, since the great lapse of Adam,
his posterity had been in thrall. It has been justly remarked
by Brown, that in the writings of Malebranche, as in all
theological metaphysicians of the Catholic church, we perceive the commanding influence of Augustin.[g] From him,
rather than, in the first instance, from Plato or Plotinus, it
may be suspected that Malebranche, who was not very
learned in ancient philosophy, derived the manifest tinge of

---

[f] L. iii. c. 6.

[g] Philosophy of the Human Mind,
Lecture xxx. Brown's own position,
that 'the idea *is* the mind,' seems to
me as paradoxical, in expression at
least, as anything in Malebranche.

[Brown meant to guard against the
notion of Berkeley and Malebranche, that
ideas are any how separable from the
mind, or capable of being considered as
real being. But he did not sufficiently
distinguish between the percipient and
the perception, or what M. de Rémusat
has called, le moi observé par le moi.
As for the word modification, which we
owe to Malebranche, though it does not
well express his own theory of independent ideas, I cannot help agreeing
with Locke: 'What service does that

word do us in one case or the other,
when it is only a new word brought in
without any new conception at all? For
my mind, when it sees a colour or figure,
is altered, I know, from the not having
such or such a perception to the having
it; but when, to explain this, I am told
that either of these perceptions is a
modification of the mind, what do I conceive more than that, from not having
such a perception, my mind is come to
have such a perception? Which is what
I as well knew before the word "modification" was made use of, which by its
use has made me conceive nothing more
than what I conceived before.' Examination of Malebranche's theory, in
Locke's works, vol. iii. p. 427, ed. 1719.
—1847.

Platonism, that, mingling with his warm admiration of
Descartes, has rendered him a link between two famous
systems, not very harmonious in their spirit and turn of
reasoning. But his genius, more clear, or at least disciplined
in a more accurate logic, than that of Augustin, taught him
to dissent from that father by denying objective reality to
eternal truths, such as that two and two are equal to four;
descending thus one step from unintelligible mysticism.

56. 'Let us repose,' he concludes, 'in this tenet, that God
is the intelligible world, or the place of spirits, like as the
material world is the place of bodies; that it is from his
power they receive all their modifications; that it is in his
wisdom they find all their ideas; and that it is by his love
they feel all their well-regulated emotions. And since his
power and his wisdom and his love are but himself, let us
believe with St. Paul, that he is not far from each of us, and
that in him we live, and move, and have our being.' But
sometimes Malebranche does not content himself with these
fine effusions of piety. His theism, as has often been the
case with mystical writers, expands till it becomes as it were
dark with excessive light, and almost vanishes in its own
effulgence. He has passages that approach very closely to
the pantheism of Jordano Bruno and Spinosa; one especially,
wherein he vindicates the Cartesian argument for a being of
necessary existence in a strain which perhaps renders that
argument less incomprehensible, but certainly cannot be said,
in any legitimate sense, to establish the existence of a Deity.[h]

57. It is from the effect which the invention of so original
and striking an hypothesis, and one that raises such magnificent conceptions of the union between the Deity and the
human soul, would produce on a man of an elevated and
contemplative genius, that we must account for Malebranche's
forgetfulness of much that he has judiciously said in part of
his treatise, on the limitation of our faculties and the imperfect knowledge we can attain as to our intellectual nature.
For, if we should admit that ideas are substances, and not
accidents of the thinking spirit, it would still be doubtful
whether he has wholly enumerated, or conclusively refuted,

---

[h] L. iii. c. 8.

the possible hypotheses as to their existence in the mind. And his more direct reasonings labour under the same difficulty from the manifest incapacity of our understandings to do more than form conjectures and dim notions of what we can so imperfectly bring before them.

58. The fourth and fifth books of the Recherche de la Vérité treat of the natural inclinations and passions, and of the errors which spring from those sources. These books are various and discursive, and very characteristic of the author's mind; abounding with a mystical theology, which extends to an absolute negation of secondary causes, as well as with poignant satire on the follies of mankind. In every part of his treatise, but especially in these books, Malebranche pursues with unsparing ridicule two classes, the men of learning, and the men of the world. With Aristotle and the whole school of his disciples he has an inveterate quarrel, and omits no occasion of holding them forth to contempt. This seems to have been in a great measure warranted by their dogmatism, their bigotry, their pertinacious resistance to modern science, especially to the Cartesian philosophy, which Malebranche in general followed. ' Let them,' he exclaims, ' prove, if they can, that Aristotle, or any of themselves, has deduced one truth in physical philosophy from any principle peculiar to himself, and we will promise never to speak of him but in eulogy.'[1] But, until this gauntlet should be taken up, he thought himself at liberty to use very different language. ' The works of the Stagirite,' he observes, ' are so obscure and full of indefinite words, that we have a colour for ascribing to him the most opposite opinions. In fact, we make him say what we please, because he says very little, though with much parade; just as children fancy bells to say anything, because they make a great noise, and in reality say nothing at all.'

59. But such philosophers are not the only class of the learned he depreciates. Those who pass their time in gazing through telescopes, and distribute provinces in the moon to their friends, those who pore over worthless books, such as the Rabbinical and other Oriental writers, or compose folio volumes on the animals mentioned in Scripture, while they can hardly

---

[1] L. iv. c. 3.

tell what are found in their own province, those who accu-
mulate quotations to inform us not of truth, but of what
other men have taken for truth, are exposed to his sharp,
but doubtless exaggerated and unreasonable ridicule.   Malebranche, like many men of genius, was much too intolerant
of what might give pleasure to other men, and too narrow
in his measure of utility.   He seems to think little valuable
in human learning but metaphysics and algebra.[k] From the
learned he passes to the great, and after enumerating the
circumstances which obstruct their perception of truth, comes
to the blunt conclusion that men ' much raised above the
rest by rank, dignity, or wealth, or whose minds are occupied in gaining these advantages, are remarkably subject to
error, and hardly capable of discerning any truths which
lie a little out of the common way.'[m]

60. The sixth and last book announces a method of directing our pursuit of truth, by which we may avoid the many
errors to which our understandings are liable.   It promises
to give them all the perfection of which our nature is capable,
by prescribing the rules we should invariably observe.   But
it must, I think, be confessed that there is less originality in
this method than we might expect.   We find, however, many
acute and useful, if not always novel, observations on the
conduct of the understanding, and it may be reckoned among
the books which would supply materials for what is still
wanting to philosophical literature, an ample and useful logic.
We are so frequently inattentive, he observes, especially to
the pure ideas of the understanding, that all resources
should be employed to fix our thoughts.   And for this pur-

---

[k] It is rather amusing to find that,
while lamenting the want of a review of
books, he predicts that we shall never
see one, on account of the prejudice of
mankind in favour of authors. The pro-
phecy was falsified almost at the time.
On regarde ordinairement les auteurs
comme des hommes rares et extraor-
dinaires, et beaucoup élevés au-dessus
des autres ; on les révère donc au lieu
de les mépriser et de les punir. Ainsi
il n'y a guères d'apparence que les
hommes érigent jamais un tribunal pour
examiner et pour condamner tous les
livres, qui ne font que corrompre la

raison. c. 8.
La plupart des livres de certains savans
ne sont fabriqués qu'à coups de diction-
naires, et ils n'ont guères lu que les
tables des livres qu'ils citent, ou quelques
lieux communs, ramassés de différens
auteurs.   On n'oseroit entrer d'avan-
tage dans le détail de ces choses, ni en
donner des exemples, de peur de choquer
des personnes aussi fières et aussi bi-
lieuses que sont ces faux savans ; car on
ne prend pas plaisir à se faire injurier en
Grec et en Arabe.
[m] C. 9.

pose we may make use of the passions, the senses, or the imagination, but the second with less danger than the first, and the third than the second. Geometrical figures he ranges under the aids supplied to the imagination rather than to the senses. He dwells much at length on the utility of geometry in fixing our attention, and of algebra in compressing and arranging our thoughts. All sciences, he well remarks (and I do not know that it had been said before), which treat of things distinguishable by more or less in quantity, and which consequently may be represented by extension, are capable of illustration by diagrams. But these, he conceives, are inapplicable to moral truths, though sure consequences may be derived from them. Algebra, however, is far more useful in improving the understanding than geometry, and is in fact, with its sister arithmetic, the best means that we possess.[n] But as men like better to exercise the imagination than the pure intellect, geometry is the more favourite study of the two.

61. Malebranche may, perhaps, be thought to have occupied too much of our attention at the expense of more popular writers. But for this very reason, that the Recherche de la Vérité is not at present much read, I have dwelt long on a treatise of so great celebrity in its own age, and which, even more perhaps than the metaphysical writings of Descartes, has influenced that department of philosophy. Malebranche never loses sight of the great principle of the soul's immateriality, even in his long and

Character of Malebranche.

---

[n] L. vi. c. 4. All conceptions of abstract ideas, he justly remarks in another place, are accompanied with some imagination, though we are often not aware of it; because these ideas have no natural images or traces associated with them, but such only as the will of man or chance has given. Thus in analysis, however general the ideas, we use letters and signs, always associated with the ideas of the things, though they are not really related, and for this reason do not give us false and confused notions. Hence, he thinks, the ideas of things which can only be perceived by the understanding may become associated with the traces on the brain, l. v. c. 2. This is evidently as applicable to language as it is to algebra.

Cudworth has a somewhat similar remark in his Immutable Morality, that the cogitations we have of corporeal things are usually, in his technical style, both noematical and phantasmatical together, the one being as it were the soul, and the other the body of them. 'Whenever we think of a phantasmatical universal or universalised phantasm, or a thing which we have no clear intellection of (as, for example, of the nature of a rose in general), there is a complication of something noematical and something phantasmatical together; for phantasms themselves as well as sensations are always individual things.' p. 143.—[See also the quotation from Gassendi, supra, § 15.—1842.]

rather hypothetical disquisitions on the instrumentality of the brain in acts of thought; and his language is far less objectionable on this subject than that of succeeding philosophers. He is always consistent and clear in distinguishing the soul itself from its modifications and properties. He knew well and had deeply considered the application of mathematical and physical science to the philosophy of the human mind. He is very copious and diligent in illustration, and very clear in definition. His principal errors, and the sources of them in his peculiar temperament, have appeared in the course of these pages. And to these we may add his maintaining some Cartesian paradoxes, such as the system of vortices, and the want of sensation in brutes. The latter he deduced from the immateriality of a thinking principle, supposing it incredible, though he owns it had been the tenet of Augustin, that there could be an immaterial spirit in the lower animals, and also from the incompatibility of any unmerited suffering with the justice of God.° Nor was Malebranche exempt from some prejudices of scholastic theology; and though he generally took care to avoid its technical language, is content to repel the objection to his denial of all secondary causation from its making God the sole author of sin, by saying that sin, being a privation of righteousness, is negative, and consequently requires no cause.

62. Malebranche bears a striking resemblance to his great contemporary Pascal, though they were not, I be- Compared lieve, in any personal relation to each other, nor with Pascal. could either have availed himself of the other's writings. Both of ardent minds, endowed with strong imagination and lively wit, sarcastic, severe, fearless, disdainful of popular opinion and accredited reputations; both imbued with the notion of a vast difference between the original and actual state of man, and thus solving many phænomena of his being; both, in different modes and degrees, sceptical, and rigorous in the exaction of proof; both undervaluing all human knowledge beyond the regions of mathematics; both

---

° This he had borrowed from a maxim of Augustin : sub justo Deo quisquam nisi mereatur, miser esse non potest; whence, it seems, that father had in- ferred the imputation of original sin to infants; a happy mode of escaping the difficulty.

of rigid strictness in morals, and a fervid enthusiastic piety. But in Malebranche there is a less overpowering sense of religion; his eye roams unblenched in the light, before which that of Pascal had been veiled in awe; he is sustained by a less timid desire of truth, by greater confidence in the inspirations that are breathed into his mind; he is more quick in adopting a novel opinion, but less apt to embrace a sophism in defence of an old one; he has less energy, but more copiousness and variety.

63. Arnauld, who, though at first in personal friendship with Malebranche, held no friendship in a balance with his steady love of truth, combated the chief points of the other's theory in a treatise on True and False Ideas. This work I have never had the good fortune to see; it appears to assail a leading principle of Malebranche, the separate existence of ideas, as objects in the mind, independent and distinguishable from the sensation itself. Arnauld maintained, as Reid and others have since done, that we do not perceive or feel ideas, but real objects, and thus led the way to a school which has been called that of Scotland, and has had a great popularity among our later metaphysicians. It would require a critical examination of his work, which I have not been able to make, to determine precisely what were the opinions of this philosopher.[p]

Arnauld on true and false ideas.

64. The peculiar hypothesis of Malebranche, that we see all things in God, was examined by Locke in a short piece, contained in the collection of his works. It will readily be conceived that two philosophers, one eminently mystical, and endeavouring upon this highly transcendental theme to grasp in his mind and express in his language something beyond the faculties of man, the other as characteristically averse to mystery, and slow to admit anything without proof, would have hardly any common ground even to fight upon. Locke, therefore, does little else than complain that he cannot understand what Malebranche has advanced; and most of his

---

[p] Brucker. Buhle. Reid's Intellectual Powers. [But see what Sir W. Hamilton has said in Edinb. Rev. vol. lii. and in his edition of Reid, p. 296 et alibi. Though Arnauld denied the *separate* existence of ideas, as held by Malebranche, he admitted them as modifications of the mind, and supposed, like Descartes and most others, that perception of external objects is representation, and not intuition.—1847.]

readers will probably find themselves in the same position.

65. He had, however, an English supporter of some celebrity in his own age, Norris; a disciple, and one of the latest we have had, of the Platonic school of Norris. Henry More. The principal metaphysical treatise of Norris, his Essay on the Ideal World, was published in two parts, 1701 and 1702. It does not therefore come within our limits. Norris is more thoroughly Platonic than Malebranche, to whom, however, he pays great deference, and adopts his fundamental hypothesis of seeing all things in God. He is a writer of fine genius and a noble elevation of moral sentiments, such as predisposes men for the Platonic schemes of theosophy. He looked up to Augustin with as much veneration as to Plato, and respected, more perhaps than Malebranche, certainly more than the generality of English writers, the theological metaphysicians of the schools. With these he mingled some visions of a later mysticism. But his reasonings will seldom bear a close scrutiny.

66. In the Thoughts of Pascal we find many striking remarks on the logic of that science with which he was peculiarly conversant, and upon the general Pascal. foundations of certainty. He had reflected deeply upon the sceptical objections to all human reasoning, and, though sometimes out of a desire to elevate religious faith at its expense, he seems to consider them unanswerable, he was too clear-headed to believe them just. 'Reason,' he says, 'confounds the dogmatists, and nature the sceptics.'[q] 'We have an incapacity of demonstration, which the one cannot overcome; we have a conception of truth which the others cannot disturb.'[r] He throws out a notion of a more complete method of reasoning than that of geometry, wherein every thing shall be demonstrated, which however he holds to be unattainable;[s] and perhaps on this account he might think the cavils of pyrrhonism invincible by pure reason. But as he afterwards admits that we may have a full certainty of propositions that cannot be demonstrated, such as the infinity of number and space, and that such incapability

---

[q] Œuvres de Pascal, vol. i. p. 205.   [s] Pensées de Pascal, part i. art. 2.
[r] P. 208.

of direct proof is rather a perfection than a defect, this notion of a greater completeness in evidence seems neither clear nor consistent.[t]

67. Geometry, Pascal observes, is almost the only subject as to which we find truths wherein all men agree. And one cause of this is that geometers alone regard the true laws of demonstration. These as enumerated by him are eight in number. 1. To define nothing which cannot be expressed in clearer terms than those in which it is already expressed : 2. To leave no obscure or equivocal terms undefined : 3. To employ in the definition no terms not already known : 4. To omit nothing in the principles from which we argue unless we are sure it is granted : 5. To lay down no axiom which is not perfectly evident : 6. To demonstrate nothing which is as clear already as we can make it : 7. To prove everything in the least doubtful, by means of self-evident axioms, or of propositions already demonstrated : 8. To substitute mentally the definition instead of the thing defined. Of these rules, he says, the first, fourth, and sixth are not absolutely necessary in order to avoid error, but the other five are indispensable. Yet, though they may be found in books of logic, none but the geometers have paid any regard to them. The authors of these books seem not to have entered into the spirit of their own precepts. All other rules than those he has given are useless or mischievous ; they contain, he says, the whole art of demonstration.[u]

68. The reverence of Pascal, like that of Malebranche, for what is established in religion does not extend to philosophy. We do not find in them, as we may sometimes perceive in the present day, all sorts of prejudices against the liberties of the human mind clustering together like a herd of bats, by an instinctive association. He has the same idea as Bacon, that the ancients were properly the children among mankind. Not only each man, he says, advances daily in science, but all men collectively make a constant progress, so that all generations of mankind during so many ages may be considered as one man, always subsisting and always

---

Comme la cause qui les rend incapables de démonstration n'est pas leur obscurité, mais au contraire leur extrême évidence, ce manque de preuve n'est pas un défaut, mais plutôt une perfection.

[u] Œuvres de Pascal, i. 66.

learning; and the old age of this universal man is not to be sought in the period next to his birth, but in that which is most removed from it. Those we call ancients were truly novices in all things; and we who have added to all they knew the experience of so many succeeding ages, have a better claim to that antiquity which we revere in them. In this, with much ingenuity and much truth, there is a certain mixture of fallacy, which I shall not wait to point out.

69. The genius of Pascal was admirably fitted for acute observation on the constitution of human nature, if he had not seen everything through a refracting medium of religious prejudice. When this does not interfere to bias his judgment he abounds with fine remarks, though always a little tending towards severity. One of the most useful and original is the following : ' When we would show anyone that he is mistaken, our best course is to observe on what side he considers the subject, for his view of it is generally right on this side, and admit to him that he is right so far. He will be satisfied with this acknowledgment that he was not wrong in his judgment, but only inadvertent in not looking at the whole of the case. For we are less ashamed of not having seen the whole, than of being deceived in what we do see ; and this may perhaps arise from an impossibility of the understanding's being deceived in what it does see, just as the perceptions of the senses, as such, must be always true.' [x]

70. The Cartesian philosophy has been supposed to have produced a metaphysician very divergent in most of his theory from that school, Benedict Spinosa. *Spinosa's Ethics.* No treatise is written in a more rigidly geometrical method than his Ethics. It rests on definitions and axioms, from which the propositions are derived in close, brief, and usually perspicuous demonstrations. The few explanations he has thought necessary are contained in scholia. Thus a fabric is erected, astonishing and bewildering in its entire effect, yet so regularly constructed, that the reader must pause, and return on his steps to discover an error in the workmanship,

---

[x] Œuvres de Pascal, p. 149. Though Pascal here says that the perceptions of the senses are always true, we find the contrary asserted in other passages ; he is not uniformly consistent with himself.

while he cannot also but acknowledge the good faith and intimate persuasion of having attained the truth, which the acute and deep-reflecting author everywhere displays.

71. Spinosa was born in 1632 ; we find by his correspon-
Its general
originality. dence with Oldenburg in 1661, that he had already developed his entire scheme, and in that with De Vries in 1663, the propositions of the Ethics are alluded to numerically, as we now read them.[y] It was therefore the fruit of early meditation, as its fearlessness, its general disregard of the slow process of observation, its unhesitating dogmatism, might lead us to expect. In what degree he had availed himself of prior writers is not evident ; with Descartes and Lord Bacon he was familiar, and from the former he had derived some leading tenets ; but he observes both in him and Bacon what he calls mistakes as to the first cause and origin of things, their ignorance of the real nature of the human mind, and of the true sources of error.[z] The pantheistic theory of Jordano Bruno is not very remote from that of Spinosa ; but the rhapsodies of the Italian, who seldom aims at proof, can hardly have supplied much to the subtle mind of the Jew of Amsterdam. Buhle has given us an exposition of the Spinosistic theory.[a] But several propositions in this I do not find in the author, and Buhle has at least, without any necessity, entirely deviated from the arrangement he found in the Ethics. This seems as unreasonable in a work so rigorously systematic, as it would be in the elements of Euclid ; and I believe the following pages will prove more faithful to the text. But it is no easy task to translate and abridge a writer of such extraordinary conciseness as well as subtlety ; nor is it probable that my attempt will be intelligible to those who have not habituated themselves to metaphysical inquiry.

72. The first book or part of the Ethics is entitled Con-
View of his
metaphysi-
cal theory. cerning God, and contains the entire theory of Spinosa. It may even be said that this is found in a few of the first propositions ; which being granted, the rest

---

[y] Spinosæ Opera Posthuma, p. 398, 460.

[z] Cartes et Bacon tam longè a cognitione primæ causæ et originis omnium rerum aberrarunt. . . . Veram naturam humanæ mentis non cognoverunt . . . .

veram causam erroris nunquam operati sunt.

[a] Hist. de la Philosophie, vol. iii. p. 440.

could not easily be denied; presenting as they do, little more than new aspects of the former, or evident deductions from them. Upon eight definitions and seven axioms reposes this philosophical superstructure. A substance, by the third definition, is that, the conception of which does not require the conception of anything else as antecedent to it.[b] The attribute of a substance is whatever the mind perceives to constitute its essence.[c] The mode of a substance is its accident or affection, by means of which it is conceived.[d] In the sixth definition he says, I understand by the name of God a being absolutely infinite; that is, a substance consisting of infinite attributes, each of which expresses an eternal and infinite essence. Whatever expresses an essence, and involves no contradiction, may be predicated of an absolutely infinite being.[e] The most important of the axioms are the following: From a given determinate cause the effect necessarily follows; but if there be no determinate cause, no effect can follow.—The knowledge of an effect depends upon the knowledge of the cause, and includes it.—Things that have nothing in common with each other cannot be understood by means of each other; that is, the conception of one does not include that of the other.—A true idea must agree with its object.[f]

73. Spinosa proceeds to his demonstrations upon the basis of these assumptions alone. Two substances, having different attributes, have nothing in common with each other; and hence one cannot be the cause of the other, since one may be conceived without involving the conception of the other; but an effect cannot be conceived without involving the knowledge of the cause.[g] It seems to be in this fourth axiom, and

---

[b] Per substantiam intelligo id quod in se est, et per se concipitur; hoc est, id cujus conceptus non indiget conceptu alterius rei, a quo formari debeat. The last words are omitted by Spinosa in a letter to De Vries (p. 463), where he repeats this definition.

[c] Per attributum intelligo id quod intellectus de substantiâ percipit, tanquam ejusdem essentiam constituens.

[d] Per modum intelligo substantiæ affectiones, sive id, quod in alio est, per quod etiam concipitur.

[e] Per Deum intelligo Ens absolutè infinitum, hoc est, substantiam constantem infinitis attributis, quorum unumquodque æternam et infinitam essentiam exprimit. Dico absolutè infinitum, non autem in suo genere; quicquid enim in suo genere tantum infinitum est, infinita de eo attributa negare possumus; quod autem absolutè infinitum est, ad ejus essentiam pertinet, quicquid essentiam exprimit et negationem nullam involvit.

[f] Axiomata, iii. iv. v. and vi.

[g] Prop. ii. and iii.

in the proposition grounded upon it, that the fundamental
fallacy lurks. The relation between a cause and effect is surely
something different from our perfect comprehension of it, or
indeed from our having any knowledge of it at all; much
less can the contrary assertion be deemed axiomatic. But if
we should concede this postulate, it might perhaps be very
difficult to resist the subsequent proofs, so ingeniously and
with such geometrical rigour are they arranged.

74. Two or more things cannot be distinguished, except by
the diversity of their attributes, or by that of their modes.
For there is nothing out of ourselves except substances and
their modes. But there cannot be two substances of the same
attribute, since there would be no means of distinguishing
them except their modes or affections; and every substance,
being prior in order of time to its modes, may be considered
independently of them; hence two such substances could
not be distinguished at all. One substance therefore cannot
be the cause of another; for they cannot have the same attribute, that is, anything in common with one another.[h] Every
substance therefore is self-caused; that is, its essence implies
its existence.[i] It is also necessarily infinite, for it would
otherwise be terminated by some other of the same nature
and necessarily existing; but two substances cannot have the
same attribute, and therefore cannot both possess necessary
existence.[k] The more reality or existence any being possesses,
the more attributes are to be ascribed to it. This, he says,
appears by the definition of an attribute.[m] The proof however
is surely not manifest, nor do we clearly apprehend what he
meant by degrees of reality or existence. But of this theorem
he was very proud. I look upon the demonstration, he says
in a letter, as capital (palmariam), that the more attributes we
ascribe to any being, the more we are compelled to acknowledge its existence; that is, the more we conceive it as true
and not a mere chimera.[n] And from this he derived the real
existence of God, though the former proof seems collateral to
it. God, or a substance consisting of infinite attributes, each
expressing an eternal and infinite power, necessarily exists.[o]

---

[h] Prop. vi.   [i] Prop. vii.   [n] P. 463. This is in the letter to De
[k] Prop. viii.   [m] Prop. ix.   Vries, above quoted.   [o] Prop. xi.

For such an essence involves existence. And, besides this, if
anything does not exist, a cause must be given for its non-
existence, since this requires one as much as existence itself.[p]
The cause may be either in the nature of the thing, as, e. gr.
a square circle cannot exist by the circle's nature, or in something extrinsic. But neither of these can prevent the existence of God. The later propositions in Spinosa are chiefly
obvious corollaries from the definitions and a few of the first
propositions which contain the whole theory, which he proceeds to expand.

75. There can be no substance but God. Whatever is, is
in God, and nothing can be conceived without God.[q] For he
is the sole substance, and modes cannot be conceived without
a substance ; but besides substance and mode nothing exists.
God is not corporeal, but body is a mode of God, and therefore uncreated. God is the permanent, but not the transient
cause of all things.[r] He is the efficient cause of their essence,
as well as their existence, since otherwise their essence might
be conceived without God, which has been shown to be absurd.
Thus particular things are but the affections of God's attributes, or modes in which they are determinately expressed.[s]

76. This pantheistic scheme is the fruitful mother of many
paradoxes, upon which Spinosa proceeds to dwell. There is
no contingency, but every thing is determined by the necessity of the divine nature, both as to its existence and operation ; nor could any thing be produced by God otherwise than
as it is.[t] His power is the same as his essence ; for he is the
necessary cause both of himself and of all things, and it is as
impossible for us to conceive him not to act as not to exist.[u]
God, considered in the attributes of his infinite substance, is
the same as nature, that is, *natura naturans* ; but nature, in
another sense, or *natura naturata*, expresses but the modes
under which the divine attributes appear.[x] And intelligence,
considered in act, even though infinite, should be referred to
natura naturata ; for intelligence, in this sense, is but a mode

---

[p] If twenty men exist, neither more
nor less, an extrinsic reason must be
given for this precise number, since the
definition of a man does not involve it.
Prop. viii. Schol. ii.

[q] Prop. xiv.

[r] Deus est omnium rerum causa im-

manens, sed non transiens. Prop. xviii.

[s] Prop. xxv. and coroll.

[t] Prop. xxix.—xxxiii.

[u] Prop. xxxix., and part ii. prop. iii.
Schol.

[x] Schol. in prop. xxix.

of thinking, which can only be conceived by means of our conception of thinking in the abstract, that is, by an attribute of God.[y] The faculty of thinking, as distinguished from the act, as also those of desiring, loving, and the rest, Spinosa explicitly denies to exist at all.

77. In an appendix to the first chapter, De Deo, Spinosa controverts what he calls the prejudice about final causes. Men are born ignorant of causes, but merely conscious of their own appetites, by which they desire their own good. Hence they only care for the final cause of their own actions or those of others, and inquire no farther when they are satisfied about these. And finding many things in themselves and in nature, serving as means to a certain good, which things they know not to be provided by themselves, they have believed that some one has provided them, arguing from the analogy of the means which they in other instances themselves employ. Hence they have imagined gods, and these gods they suppose to consult the good of men in order to be worshipped by them, and have devised every mode of superstitious devotion to insure the favour of these divinities. And finding in the midst of so many beneficial things in nature not a few of an opposite effect, they have ascribed them to the anger of the gods on account of the neglect of men to worship them; nor has experience of calamities falling alike on the pious and impious cured them of this belief, choosing rather to acknowledge their ignorance of the reason why good and evil are thus distributed, than to give up their theory. Spinosa thinks the hypothesis of final causes refuted by his proposition that all things happen by eternal necessity. Moreover, if God were to act for an end, he must desire something which he wants; for it is acknowledged by theologians that he acts for his own sake, and not for the sake of things created.

78. Men having satisfied themselves that all things were created for them, have invented names to distinguish that as good which tends to their benefit; and believing themselves free, have gotten the notions of right and wrong, praise and dispraise. And when they can easily apprehend and recollect the relations of things, they call them well ordered, if not, ill ordered; and then say that God created all things

---

[y] Prop. xxxi. The atheism of Spinosa is manifest from this single proposition.

in order, as if order were anything except in regard to our imagination of it; and thus they ascribe imagination to God himself, unless they mean that he created things for the sake of our imagining them.

79. It has been sometimes doubted whether the Spinosistic philosophy excludes altogether an infinite intelligence. That it rejects a moral providence or creative mind is manifest in every proposition. His Deity could at most be but a cold passive intelligence, lost to our understandings and feelings in its metaphysical infinity. It was not, however, in fact so much as this. It is true that in a few passages we find what seems at first a dim recognition of the fundamental principle of theism. In one of his letters to Oldenburg, he asserts an infinite power of thinking, which, considered in its infinity, embraces all nature as its object, and of which the thoughts proceed according to the order of nature, being its correlative ideas.[z] But afterwards he rejected the term, power of thinking, altogether. The first proposition of the second part of the Ethics, or that entitled On the Mind, runs thus : Thought is an attribute of God, or, God is a thinking being. Yet this, when we look at the demonstration, vanishes in an abstraction destructive of personality.[a] And in fact we cannot reflect at all on the propositions already laid down by Spinosa, without perceiving that they annihilate every possible hypothesis in which the being of a God can be intelligibly stated.

80. The second book of the Ethics begins, like the first, with definitions and axioms. Body he defines to be a certain and determinate mode expressing the essence of God, considered as extended. The essence of anything he defines to be that, according to the affirmation or negation of which

---

[z] Statuo dari in naturâ potentiam infinitam cogitandi quæ quatenus infinita in se continet totam naturam objectivè, et cujus cogitationes procedunt eodem modo ac natura, ejus nimirum edictum. p. 441. In another place he says, perhaps at some expense of his usual candour, Agnosco interim, id quod summam mihi præbet satisfactionem et mentis tranquillitatem, cuncta potentia Entis summè perfecti et ejus immutabili ita fieri decreto. p. 498. What follows is in the same strain. But Spinosa had wrought himself up, like Bruno, to a mystical personification of his infinite unity.

[a] Singulares cogitationes, sive hæc et illa cogitatio, modi sunt, qui Dei naturam certo et determinato modo exprimunt. Competit ergo Dei attributum, cujus conceptum singulares omnes cogitationes involvunt, per quod etiam concipiuntur. Est igitur cogitatio unum ex infinitis Dei attributis quod Dei æternam et infinitam essentiam exprimit, sive Deus est res cogitans.

the thing exists or otherwise.   An idea is a conception which
the mind forms as a thinking being.   And he would rather
say conception than perception, because the latter seems to
imply the presence of an object.   In the third axiom he says,
Modes of thinking, such as love, desire, or whatever name
we may give to the affections of the mind, cannot exist without an idea of their object, but an idea may exist with no
other mode of thinking.[b]   And in the fifth : We perceive no
singular things besides bodies and modes of thinking; thus
distinguishing, like Locke, between ideas of sensation and of
reflection.

81. Extension, by the second proposition, is an attribute
of God as well as thought.   As it follows from the infinite
extension of God, that all bodies are portions of his substance, inasmuch as they cannot be conceived without it, so
all particular acts of intelligence are portions of God's infinite intelligence, and thus all things are in him.   Man is
not a substance, but something which is in God, and cannot
be conceived without him; that is, an affection or mode of
the divine substance expressing its nature in a determinate
manner.[c]   The human mind is not a substance, but an idea
constitutes its actual being, and it must be the idea of an
existing thing.[d]   In this he plainly loses sight of the percipient in the perception ; but it was the inevitable result of
the fundamental sophisms of Spinosa to annihilate personal
consciousness.   The human mind, he afterwards asserts, is
part of the infinite intellect of God ; and when we say, the
mind perceives this or that, it is only that God, not as infinite,
but so far as he constitutes the essence of the human mind,
has such or such ideas.[e]

82. The object of the human mind is body actually existing.[f]   He proceeds to explain the connexion of the human
body with the mind, and the association of ideas.   But in

---

[b] Modi cogitandi, ut amor, cupiditas,
vel quocunque nomine affectus animi in-
signiuntur, non dantur nisi in eodem
individuo detur idea rei amatæ, deside-
ratæ, &c.   At idea dari potest, quamvis
nullus alius detur cogitandi modus.

[c] Prop. x.

[d] Quod actuale mentis humanæ esse
constituit, nihil aliud est quam idea rei

alicujus singularis actu existentis. This
is an anticipation of what we find in
Hume's Treatise on Human Nature, the
negation of a substance, or Ego, to
which paradox no one can come except
a professed metaphysician.

[e] Prop. xi., coroll.

[f] Prop. xiii.

all this, advancing always synthetically and by demonstration, he becomes frequently obscure if not sophistical. The idea of the human mind is in God, and is united to the mind itself in the same manner as the latter is to the body.[g] The obscurity and subtilty of this proposition are not relieved by the demonstration; but in some of these passages we may observe a singular approximation to the theory of Malebranche. Both, though with very different tenets on the highest subjects, had been trained in the same school; and if Spinosa had brought himself to acknowledge the personal distinctness of the Supreme Being from his intelligent creation, he might have passed for one of those mystical theosophists who were not averse to an objective pantheism.

83. The mind does not know itself, except so far as it receives ideas of the affections of the body.[h] But these ideas of sensation do not give an adequate knowledge of an external body, nor of the human body itself.[i] The mind therefore has but an inadequate and confused knowledge of anything, so long as it judges only by fortuitous perceptions; but may attain one clear and distinct by internal reflection and comparison.[k] No positive idea can be called false; for there can be no such idea without God, and all ideas in God are true, that is, correspond with their object.[m] Falsity, therefore, consists in that privation of truth, which arises from inadequate ideas. An adequate idea he has defined to be one which contains no incompatibility, without regard to the reality of its supposed correlative object.

84. All bodies agree in some things, or have something in common: of these all men have adequate ideas;[n] and this is the origin of what are called common notions, which all men possess; as extension, duration, number. But to explain the nature of universals, Spinosa observes, that the human body can only form at the same time a certain number of distinct images; if this number be exceeded, they become confused; and as the mind perceives distinctly just

---

[g] Mentis humanæ datur etiam in Deo idea, sive cognitio, quæ in Deo eodem modo sequitur, et ad Deum eodem modo refertur, ac idea sive cognitio corporis humani. Prop. xx. Hæc mentis idea eodem modo unita est menti, ac ipsa mens unita est corpori.

[h] Prop. xxiii.
[i] Prop. xxv.
[k] Schol., prop. xxix.
[m] Prop. xxxii. xxxiii. xxxv.
[n] Prop. viii.

so many images as can be formed in the body, when these are confused the mind will also perceive them confusedly, and will comprehend them under one attribute, as Man, Horse, Dog; the mind perceiving a number of such images, but not their differences of stature, colours, and the like. And these notions will not be alike in all minds, varying according to the frequency with which the parts of the complex image have occurred. Thus those who have contemplated most frequently the erect figure of man will think of him as a perpendicular animal, others as two-legged, others as unfeathered, others as rational. Hence so many disputes among philosophers who have tried to explain natural things by mere images.[o]

85. Thus we form universal ideas; first by singulars, represented by the senses confusedly, imperfectly, and disorderly; secondly, by signs, that is, by associating the remembrance of things with words; both of which he calls imagination, or primi generis cognitio; thirdly, by what he calls reason, or secundi generis cognitio; and fourthly, by intuitive knowledge, or tertii generis cognitio.[p] Knowledge of the first kind, or imagination, is the only source of error; the second and third being necessarily true.[q] These alone enable us to distinguish truth from falsehood. Reason contemplates things not as contingent but necessary; and whoever has a true idea, knows certainly that his idea is true. Every idea of a singular existing thing involves the eternal and infinite being of God. For nothing can be conceived without God, and the ideas of all things, having God for their cause, considered under the attribute of which they are modes, must involve the conception of the attribute, that is, the being of God.[r]

86. It is highly necessary to distinguish images, ideas, and words, which many confound. Those who think ideas consist in images which they perceive, fancy that ideas of which we can form no image are but arbitrary figments. They look at ideas as pictures on a tablet, and hence do not understand that an idea, as such, involves an affirmation or negation. And those who confound words with ideas, fancy they can

---

[o] Schol., prop. xl.
[p] Schol. ii., prop. xl.

[q] Prop. xli. xlii. et sequent.
[r] Prop. xlv.

will something contrary to what they perceive, because they can affirm or deny it in words. But these prejudices will be laid aside by him who reflects that thought does not involve the conception of extension; and therefore that an idea, being a mode of thought, neither consists in images nor in words, the essence of which consists in corporeal motions, not involving the conception of thought.[s]

87. The human mind has an adequate knowledge of the eternal and infinite being of God. But men cannot imagine God as they can bodies, and hence have not that clear perception of his being which they have of that of bodies, and have also perplexed themselves by associating the word God with sensible images, which it is hard to avoid. This is the chief source of all error, that men do not apply names to things rightly. For they do not err in their own minds, but in this application; as men who cast up wrong see different numbers in their minds from those in the true result.[t]

88. The mind has no free will, but is determined by a cause, which itself is determined by some other, and so for ever. For the mind is but a mode of thinking, and therefore cannot be the free cause of its own actions. Nor has it any absolute faculty of loving, desiring, understanding; these being only metaphysical abstractions.[u] Will and understanding are one and the same thing; and volitions are only affirmations or negations, each of which belongs to the essence of the idea affirmed or denied.[x] In this there seems to be not only an extraordinary deviation from common language, but an absence of any meaning which, to my apprehension at least, is capable of being given to his words. Yet we have seen something of the same kind said by Malebranche; and it will also be found in a recently published work of Cudworth,[y] a writer certainly uninfluenced by either of these, so that it may be suspected of having some older authority.

89. In the third part of this treatise, Spinosa comes to the consideration of the passions. Most who have written

---

[s] Schol. prop. xlix.

[t] Prop. xlvii. Atque hinc pleræque oriuntur controversiæ, nempe, quia homines mentem suam non recte explicant, vel quia alterius mentem male interpretantur.

[u] Prop. xlviii.

[x] Prop. xlix.

[y] See Cudworth's Treatise on Freewill (1838), p. 20, where the will and understanding are purposely, and, I think, very erroneously confounded.

on moral subjects, he says, have rather treated man as some-
Spinosa's
theory of
action and
passion. thing out of nature, or as a kind of imperium in
imperio, than as part of the general order.   They
have conceived him to enjoy a power of disturbing
that order by his own determination, and ascribed his weakness and inconstancy not to the necessary laws of the system,
but to some strange defect in himself, which they cease not
to lament, deride, or execrate.   But the acts of mankind,
and the passions from which they proceed, are in reality but
links in the series, and proceed in harmony with the common
laws of universal nature.

90. We are said to act when any thing takes place within
us, or without us, for which we are an adequate cause; that
is, when it may be explained by means of our own nature
alone.   We are said to be acted upon, when any thing takes
place within us which cannot wholly be explained by our own
nature.   The affections of the body which increase or diminish its power of action, and the ideas of those affections, he
denominates passions (affectus).   Neither the body can determine the mind to thinking, nor can the mind determine
the body to motion or rest.   For all that takes place in body
must be caused by God, considered under his attribute of
extension, and all that takes place in mind must be caused
by God under his attribute of thinking.   The mind and body
are but one thing, considered under different attributes; the
order of action and passion in the body being the same in
nature with that of action and passion in the mind.   But
men, though ignorant how far the natural powers of the body
reach, ascribe its operations to the determination of the
mind, veiling their ignorance in specious words.   For if they
allege that the body cannot act without the mind, it may be
answered that the mind cannot think till it is impelled by
the body, nor are the volitions of the mind any thing else
than its appetites, which are modified by the body.

91. All things endeavour to continue in their actual being;
this endeavour being nothing else than their essence, which
causes them to be, until some exterior cause destroys their
being.   The mind is conscious of its own endeavour to continue as it is, which is in other words the appetite that seeks
self-preservation; what the mind is thus conscious of seek-

ing, it judges to be good, and not inversely. Many things increase or diminish the power of action in the body, and all such things have a corresponding effect on the power of thinking in the mind. Thus it undergoes many changes, and passes through different stages of more or less perfect power of thinking. Joy is the name of a passion, in which the mind passes to a greater perfection or power of thinking; grief, one in which it passes to a less. Spinosa, in the rest of this book, deduces all the passions from these two and from desire; but as the development of his theory is rather long, and we have already seen that its basis is not quite intelligible, it will be unnecessary to dwell longer upon the subject. His analysis of the passions may be compared with that of Hobbes.

92. Such is the metaphysical theory of Spinosa, in as concise a form as I have found myself able to derive it from his Ethics. It is a remarkable proof, and his moral system will furnish another, how an undeviating adherence to strict reasoning may lead a man of great acuteness and sincerity from the paths of truth. Spinosa was truly, what Voltaire has with rather less justice called Clarke, a reasoning machine. A few leading theorems, too hastily taken up as axiomatic, were sufficient to make him sacrifice, with no compromise or hesitation, not only every principle of religion and moral right, but the clear intuitive notions of common sense. If there are two axioms more indisputable than any others, they are that ourselves exist, and that our existence, simply considered, is independent of any other being. Yet both these are lost in the pantheism of Spinosa, as they had always been in that delusive reverie of the imagination. In asserting that the being of the human mind consists in the idea of an existing thing presented to it, this subtle metaphysician fell into the error of the school which he most disdained, as deriving all knowledge from perception, that of the Aristotelians. And, extending this confusion of consciousness with perception to the infinite substance, or substratum of particular ideas, he was led to deny it the self, or conscious personality, without which the name of Deity can only be given in a sense deceptive of the careless reader, and inconsistent with the use of language. It was an equally

Character of Spinosism.

legitimate consequence of his original sophism to deny all
moral agency, in the sense usually received, to the human
mind, and even, as we have seen, to confound action and
passion themselves, in all but name, as mere phenomena in
the eternal sequence of things.

93. It was one great error of Spinosa to entertain too arrogant a notion of the human faculties, in which, by dint of his
own subtle demonstrations, he pretended to show a capacity
of adequately comprehending the nature of what he denominated God. And this was accompanied by a rigid dogmatism,
no one proposition being stated with hesitation, by a disregard of experience, at least as the basis of reasoning, and by
an uniform preference of the synthetic method. Most of
those, he says, who have turned their minds to those subjects
have fallen into error, because they have not begun with the
contemplation of the divine nature, which both in itself and
in order of knowledge is first, but with sensible things, which
ought to have been last. Hence he seems to have reckoned
Bacon, and even Descartes, mistaken in their methods.

94. All pantheism must have originated in overstraining
the infinity of the divine attributes till the moral part of religion was annihilated in its metaphysics. It was the corruption, or rather, if we may venture the phrase, the suicide of
theism ; nor could this theory have arisen, except where we
know it did arise, among those who had elevated their conceptions above the vulgar polytheism that surrounded them
to a sense of the unity of the Divine nature.

95. Spinosa does not essentially differ from the pantheists
of old. He conceived, as they had done, that the infinity of
God required the exclusion of all other substance ; that he
was infinite *ab omni parte*, and not only in certain senses.
And probably the loose and hyperbolical tenets of the schoolmen, derived from ancient philosophy, ascribing, as a matter
of course, a metaphysical infinity to all the divine attributes,
might appear to sanction those primary positions, from which
Spinosa, unfettered by religion, even in outward profession,
went on ' sounding his dim and perilous track ' to the paradoxes that have thrown discredit on his name. He had certainly built much on the notion that the essence or definition
of the Deity involved his actuality or existence, to which
Descartes had given vogue.

96. Notwithstanding the leading errors of this philosopher, his clear and acute understanding perceived many things which baffle ordinary minds. Thus he well saw and well stated the immateriality of thought. Oldenburg, in one of his letters, had demurred to this, and reminded Spinosa that it was still controverted whether thought might not be a bodily motion. ' Be it so,' replied the other, ' though I am far from admitting it; but at least you must allow that extension, so far as extension, is not the same as thought.'[x] It is from inattention to this simple truth that all materialism, as it has been called, has sprung. Its advocates confound the union between thinking and extension or matter (be it, if they will, an indissoluble one) with the identity of the two, which is absurd and inconceivable. ' Body,' says Spinosa, in one of his definitions, ' is not terminated by thinking, nor thinking by body.'[a] This also does not ill express the fundamental difference of matter and mind; there is an incommensurability about them which prevents one from bounding the other, because they can never be placed in juxta-position.

97. England, about the era of the Restoration, began to make a struggle against the metaphysical creed of the Aristotelians, as well as against their natural philosophy. Glanvil's Scepsis Scientifica. A remarkable work, but one so scarce as to be hardly known at all, except by name, was published by Glanvil in 1661, with the title The Vanity of Dogmatizing. A second edition, in 1665, considerably altered, is entitled Scepsis Scientifica.[b] This edition has a dedication to the Royal Society, which comes in place of a fanciful preface, wherein he had expatiated on the bodily and mental perfections of his protoplast, the father of mankind.[c] But in proportion

---

[x] At ais, forte cogitatio est actus corporeus. Sit, quamvis nullus concedam; sed hoc unum non negabis, extensionem, quoad extensionem, non esse cogitationem. Epist. iv.

[a] Corpus dicitur finitum, quia aliud semper majus concipimus. Sic cogitatio alia cogitatione terminatur. At corpus non terminatur cogitatione, nec cogitatio corpore.

[b] This book, I believe, especially in the second edition, is exceedingly scarce. The editors, however, of the Biographia Britannica, art. Glanvil, had seen it, and also Dugald Stewart. The first edition, or Vanity of Dogmatizing, is in the Bodleian Catalogue, and both are in the British Museum.

[c] Thus, among other extravagances worthy of the Talmud, he says, 'Adam needed no spectacles. The acuteness of his natural optics (if conjecture may have credit) showed him much of the celestial magnificence and bravery without a Galileo's tube; and it is most probable that his naked eyes could reach near as much of this upper world as we with all the advantages of art. It may be it was as absurd even in the judgment of his senses, that the sun and stars

to the extravagant language he employs to extol Adam before
his lapse, is the depreciation of his unfortunate posterity, not,
as common among theologians, with respect to their moral
nature, but to their reasoning faculties. The scheme of
Glanvil's book is to display the ignorance of man, and especially to censure the Peripatetic philosophy of the schools.
It is, he says, captious and verbal, and yet does not adhere
itself to any constant sense of words, but huddles together
insignificant terms and unintelligible definitions; it deals
with controversies, and seeks for no new discovery or physical
truth. Nothing, he says, can be demonstrated but when the
contrary is impossible, and of this there are not many instances. He launches into a strain of what may be called
scepticism, but answered his purpose in combating the dogmatic spirit still unconquered in our academical schools.
Glanvil had studied the new philosophy, and speaks with
ardent eulogy of ' that miracle of men, the illustrious Descartes.' Many, if not most, of his own speculations are
tinged with a Cartesian colouring. He was, however, far
more sceptical than Descartes, or even than Malebranche.
Some passages from so rare and so acute a work may deserve
to be chosen, both for their own sakes, and in order to display the revolution which was at work in speculative philosophy.

98. ' In the unions which we understand the extremes are
reconciled by interceding participations of natures, which
have somewhat of either. But body and spirit stand at such
a distance in their essential compositions, that to suppose an
uniter of a middle construction that should partake of some
of the qualities of both, is unwarranted by any of our faculties,
yea most absonous to our reasons; since there is not any the
least affinity betwixt length, breadth, and thickness, and
apprehension, judgment, and discourse; the former of which
are the most immediate results, if not essentials of matter,
the latter of spirit.'[d]

99. ' How is it, and by what art does it (the soul) read

---

should be so very much less than this
globe, as the contrary seems in ours;
and it is not unlikely that he had as clear
a perception of the earth's motion as we
have of its quiescence.' P. 5, edit. 1661.

In the second edition, he still adheres to
the hypothesis of intellectual degeneracy,
but states it with less of rhapsody.

[d] Scepsis Scientifica, p. 16. We have
just seen something similar in Spinosa.

that such an image or stroke in matter (whether that of her
vehicle or of the brain, the case is the same) signifies such
an object?   Did we learn an alphabet in our embryo state?
And how comes it to pass that we are not aware of any such
congenite apprehensions?   We know what we know; but do
we know any more?   That by diversity of motions we should
spell out figures, distances, magnitudes, colours, things not
resembled by them, we must attribute to some secret deduction.
But what this deduction should be, or by what medium this
knowledge is advanced, is as dark as ignorance.   One that
hath not the knowledge of letters may see the figures, but
comprehends not the meaning included in them; an infant
may hear the sounds and see the motion of the lips, but hath
no conception conveyed by them, not knowing what they are
intended to signify.   So our souls, though they might have
perceived the motions and images themselves by simple sense,
yet without some implicit inference it seems inconceivable
how by that means they should apprehend their antitypes.
The striking of divers filaments of the brain cannot well be
supposed to represent distances, except some kind of inference be allotted us in our faculties; the concession of
which will only stead us as a refuge for ignorance, when we
shall meet what we would seem to shun.'[e]   Glanvil, in this
forcible statement of the heterogeneity of sensations with
the objects that suggest them, has but trod in the steps of
the whole Cartesian school, but he did not mix this up with
those crude notions that halt half way between immaterialism
and its opposite; and afterwards well exposes the theories of
accounting for the memory by means of images in the brain,
which, in various ways, Aristotle, Descartes, Digby, Gassendi,
and Hobbes had propounded, and which we have seen so
favourite a speculation of Malebranche.

100.   It would be easy to quote many paragraphs of uncommon vivacity and acuteness from this forgotten treatise.
The style is eminently spirited and eloquent; a little too
figurative, like that of Locke, but less blameably, because
Glanvil is rather destroying than building up.   Every bold
and original thought of others finds a willing reception in
Glanvil's mind, and his confident impetuous style gives them

• P. 22, 23.

an air of novelty which makes them pass for his own. He stands forward as a mutineer against authority, against educational prejudice, against reverence for antiquity.[f] No one thinks more intrepidly for himself; and it is probable that, even in what seems mere superstition, he had been rather misled by some paradoxical hypothesis of his own ardent genius, than by slavishly treading in the steps of others.[g]

101. Glanvil sometimes quotes Lord Bacon, but he seems to have had the ambition of contending with the Novum Organum in some of his brilliant passages, and has really developed the doctrine of *idols* with uncommon penetration, as well as force of language. 'Our initial age is like the melted wax to the prepared seal, capable of any impression from the documents of our teachers. The half-moon or cross are indifferent to its reception; and we may with equal facility write on this *rasa tabula* Turk or Christian. To determine this indifference our first task is to learn the creed of our country, and our next to maintain it. We seldom examine our receptions, more than children do their catechisms, but by a careless greediness swallow all at a venture. For implicit faith is a virtue, where orthodoxy is the object. Some will not be at the trouble of a trial, others are scared from attempting it. If we do, 'tis not by a sunbeam or ray of light, but by a flame that is kindled by our affections, and fed by the fuel of our anticipations. And thus, like the hermit,

---

[f] 'Now if we inquire the reason why the mathematics and mechanic arts have so much got the start in growth of other sciences, we shall find it probably resolved into this as one considerable cause, that their progress hath not been retarded by that reverential awe of former discoveries, which hath been so great a hinderance to theoretical improvements. For, as the noble Lord Verulam hath noted, we have a mistaken apprehension of antiquity, calling that so which in truth is the world's non-age. Antiquitas sæculi est juventus mundi. 'Twas this vain idolizing of authors which gave birth to that silly vanity of impertinent citations, and inducing authority in things neither requiring nor deserving it.—Methinks it is a pitiful piece of knowledge that can be learned from an index, and a poor ambition to be rich in the inventory of another's treasure. To boast a memory, the most that these pedants can aim at, is but a humble ostentation.' P. 104.

[g] 'That the fancy of one man should bind the thoughts of another, and determine them to their particular objects, will be thought impossible; which yet, if we look deeply into the matter, wants not its probability.' P. 146. He dwells more on this, but the passage is too long to extract. It is remarkable that he supposes a subtle ether (like that of the modern Mesmerists) to be the medium of communication in such cases; and had also a notion of explaining these sympathies by help of the anima mundi, or mundane spirit.

we think the sun shines no where but in our cell, and all the
world to be darkness but ourselves. We judge truth to be
circumscribed by the confines of our belief and the doctrines we were brought up in.'[h] Few books, I think, are
more deserving of being reprinted than the Scepsis Scientifica
of Glanvil.

102. Another bold and able attack was made on the ancient
philosophy by Glanvil in his 'Plus Ultra, or the His Plus
Progress and Advancement of Knowledge since the Ultra.
Days of Aristotle. 1668.' His tone is peremptory and imposing, animated and intrepid, such as befits a warrior in
literature. Yet he was rather acute by nature than deeply
versed in learning, and talks of Vieta and Descartes's algebra so as to show he had little knowledge of the science, or
of what they had done for it.[i] His animosity against Aristotle is unreasonable, and he was plainly an incompetent
judge of that philosopher's general deserts. Of Bacon and
Boyle he speaks with just eulogy. Nothing can be more free
and bold than Glanvil's assertion of the privilege of judging
for himself in religion;[k] and he had doubtless a perfect right
to believe in witchcraft.

103. George Dalgarno, a native of Aberdeen, conceived, and
as it seemed to him, carried into effect, the idea of Dalgarno.
an universal language and character. His Ars Sig-
norum, vulgo Character Universalis et Lingua Philosophica,
Lond. 1661, is dedicated to Charles II. in this philosophical
character, which must have been as great a mystery to the
sovereign as to his subjects. This dedication is followed by
a royal proclamation in good English, inviting all to study
this useful art, which had been recommended by divers learned
men, Wilkins, Wallis, Ward, and others, 'judging it to be of
singular use for facilitating the matter of communication
and intercourse between people of different languages.' The
scheme of Dalgarno is fundamentally bad, in that he assumes
himself, or the authors he follows, to have given a complete
distribution of all things and ideas; after which his language
is only an artificial scheme of symbols. It is evident that
until objects are truly classified, a representative method of
signs can only rivet and perpetuate error. We have but to

ʰ P. 95.   ˡ Plus Ultra, p. 24 and 33.   ᵏ P. 142.

look at his tabular synopsis to see that his ignorance of physics, in the largest sense of the word, renders his scheme deficient; and he has also committed the error of adopting the combinations of the ordinary alphabet, with a little help from the Greek, which, even with his slender knowledge of species, soon leave him incapable of expressing them. But Dalgarno has several acute remarks; and it deserves especially to be observed, that he anticipated the famous discovery of the Dutch philologers, namely, that all other parts of speech may be reduced to the noun, dexterously, if not successfully, resolving the verb-substantive into an affirmative particle.[m]

104. Wilkins, bishop of Chester, one of the most ingenious men of his age, published in 1668 his Essay towards a Philosophical Language, which has this advantage over that of Dalgarno, that it abandons the alphabet, and consequently admits of a greater variety of characters. It is not a new language, but a more analytical scheme of characters for English. Dalgarno seems to have known something of it, though he was the first to publish, and glances at ' a more difficult way of writing English.' Wilkins also intimates that Dalgarno's compendious method would not succeed. His own has the same fault of a premature classification of things: and it is very fortunate that neither of these ingenious but presumptuous attempts to fasten down the progressive powers of the human mind by the cramps of association had the least success.[n]

Wilkins.

105. But from these partial and now very obscure endeavours of English writers in metaphysical philosophy we come at length to the work that has eclipsed every other, and given to such inquiries whatever popularity they ever possessed, the Essay of Locke on the

Locke on Human Understanding.

---

[m] Tandem mihi affulsit clarior lux; accuratius enim examinando omnium notionum analysin logicam, percepi nullam esse particulam quæ non derivetur a nomine aliquo prædicamentali, et omnes particulas esse vere casus seu modos notionum nominalium. P. 120. He does not seem to have arrived at this conclusion by etymological analysis, but by his own logical theories.

The verb-substantive, he says, is equivalent to *ita.* Thus, Petrus est in domo, means, Petrus—ita—in domo. That is, it expresses an idea of apposition or

conformity between a subject and predicate. This is a theory to which a man might be led by the habit of considering propositions logically, and thus reducing all verbs to the verb-substantive; and it is not deficient, at least, in plausibility.

[n] Dalgarno, many years afterwards, turned his attention to a subject of no slight interest, even in mere philosophy, the instruction of the deaf and dumb. His Didascalocophus is perhaps the first attempt to found this on the analysis of language. But it is not so philosophical as what has since been effected.

Human Understanding.   Neither the writings of Descartes, as I conceive, nor perhaps those of Hobbes, so far as strictly metaphysical, had excited much attention _Its merits._ in England beyond the class of merely studious men.   But the Essay on Human Understanding was frequently reprinted within a few years from its publication, and became the acknowledged code of English philosophy.[o]   The assaults it had to endure in the author's lifetime, being deemed to fail, were of service to its reputation; and considerably more than half a century was afterwards to elapse before any writer in our language (nor was the case very different in France, after the patronage accorded to it by Voltaire) could with much chance of success question any leading doctrine of its author. Several circumstances no doubt conspired with its intrinsic excellence to establish so paramount a rule in an age that boasted of peculiar independence of thinking, and full of intelligent and inquisitive spirits.   The sympathy of an English public with Locke's tenets as to government and religion was among the chief of these; and the re-action that took place in a large portion of the reading classes towards the close of the eighteenth century turned in some measure the tide even in metaphysical disquisition.   It then became fashionable sometimes to accuse Locke of preparing the way for scepticism; a charge which, if it had been truly applicable to some of his opinions, ought rather to have been made against the long line of earlier writers with whom he held them in common; sometimes, with more pretence, to allege that he had conceded too much to materialism; sometimes to point out and exaggerate other faults and errors of his Essay, till we have seemed in danger of forgetting that it is perhaps the first, and still the most complete chart of the human mind which has been laid down, the most ample repertory of truths relating to our intellectual being, and the one book which we are still compelled to name as the most important

---

[o] It was abridged at Oxford, and used by some tutors as early as 1695. But the heads of the university came afterwards to a resolution to discourage the reading of it. Stillingfleet, among many others, wrote against the Essay; and Locke, as is well known, answered the bishop. I do not know that the latter makes altogether so poor a figure as has been taken for granted; but the defence of Locke will seem in most instances satisfactory. Its success in public opinion contributed much to the renown of his work; for Stillingfleet, though not at all conspicuous as a philosopher, enjoyed a great deal of reputation. and the world can seldom understand why a man who excels in one province of literature should fail in another.

in metaphysical science.[p]　Locke had not, it may be said, the luminous perspicacity of language we find in Descartes, and, when he does not soar too high, in Malebranche; but he had more judgment, more caution, more patience, more freedom from paradox, and from the sources of paradox, vanity and love of system, than either.　We have no denial of sensation to brutes, no reference of mathematical truths to the will of God, no oscillation between the extremes of doubt and of positiveness, no bewildering mysticism.　Certainly neither Gassendi nor even Hobbes could be compared with him; and it might be asked of the admirers of later philosophers, those of Berkeley, or Hume, or Hartley, or Reid, or Stewart, or Brown, without naming any on the continent of Europe, whether, in the extent or originality of their researches, any of these names ought to stand on a level with that of Locke. One of the greatest whom I have mentioned, and one who, though candid towards Locke, had no prejudice whatever in his favour, has extolled the first two books of the Essay on Human Understanding, which yet he deems in many respects inferior to the third and fourth, as ' a precious accession to the theory of the human mind; as the richest contribution of well-observed and well-described facts which was ever bequeathed by a single individual; and as the indisputable, though not always acknowledged, source of some of the most refined conclusions with respect to the intellectual phænomena, which have been since brought to light by succeeding inquirers.' [q]

---

[p] [The first endeavour completely to analyse the operations of the human understanding was made by Hobbes, in his Treatise of Human Nature; for, important as are the services of Descartes to psychology, he did not attempt to give a full scheme.　Gassendi, in his different writings, especially in the Syntagma Philosophicum, seems to have had as extensive an object in view; but his investigation was neither so close, nor perhaps so complete, as that of our countryman. Yet even in this remarkable work of Hobbes, we find accounts of some principal faculties of the mind so brief and unsatisfactory, and so much wholly omitted, that Locke can hardly be denied the praise of having first gone painfully over the whole ground, and, as far

as the merely intellectual part of man is concerned, explained in a great degree the various phænomena of his nature and the sources of his knowledge.　Much allowance ought to be made by every candid reader for the defects of a book which was written with so little aid from earlier inquirers, and displays throughout so many traces of an original mind. The bearings in our first voyages of discovery were not all laid down as correctly as at present.　It is not pleasant to observe, that neither on the continent, nor, what is much worse, in Britain, has sufficient regard been paid to this consideration.—1847.]

[q] Stewart's Preliminary Dissertation to Encyclopædia Britannica, part ii.

[No one seems to have so much anti-

106. It would be an unnecessary prolixity to offer in this
place an analysis of so well-known a book as the
Essay on the Human Understanding.   Few have
turned their attention to metaphysical inquiries without
reading it.   It has however no inconsiderable faults, which,
though much over-balanced, are not to be passed over in a
general eulogy.   The style of Locke is wanting in philosophical precision ; it is a good model of the English language ;
but too idiomatic and colloquial, too indefinite and figurative, for the abstruse subjects with which he has to deal.
We miss in every page the translucent simplicity of his great
French predecessors.   This seems to have been owing, in a
considerable degree, to an excessive desire of popularising
the subject, and shunning the technical pedantry which had
repelled the world from intellectual philosophy.   Locke
displays in all his writings a respect which can hardly be too
great, for men of sound understanding unprejudiced by
authority, mingled with a scorn, perhaps a little exaggerated,
of the gown-men or learned world; little suspecting that
the same appeal to the people, the same policy of setting up
equivocal words and loose notions, called the common sense
of mankind, to discomfit subtle reasoning, would afterwards
be turned against himself, as it was, very unfairly and
unsparingly, by Reid and Beattie.   Hence he falls a little
into a laxity of phrase, not unusual, and not always important, in popular and practical discourse, but an inevitable
source of confusion in the very abstract speculations which
his Essay contains.   And it may perhaps be suspected,
without disparagement to his great powers, that he did not
always preserve the utmost distinctness of conception, and
was liable, as almost every other metaphysician has been, to
be entangled in the ambiguities of language.

Its defects.

---

cipated Locke, if we can wholly rely on
the analysis of a work unpublished, and
said to be now lost, as Father Paul Sarpi.
This is a short treatise, entitled Arte di
ben Pensare, an extract from the analysis
of which by Marco Foscarini is given in
Sarpi's Life, by Bianchi Giovini, vol. i.
p. 81.   We have here not only the derivation of ideas from sense, but from reflection ; the same theory as to substance,
the formation of genera and species, the
association of ideas, the same views as to
axioms and syllogisms.   But as the Italian who has given us this representation
of Father Paul's philosophy had Locke
before him, and does not quote his own
author's words, we may suspect that he
has somewhat exaggerated the resemblance.   I do not think that any nation
is more prone to claim every feather from
the wings of other birds.—1847.]

107. The leading doctrine of Locke, as is well known, is
Origin of   the derivation of all our *simple* ideas from sensation
ideas, ac-
cording to   and from reflection. The former present, compa-
Locke.
             ratively, no great difficulty; but he is not very clear
or consistent about the latter. He seems in general to limit
the word to the various operations of our own minds in
thinking, believing, willing, and so forth. This, as has been
shown formerly, is taken from, or at least coincident with,
the theory of Gassendi in his Syntagma Philosophicum. It
is highly probable that Locke was acquainted with that
work; if not immediately, yet through the account of the
philosophy of Gassendi, published in English by Dr. Charle-
ton, in 1663, which I have not seen, or through the excellent
and copious abridgment of the Syntagma by Bernier. But
he does not strictly confine his ideas of reflection to this
class. Duration is certainly no mode of thinking; yet the
idea of duration is reckoned by Locke among those with
which we are furnished by reflection. The same may perhaps be said, though I do not know that he expresses himself
with equal clearness, as to his account of several other ideas,
which cannot be deduced from external sensation, nor yet
can be reckoned modifications or operations of the soul
itself; such as number, power, existence.[r]

---

[r] [Upon more attentive consideration
of all the passages wherein Locke speaks
of ideas derived from reflection, I entertain no doubt but that Stewart is right,
and some of Locke's opponents in the
wrong. He evidently meant, that by
reflecting on the operations of our own
minds, as well as on our bodily sensations,
divers new simple ideas are suggested to
us, which are not in themselves either
such operations, or such sensations. These
'simple ideas convey themselves into the
mind by all the ways of sensation and
reflection;' and he enumerates pleasure
and pain, power, existence, unity; to
which he afterwards adds duration.
'Reflection on the appearance of several
ideas, one after another, in our minds,
is that which furnishes us with the idea
of succession. And the distance between
any parts of that succession, or between
the appearance of new ideas in our minds,
is that we call duration.' B. ii. ch. 14,
§ 3. So of number, or unity, which he
takes for the basis of the idea of number.

'Amongst all the ideas we have, as there
is none suggested to the mind by more
ways, so is there none more simple than
that of unity, or one; it has no shadow
of variety or composition in it; every object our senses are employed about, every
idea in our understandings, every thought
of our minds, brings this idea along with
it.' Ch. x. § 1. Thus we have proofs,
and more might easily be alleged, that
Locke really admitted the understanding
to be so far the source of new simple
ideas, that several of primary importance
arise in our minds, on the *suggestion* of
the senses, or of our observing the inward
operations of our minds, which are not
strictly to be classed themselves as suggestions, or as acts of consciousness. And
when we remember also, that the power
of the understanding to compound simple
ideas is a leading part of his system, and
also that certain ideas, which others take
for simple, are reckoned by him, whether
rightly or no, to be complex, we may be
forced to admit that the outcry raised

108. Stewart has been so much struck by this indefinite- Vague use
ness, with which the phrase ' ideas of reflection ' of the word
has been used in the Essay on the Human Under- idea.
standing, that he ' does not think, notwithstanding some
casual expressions which may seem to favour the contrary
supposition, that Locke would have hesitated for a moment

against Locke as a teacher of the sensualist school has been chiefly founded on
inattention to his language, and to some
inaccuracy in it. Stewart had already
stated the true doctrine as to ideas of reflection. ' In such cases all that can be
said is, that the exercise of a particular
faculty furnishes the occasion on which
certain simple notions are, by the laws
of our constitution, presented to our
thoughts ; nor does it seem possible for
us to trace the origin of a particular notion any farther, than to ascertain what
the nature of the occasion was, which, in
the first instance, introduced it to our
acquaintance.' Philos. Essays, I. chap.
ii. It is true, that he proceeds to impute
a different theory to Locke; namely,
that consciousness is exclusively the
source of all our knowledge ; which he
takes to mean, that all our original ideas
may be classed under acts of consciousness, as well as suggested by it. But in
his Dissertation, we have seen that he
takes a more favourable view of the
Essay on the Human Understanding in
this great question of the origin of our
ideas, and, as it now appears to me, beyond dispute a more true one. The want
of precision, so unhappily characteristic
of Locke, has led to this misapprehension
of his meaning. But surely no one can
believe, hardly the most depreciating
critic of Locke at Paris or Oxford, that
he took duration and number for actual
operations of the mind, such as doubting
or comparing. Price had long since
admitted, that Locke had no other meaning than that our ideas are derived, immediately or ultimately, from sensation
or reflection, or, in other words, ' that
they furnish us with all the subjects,
materials, and occasions of knowledge,
comparison, and internal perception.
This however by no means renders them
in any proper sense the source of all our
ideas.' Price's Dissertations on Morals,
p. 16.
   Cousin enumerates, as simple ideas not
derived from sensation or reflection,
space, duration, infinity, identity, sub-

stance, cause, and right. Locke would
have replied, that the idea of space, as
mere definite extension, was derived from
sensation, and that of space generally, or
what he has called expansion, was not
simple, but complex ; that those of duration, cause (or power), and identity,
were furnished by reflection ; that the
idea of right is not simple, and that
those of substance and infinity are
hardly formed by the mind at all. He
would add existence and unity to the
list, both, according to him, derived
from reflection.
   M. Cousin has by no means done justice to Locke as to the idea of *cause.*
' On sait que Locke, après avoir affirmé
dans un chapitre sur l'idée de cause et
d'effet, que cette idée nous est donnée
par la sensation, s'avise, dans un chapitre
différent sur la puissance, d'une toute
autre origine, bien qu'il s'agisse, au fond,
de la même idée, il trouve cette origine
nouvelle dans la réflexion appliquée à la
volonté,' &c. Fragmens Philosophiques,
p. 83. Now, in the first place, the chapter on Power, in the Essay on the Human Understanding, B. ii. ch. 21, comes
before and not after that on Cause and
Effect, ch. 26. But it is more important to observe, that in the latter chapter, and at the close of the 25th, Locke
distinctly says, that the idea is ' derived
from the two fountains of all our knowledge, sensation and reflection,' and,
' that this relation, how comprehensive
soever, terminates at last in them.' It
is also to be kept in mind, that he is here
speaking of physical causes : but in his
chapter on Power, of efficient ones, and
principally of the human mind; intimating also his opinion, that matter is
destitute of active power; that is, of
efficient causation. The form *on sait* is,
as *on sait,* a common mode of introducing
any questionable position. It does not
follow from this, that Locke's expressions
in the 26th chapter, on Cause and Effect,
are altogether the best ; but they must
be considered in connection with his long
chapter on Power.—1847.]

to admit with Cudworth and Price, that the understanding is the source of new ideas.'[a] And though some might object that this is too much in opposition, not to casual expressions, but to the whole tenour of Locke's Essay, his language concerning substance almost bears it out. Most of the perplexity which has arisen on this subject, the combats of some metaphysicians with Locke, the portentous errors into which others have been led by want of attention to his language, may be referred to the equivocal meaning of the word idea. The Cartesians understood by this whatever is the object of thought, including an intellection as well as an imagination. By an intellection they meant that which the mind conceives to exist, and to be the subject of knowledge, though it may be unimaginable and incomprehensible. Gassendi and Locke (at least in this part of his essay) limit the word idea to something which the mind sees and grasps as immediately present to it. 'That,' as Locke not very well expresses it, ' which the mind is applied about while thinking being the ideas that are there.' Hence he speaks with some ridicule of ' men who persuade themselves that they have clear comprehensive ideas of infinity.' Such men can hardly have existed; but it is by annexing the epithets clear and comprehensive, that he shows the dispute to be merely verbal. For that we know the existence of infinites as objectively real, and can reason upon them, Locke would not have denied; and it is this knowledge to which others gave the name of idea.

109. The different manner in which this all-important word was understood by philosophers is strikingly shown when they make use of the same illustration. Arnauld, if he is author of L'Art de Penser, mentions the idea of a chiliagon, or figure of 1000 sides, as an instance of the distinction between that which we imagine and that which we conceive or understand. Locke has employed the same instance to exemplify the difference between clear and obscure ideas. According to the former, we do not imagine a figure with 1000 sides at all: according to the latter, we form a confused image of it. We have an idea of such a figure, it

---

[a] Prelim. Dissertation.

is agreed by both; but in the sense of Arnauld, it is an idea of the understanding alone; in the sense of Locke, it is an idea of sensation, framed, like other complex ideas, by putting together those we have formerly received, though we may never have seen the precise figure. That the word suggests to the mind an image of a polygon with many sides is indubitable; but it is urged by the Cartesians, that as we are wholly incapable of distinguishing the exact number, we cannot be said to have, in Locke's sense of the word, any idea, even an indistinct one, of a figure with 1000 sides; since all we do imagine is a polygon. And it is evident that in geometry we do not reason from the properties of the image, but from those of a figure which the understanding apprehends. Locke, however, who generally preferred a popular meaning to one more metaphysically exact, thought it enough to call this a confused idea. He was not, I believe, conversant with any but elementary geometry. Had he reflected upon that which in his age had made such a wonderful beginning, or even upon the fundamental principles of it, which might be found in Euclid, the theory of infinitesimal quantities, he must, one would suppose, have been more puzzled to apply his narrow definition of an idea. For what image can we form of a differential, which can pretend to represent it in any other sense than as $d\,x$ represents it, by suggestion, not by resemblance?

110. The case is however much worse when Locke deviates, as in the third and fourth books he constantly does, from this sense that he has put on the word idea, and takes it either in the Cartesian meaning, or in one still more general and popular. Thus, in the excellent chapter on the abuse of words, he insists upon the advantage of using none without clear and distinct ideas; he who does not this ' only making a noise without any sense or signification.' If we combine this position with that in the second book, that we have no clear and distinct idea of a figure with 1000 sides, it follows with all the force of syllogism, that we should not argue about a figure of 1000 sides at all, nor, by parity of reason, about many other things of far higher importance. It will be found, I incline to think, that the large use of the word idea for that about which we have some knowledge, without

limiting it to what can be imagined, pervades the third and fourth books. Stewart has ingeniously conjectured that they were written before the second, and probably before the mind of Locke had been much turned to the psychological analysis which that contains. It is however certain that in the Treatise upon the Conduct of the Understanding, which was not published till after the Essay, he uses the word idea with full as much latitude as in the third and fourth books of the latter. We cannot, upon the whole, help admitting that the story of a lady who, after the perusal of the Essay on the Human Understanding, laid it down with a remark, that the book would be perfectly charming were it not for the frequent recurrence of one very hard word, *idea*, though told, possibly, in ridicule of the fair philosopher, pretty well represents the state of mind in which many at first have found themselves.[t]

111. Locke, as I have just intimated, seems to have possessed but a slight knowledge of geometry; a science which, both from the clearness of the illustrations it affords, and from its admitted efficacy in rendering the logical powers acute and cautious, may be reckoned, without excepting physiology, the most valuable of all to the metaphysician. But it did not require any geometrical knowledge, strictly so called, to avoid one material error into which he has fallen ; and which I mention the rather, because even Descartes, in one place, has said something of the same kind ; and I have met with it not only in Norris very distinctly and positively, but, more or less, in many or most of

An error as to geometrical figure.

---

[t] [The character of Locke's philosophical style, as given by a living philosopher by no means favourable to him, is perhaps too near the truth. 'In his *language*, Locke is, of all philosophers, the most figurative, ambiguous, vacillating, various, and even contradictory, as has been noticed by Reid and Stewart, and by Brown himself; indeed, we believe, by every author who has had occasion to comment on this philosopher. The opinions of such a writer are not, therefore, to be assumed from isolated and casual expressions, which themselves require to be interpreted on the general analogy of his system.' Edinb. Rev. (Sir William Hamilton), vol. lii. p. 189. I am happy to cite another late writer of high authority, in favour of the *general* character of Locke as a philosopher. 'Few among the great names in philosophy,' says Mr. Mill, 'have met with a harder measure of justice from the present generation than Locke, the unquestioned founder of the analytical philosophy of mind.' Perhaps Descartes and Hobbes, not to mention Gassendi, might contest the palm as *founders* of psychological analysis, but Mr. Mill justly gives to Locke the preference over Hobbes, who has been sometimes overrated of late, 'not only in sober judgment, but even in profundity and original genius.' System of Logic, vol. i. p. 150. —1847.]

those who have treated of the metaphysics or abstract principles of geometry. 'I doubt not,' says Locke,[u] 'but it will
be easily granted that the knowledge we have of mathematical truths is not only certain but real knowledge, and
not the bare empty vision of vain insignificant chimeras of
the brain ; and yet if we well consider, we shall find, that it
is only of our own ideas. The mathematician considers the
truth and properties belonging to a rectangle or circle only
as they are in idea in his own mind ; for it is possible he
never found either of them existing mathematically, that is,
precisely true, in his life. . . . . All the discourses of the
mathematicians about the squaring of a circle, conic sections,
or any other part of mathematics, concern not the existence of
any of those figures ; but their demonstrations, which depend
on their ideas, are the same, whether there be any square
or circle in the world or no.' And the inference he draws
from this is, that moral as well as mathematical ideas, being
archetypes themselves, and so adequate and complete ideas,
all the agreement or disagreement which he shall find in
them will produce real knowledge, as well as in mathematical
figures.

112. It is not perhaps necessary to inquire how far, upon
the hypothesis of Berkeley, this notion of mathematical
figures, as mere creations of the mind, could be sustained.
But on the supposition of the objectivity of space, as truly
existing without us, which Locke undoubtedly assumes, it is
certain that the passage just quoted is entirely erroneous,
and that it involves a confusion between the geometrical
figure itself and its delineation to the eye. A geometrical
figure is a portion of space contained in boundaries, determined by given relations. It exists in the infinite round
about us, as the statue exists in the block.[x] No one can
doubt, if he turns his mind to the subject, that every point

---

[u] B. iv. c. 8.

[x] Michael Angelo has well conveyed
this idea in four lines, which I quote
from Corniani : —

    Non ha l' ottimo artista alcun concetto,
    Che un marmo solo in se non circonscriva
    Col suo soverchio, e solo a quello arriva
    La mano che obbedisce all' intelleto.

The geometer uses not the same obedient

hand, but he equally feels and perceives
the reality of that figure which the broad
infinite around him comprehends *col suo
soverchio*.

[Cicero has a similar expression:—
Quasi non in omni marmore necesse sit
inesse vel Praxitelia capita ! illa enim
ipsa efficiuntur detractione. De Divi-
natione, ii. 21.—1842.]

in space is equidistant, in all directions, from certain other points. Draw a line through all these, and you have the circumference of a circle; but the circle itself and its circumference exist before the latter is delineated. Thus the orbit of a planet is not a regular geometrical figure, because certain forces disturb it. But this disturbance means only a deviation from a line which exists really in space, and which the planet would actually describe, if there were nothing in the universe but itself and the centre of attraction. The expression therefore of Locke, ' whether there be any square or circle existing in the world or no,' is highly inaccurate, the latter alternative being an absurdity. All possible figures, and that ' in number numberless,' exist every where; nor can we evade the perplexities into which the geometry of infinites throws our imagination, by considering them as mere beings of reason, the creatures of the geometer, which I believe some are half disposed to do, nor by substituting the vague and unphilosophical notion of indefinitude for a positive objective infinity.[y]

---

[y] [The confusion, as it appears to me, between sensible and real figure in geometry, I have found much more general in philosophical writers than I was aware of when this passage was first committed to the press. Thus M. Cousin: ' Il n'existe, dans la nature, que des figures imparfaites, et la géométrie a pour condition d'opérer sur des figures parfaites, sur le triangle parfait, le cercle parfait, &c.; c'est à dire, sur des figures qui n'ont pas d'existence réelle, et qui sont des pures conceptions de l'esprit.' Hist. de la Philos., vol. ii. p. 311. If by figure we mean only visible circumference, this is very true. But the geometer generally reasons, not upon the boundaries, but upon the extension, superficial or solid, comprehended within them; and to this extension itself we usually give the name of figure. Again, 'It is not true,' says Mr. Mill, ' that a circle exists, or can be described, which has all its radii exactly equal.' System of Logic, vol. i. p. 200. Certainly such a circle cannot be described, but in every geometrical sense it really exists. Hence he asserts 'the character of necessity, ascribed to mathematics, to be a mere illusion; nothing exists conformable to the definitions, nor is even possible.' P. 296.

It follows, of course, that a straight line is impossible; which is perfectly true, if it must be drawn with a ruler. But is it not surprising that so acute a writer as Mr. Mill can think any thing impossible, in a metaphysical sense, which implies no contradiction, and is easily conceived? He must have used possible in a sense limited to human execution.

Another eminent reasoner has gone the full lengths of this paradox. ' It has been rightly remarked by Dugald Stewart, that mathematical propositions are not properly true or false, in the same sense as any proposition respecting real fact is so called, and hence the truth, such as it is, of such propositions is necessary and eternal; since it amounts only to this, that any complex notion which you have arbitrarily formed must be exactly conformable to itself.' Whateley's Elements of Logic, 3rd edit., p. 229. And thus a celebrated writer who began in that school, though he has since traversed the diameter of theology: ' We are able to define the creations of our own minds, for they are what we make them; but it were as easy to create what is real, as to define it.' Newman's Sermons before the University of Oxford, p. 333.

113. The distinction between ideas of mere sensation and those of intellection, between what the mind comprehends,

The only meaning we can put on such assertions is, that geometry is a mere pastime of the mind, an exercise of logic, in which we have only to take care that we assign no other properties to the imaginary figures which answer to the syllogistic letters, A, B, and C, than such as are contained in their definition, without any objective truth whatever, or relation to a real external universe. The perplexities into which mathematicians have been thrown by the metaphysical difficulties of their science, must appear truly ludicrous, and such as they have manufactured for themselves. But the most singular circumstance of all is, that nature is regulated by these arbitrary definitions; and that the truths of geometry, *such as they are*, enable us to predict the return of Uranus or Neptune to the same place in the heavens after the present generation are in their graves. A comet leaves its perihelion, and pursues its path through the remote regions of space; the astronomer foretells its return by the laws of a geometrical figure, and if it come a few days only before the calculated moment, has recourse to the hypothesis of some resistance which has diminished its orbit; so sure is he that the projectile force, and that of gravity, act in lines geometrically straight.

The source of this paradox appears to be a too hasty and rather inaccurate assumption, that geometry depends upon definitions. But though we cannot argue except according to our definitions, the real subject of the science is not those terms, but the properties of the things defined. We conceive a perfect circle to be not only a possible but a real figure; that its radii are equal, belongs to the idea, not to the words by which we define it. Men might reason by themselves on geometry without any definitions; or, if they could not, the truths of the science would be the same.

The universal and necessary belief of mankind is, that we are placed in the midst of an unbounded ocean of space. On all sides of us, and in three dimensions, this is spread around. We cannot conceive it to be annihilated, or to have had a beginning. Innumerable objects of our senses, themselves extended, that is, occupying portions of this space, but

portions not always the same, float within it. And as we find other properties than mere extension in these objects, by which properties alone they are distinguishable from the surrounding space, we denominate them bodies, or material substances. Considered in its distinction from this space, their own proper extension has boundaries by which they come under the relation of figure; and thus all bodies are figured. But we do not necessarily limit this word to material substances. The mind is not only perfectly capable of considering geometrical figures, that is, particular portions of the continuous extension which we call absolute space, by themselves, as measured by the mutual distances of their boundaries, but is intuitively certain that such figures are real, that extension is divisible into parts, and that there must be everywhere in the surrounding expanse triangles and circles mathematically exact, though any diagram which we can delineate will be more or less incorrect. 'Space,' says Sir John Herschel (if we may name him), 'in its ultimate analysis, is nothing but an assemblage of distances and directions.' Quarterly Review, June, 1841, quoted in Mill's Logic, i. 324. This is very forcibly expressed, if not with absolute precision; for distance is perhaps, in strictness, rather the measure of space than space itself. It is suggested by every extended body, the boundaries whereof must be distant one from another, and it is suggested also by the separation of these bodies, which, when not in contact, are perceived to have intervals between them. But these intervals are not necessarily filled by other bodies, nor even by light; as when we perceive stars, and estimate their distances from one another, in a moonless night. The mere ideas of distance and direction seem to be simple, or rather modes of the simple idea extension; and for this reason no definition can be given of a straight line. It is the measure of distance itself which the mind intuitively apprehends to be but one, and that the shortest line which can be drawn.

'The only clear notion,' says Herschel, 'we can form of straightness, is, uniformity of direction.' And as the

and what it conceives without comprehending, is the point of divergence between the two sects of psychology which still exist

line itself is only imaginary, or, if it be drawn, is but the representative of distance or length, it cannot have, as such, any other dimension. Though we know that a material line must have breadth, it is not a mere abstraction of the geometer to say, that the distance of an object from the eye has no breadth, but it would be absurd to say the contrary.

The definition of a mathematical figure involves only its possibility. But our knowledge of extension itself, as objectively real, renders all figures true beings, not *entia rationis*, but actual beings, portions of one infinite continuous extension. They exist in space, to repeat the metaphor (which indeed is no metaphor, but an instance), as the statue exists in the block. Extension, perhaps, and figure, are rather the conditions under which bodies, whatever else they may be, are presented to our senses, than, in perfect strictness of expression, the essentials of body itself. They have been called by Stewart, the mathematical properties of matter. Certain it is that they remain when the body is displaced; and would remain were it annihilated. And it is with the relation of bodies to space absolute, that the geometer has to deal ; never, in his pure science, with their material properties.

What, then, is the meaning of what we sometimes read, that there is no such thing as a circle or a triangle in nature ? If we are to understand the physical universe, the material world, which is the common sense, this may perhaps be true ; but what, then, has the geometer to do with nature ? If we include absolute space under the word nature, I must entirely deny the assertion. Can we doubt that portions of space, or points, exist in every direction at the same distance from any other assignable point or portion of space? I cannot draw a radius precisely a foot long ; but I can draw a line more than eleven inches in length, and can produce this till it is more than twelve. At some point or other, it has been exactly the length of a foot. The want of precise uniformity of direction may be overcome in the same way ; there is a series of points along which the line might have been directed, so as to be perfectly uniform ; just as in the orbit of a planet

round the sun, disturbed as it is by the attraction of a third body at every point, there is yet at every point a line, called the instantaneous ellipse, along which the path of the body might by possibility have proceeded in a geometrical curve. Let the mind once fix itself on the idea of continuous extension, and its divisibility into parts mathematically equal, or in mathematical ratios, must appear necessary.

Geometry, then, is not a science of reasoning upon definitions, such as we please to conceive, but on the relations of space ; of space, an objective being, according at least to human conceptions, space, the bosom of nature, that which alone makes all things sensibly without us ; made known to us by a primary law of the understanding, as some hold ; by experience of sensation, or inference from it, as others maintain ; but necessary, eternal, the basis of such demonstration as no other science possesses ; because in no other do we perceive an absolute impossibility, an impossibility paramount, speaking reverently, to the Creator's will, that the *premises* of our reasoning might have been different from what they are. The definitions of geometrical figures no more constitute their essence than those of a plant or a mineral. Whether geometrical *reasoning* is built on the relations of parts of space, merely as defined in words, is another question ; it certainly appears to me, that definitions supply only the terms of the proposition ; and that without a knowledge, verbal or implied, of the axioms, we could not deduce any conclusions at all. But this affects only the logic of the theorem, the process by which the relations of space are unfolded to the human understanding. I cannot for a moment believe, that the distinguished philosopher, who has strenuously argued for the deduction of geometry from definitions, meant any more than to oppose them to axioms. That they are purely arbitrary, that they are the creatures of the mind, like harpies and chimæras, he could hardly have thought, being himself habituated to geometrical studies. But the language of Stewart is not sufficiently guarded ; and he has served as an authority to those who have uttered so singular a paradox. 'From what prin-

in the world.   Nothing is in the intellect which has not before
been in the sense, said the Aristotelian schoolmen.   Every

ciple,' says Stewart, 'are the various
properties of the circle derived, but from
the definition of a circle? from what
principle the properties of the parabola
or ellipse, but from the definitions of
these curves? A similar observation may
be extended to all the other theorems
which the mathematician demonstrates.'
Vol. ii. p. 41. The properties of a circle
or the other curves, we answer, are derived from that leading property which
we express in the definition. But surely
we can make use of no definition, which
does not declare a real property. We
might impose a name on a quadrilateral
figure with equal angles and sides not
parallel; but could we draw an inference
from it? And why could we not, but
because we should be restrained by its
incompatibility with our necessary conceptions of the relations of space? It is
these primary conceptions to which our
definitions must conform. Definitions
of figure, at least in all but the most
familiar, are indispensable, in order to
make us apprehend particular relations
of distance, and to keep our reasonings
clear from confusion; but this is only the
common province of language.

In this I have the satisfaction of finding myself supported by the authority
of Dr. Whewell. 'Supposing,' he observed in his Thoughts on the Study of
the Mathematics, 'we could get rid of
geometrical axioms altogether, and deduce our reasoning from definitions alone,
it must be allowed, I think, that still our
geometrical propositions would probably depend, not on the definitions, but
on the act of mind by which we fix
upon such definitions; in short, on our
conception of *space*. The axiom, that
two straight lines cannot enclose space,
is a self-evident truth, and founded upon
our faculty of apprehending the properties of space, and of conceiving a straight
line. . . . We should present a false view
of the nature of geometrical truth if we
were to represent it as resting upon definitions, and should overlook or deny the
faculty of the mind, and the intellectual
process which is implied in our fixing
upon such definitions. The foundation
of all the properties of straight lines is
certainly not the definition, but the conception of a straight line, and in the same
manner the foundation of all geometrical

truth resides in our general conceptions
of space.' P. 151.

That mathematical truths (a position
of Stewart commended by Whately) are
not properly called matters of fact,
is no new distinction. They are not
γενόμενα; they have no being in time,
as matters of fact have; they are ὄντα,
beings of a higher order than any facts,
but still realities, and, as some philosophers have held, more truly real than
any created essence. But Archbishop
Whately is a nominalist of the school of
Hobbes. Mr. Mill, who is an avowed
conceptualist, has said : 'Every proposition which conveys real information, asserts a matter of fact dependent on the
laws of nature, and not upon artificial
classification.' Vol. i. p. 237. But here
he must use matter of fact in a loose
sense; for he would certainly admit mathematical theorems to convey real information; though I do not agree with
him that they are, in propriety of language, dependent on the laws of nature.
He observes on the archbishop's position,
that the object of reasoning is to expand
the assertions wrapped up in those with
which we set out, that 'it is not easy to
see how such a science as geometry can be
said to be wrapped up in a few definitions
and axioms.' P. 297. Whether this be a
sufficient answer to the archbishop or
no, it shows that Mr. Mill considers mathematical propositions to convey real
science.

Two opposite errors are often found
in modern writers on the metaphysics of
geometry; the one, that which has just
been discussed, the denial of absolute
reality to mathematical truths; the other
wholly opposite, yet which equally
destroys their prerogative; I mean the
theory that they are only established by
induction. As in the first they are no
facts in any sense, not real truths, so in
the other they are mere facts. But, indeed, both these opinions, divergent as
they seem, emanate from the ultra-no-
minalist school, and they sometimes are
combined in the same writer. Mr. Mill
and Mr. De Morgan have lent their great
authority to the second doctrine, which
was revived from Hobbes, fifty years
since, by Dr. Beddoes, in a tract on Demonstrative Evidence, which I have
heard attributed, in part, to Professor

idea has its original in the senses, repeated the disciple of Epicurus, Gassendi. Locke indeed, as Gassendi had done

Leslie, a supporter of the same theory. Sir William Hamilton exclaims upon the position of two writers in the suite of Archbishop Whately, that it is by induction all axioms are known; such as, 'A whole is greater than its parts.' 'Is such the Oxford metaphysics?' Edinb. Rev. vol. lvii. p. 232. But though the assertion seems more monstrous, when applied to such an axiom as this, it is substantially found in many writers of deserved fame; nor is it either a metaphysics of Oxford growth, or very likely to be well received there. The Oxford error at present, that at least of the dominant school, seems to be the very reverse; a strong tendency to absolute Platonic realism. This has had, cause or effect, something to do with the apotheosis of the *Church*, which implies reality, a step to personality.

It seems to follow from this inductive theory, that we believe two straight lines not to include a space, because we have never seen them do so, or heard of any one who has; and as mere induction is confessed to be no basis of certain truth, we must admit mathematical demonstration to differ only in degree of positive evidence from probability. As the passage in my text to which this note refers bears no relation to this second opinion, I shall not dwell upon it farther than to remark, that it seems strange to hear that two straight lines are only proved by observation not to include a space, when we are told in the same breath that no straight lines exist, and consequently that any which we may take for straight would be found, on a more accurate examination, to include a space between them. But, reverting to the subject of the former part of this note, it may be observed that our conception that two straight lines cannot include a space is a homage to the reality of geometrical figure, for experience has not given it; all we learn from experience is, that the nearer to straightness two lines are drawn, the less space they include; and even here the reasoning is in the inverse order, the less space they include, the more they approach to straight, that is the nearer to uniformity is their direction.

In all this I have assumed the reality of space, according to the usual apprehen-

sion of mankind. With the transcendental problem, raised by the Kantian school, it seems unnecessary to meddle. We know at least that we acknowledge the objectivity of space by a condition of our understandings; we know that others with whom we converse have the like conceptions of it; we have every reason to believe that inferior animals judge of extension, distance, and direction, by sensations and inferences analogous to our own; we predict the future, in calculating the motions of heavenly and terrestrial bodies, on the assumption that space is no fiction of the brain, its portions and measured distances no creations of an arbitrary definition. Locke, I am aware, in one of the miscellaneous papers published by Lord King (Life of Locke, vol. ii. p. 175), bearing the date 1677, says: ' Space in itself seems to be nothing but a capacity or possibility for extended beings or bodies to be or exist;' and, ' The space where a real globe of a foot diameter exists, though we imagine it to be really something, to have a real existence before and after its [the globe's] existence, there in truth is really nothing.' And finally, ' though it be true that the black lines drawn on a rule have the relation one to another of an inch distance, they being real sensible things; and though it be also true that I, knowing the idea of an inch, can imagine that length without imagining body, as well as I can imagine a figure without imagining body, yet it is no more true that there is any real distance in that which we call imaginary space, than that there is any real figure there.' P. 185.

I confess myself wholly at a loss how to reconcile such notions of space and distance, not only with geometry, but dynamics; the idea of velocity involving that of mere extension in a straight line, without the conception, necessarily implied, of any body except the moving one. But it is worthy of remark, that Locke appears to have modified his doctrine here delivered, before he wrote the Essay on the Human Understanding; where he argues at length, in language adapted to the common belief of the reality of space, and once only observes that some may ' take it to be only a relation resulting from the existence of other beings at a distance, while others

before him, assigned another origin to one class of ideas ; but these were few, in number, and in the next century two writers of considerable influence, Hartley and Condillac, attempted to resolve them all into sensation. The ancient school of the Platonists, and even that of Descartes, who had distinguished innate ideas, or at least those spontaneously

---

understand the words of Solomon and St. Paul in a literal sense' (b. ii. c. 13, § 27); by which singular reference to Scripture he may perhaps intimate that he does not perceive the force of the metaphysical argument. I think it not impossible that the reading of Newton, who has so emphatically pronounced himself for the real existence of absolute space, had so far an effect upon the mind of Locke, that he did not commit himself to an opposite hypothesis. Except with a very few speculative men, I believe the conviction, that space exists truly and independently around us, to be universal in mankind.

Locke was a philosopher, equally bold in following up his own inquiries, and cautious in committing them, except as mere conjectures, to the public. Perhaps an instance might be given from the remarkable anticipation of the theory of Boscovich as to the nature of matter, which Stewart has sagaciously inferred from a passage in the Essay on the Human Understanding. But if we may trust an anecdote in the Bibliothèque raisonnée, vol. iv. p. 350, on the authority of Coste, the French translator of that work, Newton conceived the idea of Boscovich's theory, and suggested it to Locke. The quotation is in the words of the translator :—

'Ici M. Locke excite notre curiosité sans vouloir la satisfaire. Bien des gens s'étant imaginés qu'il m'avait communiqué cette manière d'expliquer la création de la matière, me prièrent, peu de temps après que ma traduction eut vu le jour, de leur en faire part ; mais je fus obligé de leur avouer que M. L. m'en avait fait un secret à moi-même. Enfin, longtemps après sa mort, M. le Chevalier Newton, à qui je parlais, par hasard, de cet endroit du livre de M. Locke, me découvrit tout le mystère. Souriant, il me dit d'abord, que c'était lui-même qui avait imaginé cette manière d'expliquer la création de la matière ; que la pensée lui en était venue dans l'esprit un jour qu'il vint à tomber sur cette question

avec M. L. et un seigneur anglais plein de vie, et qui n'est pas moins illustre par l'étendue de ses lumières que par sa naissance. Et voici comment il leur expliqua sa pensée. " On pouvait," dit-il, " se former, en quelque manière, une idée de la création de la matière, en supposant que Dieu eût empêché par sa puissance, que rien ne pût entrer dans une certaine portion de l'espace pur, que, de sa nature, est pénétrable, éternel, nécessaire, infini ; car dès-là cette portion d'espace aurait l'impénétrabilité, l'une des qualités essentielles à la matière. Et comme l'espace pur est absolument uniforme, on n'a qu'à supposer que Dieu aurait communiqué cette espèce d'impénétrabilité à une autre pareille portion de l'espace, et cela nous donnerait, en quelque sorte, une idée de la mobilité de la matière, autre qualité qui lui est aussi très essentielle." Nous voilà maintenant délivrés de chercher ce que M. L. avait trouvé bon de cacher à ses lecteurs.' Bibl. raisonnée, vol. iv. p. 349.

It is unnecessary to observe what honour the conjecture of Stewart does to his sagacity ; for he was not very likely to have fallen on this passage in an old review little read, nor was he a man to conceal the obligation, had he done so. The theory of Boscovich, or, as we may perhaps now say, of Newton, has been lately supported, with abundance of new illustration, by the greatest genius in philosophical discovery whom this age and country can boast. I will conclude with throwing out a suggestion, whether, on the hypothesis that matter is only a combination of forces, attractive or repulsive, and varying in different substances or bodies, as they are vulgarly called, inasmuch as all forces are capable of being mathematically expressed, there is not a proper formula belonging to each body, though of course not assignable by us, which might be called its equation, and which, if known, would be the definition of its essence, as strictly as that of a geometrical figure.—1847.]

suggesting themselves on occasion of visible objects, from those strictly belonging to sense, lost ground both in France and England; nor had Leibnitz, who was deemed an enemy to some of our great English names, sufficient weight to restore it. In the hands of some who followed in both countries, the worst phrases of Locke were preferred to the best; whatever could be turned to the account of pyrrhonism, materialism, or atheism, made a figure in the Epicurean system of a popular philosophy.[z] The German metaphysicians from the time of Kant deserve at least the credit of having successfully withstood this coarse sensualism, though they may have borrowed much that their disciples take for original, and added much that is hardly better than what they have overthrown. France has also made a rapid return, since the beginning of this century, and with more soundness of judgment than Germany, towards the doctrines of the Cartesian school. Yet the opposite philosophy to that which never rises above sensible images is exposed to a danger of its own; it is one which the infirmity of the human faculties renders perpetually at hand; few there are who in reasoning on subjects where we cannot attain what Locke has called 'positive comprehensive ideas' are secure from falling into

---

[z] ['Locke,' says M. Cousin, 'has certainly not confounded sensation with the faculties of the mind; he expressly distinguishes them, but he makes the latter play a secondary and insignificant part, and concenters their action on sensible *data*; it was but a step from thence to confound them with sensibility; and we have here the feeble germ of a future theory, that of transformed sensation, of sensation as the only principle of all the operations of the mind. Locke, without knowing or designing it, has opened the road to this exclusive doctrine, by adding nothing to sensation but faculties whose whole business is to exercise themselves upon it, with no peculiar or original power.' Hist. de la Philos. vol. ii. p. 137.

If the powers of combining, comparing, and generalising the ideas originally derived from sense are not to be called peculiar and original, this charge might be sustained. But though Locke had not the same views of the active and self-originated powers of the mind which have

been taken by others, if he derived some ideas from sense to which a different source has been assigned, it seems too much to say that he makes the faculties play a secondary and insignificant part; when the part he attributes to them is that of giving us all our knowledge beyond that of mere simple sense; and, to use his own analogy, being to sensation what the words of a language, in all their combinations, are to the letters which compose them. M. Cousin, and the other antagonists of Locke, will not contend that we could have had any knowledge of geometry or arithmetic without sensation; and Locke has never supposed that we could have so much as put two ideas of extension or number together without the active powers of the mind. In this point I see no other difference between the two schools, than that one derives a few ideas from sense, which the other cannot trace to that source; and this is hardly sufficient to warrant the depreciation of Locke as a false and dangerous guide in philosophy.—1847.]

mere nonsense and repugnancy. In that part of physics
which is simply conversant with quantity, this danger is
probably not great, but in all such inquiries as are sometimes
called transcendental, it has perpetually shipwrecked the
adventurous navigator.

114. In the language and probably the notions of Locke as
to the nature of the soul there is an indistinctness His notions
more worthy of the Aristotelian schoolmen than of as to the soul,
one conversant with the Cartesian philosophy. 'Bodies,' he
says, 'manifestly produce ideas in us by impulse, the only
way which we can conceive bodies to operate in. If, then,
external objects be not united to our minds, when they
produce ideas in it, and yet we perceive these original
qualities in such of them as singly fall under our senses, it is
evident that some motion must be thence continued by our
nerves, or animal spirits, by some parts of our bodies to the
brain, or the seat of sensation, there to produce in our minds
the particular ideas we have of them. And since the extension, figure, number, and motion of bodies of an observable bigness may be perceived at a distance by the sight,
it is evident some singly imperceptible bodies must come
from them to the eyes, and thereby convey to the brain some
motion which produces those ideas, which we have of them,
in us.' He so far retracts his first position afterwards, as
to admit, 'in consequence of what Mr. Newton has shown in
the Principia on the gravitation of matter towards matter,'
that God not only can put into bodies powers and ways of
operation above what can be explained from what we know of
matter, but that he has actually done so. And he promises
to correct the former passage, which however he has never
performed. In fact he seems, by the use of phrases which
recur too often to be thought merely figurative, to have supposed that something in the brain comes into local contact
with the mind. He was here unable to divest himself, any
more than the schoolmen had done, of the notion that there
is a proper action of the body on the soul in perception. The
Cartesians had brought in the theory of occasional causes
and other solutions of the phænomena, so as to avoid what
seems so irreconcilable with an immaterial principle. No
one is so lavish of a cerebral instrumentality in mental

images as Malebranche; he seems at every moment on the verge of materialism; he coquets, as it were, with an Epicurean physiology; but, if I may be allowed to continue the metaphor, he perceives the moment where to stop, and retires, like a dexterous fair one, with unsmirched honour to his immateriality. It cannot be said that Locke is equally successful.

115. In another and a well-known passage he has thrown
and its im-
materiality. out a doubt whether God might not superadd the faculty of thinking to matter; and, though he thinks it probable that this has not been the case, leaves it at last a debatable question, wherein nothing else than presumptions are to be had.   Yet he has strongly argued against the possibility of a material Deity, upon reasons derived from the nature of matter.   Locke almost appears to have taken the union of a thinking being with matter for the thinking of matter itself.   What is there, Stillingfleet well asks, like self-consciousness in matter ? 'Nothing at all,' Locke replies, 'in matter as matter.   But that God cannot bestow on some parcels of matter a power of thinking, and with it self-consciousness, will never be proved by asking how it is possible to apprehend that mere body should perceive that it doth perceive.'   But if that we call mind, and of which we are self-conscious, were thus superadded to matter, would it the less be something real?   In what sense can it be compared to an accident or quality ?   It has been justly observed that we are much more certain of the independent existence of mind than of that of matter.   But that, by the constitution of our nature, a definite organisation, or, what will be generally thought the preferable hypothesis, an organic molecule, should be a necessary concomitant of this immaterial principle, does not involve any absurdity at all, whatever want of evidence may be objected to it.

116. It is remarkable that, in the controversy with Stillingfleet on this passage, Locke seems to take for granted that there is no immaterial principle in brutes; and as he had too much plain sense to adopt the Cartesian theory of their insensibility, he draws the most plausible argument for the possibility of thought in matter by the admitted fact of sensation and voluntary motion in these animal organisations. 'It is not doubted but that the properties of a rose, a peach,

or an elephant, superadded to matter, change not the
properties of matter, but matter is in these things matter
still.' Few perhaps at present who believe in the immateriality of the human soul would deny the same to an
elephant; but it must be owned that the discoveries of
zoology have pushed this to consequences which some might
not readily adopt. The spiritual being of a sponge revolts a
little our prejudices; yet there is no resting-place, and we
must admit this, or be content to sink ourselves into a mass
of medullary fibre. Brutes have been as slowly emancipated
in philosophy as some classes of mankind have been in civil
polity; their souls, we see, were almost universally disputed
to them at the end of the seventeenth century, even by those
who did not absolutely bring them down to machinery.
Even within the recollection of many, it was common to
deny them any kind of reasoning faculty, and to solve their
most sagacious actions by the vague word instinct. We
have come of late years to think better of our humble companions; and, as usual in similar cases, the predominant
bias, at least with foreign naturalists, seems rather too much
of a levelling character.

117. No quality more remarkably distinguishes Locke than
his love of truth. He is of no sect or party, has no His love of
oblique design, such as we so frequently perceive, originality.
of sustaining some tenet which he suppresses, no submissive-
ness to the opinions of others, nor what very few lay aside,
to his own. Without having adopted certain dominant
ideas, like Descartes and Malebranche, he follows with inflexible impartiality and unwearied patience the long process
of analysis to which he has subjected the human mind. No
great writer has been more exempt from vanity, in which he
is very advantageously contrasted with Bacon and Descartes;
but he is sometimes a little sharp and contemptuous of his
predecessors. The originality of Locke is real and unaffected; not that he has derived nothing from others, which
would be a great reproach to himself or to them, but in
whatever he has in common with other philosophers there is
always a tinge of his own thoughts, a modification of the
particular tenet, or at least a peculiarity of language which
renders it not very easy of detection. 'It was not to be

expected,' says Stewart, ' that in a work so composed by
snatches, to borrow a phrase of the author, he should be able
accurately to draw the line between his own ideas and the
hints for which he was indebted to others. To those who
are well acquainted with his speculations it must appear
evident that he had studied diligently the metaphysical
writings both of Hobbes and Gassendi, and that he was no
stranger to the Essays of Montaigne, to the philosophical
works of Bacon, and to Malebranche's Inquiry after Truth.
That he was familiarly conversant with the Cartesian system
may be presumed from what we are told by his biographer,
that it was this which first inspired him with a disgust at
the jargon of the schools, and led him into that train of
thinking which he afterwards prosecuted so successfully.
I do not, however, recollect that he has any where in his
Essay mentioned the name of any one of those authors. It
is probable that when he sat down to write he found the
result of his youthful reading so completely identified with
the fruits of his subsequent reflections, that it was impossible
for him to attempt a separation of the one from the other,
and that he was thus occasionally led to mistake the treasures of memory for those of invention. That this was really
the case may be further presumed from the peculiar and
original cast of his phraseology, which, though in general
careless and unpolished, has always the merit of that
characteristical unity and raciness of style which demonstrate that while he was writing he conceived himself to be
drawing only from his own resources.' [a]

118. The writer, however, whom we have just quoted has
Defended in
two cases. not quite done justice to the originality of Locke in
more than one instance. Thus on this very passage
we find a note in these words :—' Mr. Addison has remarked
that Malebranche had the start of Locke by several years in
his notions on the subject of duration. Some other coincidences not less remarkable might be easily pointed out in the
opinions of the English and of the French philosopher.' I am
not prepared to dispute, nor do I doubt, the truth of the
latter sentence. But with respect to the notions of Male-

---

[a] Preliminary Dissertation.

branche and Locke on duration, it must be said, that they are neither the same, nor has Addison asserted them to be so.[b] The one threw out an hypothesis with no attempt at proof : the other offered an explanation of the phænomena. What Locke has advanced as to our getting the idea of duration by reflecting on the succession of our ideas seems to be truly his own. Whether it be entirely the right explanation, is another question. It rather appears to me that the internal sense, as we may not improperly call it, of duration belongs separately to each idea, and is rather lost than suggested by their succession. Duration is best perceived when we are able to detain an idea for some time without change, as in watching the motion of a pendulum. And though it is impossible for the mind to continue in this state of immobility more perhaps than about a second or two, this is sufficient to give us an idea of duration as the necessary condition of existence. Whether this be an objective or merely a subjective necessity, is an abstruse question, which our sensations do not enable us to decide. But Locke appears to have looked rather at the measure of duration, by which we divide it into portions, than at the mere simplicity of the idea itself. Such a measure, it is certain, can only be obtained through the medium of a succession in our ideas.

119. It has been also remarked by Stewart that Locke claims a discovery due rather to Descartes, namely, the impossibility of defining simple ideas. Descartes however, as well as the authors of the Port-Royal Logic, merely says that words already as clear as we can make them, do not require, or even admit of definition. But I do not perceive that he has made the distinction we find in the Essay on the Human Understanding, that the names of simple ideas are not capable of any definition, while the names of all complex ideas are so. 'It has not, that I know,' Locke says, 'been observed by any body what words are, and what words are not, capable of being defined.' The passage which I have quoted in another place, from Descartes's posthumous dialogue, even if it went to this length, was unknown to Locke ; yet he might have acknowledged that he had been in some measure anticipated in other observations by that philosopher.

---

[b] Spectator, No. 94.

120. The first book of the Essay on the Human Under-
His view of standing is directed, as is well known, against the
innate ideas. doctrine of innate ideas, or innate principles in the
mind.   This has been often censured, as combating in some
places a tenet which no one would support, and as, in other
passages, breaking upon moral distinctions themselves, by
disputing the universality of their acknowledgment.   With
respect to the former charge, it is not perhaps easy for us to
determine what might be the crude and confused notions, or
at least language, of many who held the theory of innate
ideas.   It is by no means evident that Locke had Descartes
chiefly or even at all in his view.   Lord Herbert, whom he
distinctly answers, and many others, especially the Platonists, had dwelt upon innate ideas in far stronger terms than
the great French metaphysician, if indeed he can be said to
have maintained them at all.   The latter and more important
accusation rests upon no other pretext, than that Locke must
be reckoned among those who have not admitted a moral
faculty of discerning right from wrong to be a part of our
constitution.   But that there is a law of nature imposed by
the Supreme Being, and consequently universal, has been so
repeatedly asserted in his writings, that it would imply great
inattention to question it.   Stewart has justly vindicated
Locke in this respect from some hasty and indefinite charges
of Beattie ;[c] but I must venture to think that he goes much
too far when he attempts to identify the doctrines of the Essay with those of Shaftesbury.   These two philosophers were
in opposite schools as to the test of moral sentiments.   Locke
seems always to adopt what is called the selfish system in
morals, resolving all morality into religion, and all religion
into a regard to our own interest.   And he seems to have
paid less attention to the emotions than to the intellectual
powers of the soul.

121. It would by no means be difficult to controvert other
General   tenets of this great man.   But the obligations we
praise.   owe to him for the Essay on the Human Understanding are never to be forgotten.   It is truly the first real

---

[c] [To the passages quoted by Stewart
(First Dissertation, p. 29) we may add a
letter since published, of Locke to Mr.
Tyrrell, wherein he most explicitly declares his belief, 'that there is a law of
nature knowable by the light of nature.'
King's Life of Locke, vol. i. p. 366.—
1847.]

chart of the coasts ; wherein some may be laid down incor-
rectly, but the general relations of all are perceived. And
we who find some things to censure in Locke have perhaps
learned how to censure them from himself; we have thrown
off so many false notions and films of prejudice by his help
that we are become capable of judging our master. This is
what has been the fate of all who have pushed onward the
landmarks of science ; they have made that easy for inferior
men which was painfully laboured through by themselves.
Among many excellent things in the Essay on Human Understanding, none are more admirable than much of the third
book on the nature of words, especially the three chapters
on their imperfection and abuse.[d] In earlier treatises of
logic, at least in that of Port-Royal, some of this might be
found ; but nowhere are verbal fallacies, and above all, the
sources from which they spring, so fully and conclusively
exposed.[e]

---

[d] [In former editions I had said 'the whole third book,' which Mr. Mills calls 'that immortal third book.' But we must except the sixth chapter on the names of substances, in which Locke's reasoning against the real distinction of species in the three kingdoms of nature is full of false assumptions, and cannot be maintained at all in the present state of natural history. He asks, ch. vi. § 13, 'What are the alterations may or may not be in a horse or lead, without making either of them to be of another species ?' The answer is obvious, that an animal engendered between a horse and mare, is a horse, and no other ; and that any alteration in the atomic weight of lead would make it a different species. 'I once saw a creature,' says Locke, 'that was the issue of a cat and a rat, and had the plain marks of both about it.' This cannot be true ; but if it were ? Are there therefore no mere cats and mere rats ?—1847.]

[e] [A highly-distinguished philosopher, M. Cousin, has devoted nearly a volume to the refutation of Locke, discussing almost every chapter in the second and fourth books of the Essay on Human Understanding. In many of these treatises I cannot by any means go along with the able writer ; and regret that he has taken so little pains to distinguish real from verbal differences of opinion, but has, on the contrary, had nothing so much at heart as to depreciate the glory of one whom Europe has long reckoned among the founders of metaphysical science. It may have been wrong in Locke to employ the word *idea* in different senses. But, as undoubtedly he did not always mean by it an image in the mind, what can be less fair than such passages as the following? 'Eh bien! songez-y, vous n'avez de connaissance légitime de la pensée, de la volonté, de la sensibilité, qu'à la condition que les idées que vous en ayez vous les représentent ; et ces idées doivent être des images, et par conséquent des images matérielles. Jugez dans quelle abîme d'absurdités nous voilà tombés. Pour connaître la pensée, et la volonté qui sont immatérielles, il faut que nous en ayons une image matérielle qui leur rassemble.' (Cours de l'Hist. de la Philos., vol. ii. p. 348, ed. 1829.) It ought surely to have occurred that, in proportion to the absurdity of such a proposition, was the want of likelihood that a mind eminently cautious and reflective should have embraced it.

It is not possible in a note to remark on the many passages wherein M. Cousin has dealt no fair measure to our illustrious metaphysician. But one I will not pass over. He quotes Locke for the words: 'A l'égard des esprits (nos âmes, les intelligences), [interpolation by M. Cousin

122. The same praiseworthy diligence in hunting error to
Locke's
Conduct of
Under-
standing. its lurking-places distinguishes the short treatise on the Conduct of the Understanding; which having been originally designed as an additional chapter to the Essay,[f] is as it were the ethical application of its theory, and ought always to be read with it, if indeed, for the sake of its practical utility, it should not come sooner into the course of education. Aristotle himself, and the whole of his dialectical school, had pointed out many of the sophisms

---

himself], nous ne pouvons pas plus connaître qu'il y a des esprits finis réellement existans, par les idées que nous en avons, que nous ne pouvons connaître qu'il y a des fées ou des centaures par les idées que nous nous en formons.' Voilà bien, ce me semble, le scepticisme absolu; et vous pensez peut-être que la conclusion dernière de Locke sera qu'il n'y a aucune connaissance des esprits finis, par conséquent de notre âme, par conséquent encore d'aucune des facultés de notre âme; car l'objection est aussi valable contre les phénomènes de l'âme que contre la substance. C'est là où il aurait dû aboutir; mais il ne l'ose, parce qu'il n'y a pas un philosophe à la fois plus sage et plus inconsistant que Locke. Que fait-il, Messieurs? Dans le péril où le pousse la philosophie, il abandonne sa philosophie et toute philosophie, et il en appelle au christianisme, à la révélation, à la foi; et par foi, par révélation, il n'entend pas une foi, une révélation philosophique; cette interprétation n'appartient pas au temps de Locke; il entend la foi et la révélation dans le sens propre de la théologie la plus orthodoxe; et il conclut ainsi: 'Par conséquent, sur l'existence de l'esprit nous devons nous contenter de l'évidence de la foi.' P. 350. Who could suppose that all this imputation of unlimited scepticism, not less than that of Hume, since it amounts to a doubt of the existence of our own minds, is founded on M. Cousin's misunderstanding of the word *spirit?* By spirits, or finite spirits, Locke did not mean our own minds, but created intelligences, differing from human, as the word was constantly used in theological metaphysics. The sense of the passage to which M. Cousin refers is so clear that no English reader could misconceive it; probably he was led wrong by a translation in which he found the word *esprit*.

But I really cannot imagine any translation to be so unfaithful as to remove from M. Cousin the blame of extreme carelessness. The words of Locke are, 'Concerning finite spirits, as well as several other things, we must content ourselves with the evidence of faith.' B. iv. ch. 11. But at the beginning of the same chapter he says, 'The knowledge of our own being we have by intuition.' And in the preceding, the tenth chapter, more fully: 'I think it is beyond question that man has a clear perception of his own being: he knows certainly that he exists, and that he is something. He that can doubt whether he be any thing or no, I speak not to, no more than I would argue with pure nothing, or endeavour to convince non-entity that it were something.' Compare this with M. Cousin's representation.

The name of Locke is part of our literary inheritance, which, as Englishmen, we cannot sacrifice. If, indeed, the university at which he was educated cannot discover that he is, perhaps, her chief boast, if a declaimer from that quarter presumes to speak of 'the sophist Locke,' we may console ourselves by recollecting how little influence such a local party is likely to obtain over the literary world. But the fame of M. Cousin is so conspicuous that his prejudices readily become the prejudices of many, and his misrepresentations pass with many for unanswerable criticisms. —1847.]

[f] See a letter to Molyneux, dated April, 1697. Locke's Works (fol. 1759), vol. iii. p. 539.

against which we should guard our reasoning faculties ; but
these are chiefly such as others attempt to put upon us in
dispute.   There are more dangerous fallacies by which we
cheat ourselves ; prejudice, partiality, self-interest, vanity,
inattention, and indifference to truth.   Locke, who was as
exempt from these as almost any man who has turned his
mind to so many subjects where their influence is to be suspected, has dwelled on the moral discipline of the intellect
in this treatise better, as I conceive, than any of his predecessors, though we have already seen, and it might appear
far more at length to those who should have recourse to
the books, that Arnauld and Malebranche, besides other
French philosophers of the age, had not been remiss in this
indispensable part of logic.

123. Locke throughout this treatise labours to secure the
inquirer from that previous persuasion of his own opinion,
which generally renders all his pretended investigations of
its truth little more than illusive and nugatory.   But the in-
differency which he recommends to everything except truth
itself, so that we should not even wish anything to be true
before we have examined whether it be so, seems to involve
the impossible hypothesis that man is but a purely reasoning
being.   It is vain to press the recommendation of freedom
from prejudice so far ; since we cannot but conceive some
propositions to be more connected with our welfare than
others, and consequently to desire their truth.   These exaggerations lay a fundamental condition of honest inquiry
open to the sneers of its adversaries ; and it is sufficient,
because nothing more is really attainable, first to dispossess
ourselves of the notion that our interests are concerned where
they are not, and next, even when we cannot but wish one
result of our inquiries rather than another, to be the more
unremitting in our endeavours to exclude this bias from our
reasoning.

124. I cannot think any parent or instructor justified in
neglecting to put this little treatise in the hands of a boy
about the time when the reasoning faculties become developed.   It will give him a sober and serious, not flippant
or self-conceited, independency of thinking ; and while it

teaches how to distrust ourselves and to watch those prejudices which necessarily grow up from one cause or another,
will inspire a reasonable confidence in what he has well considered, by taking off a little of that deference to authority,
which is the more to be regretted in its excess, that, like its
cousin-german, party-spirit, it is frequently united to loyalty
of heart and the generous enthusiasm of youth.

CHAPTER IV.

HISTORY OF MORAL AND POLITICAL PHILOSOPHY AND OF JURISPRUDENCE, FROM 1650 TO 1700.

Sect. I.—On Moral Philosophy.

Pascal's Provincial Letters — Taylor — Cudworth — Spinosa — Cumberland's Law of Nature—Puffendorf's Treatise on the same Subject—Rochefoucault and La Bruyère—Locke on Education—Fenelon.

1. The casuistical writers of the Roman church and especially of the Jesuit order, belong to earlier periods; Casuistry of for little room was left for anything but popular the Jesuits. compilations from large works of vast labour and accredited authority. But the false principles imputed to the latter school now raised a louder cry than before. Implacable and unsparing enemies, as well as ambitious intriguers themselves, they were encountered by a host of those who envied, feared, and hated them. Among those none were such willing or able accusers as the Jansenists whom they persecuted. Pascal, by his Provincial Letters, did more to ruin Pa-cal's Provincial Letters. the name of Jesuit than all the controversies of Pro- ters. testantism, or all the fulminations of the parliament of Paris. A letter of Antony Arnauld, published in 1655, wherein he declared that he could not find in Jansenius the propositions condemned by the pope, and laid himself open to censure by some of his own, provoked the Sorbonne, of which he was a member, to exclude him from the faculty of theology. Before this resolution was taken, Pascal came forward in defence of his friend, under a fictitious name, in the first of what have been always called Lettres Provinciales, but more accurately, Lettres écrites par Louis de Montalte à un Provincial de ses Amis.   In the first four of them he discusses the thorny problems of Jansenism, aiming chiefly to show that St. Thomas

Aquinas had maintained the same doctrine on efficacious grace which his disciples the Dominicans now rejected from another quarter. But he passed from hence to a theme more generally intelligible and interesting, the false morality of the Jesuit casuists. He has accumulated so long a list of scandalous decisions, and dwelled upon them with so much wit and spirit, and yet with so serious a severity, that the order of Loyola became a by-word with mankind. I do not agree with those who think the Provincial Letters a greater proof of the genius of Pascal than his Thoughts, in spite of the many weaknesses in reasoning which these display. The former are at present, finely written as all confess them to be, too much filled with obsolete controversy, they quote books too much forgotten, they have too little bearing on any permanent sympathies, to be read with much interest or pleasure.

2. The Jesuits had, unfortunately for themselves, no writers at that time of sufficient ability to defend them; and being disliked by many who were not Jansenists, could make little stand against their adversaries, till public opinion had already taken its line. They have since not failed to charge Pascal with extreme misrepresentation of their eminent casuists, Escobar, Busenbaum, and many others, so that some later disciples of their school have ventured to call the Provincial Letters the immortal liars (les immortelles menteuses). It has been insinuated, since Pascal's veracity is hard to attack, that he was deceived by those from whom he borrowed his quotations. But he has himself declared, in a remarkable passage, not only that, far from repenting of these letters, he would make them yet stronger if it were to be done again, but that, although he had not read all the books he has quoted, else he must have spent great part of his life in reading bad books, yet he had read Escobar twice through; and with respect to the rest, he had not quoted a single passage without having seen it in the book, and examined the context before and after, that he might not confound an objection with an answer, which would have been reprehensible and unjust:[a] it is therefore

Their truth questioned by some.

---

[a] Œuvres de Pascal, vol. i. p. 400.

impossible to save the honour of Pascal, if his quotations are
not fair.　Nor did he stand alone in his imputations on the
Jesuit casuistry.　A book called Morale des Jésuites, by
Nicolas Perrault, published at Mons in 1667, goes over the
same ground with less pleasantry, but not less learning.

3. The most extensive and learned work on casuistry which
has appeared in the English language is the Ductor　Taylor's
Dubitantium of Jeremy Taylor, published in 1660.　Ductor Dubitantium.
This, as its title shows, treats of subjective morality, or the
guidance of the conscience.　But this cannot be much discussed without establishing some principles of objective right
and wrong, some standard by which the conscience is to be
ruled.　'The whole measure and rule of conscience,' according to Taylor, ' is the law of God, or God's will signified to
us by nature or revelation; and by the several manners and
times and parts of its communication it hath obtained several
names;—the law of nature—the consent of nations—right
reason—the Decalogue—the sermon of Christ—the canons
of the apostles—the laws ecclesiastical and civil of princes
and governors—fame or the public reputation of things, expressed by proverbs and other instances and manners of
public honesty. . . . These being the full measures of right
and wrong, of lawful and unlawful, will be the rule of conscience and the subject of the present book.'

4. The heterogeneous combination of things so different in
nature and authority, as if they were all expressions　Its character
of the law of God, does not augur well for the dis-　and defects.
tinctness of Taylor's moral philosophy, and would be disadvantageously compared with the Ecclesiastical Polity of
Hooker.　Nor are we deceived in the anticipations we might
draw.　With many of Taylor's excellences, his vast fertility
and his frequent acuteness, the Ductor Dubitantium exhibits
his characteristic defects; the waste of quotations is even
greater than in his other writings, and his own exuberance
of mind degenerates into an intolerable prolixity.　His solution of moral difficulties is often unsatisfactory; after an
accumulation of arguments and authorities we have the disappointment to perceive that the knot is neither untied nor
cut; there seems a want of close investigation of principles,
a frequent confusion and obscurity, which Taylor's two chief '

faults, excessive display of erudition and redundancy of language, conspire to produce. Paley is no doubt often superficial, and sometimes mistaken; yet in clearness, in conciseness, in freedom from impertinent reference to authority, he is far superior to Taylor.

5. Taylor seems too much inclined to side with those who resolve all right and wrong into the positive will of God. The law of nature he defines to be ' the universal law of the world, or of mankind, to which we are inclined by nature, invited by consent, prompted by reason, but which is bound upon us only by the command of God.' Though in the strict meaning of the word, law, this may be truly said, it was surely required, considering the large sense which that word has obtained as coincident with moral right, that a fuller explanation should be given than Taylor has even intimated, lest the goodness of the Deity should seem something arbitrary and precarious. And though, in maintaining, against most of the scholastic metaphysicians, that God can dispense with the precepts of the Decalogue, he may be substantially right, yet his reasons seem by no means the clearest and most satisfactory that might be assigned. It may be added, that in his prolix rules concerning what he calls a probable conscience, he comes very near to the much decried theories of the Jesuits. There was indeed a vein of subtilty in Taylor's understanding which was not always without influence on his candour.

6. A treatise concerning eternal and immutable morality, by Cudworth, was first published in 1731. This may be almost reckoned a portion of his Intellectual System, the object being what he has declared to be one of those which he had there in view. This was to prove that moral differences of right and wrong are antecedent to any divine law. He wrote therefore not only against the Calvinistic school, but in some measure against Taylor, though he abstains from mentioning any recent author except Descartes, who had gone far in referring all moral distinctions to the arbitrary will of God. Cudworth's reasoning is by no means satisfactory, and rests too much on the dogmatic metaphysics which were going out of use. The nature or essence of nothing, he maintains, can depend upon the will

Cudworth's immutable morality.

of God alone, which is the efficient, but not the formal, cause
of all things; a distinction not very intelligible, but on which
he seems to build his theory.[b] For, though admitting that
moral relations have no objective existence out of the mind,
he holds that they have a positive essence, and therefore are
not nothing; whence it follows that they must be independent of will. He pours out much ancient learning, though
not so lavishly as in the Intellectual System.

7. The urgent necessity of contracting my sails in this last
period, far the most abundant as it is in the variety Nicole—La
and extent of its literature, restrains me from more Placette.
than a bare mention of several works not undeserving of
regard. The Essais de Morale of Nicole are less read than
esteemed, says a late biographer.[c] Voltaire, however, pro-
phesied that they would not perish. 'The chapter, especially,'
he proceeds, 'on the means of preserving peace among men
is a master-piece to which nothing equal has been left to us
by antiquity.'[d] These Essays are properly contained in six
volumes; but so many other pieces are added in some editions that the collection under that title is very long. La
Placette, minister of a French church at Copenhagen, has
been called the Protestant Nicole. His Essais de Morale,
in 1692 and other years, are full of a solid morality, rather
strict in casuistry, and apparently not deficient in observation, and analytical views of human nature. They were
much esteemed in their own age. Works of this kind treat
so very closely on the department of practical religion that
it is sometimes difficult to separate them on any fixed principle. A less homiletical form, a comparative absence of
Scriptural quotation, a more reasoning and observing mode
of dealing with the subject, are the chief distinctions. But
in the sermons of Barrow and some others we find a great
deal of what may be justly called moral philosophy.

8. A book by Sharrock, De Officiis secundum Rationis
Humanæ Dictata, 1660, is occasionally quoted, and Other
seems to be of a philosophical nature.[e] Velthuysen, writers.
a Dutch minister, was of more reputation. His name was
rather obnoxious to the orthodox, since he was a strenuous

---

[b] P. 15.   [c] Biog. univ.   [d] Siècle de Louis XIV.
[e] Cumberland (in præfatione) De Legibus Naturæ.

advocate of toleration, a Cartesian in philosophy, and inclined to judge for himself. His chief works are De Prin-
cipiis Justi et Decori, and De Naturali Pudore.[f] But we
must now pass on to those who have exercised a greater influence in moral philosophy, Cumberland and Puffendorf,
after giving a short consideration to Spinosa.

9. The moral system, if so it may be called, of Spinosa,

Moral
System of
Spinosa. has been developed by him in the fourth and fifth
parts of his Ethics. We are not deceived in what
might naturally be expected from the unhesitating adherence
of Spinosa to a rigorous line of reasoning, that his ethical
scheme would offer nothing inconsistent with the fundamental pantheism of his philosophy. In nature itself, he
maintains as before, there is neither perfection nor imperfection, neither good nor evil; but these are modes of speaking, adopted to express the relations of things as they appear
to our minds. Whatever contains more positive attributes
capable of being apprehended by us than another contains,
is more perfect than it. Whatever we know to be useful to
ourselves, that is good; and whatever impedes our attain-
ment of good, is evil. By this utility Spinosa does not
understand happiness, if by that is meant pleasurable sensation, but the extension of our mental and bodily capacities.
The passions restrain and overpower these capacities; and
coming from without, that is, from the body, render the
mind a less powerful agent than it seems to be. It is only,
we may remember, in a popular sense, and subject to his own
definitions, that Spinosa acknowledges the mind to be an
agent at all; it is merely so, in so far as its causes of action
cannot be referred by us to anything external. No passion
can be restrained except by a stronger passion. Hence even
a knowledge of what is really good or evil for us can of itself
restrain no passion; but only as it is associated with a perception of joy and sorrow, which is a mode of passion. This
perception is necessarily accompanied by desire or aversion;
but they may often be so weak as to be controlled by other
sentiments of the same class inspired by conflicting passions.
This is the cause of the weakness and inconstancy of many,

---

[f] Biogr. univ.   Barbeyrac's notes on Puffendorf, passim.

and he alone is wise and virtuous who steadily pursues what is useful to himself; that is, what reason points out as the best means of preserving his well-being and extending his capacities. Nothing is absolutely good, nothing therefore is principally sought by a virtuous man, but knowledge, not of things external, which gives us only inadequate ideas, but of God. Other things are good or evil to us so far as they suit our nature or contradict it; and so far as men act by reason, they must agree in seeking what is conformable to their nature. And those who agree with us in living by reason, are themselves of all things most suitable to our nature; so that the society of such men is most to be desired; and to enlarge that society by rendering men virtuous, and by promoting their advantage when they are so, is most useful to ourselves. For the good of such as pursue virtue may be enjoyed by all, and does not obstruct our own. Whatever conduces to the common society of mankind and promotes concord among them is useful to all; and whatever has an opposite tendency is pernicious. The passions are sometimes incapable of excess, but of this the only instances are joy and cheerfulness; more frequently they become pernicious by being indulged, and in some cases, such as hatred, can never be useful. We should therefore, for our own sakes, meet the hatred and malevolence of others with love and liberality. Spinosa dwells much on the preference due to a social above a solitary life, to cheerfulness above austerity, and alludes frequently to the current theological ethics with censure.

10. The fourth part of the Ethics is entitled On Human Slavery, meaning the subjugation of the reason to the passions: the fifth, On Human Liberty, is designed to show, as had been partly done in the former, how the mind or intellectual man is to preserve its supremacy. This is to be effected, not by the extinction, which is impossible, but the moderation of the passions; and the secret of doing this, according to Spinosa, is to contemplate such things as are naturally associated with affections of no great violence. We find that when we look at things simply in themselves, and not in their necessary relations, they affect us more powerfully; whence it may be inferred that we shall weaken the passion by viewing them as parts of a necessary series. We promote the same end by considering the object of the pas-

sion in many different relations, and in general, by enlarging
the sphere of our knowledge concerning it.   Hence the more
adequate ideas we attain of things that affect us, the less we
shall be overcome by the passion they excite.   But most of
all it should be our endeavour to refer all things to the idea
of God.   The more we understand ourselves and our passions,
the more we shall love God ; for the more we understand anything, the more pleasure we have in contemplating it ; and
we shall associate the idea of God with this pleasurable contemplation, which is the essence of love.   The love of God
should be the chief employment of the mind.   But God has
no passions ; therefore he who desires that God should love
him, desires in fact that he should cease to be God.   And the
more we believe others to be united in the same love of God,
the more we shall love him ourselves.

11. The great aim of the mind, and the greatest degree of
virtue, is the knowledge of things in their essence.   This
knowledge is the perfection of human nature ; it is accompanied with the greatest joy and contentment ; it leads to a
love of God, intellectual, not imaginative, eternal, because
not springing from passions that perish with the body, being
itself a portion of that infinite love with which God intellec-
tually loves himself.   In this love towards God our chief felicity consists, which is not the reward of virtue, but virtue
itself ; nor is any one happy because he has overcome the
passions, but it is by being happy, that is, by enjoying the
fulness of divine love, that he has become capable of over-
coming them.

12. These extraordinary effusions confirm what has been
hinted in another place, that Spinosa, in the midst of his
atheism, seemed often to hover over the regions of mystical
theology.   This last book of the Ethics speaks, as is evident,
the very language of Quietism.   In Spinosa himself it is not
easy to understand the meaning ; his sincerity ought not, I
think, to be called in question ; and this enthusiasm may be
set down to the rapture of the imagination expatiating in the
enchanting wilderness of its creation.   But the possibility of
combining such a tone of contemplative devotion with the
systematic denial of a Supreme Being, in any personal sense,
may put us on our guard against the tendency of mysticism,

which may again, as it has frequently, degenerate into a similar chaos.

13. The science of ethics, in the third quarter of the seventeenth century, seemed to be cultivated by three *Cumber-*
very divergent schools ; by that of the theologians, *land's*
De Legibus
who went no farther than revelation, or at least *Naturæ.*
than the positive law of God, for moral distinctions ; by that
of the Platonic philosophers, who sought them in eternal and
intrinsic relations ; and that of Hobbes and Spinosa, who reduced them all to selfish prudence. A fourth theory, which,
in some of its modifications, has greatly prevailed in the last
two centuries, may be referred to Richard Cumberland, afterwards Bishop of Peterborough. His famous work, De Legibus Naturæ Disquisitio Philosophica, was published in 1672.
It is contained in nine chapters, besides the preface or prolegomena.

14. Cumberland begins by mentioning Grotius, Selden, and
one or two more who have investigated the laws of *Analysis of*
nature *à posteriori*, that is, by the testimony of *Prolego-*
mena.
authors and the consent of nations. But as some objections
may be started against this mode of proof, which, though he
does not hold them to be valid, are likely to have some effect,
he prefers another line of demonstration, deducing the laws of
nature, as effects, from their real causes in the constitution
of nature itself. The Platonic theory of innate moral ideas,
sufficient to establish natural law, he does not admit. 'For
myself at least I may say that I have not been so fortunate
as to arrive at the knowledge of this law by so compendious
a road.' He deems it therefore necessary to begin with what
we learn by daily use and experience, assuming nothing but
the physical laws of motion shown by mathematicians, and
the derivation of all their operations from the will of a
First Cause.

15. By diligent observation of all propositions which can
be justly reckoned general moral laws of nature, he finds
that they may be reduced to one, the pursuit of the common
good of all rational agents, which tends to our own good as
part of the whole ; as its opposite tends not only to the
misery of the whole system, but to our own.[g] This tendency,

---

[g] Prolegomena, sect. 9.

he takes care to tell us, though he uses the present tense
(conducit), has respect to the most remote consequences, and
is so understood by him.   The means which serve to this end,
the general good, may be treated as theorems in a geometrical method.[h]   Cumberland, as we have seen in Spinosa, was
captivated by the apparent security of this road to truth.

16. This scheme, he observes, may at first sight want the
two requisites of a law, a legislator and a sanction.   But
whatever is naturally assented to by our minds must spring
from the author of nature.   God is proved to be the author
of every proposition which is proved to be true by the constitution of nature, which has him for its author.[i]   Nor is a
sanction wanting in the rewards, that is, the happiness which
attends the observance of the law of nature, and in the opposite effects of its neglect; and in a lax sense, though not
that of the jurists, reward as well as punishment may be included in the word sanction.[k]   But benevolence, that is, love
and desire of good towards all rational beings, includes piety
towards God, the greatest of them all, as well as humanity.[m]
Cumberland altogether abstains from arguments founded on
revelation, and is perhaps the first writer on natural law who
has done so, for they may even be found in Hobbes.   And I
think that he may be reckoned the founder of what is awkwardly and invidiously called the utilitarian school; for
though similar expressions about the common good may sometimes be found in the ancients, it does not seem to have been
the basis of any ethical system.

17. This common good, not any minute particle of it, as
the benefit of a single man, is the great end of the legislator
and of him who obeys his will.   And such human actions as
by their natural tendency promote the common good may be
called naturally good, more than those which tend only to
the good of any one man, by how much the whole is greater
than this small part.   And whatever is directed in the
shortest way to this end may be called right, as a right line
is the shortest of all.   And as the whole system of the universe, when all things are arranged so as to produce happiness, is beautiful, being aptly disposed to its end, which is
the definition of beauty, so particular actions contributing to
this general harmony may be called beautiful and becoming.[n]

------

[h] Sect. 12.   [i] Sect. 13.   [k] Sect. 14.   [m] Sect. 15.   [n] Sect. 16.

18. Cumberland acutely remarks, in answer to the objection to the practice of virtue from the evils which fall on good men, and the success of the wicked, that no good or evil is to be considered, in this point of view, which arises from mere necessity, or external causes, and not from our virtue or vice itself. He then shows that a regard for piety and peace, for mutual intercourse, and civil and domestic polity, tends to the happiness of every one; and in reckoning the good consequences of virtuous behaviour we are not only to estimate the pleasure intimately connected with it, which the love of God and of good men produces, but the contingent benefits we obtain by civil society, which we promote by such conduct.[o] And we see that in all nations there is some regard to good faith and the distribution of property, some respect to the obligation of oaths, some attachments to relations and friends. All men therefore acknowledge, and to a certain extent perform, those things which really tend to the common good. And though crime and violence sometimes prevail, yet these are like diseases in the body which it shakes off; or if, like them, they prove sometimes mortal to a single community, yet human society is immortal; and the conservative principles of common good have in the end far more efficacy than those which dissolve and destroy states.

19. We may reckon the happiness consequent on virtue as a true sanction of natural law annexed to it by its author, and thus fulfilling the necessary conditions of its definition. And though some have laid less stress on these sanctions, and deemed virtue its own reward, and gratitude to God and man its best motive, yet the consent of nations and common experience show us that the observance of the first end, which is the common good, will not be maintained without remuneration or penal consequences.

20. By this single principle of common good we simplify the method of natural law, and arrange its secondary precepts in such subordination as best conduces to the general end. Hence moral rules give way in particular cases, when they come in collision with others of more extensive importance. For all ideas of right or virtue imply a relation to the system

[o] Sect. 20.

and nature of all rational beings. And the principles thus deduced as to moral conduct are generally applicable to political societies, which in their two leading institutions, the division of property and the coercive power of the magistrate, follow the steps of natural law, and adopt these rules of polity, because they perceive them to promote the common weal.

21. From all intermixture of Scriptural authority Cumberland proposes to abstain, building only on reason and experience, since we believe the Scriptures to proceed from God because they illustrate and promote the law of nature. He seems to have been the first Christian writer who sought to establish systematically the principles of moral right independently of revelation. They are indeed taken for granted by many, especially those who adopted the Platonic language; or the schoolmen may have demonstrated them by arguments derived from reason, but seldom, if ever, without some collateral reference to theological authority. In this respect, therefore, Cumberland may be deemed to make an epoch in the history of ethical philosophy, though Puffendorf, whose work was published the same year, may have nearly equal claims to it. If we compare the Treatise on the Laws of Nature with the Ductor Dubitantium of Taylor, written a very few years before, we shall find ourselves in a new world of moral reasoning. The schoolmen and fathers, the canonists and casuists, have vanished like ghosts at the first daylight; the continual appeal is to experience, and never to authority; or if authority can be said to appear at all in the pages of Cumberland, it is that of the great apostles of experimental philosophy, Descartes or Huygens, or Harvey or Willis. His mind, liberal and comprehensive as well as acute, had been forcibly impressed with the discoveries of his own age, both in mathematical science and in what is now more strictly called physiology. From this armoury he chose his weapons, and employed them, in some instances, with great sagacity and depth of thought. From the brilliant success also of the modern analysis, as well as from the natural prejudice in favour of a mathematical method, which arises from the acknowledged superiority of that science in the determination of its proper truths, he was led to expect more from the use of similar processes in moral

reasoning than we have found justified by experience. And this analogy had probably some effect on one of the chief errors of his ethical system, the reduction, at least in theory, of the morality of actions to definite calculation.

22. The prolegomena or preface to Cumberland's treatise contains that statement of his system with which His theory expanded afterwards. we have been hitherto concerned, and which the whole volume does but expand. His manner of reasoning is diffuse, abounding in repetitions, and often excursive; we cannot avoid perceiving that he labours long on propositions which no adversary would dispute, or on which the dispute could be little else than one of verbal definition. This however is almost the universal failing of preceding philosophers, and was only put an end to, if it can be said yet to have ceased, by the sharper logic of controversy, which a more general regard to metaphysical inquiries, and a juster sense of the value of words, brought into use.

23. The question between Cumberland and his adversaries, that is, the school of Hobbes, is stated to be, whether certain propositions of immutable truth, directing the voluntary actions of men in choosing good and avoiding evil, and imposing an obligation upon them, independently of civil laws, are necessarily suggested to the mind by the nature of things and by that of mankind. And the affirmative of this question he undertakes to prove from a consideration of the nature of both; from which many particular rules might be deduced, but above all that which comprehends all the rest, and is the basis of his theory; namely, that the greatest possible bene-volence (not a mere languid desire, but an energetic principle) of every rational agent towards all the rest constitutes the happiest condition of each and of all, so far as depends on their own power, and is necessarily required for their greatest happiness; whence the common good is the supreme law. That God is the author of this law appears evident from his being the author of all nature and of all the physical laws according to which impressions are made on our minds.

24. It is easy to observe by daily experience that we have the power of doing good to others, and that no men are so happy or so secure as they who most exert this. And this may be proved synthetically and in that more rigorous

method which he affects, though it now and then leads the reader away from the simplest argument, by considering our own faculties of speech and language, the capacities of the hand and countenance, the skill we possess in sciences and in useful arts; all of which conduce to the social life of mankind and to their mutual co-operation and benefit. Whatever preserves and perfects the nature of anything, that is to be called good, and the opposite evil; so that Hobbes has crudely asserted good to respect only the agent desiring it, and consequently to be variable. In this it will be seen that the dispute is chiefly verbal.

25. Two corollaries of great importance in the theory of ethics spring from a consideration of our physical powers. The first is, that inasmuch as they are limited by their nature, we should never seek to trangress their bounds, but distinguish, as the Stoics did, things within our reach, τὰ ἐφ᾽ ἡμῖν, from those beyond it, τὰ οὐκ ἐφ᾽ ἡμῖν, thus relieving our minds from anxious passions, and turning them to the prudent use of the means assigned to us. The other is one which applies more closely to his general principle of morals; that as all we can do in respect of others, and all the enjoyment we or they can have of particular things, is limited to certain persons, as well as by space and time, we perceive the necessity of distribution, both as to things, from which spring the rights of property, and as to persons, by which our benevolence, though a general rule in itself, is practically directed towards individuals. For the conservation of an aggregate whole is the same as that of its divided parts, that is, of single persons, which requires a distributive exercise of the powers of each. Hence property and dominion, or *meum* and *tuum*, in the most general sense, are consequences from the general law of nature. Without a support from that law, according to Cumberland, without a positive tendency to the good of all rational agents, we should have no right even to things necessary for our preservation; nor have we that right, if a greater evil would be incurred by our preservation than by our destruction. It may be added, as a more universal reflection, that as all which we see in nature is so framed as to persevere in its appointed state, and as the human body is endowed with the power of throwing off whatever is noxious

and threatens the integrity of its condition, we may judge from this that the conservation of mankind in its best state must be the design of nature, and that their own voluntary actions conducing to that end must be such as the author of nature commands and approves.

26. Cumberland next endeavours, by an enlarged analysis of the mental and bodily structure of mankind, to evince their aptitude for the social virtues, that is, for the general benevolence which is the primary law of nature. We have the power of knowing these by our rational faculty, which is the judge of right and wrong, that is, of what is conformable to the great law; and by the other faculties of the mind, as well as by the use of language, we generalise and reduce to propositions the determinations of reason. We have also the power of comparison, and of perceiving analogies, by means of which we estimate degrees of good. And if we are careful to guard against deciding without clear and adequate apprehensions of things, our reason will not mislead us. The observance of something like this general law of nature by inferior animals, which rarely, as Cumberland supposes, attack those of the same species, and in certain instances live together, as if by a compact for mutual aid; the peculiar contrivances in the human body which seems designed for the maintenance of society; the possession of speech, the pathognomic countenance, the efficiency of the hand, a longevity beyond the lower animals, the duration of the sexual appetite throughout the year, with several other arguments derived from anatomy, are urged throughout this chapter against the unsocial theory of Hobbes.

27. Natural good is defined by Cumberland with more latitude than has been used by Paley and by those of a later school, who confine it to happiness or pleasurable perception. Whatever conduces to the preservation of an intelligent being, or to the perfection of his powers, he accounts to be good, without regard to enjoyment. And for this he appeals to experience, since we desire existence, as well as the extension of our powers of action, for their own sakes. It is of great importance to acquire a clear notion of what is truly good, that is, of what serves most to the happiness and perfection of every one; since all the secondary laws of nature,

that is, the rules of particular virtues, derive their authority
from this effect. These rules may be compared one with
another as to the probability, as well as the value of their
effects upon the general good ; and he anticipates greater
advantage from the employment of mathematical reasoning
and even analytical forms in moral philosophy than the different nature of the subjects would justify, even if the fundamental principle of converting the theory of ethics into
calculation could be allowed.[p]

28. A law of nature, meaning one subordinate to the great
principle of benevolence, is defined by Cumberland to be a
proposition manifested by the nature of things to the mind
according to the will of the First Cause, and pointing out an
action tending to the good of rational beings, from the performance of which an adequate reward, or from the neglect
of which a punishment, will ensue by the nature of such
rational beings. Every part of this definition he proves with
exceeding prolixity in the longest chapter, namely, the fifth,
of his treatise ; but we have already seen the foundations of
his theory upon which it rests. It will be evident to the
reader of this chapter that both Butler and Paley have been
largely indebted to Cumberland.[q] Natural obligation he
defines thus :—No other necessity determines the will to act
than that of avoiding evil and of seeking good, so far as
appears to be in our power.[r] Moral obligation is more limited,
and is differently defined.[s] But the main point, as he justly
observes, of the controversy is the connection between the
tendency of each man's actions, taking them collectively
through his life, to the good of the whole, and that to his
own greatest happiness and perfection. This he undertakes
to show, premising that it is twofold ; consisting immediately
in the pleasure attached to virtue, and ultimately in the
rewards which it obtains from God and from man. God, as

---

[p] Ea quippe tota (disciplina morum)
versatur in æstimandis rationibus virium
humanarum ad commune bonum entium
rationalium quicquam facientium, quæ
quidem variant in omni casuum possibi-
lium varietate. Cap. ii. sect. 9. The
same is laid down in several other passages. By *rationibus* we must understand
ratios ; which brings out the calculating
theory in the strongest light.

[q] A great part of the second and
third chapters of Butler's Analogy will
be found in Cumberland. See cap. v.
sect. 22.

[r] Non alia necessitas voluntatem ad
agendum determinat, quam malum in
quantum tale esse nobis constat fugiendi,
bonumque quatenus nobis apparet pro-
sequendi. Cap. v. sect. 7.

[s] Sect. 27.

a rational being, cannot be supposed to act without an end
or to have a greater end than the general good ; that is, the
happiness and perfection of his creatures.[t]　And his will may
not only be shown *à priori*, by the consideration of his essence
and attributes, but by the effects of virtue and vice in the
order of nature which he has established.　The rewards and
punishments which follow at the hands of men are equally
obvious ; and whether we regard men as God's instruments,
or as voluntary agents, demonstrate that virtue is the highest
prudence.　These arguments are urged rather tediously, and
in such a manner as not to encounter all the difficulties
which it is desirable to overcome.

29. Two objections might be alleged against this kind of
proof; that the rewards and punishments of moral actions
are too uncertain to be accounted clear proofs of the will of
God, and consequently of their natural obligation ; and that
by laying so much stress upon them we make private happiness the measure of good.　These he endeavours to repel.
The contingency of a future consequence has a determinate
value, which, if it more than compensates, for good or evil,
the evil or good of a present action, ought to be deemed
a proof given by the Author of nature that reward or punishment are annexed to the action, as much as if they were its
necessary consequences.[u]　This argument, perhaps sophistical, is an instance of the calculating method affected by
Cumberland, and which we may presume, from the then
recent application of analysis to probability, he was the first
to adopt on such an occasion.　Paley is sometimes fond of
a similar process.　But after these mathematical reasonings,
he dwells, as before, on the beneficial effects of virtue, and
concludes that many of them are so uniform as to leave no
doubt as to the intention of the Creator.　Against the charge
of postponing the public good to that of the agent, he protests that it is wholly contrary to his principle, which permits
no one to preserve his life, or what is necessary for it, at the
expense of a greater good to the whole.[x]　But his explication

---

[t] Sect. 19.

[u] Sect. 37.

[x] Sua cujusque felicitas est pars valde
exigua finis illius, quem vir verè ratio-

nalis prosequitur, et ad totum finem, sci-
licet commune bonum, cui a natura seu
a Deo intertexitur, eam tantum habet,
rationem quam habet unus homo ad ag-

of the question ends in repeating that no single man's greatest felicity can by the nature of things be inconsistent with that of all; and that every such hypothesis is to be rejected as an impossible condition of the problem. It seems doubtful whether Cumberland uses always the same language on the question whether private happiness is the final motive of action, which in this part of the chapter he wholly denies.

30. From the establishment of this primary law of universal benevolence Cumberland next deduces the chief secondary principles, which are commonly called the moral virtues. And among these he gives the first place to justice, which he seems to consider, by too lax an use of terms, or too imperfect an analogy, as comprehending the social duties of liberality, courtesy, and domestic affection. The right of property, which is the foundation of justice, he rests entirely on its necessity for the common good; whatever is required for that prime end of moral action being itself obligatory on moral agents, they are bound to establish and to maintain separate rights. And all right so wholly depends on this instrumentality to good, that the rightful sovereignty of God over his creatures is not founded on that relation which he bears to them as their Maker, much less on his mere power, but on his wisdom and goodness, through which his omnipotence works only for their happiness. But this happiness can only be attained by means of an absolute right over them in their Maker, which is therefore to be reckoned a natural law.

31. The good of all rational beings is a complex whole, being nothing but the aggregate of good enjoyed by each. We can only act in our proper spheres, labouring to do good. But this labour will be fruitless, or rather mischievous, if we do not keep in mind the higher gradations which terminate in universal benevolence. No man must seek his own advantage otherwise than that of his family permits; or provide for his family to the detriment of his country; or promote the good of his country at the expense of mankind; or serve mankind, if it were possible, without regard to the majesty

---

gregatum ex omnibus rationalibus, quæ   molem universi corporis. Sect. 23 and
minor est quam habet unica arenula ad   sect. 28.

of God.[y] It is indeed sufficient that the mind should acknowledge and recollect this principle of conduct, without
having it present on every single occasion. But where moral
difficulties arise, Cumberland contends that the general good
is the only measure by which we are to determine the lawfulness of actions, or the preference due to one above another.

32. In conclusion he passes to political authority, deriving
it from the same principles, and comments with severity and
success, though in the verbose style usual to him, on the system of Hobbes. It is, however, worthy of remark, that he
not only peremptorily declares the irresponsibility of the supreme magistrate in all cases, but seems to give him a more
arbitrary latitude in the choice of measures, so long as he
does not violate the chief negative precepts of the Decalogue,
than is consistent with his own fundamental rule of always
seeking the greatest good. He endeavours to throw upon
Hobbes, as was not uncommon with the latter's theological
opponents, the imputation of encouraging rebellion while he
seemed to support absolute power; and observes with full as
much truth that, if kings are bound by no natural law, the
reason for their institution, namely, the security of mankind, assigned by the author of the Leviathan, falls to the
ground.

33. I have gone rather at length into a kind of analysis
of this treatise because it is now very little read, and Remarks on
yet was of great importance in the annals of ethical Cumberland's theory
philosophy. It was, if not a text-book in either of our universities, concerning which I am not confident, the basis of the
system therein taught, and of the books which have had most
influence in this country. Hutcheson, Law, Paley, Priestley,
Bentham, belong, no doubt some of them unconsciously, to
the school founded by Cumberland. Hutcheson adopted the
principle of general benevolence as the standard of virtue;
but by limiting the definition of good to happiness alone, he
simplified the scheme of Cumberland, who had included conservation and enlargement of capacity in its definition. He
rejected also what encumbers the whole system of his predecessor, the including the Supreme Being among those rational

---

[y] Cap. viii. sect. 14, 15.

agents whose good we are bound to promote. The schoolmen, as well as those whom they followed, deeming it necessary to predicate metaphysical infinity of all the divine
attributes, reckoned unalterable beatitude in the number.
Upon such a subject no wise man would like to dogmatise.
The difficulties on both sides are very great, and perhaps
among the most intricate to which the momentous problem
concerning the cause of evil has given rise. Cumberland,
whose mind does not seem to have been much framed to
wrestle with mysteries, evades, in his lax verbosity, what
might perplex his readers.

34. In establishing the will of a supreme lawgiver as essential to the law of nature, he is followed by the bishop of
Carlisle and Paley, as well as by the majority of English
moralists in the eighteenth century. But while Paley deems
the recognition of a future state so essential, that he even includes in the definition of virtue that it is performed 'for the
sake of everlasting happiness,' Cumberland not only omits
this erroneous and almost paradoxical condition, but very
slightly alludes to another life, though he thinks it probable
from the stings of conscience and on other grounds; resting
the whole argument on the certain consequences of virtue
and vice in the present, but guarding justly against the supposition that any difference of happiness in moral agents can
affect the immediate question except such as is the mere result of their own behaviour. If any one had urged, like
Paley, that unless we take a future state into consideration,
the result of calculating our own advantage will either not
always be in favour of virtue, or in consequence of the violence of passion will not always seem so, Cumberland would
probably have denied the former alternative, and replied to
the other, that we can only prove the truth of our theorems
in moral philosophy, and cannot compel men to adopt them.

35. Sir James Mackintosh, whose notice of Cumberland is
rather too superficial, and hardly recognises his influence on
philosophy, observes, that 'the forms of scholastic argument
serve more to encumber his style than to insure his exactness.'[z] There is not however much of scholastic form in the

---

[z] Dissertation on Ethical Philosophy, p. 48.

treatise on the Laws of Nature, and this is expressly disclaimed in the preface. But he has, as we have intimated, a great deal too much of a mathematical line of argument which never illustrates his meaning, and has sometimes misled his judgment. We owe probably to his fondness for this specious illusion, I mean the application of reasonings upon quantity to moral subjects, the dangerous sophism that a direct calculation of the highest good, and that not relatively to particulars, but to all rational beings, is the measure of virtuous actions, the test by which we are to try our own conduct and that of others. And the intervention of general rules, by which Paley endeavoured to dilute and render palatable this calculating scheme of utility, seems no more to have occurred to Cumberland than it was adopted by Bentham.

36. Thus as Taylor's Ductor Dubitantium is nearly the last of a declining school, Cumberland's Law of Nature may be justly considered as the herald, especially in England, of a new ethical philosophy, of which the main characteristics were, first, that it stood complete in itself without the aid of revelation; secondly, that it appealed to no authority of earlier writers whatever, though it sometimes used them in illustration; thirdly, that it availed itself of observation and experience, alleging them generally, but abstaining from particular instances of either, and making, above all, no display of erudition; and, fourthly, that it entered very little upon casuistry, leaving the application of principles to the reader.

37. In the same year, 1672, a work still more generally distinguished than that of Cumberland was published at Lund, in Sweden, by Samuel Puffendorf, a Saxon by birth, who filled the chair of moral philosophy in that recently-founded university. This large treatise, On the Law of Nature and Nations, in eight books, was abridged by the author, but not without some variations, in one perhaps more useful, On the Duties of a Man and a Citizen. Both have been translated into French and English; both were long studied in the foreign universities, and even in our own. Puffendorf has been perhaps, in moral philosophy, of greater authority than Grotius, with whom he is

Puffendorff's Law of Nature and Nations.

frequently named in conjunction ; but this is not the case in international jurisprudence.

38. Puffendorf, after a very diffuse and technical chapter on

Analysis of this work. moral beings, or modes, proceeds to assert a demonstrative certainty in moral science, but seems not to maintain an inherent right and wrong in actions antecedent to all law, referring the rule of morality altogether to the divine appointment. He ends however by admitting that man's constitution being what it is, God could not without inconsistency have given him any other law than that under which he lives.[a] We discern good from evil by the understanding, which judgment when exercised on our own actions is called conscience; but he strongly protests against any such jurisdiction of conscience, independent of reason and knowledge, as some have asserted. This notion ' was first introduced by the schoolmen, and has been maintained in these latter ages by the crafty casuists for the better securing of men's minds and fortunes to their own fortune and advantage.'[b] Puffendorf was a good deal imbued with the Lutheran bigotry which did no justice to any religion but its own.

39. Law alone creates obligation; no one can be obliged except towards a superior. But to compel and to oblige being different things, it is required for this latter that we should have received some great good at the hands of a superior, or have voluntarily submitted to his will. This seems to involve an antecedent moral right, which Puffendorf's general theory denies.[c] Barbeyrac, his able and watchful commentator, derives obligation from our natural dependence on the supreme authority of God, who can punish the disobedient and reward others. In order to make laws obligatory, it is necessary, according to Puffendorf, that we should know both the law and the lawgiver's authority. Actions are good or evil, as they conform more or less to law. And, coming to consider the peculiar qualities of moral actions, he introduces the distinction of perfect and imperfect rights, objecting to that of Grotius and the Roman lawyers, expletive and distributive justice.[d] This first book of Puffen-

---

[a] C. 2.   [b] C. 3.   [c] C. 6.   [d] C. 7.

dorf is very diffuse; and some chapters are wholly omitted in the abridgment.

40. The natural state of man, such as in theory we may suppose, is one in which he was never placed, ' thrown into the world at a venture, and then left entirely to himself with no larger endowments of body or mind than such as we now discover in men.' This, however, he seems to think physically possible to have been, which I should incline to question. Man in a state of nature is subject to no earthly superior; but we must not infer thence that he is incapable of law, and has a right to everything that is profitable to himself. But, after discussing the position of Hobbes that a state of nature is a state of war, he ends by admitting that the desire of peace is too weak and uncertain a security for its preservation among mankind.[e]

41. The law of nature he derives not from consent of nations, nor from personal utility, but from the condition of man. It is discoverable by reason; its obligation is from God. He denies that it is founded on the intrinsic honesty or turpitude of actions. It was free to God whether he would create an animal to whom the present law of nature should be applicable. But supposing all things human to remain constant, the law of nature, though owing its institution to the free will of God, remains unalterable. He therefore neither agrees wholly with those who deem of this law as of one arbitrary and mutable at God's pleasure, nor with those who look upon it as an image of his essential holiness and justice. For he doubts whether the law of nature is altogether conformed to the divine attributes as to a type; since we cannot acquire a right with respect to God; so that his justice must be of a different kind from ours. Common consent, again, is an insufficient basis of natural law, few men having searched into the foundations of their assent, even if we could find a more general consent than is the case. And here he expatiates, in the style of Montaigne's school, on the variety of moral opinions.[f] Puffendorf next attacks those who resolve right into self-interest. But unfortunately he only proves that men often mistake their interest. 'It is

---

                    [e] L. ii. c. 2.   [f] C. 3.

a great mistake to fancy it will be profitable to you to take away either by fraud or violence what another man has acquired by his labour ; since others have not only the power of resisting you, but of taking the same freedom with your goods and possessions.'[g] This is evidently no answer to Hobbes or Spinosa.

42. The nature of man, his wants, his powers of doing mischief to others, his means of mutual assistance, show that he cannot be supported in things necessary and convenient to him without society, so that others may promote his interests. Hence sociableness is a primary law of nature, and all actions tending towards it are commanded, as the opposite are forbidden by that law. In this he agrees with Grotius ; and, after he had become acquainted with Cumberland's work, observes that the fundamental law of that writer, to live for the common good and show benevolence towards all men, does not differ from his own. He partly explains, and partly answers, the theory of Hobbes. From Grotius he dissents in denying that the law of nature would be binding without religion, but does not think the soul's immortality essential to it.[h] The best division of natural law is into duties towards ourselves and towards others. But in the abridged work, the Duties of a Man and a Citizen, he adds those towards God.

43. The former class of duties he illustrates with much prolixity and needless quotation,[i] and passes to the right of self-defence, which seems to be the debatable frontier between the two classes of obligation. In this chapter Puffendorf is free from the extreme scrupulousness of Grotius ; yet he differs from him, as well as from Barbeyrac and Locke, in denying the right of attacking the aggressor, where a stranger has been injured, unless where we are bound to him by promise.[k]

44. All persons, as is evident, are bound to repair wilful injury, and even that arising from their neglect ; but not where they have not been in fault.[m] Yet the civil action *ob pauperiem,* for casual damage by a beast or slave, which Grotius held to be merely of positive law, and which our own (in the only applicable case) does not recognise, Puffendorf thinks grounded on natural right. He considers several

---

[g] L. ii. c. 3.　　[h] C. 3.　　[i] C. 4.　　[k] C. 5.　　[m] L. iii. c. 1.

questions of reparation, chiefly such as we find in Grotius.
From these, after some intermediate disquisitions on moral
duties, he comes to the more extensive province of casuistry,
the obligation of promises.[n]   These, for the most part,
give perfect rights which may be enforced, though this is
not universal ; hence promises may themselves be called imperfect or perfect.   The former, or *nuda pacta,* seem to be
obligatory rather by the rules of veracity, and for the sake of
maintaining confidence among men, than in strict justice ;
yet he endeavours to refute the opinion of a jurist who held
nuda pacta to involve no obligation beyond a compensation
for damage.   Free consent and knowledge of the whole
subject are required for the validity of a promise ; hence
drunkenness takes away its obligation.[o]   Whether a minor
is bound in conscience, though not in law, has been disputed ;
the Romish casuists all denying it unless he has received an
advantage.   La Placette, it seems, after the time of Puffendorf, though a very rigid moralist, confines the obligation to
cases where the other party sustains any real damage by the
non-performance.   The world, in some instances at least,
would exact more than the strictest casuists.   Promises were
invalidated, though not always mutual contracts, by error ;
and fraud in the other party annuls a contract.   There can
be no obligation, Puffendorf maintains, without a corresponding right ; hence fear arising from the fault of the other
party invalidates a promise.   But those made to pirates or
rebels, not being extorted by fear, are binding.   Vows to God
he deems not binding, unless accepted by him ; but he thinks
that we may presume their acceptance when they serve to
define or specify an indeterminate duty.[p]   Unlawful promises
must not be performed by the party promising to commit an
evil act, and as to performance of the other party's promise,
he differs from Grotius in thinking it not binding.   Barbeyrac
concurs with Puffendorf, but Paley holds the contrary ; and
the common sentiments of mankind seem to be on that side.[q]

45. The obligations of veracity Puffendorf, after much
needless prolixity on the nature of signs and words, deduces
from a tacit contract among mankind, that words, or signs
of intention, shall be used in a definite sense which others

---

[n] L. iii. c. 5.   [o] C. 6.   [p] C. 6.   [q] C. 7.

may understand.[r] He is rather fond of these imaginary compacts. The laxer casuists are in nothing more distinguishable from the more rigid than in the exceptions they allow to the general rule of veracity. Many, like Augustin and most of the fathers, have laid it down that all falsehood is unlawful; even some of the jurists, when treating of morality, had done the same. But Puffendorf gives considerable latitude to deviations from truth, by mental reserve, by ambiguous words, by direct falsehood. Barbeyrac, in a long note, goes a good deal farther, and indeed beyond any safe limit.[s] An oath, according to these writers, adds no peculiar obligation; another remarkable discrepancy between their system and that of the theological casuists. Oaths may be released by the party in favour of whom they are made; but it is necessary to observe whether the dispensing authority is really the obligee.

46. We now advance to a different part of moral philosophy, the rights of property. Puffendorf first inquires into the natural right of killing animals for food; but does not defend it very well, resting this right on the want of mutual obligation between man and brutes. The arguments from physiology, and the manifest propensity in mankind to devour animals, are much stronger. He censures cruelty towards animals, but hardly on clear grounds; the disregard of moral emotion, which belongs to his philosophy prevents his judging it rightly.[t] Property itself in things he grounds on an express or tacit contract of mankind, while all was yet in common, that each should possess a separate portion. This covenant he supposes to have been gradually extended, as men perceived the advantage of separate possession, lands having been cultivated in common after severalty had been established in houses and movable goods; and

---

[r] L. iv. c. 1.

[s] Barbeyrac admits that several writers of authority since Puffendorf had maintained the strict obligation of veracity for its own sake; Thomasius, Buddæus, Noodt, and, above all, La Placette. His own notions are too much the other way, both according to the received standard of honourable and decorous character among men, and according to any sound theory of ethics. Lying, he says, as condemned in Scripture, always means fraud or injury to others. His doctrine is, that we are to speak the truth, or to be silent, or to feign a d dissemble, according as our own lawful interest, or that of our neighbour, may demand it. This is surely as untenable one way as any paradox in Augustin or La Placette can be the other.

[t] C. 3.

he refutes those who maintain property to be coeval with
mankind, and immediately founded on the law of nature.[u]
Nothing can be the subject of property which is incapable of
exclusive occupation; not therefore the ocean, though some
narrow seas may be appropriated.[x] In the remainder of this
fourth book he treats on a variety of subjects connected with
property, which carry us over a wide field of natural and
positive jurisprudence.

47. The fifth book of Puffendorf relates to price, and to
all contracts onerous or lucrative, according to the distinction
of the jurists, with the rules of their interpretation. It is a
running criticism on the Roman law, comparing it with right
reason and justice. Price he divides into proper and eminent; the first being what we call real value, or capacity
of procuring things desirable by means of exchange; the
second the money value. What is said on this subject
would now seem common-place and prolix; but it is rather
interesting to observe the beginnings of political economy.
Money, he thinks, was introduced by an agreement of civi-
lised nations, as a measure of value. Puffendorf, of more
enlarged views than Grotius, vindicates usury, which the
other had given up; and mentions the evasions usually
practised, such as the grant of an annuity for a limited term.

48. In the sixth book we have disquisitions on matrimony
and the rights incident to it, on paternal and on herile power.
Among other questions he raises one whether the husband
has any natural dominion over the wife. This he thinks
hard to prove, except as his sex gives him an advantage; but
fitness to govern does not create a right. He has recourse
therefore to his usual solution, her tacit or express promise
of obedience. Polygamy he deems contrary to the law of
nature, but not incest, except in the direct line. This is
consonant to what had been the general determination of
philosophers.[y] The right of parents he derives from the
general duty of sociableness, which makes preservation of
children necessary, and on the affection implanted in them by
nature; also on a presumed consent of the children in return

---

[u] C. 4. Barbeyrac more wisely denies this assumed compact, and rests the
right of property on individual occupancy.   [x] C. 5.   [y] L. vi. c. 1.

for their maintenance.[z] In a state of nature this command
belongs to the mother, unless she has waived it by a matri-
monial contract. In childhood, the fruits of the child's labour
belong to the father, though the former seems to be capable
of receiving gifts. Fathers, as heads of families, have a kind
of sovereignty, distinct from the paternal, to which adult
children residing with them are submitted. But after their
emancipation by leaving their father's house, which does not
absolutely require his consent, they are bound only to duty
and reverence. The power of a master over his servant is not
by nature, nor by the law of war, but originally by a contract
founded on necessity. War increased the number of those
in servitude. A slave, whatever Hobbes may say, is capable
of being injured by his master; but the laws of some nations
give more power to the latter than is warranted by those of
nature. Servitude implies only an obligation to perpetual
labour for a recompense (namely, at least maintenance); the
evil necessary to this condition has been much exaggerated
by opinion.[a]

49. Puffendorf and Cumberland are the two great pro-
moters, if not founders, of that school in ethics,
which, abandoning the higher ground of both philosophers and theologians, that of an intrinsic fitness and
propriety in actions, resolved them all into their conduciveness towards good. Their *utile* indeed is very different from
what Cicero has so named, which is merely personal, but it is
different also from his *honestum*. The sociableness of Puffendorf
is perhaps much the same with the general good of Cumberland, but is somewhat less comprehensive and less clear. Paley,
who had not read a great deal, had certainly read Puffendorf;
he has borrowed from him several minor illustrations, such as
the equivocal promise of Timur (called by Paley, Temures) to
the garrison of Sebastia, and the rules for division of profits in
partnership. Their minds were in some respects alike; both
phlegmatic, honest, and sincere without warmth or fancy;
yet there seems a more thorough good-nature and kindliness
of heart in our countryman. Though an ennobled German,
Puffendorf had as little respect for the law of honour as

Puffendorf and Paley compared.

---

[z] C. 2.   [a] C. 3.

Paley himself.   They do not, indeed, resemble each other in
their modes of writing; one was very laborious, the other
very indolent; one sometimes misses his mark by circuity,
the other by precipitance.   The quotations in Puffendorf are
often as thickly strewed as in Grotius, though he takes less
from the poets; but he seems not to build upon their authority, which gives them still more the air of superfluity.
His theory, indeed, which assigns no weight to any thing
but a close geometrical deduction from axioms, is incompatible with much deference to authority; and he sets aside
the customs of mankind as unstable and arbitrary.   He
has not taken much from Hobbes, whose principles are far
from his, but a great deal from Grotius.   The leading difference between the treatises of these celebrated men is that,
while the former contemplated the law that ought to be
observed among independent communities as his primary
object, to render which more evident he lays down the fundamental principles of private right or the law of nature, the
latter, on the other hand, not only begins with natural law,
but makes it the great theme of his inquiries.

50. Few books have been more highly extolled or more
severely blamed than the Thoughts or Maxims of Rochefoucault.
the Duke of la Rochefoucault.   They have, indeed,
the greatest advantages for popularity; the production of
a man less distinguished by his high rank than by his active
participation in the factions of his country at a time when
they reached the limits of civil war, and by his brilliancy
among the accomplished courtiers of Louis XIV.; concise
and energetic in expression; reduced to those short aphorisms
which leave much to the reader's acuteness, and yet save his
labour; not often obscure, and never wearisome; an evident
generalisation of long experience, without pedantry, without
method, without deductive reasonings, yet wearing an appearance at least of profundity, they delight the intelligent though
indolent man of the world, and must be read with some admiration by the philosopher.   Among the books in ancient
and modern times which record the conclusions of observing
men on the moral qualities of their fellows, a high place
should be reserved for the Maxims of Rochefoucault.

51. The censure that has so heavily fallen upon this writer

is founded on his proneness to assign a low and selfish motive
to human actions, and even to those which are most usually
denominated virtuous. It is impossible to dispute the partial
truth of this charge. Yet it may be pleaded, that many of
his maxims are not universal even in their enunciation; and
that, in others, where, for the sake of a more effective expression, the position seems general, we ought to understand
it with such limitations as our experience may suggest. The
society with which the Duke of la Rochefoucault was conversant could not elevate his notions of disinterested probity
in man, or of unblemished purity in woman. Those who call
themselves the world, it is easy to perceive, set aside, in their
remarks on human nature, all the species but themselves, and
sometimes generalise their maxims, to an amusing degree,
from the manners and sentiments which have grown up in the
atmosphere of a court or an aristocratic society. Rochefoucault was of far too reflecting a mind to be confounded
with such mere worldlings; yet he bears witness to the con-
tracted observation and the precipitate inferences which an
intercourse with a single class of society scarcely fails to
generate. The causticity of Rochefoucault is always directed
against the false virtues of mankind, but never touches the
reality of moral truths, and leaves us less injured than the
cold, heartless indifference to right which distils from the
pages of Hobbes. Nor does he deal in those sweeping
denials of goodness to human nature which are so frequently
hazarded under the mask of religion. His maxims are not
exempt from defects of a different kind ; they are sometimes
refined to a degree of obscurity, and sometimes, under an
epigrammatic turn, convey little more than a trivial meaning.
Perhaps, however, it would be just to say that one-third of
the number deserve to be remembered, as at least partially
true and useful; and this is a large proportion, if we exclude
all that are not in some measure original.

52. The Characters of La Bruyère, published in 1687,
approach to the maxims of La Rochefoucault by
La Bruyère. their refinement, their brevity, their general tendency to an unfavourable explanation of human conduct.
This nevertheless is not so strongly marked, and the picture
of selfishness wants the darkest touches of his contempo-

rary's colouring. La Bruyère had a model in antiquity, Theophrastus, whose short book of Characters he had himself translated, and prefixed to his own; a step not impolitic for his own glory, since the Greek writer, with no contemptible degree of merit, has been incomparably surpassed by his imitator. Many changes in the condition of society, the greater diversity of ranks and occupations in modern Europe, the influence of women over the other sex, as well as their own varieties of character and manners, the effects of religion, learning, chivalry, royalty, have given a range to this very pleasing department of moral literature which no ancient could have compassed. Nor has Theophrastus taken much pains to search the springs of character; his delineations are bold and clear, but merely in outline; we see more of manners than of nature, and the former more in general classes than in portraiture. La Bruyère has often painted single persons; whether accurately or no, we cannot at this time determine, but with a felicity of description which at once renders the likeness probable, and suggests its application to those we ourselves have seen. His general reflections, like those of Rochefoucault, are brilliant with antithesis and epigrammatic conciseness; sometimes perhaps not quite just or quite perspicuous. But he pleases more on the whole, from his greater variety, his greater liveliness, and his gentler spirit of raillery. Nor does he forget to mingle the praise of some with his satire. But he is rather a bold writer for his age and his position in the court, and what looks like flattery may well have been ironical. Few have been more imitated, as well as more admired, than La Bruyère, who fills up the list of those whom France has boasted as most conspicuous for their knowledge of human nature. The others are Montaigne, Charron, Pascal, and Rochefoucault; but we might withdraw the second name without injustice.

53. Moral philosophy comprehends in its literature whatever has been written on the best theory and precepts of moral education, disregarding what is confined to erudition, though this may frequently be partially treated in works of the former class. Education, notwithstanding its recognized importance, was miserably neglected in England, and quite as much, perhaps, in **every** *Education. Milton's Tractate.*

part of Europe. Schools, kept by low-born, illiberal pedants, teaching little, and that little ill, without regard to any judicious discipline or moral culture, on the one hand, or, on the other, a pretence of instruction at home under some ignorant and servile tutor, seem to have been the alternatives of our juvenile gentry. Milton raised his voice against these faulty methods in his short Tractate on Education. This abounds with bursts of his elevated spirit; and sketches out a model of public colleges, wherein the teaching should be more comprehensive, more liberal, more accommodated to what he deems the great aim of education than what was in use. 'That,' he says, 'I call a complete and generous education which fits a man to perform justly, skilfully, and magnanimously all the offices both private and public, of peace and war.' But when Milton descends to specify the course of studies he would recommend, it appears singularly ill-chosen and impracticable, nearly confined to ancient writers, even in mathematics and other subjects where they. could not be sufficient, and likely to leave the student very far from that aptitude for offices of war and peace which he had held forth as the reward of his diligence.

54. Locke, many years afterwards, turned his thoughts to education with all the advantages that a strong understanding and entire disinterestedness could give him; but, as we should imagine, with some necessary deficiencies of experience, though we hardly perceive much of them in his writings. He looked on the methods usual in his age with severity, or, some would say, with prejudice; yet I know not by what proof we can refute his testimony. In his Treatise on Education, which may be reckoned an introduction to that on the Conduct of the Understanding, since the latter is but a scheme of that education an adult person should give himself, he has uttered, to say the least, more good sense on the subject than will be found in any preceding writer. Locke was not like the pedants of his own or other ages, who think that to pour their wordy book-learning into the memory is the true discipline of childhood. The culture of the intellectual and moral faculties in their most extensive sense, the health of the body, the accomplishments which common utility or social custom has rendered

valuable, enter into his idea of the best model of education, conjointly at least with any knowledge that can be imparted by books. The ancients had written in the same spirit; in Xenophon, in Plato, in Aristotle, the noble conception which Milton has expressed, of forming the perfect man, is always predominant over mere literary instruction, if indeed the latter can be said to appear at all in their writings on this subject; but we had become the dupes of schoolmasters in our riper years, as we had been their slaves in our youth. Much has been written, and often well, since the days of Locke; but he is the chief source from which it has been ultimately derived; and though the Emile is more attractive in manner, it may be doubtful whether it is as rational and practicable as the Treatise on Education. If they have both the same defect, that their authors wanted sufficient observation of children, it is certain that the caution and sound judgment of Locke have rescued him better from error.

55. There are, indeed, from this or from other causes, several passages in the Treatise on Education to which we cannot give an unhesitating assent. _and defects._ Locke appears to have somewhat exaggerated the efficacy of education. This is an error on the right side in a work that aims at persuasion in a practical matter; but we are now looking at theoretical truth alone. 'I think I may say,' he begins, 'that of all the men we meet with, nine parts of ten are what they are, good or evil, useful or not, by their education. It is this which makes the great difference in mankind. The little or almost insensible impressions on our tender infancies have very important and lasting consequences; and there 'tis as in the fountains of some rivers, where a gentle application of the hand turns the flexible waters into channels that make them take quite contrary courses; and by this little direction given them at first in the source, they receive different tendencies, and arrive at last at very remote and distant places.' 'I imagine,' he adds soon afterwards, 'the minds of children as easily turned this or that way as water itself.'[b]

---

[b] Treatise on Education, § 2. 'The difference,' he afterwards says, 'to be found in the manners and abilities of men is owing more to their education than to anything else.' § 32.

56. This passage is an instance of Locke's unfortunate fondness for analogical parallels, which, as far as I have observed, much more frequently obscure a philosophical theorem than shed any light upon it. Nothing would be easier than to confirm the contrary proposition by such fanciful analogies from external nature. In itself, the position is hyperbolical to extravagance. It is no more disparagement to the uses of education, that it will not produce the like effects upon every individual, than it is to those of agriculture (I purposely use this sort of idle analogy), that we do not reap the same quantity of corn from every soil. Those who are conversant with children on a large scale will, I believe, unanimously deny this levelling efficacy of tuition. The variety of characters even in children of the same family, where the domestic associations of infancy have run in the same trains, and where many physical congenialities may produce, and ordinarily do produce, a moral resemblance, is of sufficiently frequent occurrence to prove that in human beings there are intrinsic dissimilitudes, which no education can essentially overcome. Among mere theorists, however, this hypothesis seems to be popular. And as many of these extend their notion of the plasticity of human nature to the effects of government and legislation, which is a sort of continuance of the same controlling power, they are generally induced to disregard past experience of human affairs, because they flatter themselves that, under a more scientific administration, mankind will become something very different from what they have been.

57. In the age of Locke, if we may confide in what he tells us, the domestic education of children must have been of the worst kind. ' If we look,' he says, ' into the common management of children, we shall have reason to wonder, in the great dissoluteness of manners which the world complains of, that there are any footsteps at all left of virtue. I desire to know what vice can be named which parents and those about children do not season them with, and drop into them the seeds of, as often as they are capable to receive them.' The mode of treatment seems to have been passionate and often barbarous severity alternating with foolish indulgence. Their spirits were often broken down, and their in-

genuousness destroyed, by the former; their habits of self-will and sensuality confirmed by the latter. This was the method pursued by parents; but the pedagogues of course confined themselves to their favourite scheme of instruction and reformation by punishment. Dugald Stewart has animadverted on the austerity of Locke's rules of education.[c] And this is certainly the case in some respects. He recommends that children should be taught to expect nothing because it will give them pleasure, but only what will be useful to them; a rule fit, in its rigid meaning, to destroy the pleasure of the present moment, in the only period of life that the present moment can be really enjoyed. No father himself, Locke neither knew how ill a parent can spare the love of his child, nor how ill a child can want the constant and practical sense of a parent's love. But if he was led too far by deprecating the mischievous indulgence he had sometimes witnessed, he made some amends by his censures on the prevalent discipline of stripes. Of this he speaks with the disapprobation natural to a mind already schooled in the habits of reason and virtue.[d] 'I cannot think any correction useful to a child where the shame of suffering for having done amiss does not work more upon him than the pain.' Esteem and disgrace are the rewards and punishments to which he principally looks. And surely this is a noble foundation for moral discipline. He also recommends that children should be much with their parents, and allowed all reasonable liberty. I cannot think that Stewart's phrase 'hardness of character,' which he accounts for by the early intercourse of Locke with the Puritans, is justly applicable to anything that we know of him; and many more passages in this very treatise might be adduced to prove his kindliness of disposition, than will appear to any judicious person over-austere. He found, in fact, everything

---

[c] Preliminary Dissertation to Encyclop. Britann.

[d] 'If severity carried to the highest pitch does prevail, and works a cure upon the present unruly distemper, it is often bringing in the room of it a worse and more dangerous disease by breaking the mind; and then, in the place of a disorderly young fellow, you have a low-spirited moped creature, who however with his unnatural sobriety he may please silly people, who commend tame inactive children, because they make no noise, nor give them any trouble; yet at last will probably prove as uncomfortable a thing to his friends, as he will be all his life an useless thing to himself and others.' § 51.

wrong; a false system of reward and punishment, a false
view of the objects of education, a false selection of studies,
false methods of pursuing them. Where so much was to be
corrected, it was perhaps natural to be too sanguine about
the effects of the remedy.

58. Of the old dispute as to public and private education
he says, that both sides have their inconveniences, but
inclines to prefer the latter, influenced, as is evident, rather
by disgust at the state of our schools than by any general
principle.[e] For he insists much on the necessity of giving a
boy a sufficient knowledge of what he is to expect in the
world. 'The longer he is kept hoodwinked, the less he will
see when he comes abroad into open daylight, and be the
more exposed to be a prey to himself and others.' But this
experience will, as is daily seen, not be supplied by a tutor's
lectures, any more than by books; nor can be given by any
course save a public education. Locke urges the necessity
of having a tutor well-bred, and with knowledge of the
world, the ways, the humours, the follies, the cheats, the
faults of the age he is fallen into, and particularly of the
country he lives in, as of far more importance than his
scholarship. 'The only fence against the world is a thorough
knowledge of it. . . . He that thinks not this of more moment to his son, and for which he more needs a governor,
than the languages and learned sciences, forgets of how
much more use it is to judge right of men and manage his
affairs wisely with them, than to speak Greek and Latin,
and argue in mood and figure, or to have his head filled with
the abstruse speculations of natural philosophy and metaphysics; nay, than to be well versed in Greek and Roman
writers, though that be much better for a gentleman, than
to be a good Peripatetic or Cartesian; because these ancient
authors observed and painted mankind well, and give the
best light into that kind of knowledge. He that goes into
the eastern parts of Asia will find able and acceptable men
without any of these; but without virtue, knowledge of the
world, and civility, an accomplished and valuable man can
be found nowhere.'[f]

---

          [e] § 70.   [f] § 94.

59. It is to be remembered, that the person whose education Locke undertakes to fashion is an English gentleman. Virtue, wisdom, breeding, and learning, are desirable for such a one in their order, but the last not so much as the rest.[g] It must be had, he says, but only as subservient to greater qualities. No objections have been more frequently raised against the scheme of Locke than on account of his depreciation of classical literature and of the study of the learned languages. This is not wholly true; Latin he reckons absolutely necessary for a gentleman, though it is absurd that those should learn Latin who are designed for trade, and never look again at a Latin book.[h] If he lays not so much stress on Greek as a gentleman's study, though he by no means would abandon it, it is because, in fact, most gentlemen, especially in his age, have done very well without it; and nothing can be deemed indispensable in education of a child, the want of which does not leave a manifest deficiency in the man. 'No man,' he observes, 'can pass for a scholar who is ignorant of the Greek language. But I am not here considering of the education of a professed scholar, but of a gentleman.'[i]

60. The peculiar methods recommended by Locke in learning languages, especially the Latin, appear to be of very doubtful utility, though some of them do not want strenuous supporters in the present day. Such are the method of interlinear translation, the learning of mere words without grammar, and above all the practice of talking Latin with a tutor who speaks it well—a phœnix whom he has not shown us where to find.[k] In general, he seems to underrate the difficulty of acquiring what even he would call a competent learning, and what is of more importance, and no rare mistake in those who write on this subject, to confound the acquisition of a language with the knowledge of its literature. The best ancient writers both in Greek and Latin furnish so much of wise reflection, of noble sentiment, of all that is beautiful and salutary, that no one who has had the happiness to know and feel what they are, will desire to see their study excluded or stinted in its just extent, wherever the

---

[g] § 138.   [h] § 189.   [i] § 195.   [k] § 165.

education of those who are to be the first and best of the
country is carried forward. And though by far the greater
portion of mankind must, by the very force of terms, remain
in the ranks of intellectual mediocrity, it is an ominous sign
of any times when no thought is taken for those who may
rise beyond it.

61. In every other part of instruction, Locke has still an
eye to what is useful for a gentleman. French he justly
thinks should be taught before Latin; no geometry is required
by him beyond Euclid, but he recommends geography, history and chronology, drawing, and what may be thought
now as little necessary for a gentleman as Homer, the jurisprudence of Grotius and Puffendorf. He strongly urges the
writing English well, though a thing commonly neglected;
and after speaking with contempt of the artificial systems of
logic and rhetoric, sends the pupil to Chillingworth for the
best example of reasoning, and to Tully for the best idea of
eloquence. 'And let him read those things that are well
writ in English to perfect his style in the purity of our language.' [m]

62. It would be to transcribe half this treatise, were we
to mention all the judicious and minute observations on the
management of children it contains. Whatever may have
been Locke's opportunities, he certainly availed himself of
them to the utmost. It is as far as possible from a theoretical
book; and in many respects the best of modern times, such
as those of the Edgeworth name, might pass for developments of his principles. The patient attention to every
circumstance, a peculiar characteristic of the genius of Locke,
is in none of his works better displayed. His rules for the
health of children, though sometimes trivial, since the
subject has been more regarded, his excellent advice as to
checking effeminacy and timorousness, his observations on
their curiosity, presumption, idleness, on their plays and
recreations, bespeak an intense, though calm love of truth
and goodness; a quality which few have possessed more
fully or known so well how to exert as this admirable philosopher.

---

[m] § 183.

63. No one had condescended to spare any thoughts for female education, till Fenelon, in 1688, published his earliest work, Sur l'Education des Filles. This was the occasion of his appointment as preceptor to the grandchildren of Louis XIV.; for much of this treatise, and perhaps the most valuable part, is equally applicable to both sexes. It may be compared with that of Locke, written nearly at the same time, and bearing a great resemblance in its spirit. Both have the education of a polished and high-bred class, rather than of scholars, before them; and Fenelon rarely loses sight of his peculiar object, or gives any rule which is not capable of being practised in female education. In many respects he coincides with our English philosopher, and observes with him that a child learns much before he speaks, so that the cultivation of his moral qualities can hardly begin too soon. Both complain of the severity of parents, and deprecate the mode of bringing up by punishment. Both advise the exhibition of virtue and religion in pleasing lights, and censure the austere dogmatism with which they were inculcated, before the mind was sufficiently developed to apprehend them. But the characteristic sweetness of Fenelon's disposition is often shown in contrast with the somewhat stern inflexibility of Locke. His theory is uniformly indulgent; his method of education is a labour of love; a desire to render children happy for the time, as well as afterwards, runs through his book, and he may perhaps be considered the founder of that school which has endeavoured to dissipate the terrors and dry the tears of childhood. 'I have seen,' he says, 'many children who have learned to read in play; we have only to read entertaining stories to them out of a book, and insensibly teach them the letters, they will soon desire to go for themselves to the source of their amusement.' 'Books should be given them well bound and gilt, with good engravings, clear types; for all that captivates the imagination facilitates study: the choice should be such as contain short and marvellous stories.' These details are now trivial, but in the days of Fenelon they may have been otherwise.

Fenelon on female education.

64. In several passages he displays not only a judicious spirit, but an observation that must have been long exercised.

'Of all the qualities we perceive in children,' he remarks,
'there is only one that can be trusted as likely to be durable,
which is sound judgment; it always grows with their growth,
if it is well cultivated; but the grace of childhood is effaced;
its vivacity is extinguished; even its sensibility is often lost,
because their own passions and the intercourse of others
insensibly harden the hearts of young persons who enter
into the world.' It is, therefore, a solid and just way of
thinking which we should most value and most improve, and
this not by any means less in girls than in the other sex,
since their duties and the occupations they are called upon
to fill do not less require it. Hence he not only deprecates
an excessive taste for dress, but, with more originality, points
out the danger of that extreme delicacy and refinement
which incapacitate women for the ordinary affairs of life,
and give them a contempt for a country life and rural
economy.

65. It will be justly thought at present, that he discourages
too much the acquisition of knowledge by women. 'Keep
their minds,' he says in one place, 'as much as you can
within the usual limits, and let them understand that the
modesty of their sex ought to shrink from science with
almost as much delicacy as from vice.' This seems, however,
to be confined to science or philosophy in a strict sense; for
he permits afterwards a larger compass of reading. Women
should write a good hand, understand orthography and the
four rules of arithmetic, which they will want in domestic
affairs. To these he requires a close attention, and even
recommends to women an acquaintance with some of the
common forms and maxims of law. Greek, Roman, and
French history, with the best travels, will be valuable, and
keep them from seeking pernicious fictions. Books also of
eloquence and poetry may be read with selection, taking
care to avoid any that relate to love; music and painting
may be taught with the same precaution. The Italian and
Spanish languages are of no use but to enlarge their knowledge of dangerous books; Latin is better as the language of
the church, but this he would recommend only for girls of
good sense and discreet conduct, who will make no display
of the acquisition.

Sect. II.—On Political Philosophy.

Puffendorf—Spinosa—Harrington's Oceana—Locke on Government—
Political Economy.

66. In the seventh book of Puffendorf's great work, he comes to political philosophy, towards which he had been gradually tending for some time; primary societies, or those of families, leading the way to the consideration of civil government.   Grotius derives the origin of this from the natural sociableness of mankind.   But this, as Puffendorf remarks, may be satisfied by the primary societies. The real cause was experience of the injuries which one man can inflict on another.[n]   And, after a prolix disquisition, he concludes that civil society must have been constituted, first, by a covenant of a number of men, each with each, to form a commonwealth, and to be bound by the majority, in which primary covenant they must be unanimous, that is, every dissentient would retain his natural liberty; next, by a resolution or decree of the majority, that certain rulers shall govern the rest; and, lastly, by a second covenant between these rulers and the rest, one promising to take care of the public weal, and the other to obey lawful commands.[o]   This covenant, as he attempts to show, exists even in a democracy, though it is less evident than in other forms.   Hobbes had admitted the first of these covenants, but denied the second; Barbeyrac, the able commentator on Puffendorf, has done exactly the reverse.   A state once formed may be conceived to exist as one person, with a single will, represented by that of the sovereign, wherever the sovereignty may be placed. This sovereignty is founded on the covenants, and is not conferred, except indirectly like every other human power, by God.   Puffendorf here combats the opposite opinion, which churchmen were as prone to hold, it seems, in Germany as in England.[p]

Puffendorf's theory of politics.

67. The legislative, punitive, and judiciary powers, those of making war and peace, of appointing magistrates, and

---

[n] L. vii. c. 1.   [o] C. 2.   [p] C. 3,

levying taxes, are so closely connected that no one can be
denied to the sovereign. As to his right in ecclesiastical
matters, Puffendorf leaves it for others to determine.[q] He
seems in this part of the work too favourable to unlimited
monarchy, declaring himself against a mixed government.
The sovereign power must be irresponsible, and cannot be
bound by the law which itself has given. He even denies
that all government is intended for the good of the governed
—a position strangely inconsistent with his theory of a
covenant—but he contends that, if it were, this end, the
public good, may be more probably discerned by the prince
than by the people.[r] Yet he admits that the exorbitances
of a prince should be restrained by certain fundamental laws,
and holds, that having accepted such, and ratified them by
oath, he is not at liberty to break them; arguing, with some
apparent inconsistency, against those who maintain such
limitations to be inconsistent with monarchy, and even re-
commending the institution of councils, without whose
consent certain acts of the sovereign shall not be valid.
This can only be reconciled with his former declaration
against a mixed sovereignty, by the distinction familiar to
our own constitutional lawyers, between the joint acts of A.
and B., and the acts of A. with B.'s consent. But this is
a little too technical and unreal for philosophical politics.
Governments not reducible to one of the three simple forms
he calls irregular; such as the Roman republic or German
empire. But there may be systems of states, or aggregate
communities, either subject to one king by different titles, or
united by federation. He inclines to deny that the majority
can bind the minority in the latter case, and seems to take it
for granted that some of the confederates can quit the league
at pleasure.[s]

68. Sovereignty over persons cannot be acquired, strictly
speaking, by seizure or occupation, as in the case of lands,
and requires, even after conquest, their consent to obey;
which will be given, in order to secure themselves from the
other rights of war. It is a problem whether, after an unjust conquest, the forced consent of the people can give a

----

      [q] C. 4.   [r] C. 6.   [s] C. 5.

lawful title to sovereignty. Puffendorf distinguishes between
a monarchy and a republic thus unjustly subdued. In the
former case, so long as the lawful heirs exist or preserve
their claim, the duty of restitution continues. But in the
latter, as the people may live as happily under a monarchy
as under a republic, he thinks that an usurper has only to
treat them well, without scruple as to his title. If he op-
presses them, no course of years will make his title lawful, or
bind them in conscience to obey, length of possession being
only length of injury. If a sovereign has been justly divested
of his power, the community becomes immediately free; but
if by unjust rebellion, his right continues till by silence he
has appeared to abandon it.[t]

69. Every one will agree that a lawful ruler must not be
opposed within the limits of his authority. But let us put
the case that he should command what is unlawful or mal-
treat his subjects. Whatever Hobbes may say, a subject may
be injured by his sovereign. But we should bear minor injuries patiently, and in the worst cases avoid personal resistance. Those are not to be listened to who assert that a
king, degenerating into a tyrant, may be resisted and punished
by his people. He admits only a right of self-defence, if he
manifestly becomes a public enemy : in all this he seems to
go quite as far as Grotius himself. The next question is as
to the right of invaders and usurpers to obedience. This, it
will be observed, he had already in some measure discussed ;
but Puffendorf is neither strict in method, nor free from repetitions. He labours much about the rights of the lawful
prince, insisting upon them, where the subjects have promised
allegiance to the usurper. This, he thinks, must be deemed
temporary, until the legitimate sovereign has recovered his
dominions. But what may be done towards promoting this
end by such as have sworn fidelity to the actual ruler, he does
not intimate.[u]

70. Civil laws are such as emanate from the supreme
power, with respect to things left indifferent by the laws of
God and nature. What chiefly belongs to them is the form
and method of acquiring rights or obtaining redress for

---

[t] C. 7.   [u] C. 8.

wrongs. If we give the law of nature all that belongs to it,
and take away from the civilians what they have hitherto en-
grossed and promiscuously treated, we shall bring the civil
law to a much narrower compass; not to say that at present
whenever the latter is deficient we must have recourse to the
law of nature, and that therefore in all commonwealths the
natural laws supply the defects of the civil.[x] He argues
against Hobbes' tenet that the civil law cannot be contrary
to the law of nature ; and that what shall be deemed theft,
murder, or adultery, depends on the former. The subject is
bound generally not to obey the unjust commands of his
sovereign ; but in the case of war he thinks it, on the whole,
safest, considering the usual difficulties of such questions,
that the subject should serve, and throw the responsibility
before God on the prince.[y] In this problem of casuistry,
common usage is wholly against the stricter theory.

71. Punishment may be defined an evil inflicted by authority upon view of antecedent transgression.[z] Hence exclusion, on political grounds, from public office, or separation of
the sick for the sake of the healthy, is not punishment. It
does not belong to distributive justice, nor is the magistrate
bound to apportion it to the malignity of the offence, though
this is usual. Superior authority is necessary to punishment;
and he differs from Grotius by denying that we have a right
to avenge the injuries of those who have no claim upon us.
Punishment ought never to be inflicted without the prospect
of some advantage from it ; either the correction of the
offender, or the prevention of his repeating the offence. But
example he seems not to think a direct end of punishment,
though it should be regarded in its infliction. It is not necessary that all offences which the law denounces should be
actually punished, though some jurists have questioned the
right of pardon. Punishments ought to be measured according to the object of the crime, the injury to the commonwealth, and the malice of the delinquent. Hence offences
against God should be deemed most criminal, and next, such
as disturb the state ; then whatever affect life, the peace or
honour of families, private property or reputation, following

---

[x] L. viii. c. 1.   [y] Id.   [z] C. 3.

the scale of the Decalogue. But though all crimes do not require equal severity, an exact proportion of penalties is not required. Most of this chapter exhibits the vacillating, indistinct, and almost self-contradictory resolutions of difficulties so frequent in Puffendorf. He concludes by establishing a great truth, that no man can be justly punished for the offence of another; not even a community for the acts of their forefathers, notwithstanding their fictitious immortality.[a]

72. After some chapters on the law of nations, Puffendorf concludes with discussing the cessation of subjection. This may ordinarily be by voluntarily removing to another state with permission of the sovereign. And if no law or custom interferes, the subject has a right to do this at his discretion. The state has not a right to expel citizens without some offence. It loses all authority over a banished man. He concludes by considering the rare case of so great a diminution of the people, as to raise a doubt of their political identity.[b]

73. The political portion of this large work is not, as will appear, very fertile in original or sagacious reflec- Politics of tion. A greater degree of both, though by no means Spinosa. accompanied with a sound theory, distinguishes the Political Treatise of Spinosa, one which must not be confounded with the Theologico-political Treatise, a very different work. In this he undertakes to show how a state under a regal or aristocratic government ought to be constituted so as to secure the tranquillity and freedom of the citizens. Whether Spinosa borrowed his theory on the origin of government from Hobbes, is perhaps hard to determine: he seems acquainted with the treatise De Cive; but the philosophical system of both was such as, in minds habituated like theirs to close reasoning, could not lead to any other result. Political theory, as Spinosa justly observes, is to be founded on our experience of human kind as it is, and on no visionary notions of an Utopia or golden age; and hence politicians of practical knowledge have written better on these subjects than philosophers. We must treat of men as liable to passions,

---

[a] C. 3.   [b] C. 11, 12.

prone more to revenge than to pity, eager to rule and to compel others to act like themselves, more pleased with having done harm to others than with procuring their own good. Hence no state wherein the public affairs are intrusted to any one's good faith can be secure of their due administration; but means should be devised that neither reason nor passion should induce those who govern to obstruct the public weal; it being indifferent by what motive men act if they can be brought to act for the common good.

74. Natural law is the same as natural power; it is that which the laws of nature, that is the order of the world, give to each individual. Nothing is forbidden by this law, except what no one desires, or what no one can perform. Thus no one is bound to keep the faith he has plighted any longer than he will, and than he judges it useful to himself; for he has not lost the power of breaking it, and power is right in natural law. But he may easily perceive that the power of one man in a state of nature is limited by that of all the rest, and in effect is reduced to nothing, all men being naturally enemies to each other; while, on the other hand, by uniting their force and establishing bounds by common consent to the natural powers of each, it becomes really more effective than while it was unlimited. This is the principle of civil government; and now the distinctions of just and unjust, right and wrong, begin to appear.

75. The right of the supreme magistrate is nothing but the collective rights of the citizens, that is, their powers. Neither he nor they in their natural state can do wrong; but after the institution of government, each citizen may do wrong by disobeying the magistrate; that, in fact, being the test of wrong. He has not to inquire whether the commands of the supreme power are just or unjust, pious or impious; that is, as to action, for the state has no jurisdiction over his judgment.

76. Two independent states are naturally enemies, and may make war on each other whenever they please. If they make peace or alliance, it is no longer binding than the cause, that is, hope or fear in the contracting parties, shall endure. All this is founded on the universal law of nature, the desire of preserving ourselves; which, whether men are conscious

of it or no, animates all their actions.   Spinosa in this, as in
his other writings, is more fearless than Hobbes ; and, though
he sometimes may throw a light veil over his abjuration of
moral and religious principle, it is frequently placed in a
more prominent view than his English precursor in the same
system had deemed it secure to exhibit.   Yet so slight is
often the connexion between theoretical tenets and human
practice, that Spinosa bore the character of a virtuous and
benevolent man.   In this treatise of politics, especially in the
broad assertion that good faith is only to be preserved so long
as it is advantageous, he leaves Machiavel and Hobbes at
some distance, and may be reckoned the most phlegmatically
impudent of the whole school.

77. The contract or fundamental laws, he proceeds, according to which the multitude transfers its right to a king
or a senate, may unquestionably be broken, when it is advantageous to the whole to do so.   But Spinosa denies to private
citizens the right of judging concerning the public good in
such a point, reserving, apparently, to the supreme magistrate an ultimate power of breaking the conditions upon which
he was chosen.   Notwithstanding this dangerous admission,
he strongly protests against intrusting absolute power to any
one man ; and observes, in answer to the common argument
of the stability of despotism, as in the instance of the Turkish
monarchy, that if barbarism, slavery, and desolation are to
be called peace, nothing can be more wretched than peace itself.   Nor is this sole power of one man a thing so possible
as we imagine ; the kings who seem most despotic trusting
the public safety and their own to counsellors and favourites,
often the worst and weakest in the state.

78. He next proceeds to his scheme of a well-regulated
monarchy, which is in some measure original and His theory of
ingenious.   The people are to be divided into fa-   a monarchy.
milies, by which he seems to mean something like the φρατρίαι
of Attica.   From each of these, councillors, fifty years of age,
are to be chosen by the king, succeeding in a rotation quin-
quennial, or less, so as to form a numerous senate.   This
assembly is to be consulted upon all public affairs, and the
king is to be guided by its unanimous opinion.   In case,
however, of disagreement, the different propositions being

laid before the king, he may choose that of the minority, provided at least one hundred councillors have recommended it.   The less remarkable provisions of this ideal polity it would be waste of time to mention; except that he advises that all the citizens should be armed as a militia, and that the principal towns should be fortified, and consequently, as it seems, in their power. A monarchy thus constituted would probably not degenerate into the despotic form. Spinosa appeals to the ancient government of Aragon, as a proof of the possibility of carrying his theory into execution.

79. From this imaginary monarchy he comes to an aristʋ-cratical republic. In this he seems to have taken Venice, the idol of theoretical politicians, as his primary model, but with such deviations as affect the whole scheme of government. He objects to the supremacy of an elective doge, justly observing that the precautions adopted in the election of that magistrate show the danger of the office itself, which was rather retained in the aristocratical polity as an ancient institution than from any persuasion of its usefulness. But the most remarkable discrepancy between the aristocracy of Spinosa and that of Venice is, that his great council, which ought, as he strongly urges, not to consist of less than 5,000, the greatness of its number being the only safeguard against the close oligarchy of a few families, is not to be hereditary, but its vacancies to be filled up by self-election. In this election, indeed, he considers the essence of aristocracy to consist, being, as is implied in its meaning, a government by the best, who can only be pronounced such by the choice of many. It is singular that he never adverts to popular representation, of which he must have known examples.   Democracy, on the contrary, he defines to be a government where political power falls to men by chance of birth, or by some means which has rendered them citizens, and who can claim it as their right, without regard to the choice of others. And a democracy, according to Spinosa, may exist, if the law should limit this privilege of power to the seniors in age, or to the elder branches of families, or to those who pay a certain amount in taxation; although the numbers enjoying it should be a smaller portion of the community than in an aristocracy of the form he has recommended.   His treatise

breaks off near the beginning of the chapters intended to
delineate the best model of democracy, which he declares to
be one wherein all persons, in their own power, and not
infamous by crime, should have a share in the public government. I do not know that it can be inferred from the writings
of Spinosa, nor is his authority, perhaps, sufficient to render
the question of any interest, to which of the three plans devised by him as the best in their respective forms, he would
have ascribed the preference.

80. The condition of France under Louis XIV. was not
very tempting to speculators on political theory. Amelot de
la Hous-
Whatever short remarks may be found in those ex- saye.
cellent writers on other subjects who distinguish this period,
we can select no one book that falls readily into this class.
For Télémaque we must find another place. It is scarcely
worth while to mention the political discourses on Tacitus,
by Amelot de la Houssaye. These are a tedious and pedantic running commentary on Tacitus, affecting to deduce
general principles, but much unlike the short and poignant
observations of Machiavel and Bacon. A whole volume on
the reign alone of Tiberius, and printed at Paris, is not likely
to repay a reader's trouble; at least I have found nothing in
it above the common level. I have no acquaintance with the
other political writings of Amelot de la Houssaye, one of
those who thought they could make great discoveries by ana-
lysing the constitution of Venice and other states.

81. England, thrown at the commencement of this period
upon the resources of her own invention to replace Harrington's
an ancient monarchy by something new, and rich Oceana.
at that time in reflecting as well as learned men, with an
unshackled press, and a growing disdain of authority as opposed to argument, was the natural soil of political theory.
The earliest fruit was Sir James Harrington's Oceana, published in 1656. This once famous book is a political allegory,
partly suggested, perhaps, by the Dodona's Grove of Howell,
or by Barclay's Argenis, and a few other fictions of the preceding age. His Oceana represents England, the history of
which is shadowed out with fictitious names. But this is
preliminary to the great object, the scheme of a new commonwealth, which, under the auspices of Olphaus Megaletor,

the Lord Archon, meaning, of course, Cromwell, not as he was, but as he ought to have been, the author feigns to have been established.   The various laws and constitutions of this polity occupy the whole work.

82. The leading principle of Harrington is that power depends on property; denying the common saying that knowledge or prudence is power.   But this property must be in land, 'because, as to property producing empire, it is required that it should have some certain root or foothold, which, except in land, it cannot have, being otherwise, as it were, upon the wing.   Nevertheless, in such cities as subsist mostly by trade, and have little or no land, as Holland and Genoa, the balance of treasure may be equal to that of land.'[c] The law fixing the balance of lands is called by him agrarian; and without an agrarian law he holds that no government, whether monarchical, aristocratic, or popular, has any long duration: this is rather paradoxical; but his distribution of lands varies according to the form of the commonwealth.   In one best constituted the possession of lands is limited to 2,000*l*. a-year, which, of course, in his time was a much greater estate than at present.

83. Harrington's general scheme of a good government is one ' established upon an equal agrarian arising into the superstructure, or three orders, the senate debating and proposing, the people resolving, and the magistracy executing, by an equal rotation through the suffrage of the people given by the ballot.'   His more particular form of polity, devised for his Oceana, it would be tedious to give in detail; the result is a moderate aristocracy; property, though under the control of his agrarian, which prevents its excess, having so great a share in the elections that it must predominate. But it is an aristocracy of what we should call the middle ranks, and might not be unfit for a small state.   In general it may be said of Harrington that he is prolix, dull, pedantic, and seldom profound; but sometimes redeems himself by just observations.   Like most theoretical politicians of that age, he had an excessive admiration for the republic of

---

[c] P. 38, edit. 1771.

Venice.[d] His other political writings are in the same spirit
as the Oceana, but still less interesting.

84. The manly republicanism of Harrington, though sometimes visionary and perhaps impracticable, shines Patriarcha
by comparison with a very opposite theory, which, of Filmer.
having been countenanced in the early part of the century by
our clergy, revived with additional favour after the Restoration. This was maintained in the Patriarcha of Sir Robert
Filmer, written, as it appears, in the reign of Charles I., but
not published till 1680, at a time when very high notions of
royal prerogative were as well received by one party as they
were indignantly rejected by another. The object, as the
author declares, was to prove that the first kings were fathers
of families; that it is unnatural for the people to govern or
to choose governors; that positive laws do not infringe the
natural and fatherly power of kings. He refers the tenet of
natural liberty and the popular origin of government to the
schoolmen, allowing that all papists and the reformed divines
have imbibed it, but denying that it is found in the fathers.
He seems, however, to claim the credit of an original hypothesis; those who have vindicated the rights of kings in
most points not having thought of this, but with one consent
admitted the natural liberty and equality of mankind. It is
certain, nevertheless, that the patriarchal theory of government as the basis of actual right was laid down as explicitly
as by himself in what is called Bishop Overall's Convocation
Book, at the beginning of the reign of James I. But this
book had not been published when Filmer wrote. His arguments are singularly insufficient; he quotes nothing but a
few irrelevant texts from Genesis; he seems not to have
known at all the strength, whatever it may be, of his own
case, and it is hardly possible to find a more trifling and
feeble work. It had however the advantage of opportunity
to be received by a party with approbation.

85. Algernon Sidney was the first who devoted his time to

---

[d] 'If I be worthy to give advice to
a man that would study politics, let him
understand Venice; he that understands
Venice right, shall go nearest to judge,
notwithstanding the difference that is in
every policy, right of any government
in the world.' Harrington's Works.
p. 292.

a refutation of this patriarchal theory, propounded as it was,
Sidney's Discourses on Government. not as a plausible hypothesis to explain the origin of civil communities, but as a paramount title, by virtue of which all actual sovereigns, who were not manifest usurpers, were to reign with an unmitigated despotism. Sidney's Discourses on Government, not published till 1698, are a diffuse reply to Filmer. They contain indeed many chapters full of historical learning and judicious reflection; yet the constant anxiety to refute that which needs no refutation renders them a little tedious. Sidney does not condemn a limited monarchy like the English, but his partiality is for a form of republic which would be deemed too aristocratical for our popular theories.

86. Locke, immediately after the Revolution, attacked the
Locke on Government. Patriarcha with more brevity, and laid down his own celebrated theory of government. The fundamental principle of Filmer is, that paternal authority is naturally absolute. Adam received it from God, exercised it over his own children, and transmitted it to the eldest born for ever. This assumption Locke combats rather too diffusely, according to our notions. Filmer had not only to show this absolute monarchy of a lineal ancestor, but his power of transmitting it in course of primogeniture. Locke denies that there is any natural right of this kind, maintaining the equality of children. The incapacity of Filmer renders his discomfiture not difficult. Locke, as will be seen, acknowledges a certain *de facto* authority in fathers of families, and possibly he might have found, as indeed he seems to admit, considerable traces of a regard to primogeniture in the early ages of the world. It is the question of natural right with which he is here concerned; and as no proof of this had been offered, he had nothing to answer.

87. In the second part of Locke's Treatise on Civil Government, he proceeds to lay down what he holds to be the true principles upon which society is founded. A state of nature is a state of perfect freedom and equality; but within the bounds of the law of nature, which obliges every one, and renders a state of liberty no state of licence. And the execution of this law, in such a state, is put into every one's hands, so that he may punish transgressors against it, not

merely by way of reparation for his own wrongs, but for those of others. ' Every offence that can be committed in the state of nature may, in the state of nature, be punished equally, and as far forth, as it may in a commonwealth.' And not only independent communities, but all men, as he thinks, till they voluntarily enter into some society, are in a state of nature.[e]

88. Whoever declares by word or action a settled design against another's life, puts himself in a state of war against him, and exposes his own life to be taken away, either by the other party, or by any one who shall espouse his cause. And he who endeavours to obtain absolute power over another may be construed to have a design on his life, or at least to take away his property. Where laws prevail, they must determine the punishment of those who injure others ; but if the law is silenced, it is hard to think but that the appeal to Heaven returns, and the aggressor may be treated as one in a state of war.[f]

89. Natural liberty is freedom from any superior power except the law of nature. Civil liberty is freedom from the dominion of any authority except that which a legislature, established by consent of the commonwealth, shall confirm. No man, according to Locke, can by his own consent enslave himself, or give power to another to take away his life. For slavery, in a strict sense, is but a continuance of the state of war between a conqueror and his captive.[g]

90. The excellent chapter on property which follows would be sufficient, if all Locke's other writings had perished, to leave him a high name in philosophy. Nothing can be more luminous than his deduction of the natural right of property from labour, not merely in gathering the fruits of the earth, or catching wild animals, but in the cultivation of land, for which occupancy is but the preliminary, and gives as it were an inchoate title. ' As much land as a man tills, plants, improves, cultivates, and can use the product of, so much is his property. He by his labour does, as it were, inclose it from the common.' Whatever is beyond the scanty limits of

---

[e] L. ii. c. 2.   [f] C. 3.   [g] C. 4.

individual or family labour, has been appropriated under the authority of civil society. But labour is the primary basis of natural right. Nor can it be thought unreasonable that labour should confer an exclusive right, when it is remembered how much of every thing's value depends upon labour alone. 'Whatever bread is more worth than acorns, wine than water, and cloth or silk than leaves, skins, or moss, that is wholly owing to labour and industry.' The superiority in good sense and satisfactory elucidation of his principle, which Locke has manifested in this important chapter over Grotius and Puffendorf, will strike those who consult those writers, or look at the brief sketch of their theories in the foregoing pages. It is no less contrasted with the puerile rant of Rousseau against all territorial property. That property owes its origin to occupancy accompanied with labour, is now generally admitted; the care of cattle being of course to be considered as one species of labour, and requiring at least a temporary ownership of the soil.[h]

91. Locke, after acutely remarking that the common arguments for the power of a father over his children would extend equally to the mother, so that it should be called parental power, reverts to the train of reasoning in the first book of this treatise against the regal authority of fathers. What they possess is not derived from generation, but from the care they necessarily take of the infant child, and during his minority; the power then terminates, though reverence, support, and even compliance are still due. Children are also held in subordination to their parents by the institutions of property, which commonly make them dependent both as to maintenance and succession. But Locke, which is worthy to be remarked, inclines to derive the origin of civil government from the patriarchal authority; one not strictly coercive, yet voluntarily conceded by habit and family consent. 'Thus the natural fathers of families, by an insensible change, became the politic monarchs of them too; and as they chanced to live long, and leave worthy and able heirs for several successions or otherwise, so they laid the foundations of hereditary or elective kingdoms.'[i]

---

[h] C. 5.   [i] C. 6.

92. The necessity that man should not live alone, produced the primary society of husband and wife, parent and
children, to which that of master and servant was early
added; whether of freemen engaging their service for hire,
or of slaves taken in just war, who are by the right of nature
subject to the absolute dominion of the captor. Such a family
may sometimes resemble a little commonwealth by its numbers, but is essentially distinct from one, because its chief
has no imperial power of life and death except over his
slaves, nature having given him none over his children,
though all men have a right to punish breaches of the law of
nature in others according to the offence. But this natural
power they quit and resign into the hands of the community,
when civil society is instituted; and it is in this union of the
several rights of its members that the legislative right of the
commonwealth consists, whether this be done by general consent at the first formation of government, or by the adhesion
which any individual may give to one already established.
By either of these ways men pass from a state of nature to
one of political society, the magistrate having now that power
to redress injuries, which had previously been each man's
right. Hence absolute monarchy, in Locke's opinion, is no
form of civil government; for there being no common authority to appeal to, the sovereign is still in a state of nature
with regard to his subjects.[k]

93. A community is formed by the unanimous consent of
any body of men; but when thus become one body, the
determination of the majority must bind the rest, else it
would not be one. Unanimity, after a community is once
formed, can no longer be required; but this consent of men
to form a civil society is that which alone did or could give
beginning to any lawful government in the world. It is idle
to object that we have no records of such an event; for few
commonwealths preserve the tradition of their own infancy;
and whatever we do know of the origin of particular states
gives indications of this mode of union. Yet he again inclines
to deduce the usual origin of civil societies from imitation of

[k] C. 7.

patriarchal authority, which having been recognised by each family in the arbitration of disputes and even punishment of offences, was transferred with more readiness to some one person, as the father and representative head of the infant community. He even admits that this authority might tacitly devolve upon the eldest son. Thus the first governments were monarchies, and those with no express limitations of power, till exposure of its abuse gave occasion to social laws, or to co-ordinate authority. In all this he follows Hooker, from the first book of whose Ecclesiastical Polity he quotes largely in his notes.[m]

94. A difficulty commonly raised against the theory of compact is, that all men being born under some government, they cannot be at liberty to erect a new one, or even to make choice whether they will obey or no. This objection Locke does not meet, like Hooker and the jurists, by supposing the agreement of a distant ancestor to oblige all his posterity. But explicitly acknowledging that nothing can bind freemen to obey any government save their own consent, he rests the evidence of a tacit consent on the enjoyment of land, or even on mere residence within the dominions of the community; every man being at liberty to relinquish his possessions, or change his residence, and either incorporate himself with another commonwealth, or, if he can find an opportunity, set up for himself in some unoccupied part of the world. But nothing can make a man irrevocably a member of one society, except his own voluntary declaration; such perhaps as the oath of allegiance, which Locke does not mention, ought to be reckoned.[n]

95. The majority having, in the first constitution of a state, the whole power, may retain it themselves, or delegate it to one or more persons.[o] And the supreme power is, in other words, the legislature, sacred and unalterable in the hands where the community have once placed it, without which no law can exist, and in which all obedience terminates. Yet this legislative authority itself is not absolute or arbitrary over the lives and fortunes of its subjects. It is the joint power of individuals surrendered to the state; but no man

---

[m] C. 8.   [n] Id.   [o] C. 10.

has power over his own life or his neighbour's property. The laws enacted by the legislature must be conformable to the will of God, or natural justice. Nor can it take any part of the subject's property without his own consent, or that of the majority. 'For if any one shall claim a power to lay and levy taxes on the people by his own authority, and without such consent of the people, he thereby invades the fundamental law of property, and subverts the end of government. For what property have I in that which another may by right take, when he pleases, to himself?' Lastly, the legislative power is inalienable; being but delegated from the people, it cannot be transferred to others.[p] This is the part of Locke's treatise which has been open to most objection, and which in some measure seems to charge with usurpation all the established governments of Europe. It has been a theory fertile of great revolutions, and perhaps pregnant with more. In some part of this chapter also, though by no means in the most practical corollaries, the language of Hooker has led onward his more hardy disciple.

96. Though the legislative power is alone supreme in the constitution, it is yet subject to the people themselves, who may alter it whenever they find that it acts against the trust reposed in it; all power given in trust for a particular end being evidently forfeited when that end is manifestly disregarded or obstructed. But while the government subsists the legislature is alone sovereign, though it may be the usage to call a single executive magistrate sovereign, if he has also a share in legislation. Where this is not the case, the appellation is plainly improper. Locke has in this chapter a remarkable passage, one perhaps of the first declarations in favour of a change in the electoral system of England. 'To what gross absurdities the following of custom, when reason has left it, may lead, we may be satisfied when we see the bare name of a town, of which there remains not so much as the ruins, where scarce so much housing as a sheepcote or more inhabitants than a shepherd is to be found, send as many representatives to the grand assembly of law-makers as a whole county, numerous in people, and powerful in riches.

p C. 11.

This strangers stand amazed at, and every one must confess needs a remedy, though most think it hard to find one, because the constitution of the legislative being the original and supreme act of the society, antecedent to all positive laws in it, and depending wholly on the people, no inferior power can alter it.' But Locke is less timid about a remedy, and suggests that the executive magistrate might regulate the number of representatives, not according to old custom but reason, which is not setting up a new legislature, but restoring an old one. 'Whatsoever shall be done manifestly for the good of the people and the establishing the government on its true foundation, is, and always will be, just prerogative;'[q] a maxim of too dangerous latitude for a constitutional monarchy.

97. Prerogative he defines to be 'a power of acting according to discretion for the public good without the prescription of the law, and sometimes even against it.' This, however, is not by any means a good definition in the eyes of a lawyer; and the word, being merely technical, ought not to have been employed in so partial if not so incorrect a sense. Nor is it very precise to say, that in England the prerogative was always largest in the hands of our wisest and best princes, not only because the fact is otherwise, but because he confounds the legal prerogative with its actual exercise. This chapter is the most loosely reasoned of any in the treatise.[r]

98. Conquest, in an unjust war, can give no right at all, unless robbers and pirates may acquire a right. Nor is any one bound by promises which unjust force extorts from him. If we are not strong enough to resist, we have no remedy save patience; but our children may appeal to Heaven, and repeat their appeals till they recover their ancestral right, which was to be governed by such a legislation as themselves approve. He that appeals to Heaven must be sure that he has right on his side, and right too that is worth the trouble and cost of his appeal, as he will answer at a tribunal that cannot be deceived. Even just conquest gives no further right than to reparation of injury; and the posterity of the vanquished, he seems to hold, can forfeit nothing by their

---

[q] C. 13.   [r] C. 14.

parent's offence, so that they have always a right to throw off
the yoke. The title of prescription, which has commonly
been admitted to silence the complaints, if not to heal the
wounds, of the injured, finds no favour with Locke.[s] But
hence it seems to follow that no state composed, as most have
been, out of the spoils of conquest, can exercise a legitimate
authority over the latest posterity of those it has incorporated. Wales, for instance, has an eternal right to shake
off the yoke of England; for what Locke says of consent to
laws by representatives, is of little weight when these must
be outnumbered in the general legislature of both countries;
and indeed the first question for the Cambro-Britons would
be to determine whether they would form part of such a
common legislation.

99. Usurpation, which is a kind of domestic conquest, gives
no more right to obedience than unjust war; it is necessary
that the people should both be at liberty to consent, and have
actually consented to allow and confirm a power which the
constitution of their commonwealth does not recognise.[t] But
tyranny may exist without usurpation, whenever the power
reposed in any one's hands for the people's benefit is abused
to their impoverishment or slavery. Force may never be
opposed but to unjust and unlawful force : in any other case,
it is condemned before God and man. The king's person is
in some countries sacred by law; but this, as Locke thinks,
does not extend to the case where, by putting himself in a
state of war with his people, he dissolves the government.[u]
A prince dissolves the government by ruling against law, by
hindering the regular assembly of the legislature, by chang-
ing the form of election, or by rendering the people subject
to a foreign power. He dissolves it also by neglecting or
abandoning it, so that the laws cannot be put into execution.
The government is also dissolved by breach of trust in either
the legislature or the prince; by the former when it usurps
an arbitrary power over the lives, liberties, and fortunes of
the subject; by the latter, when he endeavours to corrupt
the representatives or to influence the choice of the electors.
If it be objected that no government will be able long to

---

[s] C. 16   [t] C. 17.   [u] C. 18.

subsist, if the people may set up a new legislature whenever they take offence at the old one, he replies that mankind are too slow and averse to quit their old institutions for this danger to be apprehended. Much will be endured from rulers without mutiny or murmur. Nor is anything more likely to restrain governments than this doctrine of the right of resistance. It is as reasonable to tell men they should not defend themselves against robbers, because it may occasion disorder, as to use the same argument for passive obedience to illegal dominion. And he observes, after quoting some other writers, that Hooker alone might be enough to satisfy those who rely on him for their ecclesiastical polity.[x]

100. Such is, in substance, the celebrated treatise of Locke Observations on civil government, which, with the favour of poli-
on this trea-
tise.   tical circumstances, and the authority of his name, became the creed of a numerous party at home; while silently spreading the fibres from its root over Europe and America, it prepared the way for theories of political society, hardly bolder in their announcement, but expressed with more passionate ardour, from which the great revolutions of the last and present age have sprung. But as we do not launch our bark upon a stormy sea, we shall merely observe that neither the Revolution of 1688, nor the administration of William III., could have borne the test by which Locke has tried the legitimacy of government. There was certainly no appeal to the people in the former, nor would it have been convenient for the latter to have had the maxim established, that an attempt to corrupt the legislature entails a forfeiture of the intrusted power. Whether the opinion of Locke, that mankind are slow to political change, be conformable to an enlarged experience, must be judged by every one according to his reading and observation; it is at least very different from that which Hooker, to whom he defers so greatly in most of his doctrine, has uttered in the very first sentence of his Ecclesiastical Polity. For my own part I must confess, that in these latter chapters of Locke on Government I see, what sometimes appears in his other writings, that the influence of temporary circumstances on a mind a little too susceptible

---

[x] C. 19.

of passion and resentment, had prevented that calm and
patient examination of all the bearings of this extensive subject which true philosophy requires.

101. But whatever may be our judgment of this work, it
is equally true that it opened a new era of political opinion
in Europe. The earlier writings on the side of popular
sovereignty, whether those of Buchanan and Languet, of the
Jesuits, or of the English republicans, had been either too
closely dependent on temporary circumstances, or too much
bound up with odious and unsuccessful factions, to sink very
deep into the hearts of mankind. Their adversaries, with
the countenance of every government on their side, kept
possession of the field; and no later jurist, nor theologian,
nor philosopher on the continent, while they generally followed their predecessors in deriving the origin of civil society
from compact, ventured to moot the delicate problem of
resistance to tyranny, or of the right to reform a constitution,
except in the most cautious and indefinite language. We
have seen this already in Grotius and Puffendorf. But the
success of the English Revolution, the necessity which the
powers allied against France found of maintaining the title
of William, the peculiar interest of Holland and Hanover
(states at that time very strong in the literary world) in our
new scheme of government, gave a weight and authority to
principles which, without some such application, it might
still have been thought seditious to propound. Locke too,
long an exile in Holland, was intimate with Le Clerc, who
exerted a considerable influence over the Protestant part of
Europe. Barbeyrac, some time afterwards, trod nearly in
the same steps, and without going all the lengths of Locke,
did not fail to take a very different tone from the two older
writers upon whom he has commented.

102. It was very natural that the French Protesants, among
whom traditions of a turn of thinking not the most
favourable to kings may have been preserved, should,
in the hour of severe persecution, mutiny in words
and writings against the despotism that oppressed them.
Such, it appears, had been the language of those exiles, as it
is of all exiles, when an anonymous tract, entitled Avis aux
Refugiéz, was published with the date of Amsterdam, in 1690.

Avis aux Refugiéz, perhaps by Bayle.

This, under pretext of giving advice, in the event of their being permitted to return home, that they should get rid of their spirit of satire, and of their republican theories, is a bitter and able attack on those who had taken refuge in Holland. It asserts the principle of passive obedience, extolling also the King of France and his government, and censuring the English Revolution. Public rumour ascribed this to Bayle; it has usually passed for his, and is even inserted in the collection of his miscellaneous works. Some, however, have ascribed it to Pelisson, and others to Larroque; one already, and the other soon after, proselytes to the church of Rome. Basnage thought it written by the latter, and published by Bayle, to whom he ascribed the preface. This is apparently in a totally opposite strain, but not without strong suspicion of irony or ill faith. The style and manner of the whole appear to suggest Bayle; and though the supposition is very discreditable to his memory, the weight of presumption seems much to incline that way.

103. The separation of political economy from the general science which regards the well-being of communities, was not so strictly made by the earlier philosophers as in modern times. It does not follow that national wealth engaged none of their attention. Few, on the contrary, of those who have taken comprehensive views could have failed to regard it. In Bodin, Botero, Bacon, Hobbes, Puffendorf, we have already seen proofs of this. These may be said to have discussed the subject, not systematically, nor always with thorough knowledge, but with acuteness and in a philosophical tone. Others there were of a more limited range, whose habits of life and experience led them to particular departments of economical inquiry, especially as to commerce, the precious metals, and the laws affecting them. The Italians led the way; Serra has been mentioned in the last period, and a few more might find a place in this. De Witt's Interest of Holland can hardly be reckoned among economical writings; and it is said by Morhof, that the Dutch were not fond of promulgating their commercial knowledge;[y] little at least was contributed from that country, even at a later period,

Political economists.

---

[y] Polyhistor, part iii. lib. iii. § 3.

towards the theory of becoming rich. But England now took a large share in this new literature. Free, inquisitive, thriving rapidly in commerce, so that her progress even in the nineteenth century has hardly been in a greater ratio than before and after the middle of the seventeenth, if we may trust the statements of contemporaries, she produced some writers who, though few of them merit the name of philosophers, yet may not here be overlooked, on account of their influence, their reputation, or their position as links in the chain of science.

104. The first of these was Thomas Mun, an intelligent merchant in the earlier part of the century, whose posthumous treatise, England's Treasure by Foreign Trade, was published in 1664, but seems to have been written soon after the accession of Charles I.[z] Mun is generally reckoned the founder of what has been called the mercantile system. His main position is that ' the ordinary means to increase our wealth and treasure is by foreign trade, wherein we must ever observe this rule, to sell more to strangers yearly than we consume of theirs in value.'[a] We must therefore sell as cheap as possible ; it was by underselling the Venetians of late years, that we had exported a great deal of cloth to Turkey.[b] It is singular that Mun should not have perceived the difficulty of selling very cheap the productions of a country's labour, whose gold and silver were in great abundance. He was, however, too good a merchant not to acknowledge the inefficacy and impolicy of restraining by law the exportation of coin, which is often a means of increasing our treasure in the long run ; advising instead a due regard to the balance of trade, or general surplus of exported goods, by which we shall infallibly obtain a stock of gold and silver. These notions have long since been covered with ridicule ; and it is plain that, in a merely economical view, they must always be delusive. Mun, however, looked to the accumulation of a portion of this imported treasure by the state ; a resource in critical emergencies which we have

Mun on foreign trade.

---

[z] Mr. M'Culloch says (Introductory Discourse to Smith's Wealth of Nations) it had most probably been written about 1635 or 1640. I remarked some things which serve to carry it up a little higher.

[a] P. 11 (edit. 1664).
[b] P. 18.

now learned to despise, since others have been at hand, but
which in reality had made a great difference in the events of
war, and changed the balance of power between many commonwealths.   Mun was followed, about 1670, by Sir Josiah
Child, in a discourse on Trade, written on the same
principles of the mercantile system, bu   more
copious and varied.   The chief aim of Child is to effect a
reduction of the legal interest of money from six to four per
cent., drawing an erroneous inference from the increase of
wealth which had followed similar enactments.

Child on
Trade.

105. Among the many difficulties with which the government of William III. had to contend, one of the
most embarrassing was the scarcity of the precious
metals and depreciated condition of the coin.   This opened
the whole field of controversy in that province of political
economy; and the bold spirit of inquiry, unshackled by
prejudice in favour of ancient custom, which in all respects
was characteristic of that age, began to work by reasonings
on general theorems, instead of collecting insulated and
inconclusive details.   Locke stood forward on this, as on so
many subjects, with his masculine sense and habitual closeness of thinking.   His ' Considerations of the Consequences
of lowering Interest, and raising the Value of Money ' were
published in 1691.   Two further treatises are in answer to
the pamphlets of Lowndes.   These economical writings of
Locke are not in all points conformable to the modern
principles of the science.   He seems to incline rather too
much towards the mercantile theory, and to lay too much
stress on the possession of the precious metals.   From his
excellent sense, however, as well as from some expressions, I
should conceive that he only considers them, as they doubtless are, a portion of the exchangeable wealth of the nation,
and by their inconsumable nature, as well as by the constancy
of the demand for them, one of the most important.
' Riches do not consist,' he says, ' in having more gold and
silver, but in having more in proportion than the rest of the
world or than our neighbours, whereby we are enabled to
procure to ourselves a greater plenty of the conveniences of
life.'

Locke on
the Coin.

106. Locke had the sagacity to perceive the impossibility

of regulating the interest of money by law. It was an empirical proposition at that time, as we have just seen, of Sir Josiah Child, to render loans more easy to the borrower by reducing the legal rate to four per cent. The whole drift of his reasoning is against any limitation, though, from fear of appearing too paradoxical, he does not arrive at that inference. For the reasons he gives in favour of a legal limit of interest, namely, that courts of law may have some rule where nothing is stipulated in the contract, and that a few money lenders in the metropolis may not have the monopoly of all loans in England, are, especially the first, so trifling, that he could not have relied upon them ; and indeed he admits that, in other circumstances, there would be no danger from the second. But his prudence, having restrained him from speaking out, a famous writer almost a century afterwards came forward to assert a paradox, which he loved the better for seeming such, and finally to convince the thinking part of mankind.

107 Laws fixing the value of silver Locke perceived to be nugatory, and is averse to prohibiting its exportation. The value of money, he maintains, does not depend on the rate of interest, but on its plenty relatively to commodities. Hence the rate of interest, he thinks, but perhaps erroneously, does not govern the price of land ; arguing from the higher rate of land relatively to money, that is, the worst interest it gave, in the reigns of Elizabeth and James, than in his own time. But one of Locke's positions, if generally received, would alone have sufficed to lower the value of land. ' It is in vain,' he says, ' in a country whose great fund is land, to hope to lay the public charges of the government on any thing else ; there at last it will terminate.' The legislature soon proceeded to act on this mistaken theory in the annual land-tax ; an impost of tremendous severity at that time, the gross unfairness, however, of which has been compensated in later times by the taxes on personal succession.

108. In such a monetary crisis as that of his time, Locke was naturally obliged to consider the usual resource of raising the denomination of the coin. This, he truly says, would be to rob all creditors of such a proportion of their debts. It is probable that his influence, which was very con-

siderable, may have put a stop to the scheme. He contends
in his Further Considerations, in answer to a tract by
Lowndes, that clipped money should go only by weight.
This seems to have been agreed by both parties ; but Lowndes
thought the loss should be defrayed by a tax, Locke that it
should fall on the holders. Honourably for the government,
the former opinion prevailed.

109. The Italians were the first who laid any thing like a
Statistical tracts. foundation for statistics or political arithmetic ; that
which is to the political economist what general
history is to the philosopher. But their numerical reckon-
ings of population, houses, value of lands or stock, and the
like, though very curious, and sometimes taken from public
documents, were not always more than conjectural, nor are
they so full and minute as the spirit of calculation demands.
England here again took the lead, in Graunt's Observations
on the Bills of Mortality, 1661, in Petty's Political Arithmetic (posthumous in 1691), and other treatises of the same
ingenious and philosophical person, and, we may add, in the
Observations of Gregory King on the Natural and Political
State of England ; for though these were not published till
near the end of the eighteenth century, the manuscripts had
fallen into the hands of Dr. Charles Davenant, who has made
extracts from them in his own valuable contributions to
political arithmetic. King seems to have possessed a sagacity which has sometimes brought his conjectures nearer to
the mark, than from the imperfection of his data it was
reasonable to expect. Yet he supposes that the population
of England, which he estimated, perhaps rightly, at five
millions and a half, would not reach the double of that number before A.D. 2300. Sir William Petty, with a mind
capable of just and novel theories, was struck by the necessary consequences of an uniformly progressive population.
Though the rate of movement seemed to him, as in truth it
then was, much slower than we have latterly found it, he
clearly saw that its continuance would in an ascertainable
length of time overload the world. 'And then, according to
the prediction of the Scriptures, there must be wars and
great slaughter.' He conceived that, in the ordinary course
of things, the population of a country would be doubled in

two hundred years; but the whole conditions of the problem were far less understood than at present. Davenant's Essay on Ways and Means, 1693, gained him a high reputation, which he endeavoured to augment by many subsequent works, some falling within the seventeenth century. He was a man of more enlarged reading than his predecessors, with the exception of Petty, and of close attention to the statistical documents which were now more copiously published than before; but he seldom launches into any extensive theory, confining himself rather to the accumulation of facts and to the immediate inferences, generally for temporary purposes, which they supplied.

SECT. III.—ON JURISPRUDENCE.

110. IN 1667, a short book was published at Frankfort, by a young man of twenty-two years, entitled Methodi Novæ discendæ docendæque Jurisprudentiæ. The science which of all others had been deemed to require the most protracted labour, the ripest judgment, the most experienced discrimination, was, as it were, invaded by a boy, but by one who had the genius of an Alexander, and for whom the glories of an Alexander were reserved. This is the first production of Leibnitz; and it is probably in many points of view the most remarkable work that has prematurely united erudition and solidity. We admire in it the vast range of learning (for though he could not have read all the books he names, there is evidence of his acquaintance with a great number, and at least with a well-filled chart of literature), the originality of some ideas, the commanding and comprehensive views he embraces, the philosophical spirit, the compressed style in which it is written, the entire absence of juvenility, of ostentatious paradox,[c] of imagina-

Works of Leibnitz on Roman law.

---

[c] I use the epithet ostentatious, because some of his original theories are a little paradoxical; thus he has a singular notion that the right of bequeathing property by testament is derived from the immortality of the soul; the living heirs being as it were the attorneys of those we suppose to be dead. Quia mortui revera adhuc vivunt, ideo manent domini rerum, quos vero hæredes reliquerunt, concipiendi sunt ut procuratores in rem suam. In our own discussions on the law of entail, I am not aware that this argument has ever been explicitly urged, though the advocates of perpetual control seem to have none better.

tion, ardour, and enthusiasm, which, though Leibnitz did not always want them, would have been wholly misplaced on such a subject. Faults have been censured in this early performance, and the author declared himself afterwards dissatisfied with it.[d]

111. Leibnitz was a passionate admirer of the Roman jurisprudence; he held the great lawyers of antiquity second only to the best geometers for strong, and subtle, and profound reasoning; not even acknowledging, to any considerable degree, the contradictions (antinomiæ juris) which had perplexed their disciples in later times, and on which many volumes had been written. But the arrangement of Justinian he entirely disapproved; and in another work, Corporis Juris reconcinnandi Ratio, published in 1668, he pointed out the necessity and what he deemed the best method of a new distribution. This appears to be not quite like what he had previously sketched, and which was rather a philosophical than a very convenient method;[e] in this new arrangement, he proposes to retain the texts of the Corpus Juris Civilis, but in a form rather like that of the Pandects than of the Institutes; to the latter of which, followed as it has been among us by Hale and Blackstone, he was very averse.

112. There was only one man in the world who could have left so noble a science as philosophical jurisprudence for pursuits of a still more exalted nature, and for which he was still more fitted; and that man was Leibnitz himself. He passed onward to reap the golden harvests of other fields. Yet the study of law has owed much to him; he did much to unite it with moral philosophy on the one hand, and with history on the other; a great master of both, he exacted perhaps a more comprehensive course of legal studies than

---

[d] This tract, and all the other works of Leibnitz on jurisprudence, will be found in the fourth volume of his works by Dutens. An analysis by Bon, professor of law at Turin, is prefixed to the Methodi Novæ, and he has pointed out a few errors. Leibnitz says in a letter, about 1676, that his book was effusus potius quam scriptus,· in itinere, sine libris, &c., and that it contained some things he no longer would have said,

though there were others of which he did not repent. Lerminier, Hist. du Droit, p. 150.

[e] In his Methodi Novæ he divides law, in the didactic part, according to the several sources of rights; namely, 1. Nature, which gives us right over res nullius, things where there is no prior property. 2. Succession. 3. Possession. 4. Contract. 5. Injury, which gives right to reparation.

the capacity of ordinary lawyers could grasp. In England also, its conduciveness to professional excellence might be hard to prove. It is however certain that in Germany at least, philology, history, and philosophy have more or less since the time of Leibnitz marched together under the robe of law. 'He did but pass over that kingdom,' says Lerminier, 'and he has reformed and enlarged it.' [f]

113. James Godefroy was thirty years engaged on an edition of the Theodosian Code, published several years after his death, in 1665. It is by far the best edition of that body of laws, and retains a standard value in the historical department of jurisprudence. Domat, a French lawyer, and one of the Port-Royal connexion, in his Loix Civiles dans leur Ordre Naturel, the first of five volumes of which appeared in 1689, carried into effect the project of Leibnitz, by re-arranging the laws of Justinian, which, especially the Pandects, are well known to be confusedly distributed, in a more regular method, prefixing a book of his own on the nature and spirit of law in general. This appears to be an useful digest or abridgment, something like those made by Viner and earlier writers of our own text-books, but perhaps with more compression and choice; two editions of an English translation were published. Domat's Public Law, which might, perhaps, in our language, have been called constitutional, since we generally confine the epithet public to the law of nations, forms a second part of the same work, and contains a more extensive system, wherein theological morality, ecclesiastical ordinances, and the fundamental laws of the French monarchy are reduced into method. Domat is much extolled by his countrymen; but in philosophical jurisprudence, he seems to display little force or originality. Gravina, who obtained a high name in this literature at the beginning of the next century, was known merely as a professor at the close of this; but a Dutch jurist, Gerard Noodt, may deserve mention for his treatise on Usury, in 1698, wherein he both endeavours to prove its natural and religious lawfulness, and traces its history through the Roman law. Several other

Civil Jurists —Godefroy, Domat.

Noodt on Usury.

---

[f] Biogr. univ. Lerminier, Hist. du Droit, p. 142.

works of Noodt on subjects of historical jurisprudence seem
to fall within this century, though I do not find their exact
dates of publication.

114. Grotius was the acknowledged master of all who
Law of   studied the theory of international right. It was,
Nations.—
Puffendorf. perhaps, the design of Puffendorf, as we may conjecture by the title of his great work on the Law of Nature
and Nations, to range over the latter field with as assi-
duous diligence as the former. But from the length of his
prolix labour on natural law and the rights of sovereigns, he
has not more than one-twentieth of the whole volume to
spare for international questions; and this is in great measure
copied or abridged from Grotius. In some instances he dis-
agrees with his master. Puffendorf singularly denies that
compacts made during war are binding by the law of nature,
but for weak and unintelligible reasons.[g] Treaties of peace
extorted by unjust force, he denies with more reason to be
binding ; though Grotius had held the contrary.[h] The
inferior writers on the law of nations, or those who, like
Wicquefort, in his Ambassador, confined themselves to
merely conventional usages, it is needless to mention.

---

[g] B. viii. chap. 7.   [h] Chap. 8.

CHAPTER V.

HISTORY OF POETRY, FROM 1650 TO 1700.

Sect. I.—On Italian Poetry.

Filicaja—Guidi—Menzini Arcadian Society.

1. The imitators of Marini, full of extravagant metaphors, and the false thoughts usually called *concetti*, were in their vigour at the commencement of this period. But their names are now obscure, and have been overwhelmed by the change of public taste, which has condemned and proscribed what it once most applauded. This change came on long before the close of the century, though not so decidedly but that some traces of the former manner are discoverable in the majority of popular writers. The general characteristics, however, of Italian poetry were now a more masculine tone ; a wider reach of topics, and a selection of the most noble ; an abandonment, except in the lighter lyrics, of amatory strains, and especially of such as were languishing and querulous ; an anticipation, in short as far as the circumstances of the age would permit, of that severe and elevated style which has been most affected for the last fifty years. It would be futile to seek an explanation of this manlier spirit in any social or political causes ; never had Italy in these respects been so lifeless ; but the world of poets is often not the world around them, and their stream of living waters may flow, like that of Arethusa, without imbibing much from the surrounding brine. Chiabrera had led the way by the Pindaric majesty of his odes, and had disciples of at least equal name with himself.

Improved tone of Italian poetry.

2. Florence was the mother of one who did most to invigo-
rate Italian poetry, Vincenzo Filicaja; a man gifted
Filicaja.   with a serious, pure, and noble spirit, from which
congenial thoughts spontaneously arose, and with an imagination rather vigorous than fertile. The siege of Vienna in
1683, and its glorious deliverance by Sobieski, are the subjects
of six odes. The third of these, addressed to the King of
Poland himself, is generally most esteemed, though I do not
perceive that the first or second are inferior. His ode to
Rome, on Christina's taking up her residence there, is in
many parts highly poetical; but the flattery of representing
this event as sufficient to restore the eternal city from decay
is too gross. It is not on the whole so successful as those on
the siege of Vienna. A better is that addressed to Florence,
on leaving it for a rural solitude, in consequence of his poverty
and the neglect he had experienced. It breathes an injured
spirit, something like the Complaint of Cowley, with which
posterity are sure to sympathise. The sonnet of Filicaja,
'Italia mia,' is known by every one who cares for this poetry
at all. This sonnet is conspicuous for its depth of feeling,
for the spirit of its commencement, and above all, for the
noble lines with which it ends; but there are surely awkward
and feeble expressions in the intermediate part. *Armenti* for
regiments of dragoons could only be excused by frequent
usage in poetry, which, I presume, is not the case, though we
find the same word in one of Filicaja's odes. A foreigner may
venture upon this kind of criticism.

3. Filicaja was formed in the school of Chiabrera; but with
his pomp of sound and boldness of imagery he is animated by
a deeper sense both of religion and patriotism. We perceive
more the language of the heart; the man speaks in his
genuine character, not with assumed and mercenary sensibility, like that of Pindar and Chiabrera. His genius is
greater than his skill; he abandons himself to an impetuosity
which he cannot sustain, forgetful of the economy of strength
and breath, as necessary for a poet as a racehorse. He has
rarely or never any conceits or frivolous thoughts, but the
expression is sometimes rather feeble. There is a general
want of sunshine in Filicaja's poetry; unprosperous himself,
he views nothing with a worldly eye; his notes of triumph

are without brilliancy, his predictions of success are without
joy. He seems also deficient in the charms of grace and
felicity. But his poetry is always the effusion of a fine soul ;
we venerate and love Filicaja as a man, but we also acknowledge that he was a real poet.

4. Guidi, a native of Pavia, raised himself to the highest
point that any lyric poet of Italy has attained. His
odes are written at Rome from about the year 1685 Guidi.
to the end of the century. Compared with Chiabrera, or even
Filicaja, he may be allowed the superiority ; if he never rises
to a higher pitch than the latter, if he has never chosen
subjects so animating, if he has never displayed so much
depth and truth of feeling, his enthusiasm is more constant,
his imagination more creative, his power of language more
extensive and more felicitous. ' He falls sometimes,' says
Corniani, ' into extravagance, but never into affectation. . . .
His peculiar excellence is poetical expression, always brilliant
with a light of his own. The magic of his language used to
excite a lively movement among the hearers when he recited
his verses in the Arcadian society.' Corniani adds that he
is sometimes exuberant in words and hyperbolical in images.[1]

5. The ode of Guidi on Fortune appears to me at least
equal to any in the Italian language. If it has been suggested
by that of Celio Magno, entitled Iddio, the resemblance does
not deserve the name of imitation ; a nobleness of thought,
imagery, and language prevails throughout. But this is the
character of all his odes. He chose better subjects than
Chiabrera ; for the ruins of Rome are more glorious than the
living house of Medici. He resembles him, indeed, rather
than any other poet, so that it might not always be easy to
discern one from the other in a single stanza ; but Guidi is a
bolder, a more imaginative, a more enthusiastic poet. Both
adorn and amplify a little to excess ; and it may be imputed
to Guidi that he has abused an advantage which his native
language afforded. The Italian is rich in words, where the
sound so well answers to the meaning, that it is hardly possible to hear them without an associated sentiment ; their
effect is closely analogous to musical expression. Such are

[1] Vol. viii. p. 224.

the adjectives denoting mental elevation, as *superbo, altiero, audace, gagliardo, indomito, maestoso*. These recur in the poems of Guidi with every noun that will admit of them; but sometimes the artifice is a little too transparent, and though the meaning is not sacrificed to sound, we feel that it is too much enveloped in it, and are not quite pleased that a great poet should rely so much on a resource which the most mechanical slave of music can employ.

6. The odes of Benedetto Menzini are elegant and in poetical language, but such as does not seem very original, nor do they strike us by much vigour or animation of thought. The allusions to mythology, which we never find in Filicaja, and rarely in Guidi, are too frequent. Some of these odes are of considerable beauty among which we may distinguish that addressed to Magalotti, beginning, ' Un verde ramuscello in piaggia aprica.' Menzini was far from confining himself to this species of poetry; he was better known in others. As an Anacreontic poet he stands, I believe, only below Chiabrera and Redi. His satires have been preferred by some to those of Ariosto; but neither Corniani nor Salfi acquiesce in this praise. Their style is a mixture of obsolete phrases from Dante with the idioms of the Florentine populace; and, though spirited in substance, they are rather full of commonplace invective. Menzini strikes boldly at priests and governments and, what was dangerous to Orpheus, at the whole sex of women. His Art of Poetry, in five books, published in 1681, deserves some praise. As his atrabilious humour prompted, he inveighs against the corruption of contemporary literature, especially on the stage, ridiculing also the Pindaric pomp that some affected, not perhaps without allusion to his enemy Guidi. His own style is pointed, animated, sometimes poetical, where didactic verse will admit of such ornament, but a little too diffuse and minute in criticism.

Menzini.

7. These three are the great restorers of Italian poetry after the usurpation of false taste. And it is to be observed that they introduced a new manner, very different from that of the sixteenth century. Several others deserve to be mentioned, though we can only do so briefly. The Satires of Salvator Rosa, full of force and

Salvator Rosa—Redi.

vehemence, more vigorous than elegant, are such as his ardent genius and rather savage temper would lead us to expect. A far superior poet was a man not less eminent than Salvator, the philosophical and every way accomplished Redi. Few have done so much in any part of science who have also shone so brightly in the walks of taste. The sonnets of Redi are esteemed; but his famous dithyrambic, Bacco in Toscana, is admitted to be the first poem of that kind in modern language, and is as worthy of Monte Pulciano wine as the wine is worthy of it.

8. Maggi and Lemene bore an honourable part in the restoration of poetry, though neither of them is reckoned altogether to have purified himself from the infection of the preceding age. The sonnet of Pastorini on the imagined resistance of Genoa to the oppression of Louis XIV. in 1684, though not borne out by historical truth, is one of those breathings of Italian nationality which we always admire, and which had now become more common than for a century before. It must be confessed, in general, that when the protestations of a people against tyranny become loud enough to be heard, we may suspect that the tyranny has been relaxed. *Other poets.*

9. Rome was to poetry in this age what Florence had once been, though Rome had hitherto done less for the Italian muses than any other great city. Nor was this so much due to her bishops and cardinals, as to a stranger and a woman. Christina finally took up her abode there in 1688. Her palace became the resort of all the learning and genius she could assemble round her; a literary academy was established, and her revenue was liberally dispensed in pensions. If Filicaja and Guidi, both sharers of her bounty, have exaggerated her praises, much may be pardoned to gratitude, and much also to the natural admiration which those who look up to power must feel for those who have renounced it. Christina died in 1690, and her own academy could last no longer; but a phœnix sprang at once from its ashes. Crescimbeni, then young, has the credit of having planned the Society of Arcadians, which began in 1690, and has eclipsed in celebrity most of the earlier academies of Italy. Fourteen, says *Christina's patronage of letters.* *Society of Arcadians.*

Corniani, were the original founders of this society; among whom were Crescimbeni, and Gravina, and Zappi. In course of time the Arcadians vastly increased, and established colonies in the chief cities of Italy. They determined to assume every one a pastoral name and a Greek birthplace, to hold their meetings in some verdant meadow, and to mingle with all their compositions, as far as possible, images from pastoral life; images always agreeable, because they recall the times of primitive innocence. This poetical tribe adopted as their device the pipe of seven reeds bound with laurel, and their president or director was denominated general shepherd or keeper (custode generale).[k] The fantastical part of the Arcadian society was common to them with all similar institutions; and mankind has generally required some ceremonial follies to keep alive the wholesome spirit of association. Their solid aim was to purify the national taste. Much had been already done, and in great measure by their own members, Menzini and Guidi; but their influence, which was of course more felt in the next century, has always been reckoned both important and auspicious to Italian literature.

Sect. II.—On French Poetry.

La Fontaine—Boileau—Minor French Poets.

10. WE must pass over Spain and Portugal as absolutely
La Fontaine. destitute of any name which requires commemoration. In France it was very different; if some earlier periods had been not less rich in the number of versifiers, none had produced poets who have descended with so much renown to posterity. The most popular of these was La Fontaine. Few writers have left such a number of verses which, in the phrase of his country, have made their fortune, and been like ready money, always at hand for prompt quotation. His lines have at once a pro-

---

[k] Corniani, viii. 301. Tiraboschi, xi. 43. Crescimbeni, Storia d'Arcadia (reprinted by Mathias).

verbial truth and a humour of expression which render them
constantly applicable.   This is chiefly true of his Fables; for
his Tales, though no one will deny that they are lively
enough, are not reckoned so well written, nor do they supply
so much for general use.

11. The models of La Fontaine's style were partly the
ancient fabulists whom he copied, for he pretends Character
to no originality; partly the old French poets, es- of his fables.
pecially Marot.   From the one he took the real gold of his
fables themselves, from the other he caught a peculiar archness and vivacity, which some of them had possessed, perhaps,
in no less degree, but which becomes more captivating from
his intermixture of a solid and serious wisdom.   For notwithstanding the common anecdotes (sometimes, as we may
suspect, rather exaggerated) of La Fontaine's simplicity, he
was evidently a man who had thought and observed much
about human nature, and knew a little more of the world
than he cared to let the world perceive.   Many of his fables
are admirable ; the grace of the poetry, the happy inspiration that seems to have dictated the turns of expression, place
him in the first rank among fabulists.   Yet the praise of La
Fontaine should not be indiscriminate.   It is said that he
gave the preference to Phædrus and Æsop above himself,
and some have thought that in this he could not have been
sincere.   It was at least a proof of his modesty.   But, though
we cannot think of putting Phædrus on a level with La
Fontaine, were it only for this reason, that in a work designed
for the general reader (and surely fables are of this description), the qualities that please the many are to be valued
above those that please the few, yet it is true that the French
poet might envy some talents of the Roman.   Phædrus, a
writer scarcely prized enough, because he is an early school-
book, has a perfection of elegant beauty which very few have
rivalled.   No word is out of its place, none is redundant, or
could be changed for a better ; his perspicuity and ease
make every thing appear unpremeditated, yet every thing is
wrought by consummate art.   In many fables of La Fontaine
this is not the case ; he beats round the subject, and misses
often before he hits.   Much, whatever La Harpe may assert
to the contrary, could be retrenched ; in much the exigencies

of rhyme and metre are too manifest.[m]   He has, on the other
hand, far more humour than Phædrus; and, whether it be
praise or not, thinks less of his fable and more of its moral.
One pleases by enlivening, the other pleases but does not enliven; one has more felicity, the other more skill; but in
such skill there is felicity.

12. The first seven satires of Boileau appeared in 1666;
Boileau.   and these, though much inferior to his later pro-
His epistles. ductions, are characterised by La Harpe as the
earliest poetry in the French language where the mechanism
of its verse was fully understood, where the style was always
pure and elegant, where the ear was uniformly gratified.
The Art of Poetry was published in 1673, the Lutrin in 1674;
the Epistles followed at various periods.   Their elaborate
though equable strain, in a kind of poetry which, never requiring high flights of fancy, escapes the censure of mediocrity and monotony which might sometimes fall upon it,
generally excites more admiration in those who have been
accustomed to the numerous defects of less finished poets,
than it retains in a later age, when others have learned to
emulate and preserve the same uniformity.   The fame of
Pope was transcendant for this reason, and Boileau is the
analogue of Pope in French literature.

13. The Art of Poetry has been the model of the Essay on
His Art of   Criticism; few poems more resemble each other.   I
Poetry.   will not weigh in opposite scales two compositions,
of which one claims an advantage from its having been the
original, the other from the youth of its author.   Both are
uncommon efforts of critical good sense, and both are distinguished by their short and pointed language, which
remains in the memory.   Boileau has very well incorporated

---

[m] Let us take, for example, the first
lines of L'Homme et la Couleuvre.

Un homme vit une couleuvre.
Ah méchante, dit-il, je m'en vais faire un œuvre
  Agréable à tout l'univers!
  A ces mots l'animal pervers
  (C'est le serpent que je veux dire,
*Et non l'homme, on pourroit aisément s'y
      tromper)*
A ces mots le serpent se laissant attraper
Est pris, mis en un sac; et, ce qui fut le pire,
On résolut sa mort, *fût il coupable ou non.*

None of these lines appear to me very

happy; but there can be no doubt about
that in italics, which spoils the effect of
the preceding, and is feebly redundant.
The last words are almost equally bad;
no question could arise about the serpent's guilt, which had been assumed
before.   But these petty blemishes are
abundantly redeemed by the rest of the
fable, which is beautiful in choice of
thoughts and language, and may be
classed with the best in the collection.

the thoughts of Horace with his own, and given them a
skilful adaptation to his own times.   He was a bolder critic
of his contemporaries than Pope.   He took up arms against
those who shared the public favour, and were placed by half
Paris among great dramatists and poets, Pradon, Desmarests,
Brebœuf.   This was not true of the heroes of the Dunciad.
His scorn was always bitter and probably sometimes unjust;
yet posterity has ratified almost all his judgments.   False
taste, it should be remembered, had long infected the poetry
of Europe ; some steps had been lately taken to repress it ;
but extravagance, affectation, and excess of refinement are
weeds that can only be eradicated by a thorough cleansing
of the soil, by a process of burning and paring which leaves
not a seed of them in the public mind.   And when we consider the gross blemishes of this description that deform the
earlier poetry of France, as of other nations, we cannot blame
the severity of Boileau, though he may occasionally have
condemned in the mass what contained some intermixture of
real excellence.   We have become of late years in England
so enamoured of the beauties of our old writers (and certainly
they are of a superior kind), that we are sometimes more
than a little blind to their faults.

14. By writing satires, epistles, and an Art of Poetry,
Boileau has challenged an obvious comparison with Comparison
Horace.   Yet they are very unlike ; one easy, col-   with Horace.
loquial, abandoning himself to every change that arises in
his mind, the other uniform as a regiment under arms, always
equal, always laboured, incapable of a bold neglect.   Poetry
seems to have been the delight of one, the task of the other.
The pain that Boileau must have felt in writing communicates itself in some measure to the reader ; we are
fearful of losing some point, of passing over some epithet
without sufficiently perceiving its selection ; it is as with
those pictures, which are to be viewed long and attentively,
till our admiration of detached proofs of skill becomes wearisome by repetition.

15. The Lutrin is the most popular of the poems of Boileau.
Its subject is ill chosen ; neither interest nor variety The Lutrin.
could be given to it.   Tassoni and Pope have the advantage in this respect ; if their leading theme is trifling, we

lose sight of it in the gay liveliness of description and episode.
In Boileau, after we have once been told that the canons of
a church spend their lives in sleep and eating, we have no
more to learn, and grow tired of keeping company with a
race so stupid and sensual. But the poignant wit and satire,
the elegance and correctness of numberless couplets, as well
as the ingenious adaptation of classical passages, redeem
this poem, and confirm its high place in the mock-heroic
line.

16. The great deficiency of Boileau is in sensibility. Far
below Pope or even Dryden in this essential quality,
which the moral epistle or satire not only admits
but requires, he rarely quits two paths, those of
reason and of raillery. His tone on moral subjects is firm
and severe, but not very noble; a trait of pathos, a single
touch of pity or tenderness, will rarely be found. This of
itself serves to give a dryness to his poetry, and it may be
doubtful, though most have read Boileau, whether many have
read him twice.

General character of his poetry.

17. The pompous tone of Ronsard and Du Bartas had
become ridiculous in the reign of Louis XIV. Even
that of Malherbe was too elevated for the public
taste; none at least imitated that writer, though
the critics had set the example of admiring him. Boileau,
who had done much to turn away the world from imagination to plain sense, once attempted to emulate the grandi-
loquent strains of Pindar in an ode on the taking of Namur,
but with no such success as could encourage himself or others
to repeat the experiment. Yet there was no want of gravity
or elevation in the prose writers of France, nor in the
tragedies of Racine. But the French language is not very
well adapted for the higher kind of lyric poetry, while it suits
admirably the lighter forms of song and epigram. And their
poets, in this age, were almost entirely men living at Paris,
either in the court, or at least in a refined society, the most
adverse of all to the poetical character. The influence of
wit and politeness is generally directed towards rendering
enthusiasm or warmth of fancy ridiculous; and without
these no great energy of genius can be displayed. But, in

Lyric poetry lighter than before.

their proper department, several poets of considerable merit appeared.

18. Benserade was called peculiarly the poet of the court; for twenty years it was his business to compose verses for the ballets represented before the king. His skill and tact were shown in delicate contrivances to make those who supported the characters of gods and goddesses in these fictions, being the nobles and ladies of the court, betray their real inclinations, and sometimes their gallantries. He even presumed to shadow in this manner the passion of Louis for Mademoiselle La Valière, before it was publicly acknowledged. Benserade must have had no small ingenuity and adroitness; but his verses did not survive those who called them forth. In a different school, not essentially, perhaps, much more vicious than the court, but more careless of appearances, and rather proud of an immorality which it had no interest to conceal, that of Ninon l'Enclos, several of higher reputation grew up; Chapelle (whose real name was L'Huillier), La Fare, Bachaumont, Lainezer, and Chaulieu. The first, perhaps, and certainly the last of these, are worthy to be remembered. La Harpe has said, that Chaulieu alone retains a claim to be read in a style where Voltaire has so much left all others behind, that no comparison with him can ever be admitted. Chaulieu was an original genius: his poetry has a marked character, being a happy mixture of a gentle and peaceable philosophy with a lively imagination. His verses flow from his soul, and though often negligent through indolence, are never in bad taste or affected. Harmony of versification, grace and gaiety, with a voluptuous and Epicurean, but mild and benevolent, turn of thought, belong to Chaulieu, and these are qualities which do not fail to attract the majority of readers.[n]

19. It is rather singular that a style so uncongenial to the spirit of that age as pastoral poetry appears was quite as much cultivated as before. But it is still true that the spirit of the age gained the victory, and drove the shepherds from their shady bowers, though without substituting any thing more rational in the fairy tales which

Benserade.

Chaulieu.

Pastoral poetry.

---

[n] La Harpe. Bouterwek, vi. 127. Biogr. univ.

superseded the pastoral romance. At the middle of the
century, and partially till near its close, the style of D'Urfé
and Scudery retained its popularity. Three poets of the age
of Louis were known in pastoral; Segrais, Madame
Deshoulières, and Fontenelle. The first belongs
most to the genuine school of modern pastoral; he is elegant, romantic, full of complaining love; the Spanish and
French romances had been his model in invention, as Virgil
was in style. La Harpe allows him nature, sweetness, and
sentiment; but he cannot emulate the vivid colouring of
Virgil, and the language of his shepherds, though simple,
wants elegance and harmony. The tone of his pastorals
seems rather insipid, though La Harpe has quoted some
pleasing lines. Madame Deshoulières, with a purer
style than Segrais, according to the same critic,
has less genius. Others have thought her Idylls the best
in the language.° But these seem to be merely trivial
moralities addressed to flowers, brooks, and sheep, sometimes
expressed in a manner both ingenious and natural, but on
the whole too feeble to give much pleasure. Bouterwek
observes that her poetry is to be considered as that of a
woman, and that its pastoral morality would be somewhat
childish in the mouth of man; whether this says more for
the lady, or against her sex, I must leave to the reader.
She has occasionally some very pleasing and even poetical
passages.ᵖ The third among these poets of the
pipe is Fontenelle. But his pastorals, as Bouterwek
says, are too artificial for the ancient school, and too cold
for the romantic. La Harpe blames, besides this general
fault, the negligence and prosaic phrases of his style. The
best is that entitled Ismène. It is in fact a poem for the
world; yet as love and its artifices are found everywhere, we
cannot censure any passage as absolutely unfit for pastoral,
save a certain refinement which belonged to the author in
everything, and which interferes with our sense of rural
simplicity.

20. In the superior walks of poetry France had nothing of
which she has been inclined to boast. Chapelain, a man of

Margin notes: Segrais. Deshoulières. Fontenelle.

° Biogr. univ.   ᵖ Bouterwek, vi. 152.

some credit as a critic, produced his long-laboured epic, La
Pucelle, in 1656, which is only remembered by the Bad epic
poems.
insulting ridicule of Boileau. A similar fate has
fallen on the Clovis of Desmarests, published in 1684,
though the German historian of literature has extolled the
richness of imagination it shows, and observed that if those
who saw nothing but a fantastic writer in Desmarests had
possessed as much fancy, the national poetry would have
been of a higher character.[q] Brebœuf's translation of the
Pharsalia is spirited, but very extravagant.

21. The literature of Germany was now more corrupted
by bad taste than ever. A second Silesian school, German
poetry.
but much inferior to that of Opitz, was founded
by Hoffmanswaldau and Lohenstein. The first had great
facility, and imitated Ovid and Marini with some success.
The second, with worse taste, always tumid and striving at
something elevated, so that the Lohenstein swell became a
by-word with later critics, is superior to Hoffmanswaldau in
richness of fancy, in poetical invention, and in warmth of
feeling for all that is noble and great. About the end of
the century arose a new style, known by the unhappy name
spiritless (geistlos), which, avoiding the tone of Lohenstein,
became wholly tame and flat.

Sect. III.—On English Poetry.

Waller—Butler—Milton—Dryden—The Minor Poets.

22. We might have placed Waller in the former division
of the seventeenth century, with no more impropriety than we might have reserved Cowley for Waller.
the latter; both belong by the date of their writings to the
two periods. And perhaps the poetry of Waller bears rather
the stamp of the first Charles's age than of that which ensued. His reputation was great, and somewhat more durable
than that of similar poets has generally been; he did not

---

q Bouterwek, vi. 157.   287. Eichhorn, Geschichte der Cultur,
r Id., vol. x. p. 288. Heinsius, iv.   iv. 776.

witness its decay in his own protracted life, nor was it much diminished at the beginning of the next century. Nor was this wholly undeserved. Waller has a more uniform elegance, a more sure facility and happiness of expression, and, above all, a greater exemption from glaring faults, such as pedantry, extravagance, conceit, quaintness, obscurity, ungrammatical and unmeaning constructions, than any of the Caroline era with whom he would naturally be compared. We have only to open Carew or Lovelace to perceive the difference; not that Waller is wholly without some of these faults, but that they are much less frequent. If others may have brighter passages of fancy or sentiment, which is not difficult, he husbands better his resources, and though left behind in the beginning of the race, comes sooner to the goal. His Panegyric on Cromwell was celebrated. 'Such a series of verses,' it is said by Johnson, 'had rarely appeared before in the English language. Of these lines some are grand, some are graceful, and all are musical. There is now and then a feeble verse, or a trifling thought; but its great fault is the choice of its hero.' It may not be the opinion of all, that Cromwell's actions were of that obscure and pitiful character which the majesty of song rejects, and Johnson has before observed, that Waller's choice of encomiastic topics in this poem is very judicious. Yet his deficiency in poetical vigour will surely be traced in this composition; if he rarely sinks, he never rises very high, and we find much good sense and selection, much skill in the mechanism of language and metre, without ardour and without imagination. In his amorous poetry he has little passion or sensibility; but he is never free and petulant, never tedious, and never absurd. His praise consists much in negations; but in a comparative estimate, perhaps negations ought to count for a good deal.

23. Hudibras was incomparably more popular than Paradise Lost; no poem in our language rose at once to greater reputation. Nor can this be called ephemeral, like that of most political poetry. For at least half a century after its publication it was generally read, and perpetually quoted. The wit of Butler has still preserved many lines; but Hudibras now attracts compa-

Butler's Hudibras.

ratively few readers. The eulogies of Johnson seem rather
adapted to what he remembered to have been the fame of
Butler, than to the feelings of the surrounding generation;
and since his time, new sources of amusement have sprung
up, and writers of a more intelligible pleasantry have superseded those of the seventeenth century. In the fiction of
Hudibras there was never much to divert the reader, and
there is still less left at present. But what has been censured as a fault, the length of dialogue, which puts the
fiction out of sight, is in fact the source of all the pleasure
that the work affords. The sense of Butler is masculine, his
wit inexhaustible, and it is supplied from every source of
reading and observation. But these sources are often so
unknown to the reader that the wit loses its effect through
the obscurity of its allusions, and he yields to the bane of
wit, a purblind mole-like pedantry. His versification is
sometimes spirited, and his rhymes humorous; yet he wants
that ease and flow which we require in light poetry.

24. The subject of Paradise Lost is the finest that has
ever been chosen for heroic poetry; it is also *Paradise*
managed by Milton with remarkable skill. The *Lost—
Choice of*
Iliad wants completeness; it has an unity of its *subject.*
own, but it is the unity of a part where we miss the relation to a whole. The Odyssey is not imperfect in this
point of view; but the subject is hardly extensive enough
for a legitimate epic. The Æneid is spread over too long
a space, and perhaps the latter books, by the diversity of
scene and subject, lose part of that intimate connexion with
the former which an epic poem requires. The Pharsalia is
open to the same criticism as the Iliad. The Thebaid is
not deficient in unity or greatness of action; but it is one
that possesses no sort of interest in our eyes. Tasso is far
superior, both in choice and management of his subject,
to most of these. Yet the Fall of Man has a more general
interest than the Crusade.

25. It must be owned, nevertheless, that a religious epic
labours under some disadvantages; in proportion *Open to
some diffi-*
as it attracts those who hold the same tenets with *culties.*
the author, it is regarded by those who dissent from him
with indifference or aversion. It is said that the discovery

of Milton's Arianism, in this rigid generation, has already impaired the sale of Paradise Lost. It is also difficult to enlarge or adorn such a story by fiction. Milton has done much in this way; yet he was partly restrained by the necessity of conforming to Scripture.

26. The ordonnance or composition of the Paradise Lost is admirable; and here we perceive the advantage which Milton's great familiarity with the Greek theatre, and his own original scheme of the poem, had given him. Every part succeeds in an order, noble, clear, and natural. It might have been wished indeed that the vision of the eleventh book had not been changed into the colder narrative of the twelfth. But what can be more majestic than the first two books which open this great drama? It is true that they rather serve to confirm the sneer of Dryden that Satan is Milton's hero; since they develop a plan of action in that potentate, which is ultimately successful; the triumph that he and his host must experience in the fall of man being hardly compensated by their temporary conversion into serpents; a fiction rather too grotesque. But it is, perhaps, only pedantry to talk about the hero, as if a high personage were absolutely required in an epic poem to predominate over the rest. The conception of Satan is doubtless the first effort of Milton's genius. Dante could not have ventured to spare so much lustre for a ruined archangel, in an age when nothing less than horns and a tail were the orthodox creed.[s]

Its arrangement.

---

[s] Coleridge has a fine passage which I cannot resist my desire to transcribe. 'The character of Satan is pride and sensual indulgence, finding in itself the motive of action. It is the character so often seen in little on the political stage. It exhibits all the restlessness, temerity, and cunning which have marked the mighty hunters of mankind from Nimrod to Napoleon. The common fascination of man is that these great men, as they are called, must act from some great motive. Milton has carefully marked in his Satan the intense selfishness, the alcohol of egotism, which would rather reign in hell than serve in heaven. To place this lust of self in opposition to denial of self or duty, and to show what

exertions it would make, and what pains endure, to accomplish its end, is Milton's particular object in the character of Satan. But around this character he has thrown a singularity of daring, a grandeur of sufferance, and a ruined splendour, which constitute the very height of poetic sublimity.' Coleridge's Remains, p. 176.

In reading such a paragraph as this, we are struck by the vast improvement of the highest criticism, the philosophy of æsthetics, since the days of Addison. His papers in the Spectator on Paradise Lost were perhaps superior to any criticism that had been written in our language; and we must always acknowledge their good sense, their judiciousness, and the

27. Milton has displayed great skill in the delineations of Adam and Eve; he does not dress them up, after the fashion of orthodox theology, which had no spell to bind his free spirit, in the fancied robes of primitive righteousness. South, in one of his sermons, has drawn a picture of unfallen man, which is even poetical; but it might be asked by the reader, Why then did he fall? The first pair of Milton are innocent of course, but not less frail than their posterity; nor, except one circumstance, which seems rather physical intoxication than anything else, do we find any sign of depravity superinduced upon their transgression. It might even be made a question for profound theologians whether Eve, by taking amiss what Adam had said, and by self-conceit, did not sin before she tasted the fatal apple. The necessary paucity of actors in Paradise Lost is perhaps the apology of Sin and Death; they will not bear exact criticism, yet we do not wish them away.

Characters of Adam and Eve.

28. The comparison of Milton with Homer has been founded on the acknowledged pre-eminence of each in his own language, and on the lax application of the word epic to their great poems. But there was not much in common either between their genius or its products; and Milton has taken less in direct imitation from Homer than from several other poets. His favourites had rather been Sophocles and Euripides; to them he owes the structure of his blank verse, his swell and dignity of style, his grave enunciation of moral and abstract sentiment, his tone of description, neither condensed like that of Dante,

He owes less to Homer than the tragedians.

---

vast service they did to our literature, in settling the Paradise Lost on its proper level. But how little they satisfy us, even in treating of the *natura naturata*, the poem itself! and how little conception they show of the *natura naturans*, the individual genius of the author! Even in the periodical criticism of the present day, in the midst of much that is affected, much that is precipitate, much that is written for mere display, we find occasional reflections of a profundity and discrimination which we should seek in vain through Dryden or Addison, or the two Wartons, or even

Johnson, though much superior to the rest. Hurd has perhaps the merit of being the first who in this country aimed at philosophical criticism; he had great ingenuity, a good deal of reading, and a facility in applying it; but he did not feel very deeply, was somewhat of a coxcomb, and having always before his eyes a model neither good in itself, nor made for him to emulate, he assumes a dogmatic arrogance, which, as it always offends the reader, so for the most part stands in the way of the author's own search for truth.

nor spread out with the diffuseness of the other Italians and of Homer himself. Next to these Greek tragedians, Virgil seems to have been his model; with the minor Latin poets, except Ovid, he does not, I think, show any great familiarity; and though abundantly conversant with Ariosto, Tasso and Marini, we cannot say that they influenced his manner, which, unlike theirs, is severe and stately, never light, nor, in the sense we should apply the words to them, rapid and animated.[t]

29. To Dante, however, he bears a much greater likeness. Compared with Dante. He has in common with that poet an uniform seriousness, for the brighter colouring of both is but the smile of a pensive mind, a fondness for argumentative speech, and for the same strain of argument. This indeed proceeds in part from the general similarity, the religious and even theological cast of their subjects; I advert particularly to the last part of Dante's poem. We may almost say, when we look to the resemblance of their prose writings, in the proud sense of being born for some great achievement, which breathes through the Vita Nuova, as it does through Milton's earlier treatises, that they were twin spirits, and that each might have animated the other's body, that each would, as it were, have been the other, if he had lived in the other's age. As it is, I incline to prefer Milton, that is, the Paradise Lost, both because the subject is more extensive, and because the resources of his genius are more multifarious. Dante sins more against good taste, but only perhaps because there was no good taste in his time; for Milton has also too much a disposition to make the grotesque accessory to the terrible. Could Milton have written the lines on Ugolino? Perhaps he could. Those on Francesca? Not, I think, every line. Could Dante have planned such a poem as Paradise Lost? Not certainly, being Dante in 1300; but living when Milton did, perhaps he could. It is however useless to go on with questions that no one can fully answer. To compare the two poets, read two or three

---

[t] The solemnity of Milton is striking in those passages where some other poets would indulge a little in voluptuousness, and the more so, because this is not wholly uncongenial to him. A few lines in Paradise Lost are rather too plain, and their gravity makes them worse.

cantos of the Purgatory or Paradise, and then two or three
hundred lines of Paradise Lost. Then take Homer, or even
Virgil, the difference will be striking. Yet notwithstanding
this analogy of their minds, I have not perceived that Milton
imitates Dante very often, probably from having committed
less to memory while young (and Dante was not the favourite
poet of Italy when Milton was there), than of Ariosto and
Tasso.

30. Each of these great men chose the subject that suited
his natural temper and genius. What, it is curious to
conjecture, would have been Milton's success in his original
design, a British story? Far less, surely, than in Paradise
Lost; he wanted the rapidity of the common heroic poem,
and would always have been sententious, perhaps arid and
heavy. Yet even as religious poets, there are several remarkable distinctions between Milton and Dante. It has
been justly observed that, in the Paradise of Dante, he makes
use of but three leading ideas, light, music, and motion, and
that Milton has drawn Heaven in less pure and spiritual
colours.[u] The philosophical imagination of the former, in
this third part of his poem, almost defecated from all sub-
lunary things by long and solitary musing, spiritualises all
that it touches. The genius of Milton, though itself subjective, was less so than that of Dante; and he has to
recount, to describe, to bring deeds and passions before the
eye. And two peculiar causes may be assigned for this
difference in the treatment of celestial things between the
Divine Comedy and the Paradise Lost; the dramatic form
which Milton had originally designed to adopt, and his own
theological bias towards anthropomorphism, which his posthumous treatise on religion has brought to light. This
was no doubt in some measure inevitable in such a subject
as that of Paradise Lost; yet much that is ascribed to
God, sometimes with the sanction of Scripture, sometimes
without it, is not wholly pleasing; such as 'the oath that

---

[u] Quarterly Review, June, 1825.
This article contains some good and
some questionable remarks on Milton,
among the latter I reckon the proposition, that his contempt for women is
shown in the delineation of Eve; an
opinion not that of Addison or of many
others, who have thought her exquisitely
drawn.

shook Heaven's whole circumference,' and several other
images of the same kind, which bring down the Deity in a
manner not consonant to philosophical religion, however it
may be borne out by the sensual analogies or mythic sym-
bolism of Oriental writing.[x]

31. We rarely meet with feeble lines in Paradise Lost,[y]
Elevation though with many that are hard, and, in a common
of his style. use of the word, might be called prosaic. Yet few
are truly prosaic; few wherein the tone is not some way
distinguished from prose. The very artificial style of Milton,
sparing in English idiom, and his study of a rhythm, not
always the most grateful to our ears, but preserving his
blank verse from a trivial flow, is the cause of this elevation.
It is at least more removed from a prosaic cadence than the
slovenly rhymes of such contemporary poets as Chamber-
layne. His versification is entirely his own, framed on a
Latin and chiefly a Virgilian model, the pause less frequently
resting on the close of the line than in Homer, and much
less than in our own dramatic poets. But it is also possible
that the Italian and Spanish blank verse may have had some
effect upon his ear.

32. In the numerous imitations, and still more numerous
His blind- traces of older poetry which we perceive in Para-
ness. dise Lost, it is always to be kept in mind that he
had only his recollection to rely upon. His blindness seems
to have been complete before 1654; and I scarcely think
that he had begun his poem, before the anxiety and trouble

---

[x] Johnson thinks that Milton should
have secured the consistency of this poem
by keeping immateriality out of sight,
and enticing his reader to drop it from
his thoughts. But here the subject for-
bad him to preserve consistency, if indeed
there be inconsistency in supposing a
rapid assumption of form by spiritual
beings. For though the instance that
Johnson alleges of inconsistency in Satan's animating a toad was not necessary,
yet his animation of the serpent was
absolutely indispensable. And the same
has been done by other poets, who do
not scruple to suppose their gods, their
fairies or devils, or their allegorical personages, inspiring thoughts, and even

uniting themselves with the soul, as well
as assuming all kinds of form, though
their natural appearance is almost always
anthropomorphic. And, after all, Satan
does not animate a real toad, but takes
the shape of one. 'Squat like a toad
close by the ear of Eve.' But he does
enter a real serpent, so that the instance of Johnson is ill chosen. If he
had mentioned the serpent, every one
would have seen that the identity of the
animal serpent with Satan is part of the
original account.

[y] One of the few exceptions is in the
sublime description of Death, where a
wretched hemistich, 'Fierce as ten
furies,' stands as an unsightly blemish.

into which the public strife of the Commonwealth and the
Restoration had thrown him gave leisure for immortal
occupations.   Then the remembrance of early reading came
over his dark and lonely path like the moon emerging from
the clouds.   Then it was that the muse was truly his ; not
only as she poured her creative inspiration into his mind,
but as the daughter of Memory, coming with fragments of
ancient melodies, the voice of Euripides, and Homer, and
Tasso ; sounds that he had loved in youth, and treasured up
for the solace of his age.   They who, though not enduring
the calamity of Milton, have known what it is, when afar
from books, in solitude or in travelling, or in the intervals
of worldly care, to feed on poetical recollections, to murmur
over the beautiful lines whose cadence has long delighted
their ear, to recall the sentiments and images which retain
by association the charm that early years once gave them—
they will feel the inestimable value of committing to the
memory, in the prime of its power, what it will easily receive
and indelibly retain.   I know not indeed whether an educa-
cation that deals much with poetry, such as is still usual in
England, has any more solid argument among many in its
favour, than that it lays the foundation of intellectual
pleasures at the other extreme of life.

33. It is owing, in part, to his blindness, but more
perhaps to his general residence in a city, that _His passion
for music._
Milton, in the words of Coleridge, is ' not a picturesque but a musical poet ; ' or, as I would prefer to say, is
the latter more of the two.   He describes visible things, and
often with great powers of rendering them manifest, what
the Greeks called ἐνάργεια, though seldom with so much
circumstantial exactness of observation as Spenser or Dante,
but he feels music.   The sense of vision delighted his
imagination, but that of sound wrapped his whole soul in
ecstasy.   One of his trifling faults may be connected with
this, the excessive passion he displays for stringing together
sonorous names, sometimes so obscure that the reader associates nothing with them, as the word Namancos in Lycidas,
which long baffled the commentators.   Hence his catalogues,
unlike those of Homer and Virgil, are sometimes merely
ornamental and misplaced.   Thus the names of unbuilt

cities come strangely forward in Adam's vision,[z] though he has afterwards gone over the same ground with better effect in Paradise Regained. In this there was also a mixture of his pedantry. But, though he was rather too ostentatious of learning, the nature of his subject demanded a good deal of episodical ornament. And this, rather than the prece-
Faults in
Paradise
Lost.
dents he might have alleged from the Italians and others, is perhaps the best apology for what some grave critics have censured, his frequent allusions to fable and mythology. These give much relief to the severity of the poem, and few readers would dispense with them. Less excuse can be made for some affectation of science which has produced hard and unpleasing lines ; but he had been born in an age when more credit was gained by reading much than by writing well. The faults, however, of Paradise Lost are in general less to be called faults, than necessary adjuncts of the qualities we most admire, and idiosyncrasies of a mighty genius. The verse of Milton is sometimes wanting in grace, and almost always in ease ; but what better can be said of his prose ? His foreign idioms are too frequent in the one ; but they predominate in the other.

34. The slowness of Milton's advance to glory is now gene-
Its progress
to fame.
rally owned to have been much exaggerated; we might say that the reverse was nearer the truth. ' The sale of 1,300 copies in two years,' says Johnson, ' in opposition to so much recent enmity, and to a style of versification new to all and disgusting to many, was an uncommon example of the prevalence of genius. The demand did not immediately increase ; for many more readers than were supplied at first the nation did not afford. Only 3,000 were sold in eleven years.' It would hardly, however, be said, even in this age, of a poem 3,000 copies of which had been sold in eleven years that its success had been small; and some, perhaps, might doubt whether Paradise Lost, published eleven years since, would have met with a greater demand. There is sometimes a want of congeniality in public taste which no power of genius will overcome.

---

[z] Par. Lost. xi. 386.

For Milton it must be said by every one conversant with the
literature of the age that preceded Addison's famous criticism, from which some have dated the reputation of Paradise Lost, that he took his place among great poets from
the beginning. The fancy of Johnson that few dared to
praise it, and that 'the revolution put an end to the secrecy
of love,' is without foundation; the Government of Charles
II. was not so absurdly tyrannical, nor did Dryden, the
Court's own poet, hesitate, in his preface to the State of
Innocence, published soon after Milton's death, to speak of
its original, Paradise Lost, as 'undoubtedly one of the
greatest, most noble, and most sublime poems which either
this age or nation has produced.'

35. The neglect which Paradise Lost never experienced,
seems to have been long the lot of Paradise Re- Paradise
gained. It was not popular with the world ; it was Regained.
long believed to manifest a decay of the poet's genius, and
in spite of all that the critics have written, it is still but the
favourite of some whose predilections for the Miltonic style
are very strong. The subject is so much less capable of
calling forth the vast powers of his mind, that we should be
unfair in comparing it throughout with the greater poem ;
it has been called a model of the shorter epic, an action comprehending few characters and a brief space of time.[a] The
love of Milton for dramatic dialogue, imbibed from Greece,
is still more apparent than in Paradise Lost; the whole
poem, in fact, may almost be accounted a drama of primal
simplicity, the narrative and descriptive part serving rather
to diversify and relieve the speeches of the actors, than their
speeches, as in the legitimate epic, to enliven the narration.
Paradise Regained abounds with passages equal to any of
the same nature in Paradise Lost; but the argumentative
tone is kept up till it produces some tediousness, and perhaps on the whole less pains have been exerted to adorn and
elevate that which appeals to the imagination.

36. Samson Agonistes is the latest of Milton's poems;
we see in it, perhaps more distinctly than in Para- Samson
dise Regained, the ebb of a mighty tide. An air Agonistes.
of uncommon grandeur prevails throughout, but the lan-

---

[a] Todd's Milton, vol. v. p. 308.

guage is less poetical than in Paradise Lost; the vigour of
thought remains, but it wants much of its ancient eloquence,
nor is the lyric tone well kept up by the chorus; they are
too sententious, too slow in movement, and, except by the
metre, are not easily distinguishable from the other personages. But this metre is itself infelicitous; the lines
being frequently of a number of syllables not recognized in
the usage of English poetry, and, destitute of rhythmical
measure, fall into prose. Milton seems to have forgotten
that the ancient chorus had a musical accompaniment.

37. The style of Samson, being essentially that of Paradise Lost, may show us how much more the latter poem is
founded on the Greek tragedians than on Homer. In Samson
we have sometimes the pompous tone of Æschylus, more
frequently the sustained majesty of Sophocles; but the religious solemnity of Milton's own temperament, as well as
the nature of the subject, have given a sort of breadth, an
unbroken severity, to the whole drama. It is perhaps not
very popular even with the lovers of poetry; yet upon close
comparison we should find that that it deserves a higher
place than many of its prototypes. We might search the
Greek tragedies long for a character so powerfully conceived
and maintained as that of Samson himself; and it is but
conformable to the sculptural simplicity of that form of
drama which Milton adopted, that all the rest should be kept
in subordination to it. 'It is only,' Johnson says, 'by a
blind confidence in the reputation of Milton, that a drama
can be praised in which the intermediate parts have neither
cause nor consequence, neither hasten nor retard the catastrophe.' Such a drama is certainly not to be ranked with
Othello and Macbeth, or even with the Œdipus or the
Hippolytus; but a similar criticism is applicable to several
famous tragedies in the less artificial school of antiquity,
to the Prometheus and the Persæ of Æschylus, and, if we
look strictly, to not a few of the two other masters.

38. The poetical genius of Dryden came slowly to perfection. Born in 1631, his first short poems, or, as
we might rather say, copies of verses, were not
written till he approached thirty; and though some of his
dramas, not indeed of the best, belong to the next period of

Dryden. His earlier poems.

his life, he had reached the age of fifty before his high rank
as a poet had been confirmed by indubitable proof.   Yet he
had manifested a superiority to his immediate contemporaries; his Astræa Redux, on the Restoration, is well versified; the lines are seldom weak, the couplets have that
pointed manner which Cowley and Denham had taught the
world to require ; they are harmonious, but not so varied as
the style he afterwards adopted.   The Annus Mirabilis, in
1667, is of a higher cast; it is not so animated as the later
poetry of Dryden, because the alternate quatrain, in which
he followed Davenant's Gondibert, is hostile to animation;
but it is not unfavourable to another excellence, condensed
and vigorous thought.   Davenant indeed and Denham may
be reckoned the models of Dryden, so far as this can be said
of a man of original genius, and one far superior to theirs.
The distinguishing characteristic of Dryden, it has been said
by Scott, was the power of reasoning and expressing the
result in appropriate language.   This indeed was the characteristic of the two whom we have named, and so far as
Dryden has displayed it, which he eminently has done, he
bears a resemblance to them.   But it is insufficient praise
for this great poet.   His rapidity of conception and readiness
of expression are higher qualities.   He never loiters about a
single thought or image, never labours about the turn of a
phrase.   The impression upon our minds that he wrote with
exceeding ease is irresistible, and I do not know that we
have any evidence to repel it.   The admiration of Dryden
gains upon us, if I may speak from my own experience, with
advancing years, as we become more sensible of the difficulty
of his style, and of the comparative facility of that which is
merely imaginative.

39. Dryden may be considered as a satirical, a reasoning,
a descriptive and narrative, a lyric poet, and as a   Absalom and
translator.   As a dramatist we must return to him   Achitophel.
again.   The greatest of his satires is Absalom and Achitophel, that work in which his powers became fully known
to the world, and which, as many think, he never surpassed.
The admirable fitness of the English couplet for satire had
never been shown before; in less skilful hands it had been
ineffective.   He does not frequently, in this poem, carry the

sense beyond the second line, which, except when skilfully
contrived, as it often is by himself, is apt to enfeeble the
emphasis; his triplets are less numerous than usual, but
energetic.   The spontaneous ease of expression, the rapid
transitions, the general elasticity and movement, have never
been excelled.   It is superfluous to praise the discrimination
and vivacity of the chief characters, especially Shaftesbury
and Buckingham.   Satire, however, is so much easier than
panegyric, that with Ormond, Ossory, and Mulgrave he has
not been quite so successful.   In the second part of Absalom
and Achitophel, written by Tate, one long passage alone is
inserted by Dryden.   It is excellent in its line of satire, but
the line is less elevated; the persons delineated are less important, and he has indulged more his natural proneness to
virulent ribaldry.   This fault of Dryden's writings, it is just
to observe, belonged less to the man than to the age.   No
libellous invective, no coarseness of allusion, had ever been
spared towards a private or political enemy.   We read with
nothing but disgust the satirical poetry of Cleveland, Butler,
Oldham, and Marvell, or even of men whose high rank did
not soften their style, Rochester, Dorset, Mulgrave.   In
Dryden there was, for the first time, a poignancy of wit
which atones for his severity, and a discretion even in his
taunts which made them more cutting.

40. The Medal, which is in some measure a continuation
of Absalom and Achitophel, since it bears wholly
on Shaftesbury, is of unequal merit, and on the
whole falls much below the former.   In Mac Flecknoe, his
satire on his rival Shadwell, we must allow for the inferiority
of the subject, which could not bring out so much of Dryden's higher powers of mind; but scarcely one of his poems
is more perfect.   Johnson, who admired Dryden almost as
much as he could any one, has yet, from his proneness to
critical censure, very much exaggerated the poet's defects.
'His faults of negligence are beyond recital.   Such is the
unevenness of his compositions, that ten lines are seldom
found together without something of which the reader is
ashamed.'   This might be true, or more nearly true, of other
poets of the seventeenth century.   Ten good consecutive
lines will, perhaps, rarely be found, except in Denham, Dave-

*Mac Fleck-
noe.*

nant, and Waller. But it seems a great exaggeration as to
Dryden. I would particularly instance Mac Flecknoe as a
poem of about four hundred lines, in which no one will be
condemned as weak or negligent, though three or four are
rather too ribaldrous for our taste. There are also passages,
much exceeding ten lines, in Absalom and Achitophel, as
well as in the later works, the Fables, which excite in the
reader none of the shame for the poet's carelessness, with
which Johnson has furnished him.

41. The argumentative talents of Dryden appear, more or
less, in the greater part of his poetry; reason in The Hind
and Pan-
rhyme was his peculiar delight, to which he seems ther.
to escape from the mere excursions of fancy. And it is remarkable that he reasons better and more closely in poetry
than in prose. His productions more exclusively reasoning
are the Religio Laici and the Hind and Panther. The latter
is every way an extraordinary poem. It was written in the
hey-day of exultation, by a recent proselyte to a winning
side, as he dreamed it to be, by one who never spared a
weaker foe, nor repressed his triumph with a dignified moderation. A year was hardly to elapse before he exchanged
this fulness of pride for an old age of disappointment and
poverty. Yet then too his genius was unquenched, and even
his satire was not less severe.

42. The first lines in the Hind and Panther are justly reputed among the most musical in our language; Its singular
fable.
and perhaps we observe their rhythm the better
because it does not gain much by the sense; for the allegory
and the fable are seen, even in this commencement, to be
awkwardly blended. Yet, notwithstanding their evident in-
coherence, which sometimes leads to the verge of absurdity,
and the facility they give to ridicule, I am not sure that
Dryden was wrong in choosing this singular fiction. It was
his aim to bring forward an old argument in as novel a style
as he could; a dialogue between a priest and a parson would
have made but a dull poem, even if it had contained some of
the excellent paragraphs we read in the Hind and Panther.
It is the grotesqueness and originality of the fable that give
this poem its peculiar zest, of which no reader, I conceive, is
insensible; and it is also by this means that Dryden has

contrived to relieve his reasoning by short but beautiful
touches of description, such as the sudden stream of light
from heaven which announces the victory of Sedgmoor near
the end of the second book.[b]

43. The wit in the Hind and Panther is sharp, ready, and
Its reason-   pleasant, the reasoning is sometimes admirably close
ing.   and strong; it is the energy of Bossuet in verse.
I do not know that the main argument of the Roman church
could be better stated; all that has been well said for tradition and authority, all that serves to expose the inconsistencies of a vacillating Protestantism, is in the Hind's mouth.
It is such an answer as a candid man should admit to any
doubts of Dryden's sincerity. He who could argue as powerfully as the Hind may well be allowed to have thought himself in the right. Yet he could not forget a few bold thoughts
of his more sceptical days, and such is his bias to sarcasm
that he cannot restrain himself from reflections on kings and
priests when he is most contending for them.[c]

44. The Fables of Dryden, or stories modernised from
The Fables.   Boccaccio and Chaucer, are at this day probably the
                 most read and the most popular of Dryden's poems.
They contain passages of so much more impressive beauty,
and are altogether so far more adapted to general sympathy
than those we have mentioned, that I should not hesitate to
concur in this judgment. Yet Johnson's accusation of negligence is better supported by these than by the earlier poems.
Whether it were that age and misfortune, though they had
not impaired the poet's vigour, had rendered its continual
exertion more wearisome, or, as is perhaps the better supposition, he reckoned an easy style, sustained above prose, in
some places, rather by metre than expression, more fitted to
narration, we find much which might appear slovenly to
critics of Johnson's temper. The latter seems, in fact, to
have conceived, like Milton, a theory, that good writing, at
least in verse, is never either to follow the change of fashion,

---

[b] [I am indebted to a distinguished
friend for the explanation of this line,
which I had misunderstood.—1853.]

[c] By education most have been misled;
So they believe because they so were bred.

The priest continues what the nurse began,
And thus the child imposes on the man.--Part iii.

'Call you this backing of your
friends?' his new allies might have
said.

or to sink into familiar phrase, and that any deviation from
this rigour should be branded as low and colloquial. But
Dryden wrote on a different plan. He thought, like Ariosto,
and like Chaucer himself, whom he had to improve, that a
story, especially when not heroic, should be told in easy and
flowing language, without too much difference from that of
prose, relying on his harmony, his occasional inversions, and
his concealed skill in the choice of words, for its effect on the
reader. He found also a tone of popular idiom, not perhaps
old English idiom, but such as had crept into society, current
among his contemporaries; and though this has in many
cases now become insufferably vulgar, and in others looks
like affectation, we should make some allowance for the times
in condemning it. This last blemish, however, is not much
imputable to the Fables. Their beauties are innumerable;
yet few are very well chosen; some, as Guiscard and Sigismunda, he has injured through coarseness of mind, which
neither years nor religion had purified; and we want in all
the power over emotion, the charm of sympathy, the skilful
arrangement and selection of circumstance, which narrative
poetry claims as its highest graces.

45. Dryden's fame as a lyric poet depends a very little on
his Ode on Mrs. Killigrew's death, but almost en- His Odes—
tirely on that for St. Cecilia's Day, commonly called Alexander's
Alexander's Feast. The former, which is much praised by Feast.
Johnson, has a few fine lines, mingled with a far greater
number ill conceived and ill expressed; the whole composition has that spirit which Dryden hardly ever wanted, but it
is too faulty for high praise. The latter used to pass for the
best work of Dryden, and the best ode in the language.
Many would now agree with me that it is neither one nor
the other, and that it was rather over-rated during a period
when criticism was not at a high point. Its beauties indeed
are undeniable; it has the raciness, the rapidity, the mastery
of language which belong to Dryden; the transitions are animated, the contrasts effective. But few lines are highly
poetical, and some sink to the level of a common drinking
song. It has the defects as well as the merits of that poetry
which is written for musical accompaniment.

46. Of Dryden as a translator it is needless to say much.

In some instances, as in an ode of Horace, he has done ex-
His trans- tremely well; but his Virgil is, in my apprehension,
lation of
Virgil. the least successful of his chief works. Lines of
consummate excellence are frequently shot, like threads of
gold, through the web, but the general texture is of an ordinary material. Dryden was little fitted for a translator of
Virgil; his mind was more rapid and vehement than that of
his original, but by far less elegant and judicious. This
translation seems to have been made in haste; it is more
negligent than any of his own poetry, and the style is often
almost studiously, and as it were spitefully, vulgar.

47. The supremacy of Dryden from the death of Milton in
Decline of 1674 to his own in 1700 was not only unapproached
poetry from by any English poet, but he held almost a complete
the Restora-
tion. monopoly of English poetry. This latter period of
the seventeenth century, setting aside these two great names,
is one remarkably sterile in poetical genius. Under the first
Stuarts, men of warm imagination and sensibility, though
with deficient taste and little command of language, had
done some honour to our literature; though once neglected,
they have come forward again in public esteem, and if not
very extensively read, have been valued by men of kindred
minds full as much as they deserve. The versifiers of Charles
II. and William's days have experienced the opposite fate;
popular for a time, and long so far known at least by name
as to have entered rather largely into collections of poetry,
they are now held in no regard, nor do they claim much
favour from just criticism. Their object in general was to
write like men of the world; with ease, wit, sense, and spirit,
but dreading any soaring of fancy, any ardour of moral emotion, as the probable source of ridicule in their readers.
Nothing quenches the flame of poetry more than this fear of
the prosaic multitude; unless it is the community of habits
with this very multitude, a life such as these poets generally
led, of taverns and brothels, or, what came much to the
same, of the court. We cannot say of Dryden, that 'he
bears no traces of those sable streams;' they sully too much
the plumage of that stately swan, but his indomitable genius
carries him upwards to a purer empyrean. The rest are just
distinguishable from one another, not by any high gifts of

the muse, but by degrees of spirit, of ease, of poignancy of skill and harmony in versification, of good sense and acuteness. They may easily be disposed of. Cleveland is Some minor poets enumerated. sometimes humorous, but succeeds only in the lightest kinds of poetry. Marvell wrote sometimes with more taste and feeling than was usual, but his satires are gross and stupid. Oldham, far superior in this respect, ranks perhaps next to Dryden; he is spirited and pointed, but his versification is too negligent, and his subjects temporary. Roscommon, one of the best for harmony and correctness of language, has little vigour, but he never offends, and Pope has justly praised his 'unspotted bays.' Mulgrave affects ease and spirit, but his Essay on Satire belies the supposition that Dryden had any share in it. Rochester, endowed by nature with more considerable and varied genius, might have raised himself to a higher place than he holds. Of Otway, Duke, and several more, it is not worth while to give any character. The Revolution did nothing for poetry; William's reign, always excepting Dryden, is our *nadir* in works of imagination. Then came Blackmore with his epic poems of Prince Arthur and King Arthur, and Pomfret with his Choice, both popular in their own age, and both intolerable by their frigid and tame monotony in the next. The lighter poetry, meantime, of song and epigram did not sink along with the serious; the state of society was much less adverse to it. Rochester, Dorset, and some more whose names are unknown, or not easily traced, do credit to the Caroline period.

48. In the year 1699, a poem was published, Garth's Dispensary, which deserves attention, not so much for its own merit, though it comes nearest to Dryden, at whatever interval, as from its indicating a transitional state in our versification. The general structure of the couplet through the seventeenth century may be called abnormous; the sense is not only often carried beyond the second line, which the French avoid, but the second line of one couplet and the first of the next are not seldom united in a single sentence or a portion of one, so that the two, though not rhyming, must be read as a couplet. The former, when as dexterously managed as it was by Dryden, adds much to the beauty of the general versification; but the latter, a sort of

adultery of the lines already wedded to other companions at
rhyme's altar, can scarcely ever be pleasing, unless it be in
narrative poetry, where it may bring the sound nearer to
prose. A tendency, however, to the French rule of constantly terminating the sense with the couplet will be perceived to have increased from the Restoration. Roscommon
seldom deviates from it, and in long passages of Dryden
himself there will hardly be found an exception. But, perhaps, it had not been so uniform in any former production
as in the Dispensary. The versification of this once famous
mock-heroic poem is smooth and regular, but not forcible;
the language clear and neat; the parodies and allusions
happy. Many lines are excellent in the way of pointed application, and some are remembered and quoted, where few
call to mind the author. It has been remarked that Garth
enlarged and altered the Dispensary in almost every edition,
and what is more uncommon, that every alteration was for
the better. This poem may be called an imitation of the
Lutrin, inasmuch as but for the Lutrin it might probably
not have been written, and there are even particular resemblances. The subject, which is a quarrel between the physicians and apothecaries of London, may vie with that of
Boileau in want of general interest; yet it seems to afford
more diversity to the satirical poet. Garth, as has been observed, is a link of transition between the style and turn of
poetry under Charles and William, and that we find in
Addison, Prior, Tickell, and Pope, during the reign of Anne.

SECT. IV.—ON LATIN POETRY.

49. THE Jesuits were not unmindful of the credit their Latin
Latin poets
of Italy. verses had done them in periods more favourable to
that exercise of taste than the present. Even in
Italy, which had ceased to be a very genial soil, one of their
Ceva. number, Ceva, may deserve mention. His Jesus
Puer is a long poem, not inelegantly written, but
rather singular in some of its descriptions, where the poet

has been more solicitous to adorn his subject than attentive
to its proper character; and the same objection might be
made to some of its episodes.   Ceva wrote also a philosophical
poem, extolled by Corniani, but which has not fallen into my
hands.[d]   Averani, a Florentine of various erudition, Cappel-
lari, Strozzi, author of a poem on chocolate, and several
others, both within the order of Loyola and without it, cultivated Latin poetry with some success.[e]   But, though some
might be superior as poets, none were more remarkable or
famous than Sergardi, best known by some biting
satires under the name of Q. Sectanus, which he $\quad$ Sergardi.
levelled at his personal enemy Gravina.   The reputation,
indeed, of Gravina with posterity has not been affected by
such libels; but they are not wanting either in poignancy
and spirit, or in a command of Latin phrase.[f]

50. The superiority of France in Latin verse was no longer
contested by Holland or Germany.   Several poets of $\quad$ Of France
real merit belong to this period.   The first in time $\quad$ —Quillet.
was Claude Quillet, who, in his Callipædia, bears the Latin-
ised name of Leti.   This is written with much elegance of
style and a very harmonious versification.   No writer has a
more Virgilian cadence.   Though inferior to Sammarthanus,
he may be reckoned high among the French poets.   He has
been reproached with too open an exposition of some parts
of his subject; which applies only to the second book.

51. The Latin poems of Menage are not unpleasing; he
has indeed no great fire or originality, but the harmonious couplets glide over the ear, and the mind $\quad$ Menage.
is pleased to recognise the tesselated fragments of Ovid and
Tibullus.   His affected passion for Mademoiselle Lavergne
and lamentations about her cruelty are ludicrous enough,
when we consider the character of the man, as Vadius in the
Femmes Savantes of Molière.   They are perfect models of
want of truth; but it is a want of truth to nature, not to the
conventional forms of modern Latin verse.

52. A far superior performance is the poem on gardens by
the Jesuit Réné Rapin.   For skill in varying and adorning

---

[d] Corniani, viii. 214,   Salfi, xiv. 257.   xiv. 238, et post.
[e] Bibl. choisie,   vol. xxii.   Salfi,   [f] Salfi, xiv. 299.   Corniani, viii. 280.

his subject, for a truly Virgilian spirit in expression, for the
Rapin on gardens. exclusion of feeble, prosaic, or awkward lines, he
may perhaps be equal to any poet, to Sammarthanus
or to Sannazarius himself.   His cadences are generally very
gratifying to the ear, and in this respect he is much above
Vida.[g]   But his subject, or his genius, has prevented him
from rising very high; he is the poet of gardens, and what
gardens are to nature, that is he to mightier poets.   There
is also too monotonous a repetition of nearly the same images,
as in his long enumeration of flowers in the first book; the
descriptions are separately good, and great artifice is shown
in varying them; but the variety could not be sufficient to
remove the general sameness that belongs to an horticultural
catalogue.   Rapin was a great admirer of box and all topiary
works, or trees cut into artificial forms.

53. The first book of the Gardens of Rapin is on flowers,
the second on trees, the third on waters, and the fourth on
fruits.   The poem is of about 3000 lines, sustained with equable dignity.   All kinds of graceful associations are mingled
with the description of his flowers, in the fanciful style of
Ovid and Darwin; the violet is Ianthis, who lurked in val-
leys to shun the love of Apollo, and stained her face with
purple to preserve her chastity; the rose is Rhodanthe, proud
of her beauty, and worshipped by the people in the place
of Diana, but changed by the indignant Apollo to a tree,
while the populace, who had adored her, are converted into
her thorns, and her chief lovers into snails and butterflies.   A
tendency to conceit is perceived in Rapin, as in the two poets
to whom we have just compared him.   Thus, in some pretty

---

[g] As the poem of Rapin is not in the
hands of every one who has taste for
Latin poetry, I will give as a specimen
the introduction to the second book :—

Me nemora atque omnis nemorum pulcherri-
  mus ordo,
Et spatia umbrandum latè fundanda per hortum
Invitant ; hortis nam si florentibus umbra
Abfuerit, reliquo deerit sua gratia ruri.
  Vos grandes luci et silvæ aspirate canenti ;
Is mihi contingat vestro de munere ramus,
Unde sacri quando velant sua tempora vates,
Ipse et amem meritam capiti imposuisse coro-
  nam.
Jam se cantanti frondosa cacumina quercus

Inclinant, plauduntque comis nemora alta coru-
  scis.
Ipsa mihi læto fremitu, assensuque secundo
E totis plausum responsat Gallia silvis.
Nec me deinde suo teneat clamore Cithæron,
Mænalaque Arcadicis toties lustrata deabus,
Non Dodonæi saltus, silvæque Molorchi,
Aut nigris latè ilicibus nemorosa Calydne,
Et quos carminibus celebravit fabula lucos :
Una meos cantus tellus jam Franca moretur,
Quæ tot nobilibus passim lætissima silvis,
Conspicienda sui latè miracula ruris
Ostendit, lucisque solum commendat amœnis.

One or two words in these lines are
not strictly correct ; but they are highly
Virgilian, both in manner and rhythm.

lines, he supposes Nature to have ' tried her 'prentice hand' in making a convolvulus before she ventured upon a lily.[h]

54. In Rapin there will generally be remarked a certain redundancy, which fastidious critics might call tautology of expression. But this is not uncommon in Virgil. The Georgics have rarely been more happily imitated, especially in their didactic parts, than by Rapin in the Gardens ; but he has not the high flights of his prototype; his digressions are short, and belong closely to the subject; we have no plague, no civil war, no Eurydice. If he praises Louis XIV., it is more as the founder of the garden of Versailles than as the conqueror of Flanders, though his concluding lines emulate, with no unworthy spirit, those of the last Georgic.[i] It may be added, that some French critics have thought the famous poem of Delille on the same subject inferior to that of Rapin.

55. Santeul (or Santolius) has been reckoned one of the best Latin poets whom France ever produced. He began by celebrating the victories of Louis and the *Santeul.* virtues of contemporary heroes. A nobleness of thought and a splendour of language distinguish the poetry of Santeul, who furnished many inscriptions for public monuments. The hymns which he afterwards wrote for the breviary of the church of Paris have been still more admired, and at the request of others he enlarged his collection of sacred verse. But I have not read the poetry of Santeul, and give only the testimony of French critics.[k]

56. England might justly boast, in the earlier part of the century, her Milton; nay, I do not know that, with *Latin* the exception of a well-known and very pleasing *poetry in England.* poem, though perhaps hardly of classical simplicity, by Cowley on himself, Epitaphium Vivi Auctoris, we can produce anything equally good in this period. The Latin verse of Barrow is forcible and full of mind, but not sufficiently redolent of antiquity.[m] Yet versification became, about the

---

[h] Et tu rumpis humum, et multo te flore profundis,
Qui riguas inter serpis. convolvule, valles ;
Dulce rudimentum meditantis lilia quondam
Naturæ, cum sese opera ad majora pararet.

[i] Hæc magni insistens vestigia sacra Maronis,
Re super hortensi. Claro de monte canebam,
Lutetia in magna ; quo tempore Francica tellus

Rege beata suo. rebusque superba secundis,
Et sua per populos latè dare jura volentes
Cœperat, et toti jam morem imponere mundo.

[k] Baillet. Biogr. universelle.

[m] The following stanzas on an erring conscience will sufficiently prove this :—

time of the Restoration, if not the distinctive study, at least the favourite exercise, of the university of Oxford. The collection entitled Musæ Anglicanæ, published near the end of the century, contains little from any other quarter. Many of these poems relate to the political themes of the day, and eulogise the reigning king, Charles, James, or William ; others are on philosophical subjects, which they endeavour to decorate with classical phrase. Their character does not, on the whole, pass mediocrity ; they are often incorrect and somewhat turgid, but occasionally display a certain felicity in adapting ancient lines to their subject, and some liveliness of invention. The golden age of Latin verse in England was yet to come.

Tyranne vitæ, fax temeraria,
Infide dux, ignobile vinculum,
   Sidus dolosum, ænigma præsens,
    Ingenui labyrinthe voti,

Assensus errans, invalidæ potens
Mentis propago, quam vetuit Deus
   Nasci, sed ortæ principatum
    Attribuit, regimenque sanctum, &c.

CHAPTER VI.

HISTORY OF DRAMATIC LITERATURE, FROM 1650 TO 1700.

Sect. I.

Racine—Minor French Tragedians—Molière—Regnard, and other Comic
Writers.

1. FEW tragedies or dramatic works of any kind are now
recorded by historians of Italian literature : those Italian and
of Delfino, afterwards patriarch of Aquileia, which Spanish
drama.
are esteemed among the best, were possibly written before
the middle of the century, and were not published till after
its termination. The Corradino of Caraccio, in 1694, was
also valued at the time.[a] Nor can Spain arrest us longer ;
the school of Calderon in national comedy extended no doubt
beyond the death of Philip IV. in 1665, and many of his own
religious pieces are of as late a date ; nor were names wholly
wanting, which are said to merit remembrance in the feeble
reign of Charles II., but they must be left for such as make
a particular study of Spanish literature.[b] We are called to
a nobler stage.

2. Corneille belongs in his glory to the earlier period of
this century, though his inferior tragedies, more Racine's first
numerous than the better, would fall within the tragedies.
later. Fontenelle, indeed, as a devoted admirer, attributes
considerable merit to those which the general voice both of
critics and of the public had condemned.[c] Meantime, another
luminary arose on the opposite side of the horizon. The first

---

[a] Walker's Memoir on Italian Tragedy, p. 201.   Salfi, xii. 57.
[b] Bouterwek.
[c] Histoire du Théâtre françois, in
Œuvres de Fontenelle, iii. 111.   St.

Evremond also despised the French
public for not admiring the Sophonisbe
of Corneille, which he had made too
Roman for their taste.

tragedy of Jean Racine, Les Frères Ennemis, was represented in 1664, when he was twenty-five years of age. It is so far below his great works as to be scarcely mentioned, yet does not want indications of the genius they were to display. Alexandre, in 1665, raised the young poet to more distinction. It is said that he showed this tragedy to Corneille, who praised his versification, but advised him to avoid a path which he was not fitted to tread. It is acknowledged by the advocates of Racine that the characters are feebly drawn, and that the conqueror of Asia sinks to the level of a hero in one of those romances of gallantry which had vitiated the taste of France.

3. The glory of Racine commenced with the representa-
Andro-   tion of his Andromaque in 1667, which was not
maque.   printed till the end of the following year. He was
now at once compared with Corneille, and the scales long continued to oscillate. Criticism, satire, epigrams were unsparingly launched against the rising poet. But his rival pursued the worst policy by obstinately writing bad tragedies. The public naturally compare the present with the present, and forget the past. When he gave them Pertharite, they were dispensed from looking back to Cinna. It is acknowledged even by Fontenelle that, during the height of Racine's fame, the world placed him at least on an equality with his predecessor; a decision from which that critic, the relation and friend of Corneille, appeals to what he takes to be the verdict of a later age.

4. The Andromaque was sufficient to show that Racine had more skill in the management of a plot, in the display of emotion, in power over the sympathy of the spectator, at least where the gentler feelings are concerned, in beauty and grace of style, in all except nobleness of character, strength of thought, and impetuosity of language. He took his fable from Euripides, but changed it according to the requisitions of the French theatre and of French manners. Some of these changes are for the better, as the substitution of Astyanax for an unknown Molossus of the Greek tragedian, the supposed son of Andromache by Pyrrhus. 'Most of those,' says Racine himself very justly, ' who have heard of Andromache, know her only as the widow of Hector and the mother of Astyanax.

They cannot reconcile themselves to her loving another husband and another son. And he has finely improved this happy idea of preserving Astyanax, by making the Greeks, jealous of his name, send an embassy by Orestes to demand his life; at once deepening the interest and developing the plot.

5. The female characters, Andromache and Hermione, are drawn with all Racine's delicate perception of ideal beauty; the one, indeed, prepared for his hand by those great masters in whose school he had disciplined his own gifts of nature, Homer, Euripides, Virgil; the other more original and more full of dramatic effect. It was, as we are told, the fine acting of Mademoiselle de Champmelé in this part, generally reckoned one of the most difficult on the French stage, which secured the success of the play. Racine, after the first representation, threw himself at her feet in a transport of gratitude, which was soon changed to love. It is more easy to censure some of the other characters. Pyrrhus is bold, haughty, passionate, the true son of Achilles, except where he appears as the lover of Andromache. It is inconceivable and truly ridiculous that a Greek of the heroic age, and such a Greek as Pyrrhus is represented by those whose imagination has given him existence, should feel the respectful passion towards his captive which we might reasonably expect in the romances of chivalry, or should express it in the tone of conventional gallantry that suited the court of Versailles. But Orestes is far worse; love-mad, and yet talking in gallant conceits, cold and polite, he discredits the poet, the tragedy, and the son of Agamemnon himself. It is better to kill one's mother than to utter such trash. In hinting that the previous madness of Orestes was for the love of Hermione, Racine has presumed too much on the ignorance, and too much on the bad taste, of his audience. But far more injudicious is his fantastic remorse and the supposed vision of the Furies in the last scene. It is astonishing that Racine should have challenged comparison with one of the most celebrated scenes of Euripides in circumstances that deprived him of the possibility of rendering his own effective. For the style of the Andromaque, it abounds with grace and beauty; but there are, to my apprehension, more insipid and feeble

lines, and a more effeminate tone, than in his later tragedies.

6. Britannicus appeared in 1669; and in this admirable

Britannicus. play Racine first showed that he did not depend
on the tone of gallantry usual among his courtly
hearers, nor on the languid sympathies that it excites. Terror and pity, the twin spirits of tragedy, to whom Aristotle
has assigned the great moral office of purifying the passions,
are called forth in their shadowy forms to sustain the consummate beauties of his diction. His subject was original
and happy; with that historic truth which usage required,
and that poetical probability which fills up the outline of
historic truth without disguising it. What can be more
entirely dramatic, what more terrible in the sense that
Aristotle means, (that is, the spectator's sympathy with the
dangers of the innocent,) than the absolute master of the
world, like the veiled prophet of Khorasan, throwing off the
appearances of virtue, and standing out at once in the ma-
turity of enormous guilt? A presaging gloom, like that
which other poets have sought by the hacknied artifices of
superstition, hangs over the scenes of this tragedy, and
deepens at its close. We sympathise by turns with the
guilty alarms of Agrippina, the virtuous consternation of
Burrhus, the virgin modesty of Junia, the unsuspecting
ingenuousness of Britannicus. Few tragedies on the French
stage, or indeed on any stage, save those of Shakspeare, display so great a variety of contrasted characters. None,
indeed, are ineffective, except the confidante of Agrippina;
for Narcissus is very far from being the mere confidant of
Nero; he is, as in history, his preceptor in crime; and his
cold villany is well contrasted with the fierce passion of the
despot. The criticisms of Fontenelle and others on small
incidents in the plot, such as the concealment of Nero behind
a curtain that he may hear the dialogue between Junia and
Britannicus, which is certainly more fit for comedy,[d] ought
not to weigh against such excellence as we find in all the
more essential requisites of a tragic drama. Racine had
much improved his language since Andromaque; the con-

---

[d] It is, however, taken from Tacitus.

ventional phraseology about flames and fine eyes, though not
wholly relinquished, is less frequent; and if he has not here
reached, as he never did, the peculiar impetuosity of Corneille,
nor given to his Romans the grandeur of his predecessor's
conception, he is full of lines wherein, as every word is
effective, there can hardly be any deficiency of vigour.   It is
the vigour indeed of Virgil, not of Lucan.

7. In one passage, Racine has, I think, excelled Shakspeare.   They have both taken the same idea from Plutarch.
The lines of Shakspeare are in Antony and Cleopatra:—

> Thy demon, that 's the spirit that keeps thee, is
> Noble, courageous, high, unmatchable,
> Where Cæsar's is not; but near him, thy angel
> Becomes a fear, as being o'erpowered.

These are, to my apprehension, not very forcible, and obscure even to those who know, what many do not, that by
'a fear' he meant a common goblin, a supernatural being
of a more plebeian rank than a demon or angel.   The single
verse of Racine is magnificent:—

> Mon génie étonné tremble devant le sien.

8. Bérénice, the next tragedy of Racine, is a surprising
proof of what can be done by a great master; but
it must be admitted that it wants many of the   Bérénice.
essential qualities that are required in the drama.   It might
almost be compared with Timon of Athens, by the absence
of fable and movement.   For nobleness and delicacy of sentiment, for grace of style, it deserves every praise; but is
rather tedious in the closet, and must be far more so on the
stage.   This is the only tragedy of Racine, unless perhaps
we except Athalie, in which the story presents an evident
moral; but no poet is more uniformly moral in his sentiments.   Corneille, to whom the want of dramatic fable was
never any great objection, attempted the subject of Bérénice
about the same time with far inferior success.   It required
what he could not give, the picture of two hearts struggling
against a noble and a blameless love.

9. It was unfortunate for Racine that he did not more
frequently break through the prejudices of the French

theatre in favour of classical subjects. A field was open of
almost boundless extent, the mediæval history of
Europe, and especially of France herself. His predecessor had been too successful in the Cid to leave it doubtful
whether an audience would approve such an innovation at
the hands of a favoured tragedian. Racine however did not
venture on a step which in the next century Voltaire turned
so much to account, and which made the fortune of some
inferior tragedies. But considering the distance of place
equivalent, for the ends of the drama, to that of time, he
founded on an event in the Turkish history not more than
thirty years old, his next tragedy, that of Bajazet. The
greater part indeed of the fable is due to his own invention.
Bajazet is reckoned to fall below most of his other tragedies
in beauty of style; but the fable is well connected; there is
a great deal of movement, and an unintermitting interest is
sustained by Bajazet and Atalide, two of the noblest cha-
acters that Racine has drawn. Atalide has not the ingenuous
simplicity of Junie, but displays a more dramatic flow of
sentiment and not less dignity or tenderness of soul. The
character of Roxane is conceived with truth and spirit; nor
is the resemblance some have found in it to that of Hermione
greater than belongs to forms of the same type. Acomat,
the vizir, is more a favourite with the French critics; but in
such parts Racine does not rise to the level of Corneille. No
poet is less exposed to the imputation of bombastic exaggeration; yet in the two lines with which Acomat concludes
the fourth act, there is at least an approach to burlesque;
and one can hardly say that they would have been out of
place in Tom Thumb:—

> Mourons, moi, cher Osmin, comme un vizir, et toi,
> Comme le favori d'un homme tel que moi.

10. The next tragedy was Mithridate; and in this Racine
has been thought to have wrestled against Corneille
on his own ground, the display of the unconquerable mind of a hero. We find in the part of Mithridate a
great depth of thought in compressed and energetic language.
But, unlike the masculine characters of Corneille, he is not
merely sententious. Racine introduces no one for the sake

Bajazet.

Mithridate.

of the speeches he has to utter.   In Mithridates he took
what history has delivered to us, blending with it no improbable fiction according to the manners of the East.   His love
for Monime has nothing in it extraordinary, or unlike what
we might expect from the king of Pontus; it is a fierce, a
jealous, a vindictive love; the necessities of the French language alone, and the usages of the French theatre, could
make it appear feeble.   His two sons are naturally less
effective; but the loveliness of Monime yields to no female
character of Racine.   There is something not quite satisfactory in the stratagems which Mithridates employs to draw
from her a confession of her love for his son.   They are not
uncongenial to the historic character, but, according to our
chivalrous standard of heroism, seem derogatory to the
poetical.

11. Iphigénie followed in 1674. In this Racine had again
to contend with Euripides in one of his most celebrated tragedies.   He had even, in the character of   Iphigénie.
Achilles, to contend, not with Homer himself, yet with the
Homeric associations familiar to every classical scholar.   The
love, in fact, of Achilles, and his politeness towards Clytem-
nestra, are not exempt from a tone of gallantry a little repugnant to our conception of his manners.   Yet the Achilles of
Homer is neither incapable of love nor of courtesy, so that
there is no essential repugnance to his character.   That of
Iphigenia in Euripides has been censured by Aristotle as
inconsistent; her extreme distress at the first prospect of
death being followed by an unusual display of courage.
Hurd has taken upon him the defence of the Greek tragedian, and observes, after Brumoy, that the Iphigenia of
Racine being modelled rather according to the comment of
Aristotle than the example of Euripides, is so much the
worse.[e]   But his apology is too subtle, and requires too long
reflection, for the ordinary spectator; and though Shakspeare
might have managed the transition of feeling with some of
his wonderful knowledge of human nature, it is certainly
presented too crudely by Euripides, and much in the style
which I have elsewhere observed to be too usual with our

---

[e] Hurd's Commentary on Horace, vol. i. p. 115.

old dramatists. The Iphigenia of Racine is not a character, like those of Shakspeare, and of him perhaps alone, which nothing less than intense meditation can develop to the reader, but one which a good actress might compass and a common spectator understand. Racine, like most other tragedians, wrote for the stage; Shakspeare aimed at a point beyond it, and sometimes too much lost sight of what it required.

12. Several critics have censured the part of Eriphile. Yet Fontenelle, prejudiced as he was against Racine, admits that it is necessary for the catastrophe, though he cavils, I think, against her appearance in the earlier part of the play, laying down a rule, by which our own tragedians would not have chosen to be tried, and which seems far too rigid, that the necessity of the secondary characters should be perceived from their first appearance.[f] The question for Racine was in what manner he should manage the catastrophe. The *fabulous truth*, the actual sacrifice of Iphigenia, was so revolting to the mind, that even Euripides thought himself obliged to depart from it. But this he effected by a contrivance impossible on the French stage, and which would have changed Racine's tragedy to a common melodrame. It appears to me that he very happily substituted the character of Eriphile, who, as Fontenelle well says, is the hind of the fable; and whose impetuous and somewhat disorderly passions both furnish a contrast to the ideal nobleness of Iphigenia throughout the tragedy, and reconcile us to her own fate at the close.

13. Once more, in Phèdre, did the great disciple of Euripides attempt to surpass his master. In both tra-
Phèdre.   gedies the character of Phædra herself throws into
shade all the others, but with this important difference, that in Euripides her death occurs about the middle of the piece, while she continues in Racine till the conclusion. The French poet has borrowed much from the Greek, more perhaps than in any former drama, but has surely heightened the interest, and produced a more splendid work of genius. I have never read the particular criticism in which Schlegel has endeavoured to elevate the Hippolytus above the Phèdre.

---

[f] Réflexions sur la Poëtique. Œuvres de Fontenelle, vol. iii. p. 149.

Many, even among French critics, have objected to the love
of Hippolytus for Aricia, by which Racine has deviated from
the older mythological tradition, though not without the
authority of Virgil. But we are hardly tied to all the circumstance of fable; and the cold young huntsman loses
nothing in the eyes of a modern reader by a virtuous attachment. This tragedy is said to be more open to verbal criticism
than the Iphigénie; but in poetical beauty I do not know
that Racine has ever surpassed it. The description of the
death of Hippolytus is perhaps his masterpiece. It is true
that, according to the practice of our stage, long descriptions, especially in elaborate language, are out of use; but
it is not, at least, for the advocates of Euripides to blame
them.

14. The Phèdre was represented in 1677; and after this
its illustrious author seemed to renounce the stage.
His increasing attachment to the Jansenists made ^Esther.
it almost impossible, with any consistency, to promote an
amusement which they anathematised. But he was induced,
after many years, in 1689, by Madame de Maintenon, to
write Esther for the purpose of representation by the young
ladies whose education she protected at St. Cyr. Esther,
though very much praised for beauty of language, is admitted
to possess little merit as a drama. Much indeed could not
be expected in the circumstances. It was acted at St. Cyr;
Louis applauded, and it is said that the Prince de Condé
wept. The greatest praise of Esther is that it encouraged
its author to write Athalie. Once more restored to
dramatic conceptions, his genius revived from sleep ^Athalie.
with no loss of the vigour of yesterday. He was even more
in Athalie than in Iphigénie and Britannicus. This great
work, published in 1691, with a royal prohibition to represent it on any theatre, stands by general consent at the head
of all the tragedies of Racine, for the grandeur, simplicity,
and interest of the fable, for dramatic terror, for theatrical
effect, for clear and judicious management, for bold and
forcible, rather than subtle delineation of character, for
sublime sentiment and imagery. It equals, if it does not, as
I should incline to think, surpass, all the rest in the perfection of style, and is far more free from every defect, especially

from feeble politeness and gallantry, which of course the subject could not admit. It has been said that he himself gave the preference to Phèdre; but it is more extraordinary that not only his enemies, of whom there were many, but the public itself, was for some years incapable of discovering the merit of Athalie. Boileau declared it to be a masterpiece, and one can only be astonished that any could have thought differently from Boileau. It doubtless gained much in general esteem when it came to be represented by good actors; for no tragedy in the French language is more peculiarly fitted for the stage.

15. The chorus, which he had previously introduced in Esther, was a very bold innovation (for the revival of what is forgotten must always be classed as innovation), and it required all the skill of Racine to prevent its appearing in our eyes an impertinent excrescence. But though we do not, perhaps, wholly reconcile ourselves to some of the songs, which too much suggest, by association, the Italian opera, the chorus of Athalie enhances the interest as well as the splendour of the tragedy. It was indeed more full of action and scenic pomp than any he had written, and probably than any other which up to that time had been represented in France. The part of Athalie predominates, but not so as to eclipse the rest. The highpriest Joad is drawn with a stern zeal admirably dramatic, and without which the idolatrous queen would have trampled down all before her during the conduct of the fable, whatever justice might have ensued at the last. We feel this want of an adequate resistance to triumphant crime in the Rodogune of Corneille. No character appears superfluous or feeble; while the plot has all the simplicity of the Greek stage, it has all the movement and continual excitation of the modern.

16. The female characters of Racine are of the greatest beauty; they have the ideal grace and harmony of ancient sculpture, and bear somewhat of the same analogy to those of Shakspeare which that art does to painting. Andromache, Monimia, Iphigenia, we may add Junia, have a dignity and faultlessness neither unnatural nor insipid, because they are only the ennobling and purifying of human passions. They are the forms of possible excellence, not

Racine's female characters.

from individual models, nor likely perhaps to delight every reader, for the same reason that more eyes are pleased by Titian than by Raffaelle. But it is a very narrow criticism which excludes either school from our admiration, which disparages Racine out of idolatry of Shakspeare. The latter, it is unnecessary for me to say, stands out of reach of all competition. But it is not on this account that we are to give up an author so admirable as Racine.

17. The chief faults of Racine may partly be ascribed to the influence of national taste, though we must con- Racine compared with Corneille. fess that Corneille has better avoided them. Though love, with the former, is always tragic and connected with the heroic passions, never appearing singly, as in several of our own dramatists, yet it is sometimes unsuitable to the character, and still more frequently feeble and courtier-like in the expression. In this he complied too much with the times; but we must believe that he did not entirely feel that he was wrong. Corneille had, even while Racine was in his glory, a strenuous band of supporters. Fontenelle, writing in the next century, declares that time has established a decision in which most seem to concur, that the first place is due to the elder poet, the second to the younger; every one making the interval between them a little greater or less according to his taste. But Voltaire, La Harpe, and in general, I apprehend, the later French critics, have given the preference to Racine. I presume to join my suffrage to theirs. Racine appears to me the superior tragedian; and I must add that I think him next to Shakspeare among all the moderns. The comparison with Euripides is so natural that it can hardly be avoided. Certainly no tragedy of the Greek poet is so skilful or so perfect as Athalie or Britannicus. The tedious scenes during which the action is stagnant, the impertinences of useless, often perverse morality, the extinction, by bad management, of the sympathy that had been raised in the earlier part of a play, the foolish alternation of repartees in a series of single lines, will never be found in Racine. But when we look only at the highest excellences of Euripides, there is, perhaps, a depth of pathos and an intensity of dramatic effect which Racine himself has not attained. The difference between the energy and sweetness

of the two languages is so important in the comparison, that
I shall give even this preference with some hesitation.

18. The style of Racine is exquisite. Perhaps he is second
only to Virgil among all poets. But I will give the
praise of this in the words of a native critic. ' His
expression is always so happy and so natural, that it seems
as if no other could have been found ; and every word is
placed in such a manner that we cannot fancy any other
place to have suited it as well. The structure of his style is
such that nothing could be displaced, nothing added, nothing
retrenched ; it is one unalterable whole. Even his incorrect-
nesses are often but sacrifices required by good taste, nor
would anything be more difficult than to write over again a
line of Racine. No one has enriched the language with a
greater number of turns of phrase ; no one is bold with more
felicity and discretion, or figurative with more grace and
propriety ; no one has handled with more command an idiom
often rebellious, or with more skill an instrument always
difficult ; no one has better understood that delicacy of style
which must not be mistaken for feebleness, and is, in fact,
but that air of ease which conceals from the reader the labour
of the work and the artifices of the composition ; or better
managed the variety of cadences, the resources of rhythm,
the association and deduction of ideas. In short, if we consider that his perfection in these respects may be opposed to
that of Virgil, and that he spoke a language less flexible,
less poetical, and less harmonious, we shall readily believe
that Racine is, of all mankind, the one to whom nature
has given the greatest talent for versification.' [g]

19. Thomas, the younger and far inferior brother of Pierre
Corneille, was yet by the fertility of his pen, by the
success of some of his tragedies, and by a certain
reputation which two of them have acquired, the next name,
but at a vast interval, to Racine. Voltaire says he would
have enjoyed a great reputation but for that of his brother—
one of those pointed sayings which seem to convey something,
but are really devoid of meaning. Thomas Corneille is never

Beauty of his style. (margin)

Thomas Corneille— his Ariane. (margin)

---

[g] La Harpe, Éloge de Racine, as quoted by himself in Cours de Littérature,
vol. vi.

compared with his brother; and probably his brother has been rather serviceable to his name with posterity than otherwise. He wrote with more purity, according to the French critics, and it must be owned that, in his Ariane, he has given to love a tone more passionate and natural than the manly scenes of the older tragedian ever present. This is esteemed his best work, but it depends wholly on the principal character, whose tenderness and injuries excite our sympathy, and from whose lips many lines of great beauty flow. It may be compared with the Bérénice of Racine, represented but a short time before; there is enough of resemblance in the fables to provoke comparison. That of Thomas Corneille is more tragic, less destitute of theatrical movement, and consequently better chosen; but such relative praise is of little value, where none can be given, in this respect, to the object of comparison. We feel that the prose romance is the proper sphere for the display of an affection, neither untrue to nature, nor unworthy to move the heart, but wanting the majesty of the tragic muse. An effeminacy uncongenial to tragedy belongs to this play; and the termination, where the heroine faints away instead of dying, is somewhat insipid. The only other tragedy of the younger Corneille that can be mentioned is the Earl of Essex. In this he has taken greater liberties with history than his critics approve; and though love does not so much predominate as in Ariane, it seems to engross, in a style rather too romantic, both the hero and his sovereign.

20. Neither of these tragedies, perhaps, deserves to be put on a level with the Manlius of La Fosse, to which La Harpe accords the preference above all of the seventeenth century after those of Corneille and Racine. It is just to observe, what is not denied, that the author has borrowed the greater part of his story from the Venice Preserved of Otway. The French critics maintain that he has far excelled his original. It is possible that we might hesitate to own this general superiority; but several blemishes have been removed, and the conduct is perhaps more noble, or at least more fitted to the French stage. But when we take from La Fosse what belongs to another—characters strongly marked, sympathies powerfully contrasted, a de-

velopment of the plot probable and interesting, what will
remain that is purely his own ?   There will remain a vigorous tone of language, a considerable power of description,
and a skill in adapting, we may add with justice, in sometimes improving, what he found in a foreign language.   We
must pass over some other tragedies which have obtained
less honour in their native land, those of Duché, Quinault,
and Campistron.

21. Molière is perhaps, of all French writers, the one whom
his country has most uniformly admired, and in
whom her critics are most unwilling to acknowledge
faults ; though the observations of Schlegel on the defects of
Molière, and especially on his large debts to older comedy,
are not altogether without foundation.   Molière began with
L'Étourdi in 1653, and his pieces followed rapidly till his
death in 1673.   About one-half are in verse ; I shall select a
few without regard to order of time, and first one written in
prose, L'Avare.

Molière.

22. Plautus first exposed upon the stage the wretchedness
of avarice, the punishment of a selfish love of gold,
not only in the life of pain it has cost to acquire it,
but in the terrors that it brings, in the disordered state of
mind, which is haunted, as by some mysterious guilt, by the
consciousness of secret wealth.   The character of Euclio in the
Aulularia is dramatic, and, as far as we know, original ; the
moral effect requires, perhaps, some touches beyond absolute
probability, but it must be confessed that a few passages are
overcharged.   Molière borrowed L'Avare from this comedy ;
and I am not at present aware that the subject, though so
well adapted for the stage, had been chosen by any intermediate dramatist.   He is indebted not merely for the scheme
of his play, but for many strokes of humour, to Plautus.
But this takes off little from the merit of this excellent
comedy.   The plot is expanded without incongruous or improbable circumstances ; new characters are well combined
with that of Harpagon, and his own is at once more diverting
and less extravagant than that of Euclio.   The penuriousness
of the latter, though by no means without example, leaves
no room for any other object than the concealed treasure, in
which his thoughts are concentred.   But Molière had

L'Avare.

conceived a more complicated action. Harpagon does not absolutely starve the rats; he possesses horses, though he feeds them ill; he has servants, though he grudges them clothes; he even contemplates a marriage supper at his own expense, though he intends to have a bad one. He has evidently been compelled to make some sacrifices to the usages of mankind, and is at once a more common and a more theatrical character than Euclio. In other respects they are much alike ; their avarice has reached that point where it is without pride ; the dread of losing their wealth has overpowered the desire of being thought to possess it; and though this is a more natural incident in the manners of Greece than in those of France, yet the concealment of treasure, even in the time of Molière, was sufficiently frequent for dramatic probability. A general tone of selfishness, the usual source and necessary consequence of avarice, conspires with the latter quality to render Harpagon odious ; and there wants but a little more poetical justice in the conclusion, which leaves the casket in his possession.

23. Hurd has censured Molière without much justice. ' For the picture of the avaricious man, Plautus and Molière have presented us with a fantastic, unpleasing draught of the passion of avarice.' It may be answered to this that Harpagon's character is, as has been said above, not so mere a delineation of the passion as that of Euclio. But as a more general vindication of Molière, it should be kept in mind, that every exhibition of a predominant passion within the compass of the five acts of a play must be coloured beyond the truth of nature, or it will not have time to produce its effect. This is one great advantage that romance possesses over the drama.

24. L'École des Femmes is among the most diverting comedies of Molière. Yet it has in a remarkable L'École
des Femmes. degree what seems inartificial to our own taste, and contravenes a good general precept of Horace; the action passes almost wholly in recital. But this is so well connected with the development of the plot and characters, and produces such amusing scenes, that no spectator, at least on the French theatre, would be sensible of any languor. Arnolphe is an excellent modification of the type which Molière loved to

reproduce; the selfish and morose cynic whose pretended
hatred of the vices of the world springs from an absorbing regard to his own gratification. He has made him as malignant
as censorious; he delights in tales of scandal; he is pleased that
Horace should be successful in gallantry, because it degrades
others. The half-witted and ill-bred child, of whom he becomes the dupe, as well as the two idiot servants, are delineated with equal vivacity. In this comedy we find the spirited
versification, full of grace and humour, in which no one has
rivalled Molière, and which has never been attempted on the
English stage. It was probably its merit which raised a
host of petty detractors, on whom the author revenged himself in his admirable piece of satire, La Critique de l'École
des Femmes. The affected pedantry of the Hôtel Rambouillet
seems to be ridiculed in this retaliation; nothing in fact could
be more unlike than the style of Molière to their own.

25. He gave another proof of contempt for the false taste
of some Parisian circles in the Misanthrope; though
the criticism of Alceste on the wretched sonnet forms

Le Misan-
thrope.

but a subordinate portion of that famous comedy. It is generally placed next to Tartuffe among the works of Molière.
Alceste is again the cynic, but more honourable and less
openly selfish, and with more of a real disdain of vice in his
misanthropy. Rousseau, upon this account, and many others
after him, have treated the play as a vindication of insincerity
against truth, and as making virtue itself ridiculous on the
stage. This charge however seems uncandid; neither the
rudeness of Alceste, nor the misanthropy from which it springs,
are to be called virtues; and we may observe that he displays
no positively good quality beyond sincerity, unless his un-
grounded and improbable love for a coquette is to pass for
such. It is true that the politeness of Philinthe, with whom
the Misanthrope is contrasted, borders a little too closely
upon flattery; but no oblique end is in his view; he flatters
to give pleasure; and if we do not much esteem his character,
we are not solicitous for his punishment. The dialogue of
the Misanthrope is uniformly of the highest style; the female,
and indeed all the characters, are excellently conceived and
sustained: if this comedy fails of any thing at present, it is
through the difference of manners, and, perhaps, in representation, through the want of animated action on the stage.

26. In Les Femmes savantes there is a more evident personality in the characters, and a more malicious Les Femmes exposure of absurdity, than in the Misanthrope; but savantes. the ridicule, falling on a less numerous class, is not so well calculated to be appreciated by posterity. It is, however, both in reading and representation, a more amusing comedy: in no one instance has Molière delineated such variety of manners, or displayed so much of his inimitable gaiety and power of fascinating the audience with very little plot, by the mere exhibition of human follies. The satire falls deservedly on pretenders to taste and literature, for whom Molière always testifies a bitterness of scorn in which we perceive some resentment of their criticisms. The shorter piece, entitled Les Précieuses ridicules, is another shaft directed at the literary ladies of Paris. They had provoked a dangerous enemy; but the good taste of the next age might be ascribed in great measure to his unmerciful exposure of affectation and pedantry.

27. It was not easy, so late as the age of Molière, for the dramatist to find any untrodden field in the follies and vices of mankind. But one had been reserved Tartuffe. for him in Tartuffe—religious hypocrisy. We should have expected the original draft of such a character on the English stage; nor had our old writers been forgetful of their inveterate enemies, the Puritans, who gave such full scope for their satire. But choosing rather the easy path of ridicule, they fell upon the starch dresses and quaint language of the fanatical party; and where they exhibited these in conjunction with hypocrisy, made the latter more ludicrous than hateful. The Luke of Massinger is deeply and villanously dissembling, but does not wear so conspicuous a garb of religious sanctity as Tartuffe. The comedy of Molière is not only original in this character, but is a new creation in dramatic poetry. It has been doubted by some critics, whether the depth of guilt that it exhibits, the serious hatred that it inspires, are not beyond the strict province of comedy. But this seems rather a technical cavil. If subjects such as the Tartuffe are not fit for comedy, they are at least fit for dramatic representation, and some new phrase must be invented to describe their class.

28. A different kind of objection is still sometimes made to this play, that it brings religion itself into suspicion. And this would no doubt have been the case, if the contemporaries of Molière in England had dealt with the subject. But the boundaries between the reality and its false appearances are so well guarded in this comedy, that no reasonable ground of exception can be thought to remain. No better advice can be given to those who take umbrage at the Tartuffe than to read it again. For there may be good reason to suspect that they are themselves among those for whose benefit it was intended; the Tartuffes, happily, may be comparatively few, but while the Orgons and Pernelles are numerous, they will not want their harvest. Molière did not invent the prototypes of his hypocrite; they were abundant at Paris in his time.

29. The interest of this play continually increases, and the fifth act is almost crowded by a rapidity of events, not so usual on the French stage as our own. Tartuffe himself is a masterpiece of skill. Perhaps in the cavils of La Bruyère there may be some justice; but the essayist has forgotten that no character can be rendered entirely effective to an audience without a little exaggeration of its attributes. Nothing can be more happily conceived than the credulity of the honest Orgon, and his more doting mother; it is that which we sometimes witness, incurable except by the evidence of the senses, and fighting every inch of ground against that. In such a subject there was not much opportunity for the comic talent of Molière; yet in some well-known passages he has enlivened it as far as was possible. The Tartuffe will generally be esteemed the greatest effort of this author's genius; the Misanthrope, the Femmes savantes, and the Ecole des Femmes will follow in various order, according to our tastes. These are by far the best of his comedies in verse. Among those in prose we may give the first place to L'Avare, and the next either to Le Bourgeois Gentilhomme, or to George Dandin.

30. These two plays have the same objects of moral satire; on one hand the absurd vanity of plebeians in seeking the alliance or acquaintance of the nobility; on the other, the pride and meanness of the nobility themselves. They are both abundantly diverting; but the

Bourgeois Gentilhomme. George Dandin.

sallies of humour are, I think, more frequent in the first three acts of the former. The last two acts are improbable and less amusing. The shorter pieces of Molière border very much upon farce; he permits himself more vulgarity of character, more grossness in language and incident, but his farces are seldom absurd, and never dull.

31. The French have claimed for Molière, and few perhaps have disputed the pretension, a superiority over all earlier and later writers of comedy. He certainly Character of Molière. leaves Plautus, the original model of the school to which he belonged, at a vast distance. The grace and gentlemanly elegance of Terence he has not equalled; but in the more appropriate merits of comedy, just and forcible delineation of character, skilful contrivance of circumstances, and humorous dialogue, we must award him the prize. The Italian and Spanish dramatists are quite unworthy to be named in comparison; and if the French theatre has, in later times, as is certainly the case, produced some excellent comedies, we have, I believe, no reason to contradict the suffrage of the nation itself, that they owe almost as much to what they have caught from this great model, as to the natural genius of their authors. But it is not for us to abandon the rights of Shakspeare. In all things most essential to comedy, we cannot acknowledge his inferiority to Molière. He had far more invention of characters, with an equal vivacity and force in their delineation. His humour was at least as abundant and natural, his wit incomparably more brilliant; in fact, Molière hardly exhibits this quality at all.[h] The Merry Wives of Windsor, almost the only pure comedy of Shakspeare, is surely not disadvantageously compared with George Dandin or Le Bourgeois Gentilhomme, or even with L'Ecole des Femmes. For the Tartuffe or the Misanthrope it is vain to seek a proper counterpart in Shakspeare; they belong to a different state of manners. But the powers of Molière are directed with greater skill to their object; none of his energy is wasted; the spectator is not interrupted by the serious scenes of tragi-comedy, nor his attention drawn

---

[h] [A French critic upon the first edition of this work has supposed *wit* to be the same as *esprit*, and is justly astonished that I should deny the latter quality to Molière, especially after the eulogies I have been passing on him.—1842.]

aside by poetical episodes. Of Shakspeare we may justly
say that he had the greater genius, but perhaps of Molière,
that he has written the best comedies. We cannot at least
put any third dramatist in competition with him. Fletcher
and Jonson, Wycherley and Congreve, Farquhar and Sheridan, with great excellences of their own, fall short of his
merit as well as of his fame. Yet in humorous conception,
our admirable play, the Provoked Husband, the best parts of
which are due to Vanbrugh, seems to be equal to any thing
he has left. His spirited and easy versification stands of
course untouched by any English rivalry ; we may have
been wise in rejecting verse from our stage, but we have certainly given the French a right to claim all the honour that
belongs to it.

32. Racine once only attempted comedy. His wit was
quick and sarcastic, and in epigram he did not
spare his enemies. In his Plaideurs there is more
of humour and stage-effect than of wit. The ridicule
falls happily on the pedantry of lawyers and the folly of
suitors ; but the technical language is lost in great measure
upon the audience. This comedy, if it be not rather a
farce, is taken from The Wasps of Aristophanes ; and that
Rabelais of antiquity supplied an extravagance very improbably introduced into the third act of Les Plaideurs, the
trial of the dog. Far from improving the humour, which
had been amusingly kept up during the first two acts, this
degenerates into absurdity.

*Les Plai-
deurs
of Racine.*

33. Regnard is always placed next to Molière among the
comic writers of France in this, and perhaps in any
age. The plays, indeed, which entitle him to such
a rank, are but few. Of these the best is acknowledged to
be Le Joueur. Regnard, taught by his own experience, has
here admirably delineated the character of an inveterate
gamester ; without parade of morality, few comedies are
more usefully moral. We have not the struggling virtues of
a Charles Surface, which the dramatist may feign that he
may reward at the fifth act ; Regnard has better painted the
selfish ungrateful being, who, though not incapable of love,
pawns his mistress's picture, the instant after she has given
it to him, that he may return to the dice-box. Her just

*Regnard—
Le Joueur.*

abandonment, and his own disgrace, terminate the comedy
with a moral dignity which the stage does not always maintain, and which, in the first acts, the spectator does not expect. The other characters seem to me various, spirited,
and humorous ; the valet of Valère the gamester is one of
the best of that numerous class, to whom comedy has owed
so much; but the pretended marquis, though diverting, talks
too much like a genuine coxcomb of the world. Molière did
this better in Les Précieuses ridicules. Regnard is in this play
full of those gay sallies which cannot be read without laughter; the incidents follow rapidly; there is more movement
than in some of the best of Molière's comedies, and the
speeches are not so prolix.

34. Next to Le Joueur among Regnard's comedies it has
been usual to place Le Légataire, not by any means
inferior to the first in humour and vivacity, but with _{His other plays.}
less force of character, and more of the common tricks of the
stage. The moral, instead of being excellent, is of the worst
kind, being the success and dramatic reward of a gross fraud,
the forgery of a will by the hero of the piece and his servant.
This servant is however a very comical rogue, and we should
not perhaps wish to see him sent to the galleys. A similar
censure might be passed on the comedy of Regnard which
stands third in reputation, Les Menechmes. The subject, as
explained by the title, is old—twin-brothers, whose undis-
tinguishable features are the source of endless confusion ;
but what neither Plautus nor Shakspeare have thought of,
one avails himself of the likeness to receive a large sum of
money due to the other, and is thought very generous at the
close of the play when he restores a moiety. Of the plays
founded on this diverting exaggeration, Regnard's is perhaps
the best ; he has more variety of incident than Plautus; and
by leaving out the second pair of twins, the Dromio servants,
who render the Comedy of Errors almost too inextricably
confused for the spectator or reader, as well as by making
one of the brothers aware of the mistake, and a party in the
deception, he has given an unity of plot instead of a series
of incoherent blunders.

35. The Mère Coquette of Quinault appears a comedy
of great merit. Without the fine traits of nature which

we find in those of Molière, without the sallies of humour
Quinault.
Boursault. which enliven those of Regnard, with a versification perhaps not very forcible, it pleases us by a
fable at once novel, as far as I know, and natural, by the
interesting characters of the lovers, by the decency and tone
of good company, which are never lost in the manners, the
incidents, or the language. Boursault, whose tragedies are
little esteemed, displayed some originality in Le Mercure
galant. The idea is one which has not unfrequently been
imitated on the English as well as French stage, but it is
rather adapted to the shorter drama than to a regular
comedy of five acts. The Mercure galant was a famous
magazine of light periodical amusement, such as was then
new in France, which had a great sale, and is described in a
few lines by one of the characters in this piece.[i] Boursault
places his hero, by the editor's consent, as a temporary substitute in the office of this publication, and brings, in a series
of detached scenes, a variety of applicants for his notice. A
comedy of this kind is like a compound animal; a few chief
characters must give unity to the whole, but the effect is
produced by the successive personages who pass over the
stage, display their humour in a single scene, and disappear.
Boursault has been in some instances successful; but such
pieces generally owe too much to temporary sources of
amusement.

36. Dancourt, as Voltaire has said, holds the same rank
Dancourt. relatively to Molière in farce, that Regnard does in
the higher comedy. He came a little after the
former, and when the prejudice that had been created
against comedies in prose by the great success of the other
kind had begun to subside. The Chevalier à la Mode is the
only play of Dancourt that I know; it is much above farce,
and if length be a distinctive criterion, it exceeds most
comedies. This would be very slight praise, if we could not
add that the reader does not find it one page too long, that

---

[i] Le Mercure est une bonne chose :
On y trouve de tout, fable, histoire, vers, prose,
Siéges, combats, procès, mort, mariage, amour,
Nouvelles de province, et nouvelles de cour—
Jamais livre à mon gré ne fut plus nécessaire.
                                        Act i. scene 2.

The Mercure galant was established

in 1672 by one Visé; it was intended
to fill the same place as a critical record of polite literature, which the
Journal des Sçavans did in learning and
science.

the ridicule is poignant and happy, the incidents well contrived, the comic situations amusing, the characters clearly
marked. La Harpe, who treats Dancourt with a sort of
contempt, does not so much as mention this play. It is a
satire on the pretensions of a class then rising, the rich
financiers, which long supplied materials, through dramatic
caricature, to public malignity, and the envy of a less opulent
aristocracy.

37. The life of Brueys is rather singular. Born of a noble
Huguenot family, he was early devoted to Protestant
theology, and even presumed to enter the lists against   Brueys.
Bossuet. But that champion of the faith was like one of
those knights in romance, who first unhorse their rash antagonists, and then make them work as slaves. Brueys was soon
converted, and betook himself to write against his former
errors. He afterwards became an ecclesiastic. Thus far there
is nothing much out of the common course in his history.
But grown weary of living alone, and having some natural
turn to comedy, he began, rather late, to write for the stage,
with the assistance, or perhaps only under the name, of a
certain Palaprat. The plays of Brueys had some success;
but he was not in a position to delineate recent manners,
and in the only comedy with which I am acquainted, Le
Muet, he has borrowed the leading part of his story from
Terence. The language seems deficient in vivacity, which,
when there is no great naturalness or originality of character
cannot be dispensed with.

38. The French opera, after some ineffectual attempts by
Mazarin to naturalise an Italian company, was suc-   Operas of
cessfully established by Lulli in 1672. It is the   Quinault.
prerogative of music in the melodrame to render poetry its
dependent ally; but the airs of Lulli have been forgotten,
and the verses of his coadjutor Quinault remain. He is not
only the earliest, but by general consent the unrivalled poet
of French music. Boileau indeed treated him with undeserved scorn, but probably through dislike of the tone he
was obliged to preserve, which in the eyes of so stern a
judge, and one so insensible to love, appeared languid and
effeminate. Quinault nevertheless was not incapable of
vigorous and impressive poetry; a lyric grandeur distin-

guishes some of his songs; he seems to possess great felicity
of adorning every subject with appropriate imagery and sentiment; his versification has a smoothness and charm of
melody which has made some say that the lines were already
music before they came to the composer's hands; his fables,
whether taken from mythology or modern romance, display
invention and skill. Voltaire, La Harpe, Schlegel, and the
author of the life of Quinault in the Biographie universelle,
but most of all, the testimony of the public, have compensated for the severity of Boileau. The Armide is Quinault's
latest and also his finest opera.

<hr>

Sect. II.—On the English Drama.

State of the Stage after the Restoration—Tragedies of Dryden, Otway,
Southern—Comedies of Congreve and others.

39. THE troubles of twenty years, and, much more, the
Revival of fanatical antipathy to stage-plays which the pre-
the English
theatre. dominant party affected, silenced the muse of the
buskin, and broke the continuity of those works of the elder
dramatists, which had given a tone to public sentiment as to
the drama from the middle of Elizabeth's reign. Davenant
had, by a sort of connivance, opened a small house for the
representation of plays, though not avowedly so called, near
the Charter House in 1656. He obtained a patent after the
Restoration. By this time another generation had arisen,
and the scale of taste was to be adjusted anew. The fondness for the theatre revived with increased avidity; more
splendid decoration, actors probably, especially Betterton, of
greater powers, and, above all, the attraction of female performers, who had never been admitted on the older stage,
conspired with the keen appetite that long restraint produced,
and with the general gaiety, or rather dissoluteness, of
manners. Yet the multitude of places for such amusement
was not as great as under the first Stuarts. Two houses only
were opened under royal patents, granting them an exclusive
privilege, one by what was called the King's Company, in
Drury Lane, another by the Duke of York's Company, in

Lincoln's Inn Fields.   Betterton, who was called the English
Roscius, till Garrick claimed that title, was sent to Paris by
Charles II., that, taking a view of the French stage, he
might better judge of what would contribute to the improvement of our own.   It has been said, and probably with truth,
that he introduced movable scenes, instead of the fixed
tapestry that had been hung across the stage ; but this improvement he could not have borrowed from France.   The
king not only countenanced the theatre by his patronage,
but by so much personal notice of the chief actors, and so
much interest in all the affairs of the theatre, as elevated
their condition.

40. An actor of great talents is the best friend of the
great dramatists; his own genius demands theirs   Change of
for its support and display ; and a fine performer   public taste.
would as soon waste the powers of his hand on feeble music,
as a man like Betterton or Garrick represent what is insipid
or in bad taste.   We know that the former, and some of
his contemporaries, were celebrated in the great parts of our
early stage, in those of Shakspeare and Fletcher.   But the
change of public taste is sometimes irresistible by those who,
as, in Johnson's antithesis, they ' live to please, must please
to live.'   Neither tragedy nor comedy was maintained at its
proper level ; and as the world is apt to demand novelty on
the stage, the general tone of dramatic representation in
this period, whatever credit it may have done to the performers, reflects little in comparison with our golden age,
upon those who wrote for them.

41. It is observed by Scott, that the French theatre, which
was now thought to be in perfection, guided the   Its
criticism of Charles's court, and afforded the pattern   causes.
of those tragedies which continued in fashion for twenty
years after the Restoration, and which were called rhyming
or heroic plays.   Though there is a general justice in this
remark, I am not aware that the inflated tone of these plays
is imitated from any French tragedy ; certainly there was a
nobler model in the best works of Corneille.   But Scott is
more right in deriving the unnatural and pedantic dialogue
which prevailed through these performances from the
romances of Scudery and Calprenède.   These were, about,

the era of the Restoration, almost as popular among our
indolent gentry as in France; and it was to be expected that
a style would gain ground in tragedy, which is not so widely
removed from what tragedy requires, but that an ordinary
audience would fail to perceive the difference.   There is but
a narrow line between the sublime and the tumid; the man of
business or of pleasure who frequents the theatre must have
accustomed himself to make such large allowances, to put
himself into a state of mind so totally different from his
every day habits, that a little extraordinary deviation from
nature, far from shocking him, will rather show like a
further advance towards excellence.   Hotspur and Almanzor,
Richard and Aurungzebe, seem to him cast in the same
mould; beings who can never occur in the common walks of
life, but whom the tragedian has, by a tacit convention with
the audience, acquired a right of feigning like his ghosts and
witches.

42. The first tragedies of Dryden were what was called
Heroic tra- heroic, and written in rhyme; an innovation which,
gedies of
Dryden.   of course, must be ascribed to the influence of
the French theatre.   They have occasionally much vigour
of sentiment and much beautiful poetry, with a versification sweet even to lusciousness.   The Conquest of Grenada
is, on account of its extravagance, the most celebrated of
these plays; but it is inferior to the Indian Emperor, from
which it would be easy to select passages of perfect elegance.   It is singular that although the rhythm of dramatic
verse is commmonly permitted to be the most lax of any,
Dryden has in this play availed himself of none of his
wonted privileges.   He regularly closes the sense with the
couplet, and falls into a smoothness of cadence which, though
exquisitely mellifluous, is perhaps too uniform.   In the Conquest of Grenada the versification is rather more broken.

43. Dryden may probably have been fond of this species
His later   of tragedy, on account of his own facility in
tragedies.   rhyming, and his habit of condensing his sense.
Rhyme, indeed, can only be rejected in our language from
the tragic scene, because blank verse affords wider scope for
the emotions it ought to excite; but for the tumid rhapsodies
which the personages of his heroic plays utter, there can be

no excuse. He adhered to this tone, however, till the change in public taste, and especially the ridicule thrown on his own plays by the Rehearsal, drove him to adopt a very different, though not altogether faultless, style of tragedy. His principal works of this latter class are All for Love, in 1678, the Spanish Friar, commonly referred to 1682, and Don Sebastian, in 1690. Upon these the dramatic fame of Dryden is built; while the rants of Almanzor and Maximin are never mentioned but in ridicule. The chief excellence of the first tragedy appears to consist in the beauty of the language, that of the second in the interest of the story, and that of the third in the highly finished character of Dorax. Dorax is the best of Dryden's tragic characters, and perhaps the only one in which he has applied his great knowledge of the human mind to actual delineation. It is highly dramatic, because formed of those complex passions which may readily lead either to virtue or to vice, and which the poet can manage so as to surprise the spectator without transgressing consistency. The Zanga of Young, a part of some theatrical effect, has been compounded of this character, and of that of Iago. But Don Sebastian is as imperfect as all plays must be in which a single personage is thrown forward in too strong relief for the rest. The language is full of that rant which characterised Dryden's earlier tragedies, and to which a natural predilection seems, after some interval, to have brought him back. Sebastian himself may seem to have been intended as a contrast to Muley Moloch; but if the author had any rule to distinguish the blustering of the hero from that of the tyrant, he has not left the use of it in his reader's hands. The plot of this tragedy is ill conducted, especially in the fifth act. Perhaps the delicacy of the present age may have been too fastidious in excluding altogether from the drama this class of fables; because they may often excite great interest, give scope to impassioned poetry, and are admirably calculated for the ἀναγνώρισις, or discovery, which is so much dwelt upon by the critics; nor can the story of Œdipus, which has furnished one of the finest and most artful tragedies ever written, be well thought an improper subject even for representation. But they require, of all others, to be dexterously managed; they may make the main distress of a tragedy, but not an episode in it. Our feelings revolt at seeing, as in Don Sebastian, an incestuous passion brought forward as the make-weight of a plot, to eke out a fifth act, and to dispose of those characters whose fortune the main story has not quite wound up.

44. The Spanish Friar has been praised for what Johnson calls the 'happy coincidence and coalition of the two plots.' It is difficult to understand what can be mean by a compliment which seems either ironical or ignorant. Nothing can be more remote from the truth. The artifice of combining two distinct stories on the stage is, we may suppose, either to interweave the incidents of one into those of the other, or at least so to connect some characters with each intrigue, as to make the spectator fancy them less distinct than they are. Thus in the Merchant of Venice, the courtship of Bassanio and Portia is happily connected with the main plot of Antonio and Shylock by two circumstances : it is to set Bassanio forward in his suit that the fatal bond is first given; and it is by Portia's address that its forfeiture is explained away. The same play affords an instance of another kind of underplot, that of Lorenzo and Jessica, which is more episodical, and might perhaps be removed without any material loss to the fable ; though even this serves to account for, we do not say to palliate, the vindictive exasperation of the Jew. But to which of these do the comic scenes in the Spanish Friar bear most resemblance ? Certainly to the latter. They consist entirely of an intrigue which Lorenzo, a young officer, carries on with a rich usurer's wife ; but there is not, even by accident, any relation between his adventures and the love and murder which go forward in the palace. The Spanish Friar, so far as it is a comedy, is reckoned the best performance of Dryden in that line. Father Dominic is very amusing, and has been copied very freely by succeeding dramatists, especially in the Duenna. But Dryden has no great abundance of wit in this or any of his comedies. His jests are practical, and he seems to have written more for the eye than the ear. It may be noted as a proof of this, that his stage directions are unusually full. In point of diction, the Spanish Friar in its tragic scenes, and All for Love, are certainly the best plays of Dryden. They

Spanish Friar.

are the least infected with his great fault, bombast, and
should perhaps be read over and over by those who would
learn the true tone of English tragedy. In dignity, in
animation, in striking images and figures, there are few or
none that excel them; the power indeed of impressing sympathy, or commanding tears, was seldom placed by nature
within the reach of Dryden.

45. The Orphan of Otway, and his Venice Preserved,
will generally be reckoned the best tragedies of this
period. They have both a deep pathos, springing
Otway.
from the intense and unmerited distress of women; ooth,
especially the latter, have a dramatic eloquence, rapid and
flowing, with less of turgid extravagance than we find in
Otway's contemporaries, and sometimes with very graceful
poetry. The story of the Orphan is domestic, and borrowed,
as I believe, from some French novel, though I do not at
present remember where I have read it; it was once popular
on the stage, and gave scope for good acting, but is unpleasing to the delicacy of our own age. Venice Preserved is
more frequently represented than any tragedy after those of
Shakspeare; the plot is highly dramatic in conception and
conduct; even what seems, when we read it, a defect, the
shifting of our wishes, or perhaps rather of our ill wishes,
between two parties, the senate and the conspirators, who are
redeemed by no virtue, does not, as is shown by experience,
interfere with the spectator's interest. Pierre indeed is one
of those villains for whom it is easy to excite the sympathy
of the half-principled and the inconsiderate. But the great
attraction is in the character of Belvidera; and when that
part is represented by such as we remember to have seen, no
tragedy is honoured by such a tribute, not of tears alone, but
of more agony than many would seek to endure. The versification of Otway, like that of most in this period, runs almost to
an excess into the line of eleven syllables, sometimes also
into the *sdrucciolo* form, or twelve syllables with a dactylic
close. These give a considerable animation to tragic verse.

46. Southern's Fatal Discovery, latterly represented under
the name of Isabella, is almost as familiar to the
lovers of our theatre as Venice Preserved itself; and
Southern.
for the same reason, that whenever an actress of great tragic

powers arises, the part of Isabella is as fitted to exhibit them
as that of Belvidera. The choice and conduct of the story
are, however, Southern's chief merits; for there is little
vigour in the language, though it is natural, and free from
the usual faults of his age. A similar character may be
given to his other tragedy, Oroonoko; in which Southern
deserves the praise of having, first of any English writer,
denounced the traffic in slaves, and the cruelties of their
West Indian bondage. The moral feeling is high in this
tragedy; and it has sometimes been acted with a certain
success; but the execution is not that of a superior dramatist. Of Lee nothing need be said, but that he is,
in spite of his proverbial extravagance, a man of
poetical mind and some dramatic skill. But he has violated
historic truth in Theodosius without gaining much by invention. The Morning Bride of Congreve is written in
prolix declamation, with no power over the passions.
Johnson is well known to have praised a few lines in this
tragedy as among the finest descriptions in the language;
while others, by a sort of contrariety, have spoken of them
as worth nothing. Truth is in its usual middle path; many
better passages may be found, but they are well written and
impressive.[k]

47. In the early English comedy, we find a large intermixture of obscenity in the lower characters, nor
always confined to them, with no infrequent scenes
of licentious incident and language. But these are invariably
so brought forward as to manifest the dramatist's scorn of
vice, and to excite no other sentiment in a spectator of even
an ordinary degree of moral purity. In the plays that appeared after the Restoration, and that from the beginning, a
different tone was assumed. Vice was in her full career on
the stage, unchecked by reproof, unshamed by contrast, and
for the most part unpunished by mortification at the close.
Nor are these less coarse in expression, or less impudent in
their delineation of low debauchery, than those of the preceding period. It may be observed, on the contrary, that
they rarely exhibit the manners of truly polished life, accord-

Lee.

Congreve.

*Comedies of
Chas. II.'s
reign.*

---

[k] Mourning Bride, act ii. scene 3. Johnson's Life of Congreve.

ing to any notions we can frame of them, and are, in this
respect, much below those of Fletcher, Massinger, and Shirley.
It might not be easy perhaps to find a scene in any comedy
of Charles II.'s reign where one character has the behaviour
of a gentleman, in the sense which we attach to the word.
Yet the authors of these were themselves in the world, and
sometimes men of family and considerable station. The
cause must be found in the state of society itself, debased
as well as corrupted, partly by the example of the court,
partly by the practice of living in taverns, which became
much more inveterate after the Restoration than before.
The contrast with the manners of Paris, as far as the stage
is their mirror, does not tell to our advantage. These plays,
as it may be expected, do not aim at the higher glories of
comic writing; they display no knowledge of nature, nor
often rise to any other conception of character than is gained
by a caricature of some known class, or perhaps of some
remarkable individual. Nor do they in general deserve much
credit as comedies of intrigue; the plot is seldom invented
with much care for its development: and if scenes follow one
another in a series of diverting incidents, if the entanglements
are such as produce laughter, above all, if the personages
keep up a well-sustained battle of repartee, the purpose is
sufficiently answered. It is in this that they often excel;
some of them have considerable humour in the representation
of character, though this may not be very original, and a
good deal of wit in their dialogue.

48. Wycherley is remembered for two comedies, the Plain
Dealer and the Country Wife, the latter represented with some change, in modern times, under　Wycherley.
the name of the Country Girl. The former has been
frequently said to be taken from the Misanthrope of Molière;
but this, like many current assertions, seems to have little if
any foundation. Manly, the Plain Dealer, is, like Alceste, a
speaker of truth; but the idea is at least one which it was
easy to conceive without plagiarism, and there is not the
slightest resemblance in any circumstance or scene of the
two comedies. We cannot say the same of the Country
Wife; it was evidently suggested by L'Ecole des Femmes;
the character of Arnolphe has been copied; but even here the

whole conduct of the piece of Wycherley is his own. It is more artificial than that of Molière, wherein too much passes in description; the part of Agnes is rendered still more poignant; and among the comedies of Charles's reign, I am not sure that it is surpassed by any.

49. Shadwell and Etherege, and the famous Afra Behn, have endeavoured to make the stage as grossly immoral as their talents permitted; but the two former, especially Shadwell, are not destitute of humour. At the death of Improve- Charles it had reached the lowest point; after the ment after Revolution, it became not much more a school of the Revolu- virtue, but rather a better one of polished manners than before; and certainly drew to its service some men of comic genius whose names are now not only very familiar to our ears, as the boasts of our theatre, but whose works have not all ceased to enliven its walls.

50. Congreve, by the Old Bachelor, written, as some have said, at twenty-one years of age, but in fact not Congreve. quite so soon, and represented in 1693, placed himself at once in a rank which he has always retained. Though not, I think, the first, he is undeniably among the first names. The Old Bachelor was quickly followed by the Double Dealer, and that by Love for Love, in which he reached the summit of his reputation. The last of his four comedies, the Way of the World, is said to have been coldly received; for which it is hard to assign any substantial cause unless it be some want of sequence in the plot. The peculiar excellence of Congreve is his wit, incessantly sparkling from the lips of almost every character, but on this account it is accompanied by want of nature and simplicity. Nature indeed and simplicity do not belong as proper attributes to that comedy which, itself the creature of an artificial society, has for its proper business to exaggerate the affectation and hollowness of the world. A critical code which should require the comedy of polite life to be natural would make it intolerable. But there are limits of deviation from likeness which even caricature must not transgress; and the type of truth should always regulate the playful aberrations of an inventive pencil. The manners of Congreve's comedies are not, to us at least, like those of reality; I am not sure that we have any cause

to suppose that they much better represent the times in which
they appeared.   His characters, with an exception or two, are
heartless and vicious ; which, on being attacked by Collier, he
justified, probably by an afterthought, on the authority of
Aristotle's definition of comedy ; that it is μίμησις φαυλοτέρων,
an imitation of what is the worse in human nature.[m]   But it
must be acknowledged that, more than any preceding writer
among us, he kept up the tone of a gentleman ; his men of
the world are profligate, but not coarse ; he rarely, like Shadwell, or even Dryden, caters for the populace of the theatre
by such indecencies as they must understand ; he gave, in
fact, a tone of refinement to the public taste, which it never
lost, and which, in its progression, has almost banished his
own comedies from the stage.

51. Love for Love is generally reputed the best of these.
Congreve has never any great success in the con- _Love for_
ception or management of his plot; but in this _Love._
comedy there is least to censure ; several of the characters
are exceedingly humorous ; the incidents are numerous and
not complex; the wit is often admirable.   Angelica and Miss
Prue, Ben and Tattle, have been repeatedly imitated ; but
they have, I think, a considerable degree of dramatic originality in themselves.   Johnson has observed that ' Ben the
sailor is not reckoned over natural, but he is very diverting.'
Possibly he may be quite as natural a portrait of a mere
sailor, as that to which we have become used in modern
comedy.

52. The Way of the World I should perhaps incline to
place next to this; the coquetry of Millamant, not _His other_
without some touches of delicacy and affection, the _comedies._
impertinent coxcombry of Petulant and Witwood, the
mixture of wit and ridiculous vanity in Lady Wishfort, are
amusing to the reader.   Congreve has here made more use
than, as far as I remember, had been common in England, of
the all-important soubrette, on whom so much depends in
French comedy.   The manners of France happily enabled
her dramatists to improve what they had borrowed with

---

[m] Congreve's Amendments of Mr. Collier's false citations.

signal success from the ancient stage, the witty and artful
servant, faithful to his master while he deceives every one
besides, by adding this female attendant, not less versed in
every artifice, nor less quick in repartee. Mincing and
Foible, in this play of Congreve, are good specimens of the
class; but speaking with some hesitation, I do not think they
will be found, at least not so naturally drawn, in the comedies
of Charles's time Many would perhaps, not without cause,
prefer the Old Bachelor, which abounds with wit, but seems
rather deficient in originality of character and circumstance.
The Double Dealer is entitled to the same praise of wit, and
some of the characters, though rather exaggerated, are
amusing; but the plot is so entangled towards the conclusion, that I have found it difficult, even in reading, to comprehend it.

53. Congreve is not superior to Farquhar and Vanbrugh,
Farquhar.   if we might compare the whole of their works.
Vanbrugh.   Never has he equalled in vivacity, in originality of
contrivance, or in clear and rapid development of intrigue,
the Beaux' Stratagem of the one, and much less the admirable delineation of the Wronghead family in the Provoked
Husband of the other. But these were of the eighteenth
century. Farquhar's Trip to the Jubilee, though once a
popular comedy, is not distinguished by more than an easy
flow of wit, and perhaps a little novelty in some of the
characters; it is indeed written in much superior language
to the plays anterior to the Revolution. But the Relapse
and the Provoked Wife of Vanbrugh have attained a considerable reputation. In the former, the character of Amanda
is interesting; especially in the momentary wavering and
quick recovery of her virtue. This is the first homage that
the theatre had paid, since the Restoration, to female
chastity; and notwithstanding the vicious tone of the other
characters, in which Vanbrugh has gone as great lengths as
any of his contemporaries, we perceive the beginnings of a
re-action in public spirit, which gradually reformed and elevated the moral standard of the stage.[n] The Provoked Wife,

---

[n] This purification of English comedy
has sometimes been attributed to the
effects of a famous essay by Collier on
the immorality of the English stage.
But if public opinion had not been prepared to go along, in a considerable

though it cannot be said to give any proofs of this sort of improvement, has some merit as a comedy; it is witty and animated, as Vanbrugh usually was; the character of Sir John Brute may not have been too great a caricature of real manners, such as survived from the debased reign of Charles; and the endeavour to expose the grossness of the older generation was itself an evidence that a better polish had been given to social life.

---

degree, with Collier, his animadversions could have produced little change. In point of fact, the subsequent improvement was but slow, and, for some years, rather shown in avoiding coarse indecencies than in much elevation of sentiment. Steele's Conscious Lovers is the first comedy which can be called moral; Cibber, in those parts of the Provoked Husband that he wrote, carried this farther, and the stage afterwards grew more and more refined, till it became languid and sentimental.

CHAPTER VII.

HISTORY OF POLITE LITERATURE IN PROSE
FROM 1650 TO 1700.

Sect. I.

Italy—High Refinement of French Language—Fontenelle—St. Evremond—
Sévigné—Bouhours and Rapin—Miscellaneous Writers—English Style
—and Criticism—Dryden.

1. If Italy could furnish no long list of conspicuous names
Low state of literature in Italy. in this department of literature to our last period,
she is far more deficient in the present. The Prose
Fiorentine of Dati, a collection of what seemed the best
specimens of Italian eloquence in this century, served chiefly
to prove its mediocrity; nor has that editor, by his own panegyric on Louis XIV., or any other of his writings, been able
to redeem its name.[a] The sermons of Segneri have already
been mentioned ; the eulogies bestowed on them seem to be
founded, in some measure, on the surrounding barrenness.
The letters of Magalotti, and still more of Redi, themselves
philosophers, and generally writing on philosophy, seem to
do more credit than anything else to this period.[b]

2. Crescimbeni, the founder of the Arcadian Society, has
Crescimbeni. made an honourable name by his exertions to purify
the national taste, as well as by his diligence in preserving the memory of better ages than his own. His History
of National Poetry is a laborious and useful work, to which
I have sometimes been indebted. His treatise on the beauty
of that poetry is only known to me through Salfi. It is
written in dialogue, the speakers being Arcadians. Anxious
to extirpate the school of the Marinists, without falling back
altogether into that of Petrarch, he set up Costanzo as a

---

[a] Salfi, xiv. 25. Tiraboschi, xi. 412.   [b] Salfi, xiv. 17. Corniani, viii. 71.

model of poetry. Most of his precepts, Salfi observes, are
very trivial at present; but, at the epoch of its appearance,
his work was of great service towards the reform of Italian
literature.[c]

3. This period, the second part of the seventeenth century,
comprehends the most considerable, and in every
sense the most important and distinguished portion
of what was once called the great age in France, the reign of
Louis XIV. In this period the literature of France was
adorned by its most brilliant writers; since, notwithstanding
the genius and popularity of some who followed, we generally
find a still higher place awarded by men of fine taste to
Bossuet and Pascal than to Voltaire and Montesquieu. The
language was written with a care that might have fettered
the powers of ordinary men, but rendered those of such as
we have mentioned more resplendent. The laws of taste and
grammar, like those of nature, were held immutable; it was
the province of human genius to deal with them, as it does
with nature, by a skilful employment, not by a preposterous
and ineffectual rebellion against their control. Purity and
perspicuity, simplicity and ease, were conditions of good
writing; it was never thought that an author, especially in
prose, might transgress the recognised idiom of his mother-
tongue, or invent words unknown to it, for the sake of effect
or novelty; or, if in some rare occurrence so bold a course
might be forgiven, these exceptions were but as miracles
in religion, which would cease to strike us, or be no miracles
at all, but for the regularity of the laws to which they bear
witness even while they infringe them. We have not thought
it necessary to defer the praise which some great French
writers have deserved on the score of their language for this
chapter. Bossuet, Malebranche, Arnauld, and Pascal have
already been commemorated; and it is sufficient to point out
two causes in perpetual operation during this period which
ennobled and preserved in purity the literature of France;
one, the salutary influence of the Academy, the other, that
emulation between the Jesuits and Jansenists for public
esteem, which was better displayed in their politer writings,

Age of
Louis XIV.
in France.

---

[c] Salfi, xiii. 450.

than in the abstruse and endless controversy of the five propositions. A few remain to be mentioned; and as the subject of this chapter, in order to avoid frequent subdivisions,
is miscellaneous, the reader must expect to find that we do
not, in every instance, confine ourselves to what he may consider as polite letters.

4. Fontenelle, by the variety of his talents, by their appli-
Fontenelle cation to the pursuits most congenial to the intel-
—his cha-
racter. lectual character of his contemporaries, and by that
extraordinary longevity which made those contemporaries
not less than three generations of mankind, may be reckoned
the best representative of French literature. Born in 1657,
and dying within a few days of a complete century, in 1757,
he enjoyed the most protracted life of any among the modern
learned; and that a life in the full sunshine of Parisian
literature, without care and without disease. In nothing
was Fontenelle a great writer; his mental and moral disposition resembled each other; equable, without the capacity
of performing, and hardly of conceiving, anything truly elevated, but not less exempt from the fruits of passion, from
paradox, unreasonableness, and prejudice. His best productions are, perhaps, the eulogies on the deceased members
of the Academy of Sciences, which he pronounced during
almost forty years, but these nearly all belong to the eighteenth century; they are just and candid, with sufficient,
though not very profound, knowledge of the exact sciences,
and a style pure and flowing, which his good sense had freed
from some early affectation, and his cold temper as well as
sound understanding restrained from extravagance. In his
first works we have symptoms of an infirmity belonging more
frequently to age than to youth; but Fontenelle was never
young in passion. He there affects the tone of somewhat
pedantic and frigid gallantry which seems to have survived
the society of the Hôtel Rambouillet who had countenanced
it, and which borders too nearly on the language which
Molière and his disciples had well exposed in their coxcombs
on the stage.

5. The Dialogues of the Dead, published in 1683, are condemned by some critics for their false taste and perpetual
strain at something unexpected and paradoxical. The lead-

ing idea is, of course, borrowed from Lucian; but Fontenelle has aimed at greater poignancy by contrast; the ghosts in his dialogues are exactly those who had least in common with each other in life, and the general object is to bring, by some happy analogy which had not occurred to the reader, or by some ingenious defence of what he had been accustomed to despise, the prominences and depressions of historic characters to a level. This is what is always well received in the kind of society for which Fontenelle wrote; but if much is mere sophistry in his dialogues, if the general tone is little above that of the world, there is also, what we often find in the world, some acuteness and novelty, and some things put in a light which it may be worth while not to neglect.

His Dialogues of the Dead.

6. Fenelon, not many years afterwards, copied the scheme, though not the style, of Fontenelle in his own Dialogues of the Dead, written for the use of his pupil the Duke of Burgundy. Some of these dialogues are not truly of the dead; the characters speak as if on earth, and with earthly designs. They have certainly more solid sense and a more elevated morality than those of Fontenelle, to which La Harpe has preferred them. The noble zeal of Fenelon not to spare the vices of kings, in writing for the heir of one so imperious and so open to the censure of reflecting minds, shines throughout these dialogues; but designed as they were for a boy, they naturally appear in some places rather superficial.

Those of Fenelon.

7. Fontenelle succeeded better in his famous dialogues on the Plurality of Worlds, Les Mondes; in which, if the conception is not wholly original, he has at least developed it with so much spirit and vivacity, that it would show as bad taste to censure his work, as to reckon it a model for imitation. It is one of those happy ideas which have been privileged monopolies of the first inventor; and it will be found accordingly that all attempts to copy this whimsical union of gallantry with science have been insipid almost to a ridiculous degree. Fontenelle throws so much gaiety and wit into his compliments to the lady whom he initiates into his theory, that we do not confound them with the nonsense of coxcombs; and she is her-

Fontenelle's Plurality of Worlds.

self so spirited, unaffected, and clever, that no philosopher could be ashamed of gallantry towards so deserving an object. The fascinating paradox, as then it seemed, though our children are now taught to lisp it, that the moon, the planets, the fixed stars, are full of inhabitants, is presented with no more show of science than was indispensable, but with a varying liveliness that, if we may judge by the consequences, has served to convince as well as amuse. The plurality of worlds had been suggested by Wilkins, and probably by some Cartesians in France; but it was first rendered a popular tenet by this agreeable little book of Fontenelle, which had a great circulation in Europe. The ingenuity with which he obviates the difficulties that he is compelled to acknowledge, is worthy of praise; and a good deal of the popular truths of physical astronomy is found in these dialogues.

8. The History of Oracles, which Fontenelle published in 1687, is worthy of observation as a sign of the His History of Oracles. change that was working in literature. In the provinces of erudition and of polite letters, long so independent, perhaps even so hostile, some tendency towards a coalition began to appear. The men of the world especially, after they had acquired a free temper of thinking in religion, and become accustomed to talk about philosophy, desired to know something of the questions which the learned disputed; but they demanded this knowledge by a short and easy road, with no great sacrifice of their leisure or attention. Fontenelle, in the History of Oracles, as in the dialogues on the Plurality of Worlds, prepared a repast for their taste. A learned Dutch physician, Van Dale, in a dull work, had taken up the subject of the ancient oracles, and explained them by human imposture instead of that of the devil, which had been the more orthodox hypothesis. A certain degree of paradox, or want of orthodoxy, already gave a zest to a book in France; and Fontenelle's lively manner, with more learning than good society at Paris possessed, and about as much as it could endure, united to a clear and acute line of argument, created a popularity for his History of Oracles, which we cannot reckon altogether unmerited.[d]

---

[d] I have not compared, or indeed read, Dale's work; but I rather suspect that some of the reasoning, not the learning, of Fontenelle is original.

9. The works of St. Evremond were collected after his death in 1705; but many had been printed before, St. Evremond. and he evidently belongs to the latter half of the seventeenth century. The fame of St. Evremond as a brilliant star, during a long life, in the polished aristocracy of France and England, gave for a time a considerable lustre to his writings, the greater part of which are such effusions as the daily intercourse of good company called forth. In verse or in prose, he is the gallant friend, rather than lover, of ladies who, secure probably of love in some other quarter, were proud of the friendship of a wit. He never, to do him justice, mistakes his character, which, as his age was not a little advanced, might have incurred ridicule. Hortense Mancini, Duchess of Mazarin, is his heroine; but we take little interest in compliments to a woman neither respected in her life, nor remembered since. Nothing can be more trifling than the general character of the writings of St. Evremond; but sometimes he rises to literary criticism, or even civil history; and on such topics he is clear, unaffected, cold, without imagination or sensibility; a type of the frigid being whom an aristocratic and highly polished society is apt to produce. The chief merit of St. Evremond is in his style and manner. He has less wit than Voiture, who contributed to form him, or than Voltaire, whom he contributed to form; but he shows neither the effort of the former, nor the restlessness of the latter. Voltaire, however, when he is most quiet, as in the earliest and best of his historical works, seems to bear a considerable resemblance to St. Evremond, and there can be no doubt that he was familiar with the latter's writings.

10. A woman has the glory of being full as conspicuous in the graces of style as any writer of this famous Madame de age. It is evident that this was Madame de Sévigné. Sévigné. Her letters indeed were not published till the eighteenth century, but they were written in the midday of Louis's reign. Their ease and freedom from affectation are more striking by contrast with the two epistolary styles which had been most admired in France, that of Balzac, which is laboriously tumid, and that of Voiture, which becomes insipid by dint of affectation. Every one perceives that in the

Letters of a mother to her daughter the public, in a strict sense, is not thought of; and yet the habit of speaking and writing what men of wit and taste would desire to hear and read, gives a certain mannerism, I will not say air of effort, even to the letters of Madame de Sévigné. The abandonment of the heart to its casual impulses is not so genuine as in some that have since been published. It is at least clear that it is possible to become affected in copying her unaffected style; and some of Walpole's letters bear witness to this. Her wit and talent of painting by single touches are very eminent; scarcely any collection of letters, which contain so little that can interest a distant age, are read with such pleasure; if they have any general fault, it is a little monotony and excess of affection towards her daughter, which is reported to have wearied its object, and, in contrast with this, a little want of sensibility towards all beyond her immediate friends, and a readiness to find something ludicrous in the dangers and sufferings of others.[e]

11. The French Academy had been so judicious both in the choice of its members, and in the general tenor of its proceedings, that it stood very high in public esteem, and a voluntary deference was commonly shown to its authority. The favour of Louis XIV., when he grew to manhood, was accorded as amply as that of Richelieu. The Academy was received by the king, when they approached him publicly, with the same ceremonies as the superior courts of justice. This body had, almost from its commencement, undertaken a national dictionary, which should carry the language to its utmost perfection, and trace a road to the

The French Academy.

---

[e] The proofs of this are numerous enough in her letters. In one of them she mentions, that a lady of her acquaintance, having been bitten by a mad dog, had gone to be dipped in the sea, and amuses herself by taking off the provincial accent, with which she will express herself on the first plunge. She makes a jest of La Voisin's execution; and though that person was as little entitled to sympathy as any one, yet when a woman is burned alive, it is not usual for another woman to turn it into drollery.

Madame de Sévigné's taste has been

arraigned for slighting Racine; and she has been charged with the unfortunate prediction: Il passera comme le café. But it is denied that these words can be found, though few like to give up so diverting a miscalculation of futurity. In her time, Corneille's party was so well supported, and he deserved so much gratitude and reverence, that we cannot much wonder at her being carried a little too far against his rival. Who has ever seen a woman just towards the rivals of her friends, though many are just towards their own?

highest eloquence that depended on purity and choice of words ; more than this could not be given by man.   The work proceeded very slowly ; and dictionaries were published in the meantime, one by Richelet in 1680, another by Furetière. The former seems to be little more than a glossary of technical or otherwise doubtful words ;[f] but the latter, though pretending to contain only terms of art and science, was found, by its definitions and by the authorities it quoted, to interfere so much with the project of the academicians, who had armed themselves with an exclusive privilege, that they not only expelled Furetière from their body, on the allegation that he had availed himself of materials intrusted to him by the Academy for its own dictionary, but instituted a long process at law to hinder its publication. This was in 1685, and the dictionary of Furetière only appeared after his death, at Amsterdam in 1690.[g] Whatever may have been the delinquency, moral or legal, of this compiler, his dictionary is praised by Goujet as a rich treasure, in which almost everything is found that we can desire for a a sound knowledge of the language.   It has been frequently reprinted, and continued long in esteem.   But the dictionary of the Academy, which was published in 1694, claimed an authority to which that of a private man could not pretend. Yet the first edition seems to have rather disappointed the public expectation. Many objected to the want of quotations, and to the observance of an orthography that had become obsolete. The Academy undertook a revision of its work in 1700 ; and finally, profiting by the public opinion on which it endeavoured to act, rendered this dictionary the most received standard of the French language.[h]

12. The Grammaire générale et raisonnée of Lancelot, in which Arnauld took a considerable share, is rather a treatise on the philosophy of all language than one peculiar to the French. ' The best critics,' says Baillet, ' acknowledged that there is nothing written by either the ancient or the modern grammarians with so much justness

French Grammars.

---

[f] Goujet, Baillet, n. 762.

[g] Pelisson, Hist. de l'Académie (continuation par Olivet), p. 47. Goujet,

Bibliothèque française, i. 232, et post. Biogr. univ., art. Furetière.

[h] Pelisson, p. 69. Goujet, p. 261.

and solidity.'[i]   Vigneul-Marville bestows upon it an almost equal eulogy.[k]   Lancelot was copied in a great degree by Lami, in his Rhetoric or Art of Speaking, with little of value that is original.[m]   Vaugelas retained his place as the founder of sound grammatical criticism, though his judgments have not been uniformly confirmed by the next generation.   His remarks were edited with notes by Thomas Corneille, who had the reputation of an excellent grammarian.[n]   The observations of Ménage on the French language, in 1675 and 1676, are said to have the fault of reposing too much on obsolete authorities, even those of the sixteenth century, which had long been proscribed by a politer age.[o]   Notwithstanding the zeal of the Academy, no critical laws could arrest the revolutions of speech.   Changes came in with the lapse of time, and were sanctioned by the imperious rule of custom. In a book on grammar, published as early as 1688, Balzac and Voiture, even Patru and the Port-Royal writers, are called semi-moderns;[p] so many new phrases had since made their way into composition, so many of theirs had acquired a certain air of antiquity.

13. The genius of the French language, as it was estimated in this age by those who aspired to the character of good critics, may be learned from one of the dialogues in a work of Bouhours, Les Entretiens d'Ariste et d'Eugène.   Bouhours was a Jesuit who affected a polite and lively tone, according to the fashion of his time, so as to warrant some degree of ridicule ; but a man of taste and judgment, whom, though La Harpe speaks of him with disdain, his contemporaries quoted with respect.   The first, and the most interesting at present, of these conversations, which are feigned to take place between two gentlemen of literary taste, turns on the French language.[q]   This he pre-

Bouhours' Entretiens d'Ariste et d'Eugène.

---

[i] Jugemens des Sçavans, n. 606. Goujet copies Baillet's words.

[k] Mélanges de Littérature, i. 124.

[m] Goujet, i. 56.   Gibert, p. 351.

[n] Goujet, i. 146.   Biogr. univ.

[o] Id. 153.

[p] Bibliothèque universelle, xv. 351. Perrault makes a similar remark on Patru.

[q] Bouhours points out several inno-

vations which had lately come into use. He dislikes *avoir des ménagemens*, or *avoir de la considération*, and thinks these phrases would not last; in which he was mistaken.   *Tour de visage* and *tour d'esprit* were new : the words *fonds, mesures, amitiés, compte,* and many more, were used in new senses.   Thus also *assez* and *trop* ; as the phrase, *je ne suis pas trop de votre avis.*   It seems on re-

sumes to be the best of all modern; deriding the Spanish for
its pomp, the Italian for its finical effeminacy.[r] The French
has the secret of uniting brevity with clearness and purity
with politeness. The Greek and Latin are obscure where they
are concise. The Spanish is always diffuse. The Spanish
is a turbid torrent, often overspreading the country with
great noise; the Italian a gentle rivulet, occasionally given
to inundate its meadows; the French a noble river, enriching
the adjacent lands, but with an equal majestic course of
waters that never quits its level.[s] Spanish again he compares
to an insolent beauty, that holds her head high, and takes
pleasure in splendid dress; Italian to a painted coquette,
always attired to please; French to a modest and agreeable
lady, who, if you may call her a prude, has nothing uncivil
or repulsive in her prudery. Latin is the common mother;
but while Italian has the sort of likeness to Latin which an
ape bears to a man, in French we have the dignity, politeness,
purity, and good sense of the Augustan age. The French
have rejected almost all the diminutives once in use, and do
not, like the Italians, admit the right of framing others.
This language does not tolerate rhyming sounds in prose, nor
even any kind of assonance, as *amertume* and *fortune*, near
together. It rejects very bold metamorphors, as the zenith
of virtue, the *apogée* of glory; and it is remarkable that its
poetry is almost as hostile to metaphor as its prose.[t] 'We
have very few words merely poetical, and the language of
our poets is not very different from that of the world.
Whatever be the cause, it is certain that a figurative style
is neither good among us in verse nor in prose.' This is
evidently much exaggerated, and in contradiction to the
known examples, at least, of dramatic poetry. All affectation
and labour, he proceeds to say, are equally repugnant to a
good French style. 'If we would speak the language well,
we should not try to speak it too well. It detests excess of

---

flection, that some of the expressions he
animadverts upon must have been affected while they were new, being in opposition to the correct meaning of words;
and it is always curious, in other languages as well as our own, to observe
the comparatively recent *nobility* of

many things quite established by present
usage. Entretiens d'Ariste et d'Eugène,
p. 95.
  [r] P. 52 (edit, 1671).
  [s] P. 77.
  [t] P. 60.

ornament; it would almost desire that words should be as it
were naked; their dress must be no more than necessity and
decency require. Its simplicity is averse to compound words;
those adjectives which are formed by such a juncture of two
have long been exiled both from prose and verse.' 'Our own
pronunciation,' he affirms, ' is the most natural and pleasing of
any. The Chinese and other Asiatics sing; the Germans
rattle (rallent); the Spaniards spout; the Italians sigh;
the English whistle; the French alone can properly be said
to speak; which arises in fact from our not accenting any
syllable before the penultimate. The French language is
best adapted to express the tenderest sentiments of the heart;
for which reason our songs are so impassioned and pathetic,
while those of Italy and Spain are full of nonsense. Other
languages may address the imagination, but ours alone
speaks to the heart, which never understands what is said in
them.'[u] This is literally amusing; and with equal patriotism,
Bouhours in another place has proposed the question,
whether a German can, by the nature of things, possess any
wit?

14. Bouhours, not deficient, as we may perceive, in self-
confidence and proneness to censure, presumed to
turn into ridicule the writers of Port-Royal, at that
time of such distinguished reputation as threatened to eclipse
the credit which the Jesuits had always preserved in polite
letters. He alludes to their long periods and the exaggerated
phrases of invective which they poured forth in controversy.[x]
But the Jansenist party was well able to defend itself.
Barbier d'Aucour retaliated on the vain Jesuit by his Sentimens de Cléanthe sur les Entretiens d'Ariste et d'Eugène.
It seems to be the general opinion of French critics, that he
has well exposed the weak parts of his adversary, his affected

Attacked by Barbier d'Aucour.

---

[u] P. 68.

[x] P. 150. Vigneul-Marville observes
that the Port-Royal writers formed their
style originally on that of Balzac (vol. i.
p. 107; and that M. d'Andilly, brother
of Antony Arnauld, affected at one
time a grand and copious manner like
the Spaniards, as being more serious
and imposing, especially in devotional
writings; but afterwards finding the
French were impatient of this style,

that party abandoned it for one more
concise, which it is by no means less
difficult to write well. p. 139. Baillet
seems to refer their love of long periods
to the famous advocate Le Maistre, who
had employed them in his pleadings, not
only as giving more dignity, but also
because the public taste at that time
favoured them. Jugemens des Sçavans,
n. 953.

air of the world, the occasional frivolity and feebleness of his observations; yet there seems something morose in the censures of the supposed Cleanthe, which renders this book less agreeable than that on which it animadverts.

15. Another work of criticism by Bouhours, La Manière de Bien Penser, which is also in dialogue, contains La Maniere de Bien Penser. much that shows acuteness and delicacy of discrimination; though his taste was deficient in warmth and sensibility, which renders him somewhat too strict and fastidious in his judgments. He is an unsparing enemy of obscurity, exaggeration, and nonsense, and laughs at the hyperbolical language of Balzac, while he has rather overpraised Voiture.[y] The affected inflated thoughts, of which the Italian and Spanish writers afford him many examples, Bouhours justly condemns, and by the correctness of his judgment may deserve, on the whole, a respectable place in the second order of critics.

16. The Réflexions sur l'Eloquence et sur la Poësie of Rapin, another Jesuit, whose Latin poem on Gardens Rapin's Reflections on Eloquence and Poetry. has already been praised, are judicious, though perhaps rather too diffuse; his criticism is what would appear severe in our times; but it was that of a man formed by the ancients, and who lived also in the best and most critical age of France. The reflections on poetry are avowedly founded on Aristotle, but with much that is new, and with examples from modern poets to confirm and illustrate it. The practice at this time in France was to depreciate

---

[y] Voiture, he says, always takes a tone of raillery when he exaggerates. Le faux devient vrai à la faveur de l'ironie, p. 29. But we can hardly think that Balzac was not gravely ironical in some of the strange hyperboles which Bouhours quotes from him.

In the fourth dialogue, Bouhours has many just observations on the necessity of clearness. An obscurity arising from allusion to things now unknown, such as we find in the ancients, is rather a misfortune than a fault; but this is no excuse for one which may be avoided, and arises from the writer's indistinctness of conception or language. Cela n'est pas intelligible, dit Philinthe (after hearing a foolish rhapsody extracted from a fune-

ral sermon on Louis XIII.). Non, répondit Eudoxe, ce n'est pas tout-à-fait de galimatias, ce n'est que du phébus. Vous mettez donc, dit Philinthe, de la différence entre le galimatias et le phébus? Oui, repartit Eudoxe, le galimatias renferme une obscurité profonde, et n'a de soi-même nul sens raisonnable. Le phébus n'est pas si obscur, et a un brillant qui signifie, ou semble signifier quelque chose; le soleil y entre d'ordinaire, et c'est peut-être ce qui a donné lieu en notre langue au nom de phébus. Ce n'est pas que quelquefois le phébus ne devienne obscur, jusqu'à n'être pas entendu; mais alors le galimatias s'en joint; ce ne sont que brillans et que ténèbres de tous côtés. p. 342.

the Italians; and Tasso is often the subject of Rapin's censure; for want, among other things, of that grave and majestic character which epic poetry demands. Yet Rapin is not so rigorous, but that he can blame the coldness of modern precepts in regard to French poetry, After condemning the pompous tone of Brebœuf in his translation of the Pharsalia, he remarks that ' we have gone since to an opposite extreme by too scrupulous a care for the purity of the language; for we have begun to take from poetry its force and dignity by too much reserve and a false modesty, which we have established as characteristics of our language, so as to deprive it of that judicious boldness which true poetry requires; we have cut off the metaphors and all those figures of speech which give force and spirit to words, and reduced all the artifices of words to a pure regular style which exposes itself to no risk by bold expression. The taste of the age, the influence of women who are naturally timid, that of the court which had hardly anything in common with the ancients, on account of its usual antipathy for learning, accredited this manner of writing.'[z] In this Rapin seems to glance at the polite but cold criticism of his brother Jesuit, Bouhours.

17. Rapin, in another work of criticism, the Parallels of Great Men of Antiquity, has weighed in the scales of his own judgment Demosthenes and Cicero, Homer and Virgil, Thucydides and Livy, Plato and Aristotle. Thus eloquence, poetry, history, and philosophy pass under review. The taste of Rapin is for the Latins; Cicero he prefers to Demosthenes, Livy on the whole to Thucydides, though this he leaves more to the reader; but is confident that none except mere grammarians have ranked Homer above Virgil.[a] The loquacity of the older poet, the frequency of his moral reflections, which Rapin thinks misplaced in an epic poem, his similes, the sameness of his transitions, are treated very freely; yet he gives him the preference over Virgil for grandeur and nobleness of narration, for his epithets, and the splendour of his language. But he is of opinion that Æneas is a much finer character than Achilles. These two epic poets he holds, however, to be the

His Parallels of Great Men.

---

[z] P. 147.   [a] P. 158.

greatest in the world; as for all the rest, ancient and modern, he enumerates them one after another, and can find little but faults in them all.[b] Nor does he esteem dramatic and lyric poets, at least modern, much better.

18. The treatise on Epic Poetry by Bossu was once of some reputation. An English poet has thought fit to say that we should have stared, like Indians, at Homer, if Bossu had not taught us to understand him.[c] The book is, however, long since forgotten; and we fancy that we understand Homer not the worse. It is in six books, which treat of the fable, the action, the narration, the manners, the machinery, the sentiments and expressions of an epic poem. Homer is the favourite poet of Bossu, and Virgil next to him; this preference of the superior model does him some honour in a generation which was becoming insensible to its excellence. Bossu is judicious and correct in taste, but without much depth, and he seems to want the acuteness of Bouhours.

Bossu on epic poetry.

19. Fontenelle is a critic of whom it may be said that he did more injury to fine taste and sensibility in works of imagination and sentiment, than any man without his good sense and natural acuteness could have done. He is systematically cold; if he seems to tolerate any flight of the poet, it is rather by caprice than by a genuine discernment of beauty; but he clings with the unyielding claw of a cold-blooded animal, to the faults of great writers, which he exposes with reason and sarcasm. His Reflections on Poetry relate mostly to dramatic composition, and to that of the French stage. Theocritus is his victim in the Dissertation on Pastoral Poetry; but Fontenelle gave the Sicilian his revenge; he wrote pastorals himself; and we have altogether forgotten, or, when we again look at, can very partially approve, the idylls of the Boulevards, while those Doric dactyls of Theocritus linger still, like what Schiller has called soft music of yesterday, from our schoolboy reminiscences on our aged ears.

Fontenelle's critical writings.

20. The reign of mere scholars was now at an end; no worse name than that of pedant could be imposed on those

---

[b] P. 175.

[c] Had Bossu never writ, the world had still,
Like Indians, view'd this mighty piece of wit,
MULGRAVE'S *Essay on Poetry.*

who sought for glory; the admiration of all that was na-
Preference of tional in arts, in arms, in manners, as well as in
French lan-
guage to
Latin. speech, carried away like a torrent those prescriptive
titles to reverence which only lingered in colleges.
The superiority of the Latin language to French had long
been contested; even Henry Stephens has a dissertation in
favour of the latter; and in this period, though a few resolute
scholars did not retire from the field, it was generally held
either that French was every way the better means of expressing our thoughts, or at least so much more convenient as to
put nearly an end to the use of the other. Latin had been
the privileged language of stone; but Louis XIV., in consequence of an essay by Charpentier, in 1676, replaced the
inscriptions on his triumphal arches by others in French.[d]
This of course does not much affect the general question
between the two languages.

21. But it was not in language alone that the ancients
General
superiority
of ancients
disputed. were to endure the aggression of a disobedient posterity. It had long been a problem in Europe
whether they had not been surpassed; one perhaps
which began before the younger generations could make good
their claim. But time, the nominal ally of the old possessors,
gave his more powerful aid to their opponents; every age saw
the proportions change, and new men rise up to strengthen
the ranks of the assailants. In mathematical science, in
natural knowledge, the ancients had none but a few mere
pedants, or half-read lovers of paradox, to maintain their
superiority; but in the beauties of language, in eloquence and
poetry, the suffrage of criticism had long been theirs. It
Charles
Perrault. seemed time to dispute even this. Charles Perrault,
a man of some learning, some variety of acquirement,
and a good deal of ingenuity and quickness, published, in
1687, his famous 'Parallel of the Ancients and Moderns
in all that regards Arts and Sciences.' This is a series of
dialogues, the parties being, first, a president, deeply learned
and prejudiced in all respects for antiquity; secondly, an
abbé, not ignorant, but having reflected more than read, cool
and impartial, always made to appear in the right, or, in

---

[d] Goujet, i. 13.

other words, the author's representative; thirdly, a man of
the world, seizing the gay side of every subject, and apparently brought in to prevent the book from becoming dull.
They begin with architecture and painting, and soon make
it clear that Athens was a mere heap of pigsties in comparison with Versailles; the ancient painters fare equally ill.
They next advance to eloquence and poetry, and here, where
the strife of war is sharpest, the defeat of antiquity is chanted
with triumph.   Homer, Virgil, Horace are successively
brought forward for severe and often unjust censure: but of
course it is not to be imagined that Perrault is always in the
wrong; he had to fight against a pedantic admiration which
surrenders all judgment; and having found the bow bent too
much in one way, he forced it himself too violently into
another direction.   It is the fault of such books to be one-
sided; they are not unfrequently right in censuring blemishes,
but very uncandid in suppressing beauties.   Homer has been
worst used by Perrault, who had not the least power of
feeling his excellence; but the advocate of the newer age in
his dialogue admits that the Æneid is superior to any modern
epic.   In his comparison of eloquence Perrault has given
some specimens of both sides in contrast; comparing by
means however of his own versions, the funeral orations of
Pericles and Plato with those of Bourdaloue, Bossuet, and
Fléchier, the description by Pliny of his country seat with
one by Balzac, an epistle of Cicero with another of Balzac.
These comparisons were fitted to produce a great effect
among those who could neither read the original text, nor
place themselves in the midst of ancient feelings and habits.
It is easy to perceive that a vast majority of the French in
that age would agree with Perrault; the book was written
for the times.

22. Fontenelle, in a very short digression on the ancients
and moderns, subjoined to his Discourse on Pastoral
Poetry, followed the steps of Perrault.   'The whole   Fontenelle.
question as to pre-eminence between the ancients and
moderns,' he begins, 'reduces itself into another, whether
the trees that used to grow in our woods were larger than
those which grow now.   If they were, Homer, Plato,
Demosthenes, cannot be equalled in these ages; but if our

trees are as large as trees were of old, then there is no reason why we may not equal Homer, Plato, and Demosthenes. The sophistry of this is glaring enough ; but it was logic for Paris. In the rest of this short essay there are the usual characteristics of Fontenelle, cool good sense, and an incapacity, by natural privation, of feeling the highest excellence in works of taste.

23. Boileau, in observations annexed to his translation Boileau's of Longinus, as well as in a few sallies of his poetry, defence of antiquity. defended the great poets, especially Homer and Pindar, with dignity and moderation ; freely abandoning the cause of antiquity where he felt it to be untenable. Perrault replied with courage, a quality meriting some praise where the adversary was so powerful in sarcasm and so little accustomed to spare it ; but the controversy ceased in tolerable friendship.

24. The knowledge of new accessions to literature which First Re- its lovers demanded, had hitherto been communi- views— Journal des cated only through the annual catalogues published Sçavans. at Frankfort or other places. But these lists of titlepages were unsatisfatory to the distant scholar, who sought to become acquainted with the real progress of learning, and to know what he might find it worth while to purchase. Denis de Sallo, a member of the parliament of Paris, and not wholly undistinguished in literature, though his other works are not much remembered, by carrying into effect a happy project of his own, gave birth, as it were, to a mighty spirit which has grown up in strength and enterprise, till it has become the ruling power of the literary world. Monday, the 5th of January, 1665, is the date of the first number of the first review, the Journal des Sçavans, published by Sallo under the name of the Sieur de Hedouville, which some have said to be that of his servant.[e] It was printed weekly, in a duodecimo or

---

[e] Camusat, in his Histoire critique des Journaux, in two volumes, 1734, which, notwithstanding its general title, is chiefly confined to the history of the Journal des Sçavans, and wholly to such as appeared in France, has not been able to clear up this interesting point ; for there are not wanting those who assert that Hedouville was the name of an es- tate belonging to Sallo ; and he is called in some public description, without reference to the journal, Dominus de Sallo d'Hedouville in Parisiensi curia senator. Camusat, i. 13. Notwithstanding this, there is evidence that leads us to the valet ; so that 'amplius deliberandum censeo ; Res magna est.'

sexto-decimo form, each number containing from twelve to sixteen pages. The first book ever reviewed (let us observe the difference of subject between that and the last, whatever the last may be) was an edition of the works of Victor Vitensis and Vigilius Tapsensis, African bishops of the fifth century, by Father Chiflet, a Jesuit.[f] The second is Spelman's Glossary. According to the prospectus prefixed to the Journal des Sçavans, it was not designed for a mere review, but a literary miscellany; composed, in the first place, of an exact catalogue of the chief books which should be printed in Europe; not content with the mere titles, as the majority of bibliographers had hitherto been, but giving an account of their contents, and their value to the public; it was also to contain a necrology of distinguished authors, an account of experiments in physics and chemistry, and of new discoveries in arts and sciences, with the principal decisions of civil and ecclesiastical tribunals, the decrees of the Sorbonne and other French or foreign universities; in short, whatever might be interesting to men of letters. We find therefore some piece of news, more or less of a literary or scientific nature, subjoined to each number. Thus in the first number we have a double-headed child born near Salisbury; in the second, a question of legitimacy decided in the parliament of Paris; in the third, an experiment on a new ship or boat constructed by Sir William Petty; in the fourth, an account of a discussion in the college of Jesuits on the nature of comets. The scientific articles, which bear a large proportion to the rest, are illustrated by engravings. It was complained that the Journal des Sçavans did not pay much regard to polite or amusing literature; and this led to the publication of the Mercure galant, by Visè, which gave reviews of poetry and of the drama.

25. Though the notices in the Journal des Sçavans are very short, and when they give any character, for the most part of a laudatory tone, Sallo did not fail to raise up enemies by the mere assumption of power which a reviewer

---

[f] Victoris Vitensis et Vigilii Tapsensis, Provinciæ Bisacenæ Episcoporum Opera, edente R. P. Chifletio, Soc. Jesu. Presb., in 4to Divione. The critique, if such it be, occupies but two pages in small duodecimo. That on Spelman's Glossary, which follows, is but in half a page.

is prone to affect. Menage, on a work of whose he had
made some criticism, and by no means, as it appears, without justice, replied in wrath ; Patin and others rose up as
injured authors against the self-erected censor ; but he made
more formidable enemies by some rather blunt declarations
of a Gallican feeling, as became a counsellor of the parliament
of Paris, against the court of Rome; and the privilege of
publication was soon withdrawn from Sallo.[g] It is said that
he had the spirit to refuse the offer of continuing the journal
under a previous censorship ; and it passed into other hands,
those of Gallois, who continued it with great success.[h] It is
remarkable that the first review, within a few months of its
origin, was silenced for assuming too imperious an authority
over literature, and for speaking evil of dignities. ' In cunis
jam Jove dignus erat.' The Journal des Sçavans, incomparably the most ancient of living reviews, is still conspicuous
for its learning, its candour, and its freedom from those stains
of personal and party malice which deform more popular
works.

26. The path thus opened to all that could tempt a man
Reviews   who made writing his profession—profit, celebrity,
established
by Bayle.   a perpetual appearance in the public eye, the facility
of pouring forth every scattered thought of his own, the
power of revenge upon every enemy—could not fail to tempt
more conspicuous men than Sallo or his successor Gallois.
Two of very high reputation, at least of reputation that hence
became very high, entered it, Bayle and Le Clerc.   The
former, in 1684, commenced a new review, Nouvelles de la
République des Lettres. He saw, and was well able to improve, the opportunities which periodical criticism furnished
to a mind eminently qualified for it; extensively, and, in
some points, deeply learned ; full of wit, acuteness, and a
happy talent of writing in a lively tone without the insipidity
of affected politeness. The scholar and philosopher of Rotterdam had a rival, in some respects, and ultimately an

---

[g] Camusat, p. 28.   Sallo had also
attacked the Jesuits.
[h] Éloge de Gallois, par Fontenelle,
in the latter's works, vol. v. p. 168.
Biographie universelle, arts. Sallo and
Gallois. Gallois is said to have been a
coadjutor of Sallo from the beginning,
and some others are named by Camusat
as its contributors, among whom were
Gombervillo and Chapelain.

adversary, in a neighbouring city.   Le Clerc, settled at Amsterdam as professor of belles lettres and of Hebrew and Le in the Arminian seminary, undertook in 1686, at the Clerc. age of twenty-nine, the first of those three celebrated series of reviews, to which he owes so much of his fame.   This was the Bibliothèque universelle, in all the early volumes of which La Croze, a much inferior person, was his coadjutor, published monthly in a very small form.   Le Clerc had afterwards a disagreement with La Croze, and the latter part of the Bibliothèque universelle (that after the tenth volume) is chiefly his own.   It ceased to be published in 1693, and the Bibliothèque choisie, which is perhaps even a more known work of Le Clerc, did not commence till 1703.   But the fulness, the variety, the judicious analysis and selection, as well as the value of the original remarks, which we find in the Bibliothèque universelle, render it of signal utility to those who would embrace the literature of that short but not unimportant period which it illustrates.

27. Meantime a less brilliant, but by no means less erudite, review, the Leipsic Acts, had commenced in Ger- Leipsic many. The first volume of this series was published Acts. in 1682. But being written in Latin, with more regard to the past than to the growing state of opinions, and consequently almost excluding the most attractive, and indeed the most important subjects, with a Lutheran spirit of unchangeable orthodoxy in religion, and with an absence of anything like philosophy or even connected system in erudition, it is one of the most unreadable books, relatively to its utility in learning, which has ever fallen into my hands. Italy had entered earlier on this critical career; the Giornale de' Litterati was begun at Rome in 1668; the Giornale Veneto de' Litterati at Venice in 1671. They continued for some time ; but with less conspicuous reputation than those above mentioned. The Mercure savant, published at Amsterdam, in 1684, was an indifferent production, which induced Bayle to set up his own Nouvelles de la République des Lettres in opposition to it. Two reviews were commenced in the German language within the seventeenth century, and three in English. The first of these latter was the Weekly Memorials for the Ingenious, London, 1682. This, I believe, lasted but

a short time.   It was followed by one, entitled The Works
of the Learned, in 1691 ; and by another, called History of
the Works of the Learned, in 1699.[i]

28. Bayle had first become known in 1682, by the Pensées
Bayle's Thoughts on the Comet. diverses sur la Comète de 1680 ; a work which I am
not sure that he ever decidedly surpassed.   Its pur-
pose is one hardly worthy, we should imagine, to
employ him ; since those who could read and reason were not
likely to be afraid of comets, and those who could do neither
would be little the better for his book.   But with this osten-
sible aim Bayle had others in view ; it gave scope to his keen
observation of mankind, if we may use the word observation
for that which he chiefly derived from modern books, and to
the calm philosophy which he professed.   There is less of the
love of paradox, less of a cavilling pyrrhonism, and though
much diffuseness, less of pedantry and irrelevant instances in
the Pensées diverses than in his greater work.   It exposed
him, however, to controversy ; Jurieu, a French minister in
Holland, the champion of Calvinistic orthodoxy, waged a war
that was only terminated with their lives ; and Bayle's defence of the Thoughts on the Comet is full as long as the
original performance, but far less entertaining.

29. He now projected an immortal undertaking, the His-
His Dictionary. torical and Critical Dictionary.   Moreri, a laborious
scribe, had published, in 1673, a kind of encyclopedic
dictionary, biographical, historical, and geographical ; Bayle
professed to fill up the numerous deficiencies, and to rectify
the errors of this compiler.   It is hard to place his dictionary,
which appeared in 1694, under any distinct head in a literary

---

[i] Jugler, Hist. Litteraria, cap. 9.
Bibliothèque universelle, xiii. 41.—
[The first number of Weekly Memorials
for the Ingenious is dated Jan. 16,
1681-2, and the first book reviewed is,
Christiani Liberii Βιϐλιοφιλια, Utrecht,
1681. The editor proposes to transcribe
from the Journal des Sçavans whatever
is most valuable, and by far the greater
part of the articles relate to foreign
books.   This review seems to have
lasted but a year ; at least there is only
one volume in the British Museum.
The Universal Historical Bibliothèque,
which began in January, 1686, and expired in March, is scarcely worth no-

tice ; it is professedly a compilation from
the foreign reviews.   The History of
the Works of the Learned, published
monthly from 1699 to 1711, is much
more respectable ; though in this also a
very large proportion is given to foreign
works, and probably on the credit of continental journals.   The books reviewed
are numerous and commonly of a learned
class.   The accounts given of them are
chiefly analytical, the reviewer seldom
interposing his judgment : if any bias is
perceptible, it is towards what was then
called the liberal side ; but for the most
part the rule adopted is to speak favourably of every one.— 1842.]

classification which does not make a separate chapter for
lexicography. It is almost equally difficult to give a general
character of this many-coloured web, which great erudition
and still greater acuteness and strength of mind wove for
the last years of the seventeenth century. The learning of
Bayle was copious, especially in what was most peculiarly
required, the controversies, the anecdotes, the miscellaneous
facts and sentences, scattered over the vast surface of literature for two preceding centuries. In that of antiquity he
was less profoundly versed, yet so quick in application of his
classical stores, that he passes for a better scholar than he
was. His original design may have been only to fill up the
deficiencies of Moreri; but a mind so fertile and excursive
could not be restrained in such limits. We may find, however, in this an apology for the numerous omissions of Bayle,
which would, in a writer absolutely original, seem both capricious and unaccountable. We never can anticipate with
confidence that we shall find any name in his dictionary.
The notes are most frequently unconnected with the life to
which they are appended ; so that, under a name uninteresting to us, or inapposite to our purpose, we may be led into
the richest vein of the author's fine reasoning or lively wit.
Bayle is admirable in exposing the fallacies of dogmatism,
the perplexities of philosophy, the weaknesses of those who
affect to guide the opinions of mankind. But, wanting the
necessary condition of good reasoning, an earnest desire to
reason well, a moral rectitude from which the love of truth
must spring, he often avails himself of petty cavils, and becomes dogmatical in his very doubts. A more sincere spirit
of inquiry could not have suffered a man of his penetrating
genius to acquiesce, even contingently, in so superficial a
scheme as the Manichean. The sophistry of Bayle, however,
bears no proportion to his just and acute observations. Still
less excuse can be admitted for his indecency, which almost
assumes the character of monomania, so invariably does it
recur, even where there is least pretext for it.

30. The Jugemens des Sçavans by Baillet, published in
1685 and 1686, the Polyhistor of Morhof in 1689, Baillet,
are certainly works of criticism as well as of bibli- Morhof.
ography. But neither of these writers, especially the latter,

are of much authority in matters of taste; their erudition was very extensive, their abilities respectable, since they were able to produce such useful and comprehensive works; but they do not greatly serve to enlighten or correct our judgments, nor is the original matter in any considerable proportion to that which they have derived from others. I have taken notice of both these in my preface.

31. France was very fruitful of that miscellaneous litera-

The Ana.

ture which, desultory and amusing, has the advantage of remaining better in the memory than more systematic books, and in fact is generally found to supply the man of extensive knowledge with the materials of his conversation, as well as to fill the vacancies of his deeper studies. The memoirs, the letters, the travels, the dialogues and essays, which might be ranged in so large a class as that we now pass in review, are too numerous to be mentioned, and it must be understood that most of them are less in request even among the studious than they were in the last century. One group has acquired the distinctive name of Ana; the reported conversation, the table-talk of the learned. Several of these belong to the last part of the sixteenth century, or the first of the next; the Scaligerana, the Perroniana, the Pithæana, the Naudæana, the Casauboniana; the last of which are not conversational, but fragments collected from the common-place books and loose papers of Isaac Casaubon. Two collections of the present period are very well known; the Menagiana, and the Mélanges de Littérature par Vigneul-Marville; which differs indeed from the rest in not being reported by others, but published by the author himself; yet comes so near in spirit and manner, that we may place it in the same class. The Menagiana has the common fault of these Ana, that it rather disappoints expectation, and does not give us as much new learning as the name of its author seems to promise; but it is amusing, full of light anecdote of a literary kind, and interesting to all who love the recollections of that generation. Vigneul-Marville is an imaginary person; the author of the Mélanges de Littérature is D'Argonne, a Benedictine of Rouen. This book has been much esteemed; the mask gives courage to the author, who writes, not unlike a Benedictine, but with a general tone of independent think-

ing, united to good judgment and a tolerably extensive
knowledge of the state of literature. He had entered into
the religious profession rather late in life. The Chevræana
and Segraisiana, especially the latter, are of little value. The
Parrhasiana of Le Clerc are less amusing and less miscellaneous than some of the Ana; but in all his writings there is
a love of truth and a zeal against those who obstruct inquiry,
which to congenial spirits is as pleasing as it is sure to render
him obnoxious to opposite tempers.

32. The characteristics of English writers in the first division of the century were not maintained in the English
second, though the change, as was natural, did not style in this
period.
come on by very rapid steps. The pedantry of unauthorised
Latinisms, the affectation of singular and not generally intelligible words from other sources, the love of quaint phrases,
strange analogies, and ambitious efforts at antithesis, gave
way by degrees; a greater ease of writing was what the
public demanded, and what the writers after the Restoration
sought to attain; they were more strictly idiomatic and
English than their predecessors. But this ease sometimes
became negligence and feebleness, and often turned to coarseness and vulgarity. The language of Sévigné and Hamilton
is eminently colloquial; scarce a turn occurs in their writings
which they would not have used in familiar society; but
theirs was the colloquy of the gods, ours of men: their idiom,
though still simple and French, had been refined in the
saloons of Paris, by that instinctive rejection of all that is
low which the fine tact of accomplished women dictates;
while in our own contemporary writers, with little exception,
there is what defaces the dialogue of our comedy, a tone not
so much of provincialism, or even of what is called the language of the common people, as of one much worse, the dregs
of vulgar ribaldry, which a gentleman must clear from his
conversation before he can assert that name. Nor was this
confined to those who led irregular lives; the general manners being unpolished, we find in the writings of the clergy,
wherever they are polemic or satirical, the same tendency
to what is called *slang*; a word which, as itself belongs to
the vocabulary it denotes, I use with some unwillingness.
The pattern of bad writing in this respect was Sir Roger

L'Estrange; his Æsop's Fables will present everything that is hostile to good taste; yet by a certain wit and readiness in raillery L'Estrange was a popular writer, and may even now be read, perhaps, with some amusement. The translation of Don Quixote, published in 1682, may also be specified as incredibly vulgar, and without the least perception of the tone which the original author has preserved.

33. We can produce nevertheless several names of those who laid the foundations at least, and indeed fur-
Hobbes.
nished examples, of good style; some of them among the greatest, for other merits, in our literature. Hobbes is perhaps the first of whom we can strictly say that he is a good English writer; for the excellent passages of Hooker, Sidney, Raleigh, Bacon, Taylor, Chillingworth, and others of the Elizabethan or the first Stuart period are not sufficient to establish their claim; a good writer being one whose composition is nearly uniform, and who never sinks to such inferiority or negligence as we must confess in most of these. To make such a writer, the absence of gross faults is full as necessary as actual beauties; we are not judging as of poets, by the highest flight of their genius, and forgiving all the rest, but as of a sum of positive and negative quantities, where the latter counterbalance and efface an equal portion of the former. Hobbes is clear, precise, spirited, and, above all, free, in general, from the faults of his predecessors; his language is sensibly less obsolete; he is never vulgar, rarely, if ever, quaint or pedantic.

34. Cowley's prose, very unlike his verse, as Johnson has observed, is perspicuous and unaffected. His few
Cowley.
essays may even be reckoned among the earliest models of good writing. In that, especially, on the death of Cromwell, till, losing his composure, he falls a little into the vulgar style towards the close, we find an absence of pedantry, an ease and graceful choice of idiom, an unstudied harmony of periods, which had been perceived in very few writers of the two preceding reigns. 'His thoughts,' says Johnson, 'are natural, and his style has a smooth and placid equability which has never yet attained its due commendation. Nothing is far-sought or hard-laboured; but all is easy without feeble-ness, and familiar without grossness.'

35. Evelyn wrote in 1651 a little piece, purporting to be an account of England by a Frenchman. It is very severe on our manners, especially in London; his abhorrence of the late revolutions in church and state conspiring with his natural politeness, which he had lately improved by foreign travel. It is worth reading as illustrative of social history; but I chiefly mention it here on account of the polish and gentlemanly elegance of the style, which very few had hitherto regarded in such light compositions. An answer by some indignant patriot has been reprinted together with this pamphlet of Evelyn, and is a good specimen of the bestial ribaldry which our ancestors seem to have taken for wit.[k] The later writings of Evelyn are such as his character and habits would lead us to expect, but I am not aware that they often rise above that respectable level, nor are their subjects such as to require an elevated style.

36. Every poem and play of Dryden, as they successively appeared, was ushered into the world by one of those prefaces and dedications which have made him celebrated as a critic of poetry and a master of the English language. The Essay on Dramatic Poesy, and its subsequent Defence, the Origin and Progress of Satire, the Parallel of Poetry and Painting, the Life of Plutarch, and other things of minor importance, all prefixed to some more extensive work, complete the catalogue of his prose. The style of Dryden was very superior to any that England had seen. Not conversant with our old writers, so little, in fact, as to find the common phrases of the Elizabethan age unintelligible,[m] he followed the taste of Charles's reign in emulating the politest and most popular writers in the French language. He seems to have formed himself on Montaigne, Balzac, and Voiture; but so ready was his invention, so vigorous his judgment, so complete his mastery over his native tongue, that, in point of style, he must be reckoned above all the three. He had the ease of Montaigne without his negligence and embarrassed structure of periods; he had the dignity of

Evelyn.

Dryden.

---

[k] Both these will be found in the late edition of Evelyn's Miscellaneous Works.

[m] Malone has given several proofs of this. Dryden's Prose Works, vol. i. part 2, p. 136, et alibi. Dryden thought expressions wrong and incorrect in Shakspeare and Jonson, which were the current language of their age.

Balzac, with more varied cadences, and without his hyperbolical tumour; the unexpected turns of Voiture without his affectation and air of effort. In the dedications, especially, we find paragraphs of extraordinary gracefulness, such as possibly have never been surpassed in our language. The prefaces are evidently written in a more negligent style; he seems, like Montaigne, to converse with the reader from his arm-chair, and passes onward with little connexion from one subject to another.[n] In addressing a patron, a different line is observable; he comes with the respectful air which the occasion seems to demand; but, though I do not think that Dryden ever, in language, forgets his own position, we must confess that the flattery is sometimes palpably untrue, and always offensively indelicate. The dedication of the Mock Astrologer to the Duke of Newcastle is a masterpiece of fine writing; and the subject better deserved these lavish commendations than most who received them. That of the State of Innocence to the Duchess of York is also very well written; but the adulation is excessive. It appears to me that, after the Revolution, Dryden took less pains with his style; the colloquial vulgarisms, and these are not wanting even in his earlier prefaces, become more frequent; his periods are often of more slovenly construction; he forgets even in his dedications that he is standing before a lord. Thus, remarking on the account Andromache gives to Hector of her own history, he observes, in a style rather unworthy of him, ' The devil was in Hector if he knew not all this matter as well as she who told it him, for she had been his bed-fellow for many years together; and if he knew it then, it must be confessed that Homer in this long digression has rather given us his own character than that of the fair lady whom he paints.'[o]

37. His Essay on Dramatic Poesy, published in 1668, was

His Essay on Dramatic Poesy.   reprinted sixteen years afterwards, and it is curious to observe the changes which Dryden made in the expression. Malone has carefully noted all these; they show both the care the author took with his own style, and the change

---

[n] This is his own account. ' The nature of a preface is rambling, never wholly out of the way, nor in it. . . . This I have learned from the practice of honest Montaigne.' Vol. iii. p. 605.

[o] Vol. iii. p. 286. This is in the dedication of his third Miscellany to Lord Ratcliffe.

which was gradually working in the English language.[p]
The Anglicism of terminating the sentence with a preposition is rejected.[q]   Thus 'I cannot think so contemptibly of
the age I live in,' is exchanged for ' the age in which I live.'
' A deeper expression of belief than all the actor can persuade
us to, is altered, ' can insinuate into us.'   And, though the
old form continued in use long after the time of Dryden, it
has of late years been reckoned inelegant, and proscribed
in all cases, perhaps with an unnecessary fastidiousness, to
which I have not uniformly deferred; since our language is
of a Teutonic structure, and the rules of Latin or French
grammar are not always to bind us.

38. This Essay on Dramatic Poesy is written in dialogue;
Dryden himself, under the name of Neander, being Improvements in
probably one of the speakers.   It turns on the use his style.
of rhyme in tragedy, on the observation of the unities, and
on some other theatrical questions.   Dryden, at this time,
was favourable to rhymed tragedies, which his practice supported.   Sir Robert Howard having written some observations on that essay, and taken a different view as to rhyme,
Dryden published a defence of his essay in a masterly style
of cutting scorn, but one hardly justified by the tone of the
criticism, which had been very civil towards him ; and as he
was apparently in the wrong, the air of superiority seems the
more misplaced.

39. Dryden, as a critic, is not to be numbered with those
who have sounded the depths of the human mind, His critical
hardly with those who analyse the language and sen- character.
timents of poets, and teach others to judge by showing why
they have judged themselves.   He scatters remarks sometimes too indefinite, sometimes too arbitrary ; yet his pre-
dominating good sense colours the whole ; we find in them

---

[p] Vol. i. pp. 136-142.

[q] ' The preposition in the end of the
sentence, a common fault with him
(Ben Jonson), and which I have but
lately observed in my own writings.'
p. 237. The form is, in my opinion,
sometimes emphatic and spirited, though
its frequent use appears slovenly. I
remember my late friend, Mr. Richard
Sharp, whose good taste is well known,
used to quote an interrogatory of Hooker :
' Shall there be a God to swear by, and
none to pray to ? ' as an instance of the
force which this arrangement, so eminently idiomatic, sometimes gives. In
the passive voice, I think it better than
in the active ; nor can it always be dispensed with, unless we choose rather the
feeble encumbering pronoun *which*.

no perplexing subtilty, no cloudy nonsense, no paradoxes and heresies in taste to revolt us. Those he has made on translation in the preface to that of Ovid's Epistles are valuable. 'No man,' he says, 'is capable of translating poetry, who, besides a genius *to* that art, is not a master both of his author's language and of his own. Nor must we understand the language only of the poet, but his particular turn of thoughts and expression, which are the characters that distinguish and as it were individuate him from all other writers.'[r] We cannot pay Dryden the compliment of saying that he gave the example as well as precept, especially in his Virgil. He did not scruple to copy Segrais in his discourse on Epic Poetry. 'Him I follow, and what I borrow from him am ready to acknowledge *to* him; for, impartially speaking, the French are as much better critics than the English as they are worse poets.'[s]

40. The greater part of his critical writings relates to the drama; a subject with which he was very conversant; but he had some considerable prejudices: he seems never to have felt the transcendent excellence of Shakspeare; and sometimes perhaps his own opinions, if not feigned, are biassed by that sort of self-defence to which he thought himself driven in the prefaces to his several plays. He had many enemies on the watch; the Duke of Buckingham's Rehearsal, a satire of great wit, had exposed to ridicule the heroic tragedies,[t] and many were afterwards ready to forget the merits of the poet in the delinquencies of the politician. 'What Virgil wrote,' he says, 'in the vigour of his age, in plenty and in ease, I have undertaken to translate in my declining years; struggling with wants, oppressed by sickness, curbed in my genius, liable to be misconstrued in all I write; and my judges, if they are not very equitable, already prejudiced against me by the lying character which has been given them of my morals.'[u]

---

[r] Vol. iii. p. 19.

[s] P. 460.

[t] This comedy was published in 1672; the parodies are amusing; and though parody is the most unfair weapon that ridicule can use, they are in most instances warranted by the original. Bayes, whether he resembles Dryden or not, is a very comic personage: the character is said by Johnson to have been sketched for Davenant; but I much doubt this report; Davenant had been dead some years before the Rehearsal was published, and could have been in no way obnoxious to its satire.

[u] Vol. iii. p. 557.

41. Dryden will hardly be charged with abandoning too hastily our national credit, when he said the French Rymer on Tragedy. were better critics than the English. We had scarcely anything worthy of notice to allege beyond his own writings. The Theatrum Poetarum by Philips, nephew of Milton, is superficial in every respect. Thomas Rymer, best known to mankind as the editor of the Fœdera, but a strenuous advocate for the Aristotelian principles in the drama, published in 1678 'the Tragedies of the last Age considered and examined by the Practice of the Ancients, and by the Common Sense of all Ages.' This contains a censure of some plays of Beaumont and Fletcher, Shakspeare and Jonson. ' I have chiefly considered the fable or plot, which all conclude to be the soul of a tragedy, which with the ancients is always found to be a reasonable soul, but with us for the most part a brutish, and often worse than brutish.'[x] I have read only his criticisms on the Maid's Tragedy, King and No King, and Rollo; and as the conduct and characters of all three are far enough from being invulnerable, it is not surprising that Rymer has often well exposed them.

42. Next to Dryden, the second place among the polite writers of the period from the Restoration to the Sir William Temple's Essays. end of the century has commonly been given to Sir Willian Temple. His Miscellanies, to which principally this praise belongs, are not recommended by more erudition than a retired statesman might acquire with no great expense of time, nor by much originality of reflection. But if Temple has not profound knowledge, he turns all he possesses well to account; if his thoughts are not very striking, they are commonly just. He has less eloquence than Bolingbroke, but is also free from his restlessness and ostentation. Much also which now appears superficial in Temple's historical surveys, was far less familiar in his age; he has the merit of a comprehensive and a candid mind. His style, to which we should particularly refer, will be found in comparison with his contemporaries highly polished, and sustained with more equability than they preserve, remote from anything either pedantic or humble. The periods are studiously rhythmical;

---

[x] P. 4.

yet they want the variety and peculiar charm that we admire in those of Dryden.

43. Locke is certainly a good writer, relatively to the
Style of Locke. greater part of his contemporaries; his plain and manly sentences often give us pleasure by the wording alone. But he has some defects; in his Essay on the Human Understanding he is often too figurative for the subject. In all his writings, and especially in the Treatise on Education, he is occasionally negligent, and though not vulgar, at least according to the idiom of his age, slovenly in the structure of his sentences as well as the choice of his words; he is not, in mere style, very forcible, and certainly not very elegant.

44. The Essays of Sir George Mackenzie are empty and
Sir George Mackenzie's Essays. diffuse; the style is full of pedantic words to a degree of barbarism; and though they were chiefly written after the Revolution, he seems to have wholly formed himself on the older writers, such as Sir Thomas Browne, or even Feltham. He affects the obsolete and unpleasing termination of the third person of the verb in *eth*, which was going out of use even in the pulpit, besides other rust of archaism.[y] Nothing can be more unlike the manner of Dryden, Locke, or Temple. In his matter he seems a mere declaimer, as if the world would any longer endure the trivial morality which the sixteenth century had borrowed from Seneca, or the dull ethics of sermons. It is probable that, as Mackenzie was a man who had seen and read much, he must have some better passages than I have found in glancing
Andrew Fletcher. shortly at his works. His countryman, Andrew Fletcher, is a better master of English style; he writes with purity, clearness, and spirit; but the substance is so much before his eyes, that he is little solicitous about language. And a similar character may be given to many of the political tracts in the reign of William. They are well expressed for their purpose; their English is perspicuous, unaffected, often forcible, and upon the whole much superior

---

[y] [It must be confessed that instances of this termination, though not frequent, may be found in the first years of George III., or even later. In the auxiliary *hath*, it is scarcely yet disused, at least in very grave writings. But the unpleasing sound of *th* is a sufficient objection.—1842.]

to that of similar writings in the reign of Charles; but
they do not challenge a place of which their authors never
dreamed; they are not to be counted in the polite literature
of England.

45. I may have overlooked, or even never known, some
books of sufficient value to deserve mention; and I regret
that the list of miscellaneous literature should be so short.
But it must be confessed that our golden age did not begin
before the eighteenth century, and then with him who has
never since been rivalled in grace, humour, and invention.
Walton's Complete Angler, published in 1653, seems   Walton's
by the title a strange choice out of all the books of   Complete Angler.
half a century; yet its simplicity, its sweetness, its natural
grace, and happy intermixture of graver strains with the
precepts of angling, have rendered this book deservedly
popular, and a model which one of the most famous among
our late philosophers, and a successful disciple of Isaac
Walton in his favourite art, has condescended to imitate.

46. A book, not indeed remarkable for its style, but one
which I could hardly mention in any less miscel-   Wilkins's
laneous chapter than the present, though, since it   New World.
was published in 1638, it ought to have been mentioned before, is Wilkins's ' Discovery of a New World, or a Discourse
tending to prove that it is probable there may be another
habitable World in the Moon, with a Discourse concerning
the Possibility of a Passage thither.' This is one of the
births of that inquiring spirit, that disdain of ancient prejudice, which the seventeenth century produced. Bacon was
undoubtedly the father of it in England; but Kepler, and
above all Galileo, by the new truths they demonstrated, made
men fearless in investigation and conjecture. The geographical discoveries indeed of Columbus and Magellan had prepared the way for conjectures, hardly more astonishing in
the eyes of the vulgar than those had been. Wilkins accordingly begins by bringing a host of sage writers who had denied
the existence of antipodes. He expressly maintains the
Copernican theory, but admits that it was generally reputed
a novel paradox. The arguments on the other side he meets
at some length, and knew how to answer, by the principles
of compound motion, the plausible objection that stones falling

from a tower were not left behind by the motion of the earth.
The spots in the moon he took for sea, and the brighter parts
for land.   A lunar atmosphere he was forced to hold, and
gives reasons for thinking it probable.   As to inhabitants he
does not dwell long on the subject.   Campanella, and long
before him Cardinal Cusanus, had believed the sun and moon
to be inhabited,[z] and Wilkins ends by saying: 'Being content for my own part to have spoken so much of it as may
conduce to show the opinion of others concerning the inhabitants of the moon, I dare not myself affirm anything of
these Selenites, because I know not any ground whereon to
build any probable opinion.   But I think that future ages
will discover more, and our posterity perhaps may invent
some means for our better acquaintance with those inhabitants.'   To this he comes as his final proposition, that it may
be possible for some of our posterity to find out a conveyance
to this other world; and if there be inhabitants there, to
have communication with them.   But this chapter is the
worst in the book, and shows that Wilkins, notwithstanding
his ingenuity, had but crude notions on the principles of
physics.   He followed this up by what I have not seen, a 'Discourse concerning a new Planet; tending to prove that it is
possible our Earth is one of the Planets.'   This appears to
be a regular vindication of the Copernican theory, and was
published in 1640.

47. The cause of antiquity, so rudely assailed abroad by
Antiquity   Perrault and Fontenelle, found support in Sir Wil-
defended by
Temple.   liam Temple, who has defended it in one of his essays with more zeal than prudence or knowledge of the
various subjects on which he contends for the rights of the
past.   It was in fact such a credulous and superficial view as
might have been taken by a pedant of the sixteenth century.
For it is in science, taking the word largely, full as much as
in works of genius, that he denies the ancients to have been
surpassed.   Temple's Essay, however, was translated into

---

[z] Suspicamur in regione solis magis
esse solares, claros et illuminatos intel-
lectuales habitatores, spiritualiores etiam
quam in luna, ubi magis lunatici, et in
terra magis materiales et crassi, ut illi
intellectualis naturæ solares sint multum
in actu et parum in potentiâ, terreni vero
magis in potentiâ et parum in actu,
lunares in medio fluctuantes, &c. Cusanus apud Wilkins, p. 103 (edit. 1802).

French, and he was supposed by many to have made a brilliant vindication of injured antiquity. But it was soon refuted in the most solid book that was written in any Wotton's country upon this famous dispute. William Wotton Reflections. published in 1694 his Reflections on ancient and modern Learning.[a] He draws very well in this the line between Temple and Perrault, avoiding the tasteless judgment of the latter in poetry and eloquence, but pointing out the superiority of the moderns in the whole range of physical science.

Sect. II.—On Fiction.

French Romances—La Fayette and others—Pilgrim's Progress—
Turkish Spy.

48. SPAIN had about the middle of this century a writer of various literature, who is only known in Europe by Quevedo's his fictions, Quevedo. His Visions and his Life of Visions. the great Tacaño were early translated, and became very popular.[b] They may be reckoned superior to any thing in comic romance, except Don Quixote, that the seventeenth century produced; and yet this commendation is not a high one. In the picaresque style, the life of Tacaño is tolerably amusing; but Quevedo, like others, has long since been surpassed. The Sueños, or Visions, are better; they show spirit and sharpness with some originality of invention. But Las Zahurdas de Pluton, which, like the other Visions, bears a general resemblance to the Pilgrim's Progress, being an allegorical dream, is less powerfully and graphically written; the satire is also rather too obvious. 'Lucian,' says Bou-

---

[a] Wotton had been a boy of astonishing precocity; at six years old he could readily translate Latin, Greek, and Hebrew; at seven he added some knowledge of Arabic and Syriac. He entered Catherine Hall, Cambridge, in his tenth year; at thirteen, when he took the degree of bachelor of arts, he was acquainted with twelve languages. There being no precedent of granting a degree to one so young, a special record of his extraordinary proficiency was made in the registers of the university. Monk's Life of Bentley, p. 7.

[b] The translation of this, 'made English by a person of honour,' takes great liberties with the original, and endeavours to excel it in wit by means of frequent interpolation.

terwek, 'furnished him with the original idea of satirical
visions; but Quevedo's were the first of their kind in modern
literature. Owing to frequent imitations, their faults are no
longer disguised by the charm of novelty, and even their
merits have ceased to interest.' [c]

49. No species of composition seems less adapted to the
French
heroic
romances. genius of the French nation in the reign of Louis
XIV. than the heroic romances so much admired in
its first years. It must be confessed that this was but the
continuance, and in some respect, possibly, an improvement
of a long-established style of fiction. But it was not fitted
to endure reason or ridicule, and the societies of Paris knew
the use of both weapons. Molière sometimes tried his wit
upon the romances; and Boileau, rather later in the day,
when the victory had been won, attacked Mademoiselle
Scuderi with his sarcastic irony in a dialogue on the heroes
of her invention.

50. The first step in descending from the heroic romance
Novels of
Madame
La Fayette. was to ground not altogether dissimilar. The feats
of chivalry were replaced by less wonderful adven-
tures; the love became less hyperbolical in expression, though
not less intensely engrossing the personages; the general
tone of manners was lowered down better to that of nature,
or at least of an ideality which the imagination did not reject; a style already tried in the minor fictions of Spain.
The earliest novels that demand attention in this line are
those of the Countess de la Fayette, celebrated, while Mademoiselle de la Vergne, under the name of Laverna in the
Latin poetry of Menage.[d] Zayde, the first of these, is entirely in the Spanish style; the adventures are improbable,
but various and rather interesting to those who carry no
scepticism into fiction; the language is polished and agreeable, though not very animated; and it is easy to perceive
that while that kind of novel was popular, Zayde would
obtain a high place. It has however the usual faults; the

---

[c] Hist. of Spanish Literature, p. 471.

[d] The name Laverna, though well-
sounding, was in one respect unlucky,
being that given by antiquity to the god-
dess of thieves. An epigram on Menage,
almost, perhaps, too trite to be quoted,
is *piquant* enough:—

Lesbia nulla tibi, nulla est tibi dicta Corinna;
  Carmine laudatur Cynthia nulla tuo.
Sed cum doctorum compilas scrinia vatum,
  Nil mirum, si sit culta Laverna tibi.

story is broken by intervening narratives, which occupy too large a space ; the sorrows of the principal characters excite, at least as I should judge, little sympathy ; and their sentiments and emotions are sometimes too much refined in the alembic of the Hôtel Rambouillet. In a later novel, the Princess of Cleves, Madame La Fayette threw off the affectation of that circle to which she had once belonged, and though perhaps Zayde is, or was in its own age, the more celebrated novel, it seems to me that in this she has excelled herself. The story, being nothing else than the insuperable and insidious, but not guilty, attachment of a married lady to a lover, required a delicacy and correctness of taste which the authoress has well displayed in it. The probability of the incidents, the natural course they take, the absence of all complication and perplexity, give such an inartificial air to this novel, that we can scarcely help believing it to shadow forth some real event. A modern novelist would probably have made more of the story ; the style is always calm, sometimes almost languid ; a tone of decorous politeness, like that of the French stage, is never relaxed ; but it is precisely by this means that the writer has kept up a moral dignity, of which it would have been so easy to lose sight. The Princess of Cleves is perhaps the first work of mere invention (for though the characters are historical, there is no known foundation for the story) which brought forward the manners of the aristocracy ; it may be said, the contemporary manners ; for Madame La Fayette must have copied her own times. As this has become a popular style of fiction, it is just to commemorate the novel which introduced it.

51. The French have few novels of this class in the seven-teenth century which they praise ; those of Madame Villedieu, or Des Jardins, may deserve to be excepted ; *Scarron's Roman Comique.* but I have not seen them. Scarron, a man deformed and diseased, but endowed with vast gaiety, which generally exuberated in buffoon jests, has the credit of having struck out into a new path by his Roman Comique. The Spaniards however had so much like this that we cannot perceive any great originality in Scarron. The Roman Comique is still well known, and if we come to it in vacant moments, will serve its end in amusing us ; the story and characters have

no great interest, but they are natural; yet, without the
least disparagement to the vivacity of Scarron, it is still true
that he has been left at an immense distance in observation
of mankind, in humorous character, and in ludicrous effect,
by the novelists of the eighteenth and nineteenth centuries.
It is said that Scarron's romance is written in a pure style;
and some have even pretended that he has not been without
effect in refining the language. The Roman Bourgeois of
Furetière appears to be a novel of middle life; it had some
reputation, but I cannot speak of it with any knowledge.

52. Cyrano de Bergerac had some share in directing the
public taste towards those extravagances of fancy
Cyrano de
Bergerac.
which were afterwards highly popular. He has
been imitated, as some have observed, by Swift and Voltaire,
and I should add, to a certain degree, by Hamilton; but all
the three have gone far beyond him. He is not himself a
very original writer. His Voyage to the Moon, and History
of the Empire of the Sun, are manifestly suggested by the
True History of Lucian; and he had modern fictions, especially the Voyage to the Moon by Godwin, mentioned in our
last volume, which he had evidently read, to imp the wings
of an invention not perhaps eminently fertile. Yet Bergerac
has the merit of being never wearisome; his fictions are well
conceived, and show little effort, which seems also the character of his language in this short piece; though his letters
had been written in the worst style of affectation, so as to
make us suspect that he was turning the manner of some
contemporaries into ridicule. The novels of Segrais,
Segrais.
such at least as I have seen, are mere pieces of light
satire, designed to amuse by transient allusions the lady by
whom he was patronised, Mademoiselle de Montpensier. If
they deserve any regard at all, it is as links in the history of
fiction between the mock-heroic romance, of which Voiture
had given an instance, and the style of fantastic invention,
which was perfected by Hamilton.

53. Charles Perrault may, so far as I know, be said to have
invented a kind of fiction which became extremely
Perrault.
popular, and has had, even after it ceased to find
direct imitators, a perceptible influence over the lighter literature of Europe. The idea was original, and happily exe-

cuted. Perhaps he sometimes took the tales of children, such as the tradition of many generations had delivered them; but much of his fairy machinery seems to have been his own, and I should give him credit for several of the stories, though it is hard to form a guess. He gave to them all a real interest, as far as could be, with a naturalness of expression, an arch naïveté, a morality neither too obvious nor too refined, and a slight poignancy of satire on the world, which render the Tales of Mother Goose almost a counterpart in prose to the Fables of La Fontaine.

54. These amusing fictions caught the fancy of an indolent but not stupid nobility. The court of Versailles and all Paris resounded with fairy tales; it became the popular style for more than half a century. But few of these fall within our limits. Perrault's immediate followers, Madame Murat and the Countess d'Aunoy, especially the latter, have some merit; but they come very short of the happy simplicity and brevity we find in Mother Goose's Tales. It is possible that Count Antony Hamilton may have written those tales which have made him famous before the end of the century, though they were published later. But these, with many admirable strokes of wit and invention, have too forced a tone in both these qualities; the labour is too evident, and, thrown away on such trifling, excites something like contempt; they are written for an exclusive coterie, not for the world; and the world in all such cases will sooner or later take its revenge. Yet Hamilton's tales are incomparably superior to what followed; inventions alternately dull and extravagant, a style negligent or mannered, an immorality passing onward from the licentiousness of the Regency to the debased philosophy of the ensuing age, became the general characteristics of these fictions, which finally expired in the neglect and scorn of the world.

55. The Télémaque of Fenelon, after being suppressed in France, appeared in Holland clandestinely without the author's consent in 1699. It is needless to say that it soon obtained the admiration of Europe, and perhaps there is no book in the French language that has been more read. Fenelon seems to have conceived that, metre not being essential, as he assumed, to poetry, he had, by imitating

the Odyssey in Télémaque, produced an epic of as legitimate a character as his model. But the boundaries between epic poetry, especially such epics as the Odyssey, and romance were only perceptible by the employment of verse in the former; no elevation of character, no ideality of conception, no charm of imagery or emotion had been denied to romance. The language of poetry had for two centuries been seized for its use. Télémaque must therefore take its place among romances; but still it is true that no romance had breathed so classical a spirit, none had abounded so much with the richness of poetical language, (much in fact of Homer, Virgil, and Sophocles having been woven in with no other change than verbal translation,) nor had any preserved such dignity in its circumstances, such beauty, harmony, and nobleness in its diction. It would be as idle to say that Fenelon was indebted to D'Urfè and Calprenède, as to deny that some degree of resemblance may be found in their poetical prose. The one belonged to the morals of chivalry, generous but exaggerated: the other, to those of wisdom and religion. The one has been forgotten because its tone is false; the other is ever admired, and is only less regarded because it is true in excess, because it contains too much of what we know. Télémaque, like some other of Fenelon's writings, is to be considered in reference to its object; an object of all the noblest, being to form the character of one to whom many must look up for their welfare, but still very different from the inculcation of profound truth. The beauties of Télémaque are very numerous, the descriptions, and indeed the whole tone of the book, have a charm of grace something like the pictures of Guido; but there is also a certain languor which steals over us in reading, and though there is no real want of variety in the narration, it reminds us so continually of its source, the Homeric legends, as to become rather monotonous. The abandonment of verse has produced too much diffuseness; it will be observed if we look attentively, that where Homer is circumstantial, Fenelon is more so; in this he sometimes approaches the minuteness of the romancers. But these defects are more than compensated by the moral, and even æsthetic excellence of this romance.

56. If this most fertile province of all literature, as we

have now discovered it to be, had yielded so little even in France, a nation that might appear eminently fitted to explore it, down to the close of the seventeenth century, we may be less surprised at the deficiency of our own country. Yet the scarcity of original fiction in England was so great as to be inexplicable by any reasoning. The public taste was not incapable of being pleased; for all the novels and romances of the Continent were readily translated. The manners of all classes were as open to humorous de - scription, the imagination was as vigorous, the heart as susceptible, as in other countries. But not only we find nothing good; it can hardly be said that we find anything at all that has ever attracted notice in English romance. The Parthenissa of Lord Orrery, in the heroic style, and the short novels of Afra Behn, are nearly as many, perhaps, as could be detected in old libraries. We must leave the beaten track before we can place a single work in this class.

Deficiency of English romances.

57. The Pilgrim's Progress essentially belongs to it, and John Bunyan may pass for the father of our novelists. His success in a line of composition like the spiritual romance or allegory, which seems to have been frigid and unreadable in the few instances where it had been attempted, is doubtless enhanced by his want of all learning and his low station in life. He was therefore rarely, if ever, an imitator; he was never enchained by rules. Bunyan possessed in a remarkable degree the power of representation; his inventive faculty was considerable, but the other is his distinguishing excellence. He saw, and makes us see, what he describes; he is circumstantial without prolixity, and in the variety and frequent change of his incidents, never loses sight of the unity of his allegorical fable. His invention was enriched, and rather his choice determined, by one rule he had laid down to himself, the adaptation of all the incidental language of Scripture to his own use. There is scarce a circumstance or metaphor in the Old Testament which does not find a place, bodily and literally, in the story of the Pilgrim's Progress; and this peculiar artifice has made his own imagination appear more creative than it really is. In the conduct of the romance no rigorous attention to the propriety of the allegory seems to have been uniformly pre-

Pilgrim's Progress.

served. Vanity Fair, or the cave of the two giants, might, for anything we see, have been placed elsewhere; but it is by this neglect of exact parallelism that he better keeps up the reality of the pilgrimage, and takes off the coldness of mere allegory. It is also to be remembered that we read this book at an age when the spiritual meaning is either little perceived or little regarded. In his language, nevertheless, Bunyan sometimes mingles the signification too much with the fable; we might be perplexed between the imaginary and the real Christian; but the liveliness of narration soon brings us back, or did at least when we were young, to the fields of fancy. Yet the Pilgrim's Progress, like some other books, has of late been a little overrated; its excellence is great, but it is not of the highest rank, and we should be careful not to break down the landmarks of fame, by placing the John Bunyans and the Daniel De Foes among the Dii Majores of our worship.

58. I am inclined to claim for England not the invention, but, for the most part, the composition of another book, which, being grounded on fiction, may be classed here, The Turkish Spy. A secret emissary of the Porte is supposed to remain at Paris in disguise for above forty years, from 1635 to 1682. His correspondence with a number of persons, various in situation, and with whom therefore his letters assume various characters, is protracted through eight volumes. Much, indeed most, relates to the history of those times and to the anecdotes connected with it; but in these we do not find a large proportion of novelty. The more remarkable letters are those which run into metaphysical and theological speculation. These are written with an earnest seriousness, yet with an extraordinary freedom, such as the feigned garb of a Mohammedan could hardly have exempted from censure in Catholic countries. Mahmud, the mysterious writer, stands on a sort of eminence above all human prejudice; he was privileged to judge as a stranger of the religion and philosophy of Europe; but his bold spirit ranges over the field of Oriental speculation. The Turkish Spy is no ordinary production, but contains as many proofs of a thoughtful, if not very profound mind, as any we can find. It suggested the Persian Letters to Montesquieu, and the Jewish to Argens; the former deviating from his

Turkish Spy.

model with the originality of talent, the latter following it
with a more servile closeness. Probability, that is, a resemblance to the personated character of an Oriental, was not to
be attained, nor was it desirable, in any of these fictions;
but Mahmud has something not European, something of a
solitary insulated wanderer, gazing on a world that knows
him not, which throws, to my feelings, a striking charm over
the Turkish Spy; while the Usbek of Montesquieu has become more than half Parisian; his ideas are neither those of
his birthplace, nor such as have sprung up unbidden from
his soul, but those of a polite, witty, and acute society; and
the correspondence with his harem in Persia which Montesquieu has thought attractive to the reader, is not much more
interesting than it is probable, and ends in the style of a
common romance. As to the Jewish Letters of Argens, it is
far inferior to the Turkish Spy, and, in fact, rather an insipid
book.

59. It may be asked why I dispute the claim made by all
the foreign biographers in favour of John Paul Ma- Chiefly of
rana, a native of Genoa, who is asserted to have English
published the first volume of the Turkish Spy at Paris in
1684, and the rest in subsequent years.[e] But I am not disputing that Marana is the author of the thirty letters published in 1684, and of twenty more in 1686, which have been
literally translated into English, and form about half the
first volume in English of our Turkish Spy.[f] Nor do I doubt
in the least that the remainder of that volume had a French
original, though I have never seen it. But the later volumes
of the Espion Turc, in the edition of 1696, with the date of

---

[e] The first portion was published at
Paris, and also at Amsterdam. Bayle
gives the following account :—Cet ouvrage a été contrefait à Amsterdam du
consentement du libraire de Paris qui
l'a le premier imprimé. Il sera composé
de plusieurs petits volumes qui contien-
dront les évènemens les plus considéra-
bles de la chrétienté en général, et de la
France en particulier, depuis l'année
1637 jusqu'en 1682. Un Italien natif
de Gênes, Marana, donne ces relations
pour des lettres écrites aux ministres de
la Porte par un espion turc qui se tenoit
caché à Paris. Il prétend les avoir

traduites de l'Arabe en Italien ; et il
raconte fort en long comment il les a
trouvées. On soupçonne avec beaucoup
d'apparence, que c'est un tour d'esprit
italien, et une fiction ingénieuse sem-
blable à celle dont Virgile s'est servi
pour louer Auguste, etc. Nouvelles de
la République des Lettres, mars 1684 ;
in Œuvres diverses de Bayle, vol. i.
p. 20. The Espion turc is not to be
traced in the index to the Journal des
Sçavans ; nor is it noticed in the Bibliothèque universelle.

[f] Salfi, xiv. 61. Biogr. univers.

Cologne, which, according to Barbier, is put for Rouen,[g] are avowedly translated from the English. And to the second volume of our Turkish Spy, published in 1691, is prefixed an account, not very credible, of the manner in which the volumes subsequent to the first had been procured by a traveller, in the original Italian: no French edition, it is declared, being known to the booksellers. That no Italian edition ever existed is, I apprehend, now generally admitted; and it is to be shown by those who contend for the claims of Marana to seven out of the eight volumes, that they were published in France before 1691 and the subsequent years, when they appeared in English. The Cologne or Rouen edition of 1696 follows the English so closely, that it has not

---

[g] Dictionnaire des Anonymes, vol. i. p. 406. Barbier's notice of L'Espion dans les cours des princes chrétiens ascribes four volumes out of six, which appear to contain as much as our eight volumes, to Marana, and conjectures that the last two are by another hand; but does not intimate the least suspicion of an English original. And as his authority is considerable, I must fortify my own opinion by what evidence I can find.

The preface to the second volume (English) of the Turkish Spy begins thus. 'Three years are now elapsed since the first volume of letters written by a Spy at Paris was published in English. And it was expected that a second should have come out long before this. The favourable reception which that found amongst all sorts of readers would have encouraged a speedy translation of the rest, had there been extant any French edition of more than the first part. *But after the strictest inquiry none could be heard of*; and, as for the Italian, our booksellers have not that correspondence in those parts as they have in the more neighbouring countries of France and Holland. So that it was a work despaired of to recover any more of this Arabian's memoirs. We little dreamed that the Florentines had been so busy in printing and so successful in selling the continued translation of these Arabian epistles, till it was the fortune of an English gentleman to travel in those parts last summer, and discover the happy news. I will not forestall his letter, which is annexed to this preface.' A pretended letter with the signature of

Daniel Saltmarsh follows, in which the imaginary author tells a strange tale of the manner in which a certain learned physician of Ferrara, Julio de Medici, descended from the Medicean family, put these volumes in the Italian language into his hands. This letter is dated Amsterdam, Sept. 9, 1690, and as the preface refers it to the last summer, I hence conclude that the first edition of the second volume of the Turkish Spy was in 1691; for I have not seen that, nor any other edition earlier than the fifth, printed in 1702.

Marana is said by Salfi and others to have left France in 1689, having fallen into a depression of spirits. Now the first thirty letters, about one thirty-second part of the entire work, were published in 1684, and about an equal length in 1686. I admit that he had time to double these portions, and thus to publish one-eighth of the whole; but is it likely that between 1686 and 1689 he could have given the rest to the world? If we are not struck by this, is it likely that the English translator should have fabricated the story above-mentioned, when the public might know that there was actually a French original which he had rendered? The invention seems without motive. Again, how came the French edition of 1696 to be an avowed translation from the English, when, according to the hypothesis of M. Barbier, the volumes of Marana had all been published in France? Surely, till these appear, we have reason to suspect their existence; and the *onus probandi* lies *now* on the advocates of Marana's claim.

given the original letters of the first volume, published with
the name of Marana, but rendered them back from the translation.

60. In these early letters, I am ready to admit, the scheme
of the Turkish Spy may be entirely traced. Marana appears
not only to have planned the historical part of the letters,
but to have struck out the more original and striking idea of
a Mohammedan wavering with religious scruples, which the
English continuator has followed up with more philosophy
and erudition. The internal evidence for their English origin,
in all the latter volumes, is to my apprehension exceedingly
strong; but I know the difficulty of arguing from this to
convince a reader. The proof we demand is the production of these volumes in French, that is, the specification of
some public or private library where they may be seen, in
any edition anterior to 1691, and nothing short of this can
be satisfactory evidence.[h]

---

[h] I shall now produce some direct
evidence for the English authorship of
seven out of eight parts of the Turkish
Spy.
  ‘ In the life of Mrs. Manley, published under the title of “ The Adventures of Rivella,” printed in 1714, in
pages 14 and 15, it is said, That her
father, Sir Roger Manley, was the genuine author of the first volume of the
Turkish Spy. Dr. Midgley, an ingenious physician, related to the family by
marriage, had the charge of looking over
his papers, among which he found that
manuscript, which he easily reserved to
his proper use ; and both by his own pen
and the assistance of some others continued the work until the eighth volume,
without ever having the justice to name
the author of the first.’ MS. note in the
copy of the Turkish Spy (edit. 1732) in
the British Museum.
  Another MS. note in the same volume gives the following extract from
Dunton’s Life and Errors :—‘ Mr. Bradshaw is the best accomplished hackney
writer I have met with ; his genius
was quite above the common size, and
his style was incomparably fine. . . . So
soon as I saw the first volume of the
Turkish Spy, the very style and manner
of writing convinced me that Bradshaw
was the author. . . . Bradshaw’s wife
owned that Dr. Midgley had engaged

him in a work which would take him
some years to finish, for which the Doctor was to pay him 40s. per sheet . . .
so that ’tis very probable (for I cannot
swear I saw him write it) that Mr. William Bradshaw was the author of the
Turkish Spy ; were it not for this discovery, Dr. Midgley had gone off with
the honour of that performance.’ It thus
appears that in England it was looked
upon as an original work ; though the
authority of Dunton is not very good for
the facts he tells, and that of Mrs. Manley
much worse. But I do not quote them
as evidence of such facts, but of common
report. Mrs. Manley, who claims for her
father the first volume, certainly written
by Marana, must be set aside ; as to
Dr. Midgley and Mr. Bradshaw, I know
nothing to confirm or refute what is here
said.
  [The hypothesis of these notes, that
all the Turkish Spy, after the first of *our*
eight volumes, is of English origin, has
been controverted in the Gentleman’s
Magazine by persons of learning and
acuteness. I would surrender my own
opinion, if I could see sufficient grounds
for doing so ; but as yet Marana’s pretensions are not substantiated by the
evidence which I demanded, the proof
of any edition in French anterior to that
of our Turkish Spy, the second volume
of which (there is no dispute about

61. It would not, perhaps, be unfair to bring within the
Swift's Tale of a Tub. pale of the seventeenth century an effusion of genius, sufficient to redeem our name in its annals of fiction. The Tale of a Tub, though not published till 1704, was chiefly written, as the author declares, eight years before; and the Battle of the Books subjoined to it has every appearance of recent animosity against the opponents of Temple and Boyle, in the question of Phalaris. The Tale of a Tub is, in my apprehension, the masterpiece of Swift; certainly Rabelais has nothing superior, even in invention, nor any thing so condensed, so pointed, so full of real meaning, of biting satire, of felicitous analogy. The Battle of the Books is such an improvement of the similar combat in the Lutrin, that we can hardly own it is an imitation.

Marana's authorship of the first) appeared in 1691, with a preface denying the existence of a French original. Those who have had recourse to the arbitrary supposition that Marana communicated his manuscript to some English translator, who published it as his own, should be aware that a mere possibility, without a shadow of evidence, even if it served to explain the facts, cannot be received in historical criticism as truth.—1842.]

CHAPTER VIII.

HISTORY OF PHYSICAL AND OTHER LITERATURE, FROM 1650 TO 1700.

Sect. I.—On Experimental Philosophy.

Institutions for Science at Florence—London—Paris—Chemistry—Boyle and others.

1. WE have now arrived, according to the method pursued in corresponding periods, at the history of mathe- Reasons for matical and physical science in the latter part of omitting mathe- the seventeenth century. But I must here entreat matics. my readers to excuse the omission of that which ought to occupy a prominent situation in any work that pretends to trace the general progress of human knowledge. The length to which I have found myself already compelled to extend these volumes, might be an adequate apology; but I have one more insuperable in the slightness of my own acquaintance with subjects so momentous and difficult, and upon which I could not write without presumptuousness and much peril of betraying ignorance. The names, therefore, of Wallis and Huygens, Newton and Leibnitz, must be passed with distant reverence.

2. This was the age, when the experimental philosophy, to which Bacon had held the torch, and which had Academy del already made considerable progress, especially in Cimento. Italy, was finally established on the ruins of arbitrary figments and partial inductions. This philosophy was signally indebted to three associations, the eldest of which did not endure long; but the others have remained to this day, the perennial fountains of science ; the Academy del Cimento at

Florence, the Royal Society of London, the Academy of Sciences at Paris. The first of these was established in 1657, with the patronage of the Grand Duke Ferdinand II., but under the peculiar care of his brother Leopold. Both were, in a manner at that time remarkable, attached to natural philosophy ; and Leopold, less engaged in public affairs, had long carried on a correspondence with the learned of Europe. It is said that the advice of Viviani, one of the greatest geometers that Europe has produced, led to this institution. The name which this Academy assumed gave promise of their fundamental rule, the investigation of truth by experiment alone. The number of Academicians was unlimited, and all that was required as an article of faith was the abjuration of all faith, a resolution to inquire into truth without regard to any previous sect of philosophy. This Academy lasted unfortunately but ten years in vigour ; it is a great misfortune for any literary institution to depend on one man, and especially on a prince, who, shedding a factitious, as well as sometimes a genuine lustre round it, is not easily replaced without a diminution of the world's regard. Leopold, in 1667, became a cardinal, and was thus withdrawn from Florence ; others of the Academy del Cimento died or went away, and it rapidly sunk into insignificance. But a volume containing reports of the yearly experiments it made, among others the celebrated one proving, as was then supposed, the incompressibility of water, is generally esteemed.[a]

3. The germ of our Royal Society may be traced to the year 1645, when Wallis, Wilkins, Glisson, and others less known, agreed to meet weekly at a private house in London, in order to converse on subjects connected with natural, and especially experimental philosophy. Some of these soon afterwards settled in Oxford ; and thus arose two little societies in connexion with each other, those at Oxford being recruited by Ward, Petty, Willis, and Bathurst. They met at Petty's lodgings till he removed to Ireland in 1652 ; afterwards at those of Wilkins in Wadham College till he became Master of Trinity College, Cambridge,

Royal Society.

---

[a] Galluzzi, Storia del Gran Ducato, vol. vii. p. 240. Tiraboschi, xi. 204. Corniani, viii. 29.

in 1659; about which time most of the Oxford philosophers came to London, and held their meetings in Gresham College. They became more numerous after the Restoration, which gave better hope of a tranquillity indispensable for science; and, on the 28th of November, 1660, agreed to form a regular society which should meet weekly for the promotion of natural philosophy; their registers are kept from this time.[b] The king, rather fond himself of these subjects, from the beginning afforded them his patronage; their first charter is dated 15th July, 1662, incorporating them by the style of the Royal Society, and appointing Lord Brouncker the first president, assisted by a council of twenty, the conspicuous names among which are Boyle, Kenelm Digby, Wilkins, Wren, Evelyn, and Oldenburg.[c] The last of these was secretary, and editor of the Philosophical Transactions, the first number of which appeared March 1, 1665, containing sixteen pages in quarto. These were continued monthly, or less frequently, according to the materials he possessed. Oldenburg ceased to be the editor in 1667, and was succeeded by Grew, as he was by Hooke. These early transactions are chiefly notes of conversations and remarks made at the meetings, as well as of experiments either then made or reported to the Society.[d]

4. The Academy of Sciences at Paris was established in 1666, under the auspices of Colbert. The king assigned to them a room in the royal library for their meetings. Those first selected were all mathematicians; but other departments of science, especially chemistry and anatomy, afterwards furnished associates of considerable name. It seems, nevertheless, that this Academy did not cultivate experimental philosophy with such unremitting zeal as the Royal Society, and that abstract mathematics have always borne a larger proportion to the rest of their inquiries. They published in this century ten volumes, known as Anciens Mémoires de l'Académie. But near its close, in 1697, they received a regular institution from the king, organising them in a manner analogous to the two other great literary found-

Academy of Sciences at Paris.

---

[b] Birch's Hist. of Royal Society, vol. i. p. 1.
[c] Id. p. 88.
[d] Id. vol. ii. p. 18. Thomson's Hist. of Royal Society, p. 7.

ations, the French Academy, and that of Inscriptions and Belles Lettres.[e]

5. In several branches of physics, the experimental philo-
State of
Chemistry.
sopher is both guided and corrected by the eternal laws of geometry. In others he wants this aid, and, in the words of his master, ' knows and understands no more concerning the order of nature, than, as her servant and interpreter, he has been taught by observation and tentative processes.' All that concerns the peculiar actions of bodies on each other was of this description; though, in our own times, even this has been in some degree brought under the omnipotent control of the modern analysis. Chemistry, or the science of the molecular constituents of bodies, manifested in such peculiar and reciprocal operations, had never been rescued from empirical hands till this period. The transmutation of metals, the universal medicine, and other inquiries utterly unphilosophical in themselves, because they assumed the existence of that which they sought to discover, had occupied the chemists so much that none of them had made any further progress than occasionally by some happy combination or analysis, to contribute an useful preparation to pharmacy, or to detect an unknown substance. Glauber and Van Helmont were the most active and ingenious of these elder chemists; but the former has only been remembered by having long given his name to sulphate of soda, while the latter wasted his time on experiments from which he knew not how to draw right inferences, and his powers on hypotheses which a sounder spirit of the inductive philosophy would have taught him to reject.[f]

6. Chemistry, as a science of principles, hypothetical, no
Becker.
doubt, and in a great measure unfounded, but cohering in a plausible system, and better than the reveries of the Paracelsists and Behmenists, was founded by Becker in Germany, by Boyle and his contemporaries of the Royal Society in England. Becker, a native of Spire, who, after wandering from one city of Germany to another, died in London, in 1685, by his Physica Subterranea, published

---

[e] Fontenelle, vol. v. p. 23. Montu-   [f] Thomson's Hist. of Chemistry
cla, Hist. des Mathématiques, vol. ii.   i. 183.
p. 557.

in 1669, laid the foundation of a theory, which having in the next century been perfected by Stahl, became the creed of philosophy till nearly the end of the last century. 'Becker's theory,' says an English writer, 'stripped of everything but the naked statement, may be expressed in the following sentence: besides water and air, there are three other substances, called earths, which enter into the composition of bodies; namely, the fusible or vitrifiable earth, the inflammable or sulphureous, and the mercurial. By the intimate combination of earths with water is formed an universal acid, from which proceed all other acid bodies; stones are produced by the combination of certain earths, metals by the combination of all the three earths in proportions which vary according to the metal.'[g]

7. No one Englishman of the seventeenth century, after Lord Bacon, raised to himself so high a reputation in experimental philosophy as Robert Boyle; it has *Boyle.* even been remarked, that he was born in the year of Bacon's death, as the person destined by nature to succeed him. An eulogy which would be extravagant, if it implied any parallel between the genius of the two; but hardly so, if we look on Boyle as the most faithful, the most patient, the most successful disciple who carried forward the experimental philosophy of Bacon. His works occupy six large volumes in quarto. They may be divided into theological or metaphysical and physical or experimental. Of the former, we may mention as the most philosophical, his Disquisition into the Final Causes of Natural Things, his Free Inquiry into the received Notion of Nature, his Discourse of Things above Reason, his Considerations about the Reconcilableness of Reason and Religion, his Excellency of Theology, and his Considerations on the Style of the Scriptures; but the latter, his chemical and experimental writings, form more than two-thirds of his prolix works.

8. The metaphysical treatises, to use that word in a large sense, of Boyle, or rather those concerning Natural *His meta-physical works.* Theology, are very perspicuous, very free from system, and such as bespeak an independent lover of truth.

---

[g] Thomson's Hist. of Royal Society, p. 468.

His Disquisition on Final Causes was a well-timed vindication of that palmary argument against the paradox of the
Cartesians, who had denied the validity of an inference from
the manifest adaptation of means to ends in the universe to
an intelligent Providence. Boyle takes a more philosophical
view of the principle of final causes than had been found in
many theologians, who weakened the argument itself by the
presumptuous hypothesis, that man was the sole object of
Providence in the creation.[h] His greater knowledge of
physiology led him to perceive that there are both animal,
and what he calls cosmical ends, in which man has no
concern.

9. The following passage is so favourable a specimen of
Extract
from one
of them. the philosophical spirit of Boyle, and so good an
illustration of the theory of *idols* in the Novum Or-
ganum, that, although it might better, perhaps, have deserved
a place in a former chapter, I will not refrain from inserting
it :—' I know not,' he says, in his Free Inquiry into the received Notion of Nature, ' whether it be a prerogative in the
human mind, that as it is itself a true and positive being, so
is it apt to conceive all other things as true and positive
beings also ; but whether or no this propensity to frame such
kind of ideas supposes an excellency, I fear it occasions mistakes, and makes us think and speak after the manner of
true and positive beings, of such things as are but chimerical,
and some of them negations or privations themselves ; as
death, ignorance, blindness, and the like. It concerns us
therefore to stand very carefully upon our guard, that we be
not insensibly misled by such an innate and unheeded temp-
tation to error, as we bring into the world with us.'[i]

10. Boyle improved the air-pump and the thermometer,
His merits
in physics
and chemis-
try. though the latter was first made an accurate instrument of investigation by Newton. He also dis-
covered the law of the air's elasticity, namely, that
its bulk is inversely as the pressure upon it. For some of
the principles of hydrostatics we are indebted to him, though
he did not possess much mathematical knowledge. The
Philosophical Transactions contain several valuable papers

---

[h] Boyle's Works, vol. v. p. 394.   [i] Vol. v. p. 161.

by him on this science.[k] By his ' Sceptical Chemist,' published in 1661, he did much to overturn the theories of Van
Helmont's school, that commonly called of the iatro-chemists,
which was in its highest reputation; raising doubts as to
the existence not only of the four elements of the peripatetics,
but of those which these chemists had substituted. Boyle
holds the elements of bodies to be atoms of different shapes
and sizes, the union of which gives origin to what are vulgarly
called elements.[m] It is unnecessary to remark that this is
the prevailing theory of the present age.

11. I shall borrow the general character of Boyle and of
his contemporaries in English chemistry from a General
modern author of credit. ' Perhaps Mr. Boyle may character of Boyle.
be considered as the first person neither connected with
pharmacy nor mining, who devoted a considerable degree of
attention to chemical pursuits. Mr. Boyle, though in common with the literary men of his age he may be accused of
credulity, was both very laborious and intelligent; and his
chemical pursuits, which were various and extensive, and
intended solely to develop the truth without any regard to
previously conceived opinions, contributed essentially to set
chemistry free from the trammels of absurdity and superstition in which it had been hitherto enveloped, and to recommend it to philosophers as a science deserving to be studied
on account of the important information which it was qualified to convey. His refutation of the alchemistical opinions
respecting the constituents of bodies, his observations on
cold, on the air, on phosphorus, and on ether, deserve particularly to be mentioned as doing him much honour. We
have no regular account of any one substance or of any class
of bodies in Mr. Boyle, similar to those which at present are
considered as belonging exclusively to the science of chemistry. Neither did he attempt to systematise the phenomena,
nor to subject them to any hypothetical explanation.

12. ' But his contemporary Dr. Hooke, who had a particular predilection for hypothesis, sketched in his Of Hooke
Micrographia a very beautiful theoretical explana- and others.
tion of combustion, and promised to develop his doctrine

---

[k] Thomson's Hist. of Royal Society,   [m] Thomson's Hist. of Chemistry, i.
pp. 400, 411.   205.

more fully in a subsequent book; a promise which he never fulfilled; though in his Lampas, published about twenty years afterwards, he has given a very beautiful explanation of the way in which a candle burns. Mayow, in his Essays, published at Oxford about ten years after the Micrographia, embraced the hypothesis of Dr. Hooke without acknowledgment; but clogged it with so many absurd additions of his own as greatly to obscure its lustre and diminish its beauty. Mayow's first and principal Essay contains some happy experiments on respiration and air, and some fortunate conjectures respecting the combustion of the metals; but the most valuable part of the whole is the chapter on affinities, in which he appears to have gone much farther than any other chemist of his day, and to have anticipated some of the best established doctrines of his successors. Sir Isaac Newton, to whom all the sciences lie under such great obligations, made two most important contributions to chemistry, which constitute as it were the foundation stones of its two great divisions. The first was pointing out a method of graduating thermometers, so as to be comparable with each other in whatever part of the world observations with them are made. The second was by pointing out the nature of chemical affinity, and showing that it consisted in an attraction by which the constituents of bodies were drawn towards each other and united; thus destroying the previous hypothesis of the hooks, and points, and rings, and wedges, by means of which the different constituents of bodies were conceived to be kept together.'[n]

13. Lemery, a druggist at Paris, by his Cours de Chymie in 1675, is said to have changed the face of the science; the change nevertheless seems to have gone no deeper. 'Lemery,' says Fontenelle, 'was the first who dispersed the real or pretended obscurities of chemistry, who brought it to clearer and more simple notions, who abolished the gross barbarisms of its language, who promised nothing but what he knew the art could perform; and to this he owed the success of his book. It shows not only a sound understanding, but some greatness of soul, to strip

Lemery.

---

[n] Thomson's Hist. of Royal Society, p. 466.

one's own science of a false pomp.'° But we do not find that
Lemery had any novel views in chemistry, or that he claims
with any irresistible pretension the title of a philosopher. In
fact, his chemistry seems to have been little more than pharmacy.

Sect. II.—On Natural History.

Zoology—Ray—Botanical Classifications—Grew—Geological Theories.

14. The accumulation of particular knowledge in Natural
History must always be progressive, where any　Slow pro-
regard is paid to the subject; every traveller in　zoology.
remote countries, every mariner may contribute some observation, correct some error, or bring home some new species.
Thus zoology had made a regular advance from the days of
Conrad Gesner; yet with so tardy a step, that, reflecting on
the extensive intercourse of Europe with the Eastern and
Western world, we may be surprised to find how little
Jonston, in the middle of the seventeenth century, had added,
even in the most obvious class, that of quadrupeds, to the
knowledge collected one hundred years before. But hitherto
zoology, confined to mere description, and that often careless
or indefinite, unenlightened by anatomy, unregulated by
method, had not merited the name of a science. That name
it owes to John Ray.

15. Ray first appeared in Natural History as the editor
of the Ornithology of his highly accomplished friend　Before Ray.
Francis Willoughby, with whom he had travelled
over the Continent. This was published in 1676; and the
History of Fishes followed in 1686. The descriptions are
ascribed to Willoughby, the arrangement to Ray, who might
have considered the two works as in great part his own,
though he has not interfered with the glory of his deceased
friend. Cuvier observes, that the History of Fishes is the
more perfect work of the two, that many species are described

---

° Éloge de Lemery, in Œuvres de Fontenelle, v. 361. Biogr. universelle.

which will not be found in earlier ichthyologists, and that those of the Mediterranean especially are given with great precision.[p]

16. Among the original works of Ray we may select the Synopsis Methodica Animalium Quadrupedum et Serpentini Generis, published in 1693. This book makes an epoch in zoology, not for the additions of new species it contains, since there are few wholly such, but as the first classification of animals that can be reckoned both general and grounded in nature. He divides them into those with blood and without blood. The former are such as breathe through lungs, and such as breathe through gills. Of the former of these some have a heart with two ventricles, some have one only. And among the former class of these some are viviparous, some oviparous. We thus come to the proper distinction of Mammalia. But in compliance with vulgar prejudice, Ray did not include the cetacea in the same class with quadrupeds, though well aware that they properly belonged to it, and left them as an order of fishes.[q] Quadrupeds he was the first to divide into *ungulate* and *unguiculate*, hoofed and clawed, having himself invented the Latin words.[r] The former are *solidipeda, bisulca,* or *quadrisulca*; the latter are *bifida* or *multifida*; and these latter with undivided, or with partially divided toes; which latter again may have broad claws, as monkeys, or narrow claws; and these with narrow claws he arranges according to their teeth, as either *carnivora* or *leporina,* now generally called *rodentia.* Besides all these quadrupeds which he calls *analoga,* he has a general division called *anomala,* for those without teeth, or with such peculiar arrangements of teeth, as we find in the insectivorous genera, the hedgehog and mole.[s]

His Synopsis of Quadrupeds.

17. Ray was the first zoologist who made use of comparative anatomy; he inserts at length every account of dissections that he could find; several had been made at Paris. He does not appear to be very anxious

Merits of this work.

---

[p] Biographie universelle, art. Ray.

[q] Nos ne a communi hominum opinione nimis recedamus, et ut affectatæ novitatis notam evitemus, cetaceum aquatilium genus, quamvis cum quadrupedibus viviparis in omnibus fere præterquam in pilis et pedibus et elemento in quo degunt convenire videantur, piscibus annumerabimus. p. 55.

[r] P. 50.   [s] P. 56.

about describing every species; thus in the simian family he omits several well known.[t] I cannot exactly determine what quadrupeds he has inserted that do not appear in the earlier zoologists; according to Linnæus, in the twelfth edition of the Systema Naturæ, if I have counted rightly, they amount to thirty-two; but I have found him very careless in specifying the synonyms of his predecessors, and many for which he only quotes Ray, are in Gesner or Jonston. Ray has however much the advantage over these in the brevity and closeness of his specific characters. 'The particular distinction of his labours,' says Cuvier, 'consists in an arrangement more clear, more determinate than those of any of his predecessors, and applied with more consistency and precision. His distribution of the classes of quadrupeds and birds has been followed by the English naturalists almost to our own days; and we find manifest traces of that he has adopted as to the latter class in Linnæus, in Brisson, in Buffon, and in all other ornithologists.'[u]

18. The bloodless animals, and even those of cold blood, with the exception of fishes, had occupied but little attention of any good zoologists till after the middle of the century. They were now studied with considerable success. Redi, established as a physician at Florence, had yet time for that various literature which has immortalised his name. He opposed, and in a great degree disproved by experiment, the prevailing doctrine of the equivocal generation of insects, or that from corruption; though where he was unable to show the means of reproduction, he had recourse to a paradoxical hypothesis of his own. Redi also enlarged our knowledge of intestinal animals, and made some good experiments on the poison of vipers.[x] Malpighi, who combated, like Redi, the theory of the reproduction of organized bodies from mere corruption, has given one of the most

Redi.

---

[t] Hoc genus animalium tum caudatorum tum cauda carentium species valde numerosæ sunt; non tamen multæ apud autores fide dignos descriptæ occurrunt. He only describes those species he has found in Clusius or Marcgrave, and what he calls Parisiensis, such, I presume, as

he had found in the Memoirs of the Académie des Sciences. But he does not mention the Simia Inuus, or the S. Hamadryas, and several others of the most known species.

[u] Biogr. univ.

[x] Biogr. univ. Tiraboschi, xi. 252.

complete treatises on the silkworm that we possess.[y] Swam-

Swammer-
dam. merdam, a Dutch naturalist, abandoned his pursuits
in human anatomy to follow up that of insects, and
by his skill and patience in dissection made numerous discoveries in their structure. His General History of Insects,
1669, contains a distribution into four classes, founded on
their bodily forms and the metamorphoses they undergo. A
posthumous work, Biblia Naturæ, not published till 1738,
contains, says the Biographie universelle, 'a multitude of
facts wholly unknown before Swammerdam; it is impossible
to carry farther the anatomy of these little animals, or to be
more exact in the description of their organs.'

19. Lister, an English physician, may be reckoned one of
Lister. those who have done most to found the science of
conchology by his Historia sive Synopsis Conchyli-
orum, in 1685; a work very copious and full of accurate
delineations; and also by his three treatises on English
animals, two of which relate to fluviatile and marine shells.
The third, which is on spiders, is not less esteemed in ento-
mology. Lister was also perhaps the first to distinguish the
specific characters, such at least as are now reckoned specific,
though probably not in his time, of the Asiatic and African
elephant. 'His works in natural history and comparative
anatomy are justly esteemed, because he has shown himself
an exact and sagacious observer, and has pointed out with
correctness the natural relations of the animals that he describes.'[z]

20. The beautiful science which bears the improper name
Comparative
anatomy. of comparative anatomy had but casually occupied
the attention of the medical profession.[a] It was to
them, rather than to mere zoologists, that it owed, and
indeed strictly must always owe, its discoveries, which had
hitherto been very few. It was now more cultivated; and
the relations of structure to the capacities of animal life be-

---

[y] Biogr. univ. Tiraboschi, xi. 252.
[z] Biogr. univ. Chalmers.
[a] It is most probable that this term
was originally designed to express a
comparison between the human structure and that of brutes, though it might
also mean one between different species
of the latter. In the first sense it is
never now used, and the second is but a
part, though an important one, of the
science. *Zootomy* has been suggested
as a better name, but it is not quite
analogical to anatomy; and on the whole
it seems as if we must remain with
the old word, protesting against its
propriety.

came more striking, as their varieties were more fully understood; the grand theories of final causes found their most
convincing arguments. In this period, I believe, comparative anatomy made an important progress, which in the
earlier part of the eighteenth century was by no means
equally rapid. France took the lead in these researches.
'The number of papers on comparative anatomy,' says Dr.
Thomson, 'is greater in the Memoirs of the French Academy
than in our national publication. This was owing to the
pains taken during the reign of Louis XIV. to furnish the
Academy with proper animals, and the number of anatomists
who received a salary, and of course devoted themselves to
anatomical subjects.' There are, however, about twenty
papers in the Philosophical Transactions before 1700 on this
subject.[b]

21. Botany, notwithstanding the gleams of philosophical
light which occasionally illustrate the writings of
Cæsalpin and Columna, had seldom gone farther   Botany.
than to name, to describe, and to delineate plants with a
greater or less accuracy and copiousness. Yet it long had
the advantage over zoology, and now, when the latter made
a considerable step in advance, it still continued to keep
ahead. This is a period of great importance in botanical
science. Jungius of Hamburgh, whose posthumous
Isagoge Phytoscopica was published in 1679, is said   Jungius.
to have been the first in the seventeenth century who led the
way to a better classification than that of Lobel; and Sprengel thinks that the English botanists were not unacquainted
with his writings; Ray indeed owns his obligations to
them.[c]

22. But the founder of classification, in the eyes of the
world, was Robert Morison, of Aberdeen, professor
of botany at Oxford; who, by his Hortus Blesensis,   Morison.
in 1669; by his Plantarum Umbelliferarum Distributio
Nova, in 1672; and chiefly by his great work, Historia
Plantarum Universalis, in 1678, laid the basis of a systematic classification, which he partly founded, not on trivial

---

[b] Thomson's Hist. of Royal Society,   [c] Sprengel, Hist. Rei Herbariæ, vol.
p. 114.   ii. p. 32.

distinctions of appearance, as the older botanists, but, as
Cæsalpin had first done, on the fructifying organs. He has
been frequently charged with plagiarism from that great
Italian, who seems to have suffered, as others have done, by
failing to carry forward his own luminous conceptions into
such details of proof as the world justly demands; another
instance of which has been seen in his very striking passages
on the circulation of the blood. Sprengel, however, who
praises Morison highly, does not impute to him this injustice
towards Cæsalpin, whose writings might possibly be unknown
in Britain.[d]　And it might be observed also, that Morison
did not, as has sometimes been alleged, establish the fruit as
the sole basis of his arrangement. Out of fifteen classes,
into which he distributes all herbaceous plants, but seven
are characterised by this distinction.[e]　‘The examination of
Morison's works,’ says a late biographer, ‘will enable us to
judge of the service he rendered in the reformation of
botany. The great botanists, from Gesner to the Bauhins,
had published works, more or less useful by their discoveries,
their observations, their descriptions, or their figures. Gesner
had made a great step in considering the fruit as the principal
distinction of genera. Fabius Columna adopted this view;
Cæsalpin applied it to a classification which should be regarded as better than any that preceded the epoch of which
we speak. Morison had made a particular study of fruits,
having collected 1500 different species of them, though he
did not neglect the importance of the natural affinities of
other parts. He dwells on this leading idea, insists on the
necessity of establishing generic characters, and has founded
his chief works on this basis. He has therefore done real
service to the science; nor should the vanity which has
made him conceal his obligations to Cæsalpin induce us
to refuse him justice.’[f]　Morison speaks of his own theory
with excessive vanity, and depreciates all earlier botanists
as full of confusion. Several English writers have been
unfavourable to Morison, out of partiality to Ray, with whom
he was on bad terms; but Tournefort declares that if he

---

[d] Sprengel, p. 34.
[e] Pulteney, Historical Progress of
Botany in England, vol. i. p. 307.
[f] Biogr. universelle.

had not enlightened botany, it would still have been in darkness.

23. Ray in his Methodus Plantarum Nova, 1682, and in his Historia Plantarum Universalis, in three vo- Ray. lumes, the first published in 1686, the second in 1688, and the third, which is supplemental, in 1704, trod in the steps of Morison, but with more acknowledgment of what was due to others, and with some improvements of his own. He described 6,900 plants, many of which are now considered as varieties.[g] In the botanical works of Ray we find the natural families of plants better defined, the difference of complete and incomplete flowers more precise, and the grand division of monocotyledons and dicotyledons fully established. He gave much precision to the characteristics of many classes, and introduced several technical terms, very useful for the perspicuity of botanical language; finally, he established many general principles of arrangement which have since been adopted.[h] Ray's method of classification was principally by the fruit, though he admits its imperfections. ' In fact, his method,' says Pulteney, ' though he assumes the fruit as the foundation, is an elaborate attempt, for that time, to fix natural classes.'[i]

24. Rivinus, in his Introductio in Rem Herbariam, Leipsic, 1690, a very short performance, struck into a Rivinus. new path, which has modified to a great degree the systems of later botanists. Cæsalpin and Morison had looked mainly to the fruit as the basis of classification; Rivinus added the flower, and laid down as a fundamental rule that all plants which resemble each other both in the flower and in the fruit ought to bear the same generic name.[k] In some pages of this introduction we certainly find the basis of the Critica Botanica of Linnæus.[m] Rivinus thinks the arrangement of Cæsalpin the best, and that Morison has only spoiled what he took; of Ray he speaks in terms of eulogy, but blames some part of his method. His own is primarily founded on the flower, and thus he forms eighteen classes, which, by considering the differences of the fruits, he sub-

g Pulteney. The account of Ray's life and botanical writings in this work occupies nearly 100 pages.

h Biogr. universelle.
k Biogr. universelle.

i P. 259.
m Id.

divides into ninety-one genera. The specific distinctions he founded on the general habit and appearance of the plant. His method is more thoroughly artificial, as opposed to natural; that is, more established on a single principle, which often brings heterogeneous plants and families together, than that of any of his predecessors; for even Ray had kept the distinction of trees from shrubs and herbs, conceiving it to be founded in their natural fructification. Rivinus set aside wholly this leading division. Yet he had not been able to reduce all plants to his method, and admitted several anomalous divisions.[n]

25. The merit of establishing an uniform and consistent system was reserved for Tournefort. His Élémens de la Botanique appeared in 1694; the Latin translation, Institutiones Rei Herbariæ, in 1700. Tournefort, like Rivinus, took the flower or corolla as the basis of his system; and the varieties in the structure, rather than number, of the petals furnish him with his classes. The genera—for like other botanists before Linnæus he has no intermediate division—are established by the flower and fruit conjointly, or now and then by less essential differences, for he held it better to constitute new genera than, as others had done, to have anomalous species. The accessory parts of a plant are allowed to supply specific distinctions. But Tournefort divides vegetables, according to old prejudice—which it is surprising that, after the precedent of Rivinus to the contrary, he should have regarded—into herbs and trees; and thus he has twenty-two classes. Simple flowers, monopetalous or polypetalous, form eleven of these; composite flowers, three; the apetalous, one; the cryptogamous, or those without flower or fruit, make another class; shrubs or *suffrutices* are placed in the seventeenth; and trees, in five more, are similarly distributed, according to their floral characters.[o] Sprengel extols much of the system of Tournefort, though he disapproves of the selection of a part so often wanting as the corolla for the sole basis; nor can its various forms be comprised in Tournefort's classes. His orders are well marked,

Tournefort.

---

[n] Biogr. univ. Sprengel, p. 56.
[o] Biogr. univ. Thomson's Hist. of Royal Society, p. 34. Sprengel, p. 64.

according to the same author; but he multiplied both his genera and species too much, and paid too little attention to the stamina.   His method was less repugnant to natural affinities and more convenient in practice than any which had come since Lobel.   Most of Tournefort's generic distinctions were preserved by Linnæus, and some which had been abrogated without sufficient reason have since been restored.[p] Ray opposed the system of Tournefort, but some have thought that in his later works he came nearer to it, so as to be called magis corollista quam fructista.[q] This, however, is not acknowledged by Pulteney, who has paid great attention to Ray's writings.

26. The classification and description of plants constitute what generally is called botany.   But these began now to be studied in connexion with the anatomy and physiology of the vegetable world; terms not merely analogical, because as strictly applicable as to animals, but which had never been employed before the middle of the seventeenth century.   This interesting science is almost wholly due to two men, Grew and Malpighi.   Grew first directed his thoughts towards the anatomy of plants in 1664, in consequence of reading several books of animal anatomy, which suggested to him that plants, being the works of the same Author, would probably show similar contrivances.   Some had introduced observations of this nature, as Highmore, Sharrock, and Hooke, but only collaterally; so that the systematic treatment of the subject, following the plant from the seed, was left quite open for himself. In 1670, he presented the first book of his work to the Royal Society, who next year ordered it to be printed.   It was laid before the society in print, December, 1671; and on the same day a manuscript by Malpighi on the same subject was read.   They went on from this time with equal steps; Malpighi, however, having caused Grew's book to be translated for his own use.   Grew speaks very honourably of Malpighi, and without claiming more than the statement of facts permits him.[r]

Vegetable physiology.

Grew.

---

[p] Biogr. universelle.
[q] Id.
[r] Pulteney. Chalmers. Biogr. univ.

Sprengel calls Grew's book opus absolutum et immortale.

27. The first book of his Anatomy of Plants, which is the
His Ana-
tomy of
Plants. title given to three separate works, when published
collectively in 1682, contains the whole of his phy-
siological theory, which is developed at length in those that
follow. The nature of vegetation and its processes seem
to have been unknown when he began ; save that common
observation and the more accurate experience of gardeners
and others must have collected the obvious truths of vegetable anatomy. He does not quote Cæsalpin, and may have
been unacquainted with his writings. No man perhaps who
created a science has carried it farther than Grew ; he is so
close and diligent in his observations, making use of the
microscope, that comparatively few discoveries of great importance have been made in the mere anatomy of plants since
his time ;[s] though some of his opinions are latterly disputed
by Mirbel and others of a new botanical school.

28. The great discovery ascribed to Grew is of the sexual
He discovers
the sexual
system. system in plants. He speaks thus of what he calls
the attire, though rather, I think, in obscure terms :
—'The primary and chief use of the attire is such as hath
respect to the plant itself, and so appears to be very great
and necessary. Because even those plants which have no
flower or foliature, are yet some way or other attired, either
with the seminiform or the floral attire. So that it seems to
perform its service to the seeds as the foliature to the fruit.
In discourse hereof with our learned Savilian professor Sir
Thomas Millington, he told me he conceived that the attire
doth serve, as the male, for the generation of the seed. I
immediately replied that I was of the same opinion, and
gave him some reasons for it, and answered some objections
which might oppose them. But withal, in regard every
plant is ἀρρενόθηλυς, or male and female, that I was also of
opinion that it serveth for the separation of some parts as
well as the affusion of others.'[t] He proceeds to explain his
notion of vegetable impregnation. It is singular that he
should suppose all plants to be hermaphrodite, and this
shows he could not have recollected what had long been

---

[s] Biogr. universelle.
[t] Book iv. ch. 1. He had hinted at some 'primary and private use of the attire,' in book i. ch. 5.

known as to the palm, or the passages in Cæsalpin relative to the subject.

29. Ray admitted Grew's opinion cautiously at first: Nos ut verisimilem tantum admittimus. But in his Camerarius Sylloge Stirpium, 1694, he fully accedes to it. The this. real establishment of the sexual theory, however, is due to Camerarius, professor of botany at Tubingen, whose letter on that subject, published 1694, in the work of another, did much to spread the theory over Europe. His experiments, indeed, were necessary to confirm what Grew had rather hazarded as a conjecture than brought to a test; and he showed that flowers deprived of their stamina do not produce seeds capable of continuing the species.[u] Woodward, in the Philosophical Transactions, illustrated the nutrition of plants, by putting sprigs of vegetables in phials filled with water, and after some time determining the weight they had gained and the quantity they had imbibed.[x] These experiments had been made by Van Helmont, who had inferred from them that water is convertible into solid matter.[y]

30. It is just to observe that some had preceded Grew in vegetable physiology. Aromatari, in a letter of Predecessors only four pages, published at Venice in 1625, on of Grew. the generation of plants from seeds, which was reprinted in the Philosophical Transactions, showed the analogy between grains and eggs, each containing a minute organised embryo, which employs the substances enclosing it for its own development. Aromatari has also understood the use of the cotyledons.[z] Brown, in his Inquiry into Vulgar Errors, has remarks on the budding of plants, and on the quinary number which they affect in their flower. Kenelm Digby, according to Sprengel, first explained the necessity in vegetation for oxygen, or vital air, which had lately been discovered by Bathurst.[a] Hooke carried the discoveries hitherto made in vegetable anatomy much further in his Micrographia. Shar-

[u] Sprengel. Biogr. univ. Pulteney, p. 338.

[x] Thomson's Hist. of Royal Society, p. 58.

[y] Thomson's Hist. of Chemistry.

[z] Sprengel. Biogr. univ.

[a] Sprengel, iii. 176. [It will be un-derstood that the name oxygen, though Sprengel uses it, is modern; and also that this gas is properly said to have been discovered in 1774 by Priestley, who exhibited it in a separate state.— 1842.]

rock and Lister contributed some knowledge, but they were
rather later than Grew.   None of these deserve such
a place as Malpighi, who, says Sprengel, was not inferior to Grew in acuteness, though, probably, through some
illusions of prejudice, he has not so well understood and explained many things.   But the structure and growth of seeds
he has explained better, and Grew seems to have followed
him.   His book is also better arranged and more concise.[b]
The Dutch did much to enlarge botanical science.   The
Hortus Indicus Malabaricus of Rheede, who had been a
governor in India, was published at his own expense in
twelve volumes, the first appearing in 1686; it contains an
immense number of new plants.[c]   The Herbarium Amboi-
nense of Rumphius was collected in the seventeenth century,
though not published till 1741.[d]   Several botanical gardens
were formed in different countries; among others that of
Chelsea was opened in 1686.[e]

Malpighi.

31. It was impossible that men of inquiring tempers
should not have been led to reflect on those remarkable phenomena of the earth's visible structure, which being in course of time accurately registered and
arranged, have become the basis of that noble science, the
boast of our age, geology.   The first thing which must strike
the eyes of the merest clown, and set the philosopher thinking, is the irregularity of the surface of our globe; the more
this is observed, the more signs of violent disruption appear.
Some, indeed, of whom Ray seems to have been one,[f] were
so much impressed by the theory of final causes, that, perceiving the fitness of the present earth for its inhabitants,
they thought it might have been created in such a state of
physical ruin.   But the contrary inference is almost irresistible.   A still more forcible argument for great revolutions in
the history of the earth is drawn from a second phænomenon
of very general occurrence, the marine and other fossil relics
of organised beings, which are dug up in strata far remote
from the places where these bodies could now exist.   It was

Early no-
tions of
geology.

---

[b] Sprengel, p. 15.
[c] Biogr. univ. The date of the first
volume is given erroneously in the B. U.
[d] Id.

[e] Sprengel.   Pulteney.
[f] See Ray's Three Physico-Theolo-
gical Discourses on the Creation, Deluge,
and final Conflagration. 1692.

common to account for them by the Mosaic deluge.   But the
depth at which they are found was incompatible with this
hypothesis.   Others fancied them to be not really organised,
but sports of nature, as they were called, the casual resemblances of shells and fishes in stone.   The Italians took the
lead in speculating on these problems; but they could only
arrive now and then at a happier conjecture than usual, and
do not seem to have planned any scheme of explaining the
general structure of the earth.[g]   The Mundus Subterraneus
of Athanasius Kircher, famous for the variety and originality
of his erudition, contains probably the geology of his age, or
at least his own.   It was published in 1662.   Ten out of
twelve books relate to the surface or the interior of the earth,
and to various terrene productions; the remaining two to
alchemy and other arts connected with mineralogy.   Kircher
seems to have collected a great deal of geographical and
geological knowledge.   In England, the spirit of observation
was so strong after the establishment of the Royal Society,
that the Philosophical Transactions, in this period, contain
a considerable number of geognostic papers, and the genius
of theory was aroused, though not at first in his happiest
mood.[h]

32. Thomas Burnet, master of the Charterhouse, a man
fearless and somewhat rash, with more imagination Burnet's
than philosophy, but ingenious and eloquent, pub- Earth. Theory of
lished in 1694 his Theoria Telluris Sacra, which he afterwards
translated into English.   The primary question for the early
geologists had always been how to reconcile the phænomena
with which they were acquainted to the Mosaic narratives of
the creation and deluge.   Every one was satisfied that his
own theory was the best; but in every case it has hitherto
proved, whatever may take place in future, that the proposed
scheme has neither kept to the letter of Scripture nor to the
legitimate deductions of philosophy.   Burnet gives the reins
to his imagination more than any other writer on that which,
if not argued upon by inductive reasoning, must be the
dream of one man, little better in reality, though it may be
more amusing, than the dream of another.   He seems to be

eminently ignorant of geological facts, and has hardly ever recourse to them as evidence. And accordingly, though his book drew some attention as an ingenious romance, it does not appear that he made a single disciple. Whiston opposed Burnet's theory, but with one not less unfounded, nor with less ignorance of all that required to be known. Hooke, Lister, Ray, and Woodward came to the subject with more philosophical minds, and with a better insight into the real phænomena. Hooke seems to have displayed his usual sagacity in conjecture ; he saw that the common theory of explaining marine fossils by the Mosaic deluge would not suffice, and perceived that, at some time or other, a part of the earth's crust must have been elevated and another part depressed by some subterraneous power. Lister was aware of the continuity of certain strata over large districts, and proposed the construction of geological maps. Woodward had a still more extensive knowledge of stratified rocks ; he was in a manner the founder of scientific mineralogy in England, but his geological theory was not less chimerical than those of his contemporaries.[i] It was first published in the Philosophical Transactions for 1695.[k]

33. The Protogæa of Leibnitz appears, in felicity of conjecture and minute attention to facts, far above any of these. But this short tract was only published in 1749, and on reading it I have found an intimation that it was not written within the seventeenth century. Yet I cannot refrain from mentioning that his hypothesis supposes the gradual cooling of the earth from igneous fusion ; the formation of a vast body of water to cover the surface, a part of his theory but ill established, and apparently the weakest of the whole ; the subsidence of the lower parts of the earth, which he takes to have been once on the level of the highest mountains, by the breaking in of vaulted caverns within its bosom ;[m] the deposition of sedimentary strata from inunda-

Other geologists.

Protogæa of Leibnitz.

---

[i] Lyell, p. 31.

[k] Thomson, p. 207.

[m] Sect. 21. He admits also a partial elevation by intumescence, but says, ut vastissimæ Alpes ex solidâ jam terrâ eruptione surrexerint, minus consentaneum puto. Scimus tamen et in illis deprehendi reliquias maris. Cum ergo alterutrum factum oporteat, credibilius multo arbitror defluxisse aquas spontaneo nisu, quam ingentem terrarum partem incredibili violentiâ tam alte ascendisse. Sect. 22.

tions, their induration, and the subsequent covering of these
by other strata through fresh inundations; with many other
notions which have been gradually matured and rectified in
the process of the science.[n] No one can read the Protogæa
without perceiving that of all the early geologists, or indeed
of all down to a time not very remote, Leibnitz came nearest
to the theories which are most received in the English school
at this day. It is evident that if the literal interpretation of
Genesis, by a period of six natural days, had not restrained
him, he would have gone much farther in his views of the
progressive revolutions of the earth.[o] Leibnitz had made
very minute inquiries, for his age, into fossil species, and
was aware of the main facts which form the basis of modern
geology.[p]

Sect. III.—On Anatomy and Medicine.

34. Portal begins the history of this period, which occupies
more than 800 pages of his voluminous work, by announcing
it as the epoch most favourable to anatomy : in less than fifty
years the science put on a new countenance ; nature is interrogated, every part of the body is examined with an observing spirit ; the mutual intercourse of nations diffuses the
light on every side ; a number of great men appear, whose
genius and industry excite our admiration.[q] But for this
very reason I must, in these concluding pages, glide over a
subject rather foreign to my own studies, and to those of the

---

[n] Facies teneri adhuc orbis sæpius
novata est; donec quiescentibus causis atque æquilibratis, consistentior emergeret
status rerum. Unde jam duplex origo
intelligitur firmorum corporum ; una
cum ignis fusione refrigescerent, altera
cum reconcrescerent ex solutione aqua-
rum. Neque igitur putandum est *lapides
ex solâ esse fusione.* Id enim potissi-
mum de primâ tantum massâ ex terræ
basi accipio ; Nec dubito, postea mate-
riam liquidam in superficie telluris pro-
currentem, quiete mox redditâ, ex ra-
mentis subactis ingentem materiæ vim
deposuisse, quorum alia varias terræ species formarunt, alia in saxa induruere, e
quibus strata diversa sibi super imposita
diversas præcipitationum vices atque in-
tervalla testantur. Sect. 4.

This he calls the incunabula of the
world, and the basis of a new science,
which might be denominated ' naturalis
geographia.' But wisely adds, licet con-
spirent vestigia veteris mundi in præsenti
facie rerum, tamen rectius omnia defi-
nient posteri, ubi curiositas eo proces-
serit, ut per regiones procurrentia soli
genera et strata describant. Sect. 5.

[o] See sect. 21, et alibi.

[p] Sect. 24, et usque ad finem libri.

[q] Hist. de l'Anatomie, vol. iii. p. 1.

generality of my readers, with a very brief enumeration of
names.

35. The Harveian theory gained ground, though obstinate
Circulation
of blood
established. prejudice gave way but slowly. It was confirmed
by the experiment of transfusing blood, tried on
dogs, at the instance of Sir Christopher Wren, in 1657, and
repeated by Lower in 1661.[r] Malpighi in 1661, and Leeuwenhoek in 1690, by means of their microscopes, demonstrated the circulation of the blood in the smaller vessels, and
rendered visible the anastomoses of the arteries and veins,
upon which the theory depended.[s] From this time it seems
to have been out of doubt. Pecquet's discovery of the thoracic duct (or rather of its uses, as a reservoir of the chyle
from which the blood is elaborated, for the canal itself had
been known to Eustachius), stands next to that of Harvey,
which would have thrown less light on physiology without
it, and, like his, was perseveringly opposed.[t]

36. Willis, a physician at Oxford, is called by Portal,
Willis.
Vieussens. who thinks all mankind inferior to anatomists, one
of the greatest geniuses that ever lived; his bold
systems have given him a distinguished place among phy-
siologers.[u] His Anatomy of the Brain, in which, however,
as in his other works, he was much assisted by an intimate
friend and anatomist of the first character, Lower, is, according to the same writer, a masterpiece of imagination and
labour. He made many discoveries in the structure of the
brain, and has traced the nerves from it far better than his
predecessors, who had in general very obscure ideas of their
course. Sprengel says that Willis is the first who has
assigned a peculiar mental function to each of the different
parts of the brain; forgetting, as it seems, that this hypothesis, the basis of modern phrenology, had been generally
received, as I understand his own account, in the sixteenth
century.[x] Vieussens of Montpellier carried on the discoveries
in the anatomy of the nerves in his Neurographia Universalis,
1684; tracing those arising from the spinal marrow, which

---

[r] Sprengel, Hist. de la Médecine, vol.
iv. p. 120.
  [s] Ibid. p. 126, 142.
  [t] Portal. Sprengel.

[u] P. 88. Biogr. univ.
  [x] Sprengel, vol. iv. p. 250. Compare
vol. iii. p. 204.

Willis had not done, and following the minute ramifications of those that are spread over the skin.[y]

37. Malpighi was the first who employed good microscopes in anatomy, and thus revealed the secrets, we may say, of an invisible world, which Leeuwenhoek afterwards, probably using still better instruments, explored with surprising success. To Malpighi anatomists owe their knowledge of the structure of the lungs.[z] Graaf has overthrown many errors, and suggested many truths in the economy of generation.[a] Malpighi prosecuted this inquiry with his microscope, and first traced the progress of the egg during incubation. But the theory of evolution, as it is called, proposed by Harvey, and supported by Malpighi, received a shock by Leeuwenhoek's or Hartsoeker's discovery of spermatic animalcules, which apparently opened a new view of reproduction. The hypothesis they suggested became very prevalent for the rest of the seventeenth century, though it is said to have been shaken early in the next.[b] Borelli applied mathematical principles to muscular movements in his treatise De Motu Animalium. Though he is a better mathematician than anatomist, he produces many interesting facts, the mechanical laws are rightly applied, and his method is clear and consequent.[c] Duverney, in his Treatise on Hearing, in 1683, his only work, obtained a considerable reputation; it threw light on many parts of a delicate organ, which by their minuteness had long baffled the anatomist.[d] In Mayow's Treatise on Respiration, published in London, 1668, we find the necessity of what is now called oxygen to that function laid down; but this portion of the atmosphere had been discovered by Bathurst and Henshaw in 1654, and Hooke had shown by experiment that animals die when the air is deprived of it.[e] Ruysch, a Dutch physician, perfected the art of injecting anatomical preparations, hardly known before, and thus conferred an inestimable benefit on the science. He possessed a celebrated cabinet of natural history.[f]

Marginal notes: Malpighi. Other anatomists.

---

[y] Portal, vol. iv. p. 5. Sprengel, p. 256. Biogr. univ.
[z] Portal, vol. iii. p. 120. Sprengel, p. 578.
[a] Portal, iii. 219. Sprengel, p. 303.

[b] Sprengel, p. 309.
[c] Portal, iii. 246. Biogr. univ.
[d] Portal, p. 464. Sprengel, p. 288.
[e] Sprengel, iii. 176, 181.
[f] Id. p. 259. Biogr. univ.

38. The chemical theory of medicine which had descended
from Paracelsus through Van Helmont, was pro-
pagated chiefly by Sylvius, a physician of Holland,
who is reckoned the founder of what was called the chemiatric
school. His works were printed at Amsterdam in 1679, but
he had promulgated his theory from the middle of the century. His leading principle was that a perpetual fermenta-
tion goes on in the human body, from the deranged action of
which diseases proceed ; most of them from excess of acidity,
though a few are of alkaline origin. 'He degraded the
physician,' says Sprengel, 'to the level of a distiller or a
brewer.'[g] This writer is very severe on the chemiatric
school, one of their offences in his eyes being their recommendation of tea; 'the cupidity of Dutch merchants conspiring with their medical theories.' It must be owned that
when we find them prescribing also a copious use of tobacco,
it looks as if the trade of the doctor went hand in hand with
those of his patients. Willis, in England, was a partisan of
the chemiatrics,[h] and they had a great influence in Germany;
though in France the attachment of most physicians to the
Hippocratic and Galenic methods, which brought upon them
so many imputations of pedantry, was little abated. A second
school of medicine, which superseded this, is called the iatro-
mathematical. This seems to have arisen in Italy. Borelli's
application of mechanical principles to the muscles has been
mentioned above. These physicians sought to explain every
thing by statical and hydraulic laws ; they were therefore
led to study anatomy, since it was only by an accurate knowledge of all the parts that they could apply their mathematics.
John Bernouilli even taught them to employ the differential
calculus in explaining the bodily functions.[i] But this school
seems to have had the same leading defect as the chemiatric;
it forgot the peculiarity of the laws of organisation and life
which often render those of inert matter inapplicable. Pit-
cairn and Boerhaave were leaders of the iatro-mathematicians;
and Mead was reckoned the last of its distinguished patrons.[k]
Meantime, a third school of medicine grew up, denominated

Medical theories.

---

[g] Vol. v. p. 59.   Biogr. univ.
[h] Sprengel, p. 73.
[i] Id. p. 159.

[k] Id. p. 182.   See Biographie universelle, art. Boerhaave, for a general
criticism of the iatro-mathematicians.

the empirical; a name to be used in a good sense, as denoting their regard to observation and experience, or the
Baconian principles of philosophy. Sydenham was the first
of these in England; but they gradually prevailed, to the
exclusion of all systematic theory. The discovery of several
medicines, especially the Peruvian bark, which was first used
in Spain about 1640, and in England about 1654, contributed
to the success of the empirical physicians, since the efficacy
of some of these could not be explained on the hypotheses
hitherto prevalent.[m]

Sect. IV.—On Oriental Literature.

39. The famous Polyglott of Brian Walton was published
in 1657; but few copies appear to have been sold Polyglott of
before the restoration of Charles II. in 1660, since Walton.
those are very scarce which contain in the preface the praise
of Cromwell for having facilitated and patronised the undertaking; praise replaced in the change of times by a loyal
eulogy on the king. This Polyglott is in nine languages;
though no one book of the Bible is printed in so many.
Walton's Prolegomena are in sixteen chapters or dissertations.
His learning perhaps was greater than his critical acuteness
or good sense; such at least is the opinion of Simon and Le
Long. The former, in a long examination of Walton's Prolegomena, treats him with all the superiority of a man who
possessed both. Walton was assailed by some bigots at home
for acknowledging various readings in the Scriptures, and
for denying the authority of the vowel punctuation. His
Polyglott is not reckoned so magnificent as the Parisian edition of Le Long; but it is fuller and more convenient.[n] Ed-
mund Castell, the coadjutor of Walton in this work, published
his Lexicon Heptaglotton in 1669, upon which he had consumed eighteen years and the whole of his substance. This
is frequently sold together with the Polyglott.

[m] Sprengel, p. 413.
[n] Simon, Hist. critique du Vieux
Testament, p. 541. Chalmers. Biogr.

Britan. Biogr. univ. Brunet. Man. du
Libraire.

40. Hottinger of Zurich, by a number of works on the
Eastern languages, and especially by the Bibliotheca
Hottinger. Orientalis, in 1658, established a reputation which
these books no longer retain since the whole field of Oriental
literature has been more fully explored. Spencer,
Spencer. in a treatise of great erudition, De Legibus Hebræorum, 1685, gave some offence by the suggestion that several
of the Mosaic institutions were borrowed from the Egyptian,
though the general scope of the Jewish law was in opposition
to the idolatrous practices of the neighbouring nations. The
vast learning of Bochart expanded itself over Orien-
Bochart. tal antiquity, especially that of which the Hebrew
nation and language is the central point; but his etymological conjectures have long since been set aside, and he has
not in other respects escaped the fate of the older Orientalists.

41. The great services of Pococke to Arabic literature,
which had commenced in the earlier part of the
Pococke. century, were extended to the present. His edition
and translation of the Annals of Eutychius in 1658, that of
the History of Abulfaragius in 1663, with many other works of
a similar nature, bear witness to his industry; no Englishman
probably has ever contributed so much to that province of
learning.[o] A fine edition of the Koran, and still esteemed
the best, was due to Marracci, professor of Arabic in the Sa-
pienza or university of Rome, and published at the expense
of Cardinal Barbadigo, in 1698.[p] But France had an Orien-
talist of the most extensive learning in D'Herbelot,
D'Herbelot. whose Bibliothèque orientale must be considered as
making an epoch in this literature. It was published in
1697, after his death, by Galland, who had also some share
in arranging the materials. This work, it has been said, is
for the seventeenth century what the History of the Huns by
De Guignes is for the eighteenth; with this difference, that
D'Herbelot opened the road, and has often been copied by
his successor.[q]

42. Hyde, in his Religionis Persarum Historia, published
in 1700, was the first who illustrated in a systematic
Hyde. manner the religion of Zoroaster, which he always
represents in a favourable manner. The variety and novelty

---

[o] Chalmers. Biogr. univ.   [p] Tiraboschi, xi. 398.   [q] Biogr. univ.

of its contents gave this book a credit which in some degree
it preserves; but Hyde was ignorant of the ancient language
of Persia, and is said to have been often misled by Mohammedan authorities.[r] The vast increase of Oriental information in modern times, as has been intimated above, renders
it difficult for any work of the seventeenth century to keep
its ground. In their own times, the writings of Kircher on
China, and still more those of Ludolf on Abyssinia, which
were founded on his own knowledge of the country, claimed
a respectable place in Oriental learning. It is remarkable
that very little was yet known of the Indian languages,
though grammars existed of the Tamul, and perhaps some
others, before the close of the seventeenth century.[s]

SECT. V.—ON GEOGRAPHY AND HISTORY.

43. THE progress of geographical science long continued to
be slow. If we compare the map of the world in
1651, by Nicolas Sanson, esteemed on all sides the
Maps of the Sansons.
best geographer of his age, with one by his son in 1692, the
differences will not appear, perhaps, so considerable as we
might have expected. Yet some improvement may be detected by the eye. Thus the Caspian Sea has assumed its
longer diameter from north to south, contrary to the old map.
But the sea of Aral is still wanting. The coasts of New
Holland, except to the east, are tolerably laid down, and
Corea is a peninsula, instead of an island. Cambalu, the
imaginary capital of Tartary, has disappeared;[t] but a vast
lake is placed in the centre of that region; the Altai range
is carried far too much to the north, and the name of Siberia
seems unknown. Africa and America have nearly the same
outline as before; in the former, the empire of Monomotopa
stretches to join that of Abyssinia in about the twelfth degree
of south latitude; and the Nile still issues, as in all the old
maps, from a lake Zayre, in nearly the same parallel. The

---

[r] Biogr. univ.
[s] Eichhorn, Gesch. der Cultur, v. 269.
[t] The Cambalu of Marco Polo is probably Pekin; but the geographers frequently placed this capital of Cathay
north of the wall of China.

coasts of Europe, and especially of Scandinavia, are a little more accurate than before. The Sanson family, of whom several were publishers of maps, did not take pains enough to improve what their father had executed, though they might have had material helps from the astronomical observations which were now continually made in different parts of the world.

44. Such was the state of geography when, in 1699, De Lisle, the real founder of the science, at the age of twenty-four, published his map of the world. He had been guided by the observations, and worked under the directions of Cassini, whose tables of the emersion of Jupiter's satellites, calculated for the meridian of Bologna, in 1668, and, with much improvement, for that of Paris, in 1693, had prepared the way for the perfection of geography. The latitudes of different regions had been tolerably ascertained by observation; but no good method of determining the longitude had been known before this application of Galileo's great discovery. It is evident that the appearance of one of those satellites at Paris being determined by the tables to a precise instant, the means were given, with the help of sufficient clocks, to find the longitudinal distance of other places by observing the difference of time; and thus a great number of observations having gradually been made, a basis was laid for an accurate delineation of the surface of the globe. The previous state of geography and the imperfect knowledge which the mere experience of navigators could furnish, may be judged by the fact that the Mediterranean sea was set down with an excess of 300 leagues in length, being more than one-third of the whole. De Lisle reduced it within its bounds, and cut off at the same time 500 leagues from the longitude of Eastern Asia. This was the commencement of the geographical labours of De Lisle, which reformed, in the first part of the eighteenth century, not only the general outline of the world, but the minuter relations of various countries. His maps amount to more than one hundred sheets.[u]

De Lisle's map of the world.

----

[u] Eloge de De Lisle, in Œuvres de Fontenelle, vol. vi. p. 253. Eloge de Cassini, in vol. v. p. 328. Biogr. univ.

45. The books of travels, in the last fifty years of the seventeenth century, were far more numerous and more $\quad$ Voyages and travels. valuable than in any earlier period, but we have no space for more than a few names. Gemelli Carreri, a Neapolitan, is the first who claims to have written an account of his own travels round the world, describing Asia and America with much detail. His Giro del Mondo was published in 1699. Carreri has been strongly suspected of fabrication, and even of having never seen the countries which he describes; but his character, I know not with what justice, has been latterly vindicated.[x] The French justly boast the excellent travels of Chardin, Bernier, Thevenot, and Tavernier in the East; the account of the Indian archipelago and of China by Nieuhoff, employed in a Dutch embassy to the latter empire, is said to have been interpolated by the editors, though he was an accurate and faithful observer.[y] Several other relations of voyages were published in Holland, some of which can only be had in the native language. In English there were not many of high reputation: Dampier's Voyage Round the World, the first edition of which was in 1697, is better known than any which I can call to mind.

46. The general characteristics of historians of this period are neither a luminous philosophy, nor a rigorous $\quad$ Historians. examination of evidence. But, as before, we mention only a few names in this extensive province of literature. The History of the Conquest of Mexico by Antonio $\quad$ De Solis. De Solis is 'the last good work,' says Sismondi, perhaps too severely as to others, 'that Spain has produced; the last where purity of taste, simplicity, and truth are preserved; the imagination, of which the author had given so many proofs, does not appear.'[z] Bouterwek is not less favourable; but Robertson, who holds De Solis rather cheap as an historian, does not fail to censure even his style.

47. The French have some authors of history who by their elegance and perspicuity, might deserve notice; such $\quad$ Memoirs of De Retz. as St. Real, Father D'Orleans, and even Varillas, proverbially discredited as he is for want of veracity. The

---

[x] Tiraboschi, xi. 86. Salfi, xi. 442.   [y] Biogr. univ.
[z] Littérature du Midi, iv. 101.

Memoirs of Cardinal De Retz rise above these; their animated style, their excellent portraitures of character, their
acute and brilliant remarks, distinguish their pages, as much
as the similar qualities did their author. 'They are written,'
says Voltaire, 'with an air of greatness, an impetuosity and
an inequality which are the image of his life; his expression,
sometimes incorrect, often negligent, but almost always
original, recals continually to his readers what has been so
frequently said of Cæsar's Commertaries, that he wrote with
the same spirit that he carried on his wars.' ᵃ The Memoirs
of Grammont, by Antony Hamilton, scarcely challenge a
place as historical, but we are now looking more at the style
than the intrinsic importance of books. Every one is aware
of the peculiar felicity and fascinating gaiety which they
display.

48. The Discourse of Bossuet on Universal History is per
Bossuet on haps the greatest effort of his wonderful genius.
universal
history.   Every preceding abridgment of so immense a subject had been superficial and dry. He first irradiated the
entire annals of antiquity down to the age of Charlemagne
with flashes of light that reveal an unity and coherence
which had been lost in their magnitude and obscurity. It
is not perhaps an unfair objection that, in a history calling
itself that of all mankind, the Jewish people have obtained a
disproportionate regard; and it might be almost as reasonable, on religious grounds, to give Palestine an ampler space
in the map of the world, as, on a like pretext, to make the
scale of the Jewish history so much larger than that of the
rest of the human race. The plan of Bossuet has at least
divided his book into two rather heterogeneous portions.
But his conceptions of Greek, and still more of Roman history, are generally magnificent; profound in philosophy, with
an outline firm and sufficiently exact, never condescending to
trivial remarks or petty details; above all, written in that
close and nervous style which no one certainly in the French
language has ever surpassed. It is evident that Montesquieu
in all his writings, but especially in the Grandeur et Décadence des Romains, had the Discourse of Bossuet before his

---

ᵃ Biogr. univ., whence I take the quotation.

eyes; he is more acute, sometimes, and ingenious, and has reflected longer on particular topics of inquiry, but he wants the simple majesty, the comprehensive eagle-like glance of the illustrious prelate.

49. Though we fell short in England of the historical reputation which the first part of the century might entitle us to claim, this period may be reckoned that in which a critical attention to truth, sometimes rather too minute, but always praiseworthy, began to be characteristic of our researches into fact. The only book that I shall mention is Burnet's History of the Reformation, written in a better style than those who know Burnet by his later and more negligent work are apt to conceive, and which has the signal merit of having been the first in English, as far as I remember, which is fortified by a large appendix of documents. This, though frequent in Latin, had not been so usual in the modern languages. It became gradually very frequent and almost indispensable in historical writings, where the materials had any peculiar originality. *English historical works.* *Burnet.*

* * * * * * *

50. The change in the spirit of literature and of the public mind in general, which had with gradual and never-receding steps been coming forward in the seventeenth century, but especially in the latter part of it, has been so frequently pointed out to the readers of this and the last volume, that I shall only quote an observation of Bayle. ' I believe,' he says, ' that the sixteenth century produced a greater number of learned men than the seventeenth; and yet the former of these ages was far from being as enlightened as the latter. During the reign of criticism and philology, we saw in all Europe many prodigies of erudition. Since the study of the new philosophy and that of living languages has introduced a different taste, we have ceased to behold this vast and deep learning. But in return there is diffused through the republic of letters a more subtle understanding and a more exquisite discernment; men are now less learned but more able.'[b] The volumes which are now submitted to the public contain suffi- *General character of 17th century.*

---

[b] Dictionnaire de Bayle, art. Aconce, note D.

cient evidence of this intellectual progress both in philosophy and in polite literature.

51. I here terminate a work, which, it is hardly necessary to say, has furnished the occupation of not very few years, and which, for several reasons, it is not my intention to prosecute any farther. The length of these volumes is already greater than I had anticipated; yet I do not perceive much that could have been retrenched without loss to a part, at least, of the literary world. For the approbation which the first of them has received I am grateful; for the few corrections that have been communicated to me I am not less so; the errors and deficiencies of which I am not specially aware may be numerous; yet I cannot affect to doubt that I have contributed something to the general literature of my country, something to the honourable estimation of my own name, and to the inheritance of those, if it is for me still to cherish that hope, to whom I have to bequeath it.

Conclusion.

INDEX.

tury, 172, 257, 276. Price of, after the invention of printing, 250. Price for the hire of, in the 14th century, 253. Restraints on the sale of printed, 254. Prohibition of certain, ii. 266. Book fairs, 262, 264. Booksellers' catalogues, 264. Bookselling trade, i. 249. Mutilation of, by the visitors of Oxford, temp. Edward VI., 523. [See Printing.]

Bordone's Islands of the World, with Charts, i. 479

Borelli, 'de Motu Animalium,' iii. 601

Borghino, Raffaelle, treatise on Painting by, ii. 191

Borgia, Francis, Duke of Gandia, i. 377.

Borgo, Luca di, ii. 223

Boscan, Spanish poetry of, i. 428, ii. 106, iii. 11

Bosco, John de Sacro, his 'Treatise on the Sphere,' i. 114, 115

Bossu, on Epic Poetry, iii. 545

Bossuet, Bishop of Meaux, ii. 334, 344, iii. 281, 292. The 'Histoire Universelle' of, 256, 608. His Sermon before the Assembly of the Gallican Clergy, 259. Draws up the Four Articles. 260. His 'Exposition de la Foi Catholique,' 263. Controversial writings of, 264 n., 265. His 'Variations of the Protestant Churches,' iii. 267. Funeral discourses of, 293, 533

Botal of Asti, pupil of Fallopius, ii. 249.

Botanical gardens instituted at Naples, Marburgh, Pisa, and at Padua, i. 474. Montpellier, ii. 242. Chelsea, iii. 596.

Botany, science of, i. 474, ii. 241, 242. Poems of Rapin and Delille on gardens, iii. 494, 496. Writers on, i. 474, 475, ii. 241, 242, iii. 210, 238, 589, 594. Medical, i. 271 n.

Botero, Giovanni, his 'Ragione di Stato,' ii. 49. His 'Cosmography,' 256. On 'Political Economy,' 531

Boucher 'De justâ Henrici III. abdicatione,' ii. 44

Bouchetel, his translation of the Hecuba of Euripides, i. 447

Bouhours, critic and grammarian, iii. 19. His 'Entretiens d'Ariste et d'Eugène,' 540. Sarcasms of, 542. His 'La Manière de bien Penser,' 543

Bouillaud, the Italian astronomer, iii. 191

Bourbon, Anthony, original of Pantagruel, i. 453

—, or Borbonius, Latin poem of, iii. 50

Bourdaloue, le Père, style of his sermons, iii. 292

Courdin, the Jesuit, objections by, to the Meditations of Descartes, ii. 446

Bourgeoise, Jacques, dramatic writer, i. 447

'Bourgeois Gentilhomme' of Molière, a diverting moral satire, iii. 515

Boursault, his 'Le Mercure Galant,' iii. 518

Bouterwek, criticisms of, i. 122, 264 n., ii. 94 n., 104, 106, 112 n., 157, 160, 210, iii. 13, 23, 24 n., 64, 156, 159, et passim.

Bowles, on the Sonnets of, iii. 41 n.

Boyle, Charles, his controversy with Bentley, iii. 252

—, Robert, metaphysical works of, iii. 581. Extract from, 582. His merits in physics and chemistry, ib. His general character, 583

Bradshaw, William, literary reputation of, iii. 575 n.

Bradwardin, Archbishop, on Geometry, i. 16, 118

Brain, anatomy of the, works on, iii. 600

Bramhall, Archbishop, ii. 317 n.

Brandt's History of the Reformation in the Low Countries, i. 376, ii. 333

Brazil, Natural History, &c., of, iii. 207

Brebœuf, his 'Pharsalie,' iii. 473

Brentius, his controversy on the ubiquity of Christ's body, i. 560

Breton, English poet, ii. 126. 'Mavilla' of, 220 n.

Breton lays, discussion on, i. 35

'Brief Conceit of English Policy,' ii. 204, 531

Briggs, Henry, mathematician, iii. 174. 'Arithmetica Logarithmica' of, 179

Brisson on Roman Law, i. 533, ii. 73

'Britannia's Pastorals' of Wm. Browne, iii. 35

British Bibliographer, ii. 121, 204

Brito, Gulielmus, poetry of, i. 76

'Broken Heart, the,' Ford's play of, iii. 120

Brooke, Lord, style of his poetry, iii. 29

Broughton, Hugh, i. 571, ii. 250

Erouncker, Lord, first president of Royal Society, iii. 579

Brown, Mr. George Armitage, 'Shakspeare's autobiographical poems' by, iii. 38, 40 n.

Brown, Dr. Thomas, ii. 412

Brown's 'Philosophy of the Human Mind,' iii. 336 n.

Browne, Sir Thomas, his 'Religio Medici,' ii. 520. His 'Hydrotaphia,' 591. Inquiry into Vulgar Errors, iii. 236, 595

Falkland, Lord, translation of Chilling-worth by, ii. 326

Fallopius, the anatomist, ii. 246, 262, iii. 212

Fanaticism, its growth among some of the reformers, i. 358

Farces, i. 221. [See Drama.]

Farinacci, or Farinaceus, jurist, ii. 547

Farmer's Essay on the Learning of Shakspeare, ii. 183 n.

Farnaby, Thomas, grammarian, ii. 284

Farquhar's comedies, iii. 530

Farringdon, Hugh, abbot of Reading, i. 460

'Fatal Discovery,' play of Southern, iii. 525

Fathers, the, religious respect for their works, ii. 309, 323. Doctrine of some of the, 447

Fayette, La, Countess of, novels by, iii. 566

Feltham, Owen, 'The Resolves' of, ii. 519

Fénelon, Archbishop of Cambray, his 'Maximes des Saints,' iii. 280 n. On Female Education, 429. 'Dia-logues of the Dead' by, 534. Merit of his 'Télémaque,' 569

Ferdinand of Tuscany,plants introduced into Europe by, ii. 242

Fermat, his discoveries in algebra and geometry, iii. 178, 183, 199, 203

Fernel, his mode of measuring a degree of the meridian, i. 462. Eminent French physician, 470

Ferrara, Church of, broken up in 1550, i. 374. Duke of, botanic garden es-tablished by, ii. 242

—, Hercules I. marquis of, i. 233

—, Spanish Bible printed at, i. 585

—, Libraries of, 484, ii. 258

Ferrari, the mathematician, i. 464, ii. 219. 'Lexicon Geographicum' of, iii. 227. Syriac lexicon of, 224

Ferrarius, Octavius, on Roman dress, ii. 294, iii. 254

Ferreira, Portuguese poet, ii. 111

Ferreo, Scipio, inventor of cubic equa-tions, i. 463

Fibonacci, Leonard, the algebraist, i. 114, 243

Fichet, rector of the Sorbonne, i. 163, 236

Ficinus, Marsilius, Theology of, i. 142, 153, 202, 203. Translator of Plo-tinus, 227

Fiction, on works of, i. 452, ii. 213, iii. 155, 565. English novels, ii. 218, iii. 166. Spanish romances, ii. 216, iii. 155. Italian, i. 165, ii. 213. Moorish romances, 112

Field, on the Church, ii. 359

Fiesole, villa of Lorenzo de Medici at, i. 180

Figulus Hermannus, i. 497

Figueroa, Spanish poet, ii. 107

Filelfo, philologist, i. 102 n., 103

Filicaja, Vicenzo, his 'Siege of Vienna,' iii. 462. His 'Italia mia,' a sonnet, ib.

Filmer, Sir Robert, his 'Patriarcha,' ii. 542, iii. 441

Finée, Oronce, mathematician, i. 462

Fioravanti of Bologna, i. 161

Fiore, or Floridus, algebraist, i. 463

Fioretti, or Udeno Nisielo, writings of, iii. 132, 233

Firenzuola, satirical poet, ii. 93. Cha-racter of his prose, 191

Fischart, German poet, ii. 120

Fisher, the Jesuit, Laud's conference with, ii. 310

—, John, i. 280 n., 295 n.

Fisheries, rights to, ii. 558

Fishes, on, ii. 239, iii. 585

Flacius Illyricus, ' Centuriæ Magdebur-genses,' chiefly by, i. 560, 580

Flaminio, Italian poet, i. 374. Latin elegies of Flaminius, 442

Flavio Biondo, i. 173

Flea at Poitiers, lines on the, ii. 147 n.

Fléchier, Bishop of Nismes, iii. 164, 292. Harmony of his diction, 295

Fleming, lyric poetry of, iii. 24

—, Robert, i. 168

Fletcher, Andrew, iii. 561

—, Giles, his poems, iii. 27, 28

Fletcher's, John, 'Faithful Shepherdess,' iii. 46, 97, 108. [See Beaumont and Fletcher.]

—, Phineas, poet, i. 317. His 'Purple Island,' iii. 27, 28

Fleury, Claude, 'Ecclesiastical History' by, i. 3. 9, iii. 262.—His 'Disserta-tions,' ib.

Florence, Platonic and other academies of, i. 201, 227. The Gnomon of, i. 190 n., 191, n. Discussion on the lan-guage of, i. 458, 459, 482, ii. 208. iii. 130. The Apatisti and men of letters of, iii. 233. The Laurentian Library, i. 484, ii. 259. Poets of, iii. 464. Academy of, i. 482, ii. 208, iii. 577. The villa of Fiesole, i. 180. Machia-vel's History of, i. 417, ii. 302

Florus, lines to, by Adrian, i. 29 n.

Fludd, Robert, his Mosaic Philosophy, ii. 381

Folengo invents the Macaronic verse, ii. 96 n.

Fontaine, La, fables of, iii. 467, 468 n., 569

compared with French and Italian,
iii. 541. [See 'Learning;' 'Language.']

Latini, Brunetto, philosophical treatise
of, i. 37, 121

Latinus Latinius, his classical eminence,
i. 519

Latitudinarians, tenets of the, ii. 335,
iii. 276

Laud, Archbishop, ii. 310, 329, 344.
His addition to the Bodleian Library,
iii. 231

Laura, Petrarch's, real existence of, disputed, ii. 205

Laurentian Library, i. 178, purchased,
484

Law, early MS. books of, on parchment, i. 60, 61. Legal studies facilitated, *ib.* Unwritten feudal customs
reduced into treatises; Roman and
Civil; Codes of Theodosius and Justinian, 62, 63, 419. Study of Civil, ii.
73, iii. 433, 443. Not countenanced in
France, ii. 75. Of Nations, 76, 78,
548, iii. 434, 460. Writers on Roman Jurisprudence, ii. 73, 456. On
Public Law by Victoria, 77. Eternal, 509. Revealed, 552. On the
Law of Nature, ii. 5, 513, 536, 551,
iii. 399, 406, 413, 434, 436, 460.
Writers on Jurisprudence, ii. 70–76.
Canon Law, 76. Suarez, 'De Legibus,' ii. 506, 512, 529, 548. Leibnitz
on Roman, ib. 458. Spencer, ' De
Legibus Hebræorum,' 604. French
lawyers, ii. 73

Layamon, peculiarities in the works of,
i. 45

Lazarillo de Tormes, by Mendoza, i.
452, ii. 216

League, Catholic tenets of the, ii, 42–
45. Satire Menippée, upon the, 195

Leake, Col., Researches in the Morea,
i. 98 *n.*

Learning, retrospect of, in the Middle
Ages, i. 1. Loss of, on the fall of the
Roman Empire of the West, 2. Its
rapid decline in the sixth century, 3.
The Church an asylum for, *ib.* Profane learning obnoxious to the Christian priesthood, 4 ; their influence in
the preservation of, *ib.* Clerical education revived in the monasteries of
Ireland, 5. Classical learning revived
in the Anglo-Saxon Church, and at
York, 6, 7. Its progress in the
tenth century, 7, 9. Circumstances
that led to the revival of, 11. In the
fifteenth century, i. 109. Progress
of polite learning, arts and sciences,
524, ii. 393, iii. 248. Decline of, i.

509–519. Effects of the Reformation on, i. 309, 343. Resistance to,
293. Theological, ii. 300–306 ; of
England, i. 523, iii. 248, i. 262, 346,
351. Germany, 211, 233, 345, 509,
510, iii. 244. Italy, i. 519. Spain,
343. Scotland, 282, 531

Le Bœuf, researches of, i. 20, 23 *n.*

Lebrixa, Nebrissensis, i. 177, 343

Le Clerc, John, criticisms of, iii. 248,
274, 299. His commentary on the
Old Testament and Bibliothèques
Universelle, &c. 274. Support of
Cudworth by, 306. His series of
Reviews, 551. His 'Parrhasians,'
555. On the Duties of Ecclesiastical
Historians, i. 580. Defence of Grotius by, ii. 336. Critique du Père
Simon by, iii. 282. His influence
over Protestant Europe, 451

Lee, dramatic works of, iii. 526

Leeuwenhoek, experiments of, on the
blood, iii. 601. Discovery of spermatic animalcules, 601

Legend, Golden, i. 133

Leger's supposed forgeries, i. 29 *n.*

L'Enclos, Ninon, iii. 469

Le Grand, metaphysician, iii. 319

Leibnitz, observations of, i. 323, ii. 18,
428, 464, iii. 380. His correspondence with Bossuet on an agreement
in religion, 266. 'On Roman Law,'
457, ii. 17. 'Protogæa' of, iii. 598.
His admiration of Bacon, ii. 434

Leicester, Earl of, charges against Oxford University by, i. 525 *n.* Press of,
528. Dramatic Company of, ii. 170

Leigh's ' Critica Sacra,' ii. 359

Leipsic press, the, i. 233. The 'Leipsic Acts,' first German Review, iii.
551

Le Long, Polyglott of, iii. 603

Le Maistre, forensic speeches of, iii.
143–145, 293

Lemene, Italian poet, iii. 465

Lemery, his 'Cours de Chymie,' iii.
584

Leo Africanus, travels in Africa by, ii.
252

— X., the patron of the literati of his
age, i. 270, 297, 325, 443, 481. His
authority attacked by Luther, 300

Leon, Fra Luis Ponce de, poetry of, ii.
104

Leonard of Pisa, algebraist, i. 463, ii.
223, 226 *n.*

Leonicenus, Nicolas, physician, i. 469

—, Omnibonus, the critic, i. 179

Leonine rhymes, i. 76 and

Lepidus, comedy attributed to,
other works of, i. 222

Mazeres, mathematical works of, ii. 223 *n.*

Masius, the learned Hebraist, ii. 249

Massa of Venice, anatomist, i. 473

Massinger, Philip, his 'Virgin Martyr,' iii. 115, 120. General nature of his dramas, 115. His delineations of character, 116. His subjects, 117. Beauty of his style, *ib.* His comic powers, 118. His tragedies, *ib.* His other plays, 119. His character of Sir Giles Overreach, 116, 119. Critique on, 119, 514

Massora, the, of Levita, i. 477

Materia Medica, on, ii, 243, 248, iii. 207

Mathematical and Physical Sciences, the, i. 113, 158, 222, 462, ii. 221, 235, iii. 170. Mathematical propositions, *ib.* De Augmentis Scientiarum of Lord Bacon, ii. 399, 429. Mathematics of Descartes, 466. Mathematicians, i. 116, iii. 578. Works, i. 222. Truths, iii. 377 *n.*

Mathews, Charles, comedian, iii. 60 *n.*

Mathias, edition of Gray by, i. 32 *n.*

Matthew Paris, History by, i. 217

Matthews's Bible of 1537, i. 388

Matthiæ, Preface to his Greek Grammar, i. 504 *n.*

Mathioli, his botanical 'Commentaries on Dioscorides,' i. 475.

Maurice, Elector of Saxony, deserts the Protestant confederacy, i. 560

Maurolycus, geometrician, ii. 227. His optical tests, 232, iii. 201

Maximilian, Emperor, patronises learning, i. 293

Maxims of Rochefoucault, iii. 161, 420, 421

May, supplement to Lucan by, iii. 54. History of the Parliament by, 151

Maynard, elegance of his French poetry, iii. 20

Mayow, Essays of, iii. 584. On respiration, 601

Mazarin, Cardinal, attempts to establish an Italian Opera at Paris, iii. 519

— Bible, the, i. 156. Its beauty and scarcity, 157

Mazochius, the Roman bookseller, i. 335

Mazzoni, his treatise 'De Triplici Vitâ,' ii. 31. His defence of Dante, 208

Mead, medical theory of, iii. 602

Mechanics, true principles of the laws of, discovered by Galileo, iii. 194. Of Descartes, 197. Writers on, ii. 232

Meckerlin, German poet, iii. 23

Medals, authors on, i. 539, iii. 255. Collections of Gems and, ii. 261. [See Numismatics.]

Mede on the Apocalypse, ii. 359

Medici, Cosmo de, a patron of learning and the arts, i. 152, 153, ii. 208. His rule arbitrary and jealous, 266. Death of, i. 164

Medici, Lorenzo de, i. 164, 178, 195, 199, 201. Character of, 179. Villa of, *ib.* Botanical gardens established by, 474

—, House of, ii. 242. Expulsion of the, from Florence in 1494, i. 227

Medicine, science of, i. 468. The Greeks the founders and best teachers of, 469. Anatomy and medicine, ii. 246, iii. 212, 599. Progress towards accurate investigation, ii. 248. Transfusion of the blood, iii. 600. Medical theories, 602. Innovations in, i. 469

Medicis, Marie de, ii. 155, iii. 19

Megiser, the Lord's Prayer in forty languages, by, ii. 252

Mehus, on the Florentine literati, i. 85. His life of Traversari, i. 82

Meigret, Louis, French Grammar of, i. 460

Meiners, Comparison of the Middle Ages by, i. 3, 9, 15 *n.*, 85 *n.* His Life of Ulric Von Hutten, 298, 299

Meister-singers of Germany, i. 41, 432, iii. 23

Mela, Pomponius, Geography by, i. 228

Melanchthon, the Reformer, i. 276, 559, ii. 360. Early studies of, i. 262. A promoter of learning, i. 344, ii. 370. His advocacy of Aristotle, i. 395. Guide to the composition of Sermons by, ii. 360. His advice to Luther, i. 359 *n.* His 'Loci Communes,' 304 *n.*, 370 *n.*, 381, 577. Views on baptism, 358 *n.* Latin poetry of, 443. His approbation of the death of Servetus, 567. Style of his works, 509. His adversaries, 560. Chronicle by, i. 480. Ethics of, 408. Purity of diction and classical taste of, 341. His tenets, i. 559, ii. 332. Style of preaching, 360

Mélanges de Littérature, by d'Argonne, iii. 554

Melchior, Adam, the German biographer, i. 510

Melville, Andrew. i. 531, ii. 21, 149

Memoirs, political, ii. 48

— French, ii. 265, iii. 607

Memory, the theory of, ii. 448, 466

Mena, Juan de la, i. 265, ii. 208

— Christopher de la, iii. 14

Ménage, Latin poems of, iii. 493, 566. On the French language, 540, 549. 'Menagiana,' 554

Mendicant Friars, their disputations promoted scholastic philosophy, i. 17

Molina, his treatise on Free-will, i. 562. His Semi-Pelagian doctrine, 562 *n.*, ii. 336. His tenets, iii. 270

Molza, Italian poet, i. 442. His Latin poetry, *ib.*

'Monarchia Solipsorum,' a satire on the Jesuits,' iii. 166

Monarchy, observations of Bodin on, ii. 55, 67. [See King.] Puffendorf's theory of, iii. 437

Monasteries, suppression of, i. 353. Destruction of, no injury to learning, 354. In Ireland, 5

Money and Coin, on, iii. 417, 454. Monetary writings, ii. 531

Monk, Dr., Bishop of Gloucester, iii. 249. Life of Bentley by, 251, 252, 253, 254 *n.*, 274 *n.*, 565 *n.*

Monks attacked by Erasmus, i. 297. Despised in Germany and Switzerland, 309. Various religious orders of, in the twelfth century, 77. Invectives against, by Manzolli and Alamanni, i. 373. By Reuchlin, 298

Monstrelet, historical works of, i. 242

Montagu, Basil, remarks of, on Bacon, ii. 390 *n.*, 391, 392 *n.*

—, Mrs., her Essays, iii. 94

Montaigne, Essays of, ii. 26, 194. Their characteristics, 26. His brilliant genius, *ib.* His sprightly and rapid thoughts, 27. His independent spirit, 28. His love of ancient authors, *ib.* His critical opinions, *ib.* His good sense, 29. His moral scepticism, *ib.* Animadversions upon, 30. The charm of simplicity in his writings, 31, 269. Allusions to, i. 142, 492, iii. 283, 557. His infidelity questioned, i. 582. His egotism, ii. 31. School of, 516

Montanus, Arias, i. 584. Antwerp Polyglott by, ii. 249

Montausier, Duke de, suggests the Delphin editions of the Classics, iii. 246

—, Madame, funeral sermon on, by Fléchier, iii. 295 *n.*

Montemayor, the 'Diana' of, ii. 106, 215

Montesquieu, the 'Grandeur et Décadence,' of, ii. 526. 'L'Esprit des Loix,' 550

Montfaucon, references to his authority, i. 57

Montluc, memoirs of, ii. 258

Montpelier, school of medicine at, i. 19
— Botanical garden of, ii. 242

Montucla, quoted, i. 161, 462, 465, ii. 221, 229, 232. On the Microscope, iii. 202. 'Histoire des Mathematiques,' iii. 170 *n.*

Moon, the, Wilkins's 'Discovery of a New World' in, iii. 563

Moore's History of Ireland, i. 5 *n.*

Moors of Spain, Conde's History of the, ii. 218. Moorish Romances, i. 239, ii. 112, iii. 12 *n.* [See Romance.]

Moral Fictions popular with the Aristocracy, i. 135
— Philosophy, writers on, iii. 391

Moralities, dramatic, i. 221. In France, 221, 447. In England, 221. Used as religious satire, 449

Morals, Italian writers on, ii. 31. English writers, 32. Jesuitical scheme of, 503, 505. Theories of Hobbes and Grotius, 515

More, Henry, on Witchcraft, iii. 299. His metaphysical philosophy, ii. 447 and *n.*, iii. 309, 343

—, Sir Thomas, i. 237, 278, 360. History of Edward V. by, 320, 447. His 'Utopia,' and derivation of the word, 283 *n.*

Morel, John, his Lexicon, i. 526

—, William, his edition of Vergara's Grammar, i. 503

Moreri, French Dictionary of, iii. 552

Morgan, Professor de, on geometrical errors, i. 463

'Morgante, Maggiore' of Pulci, i. 200, iii. 8

Morhof, quotations from the 'Polyhistor' of, i. 197, 324, 345, 503, ii. 4, 275, 372, iii. 452, 554

Morin, Protestant theologian, iii. 221

Morison, Dr., Professor of Botany, iii. 589. His works, 590

Mornay, Du Plessis, writings of, i. 507 *n.*, ii. 305, 311 *n.*

Morosina, Sonnets on the death of, i. 424

Mosellanus, Peter, i. 276, 344, 361

Moses, his authorship of the Pentateuch questioned, iii. 282. Mosaic history of the Deluge, &c., 597, 598. Institutions, 604

Mosheim, his 'Ecclesiastical History,' i. 12, 304, 571, 580, iii. 270 *n.*

Mothe le Vayer, La, his Dialogues, ii. 366, 516, 527. On French eloquence, iii. 143

Mouffet, his 'Theatrum Insectorum,' iii. 207

Mousset, French poet, ii. 119 *n.*

Mulgrave, Lord, 'Essay on Poetry' by, iii. 545 *n.* Poems of, 486, 491

Mun, Thomas, on foreign trade, ii. 539, iii. 453

Munday, Anthony, translator of 'Amadis de Gaul,' and other Romances, i. 315, ii. 220

114 *n.* See also ii. 172 *n.* 176, 200, iii. 524. Remarks on the mode of spelling the poet's name, ii. 178 *n.*

Sharp, Richard, Mr., remarks of, iii. 559, *n.*

Sharrock, 'De Officiis,' &c., iii. 394

Shepherd, life of Poggio by, i. 88 *n.* 102 *n.*

'Shepherd's Kalendar,' poem of Spenser, ii. 124, 212

Sheridan, plays of, iii. 517

'Ship of Fools,' the, i. 241

Shirley, dramatic works of, iii. 124, 527

Sibilet, Thomas, the 'Art poétique' of, i. 459. His 'Iphigenia' of Euripides, 447

Sidney, Algernon, his Discourses on Government, iii. 442

Sidney, Sir Philip, ii. 81, 128, 171. His 'Arcadia,' 199, 218, 220, iii. 236. 'Defence of Poesie,' ii. 126, 171, 199, 213. 'Astrophel and Stella,' 128. Poems of, 128, iii. 556. His censure of the English drama, ii. 171. Character of his prose, 198

Sidonius, observations of, and their character, i. 20

Sienna, the 'Rozzi' of, ii. 263. 'Intronati' of, i. 482

Sigismund, Emperor, literature encouraged by, i. 103

— III., persecution of Protestants by, i. 548

Sigonius, works of, i. 335, 515, 535. 'De Consolatione,' 518. On the Athenian Polity, 536. On Roman Antiquity, 533. 'De Jure Civium Rom.' and 'De Jure Italiæ,' 535. On the antiquities of Greece, 536

Silvester's translation of the Creation, or 'La Semaine,' by Du Bartas, ii. 118. Poems ascribed to, 127, iii. 44

Simler, George, schoolmaster of Hesse, i. 262

Simon le Père, iii. 282. Critical History of, 299-603

Singers of Germany, i. 38, iii. 23

Sionita, Hebraist, iii. 222, 224

Sirmond, the historian, ii. 357

Sismondi, criticisms of, i. 27, iii. 66, 159

Sixtus V., i. 584, ii. 259. The Sistine Bible published by, i. 584

Skelton's rhymes, i. 321, 433, 448

Slavery, Bodin on, ii. 58. Grotius on, 578

Sleidan's History of the Reformation, i. 299 *n.*

Smetius, Martin, works on ancient inscriptions by, ii. 292, 293

Smiglecius, the Logician, iii. 302 *n*, 373

Smith, professor at Cambridge, i. 348

—, Adam, remarks of, ii. 589, 591

Snell, Willibrod, his 'Cyclometricus,' iii. 179. On Refraction, 202

Society, Hobbes on Civil, ii. 543

— Royal, iii. 578

Socinian academy at Racow, i. 565, ii. 337. Writers, i. 375, 565. Socinianism, ii. 335, 337. In England, iii. 278

Socinus Faustus, i. 565, ii. 337

— Lælius, founder of the sect of Socinians, i. 375, 565

Solids, the ratio of, iii. 175

Solinas, his 'Polyhistor.' ii. 286

Solis, Antonio de, 'Conquest of Mexico,' by, iii. 607

Solon, philosophy of, ii. 555

Sonnets, Italian, ii. 43, 84 *et seq.*, iii. 461-465. French, ii. 416. Of Milton, iii. 47. Of Shakspeare, 37. Of Drummond, of Hawthornden, 40. Of the Earl of Stirling, 41. Construction of, *ib.* *n.*

Sophia, Princess, iii. 266

Sophocles, style of, iii. 477, 484

Sorbonne, the, i. 236, iii. 272, 301

Soto, Peter, confessor to Charles V., i. 382, 561, ii. 512

—, Barahona, poetry of, ii. 107

—, Dominic, 'De Justitiâ,' ii. 22, 79, 82

Soul, Descartes on the immateriality of the, ii. 446, 454. On the seat of, 449. Theory of Gassendi, iii. 311. Malebranche, 332. Locke, 382

'Soul's Errand,' the, early poem, ii. 127

Sousa, Manuel Faria y, sonnets of, iii. 14

South, Dr., sermons of, iii. 297

Southampton, Lord, friend of Shakspeare, ii. 179

Southern, his 'Fatal Discovery,' iii. 526. 'Oroonoko,' 526

Southey, Mr., his edition of Hawes, i. 318. Remarks of, ii. 215. Edition of Poets by, iii. 27, 40 *n.*

Southwell, Robert, poems of, ii. 128

Sovereign, and sovereign power, the, ii. 538, 554

Spain, drama of, i. 264, 445, ii. 156, iii. 59, 67, 495. Poets and poetry of, i. 266, 428, ii. 103, 108, iii. 11. Ballads, i. 122, 239, ii. 112. Novels and romances, ii. 112, 215, iii. 12 *n.* 565.

THE END.